THE MAN
WHO GOT AWAY

THE MAN WHO GOT AWAY

THE
BUGS MORAN
STORY

A BIOGRAPHY

ROSE KEEFE

CUMBERLAND HOUSE
NASHVILLE, TENNESSEE

Copyright © 2005 by Rose Keefe

Published by
Cumberland House Publishing, Inc.
431 Harding Industrial Drive
Nashville, TN 37211-3160

Cover design: Gore Studio, Inc.
Text design: John Mitchell

Library of Congress Cataloging-in-Publication Data

Keefe, Rose.
    The man who got away : the Bugs Moran story : a biography / Rose Keefe.
        p. cm.
    Includes bibliographical references and index.
    ISBN 1-58182-443-2 (alk. paper)
    1. Moran, George Clarence 1893-1957. 2. Criminals—Illinois—Chicago—Biography. 3. Gangsters—Illinois—Chicago—Biography. 4. Organized crime—Illinois—Chicago—History—20th century.
    I. Title.
    HV6248.M67K44 2005
    364.1'06'6092—dc22

                                                                    2005005378

Printed in the United States of America

1 2 3 4 5 6 7—11 10 09 08 07 06 05

To Mario Gomes, who helped make it all happen,
and to the memory of John George Moran (1920–1959),
whom I wish I'd gotten to know before he left this world.

CONTENTS

FOREWORD

THE MAN WHO GOT AWAY. That was George "Bugs" Moran in more ways than one. An underworld legend, he survived the gun-blazing Prohibition era which witnessed the bloody rubouts of many of his gangland contemporaries. His predecessors in the North Side Gang were gunned down one by one: Dean O'Banion, Hymie Weiss, Vincent "the Schemer" Drucci. So were "Mossy" Enright, "Big Jim" Colosimo, Charles "the Ox" Reiser, Eddie Tancl, Frank Capone, "Samoots" Amatuna, "Big Tim" Murphy, Tony Lombardo, Patsy Lolordo, and "murder twins" Anselmi and Scalise. And some of the Gennas, O'Donnells, Aiellos, and Touhys, as well many of their adherents, reporter Jake Lingle, and even "Machine-Gun" Jack McGurn. All were slain in Chicago. Yet Moran outlived them all.

"A real goddamn crazy place," visiting New York mobster "Lucky" Luciano once reportedly complained about the Windy City. "No one's safe in the streets." As with most gangland quotes, the attribution is probably dubious but appropriate. Not that New York was entirely free of street warfare either. The 1920s and '30s also saw violent sendoffs for New York hoods like "Peg Leg" Lonergan, Frankie Yale, Arnold Rothstein, Vannie Higgins, Jack "Legs" Diamond, Vincent "Mad Dog" Coll and Dutch Schultz, and spawned the so-called Castellemmarese War which gruesomely defined the shape of the future five Italian crime families of the Big

Apple. The same violent struggles between rival bootleggers were going on all over America—in St. Louis, Kansas City, Cleveland, Detroit, Newark, and even the farming and coal-mining regions of downstate Illinois, where the Birger and Shelton gangs fought for control. But Chicago was America's "Capital of Gangsterdom," and nowhere were hoodlums more colorful, extravagant, daring, and murderous. It was the city in which Bugs Moran both thrived and survived.

It was where the "one way ride" and the "handshake murder" (practiced on Moran's pal Dean O'Banion) supposedly originated, and while rather dubious as "firsts," these events actually happened. It was where Moran's arch rival Al Capone ordered a seven-ton armored limousine after his sedan was riddled with bullets and his chauffeur wounded, presumably by the North Side avengers of O'Banion. Where bombings occurred weekly and sometimes daily, and elections were decided not just by balloting and bribery but by terrorism, kidnapping, and murder. And where the Thompson submachine gun made its spectacular debut, on September 25, 1925, in an unsuccessful attempt to kill "Spike" O'Donnell outside a drugstore at Sixty-third and Western Avenue. The Tommygun—the "Chicago typewriter"— became so prominently identified with Chicago that when Brooklyn mobster Frankie Yale was cut down in 1928 in New York's first machine-gun assassination, it was automatically (and correctly, as it turned out) presumed by all that the killers had come from Chicago.

Yale's demise has at least one direct link to Bugs Moran, for one of the Thompsons used in his assassination was in fact used later in the mayhem that brought Moran immortality as the ultimate underworld survivor: the St. Valentine's Day Massacre, the slaughter of the high command of Moran's North Side mob. A slaughter he narrowly missed being part of and which, curiously, has remained his legacy. A legend in his own time, Bugs Moran is today remembered chiefly as the man who escaped Al Capone's vengeance.

There are some strange parallels in the lives of these two arch enemies. Both hailed from place other than Chicago. Both were refugees from the underworlds of other cities and fled to the Windy City to avoid legal confrontations at home. Both were permanently scarred at an early age in barroom knife fights. Both rose to dominance as the major protagonists in Chicago's "beer wars," a rivalry which extended as the two mobs expanded into labor racketeering. Both survived the Prohibition era. And both were ultimately, perhaps ironically, victims of their own personal vices. Unsafe sex killed Capone, who died quietly in retirement in Florida, a syphilitic loon. Cigarettes were the likely culprits that did Moran in. His career took a downward after the massacre, but only prison could retire him from crime, and he outlived his chief rival by ten years.

But for all the spectacular publicity Moran received during his heyday, he has remained, unlike Capone, a man of mystery. Over the years various writers have either dropped vague or erroneous hints about his true background, or have ignored it altogether. He was not Irish or Polish, contrary to popular belief, nor was his real name Moran. Long before he assumed that Irish-sounding moniker, he was thriving in Chicago's crime jungle as a robber and safecracker, having arrived in the city a decade before Capone.

His years after the massacre, culminating in a return to burglary and a series of bank robberies, comprise another fascinating chapter of a life that has remained largely unexplored—until now.

Author Rose Keefe, unquestionably one of the brightest rising stars in the firmament of historical crime researchers, has turned her considerable talents to unearthing the man behind the myth. She has succeeded admirably, in a natural follow-up to her previous work *Guns and Roses*, the classic, definitive biography of Dean O'Banion. Rose has at long last lifted the veil of mystery that has surrounded George "Bugs" Moran. She has captured *The Man Who Got Away*.

Even Capone couldn't do that!

— Rick Mattix,
coauthor of
Public Enemies: America's Criminal Past, 1919-1940,
Thompson, the American Legend: The First Submachine Gun,
and *Dillinger: The Untold Story (Expanded Edition)*

ACKNOWLEDGMENTS

WHEN HE DIED IN LEAVENWORTH Penitentiary on February 25, 1957, George "Bugs" Moran became gangland's equivalent of World War II's Unknown Soldier. The death certificate contained a different name than the one he had been born with, albeit a name that the public would forever associate with Chicago during the Roaring Twenties. Warden Looney and prison chaplain Father O'Connor thought they knew whom they were burying in the frozen cemetery ground, but in truth they were just as blind to the man's real identity as the Bloomington, Illinois, police force which had arrested him as George Moran in 1912. It was a name that stuck, because after 1912 he became too well known to get away with calling himself anything else for long. By 1925 Bugs Moran was as strongly associated with Prohibition-era Chicago as were "Big Bill" Thompson, the Tommygun, bathtub gin, and Al Capone.

Separating fact from fiction when it came to researching George Moran's life was something I could never have done without assistance from the following people. All of them gave generously of their time and expertise to a bigger extent than I can ever hope to repay.

G. J. Moran broke years of silence to talk about his infamous relative. Without the photos, letters, and memories that he placed at my disposal, my task would have been harder and the results less accurate. He made accessible Moran's detailed files from the Ohio State Penitentiary and Leavenworth, which yielded both valuable information and more avenues for investigation.

Carol Horan, daughter of George Moran's youngest sister, spent hours on the phone relaying stories about the Cunin–Gobeil family and her notorious uncle. Pat and Jeanne Coonan of St. Paul, Minnesota, were also helpful with e-mailed information about the Cunin family tree and its most famous offshoot.

Mario Gomes, who maintains a popular Al Capone Web site, offered twenty-four hour support and encouragement during the months it took to write this book. So did Larry Raeder, whose knowledge of Chicago and its Prohibition-era gangsters is second to none. Larry deserves additional credit for weeding out multiple errors in the manuscript's earlier drafts, leaving me thankful as well as embarrassed. Author and crime historian Rick Mattix was another much-valued proofreader and source of moral support.

My thanks also go out to Emilienne Veinot, Doretta Kleinhauf, and Frank Cantwell, all of whom encountered George Moran as children and still remembered him with awe and affection more than seventy years later.

Allen Hermansen, nephew of Hobart Hermansen, and Mrs. Bobbie Bajoreck spent hours on the phone recounting their friendship with Moran's son John, and his years at Lake Geneva, Wisconsin.

Martha Hild and Phillip Elam of the *Dayton (OH) Daily News* provided the pictures and clippings covering the August 1946 trial of Moran, Virgil Summers, and Al Fouts for the Kurpe Payroll Robbery. Sherri Heckel and Bob Bruck of the *Owensboro (KY) Messenger–Inquirer* also assisted with photos and contemporary news accounts of Moran's 1946 arrest in Owensboro. Additional thanks to John Binder, author of the fantastic *Chicago Outfit*, for making his extensive collection of gangster images, some of which appear in this book, available to me.

The libraries and historical societies in the cities and towns where Moran or his associates made local history dug into their archives and special collections to furnish more pieces to the puzzle. I am especially grateful to the following: the staff of the Ohio State Historical Society, for copying their large file on Al Fouts; Penny Habeck of the Shawano Public Library, for providing the news accounts of the July 1932 murders of Willie Marks and Patrick Berrell; Barbara Denham of the C. E. Brehm Memorial Library in Mount Vernon, Illinois, for her assistance in tracking down the newspaper coverage of Virgil Summers's 1934 murder trial; Nikki Stallings of the Henderson, Kentucky, Public Library, for the contemporary accounts of Moran's residence and 1946 arrest there; and Bettie Spratt and Sheila Hefflin of the Daviess County Public Library, for sharing their extensive file covering Moran's time in Owensboro, Kentucky. Special thanks to Diana Dretske of the Lake County Discovery Museum in Wauconda, Illinois, for sharing her expertise on the region that Moran called home during the early thirties.

Kelly Lansing graciously answered any and all questions about the Red Wing, Minnesota, Juvenile Correctional Facility during Moran's years there, and Kelly

Vassallo from the office of the circuit court clerk of MacLean County dug up the long-buried court documents related to Moran's 1912 and 1913 arrests in Bloomington, Illinois.

I'd also like to thank Bill Helmer, a longtime friend and co-author (along with Art Bilek, who has also been helpful) of *The St. Valentine's Day Massacre: The Untold Story of the Gangland Bloodbath that Brought Down Al Capone*; Doug Hawke, who has a book about Louis Alterie in the works; Tony Navrilio, who currently runs Moran's old Lake Como Inn haunt in Lake Geneva, Wisconsin, as an upscale resort, the French Country Inn; Hymie Weiss relative Bob Koznecki and his wife, Sue; writer Allan May, who provided additional suggestions and leads; Walter Fontane, who helped me make sense of Moran's 1931 visit to St. Louis; Pat Downey, author of *Gangster City*; Tom Prior from *True Detective* magazine; Glenn Taylor, whose father-in-law played uneasy host to the FBI when Moran's house on Littlewood Drive in Owensboro was under surveillance; Verne Miller biographer Brad Smith, who answered questions about Miller's involvement in the Fox Lake Massacre; and Mari Abba, a longtime friend who helped me locate the final resting places of many Moran associates. If Mari doesn't know where they're buried, they're probably still alive.

THE MAN
WHO GOT AWAY

PROLOGUE

Chicago: Thursday, February 14, 1929, 10:30 a.m.

A DELARD CUNIN DUG HIS GLOVED hands deep into the pockets of his gray over-coat and trudged down Lincoln Park West, squinting beneath the brim of his olive-brown hat as he and his companion picked their way through the swirling mass of snow. The icy wind whistled down the dreary streets, which crawled with trolley cars, delivery trucks, and average motorists, some of whom had a hard time keeping their vehicles going while looking out for sheet ice or frost-coated trolley tracks. The precipitation was not heavy, but like the city, it was continuous and hypnotic enough to be as hazardous as any blizzard.

Cunin was not from Chicago but had lived here since 1910, and in his way became as firmly entrenched in the city's social and historical fabric as any native-born resident. His success in his chosen line of business—booze smuggling, union affairs, and sporting events like dog racing—had made him a local cause célèbre, although some would say that he had nothing to be proud of. Cunin, a Minnesotan by birth and French Canadian by descent, didn't much care. Those who derided his livelihood were the very ones who purchased his liquor and gambled without restraint at his dog tracks; as long as their hypocrisy made him rich, he relished his enemies almost as much as he did his friends.

That morning, he had an important appointment at a garage on North Clark Street, one of many locations where he conducted his business. He had promised to be there at 10:30 a.m., but an unexpectedly long appointment at the Parkway Hotel barbershop had put him almost ten minutes behind schedule. He and his associate passed other residents who hurried by without giving him a second glance. The inclement weather was not concealing him from recognition; he would have been overlooked just as casually had April sunshine been beating down from above. His name was more famous than his face; during his nearly twenty years in action, his photo had graced the Chicago papers only a handful of times. He liked it that way—in his line of work, a widely circulated picture was an impediment.

When Cunin and his companion, a longtime business associate, reached Griffin Avenue, they turned west and continued walking until they came to North Clark Street, at which point they turned northward. Although a respectable German–Irish middle class occupied the greater percentage of its apartment buildings and furnished rooms, the neighborhood consisted mostly of rooming houses, cheap cafes, storage depots, pawnshops, and other establishments designed to cater to a transient population. The two men had commenced their journey in the ritzier surroundings of the Parkway Hotel on Lincoln Park West, and a few minutes' walk had taken them to a district that supplied the city with blue-collar workers. Chicago was one huge collection of neighboring diversities, where alternate worlds were within moments of one another.

Although Valentine's Day, no matter how freezing or inclement the weather, was a celebration of love, that morning the people of Chicago acknowledged the grim reality that the next day's morning paper would carry news of a multiple killing. Two young men in the Cook County Jail had the dubious honor of knowing that, unless God or the governor intervened, February 14 would be their last day on earth.

Almost a year earlier, on April 27, 1928, seventeen-year-old Charles Walz and nineteen-year-old Anthony Grecco had entered a drugstore at 3404 North Clark Street, intending to rob it in order to obtain "jewelry and clothing" money for their girlfriends. When plainclothes police officer Arthur Esau interrupted them in mid-deed, Walz shot him and boasted afterward, "The police have been telling that I shot him twice. That's bunk. I shot three times—once in the head, once in the heart, and once in the shoulder. Sure, I killed him, and I ain't scared to say so." The public reacted violently; Esau had been the fourth police officer killed in the line of duty in April 1928, and both cops and citizens were furious with the killers' blasé attitude toward the cold-blooded murder. After a heated trial, Walz and Grecco were sentenced to die in the electric chair at midnight on February 15, the first to face death by electrocution (Cook County had recently retired its gallows). A third

4

murderer had been scheduled to join them and make it a triple event, but he had received a stay of execution the previous Saturday.

Cunin and his associate were almost at their destination when they noticed something was amiss. Parked outside the garage at 2122 North Clark was a large, seven-passenger Cadillac whose gong on the running board marked it as a police vehicle. They stopped in their tracks as they realized that their morning plans had just changed.

At the time, he probably assumed that it meant a "visit" from cops who'd either been pressured into making a token roundup of hoodlums or were about to demand a bigger payoff from Adelard's associates and had thrown in an example of a refusal consequence for good measure. Cunin would not have been pleased with either possibility, and he likely spent the remainder of the morning imagining the offending officers walking a country beat in conditions worse than the current weather. He would see to that personally—by February 1929 he had the power and the connections to pull it off.

History is not clear on whether the two men retraced their steps to the residential hotel on Lincoln Park West or ducked into a coffee shop to wait out what appeared to be a police raid on the establishment where they had business that blustery morning. Cunin never discussed it publicly, then or later.

The significance of the police car soon became all too apparent, proving that if Cunin and his companion had not turned back, they would have faced a fate worse than arrest. Before twenty-four hours had passed, headlines appeared that shocked a public long accustomed to the sensational, scandalous, and violent in their morning papers:

MASSACRE 7 OF MORAN GANG, proclaimed the *Chicago Daily News.*

FIRING SQUAD KILLS SEVEN IN BIG GANGLAND MASSACRE, cried the *Chicago Herald and Examiner.*

SEVEN SLAIN IN GANG MASSACRE, ballied the *Milwaukee Journal.*

The facts were just as incredible as the headlines they supported. That morning, five members of the Bugs Moran North Side Gang, which had been at war with "Scarface Al" Capone since the 1924 murder of the original North Side leader, Dean O'Banion, were found lying in a bloody, torn jumble in the dimly lit trucking garage at 2122 North Clark. An optometrist who had dropped in for a friendly visit with his gangster buddies and a mechanic who serviced the trucks on the premises brought the total death count to seven. One man, Frank Gusenberg, whose gunman brother Pete had been among the victims, survived the initial attack but died hours later in hospital, refusing to tell police investigators who had shot him.

When it sank in that he had narrowly escaped becoming a Cook County homicide statistic, Cunin collapsed from shock. He checked into St. Francis Hospital in Evanston, claiming severe flu symptoms, and for days frustrated the best efforts of police and journalists seeking to interview him for his role in the butchery that would achieve infamy as the "St. Valentine's Day Massacre."

5

Said officers and scribes knew Cunin as someone else: years ago, to combat anti-foreign prejudice (among other reasons based on self-preservation), he disguised his French origin by changing his name to George Moran. It was as George "Bugs" Moran that he had achieved fame and fortune as a gangster and bootlegger, and a certain amount of admiration as Al Capone's last great challenger in the Chicago bootlegging battles of the 1920s.

The "beer wars," as the press called them, had their origin in the 1924 murder of Moran's beloved boss, Dean O'Banion, but over time became less of a personal vendetta and more of a vicious rivalry of the type that bloodied Chicago history during the pre-Volstead era. There had been comparative peace in the city during the first few years of the decade, thanks to Capone mentor Johnny Torrio's success in convincing the city's numerous gangs that cooperation was the best way to derive the maximum benefit from supplying forbidden liquor to a parched and rebellious public. But smooth talk had not been enough to protect the Chicago gangs from their competitive natures and innate distrust based on racial/ethnic issues, and O'Banion, boss of the powerful North Side Gang, had been killed for bucking the Syndicate.

Cunin, known only as George "Bugs" Moran or George Morrissey, joined comrades Hymie Weiss and Vincent Drucci in making the lives of Johnny Torrio, Al Capone, and their allies the stuff of nightmares. Naturally, the Italians struck back, taking down Weiss in a machine-gun ambush in October 1926. Vincent Drucci cursed the wrong cop months later, in April 1927, and joined Weiss in Mount Carmel Cemetery, leaving Moran the last great hope of the dwindling North Side forces. Johnny Torrio had left Chicago by then, a near-fatal encounter with North Sider bullets having convinced him that he had no stomach for the war that was escalating. But there was still Capone, and Moran made sure that Big Al regretted ever coming to Chicago from New York in the first place.

"If I'd known what I was getting into," the Italian gang leader lamented to the press after yet another attempt on his life, "I'd never have left the Five Points outfit in New York."

By 1927 Bugs Moran was a Chicago landmark as the Capone gang antichrist, but he turned heads even among those who knew neither him nor his reputation. He was a gangland fashion plate, adorning his five-foot-eight, 175-pound frame in expensive blue serge suits, striped shirts and ties with a diamond stickpin, pearl-gray spats, and an off-white Fedora. When he smiled, his swarthy face lit up. No one was fooled by the outward display of gentility; toughness and a sometimes murderous disposition had gotten him where he was, and kept him there when necessary.

Adopting the motto that any enemy of Capone's was a friend of his, Moran allied with the Aiello brothers, who had been battling Capone's handpicked candidates for the presidency of the powerful Unione Siciliana in order to seize that coveted spot for the head of the clan, Joe Aiello. Despite his own aversion to the flesh trade, Moran also welcomed the support of West Side pimp and politically powerful Jack Zuta, as well as a handful of smaller underworld satellites who had one reason or another to want to strap Capone in for a one-way ride.

What the Moran-Aiello-Zuta forces lacked in numbers they more than compensated for in sheer bravado. In January 1929 Aiello and two Moran gunmen shot and killed the incumbent Unione President, Pasqualino Lolordo, a Capone minion, in the sanctity of his own home. They also attempted to bribe the chef of the Italian gang boss's favorite restaurant to put prussic acid in his soup. Anyone close to Capone was fair game; his triggerman and friend "Machine-Gun" Jack McGurn had been fired on twice by the deadly Gusenberg brothers, Bugs Moran's ace killers. Less lethal but equally frustrating to Capone were Moran's intrusions into the dog racing business, a field over which Capone had long held sway.

Considering the hateful and desperate mentalities backing the power struggle, it was only a question of time before one side made a move that would make the previous attacks look like petty shots in the dark. As news of the seven-man killing at the North Clark Street garage that cold February morning reached the public, both gangland and the police knew that Big Al's guns had spoken what they hoped would be their last piece in the five-year war.

As Cunin/Moran reclined on the hospital pillows, he sent word to Chicago Chief of Detectives John Eagan that, "We don't know what brought it on. We're facing an enemy in the dark." But when reporters finally tracked him down and questioned him in his hospital room, Moran's temper flared and his restraint broke. "Only Capone kills like that!" he insisted.

Capone, who was in Miami at the time, merely smiled when he learned of Moran's accusation. "They don't call that guy bugs for nothing."

As soon as he had collected his wits, Moran checked out of the hospital and hurried to Windsor, Ontario, where he and a handful of his remaining faithful holed up in the King Edward Hotel. The conferences they held must have been animated; not only did they, like Capone, have to devise a strategy to weather the maelstrom of public outcry over the bloody showiness of the massacre, but they also had to determine how to prevent the erosion of their businesses in the face of the Capone Syndicate's persistent invasion.

They eventually lost that battle, but not to Capone, who in 1932 was indicted in federal court for income tax evasion and handed an eleven-year sentence. As the Depression progressed and Prohibition was repealed, the wealthy, splashy gangster of the 1920s went the way of the glamorous flapper and bathtub gin: into history. The era of the outlaw, the smaller bands of two-gun bank robbers and killers such as Bonnie and Clyde, the Barkers, and Baby Face Nelson had arrived.

The former Capone mob, now known as the Outfit, among other things, adapted by assuming a cloak of invisibility and infiltrating more and more legitimate businesses. It was a coping mechanism alien to Bugs Moran, whose closest brush with gainful employment had been the takeover of the Central Cleaning Company's presidency in 1928. After spending the thirties alternating between running slot

7

machines in Lake County, operating briefly under the aegis of the Bookie Gang, and participating in a counterfeiting ring, he dusted off his sidearms and hit the bank robbery trail with men half his age, heading down a road destined to end in ten years of imprisonment and lasting inclusion in any morality story suggesting that crime does not pay.

George "Bugs" Moran was the last of the spectacular North Side Gang leaders, a colorful and violent urban dynasty that began with the rise of Dean O'Banion in 1920. Although Moran was not killed in the February bloodbath that had obviously been meant for him, his days as a mighty gangland power were numbered. Cops and journalists who prided themselves on knowing gangsters better than the hoods themselves dismissed Moran, figuring that the loss of his top men in the Clark Street garage and Capone's slow but sure absorption of the North Side would either force Bugs out of town for good or make him a vulnerable target that no red-hot seeking a reputation could resist.

Moran suffered neither predicted fate. The career that commenced in St. Paul, Minnesota, with a 1909 burglary conviction and progressed by 1929 to bootlegging, cleaning and dyeing unions, and dog racing was the outward expression of a cunning and determined survivor. Although not as cerebral as John Torrio or Hymie Weiss, Moran was street-smart in the style of the pre-World War I gangsters, those rough and tumble brawlers who relied on their instincts alone and sneered that they'd never seen a bullet yet that was afraid of brains. He had the battle scars to prove his apprenticeship in that do-or-die environment, sporting a four-inch knife scar along the right side of his neck, a multitude of bullet and stab wounds, and a crooked middle finger from a badly knit broken bone. He outlived O'Banion, Weiss, Drucci, Capone (his preference for monogamy rescued him from Capone's fate: to die a syphilitic wreck), and probably those who predicted his imminent demise back in 1929.

He was the man who got away: from an early death (the average lifespan of the Prohibition gangster was twenty-six years) and from judicial punishment for the series of underworld killings that he either committed himself or ordered done during his years at war with the Capone mob. He did not, however, escape scot-free, serving the last ten years of his life in the Ohio State and Leavenworth penitentiaries on bank robbery charges, and he did die from causes unrelated to old age: decades as a heavy smoker had left him with a lethal dose of lung cancer by 1957. Thirty years earlier, during an interview with a crusading minister who published a reform magazine, Moran insisted that he would rather die from bullets than something slow and lingering like cancer.

Irony knows no bounds.

Despite the fame that Adelard Cunin/Bugs Moran attained as Al Capone's archenemy and gangland's ultimate survivor, the man himself has been somewhat of a mystery to crime historians. His criminal record included arrests under at least three other names (Miller, Gage, and Morrissey), leading to speculation that the name on his gravestone was just another alias—a theory that research and interviews with his family have proven to be correct. Every book or anthology in which he merits a mention gives his heritage as Irish or Polish or a hybrid of both, and his choice of aliases certainly threw a smokescreen over his Gallic roots. For decades his pre-Chicago past has been hidden beneath a subterfuge of his own making; the true story is told here for the first time.

Previous books exploring and explaining the turbulent period that Chicago's underworld experienced during the 1920s report Moran's pre-Prohibition activities only to the extent of quoting his criminal record. His Minnesota childhood as the son of French immigrant parents has never been described in detail until now; his two marriages and fatherhood have been skimmed over; and his years as an independent outlaw (late 1930s to mid-'40s) have appeared as mere mentions in an epilogue. This book is the first in-depth treatment of Bugs Moran's charmed yet wacky life. In the process of telling his story, some of the twentieth century's most fascinating and bewildering gangland figures are revisited: Al Capone, Johnny Torrio, Dean O'Banion, Vincent Drucci, Earl "Hymie" Weiss, Chicago's bellowing showboat Mayor "Big Bill" Thompson, the gang-hating yet oddly pro-Moran Judge John H. Lyle, and Virgil Summers and Albert Fouts, two of the Midwest's most colorful and brazen robbers.

Although George Moran both associated with and commanded some of Chicago's most feared gangsters, those who knew him well suspected that there was as much gold in his heart as in his 1920s bank account. Judge John Lyle, who relished the vagrancy warrant as a weapon against wealthy gangsters with no "legal" means of support, recalled in his memoir, *The Dry and Lawless Years*:

> As a man Moran had interested me. In the many times he had been
> before me in court I had discerned contradictions in his makeup. He was
> guilty of many wicked acts. But also he was sharp-witted, had a keen
> sense of humor, and at times was highly emotional. I had long thought
> that of all the gangsters I had observed, Moran was the most likely to
> repent before he died and ask God's forgiveness.

History has not recorded the details of Moran's last confession, but the public record allows us to venture a guess.

1

"MAUDIT FRERES!"

S T. PAUL, MINNESOTA, IN 1885 presented attractive prospects to twenty-four-year-old Jules Cunin. A young mason who had originally emigrated from Alsace-Lorraine, he had come to America to escape the poverty and strife that had wracked his homeland while the German and French governments struggled for control. Cunin, unlike the majority of European immigrants who poured into the United States during the latter half of the nineteenth century, was fortunate enough to possess a skill that was in hot demand during the building booms that gripped the rapidly growing American cities. He and his parents, August and Mary Cunin, settled initially in the vicinity of West Fairfield Avenue, where August worked in a blacksmith shop, but shifted addresses at least once a year afterward, as was customary in the boardinghouse districts they frequented.

Transient living and a physically demanding job did nothing to refine Jules Cunin's temperament. "[Jules] was mean and nasty," a family member would later recall. "He was hard-nosed."[1]

His youngest daughter, Laurette, dissented from the general opinion. She spent a great deal of time with him in his later years, after illness and old age had mellowed and sobered him, and remembered her father as a sensitive man with a voracious love of books. "He had them all over the house," his granddaughter Carol

11

Horan (daughter of Laurette) recalled. " He was smart, could talk about anything and everything. His entire house was like a library."

Perhaps it was his bookish, intelligent side that won the heart of twenty-year-old Marie Diana Gobeil.

Born August 20, 1868, in St. Alphonse, near Chicoutimi in the Canadian province of Quebec, Marie Diana was, by all accounts, witty, vivacious, and highly intelligent. Although she only received an elementary school education, her naturally quick mind allowed her to complete the rest of her learning on her own time.[2] She also had an irrepressible sense of humor. Carol Horan remembered, "She had long, dark hair that used to hang all the way down her back when it wasn't tied up. One day she let me brush it for her. I must have been only four or five, but I remember wrapping some of her hair so tightly around the brush that my father had to cut it to get the brush out. My parents were so upset with me, but Grandma just laughed and laughed."

Marie Diana and her parents, Joseph and Josephine (Pepin) Gobeil, left St. Alphonse and its rural, highly religious environment in 1877, when she was nine years old, and moved to St. Paul, where they lodged in the French Canadian section of town. This area, whose modern boundaries are Lexington Parkway on the west, Interstate 35 E to the east, University Avenue to the south, and the tracks of the Burlington National Railway to the north, was known locally as "Frog Town" because of the national background of its inhabitants. Although Irish, Polish, Scandinavian, and German immigrants arrived in increasing numbers during the 1880s, mostly to take employment in the St. Paul and Pacific Railroad yards or in the railroad shops along Jackson Street and Philadelphia Avenue, the dominant ethnic flavor continued to be French.

French Canadians like Diana Gobeil and her family had been adding to the St. Paul melting pot since the late eighteenth century, when the American Fur Company recruited them in droves to staff the numerous trading posts throughout Minnesota. The majority contributed honorably to their adopted community; one of them, Charles Bazille, built the growing town's first frame house, in 1844. The building, constructed as a residence and warehouse for Captain Louis Robert, stood for many years at the corner of Fourth and Minnesota and was locally hailed as the oldest building in the city. Louis Robert himself, born in Missouri to French Canadian parents, played a major role in the development of the city, and has been credited by history as the man responsible for locating the state capital at St. Paul. Others used their hunting and trapping skills to obtain the furs and pelts that were the cornerstone of early St. Paul commerce, and acted as interpreters during social and business transactions between local Indian tribes and the white settlers.

Others saw fit to make their mark via less acceptable methods. Pierre Parrant, born in Sault Ste. Marie, Michigan, but descended from a long line of French Canadian trappers and fur traders, made his first appearance in St. Paul while in his early sixties. Unlike his ancestors, he derived his livelihood from a still he set up outside Fort Snelling, the area's first settlement. Parrant cheerfully sold his throat-scorching brew to the local Indians, the soldiers, and the squatters' camp (which consisted mainly of refugees from Manitoba's ill-fated Selkirk Colony) that sprang up in the shadow of the fort. The liquor was bad and made his customers feel worse, but government rationing of the better-quality merchandise left him with no shortage of business.

Parrant was by all accounts a coarse individual, who spoke deplorable English and squinted balefully at all comers with his one good eye. His blind eye was a horror to behold, being blotchy, crooked, and ringed with a sickly white around the pupil. Contemporary accounts describe his personal habits as "intemperate and licentious."

When the local Indian Agent, Major Lawrence Taliaferro, ordered him out of the area in 1835, Parrant moved his operations to a point just north of the fort's jurisdiction. After borrowing money from another Frenchman, William Beaumette, and mortgaging his land claim in the process, he defaulted on the loan and suffered eviction. After months of economic struggle, Parrant resurfaced as a saloonkeeper near Lambert's Landing, where downtown St. Paul is now located.

The pugnacious Frenchman's last act of public notoriety before leaving the district in 1844 revolved around a land claim dispute with French Canadian Michel Leclaire. Parrant had filed a claim that Leclaire insisted was part of his own land allotment, and when arguments failed, the two men went before Justice of the Peace Joseph Brown. Brown was stymied after reviewing the evidence, which showed an equally valid argument for both parties, so he offered an ingenious solution: since neither Parrant nor Leclaire had properly staked his claim to the land in question before witnesses, the first of the two to do so would win the current dispute. The result was an eight-mile race between the claimants, most of it through forest and swamp. The twenty-two-year-old Leclaire, with the advantage of youth, emerged the winner, but sixty-seven-year-old Parrant had maintained his stamina through hard living and was the loser by mere minutes. He reluctantly conceded defeat and died soon after, while en route to his native Sault Ste. Marie.[3]

By 1851 St. Paul was growing but still little more than a frontier community of tradesmen and merchants. Most of the incoming residents were attracted by the land boom and the promise of employment in the logging industry or merchant trades, St. Paul being the upper terminus of the Mississippi riverboats. Others, however, stepped from the wagons and steamboats with the full intention of depriving their fellow townspeople of the same riches that had brought them to the area.

Gamblers, prostitutes, con men, and ordinary hoodlums came in droves, taking advantage of the social disorder that normally accompanies a young town's growing pains. They became such a nuisance that one Alexander Marshall was appointed in 1851 to enforce the law in St. Paul and keep the rowdies under control. It was such a hopeless task, given the Wild West spirit that remained despite increasing urbanization, that Marshall resigned three years later. By then, St. Paul

13

had been incorporated as a city and had its own police department, a five-man squad headed by newly appointed Chief William Miller.[4]

Miller's microscopic force made a courageous attempt at keeping the peace, but the criminal element remained defiant. A new jail, built in 1857, was hard-pressed to contain all the "guests" Miller and his men were forced to bring in. Assault, murder, and thievery took place on a nightly basis, and gambling and prostitution ranked alongside logging and retail commerce as the town's most thriving businesses. Miller was permitted to hire eight more policemen, but sheer necessity prompted the formation of a forty-man vigilance committee. Both officers and volunteers encountered assault and abuse from the gangs on a nightly and even daily basis. The advent of the Civil War made things even worse, as many of the policemen enlisted in the army. If it weren't for the hurried formation of a 200-man volunteer force, the city would have fallen under a total reign of terror.

Even after Appomattox and a return to comparative prosperity, the law enforcement body of St. Paul remained hard put to do its job; the uneven topography of the city made it difficult for policemen to escort/haul their prisoners to jail night after night. The dilemma was so apparent that a sympathetic merchant began leaving his horse and wagon parked overnight at the corner of Seventh and Wabasha, inviting the harried officers to use it as a makeshift paddy wagon. By the 1870s, when the Cunin and Gobeil families settled in St. Paul, the system of law enforcement had improved, but probably from necessity; the gang situation continued to be a serious problem.

How or exactly where they met is not known, but Jules Cunin and Marie Diana, who also went by Diana or "Jenny," married in November 1889 at St. Louis, a parish known throughout St. Paul as the "French Church." Their wedding photo presents them as a striking young couple: Jules sits erect in a dark coat and striped trousers, with his thick moustache suavely groomed and a calm, thoughtful expression on his well-sculpted face, while Diana's delicate features and wasp-waisted, doll-like figure are the epitome of frail Victorian womanhood.

After a brief honeymoon they set up house at 251 Western Avenue South,[5] where August Cunin, whose wife had died the previous year, resided. Father and son worked in the same blacksmith shop while Diana kept house and prepared herself to raise a family. On August 21, 1891, she gave birth to their first child, a son whom they named Adelard Leo.[6] Five years later, in November 1896, a second boy, Cyrille, was born. A daughter, Josephine, who was affectionately known as "Finney," arrived in January 1900. Another girl, Laurette, completed the family in July 1904.[7]

The four- to five-year gap between each child was unusual for the Cunins' era and religious background and offers silent testimony that whatever their initial attraction, Jules and Diana fell out of love almost as quickly as they fell into it. No proof exists in the public record or family history that Jules maltreated his wife physically, but he is remembered today as a man with an abrasive nature that few

14

could stand, even the patient, vivacious Diana. Fear of community disapproval, a sense of religious obligation, and concern over her children's economic security kept her from leaving him, but after Laurette's birth an estrangement set in and left them married in name only.

Adelard, the eldest, was an energetic, mischievous child who refused to embrace either his father's patriarchal notion of obedience or his mother's religious devotion. Physically speaking, he was well built and had a square face with a sculpted jawline that became even more prominent when his lips were pressed tight in a stubborn pout. His chin had a pronounced dimple that gave his youthful expression an elfin cast. When calm, he had a winning smile and an easy manner that won over most adversaries, but a volatile temper made him react to most obstacles with explosive aggression. He and his father, from whom he'd inherited the hair-trigger temperament, clashed often. The whippings that Jules administered in response to what he perceived as an attack on his authority did nothing to instill humility in his son. If anything, the punishment made Adelard more stubborn and rebellious.[8]

The Cunins, like many of their European and Quebeçois counterparts, were hardworking and anticipated a similar future for Adelard and his siblings. To instill both moral and religious values, they sent the children to Catholic schools; Adelard and Cyrille received their high school educations at Creighton, an institution run by the Christian Brothers which still exists today. Cyrille, although as spirited as his brother, managed to quell his lively instincts long enough to pass successfully through the St. Paul school system and enter the stonecutter trade.

Adelard's scholastic experience was considerably rockier than that of his siblings. Scarcely a week went by at Creighton High School without one of the brothers reacting to his insubordination by administering the strap. Once, one of the brothers who taught a regular class was out sick, and a substitute was appointed to take his place. When Adelard observed the newcomer's bald head, he snickered, "I thought the moon only came out at night." The other students giggled, but Adelard was promptly hauled out of the classroom, marched down to the principal's office, and strapped. Another time, he sneered, "Maudit freres" (damned brothers) to a friend while out in the schoolyard, and was overheard by a francophone teacher who found the comment less than amusing.

"The Christian Brothers at Creighton were always beating him for misbehaving," one Cunin descendent remembered. "Then word would be sent home about whatever he did, and Jules would belt him again."[9]

No beating would have been intense enough to kill or even subdue the boy's stubborn nature. His behavior dismayed his parents, but in the local juvenile gangs, he found not only an outlet but also an admiring audience. Most of the gang members were, like himself, the children of immigrants who were caught in that bewildering and alienating boundary line between rigid and well-defined Old World customs and the less proscribed, comparatively irreverent American way of life.

In St. Paul, Adelard Cunin's name and parentage, as well as the fact that he lived within the boundaries of Frog Town, made him a "Frenchie," a "frog" in the eyes of Anglo-Saxon onlookers. He, his brother, and other boys of similar heritage would bond together and indulge in pastimes that ranged from the respectable (attending the circus and other public entertainments en masse, playing stickball in the streets, holding swimming parties at local watering holes during the heat of summer) to the destructive (breaking the windows of public buildings that they were ejected from for being noisy, shoplifting, fighting boys from rival backgrounds and territories). Negative responses to their activities from parents, police, and school authorities increased the sense of unity among the boys, instilling an "us-versus-them" mentality.

John Landesco's 1929 Illinois Crime Survey included interviews with adult gangsters who talked at length about their childhood in youth gangs. Although Landesco's work focused on Illinois in general and Cook County in particular, the stories he collected were typical of the juvenile criminal of Adelard Cunin's day. One wrote:

> When we were small we used to watch the older boys and we joined in the same things when we were a little older. There was crap shooting, pilfering, and roughhousing among them. On election night or Hallowe'en, we would burn fences or wagons or anything else we could get our hands on which would make a fire. The little fellows would steal potatoes to bake on the fire. One time we burned an old patrol wagon. . . . Later, we went to shows in a gang and would yell and holler and get put out. Sometimes after we were put out we would throw bricks at the back door of the picture show. We liked "the thrillers." The nickel shows in those days had a good many shootings and killings.

The subject confirmed that law enforcement officials were perceived as the enemy right from day one. "We could never be friendly with the cop because we were always in the wrong," he explained. "We always got out of his way quickly with the warning cry, "Jigger, the cop!"

The boys did not lack for adult role models to emulate. In 1900 St. Paul's new Chief of Police, John J. O'Connor, devised a system that turned the city into a national crooks' haven. Technically speaking, any criminal wanted for offenses in other cities would find sanctuary in St. Paul; if they "checked in" with O'Connor or his representative and agreed to commit no crimes while they remained in the city, arriving killers, robbers, and thugs could count on immunity from arrest by the local force or extradition to an outside jurisdiction. This tolerance of criminals has gone down in Minnesota history as the "O'Connor System."[10]

Explaining his attitude toward crime prevention in his city, O'Connor said, "If they behaved themselves, I let them alone. If they didn't, I got them. Under other

16

administrations there were as many thieves here as when I was chief, and they pillaged and robbed; I chose the lesser of two evils."

The occasional ruffian who took advantage of O'Connor's generosity usually ended up the recipient of a "private discussion" in the Chief's office. The conversations must have been intense ones, for when they left (or were carried out), the malefactors were physically the worse for wear.

Police officers capable of recognizing the nation's foremost crooks met all incoming trains and stopped anyone that they knew or suspected of being a thug on the lam. Knowing what to expect, most times these visitors carried jewelry and money to present to the uniformed welcome wagons and promised to check in at the nearest police station to hear the "behave or else" lecture.

A write-up in the police department souvenir book of 1904 insisted that however unorthodox the concept, in practice it worked: "Never in the history of St. Paul has human life and the property of citizens been so safe, and the virtue of women so assured."

Although O'Connor claimed that making a deal with the devil was a necessary price for peace, he set rates of his own among the local underworld. High-profile crimes like bank robbery and predatory activity such as purse snatching and mugging were discouraged because of the public reaction, but gambling and prostitution were, in the eyes of many, wanted vices. That meant that the brothels and gambling halls could do business, as long as they paid O'Connor for the privilege of operating without police harassment.

During the early years of his tenure as chief, O'Connor's cut of the St. Paul gambling and prostitution rackets was collected by William "Reddy" Griffin, a redhaired character who headquartered at the Hotel Savoy, a gamblers rendezvous on Minnesota Street. Griffin made regular rounds of all the resorts on Hill, Washington, and St. Peter streets, picking up the chief's tribute, and when necessary arranged housing for visiting gangster "dignitaries" in some "ask no questions" rooming houses along Wabasha Street. If any of these visitors failed to report their presence to the nearest police station within twelve hours, "Reddy" would go looking for them and deal with the situation accordingly.

The majority of the system adherents never saw Reddy's face except in passing; they recognized a good thing when they saw it, and only insanity or liquor ever made any of them rock the boat. It was one particular class of criminal that continued to give the local policemen a run for their badges: the native-born burglars and petty thieves who were too small-time to buy leniency.

Adelard's irrepressible personality and lively disdain for authority were bound to get him into trouble with the law one day. And that was exactly what happened in 1909, when he was eighteen. He had left school by that point and obtained employment as a driver with a local business, Elmquist Brothers.[11] Records pertaining to that period are meager, so the details are incomplete, but bored with the monotony and low pay that went hand in hand with legitimate work, Adelard and a friend robbed a St. Paul store in the downtown district and were caught as they tried to exit with the loot. It was just the type of petty crime that O'Connor's system frowned on and punished without mercy, so imprisonment was the inevitable result of the guilty plea both boys gave. As both were under age twenty-one, the judge who heard their cases sentenced them to the state juvenile correctional facility at Red Wing.

Red Wing had been housing young male offenders since its opening in October 1890. The original reform school had been located right in St. Paul, a small facility constructed in 1866 after the public protested against the practice of sending juveniles to the state prison at Stillwater. By 1886 the House of Refuge, as it was called, was so overcrowded that the state Board of Charities and Corrections recommended relocation. J. W. Brown was the first superintendent of the new institution, whose motto was, "It is better to build boys than to mend men." Archbishop John Ireland attended the laying of the cornerstone and summed up his hopes for Red Wing's rehabilitative powers:[12]

> Amid the youth there are weaklings that need particular nurturing care lest they fall by the wayside. We have advanced beyond the primary state when there was only punishment for offenses committed, and now the state takes the part of the prudent parent. It is the right and the duty of the state to come to the rescue. The money so spent is public money well spent. Prevention is cheaper than the reparation of damage done. The study of crime begets a feeling of compassion. It is not so often a malicious propensity as circumstances into which the unfortunate is thrown that causes crime.

Despite the positive hopes and Christian intentions that backed the development of Red Wing, a sordid reality lay beneath the outer veneer of daily classes and vocational training. A high percentage of the young offenders admitted to the institution had little use for Christians and even less for the low-paying trades their prison jobs prepared them for; thus, the recidivism rate was high. After J. W. Brown left his post as superintendent, his successor, F. A. Whittier, implemented a more rigid philosophy of rehabilitation. Unlike Brown, Whittier did not believe that the majority of Red Wing's inmates committed their crimes as the result of a childhood of poverty.

"Sentimentalists would have us believe that much crime is due to extreme poverty," he scoffed. "Such is not borne out by the figures, as less than 5 percent of crime can be attributed to actual want." He was convinced that moral degeneracy and lack of discipline were the primary launching pads to acts of juvenile delinquency, and so he ran the institution along military lines. The boys were outfitted in uniforms, divided into "companies," and forced to undergo daily regimentation and drilling as well as school and vocational training.

Carl Panzram, the psychopathic serial killer who was hanged at Leavenworth in 1930 after a career of sodomy and murder, was at Red Wing not long before Adelard passed through the gates. In his memoirs, Panzram, who was initially committed for breaking into a neighbor's house, recalled the brutality inflicted on boys whom the guards perceived as troublemakers.

> They used to have a large wooden block (in the paint shop, where most of the corporal punishment took place) which we were bent over and tied face downward after first being stripped naked. Then a large towel was soaked in salt water and spread on our backs from the shoulders to the knees. Then the man who was to do the whipping took a large strap about a quarter of an inch thick by four inches and about two feet long. The strap had a lot of little round holes punched through it. Every time that whip came down on our body the skin would come up through these little holes in the strap and after 25 or 30 times of this, little blisters would form and then would burst, and right there and then hell began. . . . I used to get this racket regularly, and when I was too ill to be given this sort of medicine, they used to take a smaller strap and beat me on the palms of my hands.

Panzram got back at his tormentors by setting a fire that destroyed the industrial building, laundry, tailor shop, and a few other buildings. No one knew who the culprit was until he confessed to the deed years later.

He was released in 1905 after satisfying his keepers that he had been "redeemed," but Panzram made his opinion of his "redemption" quite clear. "I was reformed all right. I had been taught by Christians how to be a hypocrite, and I had learned more about stealing, lying, hating, burning, and killing. I had learned that a boy's penis could be used for something besides to urinate with and that a rectum could be used for other purposes. . . ."[13]

Adelard, whose response to the religious tyranny and strict structure he perceived at Creighton had been anything but submissive, rebelled at being forced to wear a uniform and fall into line. He was openly confrontational and was punished accordingly. No thoughts of penance crossed his mind the entire time he spent at Red Wing; when he wasn't matching wits with his warders, he was plotting escape.

His opportunity came one night in 1909, soon after his admission to the facility. Although neither Red Wing records nor Cunin–Gobeil family stories contain all relevant details, Adelard escaped from the facility and hurried off into the dead of night. The authorities went through the usual routine of checking his parents' and other relatives' houses (Cunin family folklore describes the sudden and frequent late-night visits to Jules's residence by police officers and Red Wing officials looking for the fugitive) and sending his description to police departments in any city or town he might conceivably have gone to. But it was all in vain; he was never recaptured.

Adelard Cunin disappeared from the public record for good. The name and persona that replaced him became bigger than he had ever been.

Jules Cunin moved his family out of St. Paul at the end of 1910 to take a job in Winnipeg, Manitoba. The city was experiencing a building boom at the time, resulting in a demand for skilled labor, particularly in the mason trade. Diana Cunin, eager to reside among other French Canadians, was overjoyed when the family set up house in nearby St. Boniface. Josephine Cunin, the eldest daughter, eventually married a Winnipeg resident and settled there permanently.[14]

Adelard did not go with his family to Canada; after his escape from the state training school, his public association with the Cunin name ended. When his siblings married and had children, many of the latter never knew that they had an Uncle Adelard. Those who did had their inquiries met with vague responses that led to more confusion instead of enlightenment.

"It was a family secret talked in hush-hush—about Mom's brother Adelard," Laurette Cunin's daughter Carol would remember. Another family member, Jeanne Gobeil, asked her father about the mystery relative, only to be told, "Some skeletons are better left alone." It was not until he was in his nineties that her father, commenting on an old picture of Adelard, said, "Doesn't that kid look like a crook?"[15]

Diana Cunin, whose love for her wayward son never faltered, did remain in touch via letter. Laurette, who had been just five years old when Adelard left the family fold, would vividly recall Diana's insistence on never leaving the house on Mondays before the morning mail had arrived. "Mom guessed that she was waiting for a letter from Adelard, " Carol Horan said.

After slipping away from Red Wing, Adelard did not remain in Minnesota. He crossed the state line into Illinois and made his way to Chicago. With his outgoing personality and refusal to back down no matter how challenging or dire a situation, Cunin had no trouble making friends in his new home. The trouble was that they had police records that made his Red Wing stay seem like a long weekend in comparison.

In September 1910 Adelard joined a gang of thieves who specialized in looting the warehouses that lined the Chicago River and disposing of the merchandise through local fences.[16] Because pilfering was such a long-standing and prevalent problem, and the perpetrators were as ferocious as dock rats when cornered, building owners and managers armed their night watchmen with pistols as well as the standard-issue clubs. This precaution was Adelard's undoing: when the watchman of a warehouse he and his comrades had broken into caught them in the act, the man opened fire on them. Everyone escaped except Cunin, who took a bullet in the back, near the shoulder joint.[17]

When the police arrived, he would only tell them that his name was George Miller, a subterfuge to avoid being recognized as an escaped convict from Minnesota and returned to Red Wing. After receiving treatment for his injury at the hospital of the Bridewell correctional facility, the defiant but unconnected nineteen-year-old received a sentence of one to twenty years in Joliet Prison.

Like St. Paul, Chicago had a nationwide reputation for being a city where a criminal could buy his way out of jail time, but Adelard's lack of dispensable cash or political connections barred him from such privileges. His arrest and conviction did not even make the daily papers; Chicago found the garment worker's strike at the Hart, Schaffner, and Marx clothing manufacturers, in which 40,000 striking employees paralyzed garment production in the city, or Blanche Scott's newly won honor as the first American woman to fly an airplane solo, much more newsworthy than the incarceration of one more felon.

On September 26 Cunin, alias Miller, his arm still in a sling, joined a crew of other convicted felons on a train bound for Joliet. While armed guards stood over them, they silently watched Chicago recede into the distance. Those with brief sentences knew that they would be returning shortly; others, like Cunin/Miller, who could potentially serve twenty years, knew that it all depended on how they did their time.

Joliet Prison had been constructed in the late 1850s to help cope with the overcrowding situation at Alton State Prison. In May 1858 Joliet received its first fifty-three inmates, and Alton closed two years later, in 1860, making the new facility the sole destination for Illinois prisoners whose sentences and crimes were too severe for incarceration in local jails. By December 1872 Joliet was the largest penitentiary in the United States, with an inmate population of over 1,200. It was also a cheap source of labor for outside interests; because the state of Illinois did not want to be directly involved in prison management, Alton and later Joliet were leased to the highest bidder, who would run the institution as he saw fit and employ the inmates as a labor force.

This practice of using prisoners as bought employees continued even after 1867, when the state began appointing a three-man team of prison commissioners to oversee operations, although the highest bidder now obtained only the labor and was required to furnish all necessary equipment and raw materials. The entire system was finally abolished in 1886, when protest from the growing number of organized labor unions made the existence of cheap inmate labor a political liability.[18]

S. W. Wetmore, in an 1892 study titled *Behind the Bars at Joliet: A Peep at a Prison, Its History and Its Mysteries*, described the prison layout and system, which had changed very little by the time Adelard Cunin/George Miller, convict No. 1838, arrived to serve his sentence. He wrote:

A front view of the prison is quite imposing, the main or center building is the warden's house, which contains the offices, the guard hall,
commissioners' rooms, dining rooms, and officers' sleeping-rooms, the
whole occupying four stories, the fifth or top story being utilized as a
female prison. On either side of the warden's house extend the great
cell-house wings, each three hundred feet long, giving the prison a
frontage toward the south of nearly 1,000 feet. The cell-houses contain 900 cells, with a capacity of 1,800 convicts. Once when the
prison became over-crowded there were 1,900 prisoners confined
here, but the erection of a new prison at Chester, in 1878, relieved
this condition of affairs, and now the average prison population
remains about 1,500.

The exterior of the prison impresses the visitor, and at first sight suggests one of these castles of the olden time, those romantic structures
that withstood the ancient archers and warring elements for ages. The
battlemented walls, upon which blue-coated men with Winchester rifles
under their arms patrolling the platforms that surround the rugged but
ornamental towers help to make up the romantic picture which is finally
dispelled when the eyes rest upon the iron-barred windows, proclaiming that it is a prison.

The cells are arranged on corridors, fifty on a tier, and each block of
cells stands in the center of the cell-house with a passage-way clear
around, twenty-five feet wide. The cells are made solidly of stone and
iron, not a particle of woodwork being used in their structure. They are,
therefore, perfectly fire-proof, and it is almost an impossibility for an
inmate to cut his way out of them. Each cell is eight feet deep, four and
one-half feet wide, seven feet high, and is arranged to hold two men. A
double iron bunk—one bed above the other—stands at one side of the
cell. The beds are provided with husk mattresses, straw pillows, sheets,
and heavy woolen blankets.

There is nothing luxurious about the furnishings of a cell. A shelf at
the rear end contains a few books and papers, bottle of vinegar, small tin
boxes containing salt and pepper (for all meals are eaten in the cells), a
couple of small stools, a bit of a mirror on the wall, and down in one
corner near the iron-barred door stands a granite-ware wide-mouthed
crock for holding drinking water.

Under the bed is a couple of small wooden wash-buckets; this list of
articles constitute the only furniture; excepting that each cell is brilliantly lighted with an incandescent electric lamp which burns until
nine o'clock every night.

Joliet records indicate that Adelard was put to work in the quarry upon arrival
and initial assessment, but when his shoulder injury made heavy labor impossible,
his work detail was changed to light cleaning and patient-care chores in the prison
hospital. He did his time without any negative notations going into his record, and

in August 1911, after he'd served the minimum eleven months required for parole eligibility, he appeared before the state board of pardon and parole.

Although prisoner advocacy groups had taken the issue all the way to the U.S. Supreme Court, Illinois law required all state prisoners to receive an offer of employment before they could obtain parole, regardless of their eligibility due to good behavior or minimum amount of time served. Cunin's first parole hearing did not end in his release, but whether he was rejected by a board decision or unable to obtain a job to satisfy the condition for release is not known. The latter is certainly possible: a July 1910 article in the *Chicago Tribune* pointed out that in July 1910, only a job offer stood between 367 anxious convicts and freedom:

> Forty-three prisoners whose liberation had been decreed by the state board of paroles last February... continued to peer through the window bars upon the pond with its white pond lilies, upon the flowers, and the grass, and the trees. They were entitled to walk out, as twelve of their fellow convicts had done on Thursday . . . except for one obstacle: there was no employment awaiting them and therefore they must tarry as guests of Warden E. J. Murphy until relatives, friends, or charitable organizations came to their relief."[19]

Adelard served another eleven months without being subjected to any disciplinary proceedings, and on June 18, 1912, he was paroled into the custody of a Bloomington, Illinois, businessman.[20]

Although required to take employment in Bloomington at the man's factory, Adelard had no intention of staying in the small town any longer than legally required. His intention was to return to Chicago. He had only been there less than a year before that fateful arrest, but that was long enough to become intoxicated with the possibilities presented by the Windy City, poet Carl Sandburg's City of Big Shoulders. Chicago gave no quarter and asked none—and neither did he.

2

"THIS MIRACLE OF PARADOX AND CONGRUITY"

Hog Butcher for the World
Tool Maker, Stacker of Wheat
Player with Railroads and the Nation's Freight Handler
Stormy, husky, brawling
City of the Big Shoulders.

They tell me you are wicked and I believe them
For I have seen your painted women under the gas lamps
Luring the farm boys.
And they tell me you are crooked and I answer:
Yes, it is true, I have seen the gunman kill and go free to kill
again.

— Carl Sandburg, "City of Big Shoulders"

C HICAGO IN 1912 WAS A city that could review its eighty-plus years of existence and progress with a justified sense of pride. What had started out as a collection of cabins and low wooden commercial buildings mired in the boggy soil lining Lake Michigan was now a thriving midwestern metropolis of two million residents. The people proved themselves to be as adaptable and hardy as the city; despite being hit with such staggering disasters as the Fort Dearborn Massacre of 1812, the 1854 cholera epidemic, and the Great Chicago Fire of 1871, they managed not only to survive but also to thrive. Only New York surpassed Chicago in population size and commercial standing.

When George W. Steevens, a young English journalist, traveled to the United States in 1896 to cover that year's presidential campaign for the *London Daily Mail*, he stopped over briefly in Chicago. The noisy, aggressive, and unrepentant atmosphere of the city left him in awe. He wrote:

> Chicago! Chicago, queen and guttersnipe of cities, cynosure and cesspool of the world! Not if I had a hundred tongues, every one shouting a different language in a different key, could I do justice to her splendid chaos. The most beautiful and the most squalid, girdled with a twofold zone of parks and slums; where the keen air from lake and prairie is ever in the nostrils, and the stench of foul smoke is never out of the throat; the great port a thousand miles from the sea; the great mart which gathers up with one hand the corn and cattle of the West and deals out with the other the merchandise of the East; widely and generously planned with streets of twenty miles, where it is not safe to walk at night; where women ride straddlewise, and millionaires dine at mid-day on the Sabbath; the chosen seat of public spirit and municipal boodle, of cut-throat commerce and munificent patronage of art; the most American of American cities, and yet the most mongrel. . . . Where in all the world can words be found for this miracle of paradox and incongruity?"[1]

Steevens's double-edged admiration was brought on by the energy and chaos of a city that had become so much in a short amount of time. Barely seventy years before, the land that now contained miles of residential streets and vibrant shopping boulevards had been a howling wilderness. Elderly residents making their way past the elegant boutiques and packed tea rooms lining Michigan Avenue could remember a time when they tramped through long grass while following the same route, eyeing blanket-swaddled Indians instead of Gold Coast matrons swathed in mink. The same men and women, observing the noisy Stockyards district and the factories that flanked the river's edge like sooty brick fortresses, recalled the legions of Indian camps and prairie schooners that once occupied that space.

It was a success that would never have been predicted for Chicago during its early years. When the first white settlers arrived, the land, particularly in the sections flanking the Chicago River, was wet and marshy. The area that would one day contain the Loop, Chicago's business and financial core, was barely one inch above the level of the lake. The fetid air acquired added density from the thick bushes of skunk cabbage that lined the riverbanks. The local Indian tribes called the place "Chickagou," meaning "bad smell." Historian Herbert Asbury, observing how an alteration of the word became the future settlement's name, called it, "a symbolism which is still kept alive by the politicians and the stockyards."[2]

Two early settlements were built before 1800, one at the junction of the Chicago River's north and south branches and the other four miles south. The former prevailed and secured its position as site of the new town when Fort Dearborn was erected in the vicinity in 1803. The local commerce received a needed kickstart when John Kinzie, a silversmith and Indian trader, arrived. He had run a successful trading business in Detroit and other Michigan towns and used both his network of merchant contacts and rapport with the local Indians to breathe life into the young settlement's economy.

Kinzie, who would go down in history as the "Father of Chicago," was a hard man in business, persisting in owning slaves even though the Northwest Ordinance forbade it. When one of his human chattels ran away, Kinzie pursued him, and did not relent until the escapee pleaded his case in a New Orleans court, which reprimanded the ex-master and upheld the ordinance.[3]

Chicago received its town charter in 1833, when it was still little more than a hamlet even by that era's standards, and by 1837 the population had expanded to just over 4,000. A large enough readership existed for two city newspapers: John Calhoun's *Democrat* and T. O. Davis's *American*, the latter of which published the following unusual announcement in its August 8, 1835 edition:

NOTICE

My wife, Mary Bumley, left my house and bed on Saturday, 8th instant, without any just cause, and is supposed to have went away with another Hoosier, who probably knew her better than I did. They will be handsomely rewarded for keeping her forever.

— Jacob Reichter[4]

European immigration, initially a trickle into Chicago's mostly native-born population, became a wave during the 1850s, when the Irish, fleeing famine and persecution in their homeland, began arriving and settling in the near North Side. The earliest immigrants found work as laborers; years would pass before they found their niche in city politics and the police force. Their communities grew to envelop sections of the South and West Sides, but their greatest influence was felt between Kinzie and Erie streets, and their rowdies made the Market Street vicinity a place for respectable citizens to avoid. This particular area was known alternately as Kilgubbin or the Patch. So synonymous was it for anti-social behavior that any woman considered "a little loud" was commonly referred to as "coming from the Patch."

The Germans supplied the next infusion of farmers and small-scale entrepreneurs. They opened at least three of Chicago's earliest breweries and preferred the wide-open spaces to the crowded conditions along the waterfront. They lived in farms and cottages east of Clark and north of Chicago Avenue, and those who did

27

choose to reside in the downtown vicinity tended to occupy small houses along Clark, La Salle, and Wells streets. A focal point of the German community's social life was the German Theater at Wells and Indiana streets, where a musical society held Chicago's earliest live musical performances.

Chicago acquired a large Swedish population when Scandinavian immigrants began arriving in the city in 1846. Their poverty was so pronounced that it took at least a generation for them to find and maintain a foothold in Chicago's commercial life. In 1855, Swedish and Norwegian slum dwellers, suffering from cold and hunger, cost the city $6,000 in relief money, and at least 100 of them received a pauper's burial at public expense. As their numbers grew, the districts where they took up residence harbored not only their shops, restaurants, and Swedish-language signs but also names that broadcast the local nationality. The area bounded by Indiana, Erie, Orleans, and the Chicago River was locally referred to as Swede Town, and one large migration to Chicago Avenue earned the street the nickname "Swede Broadway."

A growing population made public improvements necessary. For years, the streets had been unpaved, and rainy season turned every thoroughfare into a dark, noxious quagmire. It was not unusual to see elegantly dressed women standing anxiously on street corners, where the sidewalk boards kept their shoes and ruffled hems out of the mess, waiting for a wagon to come along merely to get them across the street. Horses and wagon wheels becoming mired in the glue-like mud was a daily occurrence during wet weather. In some areas the streets turned to quicksand. One story (albeit a probably apocryphal one) describes a man walking along the more stable surface of a sidewalk and spotting another man in the mud up to his waist. When asked if he needed help moving, the seemingly trapped pedestrian replied, "No, thanks, I have a horse beneath me."

Rather than gradually move the city westward onto firmer ground, the citizens of Chicago opted to find a way around the problem. The solution that they eventually adopted was to raise the streets several feet by building a false surface and paving it with planks and stone. Elevation of the street levels necessitated the raising of the buildings as well, a feat accomplished by digging under the foundations, positioning iron jacks in strategic locations, and employing fifty-man teams to turn the jacks until each building had been raised to the new street level, at which time strong supporting pillars were built underneath. As newer, more attractive houses and buildings were constructed in the business district and fashionable residential areas along Lake Street, older residences were torn down entirely or at least moved to a more convenient location. Moving a house required its placement on planks and rollers while a horse team pulled it along.

Gustaf Unonius, a Swedish settler, visited Chicago in 1857 and witnessed the surreal sight of city structures being wheeled from one location to another. He wrote:

> Often the entire width of the street is blocked by a house that is out for
> a walk and extends from one side of the street to the other. . . . Moving
> the house does not necessarily mean that those living in it must move
> out. I have seen houses on the move while the families living in them
> continued with their daily tasks, keeping fire in the stove, eating their
> meals as usual, and at night quietly going to bed to wake up the next
> morning on some other street. Once a house passed my window while
> a tavern business housed in it went on as usual.

During this awkward phase few if any Chicago sidewalks were perfectly level. Walking along a downtown thoroughfare entailed climbing and descending wooden steps, their steepness depending on how far along the street-raising had progressed. Pedestrians took care not to fall off of these makeshift boardwalks into the muddy street below. Many an unsuspecting drunk staggered out of his favorite watering hole, only to stumble off of the planking and break his legs or neck. Once the entire project was completed, the newly elevated city was left with a series of dank tunnels that twisted and turned beneath the paved surface, offering a foul but effective hideout for anyone on the run from the law.

The Chicago-area land boom of the early to mid-1830s brought speculators and pioneers from the South and East pouring into the region. Among the side effects of a rapidly growing settlement was an influx of criminals among the respectable immigrants, and Chicago was no exception. The earliest miscreants were gamblers and prostitutes, lured by the daily inflow of men who were either single or had left their wives elsewhere while they investigated their prospects in the new land. Despite their presence, Chicago was remarkably quiet and orderly in the earliest years of its incorporation, and there were few violent crimes of note.

The first thief on record was a man who stole money from a fellow boarder at the Wolf Tavern. When the arresting officer searched him, the missing cash was found wadded in the toe of his sock. A brief trial held in a carpenter's shop fitted out for the occasion found him guilty of theft, but he was permitted to go free on bail pending an appeal. The man expressed his gratitude for the postponement of imprisonment by jumping bail and disappearing forever. It was, Herbert Asbury wrote, "a precedent which has been followed more or less regularly in Chicago ever since."[5]

The earliest gangs arrived in the city soon after the gamblers and daughters of joy. Citizens who were not too choosy about the type of business they were to go into realized a fortune by opening saloons to deal with this newest population segment. Soon almost every street corner in the downtown and its immediate environs hosted a saloon, groggery, or "liquor grocery," an establishment that sold more booze in the back room than cabbages over the counter. Temperance advocate John Hawkins, visiting from Washington, took stock of the phenomenon and declared that during all of his travels from state to state, he "had never seen a town which seemed so like the universal grog-shop as did Chicago." Everyone had an opinion as to whether the criminal and vagrant begat the saloon or vice versa, but the end result was an unsavory reputation for Chicago that traveled well beyond the city and even state boundaries. One daily in Jackson, Missouri, gave voice to the general perception when it noted in 1839, "the population of Chicago is said to be principally composed of dogs and loafers."

Said dogs and loafers must have had exceptional talent and ambition, for by the mid-1850s, Chicago boasted architectural, commercial, and cultural advancements on a par with anything found on the older and more established cities, such as New York. Thirty railroad lines terminated in or ran through the city, importing and exporting both goods and passengers. The waterfront was the site of a busy shipping traffic. There were elegant theaters, ballrooms, galleries, and ten first-class hotels as well as decent accommodations for more economical travelers. In twenty short years Chicago had evolved from Slab Town—a name stemming from its earliest, primitive houses with "slabbed" exteriors—to a Midwestern Gateway of 100,000 inhabitants.

But if Chicago became more robust and consequential in the scheme of things, so did the criminals. The underworld had been enjoying a growth and strengthening of its own.

The liquor groceries and tumbledown assignation houses of the early years were no more; by the 1850s they were as sentimental a notion as grandmother's fashions. Although the back-room dice games and alley brothels continued to exist, Chicago had become big enough to play host to gambling parlors and gilded houses of prostitution that encouraged a wealthier clientele. Entire regions, such as the Sands near the lakefront and Conley's Patch, were given over almost exclusively to vice. One Sands inmate, Margaret McGuiness, acquired a dubious fame for being continually drunk for five years and never having her clothes on for three. She died in 1857 of what the coroner delicately called "intemperance." He might well have included exhaustion; McGuiness rarely saw fewer than ten clients a night, sometimes as many as forty.[6]

Low-class brothels dotted Wells Street, giving it such a vile reputation that the thoroughfare was considered a disgrace to the memory of its namesake, Indian fighter Captain Billy Wells. The better class of johns and thrill seekers found more expensive and sophisticated female companionship at Mother Herrick's Prairie Queen, where they could have a cultured companion for fifty cents, unless they were game enough to participate in one of the weekly bare-knuckle prizefights for the chance of winning $2 and a night with the girl of their choice.

The fledgling underworld had a determined foe in Mayor John Wentworth, whose six-foot, seven-inch stature earned him the nickname "Long John." Wentworth targeted the miserable Sands district for eradication and carried out the task one April afternoon in 1857, when most of the area's menfolk were at the remote site of a highly anticipated dogfight. He personally led a group of law enforcement officers into the Sands and watched while the tumbledown shanties were harnessed to horse teams and hauled down one by one. A fire that broke out after he and his followers left completed the demolition job. But rather than leave Chicago, the noxious former Sands residents merely scattered throughout the city and reestablished themselves, contaminating areas where they might otherwise never have gone and creating a greater problem than they had ever posed when gathered in a small, easily avoided district.

Wentworth, ironically, contributed to the growth of Chicago's criminal element when he treated the police force like his personal security team. He hired and fired at will, in the process upsetting veteran officers and enough influential citizens to have the Illinois legislature remove control of the department from the mayor's office and invest it instead in a board of police commissioners. Wentworth responded to the perceived slight by firing the entire force, and while the newly appointed board fought to reorganize it, Chicago residents were responsible for their own lives and property.

The replacement force had a few capable officers but not enough to compensate for the inefficiency and outright corruption of the others. Chicago acquired yet another negative reputation, this one based on its lax policing system. Gangsters, gamblers, and thugs from less tolerant cities flooded in, liked what they found, and stayed. "We are beset on every side by a gang of villains!!" lamented the *Chicago Journal.*

Like any thriving community, the underworld established its own city hall in the form of Roger Plant's domain at Wells and Monroe streets, a rambling architectural curiosity that extended halfway down both streets. Plant, a five-foot-tall English immigrant, had a ferocity that more than made up for his tiny stature. Inside his kingdom, drunkenness, debauchery, and even murder took place around the clock. His wife ran a busy brothel on the premises, where customers were first enticed inside by the gilt letters WHY NOT on the outside curtains, and then stood a fifty-fifty chance of being robbed instead of serviced sexually. There were at least three saloons serving bad liquor to even worse customers. It was rumored that the building's ground floor had multiple secret entrances leading to a series of subterranean tunnels created by the earlier elevation of the city streets. The police, even those not paid by Plant to do so, gave the place a wide berth, recognizing the futility of doing anything else. One veteran officer explained, "Trying to raid those barracks would be like trying to arrest an elephant!"

Chicago's foremost criminals of the 1850s and '60s took up headquarters there: Mary Hodges, shoplifting queen; Mary Brennan, who ran a pickpocket school for girls; and Speckled Jimmy Calwell, burglar and safecracker who achieved notoriety after a failed attempt to blow up the Blue Island horsecar line. Although Roger himself quit the business after he had made a small fortune and retired to semi-respectability, at least three of his fifteen children kept the Plant name in the police blotters. His son, Roger Jr., ran a cutthroat saloon, and daughters Kitty and Daisy operated brothels well known for their depravity. Kitty's place was famous for its frequent circuses involving both women and animals.

The gamblers scored fortunes during the Civil War, when Chicago was teeming with soldiers on leave who had payroll money in hand and were eager to spend it on a good time. The most notorious gaming districts were Hairtrigger Block, a short stretch of Randolph Street between Clark and State, and Gambler's Row, which ran along Clark from Randolph to Monroe. The professional gambler was a conspicuous sight; impressionable youths, much to the dismay of their parents, copied the flashy fashions of Cap Hyman, George Trussell, and the Hankins Brothers and tagged eagerly along at their heels, listening in rapt admiration to their sucker-fleecing stories. When Cap Hyman wed brothelkeeper Annie Stafford, the happy occasion was attended not only by local color but also delegates from nearby cities like St. Louis and Detroit.

While most did well financially because of their knack for ruining the finances of others, some could be worse with money than their most pathetic customer. Theodore Cameron made a million dollars in eight years of operation, but upon his departure from Chicago, a scant 500 remained. A conspicuous segment of the gaming-house population was the gambler/operator who was both addicted and stupid; one Johnny Lawlor reacted to loss by screaming, butting his head against the wall, and tearing at his ears.

The Great Chicago Fire of October 1871—allegedly started when a cow belonging to the mother of a future gambling kingpin, "Big Jim" O'Leary, kicked over a lantern in a barn—leveled most of the city. A *Tribune* editorial that appeared the previous September had warned that for such a rapidly growing and voluminous city, Chicago's buildings included an alarming number of cheap wooden shanties, and even many of the better buildings (hotels, banks, theaters, and office blocks) were only one brick thick—portions of their facades falling into the street were a far from uncommon occurrence. DeKoven Street, where the fire originated on October 8, was located in a neighborhood constructed almost entirely of wood. Once it was underway, very few buildings could defy the raging inferno.

By the time October 10 rolled around, and the flames had been drowned by a welcome influx of rain, an estimated 300 citizens were dead and 100,000 were left homeless, a tract of land that encompassed four miles in length and two-thirds of a mile in width was a burned and barren wasteland, and almost $200 million worth of property was no more. It was a calamity that would have shattered a less resilient population, but Chicagoans, after the shock had passed, set about rebuilding their city from the ashes and making its reincarnation more prosperous and sturdy than the previous.

The underworld followed suit. The post-1871 gambling and vice districts were more organized and powerful than their predecessors. Even the judges and policemen not actively on the take from the gaming-house and resort keepers adopted a resigned attitude toward the permanence of the illegal interests. In August 1896 renowned strong-arm woman Jennie Clark appeared before Superior Court Judge James Groggin to answer charges of robbing an old man of $5. Judge Groggin ruled that any man who went into the Levee district deserved to be robbed, and that the robbers should not be punished. Clark, overjoyed, went free.

The gamblers enjoyed increased immunity when Harvey Colvin won the fall 1873 mayoral election. His predecessor, Joseph Medill, had cracked down hard on the gaming community, closing dice and betting parlors and driving key players out of Chicago. Things changed under Mayor Colvin for one key reason: the new incumbent had been backed by Michael Cassius "Big Mike" MacDonald, who also happened to be a close personal friend.

MacDonald achieved power and wealth through his numerous gambling concessions, although he had his hand in many activities. During the Civil War he organized a gang of bounty jumpers (men who joined the army to obtain the $300 enlistment bonus, deserted, and then re-enlisted under another name) and owned a string of saloons. After Colvin took office, anyone who wished to run a gambling den or swindle citizens out of their money via other means had to "see Mike" for the approval necessary for success. MacDonald endorsed any scheme or business that put a percentage in his own pocket, except for one: prostitution. He refused to deal with pimps. One MacDonald henchman explained with pride, "A crook has to be decent to work with Mike."

MacDonald's resort, the Store, occupied the northwest corner of Clark and Monroe streets, and all floors except the top two, which contained a boardinghouse for Store employees, were given over exclusively to a saloon and gambling facilities. When Harry Lawrence, one of MacDonald's partners, worried that there might not be enough hardcore gamblers to keep such a gamer's paradise open, MacDonald assured him that there was "a sucker born every minute." The quote became a universal one, attributed at times to P. T. Barnum.

Not even the arrival of a reform mayor in 1887 could tarnish MacDonald's Midas touch. The gambling kingpin merely entrusted his illegal businesses to faithful henchmen and used his fortune to purchase a newspaper (the *Chicago Globe*) and acquire a quarry that enabled him to turn a profit selling gravel and stone to the city. Once Mayor John Roche was voted out, reform having worn out its welcome, "Big Mike" shrugged off the shackles of respectability and came back stronger than ever. He formed a citywide crime syndicate that collected a tribute of up to 65 percent from any gambler or con man who wanted to operate in Chicago. Those who paid were guaranteed protection from police interference; those who didn't soon left the city for health reasons.

MacDonald ruled Chicago with an iron fist until his death in 1907. He selected the men who went into office and gave them orders once they were firmly in place. He might have gone on for much longer, given his steel will and youthful vigor, had it not been for a woman—his second wife, to be exact. More than thirty years his junior and a former playmate of his children, she'd married him after his first wife ran away to France with a defrocked priest. In February 1907 MacDonald learned to his shock that she'd been cheating on him with a much younger man—a man she shot to death for giving her a taste of her own adulterous medicine. MacDonald collapsed at the news and attending scandal but managed to collect himself long enough to place a sizeable defense fund in the hands of his wife's attorneys. She was acquitted of murder, a verdict bought by Big Mike's dollars and posthumous influence.

When the World's Fair of 1893 was still in the planning stages, Mayor Carter Harrison II supposedly went to MacDonald for his approval on the project first. The gambling boss gave the fair his full backing, delighted at the thought of the swarms of visiting suckers who would patronize his resorts. During the fair's run Chicago became even more open and laissez-faire than anyone thought possible. Herbert Asbury wrote:

> (Carter) Harrison promised during his campaign that he would give the World's Fair crowd a wide-open town, and he more than kept his word. . . . Chicago was the most wide-open town that America had ever seen, or probably ever will see. . . . Everyone in Chicago capable of reasoning knew that virtually all departments of the city government reeked of graft and bribery, but nobody felt called upon to do anything about it.

One of the earliest chroniclers of Chicago's darker side was English writer William T. Stead, who visited the World's Fair and was so appalled by the open vice and visible signs of government corruption that he stayed to gather material for the eventual work *If Christ Came to Chicago*. He wrote scathingly of police officials and beat cops collecting anywhere from $15 to $100 a week from brothels (many of which provided rental income to some of Chicago's outwardly respectable citizens); deplored the entire city blocks given over to saloons and vice dens in certain areas such as the Levee (he even published names and addresses of the brothels, probably one of the key reasons why the book sold like hotcakes); and went into detail about Mayor Harrison's mutually profitable arrangements with gambling bigwigs like Mike MacDonald. Stead made city hall the object of public scorn when he quoted a corporation lawyer as bragging, "There are sixty-eight aldermen in the city council, and sixty-six of them can be bought; this I know because I have bought them myself."[7]

Stead's findings led to public indignation and the formation of a Civic Federation of Chicago, whose aim was to expose and combat the vice and gaming interests as well as political corruption. But its bark was worse than its bite; Chicagoans may not have liked their city being publicly exposed as a grafter's paradise, but neither did they relish sporting the shackles of reform. Even Mayor John Hopkins, a straight-laced individual elected on a reform ticket, was found to be actively permitting a few gaming houses to run. When the aghast civic federation demanded an explanation, Hopkins replied tensely, "It is surprising how many reputable business men want gambling to continue. I have had representatives of prominent wholesale houses tell me that they have great difficulty in entertaining their country customers because they cannot take them around to gambling houses."

Gambling had become such a competitive business by the time of Adelard Cunin's arrival in Chicago that a full-blown gamblers war erupted. The primary combatants were Mont Tennes, the racing wire czar from the North Side, and some South and West Side competitors who resented his domination over the city's gaming industry. Tennes had exclusive rights to the Payne Telegraph Service and collected $50 to $100 a day from Chicago betting parlor owners who required Payne's racing wire results. In June 1907 the bombs started flying back and forth between both sides; Tennes's house was bombed, as were the abodes of Big Jim O'Leary and John O'Malley, both Tennes opponents.

The city air was rarely without the faint scent of discharged explosives until late 1908, when First Ward Alderman Michael Kenna, who had allegedly been paid by gamblers anxious to see the fighting end, orchestrated a truce. Tennes, his aggressive energies no longer being needed for self-preservation, organized his own news wire service, the General News Bureau, which soon put his old benefactor, Payne, out of business.

Prostitution, which Mike MacDonald and his brethren scorned as beneath them, bred a society and culture all its own. Besides the low-level dens, there were also the elegant brothels decorated with brass door signs and red window shades, such as Lou Harper's place at 219 Monroe Street. Harper frowned on the raucousness and vulgarity prevalent in most Chicago brothels during the Civil War and insisted that her girls wear evening gowns and conduct themselves as ladies. Her business thrived because she appealed to the carriage trade of pleasure-seeking males, those with money to spend on beautiful women again and again.

At the other end of the scale was Kate Hawkins's Ramrod Hall, a rambling wooden structure in which men were robbed, slugged, or worse. Scarcely a night went by without the police being called to quell a disturbance or investigate an assault or theft. Ramrod Hall surpassed its own reputation one night when one of Hawkins's girls announced she was leaving the business in order to marry. The furious madam attempted to lock the young woman in her room, but the latter's friends, who despised their employer, rushed to her aid, as did a few pimps and customers. A violent battle ensued in which fists, bottles, and bricks flew like wedding confetti. When the police arrived, they had a relatively easy job: lift the unconscious fighters off the floor and carry them into the patrol wagon. Those not unconscious or injured simply fled.

After the 1871 fire, about a dozen vice districts sprang up, all-man's-lands with such unsavory names as Coon Hollow, Satan's Mile, and Hell's Half-Acre. It was said that in the latter place, every building housed a saloon or bordello. Custom

House Place (now Federal Street) was a garish mix of Chicago's lowest dives and most elegant brothels. A visitor to the World's Fair in 1893 passed through the district and commented, "In these houses could be found every low and demoralizing phase of life that the human mind could think of. Many of these women were even lower than brutes."

It was the Levee that was to achieve nationwide notoriety. The original Levee was part of the vice district known as Satan's Mile and occupied a stretch of State Street between Van Buren and Twenty-second streets. Over time the boundaries flexed and extended, and by 1909 its outer limits were Twenty-second and Eighteenth streets on the north and south and Clark and Wabash on the east and west.

Commercial sex existed to suit every pocketbook. Bed Bug Row, at Nineteenth Street and Armour Avenue, was a dismal collection of wooden shacks where black prostitutes serviced clients at twenty-five cents a session. The Bucket of Blood and the California charged $1 for a woman, but the method of assignation was scarcely classier: girls in transparent gowns would parade before men seated on benches, waiting selection. At Black May's, patrons could watch a circus that was as obscene as they were willing to pay for. Customers of means found companionship among the better-class parlor houses, such as French Emma's, Vic Shaw's, or the Casino. For Chicago's wealthy, there was the Everleigh Club.

So famous had this latter pleasure palace become since its February 1900 opening that the German Kaiser's brother, Prince Henry, asked to see it during a 1902 visit to Chicago. The Everleigh Club was the opulent brainchild of two Kentucky sisters, Minna and Ada Lester, who had changed their surname to the more genteel-sounding Everleigh as a tribute to how their Southern belle grandmother used to sign her letters. The old lady would have been horrified to know how her trademark was applied by the granddaughters. After years spent running a successful brothel in Omaha, the girls moved to Chicago and used a $35,000 inheritance to buy Lizzie Allen's old bordello at 2131–3 South Dearborn Street.[8]

The fifty-room mansion radiated elegance and refinement despite its purpose. Exotic plants and marble statues lined the halls, gold spittoons and fountains spraying perfumed water adorned every parlor, and all of the rooms were decorated based on exotic themes: Copper, Moorish, Turkish, Chinese, Egyptian, and Japanese, to name a few. A cordon bleu chef prepared $50 meals served on gold-rimmed china. The girls, handpicked by Minna and Ada for their beauty and genteel mannerisms, greeted visitors to the club wearing jewels and gowns befitting nobility. It was only in the bedroom that the real nature of the client's visit was attended to, and some rooms had a bowl of firecrackers beside the bed, set off at the right moment to intensify the experience.

The Everleigh Club, despite jealous sabotage attempts on the part of other brothel keepers, flourished for ten years. It wasn't until the sisters published a glossy brochure that found its way to an embarrassed Mayor Harrison that they reached a point of public scandal that all of their previous payoffs to local cops and politicians could not protect them from. Rather than fight it or even close long enough for the heat to die down, Ada and Minna retired with their millions, left Chicago, and spent their remaining years in luxurious ease.

By 1912 the vice operators of Chicago had organized themselves into a mutually beneficial trust. The members worked together to regulate necessary payoffs, import girls from other houses and even other cities and states to keep their regular clients entertained with new faces, and thwart the reform measures that civic-minded groups like the Committee of Fifteen attempted to implement. In 1911, when State's Attorney John E. Wayman responded to public pressure and ordered every dive in the Levee closed, the vice trust sent their women into respectable neighborhoods to disturb the peace and seek lodging, boldly hinting that closure of the Levee meant that the social evil could no longer be contained.

The anti-vice campaign was momentarily checked by the counter-offensive, but when it started again, it settled for making the vice district less of a brilliantly lit eyesore. The trust obliged: brothels shut off the red lights and toned down the loud music, making their purpose more difficult to detect from the exterior, and smaller batches of girls were moved to "massage parlors" and discreet call flats. Johnny Torrio, originally from New York but now the greatest mind operating in the Chicago flesh trade, opened roadhouses outside the city limits when motoring became more commonplace.[9]

Reformer Kate Adams visited the Levee after its supposed shuttering and found the vice trust to be as strong and organized as ever. She credited it with ownership of at least 200 "sin parlors" and noted in a report, "The trust collects from each of the houses and pays for arrangements with the police and for political contribution. It regulates competition. . . . The houses are required to patronize certain grocery stores in the immediate vicinity, to take out all their insurance in a company represented by a powerful politician. Three doctors are especially endorsed by the trust. Cab drivers receive a percentage on money spent by customers they bring to a house."

In 1913 Mayor Carter Harrison II created a Morals Squad, which had the authority to investigate and prosecute vice offenses independently of the regular police force. Despite the fanaticism of its leader, a retired major named Funkhouser, the squad caused the vice trust only temporary setbacks. The trust was too well organized and its relationships with the police and politicians too deeply entrenched in the city's administration. Seven years later, when Prohibition descended on the land, the same organizing skill and protective arrangements would be carried over into bootlegging.

In 1910, soon after Adelard Cunin arrived in Chicago for the first time, a magazine article boasted of the city's assets and accomplishments. The writer glowed, "Chicago is noted for the greatness of its financial institutions, for the excellence of its parks and public playgrounds, for its universities, its efficient public school system, and for other educational, artistic, and morally uplifting institutions that give to Chicago an enlightened, a cultured, and a progressive citizenship."

Just as the recently passed Gilded Age had spawned its mighty financiers and social royalty, the criminal element produced its strongest leaders by 1910: Mike MacDonald, Mont Tennes, Jim O'Leary, Levee vice lord "Big Jim" Colosimo, and Alderman Johnny Rogers, who controlled and protected all gambling in his West Side territory from his seat in city hall. Those who did not work for one of these men were smaller potatoes: the footpads, stickup men, and independent operators who did not make enough to warrant the predatory attention of Tennes or O'Leary.

This was also a time when the influx of Italian immigrants into Chicago reached an all-time high. It had started in the 1890s, and by 1910, Chicago had a higher immigrant population than most other major American cities. With few exceptions, these newcomers lived in squalid conditions until they had made enough of a stake to move into better surroundings. They were hardworking and willing to do whatever it took to earn a better place in their new home than they'd been able to attain in their own land. Yet interspersed with the honest working class and the poor was a criminal element that was more likely than not fleeing police detection instead of an economically disadvantaged situation.

The Black Hand was one of the earliest examples of criminal activity that blackened the reputation of the immigrant communities of larger U.S. cities. Although popular lore linked it to organized gangs of Italian thugs, the truth is that the Black Hand consisted of small bands of terrorists who made a living preying on their wealthier compatriots. Whenever an Italian resident showed any signs of affluence, such as the purchase of a building or land, chances were that he or she would soon receive a letter in the mail demanding money. Some notes were stamped with an inky handprint, hence the name that came to be associated with this predatory practice. A victim who ignored the letter or went to the police ran the very real risk of having his or her new asset bombed or a family member kidnapped or killed. Targets usually paid the amount demanded, too frightened or too wary of American law enforcement to do otherwise.[10]

In Chicago the Black Hand activity was concentrated primarily around Oak and Taylor streets, as well as Grand and Wentworth avenues, where the larger Italian communities were located. The corner of Oak and Milton streets, in the heart of Chicago's Little Italy, earned the gruesome moniker of Death Corner after a mysterious assassin and Black Hander known as the Shotgun Man plied his trade there. At least twelve of the thirty-eight violent killings that took place on or near Death Corner between January 1910 and March 1911 were attributed to this stealthy murderer, who was never caught.

The *Chicago Daily News* estimated in May 1915 that the first three months of the year had witnessed the explosion of fifty-five bombs in the Italian areas. "A detective of experience in the Italian quarter," the article stated, "estimates that ten pay tribute to one who is sturdy enough to resist until he is warned by a bomb. Well-informed Italians have never put the year's tribute to the Black Hand at less than half a million dollars."

For the local politicians, a vote was a vote, regardless of the existence of a criminal record. Any strong-arm, thug, or murderer who might have feared prison back home found a market for his talents at election time, when rival political factions hired such muscle to intimidate voters at polling booths, steal ballot boxes, beat up stubborn election officials, and fight gangsters employed by the opposition. The Market Streeters and their juvenile counterparts, the Little Hellions, were an election-day fixture. Because of their widely known association with the reigning politicians, the police rarely interfered when they busted heads, clubbed or knifed rival sluggers, and tossed battered voters into the water troughs that lined the streets.

Newspapers and citizens groups targeted the police force for failure to cope with the gang situation and the rising crime rate in general. By one estimate, six months in 1906 averaged a burglary every three hours and a murder every day. There were honest policemen on the Chicago force, but they were in the minority because of the lax, patronage-ridden hiring methods of the day.

At the request of the City Club, Alexander Piper, a former army officer who later became deputy police commissioner of New York, made a secret study of the workings of the police force. Piper found, among other things, that at least 10 percent of the policemen were either too fat or in such poor shape health-wise to discharge their duties effectively, and at least a hundred men were morally unfit or too intemperate to hold such responsible positions. He observed that the police force as a whole was ill suited to the stemming—let alone stopping—of the underworld's reign of terror in the city.[11]

He might well have suggested that city hall be overhauled as well and transfused with honest men. Alderman Nathan Brewer was credited with the harrowing statement, "There are only three aldermen in the entire sixty-eight who are not able and willing to steal a red-hot stove." William T. Stead wrote, "We shall probably not err on the side of caution if we admit that there are ten Aldermen on the Council who have not sold their votes or received any corrupt consideration for voting away the patrimony of the people."

Harold Ickes, who acted as campaign manager for the (relatively) honest professor Charles Merriam in the 1911 mayoral campaign (which Merriam lost), noted in his autobiography that his years spent among Chicago politicians "helped to sharpen my teeth for Mussolini, Hirohito, and Hitler."[12]

Foremost among Stead's list of fifty-eight confirmed boodlers were Michael "Hinky Dink" Kenna and "Bathhouse John" Coughlin, the colorful and omnipotent aldermen of the First Ward. This influential duo, known as the unofficial Lords of the Levee, gained fortunes when they let it be known that their political power was for hire. Brothels paid them from $25 to $100 weekly for insulation from raids, more if the resort were higher-end, like the Everleigh Club. They charged $1,000 for quashing a pandering indictment, and up to $2,000 to help a white slaver escape punishment for harboring a young woman against her will. Although city hall paid them a minor stipend of $3 per council meeting they attended, their income from special votes amounted to anywhere from $5,000 to $100,000 per vote, depending upon the nature of the matter being put to the council.[13]

Visually, Kenna and Coughlin were at opposite ends of the fashion and personality spectrums. Michael Kenna, nicknamed "Hinky Dink" because his five-foot-tall, birdlike body resembled comic strip character Petey Dink, dressed in somber hues and spoke in soft tones. He was a man of few words, but what he did say was usually carefully thought out beforehand. John Coughlin, on the other hand, was a husky six-footer who decked himself out in bright pinks, lavender overcoats, and a general crazyquilt-style wardrobe that drew snickers from onlookers. Dubbed "Bathhouse John" because he once worked as a rubber in a Turkish bath, he was a liberal handshaker and backslapper who also fancied himself a songwriter and poet. Those who heard his songs wondered if he were crazy or on dope, a rumor that Kenna put to rest by assuring everyone that Coughlin was not insane, just something "they haven't found a name for yet."[14]

As laughable as Coughlin appeared, the denizens of the Levee, which lay within the boundaries of the First Ward, recognized that they needed him for survival and kept their chuckles to themselves. Pimps like James Colosimo, who'd had enough brushes with the law to know that his chances of avoiding prison were dismal without the support of bought immunity, made themselves useful to Kenna and Coughlin by organizing their fellow workers into cohesive units that delivered the votes on election day. The politicians employed the gangsters, who kept the politicians in office, ad infinitum. The snake of corruption was swallowing its tail without apparent distress—quite the opposite.

What Kenna and Coughlin provided to the Levee residents, Mayor William Hale "Big Bill" Thompson offered to the entire city's renegades. Elected mayor in 1915, Thompson was a familiar face to First Ward saloon owners and habitués, having lived in a residential hotel in the old Second Ward (which he later assisted, probably unwittingly, in amalgamating with the First). His family name was a good one in Chicago, being attached to a prosperous real estate firm that his father had founded, but the red-light district welcomed him as a sympathetic spirit when he spent varying amounts of the family fortune on drinks and female companionship.

No one who met Thompson, or for that matter lived through one of his administrations, ever forgot the experience. He was tall, husky, and in appearance and demeanor a product of the Western ranges as opposed to the Chicago social aristocracy. He cut a highly conspicuous figure strolling through the Loop with a gigantic Stetson perched atop his head, and unless he had reason to act otherwise, greeting all comers with a firm handshake and hearty slap on the back. His campaigns were masterpieces of verbal fireworks and platform juggling. Douglas Bukowski, author of *Big Bill Thompson, Chicago, and the Politics of Images*, wrote:

> Thompson . . . learned to use words the way most politicians depended
> on organization. The detail work of politics mostly bored him. Where
> other mayors sought ways to control the city council, Thompson simply
> tried to overwhelm it—and all opposition—through his demagogy."[15]

The "cowboy mayor," as he was called, was born in Boston in 1867 but was taken to Chicago the following year, before Boston's refinement could take hold in his character. William Hale Thompson Sr. invested in Chicago real estate and became wealthy beyond anticipation when the Great Fire of 1871 spared the block he owned on West Madison Street. Being one of the few landlords with property available for rent once the flames had been quenched and the smoke had dissipated, he made massive profits and invested wisely. At the time of his death in 1891, he left an estate valued at $2 million.

Billy, as his friends called the younger Thompson, showed no interest in the Yale or Exeter education that his family's money could acquire for him. Bored in the classroom, he preferred the outdoors and was in his glory when riding along Chicago's streets on horseback, imagining that the skyline was empty of towering buildings and the Loop was a wide-open range. One day, when he was fourteen, he and some friends, also on horseback, charged noisily across the State Street Bridge, pretending that they were overtaking fleeing Indian raiders. The attendants seized them, and although Thompson thumped one of them, the boys ended up arrested and jailed. Their incarceration lasted only until Thompson Sr. heard about it. Not only was Billy sprung at 2 a.m., but it took a joint effort by Mayor Harrison and the chief of police to persuade the real estate baron to abandon his demand to have every officer associated with his son's arrest dismissed.[16]

Displaying an ability to manipulate even at an early age, fifteen-year-old Billy persuaded his father to let him spend the spring to autumn months working on the Western range if he promised to maintain his business school studies in Chicago during the winter. He set off on his cowboy adventure and worked a series of menial jobs (wagon driver, cook's helper). His indulgent father bought a ranch in Nebraska in 1888, and the then-twenty-one-year-old Billy accepted the management position with joy. He made the ranch turn a healthy profit, so not much was said when he spent his off time drinking to excess, riding the range, and getting into the occasional fight, such as the barroom brawl in which he beat three attackers unconscious with a pool cue.[17]

The rural life came to an abrupt end in 1891, when Thompson Sr. died and Billy, responding to his mother's pleas, returned to Chicago to take over the family business. As soon as he could safely pass all responsibility for the day-to-day operations onto the shoulders of his father's longtime partner, Thompson moved on to something more to his liking: he joined the Chicago Athletic Club and became an avid football and water polo player. By 1900 he was coaching football by day and spending his nights wandering the Levee in the company of his boyhood cronies.

One of them, Eugene Pike, with whom he shared bachelor accommodations at the Hotel Metropole, dared him to run for the post of alderman of the Second Ward.[18]

Strange as it sounds, politics, or at least the campaigning side of it, was a prospect that Thompson found appealing. It was an arena in which the strongest and wiliest survived, and the cutthroat competition was not much different than what he'd experienced as a sportsman and coach. In what has to be termed one of the pinnacles of irony, Thompson was nominated by the ward's Republican organization in a meeting at Freiberg's, a dance hall frequented by prostitutes and killers. He was presented to the voting public as a reform candidate and impressed the constituents enough to be elected over the incumbent Charles F. Gunther.[19]

Kenna and Coughlin, the political lords of the Levee, had backed Thompson for reasons that soon became apparent. The vice district had expanded into the Second Ward, beyond their control, and Gunther had opposed a redistricting vote. Thompson was more naïve, and the cagey duo persuaded him to support the ordinance, which in effect left him without a chance at reelection, as his residence was now part of the First Ward, and Kenna and Coughlin were immobile in their tenure.

He must have been embittered by the trick, but the brief time he spent on the city council was long enough for him to appreciate the unadvertised benefits of political office, namely cash "bonuses" and "donations" given in exchange for the return of a revoked liquor license, dismissal of Mann Act violation charges, or casting a vote for a zoning or construction proposal that stood no chance of being passed otherwise. When his term as alderman ended, Thompson jumped at the offer to run for Cook County commissioner on the Republican ticket. He won, once again thanks to his knack of telling audiences exactly what they wanted to hear and convincing them that his interests were indistinguishable from theirs.

In 1915 he ran for mayor on the Republican ticket and gave voters a show that was dazzling in its inconsistency. His Democratic opponent, Robert Sweitzer, was German and a Catholic, two antecedents that Thompson bludgeoned him with during campaign speeches, anti-German sentiments being powerful at the time because of the war being waged overseas. When in front of German audiences, however, he was so ingratiating that his detractors sneered and called him "Kaiser Bill." He blasted the British before Irish voters one night and denounced the Catholic religion in Protestant wards the next. He assured the silk-stocking wards that he would "clean up this city and drive out the crooks," neglecting to mention the fact he'd told saloonkeepers, who ran the places where the crooks hung out, that he planned to oppose the Sunday closing law.

Thompson was especially genial toward black voters, long underestimated by those on the campaign trail. They remembered him as one of the aldermen who supported an ordinance establishing Chicago's first municipal playground in a black district. He played up this accomplishment before them, reminding them, "White people from nearby came over and said they wanted [the playground] in their neighborhood. I said to this, 'I see you have a fine house and yard with fences around them and nice dogs but no children; I'll build a playground for children and not poodle dogs.'"[20] He assured them that police harassment would cease under his administration. "If you want to shoot craps, go ahead and do it. When I'm mayor the police will have something better to do than break up a friendly little crap game."

Sweitzer reminded audiences that Thompson had spent his previous terms in office racing sailboats on Lake Michigan instead of giving the requisite attention to his obligations. "Who has heard of him doing anything? . . . He is a man who plays with sailboats."

Congressman Fred Lundin, who'd once made a living selling nonalcoholic juniper ade and quack medical concoctions from the back of a horse-drawn wagon, was backing Thompson in the mayoral race, and he made an equally astute comment: "He may not be big on brains, but he gets through to people." Lundin's observation proved more prophetic than Sweitzer's, as Chicago's voters elected Big Bill Thompson by the largest majority ever accorded a Republican candidate.[21]

The government that Thompson gave the people was one that only a certain segment of the population had voted for. Within eight months the only promise he succeeded in keeping was creating a "wide-open town." After a few token raids had been aimed at the Levee brothels and gambling houses, William Stead's dreaded "King Boodle" was back stronger than ever. Slot machines ran full tilt twenty-four hours a day, with payoffs to the local police station and city hall insuring that play was uninterrupted, and prostitutes plied their trade as determinedly as ever, only working out of unobtrusive call flats instead of the noisy whorehouses that drew reformer ire. The Sportsman's Club, a Republican group, was delegated to collect all the graft.

Crime statistics lunged upward, a calamity that reform Alderman Charles Merriam attributed to the police department being "just a big sewing circle." Thompson's chief of police, Charles Healy, was exposed as a grafting cop who associated regularly with Levee characters such as brothel owner and white slaver Mike "de Pike" Heitler. Among the evidence produced at the ensuing trial of Healy and eight other defendants was a notebook with some shady resorts clearly marked as "chief's places" and "can't be raided." Healy retained the high-profile defense team of Clarence Darrow and Charles Erbstein, and despite the multitudinous evidence of corruption, was acquitted.[22]

Adelard Cunin was now living and working in Bloomington under the alias of George Miller. The terms of his release from Joliet required him to report to a parole officer once a month and submit a report detailing his earnings, his living and entertainment expenses, and when and how his leisure time was spent. His employer had to countersign the report before it was handed in.

Prison and police officials had no way of keeping tabs on his acquaintances, however. If they had, he might never have had free rein to foster his association with local miscreants Louis Miller and John Brown.[23] Throughout the summer of 1912 they operated a "horse snatch" racket, breaking into stables or simply walking off with horses and buggies left unattended. They would demand a ransom for the animals' return, and usually got it, as the horse and wagon had not yet been displaced by the automobile in Bloomington, and they were careful to ask for less than a replacement mount would cost.

Such activity could not go unpunished indefinitely. In September 1912, patrolling police officers caught Cunin, Miller, and Brown in the act of transporting a stolen horse and arrested them. A search of their hideout revealed stolen property (type not specified in police reports). On September 27 they appeared in court to face charges—Cunin on two counts of receiving pilfered goods, one of grand larceny, and one of petty larceny; Miller on one count of burglary and larceny; and Brown on a single attempt to burglary charge, as he had been functioning as the lookout. To hold off his recognition as a paroled felon for as long as possible, Cunin told the court that his name was George Moran.

The charge against Brown was dismissed when Cunin/Moran and Louis Miller denied his involvement in their scheme. They pled not guilty to all charges, and bail was set at $800 for Miller and $1,200 for "George Moran." Unable to raise bail, they sat in the MacLean County Jail until their cases were heard on October 5. For reasons not entered into the record, Moran's attorney moved for a continuance until December 20, which the presiding judge granted. Soon after that court appearance, Moran's erstwhile employer contacted Joliet authorities to inform them of the young ex-convict's new troubles, and a warrant for his arrest for parole violation was issued on October 18.

On December 20 Moran withdrew his plea of not guilty, entered a guilty plea, and instructed his counsel to tell the presiding judge that he was throwing himself upon the mercy of the court. After consulting with State's Attorney Miles K. Young, the judge sentenced him to four months in the county jail on the grand larceny charge and ninety days on each of the other charges, all to run concurrently.

After his release, Cunin/Moran managed to keep off of the public record and away from Joliet authorities until June 11, 1913, when he faced a burglary and larceny charge. (It is not known what became of the parole violation warrant.) Details behind the indictment are not known, but he did opt for a jury trial and posted a $1,000 bond. When the case was heard in October, twelve Bloomington citizens duly found him guilty. That meant a return to Joliet for the standard one- to twenty-year term, but Moran attempted to dodge that bullet by telling the court that his birth date was August 21, 1893, making him only nineteen and eligible for a term at the state reformatory at Pontiac instead. At the last minute, the truth was discovered (the county clerk noting in the indictment record, "The Court finds the age of defendant George Moran to be twenty-two years as of August 21, 1913."), and on October 30, 1913, he was on his way back to the state prison.

Prison authorities were not so quick to grant a parole to Moran as a second-time offender and violator of previous parole conditions. He remained within the high stone walls of the institution until June 26, 1917, when he finally was set free.

Adelard Cunin, now calling himself George Clarence Moran, would adopt two more aliases in the years to come: George Gage and George Morrissey. But neither stuck. The changing of one's name was a routine activity among the underworld, and the transformations ran the gamut from a simple nickname that stuck (i.e., "Bugs," although these were rarely employed or supported by the individual in question) to a complete variation from the original name.

Marie Neubauer, sister of James Clark, one of the St. Valentine's Day Massacre victims, sobbed that her brother had been born Albert Kachellek but used an alias to spare his family the shame his notoriety as a Moran gangster could have brought on.[24] Rarely has the mask been so complete that it took on a life of its own and completely obliterated the original identity, as well as the history associated with that identity.

Adelard Cunin had his own reasons for letting George "Bugs" Moran represent his past, present, and future. One was an outstanding warrant in the state of Minnesota as an escaped convict. Another was a loving French Canadian mother to whom he regularly sent letters and, later, money. Like James Clark, he had a strong enough sense of family loyalty to shield his mother and siblings from any consequences of his present actions. Unlike James Clark, the subterfuge remained in place long after Cunin's death.

On November 13, 1913, two weeks after Moran returned to Joliet, delegations of anti-liquor politicians and campaigners (otherwise known as "drys") converged on Columbus, Ohio, to celebrate the twentieth anniversary of the Anti-Saloon League. The league's primary objective in the early days had been the closure of the saloons where men and women drank away their livelihoods and health, but a growing membership whose ranks included some of the country's most influential citizens made them aim higher by 1913; now nationwide Prohibition was on the agenda.[25]

Former Indiana Governor James Hanley told a crowd of spellbound onlookers, "We therefore declare for its [the liquor industry's] national annihilation by an amendment to the Federal Constitution which shall forever prohibit throughout the territory of the United States the manufacture and sale and the importation, exportation, and transportation of intoxicating liquor to be used as a beverage."

His listeners, which included delegates from the Women's Christian Temperance Union, members of the Prohibition Party, clergymen, and league sympathizers, leaped to their feet and applauded until the din drowned out the howl of the blizzard raging outside. No longer would the dry forces limit themselves to legislating temperance through local option; they had determined that the country needed total Prohibition, whether the citizenry wanted it or not.

45

John Granville Woolley, a Prohibition Party member, insisted in no uncertain terms that liquor had to be eradicated. "We will crowd it to the ropes," he warned. "We will not break away in the clinches. And when it lies dying among its bags of bloody gold and looks into our faces with its last gasp and whispers, 'Another million of revenue for just one breath of life,' we will put the heel of open-eyed national honor on its throat and say, 'NO! Down to hell and say we sent thee thither!!'"

The cause espoused by Woolley, Hanley, and their supporters was almost as old as America itself. Preachers had long been assailing the sin of drunkenness from their pulpits, but a government role in curtailing drinking went against the American ideal of personal liberty. Rum was the earliest medium of exchange in the slave trade, and taverns the preferred location for male socializing. John Adams noted in his diary in 1760, "These houses are becoming the nurseries of our legislators." He had observed firsthand that any man who opened or supported a tavern or dram shop could easily control the vote of the patrons during election time.

Some of these establishments were dives of the lowest caliber, however, so in 1734 Governor James Oglethorpe of Georgia made history's first attempt at prohibition in the United States by outlawing the importation and consumption of liquor in his state. The motive behind the ban was to get the workers out of the taverns and into the forests and fields to build up Georgia, but the reverse occurred. The colonists, chafing at the restraint, instead applied themselves to getting liquor from rumrunners who smuggled it in from South Carolina. When the ban was finally lifted nine years later, Parliament recognizing its futility, public drunkenness decreased, and respect for the law returned.[26]

Liquor consumption had long been a staple of American life. During the country's earliest years it was customary for the citizens of Portland, Maine, to cease work or play each day (save Sunday) at 11 a.m. and 4 p.m. to repair to the taverns and saloons for their twice-daily "bitters." Hard liquor was a catch-all remedy favored by the medical establishment of the day, and one life insurance company increased its premiums by 10 percent for abstainers, believing such applicants to be "thin, watery, and as mentally cranked, in that [they] repudiated the good creatures of God as found in alcoholic drinks." Quaker leader William Penn owned a Philadelphia brewery, and even the revered George Washington maintained a distillery at Mount Vernon. During Washington's first three months as president an estimated one-fourth of his entire household expenses went toward liquor.

The temporary period of prohibition in Georgia, combined with disgust over the broken family life and shattered health that prevailed among tavern habitués, encouraged dreams of nationwide temperance legislation among anti-liquor factions. In the 1830s reformers such as Reverend Justin Edwards of Boston and Reverend Lyman Beecher of Litchfield, Connecticut, pushed for total abstinence in the American citizenry through a form of religious intimidation: they glossed over physical and economic ramifications and insisted that liquor consumption was bad for the soul. When the Washington Temperance Society was founded in 1840, it operated under

46

the theory that religious conversion was the key to eliminating the alcohol problem, angering other temperance societies that believed only legislative action could combat the evil.

No less distinguished a personage than Abraham Lincoln, himself a teetotaler, believed that prohibition statutes would be legislative failures. In 1840, when a Whig member of the Illinois state legislature, he argued, "Prohibition will work great injury to the cause of temperance. It is a species of intemperance within itself, for it goes beyond the bounds of reason in that it attempts to control a man's appetite by legislation and makes a crime out of things that are not crimes. A prohibition law strikes at the very principle upon which our government was founded."

Those who advocated the outlawing of liquor production and consumption on religious grounds were derided by their fellow citizens as fanatics. It was an unfair assessment, as many preachers and their pro-temperance congregations were more concerned with the welfare of mankind than glorifying themselves by aligning with a morally lofty cause. But Thomas Poage Hunt, who believed that the future of temperance relied on proper instruction of the young and founded the all-youth Cold Water Army, was of the breed that gave the movement's detractors fuel for the fire. He wrote in his memoirs, "In a town in Pennsylvania, in which I was lecturing, a liquor-seller said he did not know how he could live if he did not sell liquor. I told him that I did not know that it was essential to the world that he should live at all."[27]

The dry forces took heart when Neal Dow, mayor of Portland, Maine, brought in a state prohibition law in June 1850. The manufacturing and selling of liquor within Maine was banned. By 1854 twelve other states and one territory had adopted similar measures. After New Hampshire went dry in 1855, however, there was a common revolt against the temperance laws, and all states except Maine repealed or modified their dry statutes. Abolition of slavery, not temperance, became the pet cause of the nation's humanitarian and religious segment.

A Massachusetts legislative committee, headed by Governor John A. Andrew, ridiculed prohibition legislation as the aim of fanatics. The Internal Revenue Law passed in 1862 confirmed the status of alcoholic beverages as a key source of government revenue, provoking angry accusations from reformers that the legislation was merely a national licensing law in disguise.

The temperance forces took on new life in the 1870s when the Women's Christian Temperance Union was founded. These determined women, many of whom had combated the liquor problem by picketing or praying in saloons, arranged for temperance programs to be taught in schools. Their educational approach was applauded for its rationality and foresight. The WCTU remained the nation's strongest temperance movement until December 1895, when the Anti-Saloon League came into being.

The league was the first dry organization to take complete control of the anti-liquor crusade. It raised money for the cause and fought both manipulative "wet" factions and politicians out to thwart their goals. The league reached the public through incessant distribution of pamphlets, opening its own publishing house in 1909 expressly for that purpose. An independent political organization, it endorsed candidates for the legislature and backed those candidates with the same resourcefulness and guile that had previously been confined to the anti-temperance faction.

The league and its satellite organizations had powerful political backing by 1913. Senator Morris Sheppard of Texas, a millionaire whose slight physique and mild speaking voice belied his boundless energy, authored the most radical Prohibition legislation. "Its benefits," he later wrote in the *Anti-Saloon League Year Book*, "will become more evident as the years separate us from the era of the nation's shame when misery, poverty, and ruin were the sad harvest of a traffic in one of the deadliest poisons known to man."[28]

It was Sheppard and Richmond Pearson Hobson from Alabama who introduced into the Senate the proposed Eighteenth Amendment to the U.S. Constitution, which had been jointly prepared by such Anti-Saloon League luminaries as Bishop James Cannon, Wayne Wheeler, and Reverend Purley Baker.

The House Judiciary Committee finally reported on the resolution in May 1914, which was also an election year, so the battle was on. Both the dry forces and prominent liquor interests such as the United States Brewers Association and the National Liquor Dealers Association pulled out all the stops and bombarded Washington with letters, threatened boycotts, and passed out millions, if not billions, of pages of literature extolling their causes and deriding that of the enemy. Although both sides had huge means at their disposal, the pro-liquor forces began to slowly lose ground for one key reason: they never claimed, or pretended to claim, that their motivation was anything other than profit. The Anti-Saloon League and Women's Christian Temperance Union had aims that were morally above reproach: the abolition of the saloon, protection of youth, and preservation of families that ran the risk of being destroyed by alcoholism.

If the brewing and distilling interests had acknowledged their own problems, such as the low dives and saloons that existed because of their product, and made their own attempt to reform/close such embarrassments, they would not have been such a villainous target for their dry opponents. Another factor that worked against them was the mostly professional ranks of their membership: beer magnates and millionaire distillers. The average American citizen who may not have wanted Prohibition did not have the campaigning options that dry citizens found in the League and the WCTU.

It was hardly surprising that the 1914 elections saw dry politicians acquire more seats in both houses of Congress. The Prohibitionists put the Hobson-Sheppard Bill up for debate mere weeks after the House of Representatives convened. Among those who spoke in front of "medical" charts depicting the destructive effects of liquor on the human system was Charles Lindbergh Sr., dry Republican congressman from Minnesota, whose famous son was to become an American icon during the next decade, when the fruits of his father's labors would make the country roar to the sound of forbidden toasts and bootlegger gunfire.[29]

The proposed bill garnered 197 votes, to 190 against, falling 61 votes short of the required two-thirds majority for passage. Disappointed but encouraged by the closeness of the voting results, the Prohibition forces intensified their efforts in the 1916 campaign. Nine more states adopted prohibition statutes. Then, in April 1917, President Woodrow Wilson called a session of Congress to declare war against Germany.

The dry forces recognized a prime opportunity in Wilson's food control bill, which was proposed to aid the war effort. They knew well that beer and liquor production used up grain, sugar, and other food items that could be put to better use feeding the soldiers who were off fighting the Kaiser. They pressed this point, as well as two others: that drinking among the armed forces would lead to military inefficiency at the worst possible time, and, in a fit of xenophobia, suggested that beer production in the United States was mostly a German endeavor, and drinking it supported the enemy. Wayne Wheeler, general counsel for the Anti-Saloon League, declared, "Kaiserism abroad and booze at home must go. Liquor is a menace to patriotism because it puts beer before country."[30]

Congressmen who supported the Anti-Saloon League amended Wilson's food control bill to bar any food items from being used to produce alcohol, and thus altered, it passed the House.

The wet forces were, predictably, furious. The *Cincinnati Enquirer* blasted what it perceived as dry manipulation in a scathing editorial: "For brazen effrontery, unmitigated gall, super-egoism, transcendent audacity, supreme impudence, commend us to the legislative committee of the prohibition lobby. Here we have the President of the United States under orders to an officious and offensive lobby."

In the latter sentence the paper referred to Wilson's asking the anti-liquor faction in Congress to let the amended food bill apply only to distilled liquor instead of beer and wine, for the President could not afford to offend the wets and have a divided Congress in the face of imminent war. The drys agreed but offered Wilson a gentle warning: "We are glad that your request applies only to the pending food legislation. It will be our purpose to urge the passage of the legislation prohibiting the waste of foodstuffs in the manufacture of beer and wines at the earliest date, either in the form of a separate bill or in connection with other war legislation."

Congress passed the food control bill, and it took effect on September 8, 1917.

The political soap opera continued, reaching its climax on January 16, 1919, two months after the armistice, when the requisite number of states ratified the Eighteenth Amendment and made it the law of the land. The wets were dismayed. With the cessation of hostilities, the patriotism angle had been removed from the dry arguments, and the wets had been expecting the issue to remain a political football for years to come. The Anti-Saloon League, WCTU, and their ancillary organizations rejoiced first, and then moved in for the kill.

Wayne Wheeler drafted the National Prohibition Act, popularly known as the Volstead Act in honor of Andrew Volstead, the senator from Minnesota (Moran's birthplace) who had introduced the measure in the House. When interviewed by the press, Volstead agreed that the penalties for violating the new law would be severe: fines could range from $500 to $2,000, and prison sentences from one year to five. Incidents that formerly had resulted in barroom brawls and hangovers could now land one in the poorhouse or jail. "It will be made even more severe after the country has learned what Prohibition means," Volstead warned.

The scheduled time of "revelation" was January 17, 1920.

3

RECIDIVISM AND THE GREAT EXPERIMENT

I T WAS A DIFFERENT WORLD that greeted George Moran upon his release from prison in 1917. The Great War had been raging in Europe since 1914, and although President Woodrow Wilson had initially indicated that the United States would not enter the fray, the 1915 sinking of the ocean liner *Lusitania* by a German U-Boat, resulting in American loss of life, had created ripples that gradually turned the tide against continued neutrality. Entry into the war was expected to happen at any time, and it finally occurred on April 6, 1917.

The country prepared to throw itself into battle. All males between the ages of eighteen and forty-five were required to register for the draft, and huge posters encouraging voluntary enlistment could be found in most public places. The Treasury Department employed Hollywood celebrities such as Douglas Fairbanks, Mary Pickford, and Charlie Chaplin to address crowds at rallies and encourage them to buy Liberty Bonds. The proceeds funded the war effort, as did a dramatic increase in taxes.

Moran, now using the identity that would belong to him for the rest of his life, paid scant attention to the appeals to his patriotism and moved into a rented room on North Clark Street, in the heart of the North Side's vice district.

North Clark had been undergoing gradual decline since the late 1880s and early '90s, when it lost its long-held status as a respectable, working-class residential district. Laborers, small-business owners, and their families did remain, but the general nature of North Clark Street was characterized by the dime museums, saloons, dance halls, and cheap all-night restaurants that encouraged and catered to a lively night life. Two entertainment spots, the Clark Street Theater and the Windsor, gratified their hard-drinking and rowdy audiences with cowboy-and-Indian dramas. Another resort, Engel's Music Hall Café, was famous for its alluring chorus girls and raunchy stage performances. Harvey Zorbaugh, author of *The Gold Coast* and *The Slum*, recounted the festive Engel's atmosphere almost thirty years later:

> The curtain rises and a pert soubrette with a very gaudy complexion and abbreviated skirts trips to the footlights and sings a song of true love, or something equally interesting. Meanwhile more drinks are ordered by everybody, and general hilarity prevails.
> The last hour is usually devoted to an opera in one act, a burlesque of the follies of the day, or anything else that will give an opportunity for the singing of "catchy" songs, the execution of intricate dances, and above all, the lavish display of feminine charms."

Zorbaugh noted that special consideration was given to wealthy visitors who could not resist the lure of unconventional entertainment.

> Another feature of Engel's, and many find it an agreeable one, is the stage boxes. These boxes are located above the stage and behind the curtain, being arranged in such a way that the persons seated therein may view all that is going forward on the stage itself and still remain invisible to the audience. With prominent citizens, or other people who like to keep their attendance at the music hall a secret, this is an advantage not to be denied.[1]

The profusion of brightly lit signs and windows earned it the disarmingly benign sobriquet, "the Little White Way." Another nickname was more accurate: "the Wilds of North Clark Street."

The mercilessly lively lights and nightlife were merely a mask for the social isolation and acts of despair and violence that gradually gave the area a bad name. On July 6, 1917, a midwife named Elizabeth Shade was arrested for performing a fatal abortion on one Helen Skoga in the former's "office" at 1310 North Clark.[2] The following September, a cabaret singer named Rae Wilson, driven out of her mind by a failing career and abusive boyfriend, threw herself out of a window in her room at the St. Regis Hotel.[3] There were other tragedies that either did not make the papers or merited only a line at the bottom of an inside page. None of these events aroused much interest in any quarter save the police and social agencies designated to combat and cope with them.

In 1917, North Clark Street was already a destination for local and incoming transients, although not yet the hobohemia it would become by the end of the 1920s. Rooms could be had for as little as a dollar a week, and anyone too broke to meet even that pathetic rent could find a nearby pawn shop low enough to accept his patched-up coat or cracked shoes. Homeless men and women humbled by hunger could drop by the Clark Street Mission for free coffee and doughnuts, as long as they didn't mind a strong dose of evangelism thrown into the menu. Many of the men came because of the "lady workers" who served the refreshments and offered encouraging words; except for the broken-down prostitutes who were more likely to give them venereal disease than any kind of real pleasure, these men had little contact with women.

Clark Street also attracted "squawkers," those who earned a living by peddling, begging, or street performing. In clement weather Moran and other pedestrians had to navigate the hordes of peddlers selling postcards, pens, pencils, and other penny items, or panhandlers who fought to catch their eye just before he or she regaled their ears with a hard-luck story. Even street hustlers had their hierarchy, and among the elite were the "black hood," a woman who cuddled a baby in her arms to elicit sympathy and money; the flopper, a male or female amputee who "flopped" along the sidewalk and begged for crutch money; and the "throw out," someone who could dislocate his joints at will and simulate various deformities. Female beggars who worked with squawkers were known as "high heelers." Peddlers usually managed just to make ends meet, but convincing squawkers could make anywhere from $10 to $50 a day.[4]

Largely because Chicago was the "Wobbly" capital of the United States, IWW sympathizers, "Reds," and other political malcontents with a grudge against the current system gathered on North Clark Street and its environs. Washington Square, between Clark and Dearborn streets, hosted nightly meetings during which propagandists climbed onto soapboxes and held forth to interested crowds on a variety of political and religious topics. The Haymarket Riot of 1886 and the subsequent executions of four radicals believed to have been behind the bombing was still within the memory of many, and a fiery speech on worker's rights and anarchism was guaranteed a quick collection of listeners. Because of the varying levels of sanity among the speakers, Washington Square acquired the nickname "Bughouse Square." Many Chicagoans never knew it by any other name.

It was an environment in which neighbors took so little interest in one another that they automatically minded their own business, which suited Moran perfectly. No one had any inclination to inform his parole officer when he began associating with ex-convict Jack King, a hulking thug known as the "man with the scar" because his right cheek bore the aftereffect of a knife battle. King had done time in the state prison for assault and burglary and since his release had made a living robbing streetcar conductors. He and Moran initially met in Joliet, when the former was completing the last months of his sentence. Before his release, King gave Moran the address of his sister's apartment on West Twenty-first Street and asked the younger man to look him up upon obtaining parole. The fact that Moran followed up on the invitation became public knowledge, thanks to a violent bank robbery that took place on July 13, 1917, mere weeks after Moran had been paroled.[5]

Early in the day, police officer Peter Bulfin drove to the Chicago City Bank and Trust Company at 6233 South Halstead Street, where he had been detailed to guard a $12,000 cash shipment destined for deposit at the Live Stock Exchange bank. Bank messenger Edward Wyatt, aided by some clerks, carried the money out of the trust company and into a waiting car, whereupon Wyatt got behind the wheel while Bulfin climbed into the front passenger seat.[6]

They failed to notice four young men, all armed, stride from around the corner of the bank and trust building and rush them. By the time Bulfin realized what was happening and reached for the gun in his hip pocket, one of the attackers thrust a pistol against his chest and fired, killing him. Wyatt threw up his hands in surrender and slid to the floor of the car, shaking in terror. Another bandit reached into the moneybox in the rear seat and took out one bag, but before more could be stolen, bank employees, some of them armed, ran to the rescue.

The foursome fled into an alley with their sole booty, a sack containing $100 in nickels. A burly truck driver who had stumbled upon the tail end of the drama attempted to intercept them but jumped back hastily at the sight of their weapons. At the end of the alley a touring car waited, its engine idling. The robbers jumped in and disappeared in a cloud of exhaust smoke.

Some time after the attack, while detectives were canvassing witnesses, the bank received a bizarre phone call. Without identifying himself, the male caller asked, "Did that policeman [Bulfin] die?" When the switchboard operator answered in the affirmative, he sneered, "Good," and hung up.

Witness descriptions of one of the assailants tallied with that of scar-faced Jack King. When shown a mug shot photo, they identified him, so the call went out to pick up King. Early on the morning of July 14, three detectives from the Twenty-second Street station located the fugitive in his sister's basement apartment on West Twenty-first Street. Jack King reacted to their arrival by lunging for a drawer later found to contain three revolvers, but the officers overpowered him. While searching the apartment, they found George Moran in the bedroom, where he had slept through the uproar. The detectives roused him, snapped cuffs on his wrists while he was still groggy, and hustled him along with King down to the Englewood police station, where Captain Ryan, who was in charge of the investigation into Bulfin's death, was waiting.

The *Tribune* suggested that the duo faced quite an ordeal from Ryan: "King and

54

George Moran . . . maintained their innocence under stress of the severest examination they have ever been subjected to."[7]

The case against the two fell through when witnesses, who had identified King from a photo, were not so sure once confronted with him in person. Moran, never picked out as a participant, was released. Whether or not the two were guilty of the robbery is not known, but Moran parted company permanently with King, the association now being a risky one, and returned to his North Clark Street stomping grounds. It did not take him long to get into trouble closer to home.

On a sultry July night, soon after being absolved of complicity in the Bulfin murder, he and a friend left a saloon and joined a crowd listening to a political speech in Bughouse Square. The air was oppressively warm, so the two men were nursing cold bottles of beer they'd brought from the saloon. Although politics was not something either of them normally found interesting, the speaker was so persuasive and magnetic that they became enthralled in spite of themselves, and when an irate heckler began puncturing the flow of the speech, Moran rounded on him.

"Shut up," he warned. "Man's got a right to speak."

The malcontent refused to back down. "So do I. Go ahead and start something then, tough guy."

Who threw the first punch is a question whose answer has been lost to history. The multitude of onlookers, hardened to brawls and other displays of public violence, turned away from the speaker and greeted the new entertainment with relish. Moran hurled his beer bottle in his opponent's face, stunning him, then closed in for a crushing grip in his powerful arms.

Suddenly, metal flashed like quicksilver through the fading evening. Twice, at least, for Moran staggered back with blood flowing freely from two serious stab wounds in his chest and the right side of his neck. What happened next is uncertain. Either his friend intervened, or the attacker lost his nerve at the sight of his grisly handiwork and fled. Moran required emergency hospitalization to prevent death from blood loss. Stitches and medication saved his life, but he was left with a four-inch neck scar that he made a point of covering with scarves and high collars.[8]

Although the event would have held little significance for Moran had he known of it at the time, a similar drama played out in New York that very summer. Frank Galluccio, a barber's assistant and former merchant seaman who now made a living as a low-level hoodlum, strolled into the Harvard Inn, a resort operated by the notorious Frankie Yale. His girlfriend and sister accompanied him. When the tall, beefy young bouncer eyed the sister, Lena, she became uncomfortable enough to ask her brother to intervene. Before Galluccio could politely ask the man to lay off, the bouncer leaned in close, his bulky shadow engulfing the small party's table, and in a voice made louder by drunkenness, told her that she had a nice ass. The furious brother, boiling with a mixture of righteous and alcohol-induced wrath, forgot all about resolving the situation nicely, and sprang to his feet, demanding an apology. The bouncer "apologized" by coming at him.

Galluccio was several inches shorter and at least thirty pounds lighter, a handicap he made up for by grabbing a knife and lunging for his attacker's throat. He missed that vital spot, but did make three facial slashes, one starting two inches in front of the left cheek, and angling four inches downward; the other two measured roughly two and a half inches and were on the left jaw and on the left side of his neck. The big man staggered back, fingers grasping at his bleeding wounds, while Galluccio and his party made a mad dash for the door.

The bouncer was rushed to the Coney Island Hospital, where thirty stitches were required to close the gaping slashes in his face and neck. When they healed, he would cover them up with talc and turn the right side of his face toward flashbulbs to avoid having the scars photographed. In later life he would be publicly identified by his disfigurement and known as "Scarface Al" Capone.[9]

Like Moran, Capone was still a low-level hoodlum in 1917. Neither was aware of the other or his injuries that summer, but the mutual ignorance was not destined to last long. Alphonse Capone and George "Bugs" Moran would see their paths cross within a few short years and follow each other almost stride for stride to underworld notoriety. Each would know the death/departure of a cherished mentor and assume control of a criminal outfit and mold it in his own personal style. In spite of, or because of, their similarities, each became the other's dark side.

After days spent recuperating in the hospital, Moran began patronizing McGovern's Cabaret at 666 North Clark Street. Run by a violent character named Bob McGovern and staffed by singing waiters whose angelic voices were a stark contrast to their brawling and punching ability, the establishment was the place to go if one were new in town or just out of prison and looking for a hookup. On a good night, one might find Mont Tennes, Big Jim O'Leary, "Hot Stove Jimmy" Quinn, or safecracking king Charles "the Ox" Reiser at the bar. On a better night, they'd need someone to bring their latest scheme to fruition and offer a promising newcomer a job. Few transactions of a legal variety went on at McGovern's, making it a target of wrath for citizens groups such as the Committee of Fifteen, which eventually padlocked the dive.

When Moran became a habitué in 1917, he made two fortuitous contacts. One was with the man who would draw him into the framework of a high-stakes safecracking and burglary gang; the other was with a charismatic individual who, although a singing waiter with a jail record at the time he met Moran, would have the entire North Side of Chicago dancing to his tune by the end of the decade.

The former, Charles Reiser, also known as "the Ox" but born Frederick Schoeps in 1882 in Elgin, Illinois, had been an independent safecracker for years, with a record dating back to 1903. He'd been arrested several times since then, both in

Seattle and Chicago, but evaded punishment by arranging the murder of any witnesses against him. The underworld grapevine had it that he had beaten his first wife to death for threatening to turn him in to the police, although an unobservant coroner attributed her demise to "accidental asphyxiation."

Only once had the Ox failed to beat the rap; in 1907 a man whom he'd assaulted with a knife ignored the potentially deadly consequences and went to the police. Reiser spent thirty days in jail when his accuser successfully evaded assassination and testified against him in court. He never met such problems the way Mont Tennes or Hot Stove Jimmy Quinn would: by making regular and growing donations to influential people on the police force, in the state's attorney's office, or in city hall. Reiser covered his blunders through free use of threats and murder, and except for the one instance mentioned, his brutal method worked for him.[10]

When not jimmying locks, emptying safes of payroll money, and using gunfire to cover his tracks, Reiser was the landlord of a clean, quiet apartment building at 1704 Otto Street. He and his family lived on the ground floor and rented out the upper level. He had remarried by then and had two children, Kenneth and Verna, with Madeline, his second wife. His tenants knew him as a friendly, easygoing landlord who did not press when rents were overdue and even allowed them to retain their apartments on credit when they suffered job loss or financial setback. They had no idea that Mr. Shopes (Schoeps), who was so understanding with them and a great husband and father to his own family, was the notorious Charles Reiser.

By 1917 the Ox was pulling bigger jobs that required weeks if not months of planning. He cast a net out for accomplices to help stake out the places beforehand and deal with potential obstacles during the actual theft, such as passersby and night watchmen. Moran was one of the core members of the safecracking gang he began assembling while the rest of the country cast its eyes and attention toward the European battlefields. What drew the Ox to the recent parolee is not known. Moran's criminal experience did not include safecracking, although he had a shaky background in nighttime burglaries and had gotten himself shot to prove it. Perhaps Reiser learned that Moran's father, like his, was originally from Alsace-Lorraine[11] and was partial to Moran because of the shared heritage. Most likely it was the recommendation and support of Moran's other acquaintance from McGovern's that resulted into his induction into the Reiser gang.

Dean O'Banion had been a singing waiter at 666 North Clark for over a year. Short at five foot four and stout without being pudgy, O'Banion's appearance successfully hid his tough nature. His light-blonde hair and smiling, clean-shaven face gave him an angelic appearance, and when he raised his sweet tenor voice to sing an Irish ballad or one of the day's popular tear-jerkers, he all but sprouted a halo in front of his listeners. He walked with a rolling limp, his left leg being an inch shorter than his right as the result of a streetcar accident. The physical handicap and cherubic appearance provided no impediment to the successful discharge of his duties, which were not limited to carting shot glasses and beer steins from one table of tough characters to another.

Although few wanted to risk the volcanic wrath of Bob McGovern by causing trouble in his place, restraint was the first casualty of too much hard liquor, and O'Banion was required to beat up and toss out many a customer he'd spent the evening serving. Sometimes he did it for personal reasons. His injured leg and wobbly gait spawned the nickname "Gimpy," but only the newcomer or the very stupid used it in his presence. When it happened, he would even the odds against a taller opponent by kicking the man in the kneecap first, to bring him down, and after leaping on top of the fallen victim, batter his face to a pulp with his fists or brass knuckles.[12]

O'Banion was tough and worked in a desperate place, but he was also a shrewd thinker and highly intelligent. An easy conversationalist, he made friends quickly and effortlessly. As a boy in Maroa, Illinois, a village 150 miles south of Chicago, he'd pushed his luck with his parents, teachers, and other adults when he teased classmates unmercifully and indulged in annoying childish pranks, but he was rarely punished because he applied his personal charm so successfully.

When his mother died of tuberculosis in 1901 and his father took him and his older brother, Floyd, to Chicago to live with their maternal grandparents, the nine-year-old O'Banion found himself in a rougher environment: Chicago's Near North Side was the habitat for some very tough Sicilian gangs. The neighborhood that his grandparents called home had once been an Irish immigrant stronghold, but by 1901 it consisted mostly of Sicilian arrivals. O'Banion, although American-born, found himself at the same disadvantage as the immigrant boys, having lived in a more laid-back and rural environment all his life.[13] Where he had once run in acres of woods and fields or strolled along a clean, placid Maroa street, he now made his way cautiously along trash-filled and crowded streets, dodging unconscious bodies and vendors' carts. The area's night skies turned red when a gashouse down by the river belched flames into the clouds, giving an aesthetic reason for the region's nickname of Little Hell. A more fitting source for the name lay in the poverty and squalor that met the eyes everywhere one looked.[14]

His father, a hardworking house painter, and grandmother attempted to ward off the seeds of criminality by sending him to the Holy Name Parochial School at Chicago Avenue and Cass streets, and securing him a place in the Holy Name Cathedral Boy's Choir, but the church made no real impression on O'Banion. Some Chicago gang histories would claim that he'd considered a career in the priesthood at one time, but O'Banion never was overly religious. He attended Holy Name School until May 1907, when an accident that would cripple him for life took place.[15]

Chicago's legions of trolley cars could be as dangerous as they were useful. According to a report published in the *Chicago Tribune* in January 1908, there were 3,430 streetcar-related deaths and injuries in 1907 alone.[16] A typical example was that of Irving Seeger on May 6, 1907. The twenty-eight-year-old cigar maker was stepping off of the corner of Randolph and Dearborn streets when his foot caught in a trolley track and he fell. Before he could get up, the streetcar came around the corner, caught him by the leg, and dragged him for twenty feet, until horrified pedestrians waved the conductor to a stop. Seeger, who suffered a fractured skull and internal injuries, died hours later in hospital. The same day, a westward-bound Division Street trolley struck one Martin Hansen and dragged him for half a block. When a woman passenger saw the extent of his injuries, she fainted.

O'Banion had been in Chicago for six years, long enough to be aware of the dangers posed by careless behavior on or around trolleys, but he had always been drawn to risky stunts. As a boy in Maroa, he had broken his arm after falling off a pair of stilts intended for an adult. In Chicago a favorite sport among his friends was "bumper-riding," or sitting on the rear fender of an idling streetcar and getting a free ride once it started. Most times a vigilant conductor or concerned passerby shooed the boys away, but one day in May 1907, no one prevented O'Banion from hitching. The result was catastrophic. The car came to a sudden stop while the boys were enjoying their ride, knocking them off their perch, then backed up suddenly. The rear wheels ran over O'Banion's left leg, pulverizing an inch of bone. Onlookers rushed him to the Chicago Emergency Hospital, where an operation saved the mangled limb but left it permanently shorter than the other.[17] After a recuperative period, O'Banion opted not to return to school, instead taking a job as a morning deliveryman for a milk company.

For social and protective purposes, O'Banion joined a youth gang called, naturally, the Little Hellions. These youngsters were as formidable as their adult counterparts, the Market Street Gang, which made an appearance every election day beating up voters, election officials, and hired goons who opposed whatever politicians had secured their services. Dean O'Banion won the respect and admiration of his fellow Hellions for his sharp mind and leader's instincts.

Although he counted sluggers, thieves, and even murderers among his acquaintances, O'Banion retained a strong devotion to his family. During a crime wave that devastated the North Side from 1901 until 1906, he escorted his grandmother, Mrs. Brophy, whenever she had to leave the house on an evening errand, carrying a gun tucked in his jacket. When his father, Charles, was nearly killed in a street attack, he extracted vengeance.

At seven o'clock on the morning of September 27, 1909, Dean got up and dressed for work as usual. Strange noises coming from his father's bedroom aroused his concern. He peered in, and reeled in horror when he saw Charles lying on the bed in a spreading pool of blood. Dean pulled himself together enough to call the police, who took the injured man to the Chicago Polyclinic Hospital.

Charles, who eventually recovered, told the officers that he had been walking home when three men stopped him and demanded money. During the scuffle that followed, the robbers stabbed him in the back and chest and stole $50 from his wallet.[18] He claimed not to know the men, but somehow the young O'Banion found out. He located two of them and beat them so badly that it was feared they might not live. They did, but when they declined to identify him, the burly seventeen-year-old went free.[19]

He served two jail terms, one at the end of 1909 for breaking into a drugstore and stealing postage stamps, and the second in 1911 for assault with a deadly weapon during a fight. The fact that he'd been caught and imprisoned did not lessen his status in the gang. Everyone was pinched sooner or later, and doing time without softening one's stay by squealing on someone was a recognized and prized mark of toughness.

When he left the Bridewell upon completion of his second jail term, O'Banion acknowledged that he needed friends in high places and cultivated the acquaintance of James Aloyisious "Hot Stove Jimmy" Quinn, a McGovern's regular and boss of the Forty-second Ward (formerly the Twenty-first) on the North Side. Quinn, although a dedicated burglar who had earned his nickname by actually trying to steal a recently heated stove, had served as city sealer under one of the five administrations of Carter Harrison II. O'Banion had joined the Little Hellions in committing election-day mayhem during his boyhood, but by openly throwing his support behind Quinn and his agendas, the young Irish-American hoodlum found himself coming into contact with the "right people." He learned who was for sale, and for how much. As a result, he never spent another day in jail, although he strayed far from the straight and narrow.[20]

O'Banion was one of those rare individuals that one either adored or hated. His friends loved him like a brother, while his enemies reddened with rage at the mere mention of his name. One of his biggest fans among the McGovern's crowd was Eugene Geary, a psychotic gunman referred to in a Chicago Crime Commission bulletin as "one of the most dangerous men in Chicago."

Geary had a reputation for violence that made the proprietors of even the toughest saloons and hangouts wince. At Polack Joe's Vestibule Café, he once threw the cash register through the mirror behind the bar and smashed the furniture and employees up merely because the singing waiter started to perform a livelier tune than the weepy Irish ballads that he loved. When the beefy bouncer at the Lambs Café attempted to eject him for rowdiness, Geary fired a shot at him and created mass panic among the customers. In 1914, patrons of a saloon at Twenty-third and Wabash watched in astonishment as he and two accomplices assaulted lawyer Samuel Foos when the latter entered the place to make a phone call. Geary held a revolver to the frightened man's head while the other two men went through his pockets and helped themselves to a wallet and watch.[21]

Whenever Geary staggered into McGovern's, maddened from drink, O'Banion would ply him with the one thing that rarely failed to calm him down: Irish ballads. Geary showed his gratitude by teaching the younger man the art of ambidextrous gunplay. He also took O'Banion along when he made sales calls to neighborhood cigar stores: Geary had invented a noxious cigar made from dried broccoli, called it "Gene Geary's Own," and demanded that the shops stock it, or else. Any proprietors who refused found themselves on the receiving end of O'Banion's street-trained fists. Geary's forced supplying was a precursor to the racketeering system of extortion and violence that would be so prevalent by 1928 that a special racket court was set up specifically to deal with such cases.[22]

Moran's friendship with O'Banion was just as deep, without psychopathology making the attachment more maudlin. Each admired the other's mischievous energy and dark sense of humor. The ornery spirit that had brought so much punishment upon him in St. Paul made Moran an appreciated part of O'Banion's circle.

That circle opened wide enough to include a nineteen-year-old Polish-American youth, Earl "Hymie" Weiss. When Weiss joined the McGovern's clique that summer of 1917, he was an embittered reject from the military. He'd volunteered for duty, having gained considerable war experience fighting other Polish youth gangs in the Bucktown neighborhood where he'd grown up, but failed the medical examination when the army physician pronounced his heart too weak for the strain of combat.[23]

Weiss privately believed that it was all bunk. Besides fighting in the ranks of the local gang, he'd lent his strong-arm talents to both unions and employers as a scab-thumper or a strikebreaker, depending on who was paying. He took the rejection more personally than his new companions did. They instantly recognized him as a sharp thinker, good organizer, and mental genius, even if temper did cloud his judgment from time to time.

Weiss was born Henry Earl Wojciechowski[24] in October 1898 in Chicago, the son of Polish immigrant Walente Wojciechowski, who ran a saloon on Austin Avenue, and his American wife, Mary. Weiss's combative instincts and explosive temper were inherited; his father had been a Coxeyite and a participant in a bloody battle between police and radicals in Buffalo, New York, in 1894.

When the financial panic of 1893 plunged the United States into the nineteenth century's most severe economic depression, Walente Wojciechowski was a steel worker in Cleveland, Ohio. He lost his job, and failure to secure another motivated him to align with the populist movement led by Jacob Coxey. He joined Coxey's parade of unemployed workers as they moved from Massillon, Ohio, toward Washington. The press and more advantaged members of the public derided the men as tramps, disease carriers, and radicals.

On August 24, 1894, a posse led by one Sheriff Taggart raided a party of 250 Coxeyites outside Buffalo. Their primary target was a man named Rybakowski, the acknowledged leader of the group. When Rybakowski's followers closed ranks around him and menaced the police with clubs, a battle erupted. Walente Wojciechowski received a scalp wound, and two of his comrades had their skulls crushed by police weapons.[25] Once Taggart's men got the upper hand, Walente and sixty-four others were marched off to the penitentiary to serve thirty-day sentences. The *New York Times* noted, "The Polish districts are greatly excited by the battle, and the streets are filled with them tonight, but the police do not anticipate any further trouble."[26]

Upon release, Wojciechowski moved his wife and three sons (Joseph, age seven; five-year-old Bruno, who would Americanize his name to Bernard; and Frederick, born in 1892) to Chicago. Two more children, Violet and Henry Earl, were born in 1895 and 1898 respectively.[27]

Despite the large family that resulted from the union, the marriage was not a happy one, and Mary separated from her husband while Violet and Earl were still young. Almost twenty years later, she admitted in probate court that she had given Earl the surname that he used until the time of his death in 1926:

Q: How many times were you married?

A: Only once.

Q: And then to whom?

A: Walente S. Wojciechowski.

Q: Is he living?

A: Yes, we were separated but not divorced.

Q: You took the name of "Weiss"?

A: Yes.[28]

Mary Weiss, like the O'Banion grandparents, sent Earl to a Catholic school, St. Malachy's. The religious atmosphere and instruction made little impression on him, although a legend would later spring up claiming that he carried a rosary constantly in his pockets and used it as a string of worry beads when not actively praying on it. He did carry around a small prayer book, a gift from one of his teachers, and thumbed through it during idle moments.[29]

Like O'Banion and Moran, he joined a gang while still young and took part in such activities as shoplifting, robbing warehouses along the waterfront, and fighting with rival gangs from Pojay Town, where another good-sized Polish colony was located. Weiss was not a large man, being at most a couple of inches taller than the diminutive O'Banion and of medium, lightly muscled build. But he possessed two qualities more prized on the streets than sheer size: speed and fearlessness. He had dark hair, flashing brown eyes, and was, from the perspective of his friends in the boy gang of his youth, Jewish in appearance. Although Catholic, Weiss was nicknamed "Hymie," and it stuck. If he disliked the moniker, it was not strongly enough for him to protest its constant use among the newsmen, police, and other gangsters after he became a regular newspaper feature.

Other members were gradually drawn into the Ox's band of safecrackers and porch climbers: Johnny Mahoney, a freelance safecracker and brother-in-law of underworld figure Tony "Mops" Volpe; former police officer Guy Wadsworth; Clarence White, a teaming contractor with a talent for murder and burglary; and

John Sheehy, who never amounted to much as a safecracker but was admired for his steel nerve. Some stayed around only for a couple of jobs or participated infrequently; Reiser, O'Banion, Weiss, and Moran were constant.

Although he refused to insulate himself by donating to a police "charity," Reiser was less stingy when it came to spending money to bring a big job to fruition. The word in Chicago was that anyone who knew about a safe recently filled with payroll money or client deposits stood to earn some cash of their own by getting the details to the Ox. If the ambitious individual could access a set of floor plans to the office where the safe was located, they stood to make even more.

Reiser once told O'Banion, "I'll pay a hundred dollars any time to score a thousand." O'Banion—and Weiss and Moran—listened. Before ten years had passed, the youthful trio would be applying the same system to learn about hidden liquor caches, and profiting well from it.

Once a location was selected, Reiser would visit the premises on a believable pretext, such as a delivery or job application, and then draw a map detailing the location of the safe and all exit and entry points. He purchased or stole sticks of dynamite and extracted nitroglycerin from them for use in blowing the safe open. On the night of the robbery, he and his accomplices would arm themselves with the usual safecracking tools: fuses, hammers, chisels, drills, laundry soap, and heavy blankets to drape over the steel box and deaden the sound of the nitro doing its work.[30]

When tackling a safe, the first approach the Reiser gang took was to knock the combination lock's exterior apparatus off and fiddle with the tumblers until the lock opened. If that failed (and the method grew less successful as cagey safe manufacturers constructed their boxes to foil it), they used a chisel to widen the hairline crack between the safe door and the box itself. When the crack was sufficiently wide, they drilled a hole large enough to pour in the nitroglycerine, then used the laundry soap to seal the rest of the crack around the door, so that the nitro wouldn't ooze out to the floor. Someone put a fuse into the freshly drilled hole after the safe had been thoroughly wrapped in blankets, while someone else touched a match to the fuse. The gang members scrambled to hide behind desks and filing cabinets before the charge went off and blasted the safe door all the way across the room.

As 1917 turned into 1918, the Reiser gang was making its mark all over Chicago. On January 29, 1918, they broke into the offices of the Western Dairy Company and helped themselves to a $2,000 payroll fund. On September 2 they slugged the night watchman at the Standard Oil Company and took $2,060 from the safe. The following night, they entered Schaeffer Brothers through the coal chute and got their hands on a $1,400 haul. On November 5 they blew open the safe at the Prudential Life Insurance Company and were rewarded for their efforts with a $3,865 payoff. They used the coal chute point of entry at least one more time, on December 3, when they entered the Borden Farm Products Company and stole $594.61.[31]

There were undoubtedly many more, but they weren't properly credited to the Reiser gang. Police only knew who to blame for the above thefts when one gang member, Johnny Mahoney, was caught and talked in order to obtain leniency from State's Attorney Robert Crowe in his own case. Mahoney had taken part in every escapade he talked about, and the fact that the gang did not use him on every job is the reason why the confirmed list is not a longer one.

In the latter part of 1918 the gang accepted a new member into its ranks, a handsome and cocksure young Sicilian who had just returned from a wartime stint in the Navy. Lodovico di Ambrosio, more commonly known as Vincent Drucci, was one of ten children born to John and Santa Rosa di Ambrosio, Sicilian immigrants who, upon arrival in Chicago, had opted to settle in the congested and vibrant yet poor Italian colony on the Near North Side.[32]

John di Ambrosio had been a stonecutter in the old country and through time and determination built up a small mosaic contracting business. His sons assisted in the enterprise once old enough to do so, but there is no evidence that Lodovico, or Drucci, had an interest or aptitude in maintaining the trade. He had run with the gangs as a boy, but more to satisfy a craving for excitement than to profit financially from burglaries or shoplifting, prompting his parents' hopes that he would settle down and join the family business. But when John died in August 1916[33] after suffering complications from a gall bladder removal operation, Drucci gradually eased himself out.

He joined the Navy when the United States announced its entry into the Great War, and upon the November 1918 cessation of hostilities found himself one of many unemployed and slightly shell-shocked young men who moved through society without really feeling connected.[34] He briefly worked for the family business, but his aggressive temper and restless work ethic severed that professional connection for good.

At the time he met O'Banion, Weiss, and Reiser, Drucci was making a living dismantling pay telephones for the coins inside, and in the learning stages of the art of safecracking. With the Reiser gang, membership hinged more upon who one knew as opposed to what skills one possessed (and of all of them, only Reiser and Hymie Weiss were anything close to completely competent). Drucci's primary asset to the gang was his fearlessness: he would fight his way through the riskiest situations without panicking or fleeing. He was also handsome, went through blondes like most men went through cigars, and had many stories of the type that continue to liven water-cooler conferences today.

Moran participated regularly right from the start and might have done so indefinitely had bad luck not struck again, as it was wont to do in his life. On November 18, 1917, Sergeants Michael Hughes and John McCauley caught him robbing a freight car. When they confronted him, he pulled out a pistol and fired three shots at Hughes, who returned fire and nicked Moran's arm with a bullet. The officers rushed him as he stumbled backward and fell, dropping his weapon in the process.[35]

After a brief struggle and a trip to the local station, Moran appeared before Judge Landis, charged with two counts of robbery. The gangster secured his freedom on a $42,000 bond posted by friends, but he failed to appear in court before Judge McGoorty on the appointed date of December 19 and forfeited the bond. His whereabouts did not remain a secret for long, once again thanks to a poor choice of associates.

At about ten twenty on the numbingly cold night of February 1, 1918, Dennis Tierney, a collector with the Illinois Central Railroad, was walking through the crowded Randolph Street station, carrying an estimated $5,000 to $10,000 in ticket receipts. M. J. Quinney, a security agent, accompanied him. The two men made rounds of all the stations every night, commencing at 8:45 p.m. with the Flossmore depot of the suburban line and collecting ticket receipts from all of the agents at all the intermediary stations between Flossmore and the Randolph Street stop. Clutching a black leather satchel containing the money, Tierney and Quinney headed for a downstairs vault, where they would leave the bag overnight.[36]

Suddenly four armed men converged on them, two seizing each man before they had left the ticket counter. During the struggle one of them struck Tierney over the head with a pistol butt, knocking him to the floor. The assailants seized the satchel containing the money and raced for one of the station exits while onlookers stared or screamed. Tierney staggered to his feet and fired one shot at the fleeing bandits, whereupon they turned and squeezed off several return rounds. One bullet struck the collector in the right breast, inflicting a mortal wound. After he fell to the station floor, the quartet ran down a flight of stairs leading to a cobblestone-paved courtyard on the west side of the station, with Quinney in pursuit.

The guard emptied his magazine pistol at them, and subsequent discovery of a bloody cap and muffler suggested that he had wounded at least one of them. A man named Hassler, who was on his way into the building when the robbers burst out into the winter air, told police that he saw one of them stumble and fall, calling out that he had been wounded.

The bandits piled into a waiting taxi, which took them north, toward Lake Street. It all happened so quickly that commuters waiting for late-night suburban trains on the outside platforms were unaware of what had transpired.

Less than an hour later, the taxi driver who had chauffeured the robbers away ran into the Warren Avenue station, wide-eyed and shaking. He told the desk sergeant about four young men having hired his taxi at Union Station and asking him to drive them to the Randolph Street depot. Once there, they told him to wait. Presuming that they were picking up a friend, he complied.

"I was only there around three minutes when I heard shots," James Pellikan said. "Then I saw three men run downstairs and all had revolvers in their hands. Two of them carried bundles. Then the man with the gray overcoat put a gun against my side and jumped into the seat beside me.

"'Drive north,' he said. 'Take orders from me, and you'll be all right. If you don't, you're a dead one. I'll croak you.'"

Pellikan did as he was told, driving north to Lake Street, turning west on State, and then north on South Water Street. He said that the man in the gray overcoat kept ordering him to drive faster, rattling him so much that he narrowly missed colliding with another car at Randolph and State. He concluded his harrowing tale with, "We were going over sixty miles an hour. After we passed through the Panhandle viaduct and were near Talman Avenue and Lake Street, the man in the gray overcoat said, 'Put her in neutral, then get out and walk down the street. Don't look back or I'll croak you.'"

Jennie King, who managed the lunch counter in the station's waiting room, told the police about two young men, both under thirty and roughly dressed, who took seats at the counter and ordered food just before the shooting went down. She was in the middle of filling their orders when she noticed a man, whom she described as five foot six, swarthy, and wearing eyeglasses, crawling under the gate that separated the lunch counter from public access. Before she could react, the man ordered Mrs. King to "get down behind the counter and keep your mouth shut." She screamed, but when he ordered her to get down and shut up a second time, she obeyed.

The two men who had ordered meals joined Mrs. King's assailant and a fourth man in the center of the waiting room seconds before Tierney and Quinney appeared. A commuter, G. W. Legare, later told the police, "I saw two men at the lunch counter walk over to the collector and his companion. There were some shouts and then . . . there was some shooting and the collector fell to the floor."

Chief of Police Mooney suspected that a gang headed by one George Raymond might be responsible. Under the alias of George Curtis, Raymond, like Moran, had been arrested in connection with the murder of Peter Bulfin but was released for lack of evidence. He had a record dating back to 1913 and had served four years in Joliet (June 1913 until March 1917) for larceny. Currently awaiting trial for complicity in a recent robbery of the Windsor Park State Bank, he was known to frequent a flat at 4140 West Monroe Street, so Mooney ordered the telephone wires tapped soon after the gang leader was released on a $35,000 bond.[37]

When a surveillance report indicated that Raymond and his gang would be attending a party at a saloon near Madison and Paulina streets, Mooney ordered a raid on the unoccupied Monroe Street hangout and another place on Flournoy Street. Detectives Crott and Ronan arrested two gang members at the Monroe

Street address, where they found both men armed and in possession of more than $300 cash. In one of the hideouts the officers found a black bag with railroad ticket stubs. Although agents for the Illinois Central Railroad, after examining the evidence, indicated that the bag and its contents were not those stolen from Tierney, the chief was positive that he was on the right track and ordered the Raymond gang picked up.

Some time after two o'clock in the afternoon, after the raids had been completed, two detective sergeants from the Fillmore Street station, Daniel O'Hara and John Norton, were walking down West Monroe, near Crawford. They spotted George Raymond, George Moran, and a companion a short distance ahead of them, apparently heading for number 4140. O'Hara nodded to his colleague.

"There are three tough birds we'd better pick up."

Raymond and the other two men spotted the officers, and instead of going into the building at 4140, turned quickly onto Crawford. John Norton told O'Hara, "Go and phone for the patrol wagon, and I'll trail them."

O'Hara ducked into a saloon to use the telephone while Norton continued after the trio who, ironically, were heading in the direction of the Fillmore Street station. When the patrol car, containing Captain Matthew Zimmer, Patrol Sergeant John McGinnis, and Detective Sergeant McCauley, left the station and went up Crawford, the gangsters realized that they were caught between the police vehicle on the south and O'Hara and Norton on the north.

Reaction was swift. All three drew pistols and began shooting. They were near the corner of Crawford and Lexington Street, so when Moran ran out of ammunition, he sprinted west on Lexington with Sergeant McGinnis and a patrolman hot on his trail. A young woman, Irene Robertson, was standing in the middle of the sidewalk when he barged into her in mid-flight, knocking her into a snowbank. One of the officers flagged down a vehicle to assist in the chase. After a few blocks, Moran, out of breath, threw down his pistol and surrendered. The third man dodged between some buildings and escaped into a network of alleys.

George Raymond also ran down Lexington but was headed off at Karlov Avenue. After zigzagging and backtracking without shaking his pursuers, he burst into a shop at 704 Crawford with the intention of seizing the proprietor as a hostage. He changed his mind when he spotted an oncoming streetcar and ran out of the shop dodging police bullets as he climbed aboard. As soon as he scanned the passengers' faces, Raymond thought he had leaped out of the frying pan into the fire; among those seated on the car was Lieutenant William Friel of the Maxwell Street station, whom he knew from past encounters.

Friel had no knowledge of the drama that was unfolding, but Raymond still panicked and shoved his smoking pistol in the lieutenant's face. "Back off, you bastard, or I'll bump you off!" he screamed, eyes bulging and sweat glistening on his reddened face. Then he suddenly spun about, pushed through the crowded aisle, and dug the gun into the frightened motorman's ribs, ordering, "Drive like hell."

Friel drew his own gun and headed for the gangster, who swore loudly and jumped off the front platform onto Crawford Avenue. The police patrol wagon pulled in front of the streetcar, which screeched to a halt. Detective Sergeant Norton made a beeline for Raymond, who fired at him and inflicted a scalp wound that sent blood showering into the officer's eyes. Undeterred, Norton kept up the pursuit. Two more bullets from Raymond's gun grazed Daniel Keefe, the patrol wagon driver.

In the midst of the smoke and gunfire Dr. James M. Hancock arrived on the scene, having just completed a patient visit. Hancock had slowed his vehicle when he saw the robber exit the streetcar, giving Raymond the opportunity to jump on the running board and try to seize the steering wheel. During the struggle that ensued, Raymond shot the physician in the forehead and left arm. Hancock slumped in the seat, badly wounded, but before the escapee could slip into the driver's seat, his police pursuers closed in and killed him.

Moran was locked up at the Fillmore Street station. When word of his arrest and the fact that he was a paroled convict appeared in the Chicago newspapers, State's Attorney Maclay Hoyne used the opportunity to criticize the state parole system and, in effect, blame the holdups and killings on lax probation officials.

"How many paroled prisoners are there right now in Chicago and Cook County?" he demanded. "How many parole agents are there? How do they look after the paroled prisoners; how do they keep track of them? How do the paroled men report? Where do agents get their information from regarding paroled men? Is it not true that they tell the men to report every so often and then are satisfied if the paroled men say, 'We're good boys, we've got jobs, we've done nothing wrong'?[38]

"This paroling of criminals has become a menace—an evil. Out of eighteen that have been paroled, only seven have been returned to prison. Where are the others? How many are in Chicago, and what are they doing?"

Moran admitted to being a friend of George Raymond but denied any association with the Illinois Central Railroad theft or the murder of Dennis Tierney. When the police learned that he was wanted as a bail-jumper, they transferred him to the Cook County Jail. On April 25 he appeared in court and succeeded in having the two counts of robbery reduced to one, but bail was denied since he had not yet been exonerated in the Tierney case, and he was returned to jail. Frustration over this outcome likely resulted in his active participation in the events of May 4.

By May, Moran's fellow prisoners at the jail included Thomas "Tommy" Touhy, a seasoned safecracker who had been awaiting trial since March 2 for a series of safe blowings; Earl Dear, under sentence of death for murdering chauffeur Rudolph Wolf while stealing Wolf's car; Lloyd Bopp and Albert Johnson, both scheduled to hang for killing police officers; and Frank Bender and Leonard Banks, who'd been convicted of robbing the Stockman's Trust and Savings Bank.

These prisoners, along with Moran, were confined in specially constructed cells on the fourth floor of the newer section of the jail, as they were considered prime escape risks. Acting Chief of Police Alcock and the state's attorney's office had both been warned that an attempt might be made to break out Earl Dear and the other condemned men, and passed the information along to jailer Will T. Davies, but what precautions Davies took are not known.

On May 4, "bath day," the guards herded the prisoners to the showers in the older section of the jail in groups of twelve. The so-called "dangerous contingent," which included Dear, Bopp, Johnson, Touhy, Moran, and Bender, were all in one gang escorted by guards George Norton, John Beggy, and Michael Lardner. While the men filled the shower room and began to soap themselves, Lardner stood watch from the doorway. Norton and Beggy chatted in the outer hallway.[39]

Suddenly, several of the men emerged from the steam, clad only in towels, and approached Lardner. "Get out of here, Mike," one of them said in urgent tones. "Beat it over to the new jail or you'll be blown to pieces."

They proceeded to push Lardner, a longtime guard popular with the prisoners, into the hallway. Touhy, Moran, Banks, and Bender grabbed George Norton and John Beggy. The three guards, shaken but unharmed, were hustled into the bathroom, where Dear, Johnson, murderer Dennis Anderson, and Bopp—the "gallows squad"—took charge of them. The four condemned men forced the captives onto the damp tile floor and sat on them while Moran, Touhy, and the Stockman's Savings robbers hurried down the hallway to a pre-arranged spot along the jail's west wall.

Suddenly there was an explosion.

An investigation revealed that prior to the shower run, nitroglycerin had been smuggled into the jail in milk bottles. While chatter from the showering prisoners had distracted the guards, Touhy had acquired the bottles, which had been secreted in the bathroom. The plotters had chosen a spot on the west wall for the nitro to breach. Once a hole was blown, it would only be a ten-foot drop and then a sprint to Illinois Street and freedom.

The explosion, however, resulted in more noise than damage. It echoed through the corridors, and the impact shook the walls, creating an uproar among the prisoners in the main jail. But the wall, which was three feet thick and fortified with steel plate, remained intact except for a ragged dent.

The horrified plotters stood there, too petrified to move. All around them and throughout the jail, pandemonium reigned. Prisoners screamed and howled in their cells while guards tried without success to calm them. More than a hundred detectives and policemen from the central station, the bureau, and the Chicago Avenue station descended on the place and cordoned it off. Deputy Sheriff Charles W. Peters took custody of Moran, Touhy, Banks, and Bender, and sent them back to their cells under escort. In the investigation that followed, six guards, including Lardner, Norton, and Beggy were charged with "cowardice" by jailer Davies and suspended from duty. It is not known what, if any, punishment other than solitary confinement was meted out to the plotters.

On May 24 Moran had his day in court on the single robbery charge. By then he had been absolved of complicity in the Tierney murder. Another George Raymond gang member had turned state's evidence and in a summer 1918 trial named Raymond and three other accomplices as the guilty parties. (In the end, because Raymond was dead, gangster Harry Emerson received a thirty-year prison sentence for the robbery and killing.[40]) The judge presiding over Moran's robbery case sentenced him to one to fourteen years at his Joliet alma mater.

The following week, on May 31, he once again joined a small group of felons on the penitentiary-bound train. It was the same routine as before: the attendant who furnished the written descriptions of the new arrivals noted Moran as "Hair— dark chestnut; eyes—yellow-azure-blue; complexion—sallow." For reasons best known to himself, Moran gave his birthplace as Canada.[41]

Things had changed, however, since the last time he had walked through the prison gates. He had friends in Chicago, friends like O'Banion and Weiss, who retained a camaraderie with Hot Stove Jimmy Quinn's old political cronies and who knew the right price for almost anything—even getting a conviction overturned or at least reviewed. Although no evidence exists to support this assertion, it's possible that O'Banion was behind the smuggling of the nitro into the jail; it was the sort of challenge the Irish-American gangster delighted in.

Two months after his arrival at Joliet, Moran was back in Chicago, albeit as a guest of the Cook County Jail. His attorney had immediately filed an appeal of the robbery conviction, resulting in his return to the city in August for a court appearance. Another inmate entered the jail at the same time, and Moran's encounter with him nearly led to another trial, this one for attempted murder.

Richard Flaherty was a police officer attached to the Cottage Grove Avenue station. On the night of August 5 he telephoned the Englewood station to report that his wife, Anna, had fallen out of bed and died suddenly. He added that she had been ill for some time and offered the opinion that heart failure had killed her. The coroner examined her body and discovered an appalling number of internal injuries. The Flahertys' five-year-old daughter, Mary, told the police, "Papa beat mamma when he came home, and she fell out of bed and he kicked her two or three times." Her testimony and the coroner's findings led to Flaherty's arrest and transportation to the county jail to await trial.

Word of his crime, not to mention his status as a former policeman, preceded him. The morning of his arrival, Flaherty, who was placed in the jail's fourth tier, joined sixty of his fellow inmates for exercise in the bullpen. Suddenly a cry arose.

"There's the copper that killed his wife. There's the copper that pinched us. Go get him, boys!"

Six prisoners, Moran included, surged forward and began striking and kicking Flaherty. Jailer Davies and the bullpen guard, a man named Mason, succeeded in rescuing the stricken ex-policeman, but not before he had lost a tooth and suffered a black eye, split lip, and facial lacerations. Moran and the other five attackers were charged with attempted murder, but when Flaherty refused to assist in prosecuting them, the charges were dropped and Moran was returned to Joliet after his Chicago court appearance.[42]

While George Moran took steps to adjust to the hopefully temporary accommodations, the world outside went through changes of its own. One major event would have powerful and permanent ramifications for America in general and Moran in particular. Prohibition descended on the land on January 17, 1920, and the young hoodlum from Minnesota would be one of the most notorious figures to emerge from the "Noble Experiment."

4

THE THINKING MAN'S GANGSTER

J OHN TORRIO HAS BEEN CALLED a man before his time. Unlike his gangster associates, who rarely thought beyond the next day or even week because of the improbability of their own futures, Torrio operated in the present but expended tremendous energy in bringing grandiose ideas and concepts to fruition. He worked toward and lived for the next big step in whatever business he undertook, but like most men whose ideas were too progressive for the society in which they dwelled, he would know more resistance and disappointment than victory.

Although a square peg in a round hole, Torrio was intelligent, and his brain had kept him alive and in command of some of New York City's most fearsome gangsters over the years. He'd been apprenticed to the seamy side of city life the way the better-class families placed their sons in clerical and manual professions to learn the trade. Born in 1882 in Orsara di Puglia, Italy, not too far from Naples, young Johnny had been brought to America by his mother at the age of two.[1] Legend has it that he took his first stumbling steps on American soil wearing a white nightdress with his poorly scrawled name pinned to the front. Not long after mother and son took up residence in the Italian quarter of New York's notorious Five Points district, Mrs. Torrio remarried. Her husband, Salvatore Caputo, put John to work in his saloon, running errands for both management and customers.

Disdaining the idea of washing beer steins and cleaning up after drunks for the rest of his life, Torrio at the age of nineteen became a boxing promoter under the pseudonym of J. T. McCarthy, using his creative brain to rig matches without detection. He was good at it, taking in enough money to pay off the local bosses, cops, and gang leaders, and open a bar on James Street. When the clientele grew large enough, he leased a nearby boarding house and store and swiftly transformed them both into a brothel and pool hall. Keeping his customers happy earned Johnny Torrio an appreciative following that by 1905 became his gang, the James Street Boys.[2]

John Torrio was the visual opposite of the broken-nose, scarred bruiser type that crowded into his bar and joined his gang. He was short, slightly built, and unless antagonized, wore a placid, rested expression. Only his eyes gave a real hint that he was anything but benign; they were dark, cold when angry, and unfathomable. He was equally untypical as a gang boss, splitting all income from robberies and gang-controlled vice equally among the participants. Torrio's business ethic was untarnished by greed. He sincerely believed that there was plenty for everyone.

The New York of Torrio's youth was a city in the grasp of the boodling political machine known as Tammany Hall, with its non-legislative muscle provided by such feared and lethal gang leaders as Monk Eastman and Paul Kelly. Making oneself known and useful to politicians and reigning gangsters was the way for an ambitious young man with few worldly prospects to climb up the underworld ladder and acquire the type of money and local prestige that would not normally come to the slum dweller. It was also a reality that the bigger gangs regarded "independents" in their territory with suspicion, and would sooner or later force the question of whether one was with them or against them.

Under Torrio's direction, the James Street Boys allied themselves with Paul Kelly's Five Points Gang. The Five Pointers practiced extortion rackets, owned or protected scores of brothels, and ran gambling games and resorts in the area between Broadway and the Bowery, and City Hall Park and Fourteenth Street. The head of this greatly feared crew of fifteen hundred battlers was Paolo Antonini Vaccarrelli, who made his name easier to pronounce and remember by changing it to Paul Kelly.

Kelly, like Torrio, was a small, dapper figure who rose through the ranks on the strength of his brain and cunning. He'd been a featherweight prizefighter during the 1890s and perfected a punch that he still put to good use if and when the occasion demanded. His pugilistic prowess was rarely needed by the time of his acquaintance with Torrio; by 1905 Kelly ran his small army from his headquarters on Great Jones Street, a garish dance hall called the New Brighton. At his side (as well as beck and call) were such head breakers as Razor Reilly and "Eat 'Em Up" Jack McManus. Anyone meeting him for the first time, unaware of his name or reputation, would have assumed him to be a successful businessman and probably a university graduate. He wore expensive but tasteful suits; spoke English, French, and Italian fluently; and read on such a wide variety of subjects that rich slummers, upon meeting him, were often intrigued in spite of themselves.[3]

74

"Big Tim" Sullivan and the other Tammany sachems valued Kelly's intelligence and self-control as much as the fifteen hundred gangsters he put at their disposal as voters and vote-getters, as the public's fascination with and fear of the Neanderthal thug type like Monk Eastman was on the decline. When Eastman was nabbed by a private detective while about to slug a rich youth he'd been trailing for blocks, Tammany recognized a primal viciousness out of control and did nothing to prevent a long prison term for the hoodlum. Kelly, more affable and restrained, continued to benefit from their association.

Torrio, in emulating the successful and powerful Paul Kelly, found his own rough edges smoothing. He could now afford to dress well and did so. He followed Kelly's example and took in more opera than vaudeville and burlesque. He put his political sponsors at their ease by presenting himself as a younger but equally civilized version of his mentor. Over time he acquired gang and political connections that allowed his businesses to flourish, first in Manhattan and then in Brooklyn. In the latter locale he maintained an office on the second floor over a restaurant, the door and windows proclaiming in bold lettering THE JOHN TORRIO ASSOCIATION.

In 1909 he received an urgent missive from Chicago. A relative, Levee vice lord Big Jim Colosimo,[4] needed his help in taking care of a situation that local muscle had been unable to eradicate. Colosimo had been receiving demands for money from a Black Hand gang who saw him as a wealthy Italian target and did not seem intimidated by his underworld standing. Big Jim had initially fought back, strangling at least one extortionist during a staged payoff meeting. But the Black Handers were too numerous and too faceless to fight easily. By 1909 they had notified Colosimo that unless he paid $50,000, he would not live to see the decade end. Big Jim needed assistance from someone just as crafty as his tormentors, who could beat them by scheming them into submission before moving in for the kill.

The plea for help came at a time when Torrio's own situation in New York was precarious. Monk Eastman's arrest and imprisonment had resulted in a temporary peace, as his successors were too busy redefining their roles in the new Monk-less Eastman gang. But in Brooklyn, where Torrio was headquartered, Irish gangsters fought Italians over waterfront racketeering and disrupted Italian-run or -protected businesses as part of their general vendetta. Johnny may not have feared the collapse of his operation, but the relentless bloodshed disgusted him. He did not want his energy divided between keeping his gambling halls and brothels going and fighting off the predatory Irish.

He decided to leave everything in the hands of deserving lieutenants and depart for Chicago. Colosimo's problem seemed pretty localized compared to the widespread, anti-Italian fighting that was ripping Brooklyn apart. Colosimo, from what he understood, was as well connected socially and politically as Kelly was in New York, and Big Jim's gratitude would surely result in an elevated place in the Chicago gang hierarchy.[5]

Upon his arrival in Chicago, Torrio conferred with Colosimo to get a thorough overview of the situation before setting a retaliation plan in motion. Identifying himself as Big Jim's representative, he sent word to the Black Handers that the Levee vice lord was unable to bear the strain of living in the shadow of death any longer and wanted to pay up. After brief negotiations, three Black Handers arrived at a railroad underpass to pick up the money that they'd been assured was forthcoming. Perhaps the night was moonless, or their greed had eclipsed the caution that the occasion called for, as they failed to notice the silent, parked carriage in the vicinity.

A hail of bullets that issued from the carriage's curtained windows spelled the end of their ambition to get rich at Colosimo's expense. Two died on the spot, the third clung to life long enough to have a smug Big Jim brought to his bedside so that he could aptly curse him as a traitor. Colosimo shrugged and left the hospital room; he had little regard for such Old World superstitions, although he did maintain a family Bible over which he required his followers to swear eternal loyalty to him.[6]

Big Jim rewarded Torrio for his efficiency by making him manager of the Saratoga, one of the flashier links in the Colosimo brothel chain. The little man from Brooklyn acted in typical fashion by taking a successful formula and making it even more profitable. In first the Saratoga and then other select houses, he had the women wear silk hair bows and dress in "rompers" that not only showed off more flesh but also projected a "little girl" image that the more lecherous visitors found irresistible. When the automobile became an American fixture, Torrio appealed to the pleasure motorist by opening roadhouses, or saloon-brothel combinations that dished up the crudest city pleasures in charming rustic environments.

The first of these vice outposts was located in Burnham, a tiny community eighteen miles from the Levee near the Illinois-Indiana border. The local police in these rural districts were easy to pay off in most instances, but Torrio further insured against trouble by constructing the roadhouse at the border's edge, so that the girls and their customers could flee any harassing Illinois lawmen by hurrying into Indiana.[7] The place did so well that two more resorts, the Speedway Inn and the Burnham Inn, were added to the village's vice holdings.

In February 1916 one of the brothels caught fire when a furnace overheated, resulting in the death of Laura Clarke, one of the working girls. Burnham authorities hastily assured Coroner Hoffman that the establishment was a rooming house run by a Chicago widow named Helen Herrald. They denied that "Porky" Torrio, as they called him, had anything to do with ownership or maintenance of the place.[8]

Finding women to staff these houses rarely posed a problem. Since the mid-1890s, girls who in a previous era would have remained at home until marriage were striking out on their own and taking jobs in offices, department stores, factories, and other places that required female labor without really valuing it. Some of these girls starved on their pathetic wages until desperation directed them into prostitution. Other women entered brothels after being seduced and abandoned by unscrupulous lovers.

Despite overwhelming evidence that pointed to economic and social crisis being at the root of the prostitution problem, the public instead obsessed over white slavery, or girls being forcibly recruited into the life. Drugged drinks and false job offers were used by procurers when they deemed the target worth it, but nowhere near as often as the press and reformers trumpeted.

In 1910 the white slavery issue set the North American reform element aflame, leading to vice investigation committees in almost every city and eventually the passage of the Mann Act, making it a federal offense to move a woman from one state to another for "immoral" purposes. Colosimo found himself in danger of being convicted under the new law in October 1912, when Rose Bruno, alias Rossi, one of his girls, whom he and partner Maurice Van Bever had sent to New York in an "exchange arrangement" with panderers there, went public with her experiences and named Colosimo as one of those behind her enslavement and transportation. Threats against her life led investigators to hide her away in Bridgeport, Connecticut, where she was kept under guard.[9]

Torrio stepped in. One day, five men showed up at the hideout bearing Department of Justice credentials and telling the police guard that further affidavits were necessary from the girl. Bruno left with them in their car and was not seen again until the following day, when two peddlers found her bullet-torn corpse sprawled in a country lane outside the town. She had been shot five times in the face. Witnesses identified her abductors as Giuseppe Amato, a Torrio associate who had operated the resort at 106 West Twenty-first Street where the girl had been shipped from, and two members of Torrio's James Street Boys. Amato was located and arrested, but the New York duo provided alibis. The young woman's murder killed the federal case against Big Jim, and a relieved Colosimo rewarded Torrio with a percentage of his vice and gambling operation.

Satisfied that he had found someone who could keep his businesses growing and handle himself in a crisis, Colosimo allowed himself to relax for the first time in years. Although he continued to oversee everything, he played less and less of a direct role in his empire's day-to-day operations. Big Jim had worked hard to rise above the menial station he had been born into, and he wanted to concentrate more on the perks than the perils of being a wealthy "businessman."

Vincenzo "Big Jim" Colosimo was born in Italy but brought to the United States by his father at the age of ten. Like most newly arrived young Italians, he did not enjoy a privileged upbringing, bypassing school in favor of a succession of low-paying jobs—boot-blacking, water boy for a railroad crew, and sweeping Chicago's grimy streets. It was in the latter occupation he found his true calling: manipulating others for his personal gain. He organized the other street sweepers in his crew into a solid voting bloc that he placed in the service of First Ward Aldermen Kenna and Coughlin. They returned the favor by awarding him a precinct captaincy.

One of Colosimo's earliest known criminal undertakings was an embezzlement scheme he hatched with one Ciraldi Frank, who had married his sister.[10] Using Frank as a front, they opened a private bank at 390 Clark Street and attracted a large Italian clientele. In March 1900, when the bank's holdings totaled $7,000, Frank and his wife fled to New Orleans, taking the money with them and leaving hundreds of bewildered compatriots destitute. Colosimo, who was questioned because of his family connection to the fugitives, assured the police that he would turn the thieves in himself if he found them. He profited from that scheme by $3,500 and quit his street inspecting position to work for the First Ward aldermen full time.

When Torrio proved adept in the precinct captain role, Kenna and Coughlin backed him in other enterprises, such as poolroom manager and saloonkeeper. They also assigned him the task of collecting the regular protection fees that the First Ward brothels paid in order to operate without police interference.

Colosimo was the ideal collection agent. Of middle height but powerful build, he had no qualms about slipping on a pair of brass knuckles and inflicting damage upon those who protested the fees. Physical violence was rarely necessary because the majority of those on his "route" were middle-aged madams who found the swarthy, brash young man handsome. One of them, Victoria Moresco, ran an average-quality bordello on Armour Avenue. In her infatuation he recognized an opportunity to stake a claim in the Levee vice trade, and he acted on it.[11]

Colosimo and Victoria Moresco were married in 1902. After the wedding he yielded to sentimentality by naming her resort the Victoria, in her honor. Together they acquired more properties, and by the time John Torrio arrived from Brooklyn to deal with the nuisance that had arisen from Big Jim's ascent into wealth, Colosimo either owned or controlled houses that ran the gamut from the fancier Victoria to the Bed Bug Row "cribs," where diseased sex could be had for twenty-five cents a session. He had an arrangement with another Levee vice lord, Maurice Van Bever, to import girls from other cities and in return export some of his own "older stock."

In 1910 Colosimo invested a chunk of his bordello income in a restaurant at 2126 South Wabash Avenue. He called it Colosimo's Café and turned it into an oasis of glamour in the heart of the seedy red light district. The café, famous for its glass-and-mahogany bar, beautiful showgirls and singers, and glittering dance floor that could be raised or lowered by hydraulic lifts, appealed to the city's rich because of its regal décor, top-notch meals prepared by a cordon bleu chef, and its location in the midst of the wicked Levee, which they'd been curious about but found no respectable reason to explore. Big Jim's public status as a successful restaurateur brought him into contact with visiting and local celebrities, many of whom became his friends, among them, Enrico Caruso, Al Jolson, Sophie Tucker, Luisa Tetrazzini.[12]

Colosimo gloried in playing the genial Italian host. He would navigate his large frame through the sea of diners, tuxedo hugging his grizzly-bear frame and hair and moustache groomed and gleaming like obsidian. He slapped men on the backs and kissed women's hands with a respectful appreciation that made matrons blush. Diamonds, a fetish of his, glittered and winked from his rings, garters, stickpin, and belt buckle. He even toted around a small chamois bag loaded with the gems, fingering and playing with them during idle moments. His silk-lined pockets contained a pearl-handled revolver and a huge wad of cash, which he would use to advance funds to gambler associates on a losing streak. The last practice earned him the nickname "Bank."

While Big Jim entertained the wealthy masses in his café, Torrio continued to supervise the day-to-day operations of the Colosimo vice and gambling empire. It was a shadowy, functional role that suited Johnny perfectly.

Approaching it as one would a regular day job, he showed up at his desk by nine o'clock each morning and one by one made the decisions that ensured the continued success of the business: transferring women between brothels, assessing the profits and losses of the gambling houses, approving the payoffs to everyone from the mayor's office down to the rookie cops whose beats included streets containing Colosimo brothels, and issuing the occasional order to put an aspiring competitor or rebellious prostitute in his or her place. He worked with a cold efficiency, the lives of the women he managed or the gamblers who ruined themselves in his games being of no special concern, and unless an emergency cropped up, was back home by six each evening. He adored his wife, Anna, and she in turn called him the "best and dearest of husbands."[13]

The vice community received a jolt in 1912, when the city's reformers made what was thought to be just another howl in the pulpits and press. A firebrand crusader led a crowd of the faithful into the heart of the Levee, picking up a score of curious followers in the procession, many of whom as a result found themselves in the red light zone for the first time and emptied their wallets finding out what all the fuss was about. This dramatic march and its attending newspaper exposure drew public attention to the depravity that went on with the tolerance if not approval of the cops and Kenna and Coughlin. State's Attorney John E. Wayman, who had regarded the prostitution and gambling as regrettable but permanent nuisances, caved in to reformer harassment and ordered a series of raids aimed at total closure of the Levee.

Torrio reacted to the raids by giving the reformers exactly what they wanted— or at least thought they did. After he, Colosimo, Maurice Van Bever, and the vice ring's other heavy-hitters called a council of war, they obligingly emptied the Levee of fallen women. Those scarlet-lipped, powdered, scantily clad ladies swarmed from their rooms and boudoirs into respectable areas of the city, banging on doors to demand lodging, sitting in family-style restaurants and turning the air blue with smoke and profanities, and in general becoming more of a social nuisance than ever.[14]

The reformers had to admit that in their zeal, they never stopped to consider where the displaced women would go after being evicted. They eased up, but only enough to allow the Levee to spring back into a feeble shadow of life. Brothels continued to do business, but gone were the days of scarlet window blinds and half-naked dances in brightly lit windows. Outwardly, the old vice zone was taken over by massage parlors, dance studios (specializing in private, intimate dance steps), and hotels whose employees knew just who to call if a male guest needed companionship for the evening.

There were setbacks in the war against the reformers. In July 1914 an unusual and fatal three-way shootout took place between Colosimo-Torrio gangsters, men from Mayor Harrison's Morals Squad, and two Chicago police officers who thought that the plainclothes morals officers were gangsters shooting it out with rivals. One of the policemen was killed while others were wounded. During the hue and cry that followed in the press, Colosimo was thrown into jail for a few hours and a warrant was issued for the arrest of John Torrio, who had actually been present during the street battle. State's Attorney Maclay Hoyne announced that he would seek indictments against both vice leaders, but nothing came of it.[15] Mayor Harrison revoked Colosimo's license for the café after police investigator Frances Willsey swore that she had been served liquor there after 1 a.m., in violation of a 1911 law directing that saloons be closed after that hour. The license was eventually restored.

In May 1919 *Tribune* reporter Morrow Krum visited one of Colosimo's suburban brothels, Burnham's Arrowhead Inn, on an undercover anti-vice assignment for his paper. He stayed in the bar section long enough to see enough post-1 a.m. drinking and general lewdness to make a scandalous story and slipped to a telephone to make a report to his editor. As he was leaving, Colosimo, who must have been doing an inspection tour, seized him on the veranda.

"You dirty rat," he hissed, "we heard you calling your office." Krum paled when the big Italian indicated that the phone in the booth had been tapped.

The reporter reeled and fell off the veranda into the road when Big Jim punched him in the mouth. Another Inn employee tackled him before he could get up, beat him severely, and sneered, "You're damned lucky to get out of here alive, rat."[16]

Krum pressed charges. A judge found Colosimo guilty of assault and ordered him to pay a $120 fine, as well as $200 for violating the state's Sunday closing law. It was a paltry punishment that only enforced the general perception that Big Jim and his syndicate were immune to justice.[17]

When Prohibition evolved from a barroom joke/fear to a looming reality, Torrio recognized it as the brainchild of a select group that believed that legislation could curb and dictate human nature. As a connoisseur of human vices, he knew that the absence of legal beer and liquor would create a huge market for illegal varieties, not to mention skyrocket the price that the parched and rebellious public would be willing to pay.

Torrio used a percentage of the profits from the vice empire to buy into local breweries and distilleries—those whose owners/directors were willing to keep them operating in the shadow of potential imprisonment. Colosimo, while not taking a leading role in these purchases and operating arrangements, approved the venture into bootlegging and let Torrio develop that new business line as he saw fit.[18]

John Torrio was not the only underworld figure in Chicago to realize that Prohibition would be the greatest gift to America's underworld since the advent of the corruptible politician. Terry Druggan and Frankie Lake, Valley Gang alumni who looked like vaudevillians in their matching horn-rimmed glasses and slightly goofy grins but killed as readily as their toughest Chicago brethren, were making arrangements to go into partnership with Joseph Stenson, scion of a local brewing family.

Druggan and Lake already had some bootlegging experience, ex-fireman Lake having made a modest profit selling five-gallon cans of homemade alcohol to Valley saloons. Stenson was no stranger to being prosecuted for bootlegging, having been arrested and fined for a violation of a wartime Prohibition law, but the money he stood to make in this new venture overshadowed the experience, and he joined forces with Druggan and Lake without thinking twice.[19]

On Chicago's North Side, Dean O'Banion was the one who organized quickly and thoroughly enough to rise to the top. At the time that the Eighteenth Amendment was adopted, he had status and rank in the city's underworld as a member of Charles Reiser's safecracking gang. Since McGovern's had been shuttered by the reformist Committee of Fifteen, O'Banion had been working as a *Herald and Examiner* slugger in the newspaper circulation wars, accepting a paycheck from William Randolph Hearst to burn newsstands carrying Colonel Robert McCormick's *Tribune*.

Joining him in threatening newsdealers and ripping *Tribunes* out of readers' hands were some of Chicago's most brutal triggermen, such as the murderous Frank McErlane. *Herald and Examiner* reporter Edward Dean Sullivan, whom O'Banion escorted into the heart of a battle zone during the July 1919 race riots, would write at length about the gangster's exploits both during and after the circulation war years in his book *Rattling the Cup on Chicago Crime*. Sullivan was open in his admiration of O'Banion, whose fast motorcycle and speed with a gun saved both their lives during that July assignment.

O'Banion got more out of his McGovern's and *Examiner* jobs than money and battle scars. He had cultivated useful friendships and connections, and by sheer force of personality had become more known and respected in the North Side hierarchy than Reiser himself. Other North Side gangsters would become involved in bootlegging, but any independence they enjoyed was short-lived. By the time Prohibition was one year old, liquor distribution and sales north of Madison Street were conducted either with O'Banion's permission or at his direction.

His big break in the bootlegging business came on the morning of December 30, 1919, when he was walking south on Wells Street on an errand, shoulders hunched against the cold and mind on the following night's celebration, which would be the last one toasted with legal champagne if the drys had anything to say about it. After crossing Randolph Street, O'Banion found his path cut off by a flatbed truck idling in the delivery alley behind the Randolph Hotel, which was still known locally by its pre-war name of the Bismarck. Several other pedestrians had the same problem, since going around the nose of the vehicle would potentially put one into the edge of oncoming Wells Street traffic. The driver showed no sign of moving; if anything, he seemed amused by the mass predicament that was becoming more widespread by the second.

Some cursed and turned back, but more waited for the truck to back up or glide onto Wells. While stamping his feet and rubbing his fingers to keep warm, O'Banion gave in to curiosity and lifted the edge of the huge tarp that covered the vehicle's contents. His eyes fell on the wooden slats of load after load of Grommes & Ullrich whiskey bottles, and just as quickly, he took his first step into the business that would make him wealthy, feared, and a legend.

Lowering the tarp, he ambled to the front of the truck and beckoned to the driver, who rolled down the window and leaned partway out to hear what he was saying. With surprising speed for someone with a pronounced limp, O'Banion jumped onto the running board of the vehicle, grabbed the other man in a headlock, and pummeled him with a fist made heavier by a roll of nickels that he always carried in anticipation of just such an opportunity. When the battered driver fell limp, O'Banion maneuvered his body out of the truck, propped him against the hotel wall, and climbed behind the wheel. He maneuvered the unwieldy vehicle out of the alley and into the early morning commuter traffic, much to the relief of the pedestrians who had made no attempt to interfere with the assault on the driver, such sights in Chicago being commonplace.

As he navigated the city streets, O'Banion acknowledged that turning this liquid gold into cash was going to require the services of an intermediary, someone with access to storage facilities for booze and truck and the connections to find customers for both. His friend and sometime associate Nails Morton came to mind.[20]

Morton, born Samuel J. Marcovitz in 1893, was a product of Chicago's Jewish ghetto on Maxwell Street. Like Vincent Drucci, the stocky, dark-complected Morton had enlisted in the American armed forces during the war, Morton going overseas to France with the 131st Illinois Infantry.[21] Years of fighting in the ghetto streets had desensitized the gangster to "combat terrors," and he earned a battlefield commission for leading a charge despite severe shrapnel wounds. When he returned to Maxwell Street a decorated war hero, he continued to do battle, but against the "Jew-baiters," gangs of malefactors who delighted in vandalizing pushcarts, assaulting Orthodox Jewish men made conspicuous by their long beards and dark garb, and leering at frightened Jewish women. Morton put enough of those troublemakers on the run to earn a reluctant respect among those of his race who regarded his livelihood with disdain.

By December 1919 Nails Morton was running a large and successful fencing operation, handling goods heisted locally, and running a "stolen car exchange" program with a Detroit gang known as the Little Jewish Navy.[22] He associated with the West Side Millers, a gang of Jewish brothers who entrenched themselves in the cleaning and dyeing unions using varying levels of violent persuasion. How he met O'Banion is not known, although it was probably through Hymie Weiss, a longtime friend.

O'Banion drove to Morton's Maxwell Street garage. It was a fortuitous decision. In exchange for a generous percentage of the total sale, Morton agreed to use his contacts among the saloonkeepers on the West Side to dispose of the whiskey, and within twenty minutes it was all sold. Even the truck was snapped up by a Morton contact at a brewery in Peoria.[23] When O'Banion left the garage, he was richer by several thousand dollars and resolute in how he planned to make his fortune. Unbeknownst to him at the time, fame was also in the cards.

January 16, 1920
A newly arrived foreigner unaware of the recent developments in American history would have assumed that Armageddon or a similarly climactic event was about to take place. Men and women from the various temperance groups were hurrying to churches and auditoriums in droves to prepare for the countdown to America's rebirth as a dry, sinless nation. Those with lower ideals ran amok through the streets, arms loaded with whatever liquor bottles would not fit into the car trunks, baby buggies, or wagons that had been pressed into service as impromptu booze trucks.

In Norfolk, Virginia, baseball-player-turned-evangelist Billy Sunday watched from his tabernacle door as a macabre cortege marched solemnly into the building: a horse-drawn hearse, accompanied by twenty pallbearers and followed by a sorrowing figure dressed as Satan. Inside the hearse was an open coffin containing an effigy of John Barleycorn.

"Good-bye, John!" Sunday bellowed for the benefit of his enthralled audience. "You were God's worst enemy. You were Hell's best friend. I hate you with a perfect hatred. I love to hate you." He promised the ten thousand congregants that the coming of Prohibition signified that "the reign of tears is over. The slums will soon be a memory. We will turn our prisons into factories and our jails into storehouses and corncribs. Men will walk upright now, women will smile, and the children will laugh. Hell will be forever for rent."[24]

In Washington's First Congregational Church, former presidential hopeful William Jennings Bryan quoted the Gospel according to St. Matthew: "They are dead which sought the young child's life." Secretary of the Navy Josephus Daniels followed Bryan to the pulpit and proclaimed, "No man living will ever see a Congress that will lessen the enforcement of that law. The saloon is as dead as slavery."[25]

Those who mourned the imminent dry spell heralded the midnight countdown with a mixture of sadness, nostalgia, and downhearted, plastic gaiety. Tom Healy, owner of the Golden Glades Restaurant in New York, had a coffin carried along the perimeter of the dance floor, around which the tables were arranged, for everyone to throw their last empty beer, wine, and shot glass into. Philadelphia publisher George Sheldon, visiting New York at that time, took over an entire dining room in the posh Hotel Park Avenue and threw an extravaganza that would be talked about for years afterward: two hundred guests, wearing black, sat in a black-walled room outfitted for the occasion with black tables, tablecloths, and candelabras. Tableware, napkins, and glasses were all black, and waiters served black caviar while a band in funereal garb played one dirge after another.[26]

Some didn't even try to make light of the occasion. When one Brooklyn resident wandered into his local saloon a few minutes after midnight and the bartender refused to serve him, the man seized a club and leveled the place, smashing up glasses, furniture, and the bones of those who worked there.[27]

He was not the only one to react drastically to the coming of the new law. One California vintner, convinced that poverty and ruin were inescapable, killed himself. The tragedy was duly noted in the press but downplayed by the lofty results that Prohibition's supporters anticipated. A pre-January 17 edition of the *St. Paul Pioneer Press* proclaimed:

> On Tuesday next the United States will go "dry." It has been the experience of those cities that have tried Prohibition that crime—petty crime, that is—declines under a dry regime. The probabilities are, however, that little by little everybody will become accustomed to the new order. . . . The best thing for the United States to do is forget as quickly as possible that it ever enjoyed the stimulation of alcohol.[28]

It was a naïve outlook that would bring wealth to many and violent death to more than just the pessimistic vintner.

5

EXIT THE OLD GUARD

T HE DISTINCTION OF PLAYING HOST to the first recorded Prohibition violation went to Chicago when, less than an hour after the Volstead Act took effect, six masked men infiltrated a railroad yard there, tied up the night watchmen, and cleared two freight cars of $100,000 worth of whiskey stamped FOR MEDICAL USE. At least two similar incidents occurred in other parts of the city before dawn broke. One gang hijacked a truck loaded with whiskey destined for a competitor, and another stole four barrels of grain alcohol from a government warehouse. On January 28 the Windy City set another record when Prohibition agents launched the first federal raid on a North Side speakeasy, the Red Lantern.[1]

John F. Kramer, the newly appointed Prohibition commissioner, warned, "We shall see to it that [liquor] is not manufactured. Nor sold, nor given away, nor hauled in anything on the surface of the earth or under the earth or in the air." To back up this grandiose intention, the secretary of the treasury had created the Prohibition Unit, composed of agents authorized to arrest anyone caught violating the Volstead Act. During the first half of 1920 enforcement was energized and intense, and by June, more than five hundred indictments for booze-related offenses were on the Chicago trial calendars.[2] Anyone found guilty of a first offense could theoretically receive a $1,000 fine and/or a year in jail, although few judges imposed punishments so severe. But as time progressed and bootleggers acquired opportunities to reach "understandings" with more flexible agents, the Prohibition Unit lost its edge as a source of fear.

Many agents chose to use their authority to make money instead of arrests. Reformers who investigated this phenomenon were quick to label the unit as corrupt without acknowledging the greater problem: that the way the unit (later the Bureau of Prohibition) was set up and run mandated corruption.

Agents rarely made more than $2,000 a year, and most averaged a salary of $1,200. Gang chiefs specializing in bootlegging could offer them several times their weekly salary to look the other way when liquor was being transported or served in the camouflaged saloons that came to be known as blind pigs or speakeasies. The unit failed to run background checks on several of the men it hired, so a portion of the enforcement body consisted of individuals scarcely more law-abiding than the bootleggers. Jerry Bohan, a New York agent, had a long record of arrests for robbery and murder, and acquired a macabre fame when he shot and killed legendary gangster Monk Eastman, with whom he'd been partnered in various crimes over the years.[3]

Those agents who did join the Prohibition Unit out of genuine sympathy with and support for the dry cause found enforcement next to impossible because they had such large territories to monitor. A paltry force of 134 agents was responsible for the entire states of Illinois and Iowa and parts of Wisconsin.[4]

One hundred thirty-four agents, even if they were all honest, would not have been enough to effectively suppress drinking in a single Chicago neighborhood. By mid-1920 the federal Prohibition administrator announced that Chicago doctors had exercised their legal right to recommend liquor for medicinal purposes and issued more than three hundred thousand prescriptions. All of the pharmaceutical needs of pre-Volstead Chicago had been easily met by four hundred drug supply houses, but after January, more than three thousand new ones cropped up, all of them eligible for a license to dispense "medicinal" alcohol.[5] Either a lot of people were getting sick, or said individuals were just drinking to their health.

The law allowed breweries to remain in operation provided that they stuck to the production of "near beer," a weak concoction that was made by first brewing full-strength beer, then siphoning off the alcohol content until it reached a level of less than 1 percent. Instead of dumping the excess alcohol, bootleggers either reintroduced it into the beer via hypodermic needles, creating a Prohibition beverage called "needle beer," or used it as the prime ingredient in making whiskey, gin, and other hard liquors.

Some dedicated imbibers tried making their own beer, wine, and liquor at home, using raw ingredients or "booze kits" cleverly disguised and sold as grape juice mixes, but unless a certain amount of skill was used, the results were substandard. Discolored corks, liquid heavy with sediment, and sour-smelling and bitter-tasting slush were all that the average amateur brewer or vintner got. One, after daring to taste his own creation, commented, "After I've had a couple of glasses I'm terribly sleepy. Sometimes my eyes don't seem to focus and my head aches. I'm not intoxicated, understand, merely feel as if I've been drawn through a knothole."[6]

John Torrio, Dean O'Banion, Terry Druggan and Frankie Lake, and Chicago's other primary gang chiefs had the resources ready to supply the demand created by those not willing to risk pain without intoxication. Torrio's specialty was beer, where O'Banion focused more on the importation of wine and hard liquors from Canada. Nails Morton, working with O'Banion, made good use of his Detroit car-exchange contacts, using them as reception agents for booze smuggled across the Canadian border.[7]

Even if the lucky discovery behind the Randolph Hotel had not occurred, O'Banion would have been motivated to get into bootlegging for another reason. The safecracking gang that had brought him riches during the war years was on the verge of unraveling.

On February 9, 1920, Johnny Mahoney and his stepbrothers John and Frank Johnston were about to step into a taxicab when a detective squad descended on them. The four officers had been on the alert for members of Reiser's gang since the burglarizing of the Western Shade Cloth Company, during which night watchman Thomas O'Donnell was killed. Squad leader Daniel Gilbert seized Mahoney, and when the Johnstons attempted to interfere, the other policemen arrested them.

Mahoney had $100 in cash and a revolver in his coat pocket. A search of a suitcase in his possession revealed two automatic handguns, a soldier's shirt and coat, two flashlights, three handkerchief masks, and four additional ammunition clips. After depositing him at the station, the squad went to his apartment at 3623 South Wells Street and found even more intriguing items: thirty ounces of nitroglycerin, two "jimmies," a crowbar, two hundred fuses with attached wires, percussion caps, two spools of steel wire, and a set of safecracking tools. The officers examined the wire and observed that it was the same type used to tie up the Western Shade Cloth employees. One of those workers told police that one assailant had worn a soldier's shirt and coat, further closing the net around Mahoney.

What the frightened safeblower told the police that day was not preserved for posterity, but rumors ran rampant that he implicated Reiser in order to save his own skin, for that night the same detective squad descended on Reiser's other home, at 3158 North Paulina Street.

Reiser was in the bathroom when his wife let the officers into the house, but when he emerged and saw the blue uniforms, he dashed across the hall and pulled a gun out from under his pillow. He aimed it at the detectives, who also drew their guns.

"You're not going to take me!" Reiser shouted. "I know you'll get me, but I'll get a couple of you first!"

Madeline Reiser and daughter Verna stood in the background, sobbing hysterically.

"Put your gun down, Charlie," squad leader Gilbert urged, keeping his voice calm. Gilbert, a former Teamster boss who years later would be exposed as a grafting

Torrio–Capone minion, was careful to maintain a respectful approach when it came to the big-league hoodlums. Mrs. Reiser, reassured by the officer's non-belligerent demeanor, flung her arms around her husband's neck and begged him to put his automatic away. Reiser pushed her aside, by now so agitated that tears were streaming down his cheeks. He insisted that he was not going to allow himself to be taken. The officers and his wife continued pleading and coaxing until he finally tossed the gun onto the bed and submitted to arrest.

Lieutenant John Loftus told reporters that the Western Shade Cloth Company robbery was as good as solved. "We'll have the watchmen [at the company] look at this pair," he said.[8]

Employees of the pillaged company failed to identify either Reiser or Mahoney. Loath to let Reiser in particular off scot-free, Loftus booked the master safecracker on a vagrancy charge, forcing him to post a $1,000 bond to gain his freedom. Mahoney took off for parts unknown, and the ensuing days were nervous and edgy ones for the Reiser gang, who were convinced that their old comrade had tried to sell the boss out. Even worse was the hostile suspicion with which the Ox now seemed to regard his own followers.

More than two weeks later, Clarence White, an old-school criminal and nitro expert with a record dating back to 1896, who had been arrested with Hymie Weiss in November 1919 on suspicion of having robbed the American Theater of $1000, was found unconscious in his dining room by his brother-in-law. A bullet wound gaped on his forehead, but he was still breathing. He died later that night at St. Anne's Hospital.[9] White's death was officially listed as a suicide, but Reiser's followers, O'Banion included, wondered. The position of the bullet entry hole suggested that if the aging safecracker had killed himself, it had been an assisted suicide.

O'Banion, whose operating territory consisted of Chicago's North Side, acknowledged that the carriage trade living in the mansions along Lake Shore Drive would be part of his customer base. Few of them were beer drinkers, so he invested more time and energy in solidifying the contacts necessary to get premium Canadian liquor past U.S. Customs and into the smoking rooms and lounges of Chicago's social elite. He also purchased the Cragin distillery once sufficient funds had been amassed.[10]

When the opportunity presented itself, O'Banion hijacked alcohol shipments en route to legitimate sources or looted government warehouses where the product was stored and sold it to bootleggers who specialized in homemade wares. He did eventually buy into local breweries, as the North Side had its fair share of the working class and slum dwellers who relished beer over cognac or champagne. For every dollar he spent on these production investments, he probably spent two paying off anyone who could possibly hinder his operation: beat cops, precinct captains, and Prohibition agents.

Next to the money he shelled out, O'Banion's greatest insulation against punishment was his highly sociable nature. It earned him friends and followers who had a personal as well as financial component in their association with him. While some writers have pointed out his easy smile and playful backslapping as the camouflage of a psychopathic personality, the truth is that O'Banion had a genuine interest in his fellow man, a byproduct of his childhood in a close-knit rural community. Unless hired to do otherwise, as he had been at both McGovern's and the *Examiner*, or he had reason to perceive someone as a threat, he had a friendly handshake for anyone who approached him.

"Dean had a lot of friends," E. Barnett, who drove a truck for the North Side Gang from 1921 until 1924, recalled in a 1988 interview. "He was someone you would go the limit for because he would do the same for you. And no matter how much money he made, he never thought he was too good for the rest of us. When he got the flower shop [on North State Street] it didn't surprise me a bit to know that he worked in it just like one of the employees, getting himself covered in dirt and crap. I couldn't tell you how many liquor shipments he helped unload. That was Dean."

O'Banion also rewarded faithful service with his organization by allowing friends and henchmen to operate semi-independently on the North Side. Rumrunner "Barefoot" Rafe Dooley told Capone biographer John Kobler, "The North Side mob gave me and my constituents, about twenty-five of them, a district, an allocation, five blocks square. This was our reward for faithful service in the past. With it went the right to distribute beer and whiskey."

Dooley admitted that O'Banion's generosity did not extend to watching the backs of his sub-vassals. "Of course, you had to protect your territory. You couldn't call for help." A two-fisted, pugnacious gunman, Dooley was capable of watching his own back, and was wealthier because of it. "They say crime don't pay. You tell that to the real hierarchy of crime and they'll laugh themselves into nervous hysteria. It don't pay only if you're apprehended. . . . If the venture succeeds, like when me and my constituents were distributing liquor on the North Side, it pays fine, very fine indeed."[11]

Like the majority of bootleggers, O'Banion reserved the "real stuff" for his wealthier customers and inflated his stock by diluting it with water, ginger ale, burnt caramel, sugar, whatever nontoxic ingredients were required to turn one case of Grommes & Ullrich whiskey into four or five and not result in drinker casualties. Too many bootleggers, however, viewed safety as secondary to profit and created their own special blends by acquiring permits to handle industrial alcohol, which was traditionally used by cosmetic firms and toilet water manufacturers to produce scented makeup and perfume. These entrepreneurs bottled it instead for sale to the thirsty masses—after it had been mixed with flavor and dyes to simulate bourbon, whiskey, or whatever label the bootlegger felt like slapping on the bottle.

It was not consumer safety that concerned John Torrio when it came to the production and sale of bootleg liquor. He worried even less about danger from law enforcement quarters, his years of experience in the vice business having taught him that police crackdowns were rare and brief. Mayor Big Bill Thompson had been elected to another term in 1919, albeit by a narrow margin; the city treasury had had a surplus when he took office in 1915, but four years later there was a $4 million deficit.[12] Anyone who could continue to put money into Thompson's pocket, either in the form of campaign contributions or bought protection, could count on silent support in city hall. The greatest dilemma that Torrio foresaw came from the other gangs.

The way he viewed it, Prohibition represented the attitude and morality of a small group that had merely been smart enough to seize a political advantage. The rest of the American population—millions of people—provided a huge enough client base to make the primary gangs of every U.S. town and city busy and rich. But Torrio knew that restraint was not the average gangster's foremost virtue, and no matter how well one gang did peddling beer and liquor in its own district, there would always be covetous, greedy glances cast beyond the boundaries, with the end result being gang wars that disrupted business and brought on crackdowns.

Noting how smoothly things had flowed in the Levee when Colosimo, Maurice Van Bever, and the other leading panderers united to thwart the reformers and strengthen the import-export system of girls from other brothels, towns, and states, Torrio envisioned a similar arrangement with Chicago's larger gangs. Ambitious and greedy though they might be, he felt sure that he would get first their attention and then their support when he outlined how cooperation would keep hijackings and murders out of the paper and the police and Prohibition agents off their backs.

The problem, the biggest obstacle to the achievement of his vision, was the man to whom he owed his current position: Big Jim Colosimo.

As Torrio proved himself more and more capable of running the Colosimo vice empire without advice or direct supervision, Big Jim let his hard edge soften enough to fall in love for the first time in his life. Colosimo's union with Victoria Moresco had been, from his perspective at least, a career move. What he felt for Dale Winter was the real thing, which in hindsight, was the worst thing.

At the time that a mutual friend introduced her to Big Jim, Dale was an attractive young actress and singer who had been supporting herself and her mother as a soloist at the South Park Avenue Methodist Church. She had been touring and appearing in live musical productions since high school; the most recent one had collapsed unexpectedly in Australia and left mother and daughter stranded. The singing job at the church kept them afloat in Chicago, but when Colosimo laid eyes on the pale, dark-haired Winter in 1917, he elevated their circumstances by hiring her to headline his club's musical entertainment.[13]

She held down both jobs, enjoying her work at the church too much to quit, but when the congregation learned of her connection to the infamous Colosimo's restaurant in January 1917, they demanded her dismissal. In a rare display of spirit, the normally mild Dale retorted, "Pooh-pooh, then, I won't sing." She explained her sharp retort to a *Tribune* reporter: "Far be it from me to cause any of the elect to leave their comfortable pews to avoid hearing a "cabaret singer."

Dale's mother threw her support behind the young woman. "She's just the bravest girl in the world. She sings in a cabaret because she is brave enough—daughter enough—to assume a little indebtedness caused by months of illness from which I am just recovered. She wouldn't choose a cabaret if better employment offered. It didn't, so she accepted what was offered. And I'm sure that's very much to her credit." [14]

Dale then worked for Big Jim full time, her lovely, ethereal stage presence and lyrical voice packing the house nightly. The big Italian and the young singer began to spend time together outside of the club, Colosimo even arranging for her to take music lessons at the Chicago Musical College. When word of her talent spread among the club patrons and she received better job offers from Broadway legend Morris Gest and the great Florenz Ziegfeld, Dale turned them down. She and Colosimo had fallen in love.

Torrio was not happy to hear that Big Jim had left Victoria to pursue the relationship with Winter. The Colosimo marriage had not been a harmonious one for years; Victoria's brother, Joe Moresco, would later tell of his brother-in-law dropping by from time to time at the cigar store where he worked, fuming from a recent quarrel with his wife, and snapping, "Joe, go down to the house and talk to that sister of yours." [15] But however volatile the relationship had become, the marriage had been the cornerstone upon which Colosimo's success in the brothel business had been built, and Victoria, as a partner, had supported and encouraged the methods he used to get to the top and stay there.

Dale Winter belonged to a more refined world, one that required Colosimo to become a shadow of the Levee powerhouse he had once been. Torrio watched with alarm as Colosimo lost the hard edge that had kept him master of the Levee for so many years and spent more time with Dale's artist friends, ignoring his political backers and underworld cronies in the process. Big Jim was transforming himself into someone befitting of such a gentle, refined young woman as the one who had captivated him so thoroughly, but in so doing, he became the target of underworld gossip that started the extortionists up again.

"Jim's getting soft."

"Jim's slipping."

Outwardly that seemed to be the case. When the Black Handers resumed their demands for money and widened their threats of violence to include Dale, he paid up without protest. He no longer had the inclination to fight.

Cupid could not have struck at a worse time as far as Torrio was concerned. He needed Colosimo to lead the foray into bootlegging and the organization (or subduing) of Chicago's other gangs, but because Big Jim had fallen in love with a decent woman for the first time in his life, it was not going to happen.

It was time for someone else to take charge.

Oblivious to his second-in-command's concerns, Colosimo sued Victoria for divorce, offering her $50,000 not to contest it. She did not protest too heavily, having seen the writing on the wall. Her youngest sister, whom the Colosimos had been raising, had told her of Dale Winter's repeated visits to their home long before the affair became public knowledge.[16] Although the cause was hopeless, Victoria didn't retreat without a parting shot: "I raised one husband for another woman, and there's nothing to it."

On March 29, 1920, Judge McGoorty granted the divorce decree, Colosimo having claimed that his wife deserted him in 1917 for refusing to take her to Europe.[17] Two months later, he and Dale Winter exchanged marriage vows. After a blissful honeymoon in French Lick, Indiana, the happy couple returned to Chicago, where Big Jim set Dale up in his Vernon Avenue mansion.

A week later, on May 11, Torrio called Colosimo to let him know that Big Jim O'Leary would be arriving at the café at 4 p.m. on the dot to discuss an incoming shipment of two truckloads of whiskey. After kissing his new bride goodbye, Big Jim climbed into his car and directed the driver to take him to the restaurant. The chauffeur would remember that Colosimo seemed agitated, muttering in Italian during the entire ride. After being dropped off at one of the café's two front doors, Colosimo crossed a small vestibule, passed through the silent restaurant, and joined his bookkeeper, Frank Camilla, in the latter's office. The two proceeded to indulge in a casual banter that was a standard exchange between them, Colosimo asking, "Hello, Frank, what's doing?" and Camilla replying, "Nothing."

When informed that no one had called for him, Big Jim seemed disturbed. He telephoned his lawyer, Rocco de Stefano, but did not find him in the office, so he left a message with the secretary and hung up. He then walked back toward the twin entrances, pausing only to exchange words with some employees setting up in the dining room.

Minutes later, Frank Camilla and the restaurant's chef, Antonio Caesarino, heard two small explosions that they initially assumed to be blown tires. While the chef checked the alley, the bookkeeper walked out one of the front doors to survey the street. Finding nothing, and realizing that the door's spring lock had latched behind him and locked him out, he walked up to the second entrance to get back inside. The moment he pushed the door open, he spotted the prone body of Big Jim on the vestibule floor, blood from head wounds puddling all over the tiles.[18]

"My God! Jim's shot!" Camilla shouted into the restaurant. He turned the lifeless form over and saw that Colosimo was dead. Someone called Dr. R. Cunningham, who ran over from his office at 2204 South State Street and confirmed that Big Jim was beyond medical aid. Cunningham was soon joined by Chief of Police John J. Garrity, Chief of Detectives Mooney, and First Deputy Alcock.

The café porter, Joseph Gabriola, offered investigators a valuable clue. Seconds after Colosimo's entry, he had been coming upstairs from the basement and saw a stranger enter the vestibule where Big Jim would later be found. After detectives interviewed him, the Chicago Police Department issued the following description of the probable killer:

> Between twenty-five and thirty years old, between five feet six inches and five feet eight inches in height, fat-faced, dark-complexioned, wearing a black derby hat, black overcoat, patent leather shoes, and white standup collar.

When Rocco de Stefano called Dale, she collapsed. She soon had another shock to contend with: because Illinois law required a year's interval between divorce and remarriage, she was not legally Big Jim's widow, and stood to lose everything he had given her. Luigi Colosimo, Big Jim's father and legitimate heir, showed some sympathy to her situation by granting her $6,000 in cash and diamonds from the estate.[19]

Torrio made a big display out of weeping and denying involvement with sobs of "Me kill Jim? Jim and me were like brothers!" Veteran officers viewed his performance with suspicion, having a thorough enough knowledge of the Colosimo operations to know that the ex-New Yorker stood to gain more from his boss's death than anyone else did. Torrio's denial had a ring of truth only in the sense that he did not kill Colosimo personally, but he was no less guilty of the crime. He had planned it, paid for it, and made sure that Big Jim would be in the wrong place at the right time.

The killer, although he was never prosecuted, was Brooklyn gangster Frankie Uale, alias Yale, whom Torrio knew from his New York days. The previous year, Torrio had given asylum in Chicago to young Al Capone, a Yale follower who was fleeing New York to escape an anticipated murder charge. Torrio remembered Capone as a fearless, intelligent Italian youth hanging around the old John Torrio Association headquarters, looking for ways to prove his gameness. The beefy twenty-year-old who arrived with his wife and young son had not lost his inclination to prove himself to men in power, and Torrio acknowledged that in doing this favor for Yale's boy, he had gained himself a devoted and determined follower. When Torrio needed someone from out of town for the Colosimo hit, to minimize the chances of premature recognition foiling the plot, he called on Yale, who obliged as much from loyalty as for the $10,000 fee.

Acting on the hunch that Colosimo's murderer was indeed an imported gunman, the Chicago Police Department sent the description to other major U.S. cities. The New York Police Department responded by sending Frankie Yale's mug shot to Chicago. The café porter looked at it and declared, "That's the man!" As soon as the sense of righteous conviction subsided, he realized what danger he was in, and a train trip to New York in the company of Chicago detectives gave him even more time to become scared. By the time he faced Yale in a police lineup, he had his response well rehearsed. It was one that sent a smiling Yale home.[20]

Big Jim Colosimo was temporarily laid to rest at the Oakwoods Cemetery chapel (pending the selection of a final burial place) on May 15 with the pomp and ceremony normally accorded royalty. The honorary pallbearers included judges, aldermen, former U.S. District Attorney Francis Borelli, Chicago Opera Ballet maestro Giacome Spadoni, and opera singer Titta Ruffo.[21] Observing how policemen and office holders fraternized with divekeepers and gamblers around the casket, the *Tribune* posed a troubling question:

> It is a strange commentary upon our system of law and justice. In how far can power derived from the life of the underworld influence institutions of law and order? It is a question worthy the thoughtful consideration of those entrusted with the establishment of law and order, and of those dependent upon and responsible for such trust.

The mile-long funeral cortege left the Vernon Avenue mansion at 9:30 a.m. and wound its way gradually toward Oakwoods Cemetery, stopping briefly in front of the shuttered café for a moment of silence. At the chapel, Dale Colosimo sobbed quietly while Rocco de Stefano attempted a eulogy. The lawyer could only manage a few words before emotion overcame him. Alderman Coughlin stepped in and finished it for him.

After the burial, Dale made a brief attempt at managing the café but sold her share to Mike "the Greek" Potzin. She left Chicago to go on the road with one musical comedy after another and finally married actor Henry Duffy in San Francisco in 1924, living out the rest of her days as an ardent Christian Scientist.[22]

As if to strengthen the notion that 1920 would be an all-over time of change in the fortunes and leadership of Chicago's primary gangs, another great leader fell barely a month after Colosimo had been buried. Patrick "Paddy the Bear" Ryan had been boss of the old Valley Gang, a fierce crew of killers, labor sluggers, and stickup men who for more than twenty years focused their activities in the West Side territory between the Cicero town limits and Chicago's Little Italy.

Ryan had been nicknamed "the Bear" because of his huge physique and the fact that he preferred to maul and claw his opponents in rough and tumble fights. He only used a gun when drunk. Knowing that he was no stranger to the art of murder, police had questioned him in connection with the 1919 slaying of Detective Sergeant James Hosna and, more recently, the assassination of labor leader Edward Coleman. Coleman, before dying, named Ryan's brother-in-law as one of his assailants.

On the morning of June 17 an unknown gunman ambushed Ryan on Racine Avenue near Fourteenth Street, emptied a pistol into him, and fled in an automobile. As Detective Sergeant Frank Kilma leaned over him, the mortally wounded gangster groaned, "I didn't think the rat would kill me." Turning to a friend, Charles Gary, he added, "I didn't think the bastard had the nerve to do it, Charlie." That was all he would say. He died on the operating table at the Columbus Extension Hospital without naming his killer.[23]

The actual murderer turned out to be another Valley gangster, Walter "the Runt" Quinlan, who, like Torrio, had aspired to his mentor's position. Unlike Torrio, however, Quinlan's own death came about as a repercussion of his ambition. On April 3, 1926, Ryan's twenty-year-old son, "John the Fox," cornered the Runt in Joseph Sindelar's saloon on Loomis Street and shot him dead.[24]

O'Banion lost a mentor of his own the very month that Ryan's death left the Valley gangsters with a change of leadership.

Gene Geary had been courting conviction and possibly execution for years. He was a confirmed alcoholic with a lust for violence, but in 1919 his mental instability became more and more pronounced. He was no longer just homicidal, but crazy and homicidal, a combination that guaranteed his downfall.

In late November 1919, cabdriver Herman Markowitz saw Geary administering a savage beating to Leonard Tripple, a driver for the Yellow Cab Company, in front of Meyer's cigar store on Twenty-second Street. On the night of the twenty-second Tripple and a colleague, Patrick Barton, went to a saloon called the Cadillac Café for a beer and ran into Geary at the bar. The gangster sneered to all present, "There's a big ——— that I had a fight with the other night." Despite Barton's effort to keep the peace, Geary seized his former victim and tried to get another battle started. Barton later testified, "I then saw Geary fire two shots, and Tripple dropped."[25]

When he realized that the man he'd shot was dead, Geary and an accomplice ran out of the saloon and boarded a streetcar without paying the fare. Passengers gasped when the gangster tossed his still-smoking revolver onto the seat beside him.

Geary was arrested, and the case went to trial in February 1920. Defending the accused killer was Thomas Nash, already a well-known criminal defense attorney, who was destined to represent Chicago's highest-ranking beer barons. Nash contended that the gun which fired the fatal shot had actually been Tripple's, and that it had gone off when Geary struggled to take it from him.

When the killer took the stand, he made statements that sounded more like responses to an admission interview to a psychiatric ward. "I don't know nothing about it," he kept insisting. "I was nutty."

Assistant State's Attorney John Prystalski asked, "Do you remember the statement you made in the state's attorney's office?"

"I never made a statement. I never signed nothing."

"But you told of the shooting?"

"I don't remember. I was nutty."

"How many shots do you say were fired?" Prystalski queried.

"Two."

"Didn't you say in the state's attorney's office that three shots were fired?" Geary crossed his arms and assumed a stubborn expression. "I was nutty."[26]

Despite Geary's failure as a witness, Thomas Nash managed to convince the jury that his client and the deceased had been mortal enemies, that Tripple had been out gunning for Geary because of the beating outside Meyer's store, and that the hunter had become the prey thanks to a badly fired bullet. They returned a not-guilty verdict. One of the jurors explained, "They were both gunmen. Both intended to kill. I believe there was too much malice in the case. We couldn't do anything but turn Geary loose."

When he realized that he had been snatched from the shadow of the noose, Geary treated the courtroom to a full-blown display of mania. He bolted over the defense table, grabbed Judge Hugo Pam's hand, and shook it. Then he hurried over to the jurors, hugging them and grabbing their hands. "God bless you all!" he cried.

Outside the Criminal Court Building, he began to sob noisily in the presence of reporters. "I never wanted to kill nobody," he insisted. "I cried for four hours when I heard that the man I shot was dead. I'm sorrier for his folks." He finished his speech with a wet-cheeked smile. "I never been convicted of a crime. If folks could only see me, they wouldn't believe all this stuff. I don't look crooked, do I?"[27]

State's Attorney Hoyne was infuriated by the acquittal. "I had hoped . . . that we would be able to hang Geary as an object lesson to others of his stripe."

The state's attorney's office got its second crack at him three months later. On May 27, 1920, more than two weeks after Big Jim Colosimo had been laid to rest, Geary walked into Jim O'Brien's Horn saloon at 4165 South Halstead Street, glassy-eyed and flushed. He clenched his pistol, extended his arm, and leveled his weapon at T. J. Fell, an attorney who had stopped at the saloon for an after-work drink. While Fell stared back, terrified, Geary paused, then shifted his aim and shot bartender Harry Reckas instead. He knew neither man, although it later came to light that Reckas had been scheduled to testify against two former Geary associates at their upcoming trial for running a $100,000 whiskey ring.[28]

The gunman hid out at the home of his girlfriend, Winifred Brooks, who had also dated gangster and circulation slugger Peter Gentleman before the latter was murdered. He sent word to authorities that "I'm sick of being annoyed by the coppers. If any of them tries to arrest me, I'll kill a couple of them."[29]

He was finally arrested on June 3, without any officer lives being lost in the process, and went to trial for murdering Reckas. Despite the best efforts of Thomas Nash and his partner Michael Ahern, this jury dealt with Geary more severely, finding him guilty. Only a miracle could have secured any other verdict, given the fact that the gangster had slain the unarmed Reckas in front of a score of witnesses.

Judge Sabath sentenced him to hang but subsequently issued a stay of execution in order to give mental health specialists time to examine the condemned man and determine the veracity of Nash and Ahern's insistence that their client was insane.

For more than a year, Edwin S. Day at the state's attorney's office and the defense team battled it out over the issue of Geary's sanity, and during that time, the racketeer's grip on reality became weaker and weaker. In February 1921 the jailer at the Cook County Jail heard Geary screaming hysterically in his cell, and upon investigation found him huddled in the corner, convinced that Reckas's ghost was in the room with him and that his enemies were boring a hole in the cell ceiling for the purpose of letting enough light in to blind him.[30]

Nash and Ahern's efforts, as well as Geary's obvious signs of increasing mental confusion, finally bore fruit. He was judged insane on September 23, 1921, thereby prohibiting his execution, and committed to the asylum for the criminally insane at Chester, Illinois. While Judge Kersten was reading out the commitment order in his courtroom, Geary became disruptive, insisting that he was someone else and that he wanted to go to see the supreme court at Springfield to have the guilty verdict overturned. As he was led away by bailiffs, he cried frantically to Thomas Nash that "they" had stuffed something in his ears, rendering him unable to hear anything further.[31]

"I haven't a friend in Chicago," he wailed before boarding the train to the asylum. "They've all deserted me like I had smallpox."

Edwin S. Day, who had led the prosecution team, died six months later, on March 28, 1922. His doctors asserted that a fatal illness had set in after a mental and physical breakdown brought on by his vigorous prosecution of the psychotic killer.[32] Day's family could take consolation in the knowledge that the actions which resulted in the loss of his own life probably saved a lot of others: Geary never killed again. He remained behind bars, first at Chester and then at the psychiatric division of Southern Illinois Penitentiary at Menard, until his death on October 21, 1942.[33]

Hymie Weiss had his own issues to contend with that eventful year of 1920.

On the afternoon of June 24 Dr. Edward Westcott was making his rounds at the Washington Boulevard Hospital when two men in their early twenties came through the door. One was supporting the other, who was barely conscious. The former helped his wounded friend into a chair in the lobby, and then hurried off before hospital staff could stop him.[34]

The injured man was bleeding heavily from a bullet wound in the chest. When Dr. Westcott and a nurse cut away his shirt, he regained consciousness long enough to beg them not to report the incident. The request aroused the suspicions of the doctor, who telephoned the Warren Avenue police station. Arriving officers searched through the mysterious patient's pockets and found papers identifying him as Frederick Weiss.

Nurses who had seen the two men come in identified his companion as Hymie Weiss after viewing police mug shots. Detectives arrested Weiss at Madison and Paulina streets at eleven o'clock that night and brought him to the nearest station, where Captain Charles Atkinson questioned him. Realizing that he had little alternative, Weiss admitted that his brother had been shot in his presence, but that it had been an accident.

"Fred was sleeping with me at my room at 41 Paulina," the North Sider explained. "There was a gun underneath the pillow and somehow it was discharged."

Physicians at the hospital insisted that the location of the wound made such a story impossible. Captain Atkinson ordered a search of Weiss's Paulina Street room, which failed to turn up any bloodstained mattress or bedding.

The case became all the more mysterious when Bernard Weiss showed up at the police station where Hymie was being held and offered yet another account of how Frederick had been injured. He said that a shot had been fired at Hymie when the North Sider had been driving on Grand Avenue the previous week, and that whoever was responsible for the botched attack must have gotten Fred by mistake during a second try.

Although Fred Weiss was not expected to pull through, he did so, and officially exonerated his notorious sibling by claiming that unseen assailants had fired at him. The truth did not become public until six years later, when Fred told a coroner's jury what the Weiss family had known all along: Earl (Hymie) had indeed shot him. Fred, an ex-soldier, had taunted his sibling about Earl's failure to serve in the military, and been rewarded for his opinion with a bullet.

After Colosimo was buried, Torrio tested the waters by approaching the politicians and Levee figures who had worked with and supported Big Jim for years, and gauging their reactions to the news that he was now head of the operation in both act and name. As he had anticipated, no one voiced any serious objection once convinced that previous partnership and payoff arrangements would continue as usual.

Aided by his New York protege Al Capone, Torrio began the slow and careful process of sizing up and approaching the city's five other primary gangs and their leaders. He did so carefully, for without their cooperation his plans for a unified bootlegging operation could not succeed.

6

MEETING THE BOYS

T HE LITTLE ITALY THAT DOMINATED Chicago's old "Bloody Nineteenth" Ward (renamed the Twenty-fifth after a 1920 rezoning) belonged to the Gennas. They were six Sicilian-born brothers who planned, operated, and struck with a combined and staggering ferocity, a multi-headed hydra both feared and obeyed by the hordes of Italian immigrants who lived in the area they dominated.

The brothers were born in Marsala, in the Sicilian province of Trapani, but arrived in the United States as young, ambitious men. Their parents, Antonio Sr. and Maria Luchari; a seventh brother, Nicola; and two sisters, Rosa Laudicina and Caterina Mariana; remained in Sicily.[1] They survived by banding together, and by adulthood had become a dangerous and efficient operating unit.

Salvatore "Sam" Genna led the way into the criminal life by scorning honest labor in favor of Black Handing. Years later he was described as the Genna Gang's "political agent," suggesting that he arranged the payoffs and represented his brothers when negotiating with political and underworld elements. Vincenzo, or Jim, operated a blind pig in the vicinity of Halstead and Taylor streets, while brother Pete operated a notorious saloon on the West Side. Mike and Angelo Genna, known respectively as "the Devil" and "Bloody Angelo," jointly delivered the bite required in that dog-eat-dog environment. Only Tony Genna would not have been recognized as a product of his environment. He studied architecture, had a love of classical literature and music, took up with a minister's daughter, and used a portion of the Genna Gang's profits to subsidize decent housing for his less fortunate countrymen.[2]

At the onset of Prohibition the Gennas obtained a permit to handle industrial alcohol and leased a three-story warehouse at 1022 Taylor Street. They sold some of it to legally approved sources, such as perfume and toilet water manufacturers, but the rest ended up undergoing enough chemical enhancement to make it look drinkable, and it was sold as rum, whiskey, and other hard liquors. It was so cheap to make that the Gennas could afford to sell it at rock-bottom prices. The result was a demand so huge that even the warehouse output could not meet it.

The brothers turned to an alcohol-production resource in their own territory. They installed five-gallon stills in the homes of Italian immigrants and paid the head of the family $15 per day to keep the fire simmering, monitor the bubbling brew, and scoop out any sediment or distillate. Each home could be counted on to produce at least 350 gallons of raw alcohol per week. The product equaled its cooking environment in filth, as the open stills attracted and killed rats and insects, and dirty household garments were known to fall off of impromptu clotheslines into the bubbling mash.

A gallon cost anywhere from 50 to 70 cents to make, and Pete and Jim Genna's former saloonkeeper cronies paid $3 to $6 a gallon. The gang's huge profits enabled it to operate without fear of legal reprisal. The Taylor Street plant earned the nickname "the police station" because blue uniforms, their pockets loaded with payoff money, were frequently seen entering and exiting the premises.[3]

The only real threat to the brothers' operation came from other bootleggers, but Angelo and Mike made such a habit of killing first and asking questions later that open confrontation was rare. Even those who suffered burns, blindness, or death of a family member due to the explosion of a poorly constructed Genna still kept silent for fear of a visit from the deadly brothers.

The gang's enforcers were the terror of Little Italy. Nervous or resentful peasants eyed them fearfully or turned away upon meeting them in the street. The most feared were "murder twins" John Scalise and Albert Anselmi, Sicilian immigrants whose warm welcome by the Gennas was due in equal parts to their killing ability and their Sicilian heritage (Anselmi was from the Genna birthplace of Marsala; Scalise was from Castelvetrano).[5] They were visual opposites, Scalise being of medium build and youthful appearance, while the balding, older Anselmi was short and overweight. Scalise had a cast to his right eye that gave him a lopsided, unnerving stare. They were famed throughout gangland for rubbing their bullets with garlic before heading out on a murder assignment, believing that if their target did not die outright, gangrene would set in and do the job more slowly and painfully.

Samuzzo "Samoots" Amatuna aped his boss Tony Genna in sporting elegant attire and worshipping the classics, particularly music, but there the resemblance ended. Unlike the dapper Genna, who rarely if ever carried a gun, Amatuna used his weapon on anyone who displeased him, two- or four-legged. On one occasion, he shot a laundry delivery-wagon horse because the laundry had returned one of his two hundred monogrammed silk shirts with a slight scorch mark. Other Genna torpedoes were Orazio "the Scourge" Tropea, who had Little Italy convinced that he possessed *il malocchio*, the evil eye; former mathematics teacher-turned-triggerman Giuseppe Nerone, alias "Il Cavaliere"; Ecola "the Eagle" Baldelli; Vito Bascone; and Filippo Gnolfo.[5]

Politicians valued the Gennas' ability to deliver the ward's Italian vote on election day and make life for opposing candidates a literal hell during the campaign period. They proved their worth to their political sponsors during the aldermanic war of 1921, during which the incumbent Johnny Powers fought off Genna-backed challenger Anthony D'Andrea for the ward seat. More than thirty men in total died during the battle. Many of the victims knew their fate well in advance; a gnarled old tree on Loomis Street was known throughout the neighborhood as "Dead Man's Tree" because anyone who found a piece of paper with his name on it tacked to the tree's base was thenceforth living on borrowed time.

Only the Catholic Church dared protest against the Genna rule. After Anthony D'Andrea was killed by two shotgun blasts in May 1921, and his bodyguard Joe Laspisa, who'd vowed to avenge him, fell beneath a hail of lead, the priest of the Church of St. Filippo Benizi made a desperate attempt to stop the murders. He posted a sign on the church doors begging his parishioners to contact the authorities with any information they might have about the slaughter of recent days. To his discouragement, the local people feared the Gennas more than church disapproval.[6]

On the West Side, south of Little Italy and adjoining Cicero, Terry Druggan and Frankie Lake ruled over the territory where Paddy the Bear's old Valley Gang had once operated with impunity. They were mirror images in every respect except height, both sporting thick-rimmed glasses, toothy grins, and jaunty hats. The shorter Druggan joined the Valley Gang after working on a garbage truck with his father long enough to decide that the honest life was for suckers. Tall, beefy Frankie Lake had worked as a railroad switchman and firefighter. He had even dabbled in bootlegging when wartime Prohibition had been in effect. They jointly owned the popular Little Bohemia Café, until Lake shot and killed former policeman Timothy Mulvihill during what Lake insisted had been a holdup attempt. Public pressure in response to the shooting shut the place down.[7]

They staked their claim in the Prohibition gold rush by partnering with Joseph Stensen in five breweries: the Gambrinus, the Standard, the George Hoffman, Pfeiffer, and Stege. It was a smart move, as the majority of the booze drinkers in their domain were workingmen who relished beer above all other intoxicants. They also dabbled in hard liquor, but usually the home-cooked stuff. To obtain the raw ingredients, they stole grain or wood alcohol. In April 1921, police arrested the duo and three accomplices (who escaped) in the act of stealing 450 gallons of grain alcohol from the Standard Toilet Goods and Pharmaceutical Company.[8]

Druggan and Lake have been credited with the execution of "Big Steve" Wisniewski, an early casualty of the now-infamous "one-way ride." A typical victim was lured into a car via force or pretense, killed in the vehicle or driven to a remote spot for execution, and then dumped. Wisniewski's death created the profile: on July 18, 1921 his hulking body was found in a patch of weeds on Half Day Road, six miles from Libertyville, Illinois. Bullet holes in his head indicated that he had died violently. An anonymous letter sent to the *Tribune* claimed that he had been kidnapped at Fourteenth and Halstead, and that the Druggan–Lake Gang was responsible.[9]

Both gang leaders were arrested on suspicion of murder, and as late as 1925, Lake County State's Attorney A. V. Smith was trying to bring them to trial. Gangland informants told police the reason for the killing was that Big Steve, who ran his own bootlegging route using the alias Steve Miller, had looted an alcohol storage warehouse that the gang had been planning to pilfer and responded to a reproach from Terry Druggan by kicking him down a flight of stairs.

The Druggan–Lake Gang would pose no problems to Torrio; they were content with what their territory offered and presented no invasion risk.

On the Southwest Side, Joe Saltis and his partner Frank McErlane controlled all the bootlegging within a grungy industrial region known as the Back o' the Yards. The yards in question were the Stockyards, where the slaughter that supported Chicago's thriving meatpacking industry kept the air rancid with the scent of freshly spilled blood and the sky dark with factory smoke.

Although known as "Polack Joe," Saltis was in fact of Slovakian descent. He had been a saloonkeeper during the days leading up to Prohibition and drew upon his experience in the booze business to buy or control a string of Stockyards watering holes. He ran beer in from Wisconsin, and made enough money to take a stab at developing his own town. He bought a Wisconsin farmhouse, built on its grounds a club that could sleep almost thirty people, and began encouraging friends and associates to relocate. By 1928 he had sixty-two people living in his township and confided to a police officer that he wanted to name the place Saltisville. The sole problem was that only twenty-six of the citizens worked for him, so he planned to hire five more voters who would enable him to get a majority vote and the right to name the town as he wished.

Although Saltis had the necessary fortitude to assume control over the Back o' the Yards saloons after the 1923 expulsion of the South Side O'Donnells, the popular perception of him was that of a slow, plodding dimwit. Ragen's Colts, a long-standing gang of rowdies that had its inception in a baseball team, considered it great fun to harass him, calling the sport "pulling Polack Joe's shirt-tail out." They underestimated him, as a half-wit would never have been able to reach the prominence that Saltis did, but considering that the Colts numbered in the hundreds, such a mistake would not have worried them.

Joe Saltis's detractors began to take him more seriously when he joined forces with two underworld powerhouses, one a top-notch killer, the other a merely competent killer but a political dynamo.

Frank McErlane, like Dean O'Banion, had fought in the newspaper circulation wars, during which a trail of bodies attested to his efficiency with a gun. He was not a particularly imposing figure, being of middle height, plump, and florid, but one look at his blue, glassy eyes was all it took to know that one was dealing with a dangerously insane individual.

He had been an auto bandit before the First World War, ambushing pedestrians, roughing them up, and driving off after stealing their valuables. In 1911 he served six months in jail for robbery, did a year for the same offense in 1912, and in March 1913 (a record year during which he was arrested twice for attempted murder, twice for robbery, and once for burglary) he was convicted of robbing one William McDonough and sentenced to serve a term of one year to life at Joliet.[12] After serving a nominal sentence he enlisted in the "newspaper wars," although his circulation soldiering never brought him as much notoriety as his off-the-job undertakings.

In 1916 McErlane did another year behind bars for attempted murder. In 1918 he kidnapped Grace Lytle, a leading witness for the state against McErlane colleague Lloyd Bopp, who had murdered policeman Herman Mallow.[13] After beating Lytle insensible and leaving her in a pool of blood along a lonely Cook County road, he fled to Los Angeles to hide out. L.A. police arrested him there in July 1918,[14] resulting in his extradition to Illinois, but he proved to be as resourceful as he was homicidal, sawing through bars in the Cook County Jail and escaping with three fellow prisoners. He supported himself while on the lam via bank robbery, holding up the United States Bank at Halstead and Sixtieth streets.

When the impulse to kill seized him, he lashed out without hesitation and covered his tracks equally violently. On May 5, 1924, he shot and killed Thaddeus Fancher, a man he did not even know, in a Crown Point, Indiana, saloon merely because a drinking crony taunted him about his shooting ability.[15] McErlane kept one step ahead of the authorities until he and a confederate managed to split open the skull of the state's star witness with an ax. The Illinois Crime Survey's pronouncement of him as "the most brutal triggerman who ever pulled a gun in Chicago" was a huge understatement.

Saltis had equally strong political backup in John "Dingbat" Oberta who, despite the Irish-sounding name, was also a Slav. He had shortened and inserted an apostrophe in his original name of Obertacz,[16] supposedly to court favor with Irish voters when he ran for office in the Thirteenth Ward. Childhood friends had nicknamed him "Dingbat" after a comic strip character, and it stuck. There the humorous side to Oberta ended. He had an excellent head for business and politics, his immaculate fashion sense turned heads on the street, and his prowess at the gentlemen's game of golf was renowned. When his longtime mentor, labor racketeer Big Tim Murphy fell before enemy bullets in 1928, Oberta moved in on Murphy's widow and married her, to absorb some of the departed Big Tim's glory and present himself as a viable successor.

The West Side O'Donnells controlled the West Side territory squeezed between Halstead and Austin Avenue and extending down to Cicero. In theory, three brothers headed the gang; in practice, the boss was William "Klondike" O'Donnell, with his lower-key brothers offering silent backup.

Klondike and his siblings acted as Cicero's unofficial rulers, sharing the privilege of bossing puppet Mayor Joseph Z. Klenha with slot-machine king Eddie Vogel and Eddie Tancl, an ex-boxer and saloonkeeper who had been a powerhouse in Cicero politics for years.[17]

Walter "the Runt" Quinlan, killer of Valley Gang leader Paddy Ryan, joined the O'Donnells after new leader Terry Druggan refused to have anything to do with him. He was delivering a shipment of beer to a Loomis Street saloon, accompanied by Klondike's brother Bernard and gunman Jim Doherty, on April 3, 1926, when a young man entered the premises, walked up to where he was making out a receipt to the saloon owner, and shot him dead. When the police began raiding O'Donnell saloons in their quest for the killer, Myles O'Donnell, another brother, broke the traditional code of silence and identified the wanted man as Paddy's twenty-year-old son, John.[18]

Ciceronians, most of whom were factory workers of Slavic descent, were less prone to bouts of reform fever than their Chicago counterparts. They may not have been vocal supporters of the town's gangster councilors, but they valued their beer and their occasional bout with Lady Luck at the slot machines, and as long as Klondike O'Donnell and his colleagues maintained opportunities to indulge in both, they were content.

Ragen's Colts, headed by Ralph Sheldon, operated in the small territory southeast of Saltis–McErlane's bailiwick, between Forty-second and Sixty-third streets. Sheldon had long suffered from tuberculosis, but physical disability did not prevent him from taking command of a gang that had its roots in the rough and tumble days of the previous century. Only nineteen in 1920, he counted among his followers the roughest gunmen and brawlers his territory had to offer: slugger and labor chief Danny Stanton; William "Gunner" McPadden, whose nickname said it all; and gambler Hugh "Stubby" McGovern. Sheldon had experienced as much as any of them, and mastered the political fix as early as his sixteenth year, when he bought his way out of a highway robbery conviction.[19]

The Colts had their origins in rowdy as opposed to criminal circumstances. In the 1890s a group of energetic Irishmen began a baseball team called the Morgan Athletic Club. Twelve years later it numbered 160 members. In 1908 Frank Ragen captured the presidency after a brawl erupted over the question of the group's leadership. The club officially became Ragen's Colts after it was sued for damaging passenger train cars on one of its annual outings, necessitating a name change. At its zenith the Colts had such a healthy membership based that a credo was spawned: "Hit me and you hit one thousand."[20]

The Colts were notorious racists.[21] One of their number, George Stauber, initiated the devastating race riots of 1919 by throwing rocks at a black youth who had made the mistake of swimming to a whites-only beach. One of his missiles struck the youngster, causing him to drown. They claimed a noble side, however; the Colts once planned to send a strike force to Oklahoma to battle the Ku Klux Klan over the Klan's anti-Catholic activities in that state.

Only one gang stood between Johnny Torrio and the uncontested success of his unity plan. This group, which originated in the far Southwest Side, was also called the O'Donnells. Like Klondike's crew, the leadership consisted of a band of brothers headed by the eldest, Edward, also known as "Spike."

A cheerful gunman who had successfully fought off two homicide prosecutions, Spike O'Donnell cut an arresting figure on the street. His six-foot-three frame, clad in plaid suits and jaunty bow ties, was a conspicuous presence wherever he went. Affable unless provoked, Spike was like Dean O'Banion in that he shook hands easily and let his magnetic personality fight his battles for him whenever possible. Whenever it was *not* possible, he made good on his favorite saying: "When arguments fail, use a blackjack."

O'Donnell's criminal record included arrests for union terrorism, bank robbery, and murder. In May 1916 he stood trial for the murder of Hugh Coogan, with whom he had supposedly quarreled over a profit split in the motion picture projectionists union.[22] Acquitted and feeling sure of his own influence, Spike presented himself as a candidate for aldermanic nomination in February 1917, but lost and compensated for the defeat by beating up one John Daly, with whom he had an argument over the election results.[23]

O'Donnell headed the gang that committed the Stockman's Trust and Savings Bank robbery in 1917, a crime for which George Moran's old comrade George Raymond had been arrested. Leonard Banks and Frank Bender, Moran's accomplices in the failed 1918 jail break, had also been in on it, and it's possible that the North Sider may have made the acquaintance of O'Donnell himself. After serving seven months for receiving $1,700 worth of stolen property, Spike was found guilty of complicity in the Stockman's job in March 1918 and sentenced to one to fourteen years at Joliet, although he remained free on appeal until 1922.[24]

O'Donnell was brazen, a trait he aptly illustrated in 1918 when he located the gang that had stolen $47,000 from the La Grange State Bank and stole a portion of the booty from them. The *Tribune*, in reporting the event, said, "Spike O'Donnell named in new version of honor among thieves."[25]

Spike had no interest in falling into line with anyone's master plan, much less that of an Italian from the East Coast. His territory included Bridgeport, Canaryville, parts of Englewood and West Englewood, and the Back o' the Yards district destined to be absorbed by the Saltis–McErlane Gang. His aggressive stance and determination to go his own way made him a potential liability, so Torrio assessed his weak spots and moved in, hoping to eliminate the problem without resorting to open warfare.

Bad things began happening to Spike and his crew. Police officers loyal to the O'Donnells suddenly found themselves transferred, and needle beer direct from Torrio breweries infiltrated O'Donnell saloons.[26] Before he could muster the resources for a counterattack, Spike lost his appeal in the old Stockman case in December 1922 and found himself en route to Joliet to commence his long-over-due sentence.

His brothers Steve, Walter, and Tommy were formidable enough with Spike at the helm, but without him, they represented no opposition. Torrio, counting on O'Donnell being out of the way for a few years at least, moved in and absorbed his territory. The Italian was not aware that Governor Len Small, who rarely needed encouragement when it came to showing leniency to powerful gangsters, had a pile of pardon requests for Spike on his desk. Some of O'Donnell's benefactors were senators, state representatives, and criminal-court judges.

Spike O'Donnell would figure in the equation sooner than Torrio anticipated. The variable he represented would endanger the Italian's formula for success.

Although some gangland histories have suggested otherwise, Torrio did not so much grant territory to the Chicago gangs as affirm the boundaries that had always been in place and suggest that co-operation and respect for those borders would make them all rich beyond their wildest dreams. Even the smaller gangs that showed some signs of independence were provided for—a small wedge of territory located between the river and the West Side O'Donnell fiefdom was split between small but tough groups captained by Claude Maddox and Marty Guilfoyle.

By common agreement each gang could obtain its beer and liquor via any source it chose except hijacking, but Torrio made the universal offer to supply beer at $50 a barrel to anyone whose resources were low.

No one offered any real objection to Johnny Torrio's approach or his ideas. Some may have scorned him as an idealist, but they all agreed that his plan would allow each gang to develop and strengthen its client base without expending valuable energy in defending it at the same time. They also concurred that he would serve as arbiter whenever disputes or suspected agreement violations arose.

Next to Torrio, who absorbed the South Side O'Donnell bailiwick and everything else south of Madison Street down to the Indiana state line, O'Banion had the largest territory. The North Side bootlegging franchise included everything north of Madison to the Chicago city limits, and was bordered on the east and west by the lake and the northwest branch of the Chicago River.

Thanks to Nails Morton, O'Banion's North Siders had a solid Canadian liquor source, and they were buying into distilleries, but their brewery holdings were minimal during Prohibition's earliest months. O'Banion and Torrio reached an agreement in which the Italian would see to it that the North Side working class was never without a steady source of beer, and O'Banion made sure that Colosimo's and the other South Side restaurants and speakeasies that valued quality over intoxication value had the finest Scotches, champagnes, and brandies available.

Torrio indulged in these exclusive negotiations with O'Banion not only to obtain a reliable liquor source but also to strengthen the personal and professional association between himself and the North Side boss. O'Banion's organizational skills were minimal, given his spirited and impulsive nature, but he had a large and devoted following in his bailiwick that did not only consist of other gangsters. Special agreements and concessions in his favor might not necessarily ensure the longevity of the inter-gang treaty, but at least it would have more of a fighting chance.

Whatever minor trouble Torrio may have anticipated from smaller-league gangs after the general amnesty agreement, he expected none at all from the police. Chief Charles Fitzmorris admitted wearily, "About 60 percent of my police are in the liquor business." Fitzmorris was the third chief appointed during Big Bill Thompson's second administration, the previous two having been exposed as corrupt and dismissed. He knew what was expected of him, despite Thompson's public declaration of his intention to clean up the city and drive out the criminals. Fitzmorris raided a few gambling resorts that had fallen behind in their protection payments, hurled suspicious-looking vagabonds into jail, and made a big show out of raiding lower-grade speakeasies. The overall effect on the Chicago crime rate was negligible, but it looked good in the press.[27]

One of the only law enforcement figures in the Thompson administration who was not openly corrupt was Robert Emmet Crowe, the state's attorney for Cook County. Crowe was a Yale graduate who made a political splash as an assistant state's attorney in the office of John Wayman when Wayman was tackling the Levee problem. He served Carter Harrison II as an assistant city corporation counsel, spent a year as a Cook County circuit court judge, and in 1919 became the youngest chief justice of the criminal court to ever hold that position. He even enjoyed some social status when he married Candida Cuneo, whose family had founded Chicago's longest-standing wholesale produce firm.[28]

Crowe was a capable jurist who never backed down from intimidating cases. When he became state's attorney, he initiated improvements to the office by hiring law school graduates who had ranked at the top of their classes, requesting that the number of judges available to the state's attorney be raised from six to twenty, and was instrumental in securing the addition of a thousand more men to the police force.

Although he was viewed as the one bright star in Thompson's tarnished cabinet, Robert Crowe was not so praiseworthy in his prosecution of gangsters. He faced many of them, both as a trial judge and as state's attorney, but never sent a single one to prison or the gallows. Outside forces, such as political insulation, shielded these men from punishment, which frustrated Crowe in his conviction attempts, but another possible explanation lay in his own use of gang support to further his ends. In January 1920, when Hymie Weiss appeared in his criminal court, Crowe railed against him from the bench before sending him home with the advice to "think of your mother and try to do better." Those who heard him excoriate the North Sider would never have guessed that the night before, O'Banion and Weiss had visited his house to discuss their support for his bid for the state's attorney's office.[29]

Crowe was dangerous to robbers and low-level thugs but would pose no serious threat to the bootleggers. Even if he did not employ gang support at the polls like every other aspirant to political office, the state's attorney had no real weapon in the war against the rumrunning gangs. By Chief Fitzmorris's own admission, the greater percentage of his police force would be too busy competing with them to keep them in line.

That point was painfully hammered home for the city's reform element on the night of August 23, 1920.[30] Nails Morton and Herschel "Hirschie" Miller, who headed a small Jewish mob on the West Side, walked into the Pekin Inn at 2700 South State Street after its 1 a.m. closing time. The Pekin, which was owned by undertaker Daniel Jackson, routinely hosted after-hours crap games, and the Beaux Arts Café upstairs supplied night revelers with liquor and live jazz until daylight, sometimes even early afternoon.

Morton had recently lost $14,000 to gambler "Nick the Greek" and was looking to win at least some of it back. While waiting for the game to amass enough players, he and Miller decided to go up to the Beaux Arts and check out the refreshments and entertainment. They ascended the stairs, entered the club, and took a table where they could see the band.

Half an hour later, Sergeant James "Pluck" Mulcahey came in through the front door, ordered a drink at the bar, and requested change for a hundred-dollar bill. Seeing the policeman's large stock of cash, the drunken Morton sidled up to him and half-jokingly said, "Gimme some ice," *ice* being underworld slang for money. Mulcahey, whose honest peers had long suspected him of cutting liquor selling deals with Hirschie Miller's crew, laughed at the display and retired with Morton to a little alcove at the rear of the club.

Those sitting in the vicinity of their table overheard a discussion about a whiskey deal and an unfair "split" just before both men raised their voices and hurled threats at each other. Morton sprang to his feet and pushed the detective to the floor. Hirschie Miller implored them to stop while café patrons eyed the intensifying dispute nervously.

Detective Sergeant William Hennessey came into the café with a friend just in time to see Mulcahey lying on the floor, wiping his bleeding mouth. Miller was holding Morton by the arms and trying to force him backward. Mulcahey, seeing his fellow officer, shouted to him, "Stick it on 'em!" Hennessey drew his gun, which caused Morton to cease his tirade and back away slowly.

The Jewish gangster did not see the chair looming behind him until he collided with it and fell backward. Seizing the advantage, Mulcahey leaped to his feet and kicked him in the head.

When Hirschie Miller pulled out his revolver and started to go to his fallen friend's rescue, Hennessey shot at him once, but the bullet missed and fractured a mirror. The bad luck that usually follows such an act was swift in coming, as Miller pumped four bullets into him and one into Mulcahey. The club patrons scrambled for the door while Hennessey's companion, an ex-Prohibition agent, called for an ambulance and police reinforcements. Both wounded officers lived long enough to name their attackers at the hospital.

Hirschie Miller and Nails Morton were arrested and tried twice for murder (once for each victim) but were acquitted both times by juries that had little sympathy for two slain detectives who patronized the sort of establishment they were duty-bound to keep closed. The Pekin Inn/Beaux Arts Café was later torn down and replaced by a courthouse and police station, but the fight that transpired there that August lingered in the public mind for a long time.

For gangland, the memory was a cause for optimism even longer.

MORAN RETURNS AND THE O'DONNELLS EXIT

B Y 1921 THE NORTH SIDE Gang had sailed through the first year of Prohibition successfully. Bootlegging was making them all rich, but not wanting to narrow the horizon in any way, O'Banion initiated an expansion into union control. His key man in this field was Daniel McCarthy, alias "Dapper Dan," who served the Journeyman Plumbers Union as its business agent. Handsome and clad in the latest men's fashions, McCarthy had an ugly temper when crossed. When a police officer came to arrest him for desertion from the army in 1918, the gangster shot him.[1]

Advice on union management and manipulation was also forthcoming from Maxie Eisen, a Morton associate who resembled Johnny Torrio in his organizational skills and business acumen. He either headed or controlled multiple unions, such as the Jewish Chicken Killers, Wholesale Fish Dealers, and the Master Butchers. He ran a popular restaurant at Roosevelt Road and Blue Island Avenue,[2] and could often be found there in an upstairs office, determining which new fish-peddling business could afford his $3,000 price for permission to operate, and which butcher shop could afford the $1,000 union dues outright or had to make arrangements for installment payments.[3]

He met adversity with brute force but rarely applied it himself. His twenty-two-year-old brother, Jack Eisen, was an accomplished gunman and slugger, and took malicious delight in smashing store windows, torching pushcarts, and beating up independent merchants who spurned the unions.[4] Despite the mayhem he created for those who opposed him, his criminal record by 1921 only consisted of a six-month sentence in the House of Correction in 1919 for petty larceny.

Eisen and his West Side partner Jacob Epstein backed O'Banion in the purchase of the Cragin Distillery, which produced denatured alcohol. Using ex-policeman Warren Levin as a front, they sold the product to bootleggers who specialized in the home-cooked, hazardous liquors.[5]

Julian "Potatoes" Kaufman was a personal O'Banion friend who provided him with advice and direction in the North Side Gang's gambling operation. Kaufman, whose nickname originated from a sideline in speculating on potato futures, was the son of millionaire commission broker Edmund Kaufman and had no need to seek the underworld for a source of income. His disdain for the law struck him at the age of thirteen, when his mother, Hattie, was shot and killed by a gang of boy bandits during a holdup gone wrong.[6] The youthful slayers got little jail time, and Julian, embittered by the trivial justice in the face of his bitter loss, determined not to let the law restrict him in how he chose to make his fortune. Kaufman moved easily in both worlds, attending business functions with his father and cabaret outings with the North Siders while assuming the same air of ease and self-assurance.

One of the North Side Gang's newest recruits was Frank Gusenberg. Gusenberg had a long and varied criminal history; his first arrest took place on September 23, 1909, when the Lincoln Park police seized him and four other young men for stalking and making suggestive remarks to young women. Under the alias of Carl Bloom, he was taken to the North Halsted police station, charged with disorderly conduct, and fined.[7]

Gusenberg soon found his calling, applying muscle in labor disputes, and did a thirty-day stretch in the Bridewell in 1911 for being a little too enthusiastic about his occupation. In June 1912 he beat up a crippled newsboy during a newspaper strike and appeared before Judge Harry Olsen. The entire time that his case was being heard, his friends and supporters cast menacing glances at prosecution witnesses and the jury, forcing Olsen to remind the latter that they could not let themselves be influenced by the hostility.

"This crowd does not represent the citizens at large," the judge said, "and the jury must be careful not to be influenced by its laughter and grimaces."[8]

Gusenberg was found guilty, but the punishment was a paltry one: $1 plus court costs. He was not so lucky four years later. In November 1916 he and other "labor goons" hired by the International Brotherhood of Electrical Workers clashed with a rival movie projectionists union, the International Alliance of Theatrical Stage Employees and Motion Picture Operators, outside the Rose Theater at 61 West Madison Street. The battle was a bloody one, with both sides armed to the teeth with knives and guns. Gusenberg came out of it with broken ribs and a concussion, but not before he beat projectionist George Heiss within an inch of his life.[9]

112

Frank's older brother Pete had an equally blemished record. He first appeared on the police blotter in 1902, when he was arrested at the age of fourteen for larceny, and went to Joliet for three years on a 1906 burglary charge. Paroled in 1909, he went back to prison the following year for a parole violation. After his release in 1911, Gusenberg evaded further arrest for the robberies, holdups, and union slugging that occupied his time for ten more years.[10]

In April 1921 his luck changed. Gusenberg joined labor racketeer Big Tim Murphy, Vincenzo Cosmano, and several others in stealing $350,000 worth of mail from the Dearborn Street station. They scouted out the location by staging a fake—and clumsy—baseball game across the street until it was time to move in.[11] The gang was arrested one by one, as everyone's identity became known, and charged with robbery. After making a plea of not guilty, Gusenberg created a sensation by eluding the novice deputy U.S. marshal assigned to escort him and walking out of the courtroom unimpeded.[12] He remained at liberty for sixteen months, missing the trial entirely. Police officers finally caught him as he was making a nighttime visit to his wife in August 1922.[13] He did almost three years in Joliet as a result of his resourcefulness.

Another newcomer was Leland Varain, alias Louis Alterie, who followed O'Banion around as doggedly as a second shadow. Handsome and outgoing, Alterie was an extrovert who had once been a police officer in Venice, California. After a mediocre career as a boxer under the name of Kid Haynes, he came to Chicago as a bodyguard for boxer Melvin Reeves, and then abandoned his employer for a better-paying career with the Valley Gang. He switched his primary allegiance to the North Side Gang after meeting and hitting it off with the equally spirited O'Banion, but he continued to pull the odd job with the Druggan–Lake crew when invited.[14]

Alterie, who was of mixed French and Mexican heritage, first came to the attention of the Chicago authorities in January 1922, when he got into an altercation with a man named Strauss at Al Tierney's café. During the heated exchange Alterie whipped out his revolver and shot Strauss through the cheek. His victim survived but declined to prosecute.[15]

Six months later, in June, he and Terry Druggan held up wealthy socialite Clara Weinberger in the vestibule of her Wayne Avenue home and robbed her and two companions of a small fortune in cash and diamonds. A woman he had jilted phoned the police and informed them that Druggan, Alterie, and the missing loot could be found in Alterie's room at the Parkway Hotel. Mrs. Weinberger positively identified Druggan as one of the assailants and felt sure that Alterie had also been present. Both men were arrested, but the charges were eventually dropped.[16]

Although new faces infused the North Side Gang as its fortunes grew, O'Banion never forgot old ones, namely George Moran. In early 1920 the North Side leader set the legal machinations in motion to get Moran's 1918 conviction overturned, hiring a lawyer to present the case to the appeals court. The maneuver worked, and Moran was finally released on bond on March 16, 1921, pending an appeal of his original conviction, and rejoined the O'Banion crew in Chicago.[17]

He moved into a rooming house at 711 West Congress Street, run by Margaret Burke Kroll, who turned a blind eye to the criminal element that comprised the majority of her boarders. Also living there were Henry Carr, a burglar who'd done time in Pontiac and had a string of burglary-related arrests in Chicago and other cities on his record, and John George, an O'Banion gangster with police and political connections of his own.

The *Chicago Evening Post*, commenting on George's career in a 1921 news item, wrote, ". . . although arrested many times on various charges, [he] was convicted but once, and then in some mysterious manner succeeded in having a term of thirty days in the Bridewell reduced to one day in jail." Those who knew of O'Banion's influence among those officials capable of reducing punishment did not find it so mysterious.

Moran did not take an active role in the organization of the O'Banion gang's North Side bootlegging empire, although he lent muscle when and where needed. His energies were focused on the type of pursuit that he had always followed: robbery, burglary, and larceny. The Kroll boarding house was a haven for men of similar inclination.

On October 7 a car drove leisurely up to the mail-loading platform of the Illinois Central Station.[18] No one from either the post office department or the railroad saw three men get out, grab five mail sacks containing $2,000 worth of women's apparel from Phillipsborn and Company, toss them into the rear seat of the vehicle, and drive away. The theft was discovered purely by chance. Barely an hour afterward, a squad car containing five police detectives was cruising along Congress Street when one of the officers saw a car parked in an alley, the mail sacks visible through the rear window.

Two men, later identified as Henry Carr and John George, were standing beside the car. When they saw the police vehicle, they bolted. Two officers jumped out and arrested Moran, who was behind the wheel of the parked car, while the others sped off after the fleeing robbers. Carr and George stopped only when bullets from the high-powered rifles carried by the cops flew dangerously close to their heads.

All three men were arrested for robbery, but the case never made it to trial. Moran was charged with larceny a month later, on November 21, and gave his name as George Gage to the arresting officers, but that too ended up stricken from the record.

Adelard Cunin no longer needed to leave a state to escape the consequences of arrest.

The North Side Gang continued to fortify its bootlegging, gambling, and union incomes with warehouse looting, hijacking, and safeblowing. Some gang historians have dismissed this practice as evidence of irresponsibility and the members' inability to focus their energies on the safer and better-paying endeavors. In reality, most of the Chicago gangs that rose to eminence during Prohibition did not completely abandon their pre-Volstead pursuits. They suspected that the dry law, in view of its overwhelming unpopularity, was not destined to last and deemed it wise to keep their skills from dulling.

On March 14, 1921, the North Siders stole twenty barrels of alcohol, valued at $5,500, from the Price Flavoring Extract Company.[19] A warrant went out for O'Banion's arrest, but the gang leader went into hiding until a nolle pros could be purchased. Although it is not known whether Moran participated in that theft, he was definitely in on the Postal Telegraph safeblowing the following June.

On the night of June 1 a watchman at the Board of Trade Building spotted suspicious movement in the Postal Telegraph Building at 332 South La Salle Street, which housed the Chicago Typographical Union. He was concerned enough to cross the street and alert the watchman there, who had noticed nothing. The two men located a policeman, Patrol Sergeant John Ryan. Directing one of the watchmen to stay down by the building entrance, Ryan and the other man quietly ascended the staircase to the second floor. Just as they pushed the door to the Typographical Union open, a small explosion went off inside and seared their eyes and nostrils with acrid smoke.

Ryan, coughing, drew his revolver and trained it on four men huddled around the blanket-swaddled safe. Charles Reiser, Dean O'Banion, Hymie Weiss, and George Moran, who'd been preparing to help themselves to the $35,000 payroll, whirled around in shock. O'Banion reached for his own gun, but Ryan was faster and knocked it from his hand. The patrol sergeant and the watchman marched the quartet down to the station, where O'Banion gave his name as Edward Sterling. Weiss was Oscar Nelson, Reiser was John Sibley, and Moran supplied yet another alias, George Morrissey. Burned money in their pockets made the police wonder whether they had been responsible for another safeblowing job discovered earlier the same evening, at Joseph Klein's feed store at 525 West Thirty-fifth Street.[20]

While John Ryan gloried in his temporary celebrity status (the *Tribune* awarded him its $100 Hero of the Month prize and he received a $300 pay raise[21]), the North Siders were charged with burglary and possession of burglar tools. When bail was set at a low amount, Henry Barrett Chamberlain of the Chicago Crime Commission made a loud and impassioned protest to Judge Frank Johnston. Johnston raised the bonds ridiculously high, setting Reiser's at $100,000, O'Banion's and Moran's at $60,000, and Weiss's at $50,000. Chamberlain, convinced that certain members of the Chicago judiciary were involved in a plot to "keep bad actors out of jail," pressed for federal warrants charging the North Siders with possession of explosives in violation of the wartime Defense of the Nation Act.

"This quartet with Charles Reiser at its head is the most dangerous in the city," he complained. "It would be a crime to allow them to escape by forfeiting their bonds should they be able to make bail."[22]

The safeblowers' attorney, John Byrne, advised State's Attorney Crowe that abnormally high bail discriminated against his clients, and he pointed out that the bond usually applied in burglary cases was much lower. Johnston reluctantly ordered a reduction. In O'Banion's case, Matt Foley of the *Chicago American* posted $5,000 to secure his freedom on the federal explosives charge, and two housewives somehow acquainted with the defendants or their counsel offered buildings they owned as security for the $40,000 bond on the other charges.[23]

By the time the case came to trial, O'Banion, Reiser, Weiss, and Moran were in a position to sit back and enjoy the legal drama as freely as the courtroom spectators. O'Banion had shelled out $30,000 to purchase an acquittal in advance, leaving him at liberty to give some of the cockiest testimony the court had ever witnessed.

"We had all met at three o'clock in the morning in the all-night Raklios restaurant here on the corner," he said. "We were having hot chocolate and chocolate éclairs. We heard a lot of racket could have been an explosion in the Postal Telegraph Building. So we climbed the fire escape to see what it was all about. Whoever was blowing the safe must have heard us coming. They got away." He said that he, Reiser, Weiss, and Moran had been standing around the smoldering safe, wondering what to do next, when the office door opened. O'Banion admitted to drawing his pistol in response. "At first I thought it might have been the thieves coming back. But when I saw it was a policeman, I put my gun down and we gave ourselves up like good citizens."[24]

The verdict: not guilty. The North Siders celebrated the acquittal by retiring to Diamond Joe Esposito's Bella Napoli Café for hours of drinking and dining. Once sufficiently drunk (even O'Banion imbibed more than he would have normally), they knocked the tables over and played a war game with their guns until the manager appealed to O'Banion to take the fun outside. A cop who rushed into the restaurant in response to the gunfire gave them the excuse they needed to depart. Thrusting their pistol muzzles against his uniformed middle, they hustled him outside and made a run for it, leaving the patrol wagon that soon arrived with no prisoners to pick up.

As the summer of 1921 progressed, O'Banion contemplated the gang's future. He had nothing to complain about in terms of how well its business interests were paying. He and his twenty-year-old wife, Viola, whom he married in February 1921[25] in an opulent ceremony held at Our Lady of Sorrows Basilica, were looking to purchase a second home closer to downtown than their current residence at 6081 Ridge Avenue, and buying a $30,000 acquittal posed no more financial strain than picking up the morning paper. One thing in particular did concern him though: Big Bill Thompson's chances of being re-elected mayor in 1923 looked dim.

In-fighting began in the Thompson camp soon after he took office, and the fissures were widening with time. Fred Lundin, his political mentor, split with him in a fit of pique after the mayor failed to consult him over Charles Fitzmorris's appointment as chief of police. Thompson had issues with Lundin too. The former congressman insisted on a monopoly over patronage and harped to all who would listen about how he was the actual power behind the mayoral throne.[26] When, in the June 1921 judicial election, Thompson advanced a slate that emphasized nothing more substantial than loyalty to himself, everyone, even the normally pro-Thompson *American*, voiced their disgust.

Johnny Torrio took the initiative in tightening connections with friends in higher places than the mayor's seat. In 1921 no less a political personage than the governor of Illinois himself, Len Small, was in dire need of the type of aid Torrio could furnish.

Small, a one-time banker and farmer from Kankakee, was indicted in July for embezzling more than $800,000 during his term as state treasurer. He had deposited the pilfered money in a fictitious bank that was nothing more than a pseudonym for his own pocket. His fate was a matter of serious concern for gangsters like Torrio and O'Banion, as Small's office was a pardon mill for convicted criminals. Everyone knew whom you were talking about in 1921 when you sang "Oh Pardon Me," a sarcastic take on the popular hit "Oh Promise Me."

Attorney General Edward Brundage, who disliked Mayor Thompson and had been fighting him for years, jumped at the chance to nail Small, whom Thompson had backed with enthusiasm in the 1920 gubernatorial election. He also had his own axe to grind with the governor, as his office had received a $700,000 budget cut. Brundage informed the public that the actual amount stolen was $819,690.31, but the arrangements that permitted the embezzlement set the total loss to the taxpayer at more than $2 million.[27]

When Small's trial commenced in Waukegan, Torrio and O'Banion emissaries traveled to the town to make the necessary promises, payoffs, and threats. They devised an ingenious scheme to ensure favorable jury selection by canvassing the homes of prospective jurors and showing them a photo album containing pictures of Governor Small. A negative reaction to Small's likeness was reported to the defense counsel, who then barred the individuals in question from the jury selection process.[28] The effort met with success when the governor was acquitted and returned to Springfield, grateful and cognizant that he owed Johnny Torrio.

On the night of October 11 Charles Reiser was at home with his wife and two children when a car pulled up outside their home at 1704 Otto Street and honked twice. Reiser parted the living room curtains and peered into the darkness for a few seconds. Recognizing the arrivals, he unlocked the front door, went down the steps, and approached the curb. While his wife watched, he leaned toward the idling vehicle and exchanged words with the occupants.[29]

Several bursts of gunfire cracked the night's stillness, followed by the screeching of tires as the car drove away at breakneck speed. Reiser, his body peppered with fourteen bullet wounds, collapsed to the sidewalk.

Neighbors assisted Madeline in rushing the injured man to Alexian Brothers Hospital. A thorough examination revealed that one bullet had struck Reiser's spine, damaging the cord badly enough to guarantee that he would never walk again. His game response surprised even the surgeon who broke the devastating news to him.

The would-be murderers, however, were still out there. When Mrs. Reiser asked for police protection, Sergeant Lawrence Cooney was detailed to stay at the Otto Street residence and play bodyguard to the family. He drove Madeline and the children to and from the hospital in the Reiser vehicle.

Madeline Reiser later claimed that during an unsupervised moment, her husband asked her to bring him a little pistol he kept in his bedroom, his reason being "there's something wrong with the handle; I want to get it fixed." She dutifully tucked the weapon into her purse and brought it when she and Verna went to visit him on October 18. Sergeant Cooney accompanied them as usual, staying downstairs in the hospital lobby while they went up to Reiser's room.

Half an hour later, Verna skipped downstairs and rejoined the policeman. "Mother's nearly ready," she said cheerily. No sooner had she spoken when three shots sounded from somewhere in the direction of Reiser's room, followed by hysterical screams from Madeline. Cooney raced up the stairs into the room and found the King of the Safecrackers lying in bed, dead from three bullets fired into his brain.

Mrs. Reiser was chalk white and gasping for air. "He shot himself!" she cried. "He asked me to get the gun for him yesterday and I did. I didn't think he would do that! He was so cheerful, and there wasn't any reason for him to kill himself."

She crumpled in a faint. After she revived, Cooney, who had doubts about the suicide theory, removed her to the Chicago Avenue station to await the verdict of the October 19 inquest. When she refused to testify, Captain Max Danner placed her under arrest, explaining to reporters, "It was the only action we could take. The deputy coroner ordered us to continue the investigation, and the only way we could hold her was to take out a warrant."[30]

The chain of bizarre events continued even after Reiser's death. A judge allowed the widow to post bond when she pleaded to attend the funeral. After a friend guaranteed the $10,000 bail, Madeline went to J. G. Waldner's undertaking establishment, where her husband's body awaited burial. The undertaker's wife, feeling sorry for her, invited her to stay in the Waldner apartment until after the funeral. Madeline Reiser tearfully accepted and then asked to use the bathroom. Thinking that she merely wanted to compose herself and reapply makeup, Mrs. Waldner directed her to it.

Seconds later, she heard groaning noises that alarmed her. Forcing the door open, the woman found Mrs. Reiser lying on the floor, arms and throat awash in blood. The distraught woman had attempted suicide with a razor. "I'm not going to let those bad men get me," she sobbed before passing out. She was taken to Grant Hospital, where doctors assured the police that she would recover.[31]

When she had her day in court, she succeeded in convincing that jury that she was no murderer, but rather a frightened widow grieving for a dead husband while fearing a return visit from the men who had failed to kill him themselves. She left the courtroom a free woman and the beneficiary of Reiser's $100,000 estate.

Ernest Schoeps, Reiser's brother, pushed for a murder investigation in December. He complained to Assistant State's Attorney Edwin S. Day that his brother could not have shot himself, since his right hand and left arm had been broken. Day, knowing that the case would be hopeless given the verdict of the coroner's jury, declined to prosecute.[32]

Although Charles Reiser's death was officially a suicide and probably uxoricide, the rumor persisted over the years that O'Banion had killed him. It was a notion that found its way into print in 1931, when Edward Doherty of the *Daily Times*, reviewing the crime, suggested that the North Sider had climbed up the hospital fire escape to avoid police detection, located Reiser's room, and shot him dead. This scenario is impossible, given the fact that Madeline Reiser was present at the time of the shooting and Sergeant Cooney arrived minutes later, robbing an assassin of the privacy necessary to do the deed and the time to successfully escape.

Although they continued to work together on safecracking jobs, O'Banion and his mentor had been gradually drifting apart since Clarence White's February 1920 death. White had been a close friend of both O'Banion and Hymie Weiss, and the likelihood that Reiser had killed him in a fit of paranoia after Johnny Mahoney's confessions did not sit well with either of them. They may not have killed the Ox, or even been in the car that sent the crippling bullets into his body, but the fact that they declined to attend his funeral speaks volumes about their regard for him by October 1921.

Who shot Reiser that cool October night, indirectly sending him to his doom? Possibly friends of Clarence White or other former associates or trial witnesses that he had killed over the years. Johnny Mahoney, whose squealing had set off Reiser's paranoia, was found murdered in an alley beside 1814 South Peoria Street in April 1921.[33] Perhaps his brother-in-law, Mops Volpe, whose connections in the Italian underworld were tight, had struck back at the probable killer in revenge.

In 1922 O'Banion and Nails Morton bought interests in the William F. Schofield florist shop at 738 North State Street. The shop was a two-story brick building just across the street from Holy Name Cathedral, where O'Banion had attended many a mass with his father and grandmother. The neighborhood was largely working class, but the presence of Michigan Avenue a short stroll away made Schofield's fancier décor less out of place.

The forty-three-year-old Schofield had been running one flower shop or another since 1896. He began his career in the business as a $3-a-week delivery boy at Gallagher's Florist Shop near Monroe and Wabash and eventually bought a tiny store of his own at 150 North Wells Street, next door to W. D. Curtin's funeral parlor. After a short stint as a soldier in the Spanish-American War, Schofield opened another florist outlet at Clark and Chestnut.[34] At one time he'd had political aspirations: in 1912, 1913, and 1914 he attempted—and failed—to secure the Democratic nomination for alderman of the Twenty-first Ward. The Municipal Voter's League noted of him in their 1914 candidate report: "Good reputation, but believed to lack ability for the position." In his initial bid for the post, O'Banion's own political mentor, Hot Stove Jimmy Quinn, had backed him.

Schofield met Dean O'Banion in 1918, when the latter began dropping into his new shop at 738 North State to buy flowers. The two hit it off so well that O'Banion hired the florist to provide $2,000 worth of blooms (150 corsages for the women, gardenias for the buttonholes of each of the men) for his February 1921 wedding. The day after the ceremony, the North Sider called Schofield from his "honeymoon suite" at the Drake Hotel, ostensibly to pay the bill.

"After we'd talked, he asked me if I wanted a partner," Schofield would remember. "He said he'd see me when he got back from his honeymoon in California."

Other matters kept O'Banion busy until the following year, when he and Morton bought into the State Street location. He also used $10,000 of his own money to back Schofield in the opening of a new shop at Broadway and Devon.[35]

Although Morton contented himself with being an absentee owner, O'Banion plunged into the day-to-day tasks of running the North State Street shop with genuine enjoyment. Schofield's was open six days a week, from 9 a.m. to 9 p.m., and anyone calling the day or night numbers might have O'Banion answer them. He maintained an office on the building's second floor, next to a smoking room loaded with stuffed leather furniture and photos of prizefighters, but more often he could be found downstairs, arranging blooms and serving customers.

Women canvassing for charity in the neighborhood found him a soft and charming touch; he rarely donated anything less than $25. Once, four fund-raisers visited him individually to solicit donations for the same cause. O'Banion gave to each one, never mentioning that he had already been approached.

O'Banion's standing in the Chicago underworld guaranteed that his shop would receive the plethora of wreath and tribute orders whenever a well-connected gangster died. Schofield's creations loomed large at any event requiring a floral tribute: ten-foot high blankets of roses, baskets stuffed with bush-sized bouquets of rare lilies, and on special funerary occasions, a life-sized wax effigy of the departed covered with hand-pressed flower petals.

Once the shop doors were locked, he continued to do business, but not the legal variety. On the morning of April 12, 1922, he and Dan McCarthy were enjoying a quiet breakfast in the coffee shop of the Hotel Sherman when Hymie Levin, an acquaintance who ran a speakeasy, rushed in. Levin paused at the door, scanned the room until he spotted them, and then hurried over.[36]

"I was hoping I'd find you here," he exclaimed before telling them about a conversation he had just overheard in his saloon. A driver for the Walter Powers Warehouse, who'd dropped in for a beer, told another customer that he had a truckload of bonded liquor that he was in the process of delivering to West Side drugstores. Levin knew that this was too good an opportunity to pass up, for O'Banion was renowned for his generosity to those who tipped him off about beer or alcohol shipments and storage spots. He would pay those among the general public who provided information 10 percent of whatever he was able to sell the product for, but he could cut in friends and associates as a partner in an even division of the profits.

O'Banion and McCarthy rose from their table and prepared to leave with Levin. At that moment, Vincent Drucci and Harry Hartman, who had once boxed under the alias of Johnny Dundee and who now operated on the fringes of the North Side Gang, strolled in. Levin eyed them nervously and commented, "I'm not sure that there's enough to go around." Drucci and Hartman assured him that they would only come along to provide muscle and not insist on a share.

After telling the waitress that they would return, the North Siders followed Levin out of the coffee shop and piled into O'Banion's car. They drew near the speakeasy just as the liquor truck was pulling away from the curb to resume the delivery trip, and followed it. Overtaking the truck at Canal Street, they pounced. O'Banion, Drucci, and Hartman got out of their car, surrounded the Jackson Express & Van Company vehicle, and ordered the driver, Joseph Goodman, to get out, run, and not look back. He hastily complied, permitting O'Banion to get behind the wheel and drive the truck to a hiding spot a block away. The North Siders and Levin regrouped at the Hotel Sherman, where O'Banion discovered to his pride that his coffee was still hot. The still-steaming brew was a testament to the speed with which he could operate.

The liquid cargo turned out to be 225 cases of whiskey consigned to the Susquemac Distilling Company. Nails Morton took the entire load off their hands for $100 per case, leaving O'Banion, McCarthy, and Levin with $7,500 each. It was excellent pay for twenty minutes' work.

They were still counting their money when warrants were issued for their arrest. Once he located a telephone, Joseph Goodman reported the hijacking to the police. At the station he identified O'Banion, Drucci, and Hartman after browsing through mug shots. He might have spared himself and the police the trouble. Alderman Titus Haffa of the Forty-third Ward posted bail for the North Siders minutes after they were brought in, and O'Banion furnished the necessary payments to have the case nolle prossed.[37]

Two months later, on the night of June 24, a watchman for the North Side Citizens Association, Nicholas Tice, spotted two men in a car parked in front of the Parkway Tea Room at 725 North Michigan Avenue. He thought nothing of it until he encountered a pedestrian who informed him that the men had just been seen leaving the supposedly closed tearoom. A suspicious Tice hurried back but found the car gone. He called the police.[38]

Investigation showed that Tice had barely missed apprehending a gang of safe-crackers. The tearoom safe had been wrapped in rugs and draperies to muffle the explosion as nitro tore open the box. The contents—$1,000 in cash, a diamond stickpin valued at $350, and $10,000 worth of stock in the Fulton Cold Storage Company—were nowhere to be found. Sergeant William T. Shanley[39] of the Chicago Avenue police station managed to lift two clean sets of fingerprints from the remains of the safe, enabling him to identify the culprits as O'Banion and Drucci.[40]

The call went out to pick them up, but they stayed out of sight for over a month. Then on September 1, Sergeants Tuohy and Katzko spied Drucci's car on Michigan Avenue and pursued him in their own vehicle. When he spotted them on his tail, Drucci stepped on the gas and sped south on the boulevard. He made for the Michigan Avenue Bridge, but as he approached, the bridge began to separate and rise to allow a steamer to pass underneath. Bells rang, warning lights flashed, and wire barriers descended.

Undeterred, Drucci ran his car through the barricades, tearing them off their hinges. A three- to four-foot gap now yawned in the middle of the slowly lifting bridge, but the North Sider vaulted his vehicle over it and made it safely to the other side. Tuohy and Katzko followed without flinching, treating motorists and pedestrians in the vicinity to a spectacle rarely seen outside the movie houses. One block away, Drucci ran into a traffic jam that forced him to abandon his auto and sprint for freedom on foot. He was caught before he went far, and police returned him to the Criminal Courts Building to face a burglary charge. He posted a $5,000 bond and went free. O'Banion turned himself in once Drucci was arrested and also walked away free on bond.[41]

It was a summer for rowdy street behavior, daring robberies, and flying automobiles. Johnny Torrio may have shaken his head as he witnessed the columns of newsprint that his North Side allies were racking up, but when young Al Capone made the *Tribune* at the end of August, he was forced to acknowledge that his own protégé was also in need of restraint.

On the morning of the thirtieth Capone and three companions were driving east on Randolph at a speed too hazardous even for that early hour.[42] All four were drunk and bleary-eyed from a wild night. At Randolph and Wabash, the Capone car crashed into a taxi and severely injured the driver, Fred Krause. His temper made even more volatile by liquor, Capone stormed out of his damaged vehicle, a deputy sheriff's badge clenched in one meaty hand and a gun in the other, and heaped threats and verbal abuse on the dazed Krause. When the motorman of a southbound streetcar attempted to intervene, Capone threatened to shoot him too.

Arriving police officers charged the raging Italian with driving while intoxicated, carrying concealed weapons, and assault with a vehicle. The visit to the station was as far as the case went. As had happened with the arrests that O'Banion and Drucci had racked up over the summer, Capone never saw the inside of a courtroom.

On December 1, 1922, the Supreme Court upheld the 1918 robbery conviction, but Moran never returned to prison.[46] His pass to freedom took the shape of $300 worth of stock in Major M. A. Messlein's engineering firm.

Messlein, who kept an office at 110 South La Salle Street, was the former head of Hope House, a refuge for ex-convicts. The major also owned a plant at 3411 Indiana Avenue, where a metal said to be cheaper than aluminum and twice as durable was manufactured. Messlein was a close personal friend of Will Colvin, head of the state Board of Pardons and Paroles, so Illinois convicts with means and the right connections found stock purchases to be the equivalent of a one-way ticket to parole and liberty. William Schofield was another Messlein acquaintance, which put the major and his influence within O'Banion's grasp.[44] Moran paid $300 to become a company stockholder and a free man. He was paroled on February 1, 1923.

Buoyed by his success in evading imprisonment, Moran started working to get Joseph Touhy, brother of his old friend Tommy, out of the state prison. Joseph and Moran met in Joliet in July 1919, when the former arrived to begin a lengthy sentence for the Christmas 1918 murder of saloonkeeper Paul Pagan. When the North Sider was freed on appeal, he promised to work on Touhy's release should his own bid for parole be successful.[45]

Both Joseph and Tommy Touhy were members of a large family later headquartered in Des Plaines and allied to the North Side Gang. They and three other brothers were sons of a Chicago police officer whose experience in handling the roughest criminals failed to prepare him for coping with his own wild brood. When James Jr., John, Joseph, Eddie, Tommy, and Roger were caught in a successive flow of misdeeds, the senior Touhy would sigh to his brother officers, "Do what you please." James Jr. was killed in 1917 while committing a robbery, but his siblings went on into safecracking, union terrorism, and bootlegging.

Moran, with the backing of the North Side Gang and Joseph's brothers, supervised the collecting of a $6,500 fund to hire a lawyer for Touhy and prepare a petition to Governor Len Small for executive clemency. How much of the money went toward the high-priced attorney and what final amount graced Small's own purse is not known, but a grateful and relieved Joseph Touhy left Joliet in October 1923, the recipient of a full pardon. This incident was one of many that led State's Attorney Robert Crowe to rail against Len Small in the press.

"Probably the worst handicap this office confronts is Len Small's parole and pardon system," he said. "He lets them out as fast as we put them in. It takes us two weeks to get the guilty man convicted and it takes the Governor two seconds to sign his name on a pardon blank. In 1923 . . . I put fifty-nine burglars and ninety-seven robbers in Joliet, and Small released eighty-eight burglars and ninety-seven robbers!"[46]

Crowe was on more of a mission than he had been when he first took office. By 1923 he had fallen out with Thompson and was less reticent when it came to inconveniencing those in power. When members of the Chicago school board alerted him to a dodgy land deal involving the board's counsel, Crowe pursued the attorney into the courtroom and succeeded in sending the man to Joliet on a one-to five-year sentence.[47] Another name figuring in that scandal was Fred Lundin, the mayor's former Fagin, whom Thompson had not spoken to in ages. Nonetheless, in the public mind, Lundin and Big Bill were joined at the political hip.

In January 1923 Thompson announced that he would not be seeking re-election that year. He knew that he stood little to no chance of success, not with all the celebrity gangsters and damning evidence about his crooked administration that confronted him and the voting public in the daily papers. Chicago was in a reform state of mind, but like most fads, it would not last. Thompson would be ready when the fervor abated.

With the cowboy mayor out of the running, Chicago prepared for a comparatively tame election. Arthur C. Lueder, postmaster of Chicago, who included State's Attorney Crowe and Senator Charles Deneen among his supporters, won the Republican primary in February. Facing him in the general election would be the Democratic candidate, sixty-one-year-old Judge William Emmet Dever, who had served four terms on the city council and in 1923 sat on the bench in the criminal branch of the superior court.

The days leading up to the election were filled with the usual mudslinging and potshots at each candidate's religion or origins. Rumors spread in the black neighborhoods that Lueder routinely discriminated against Negro employees and intended to appoint a Klansman as police chief should he win. Anti-Dever forces distributed a pamphlet that read, "If you want Rome to run our Public Schools and City Government, vote for Wm. E Dever, Democratic candidate for Mayor. He is a Roman Catholic and a member of the Knights of Columbus." Lueder's supporters also accused Dever of agreeing to back William Randolph Hearst in the publisher's intended presidential bid in exchange for a $100,000 campaign contribution.[48]

The Klan rumors proved more deadly than the threat of Rome taking over city hall; Dever won the election by a 105,000-vote margin. Sixty-six hundred of those ballots were cast in the mostly black Second and Third wards.[49]

At his inaugural, Chicago's new mayor proclaimed, "I want my administration to be remembered for something definite in the service of the city." No one doubted his sincerity. During his years in city council and on the bench, the Massachusetts-born Dever, who had worked as a tanner before taking the bar exam, had acquired a reputation as a champion of the common man and fighter for causes he believed in. Even when he did not believe in a cause, he supported it if required to do so by law. He told the public that he was not a Prohibitionist, but while the Volstead Act remained law, he would do all in his power to keep Chicago dry. "The only way to get rid of a bad law," he said, "is to enforce it."

For his chief of police, Dever chose Morgan A. Collins, an officer with thirty-five years' experience. Collins stood out on the force for his honesty, dedication to duty, and hands-on approach to fighting criminals. His original career plan had been the field of medicine, and he had actually taken a few courses at Bennett Medical College before deciding that police work was more to his liking and joining the force in 1888.[50]

Collins had an impressive record. In June 1906, when he was a lieutenant, he came across a bartender named Albert Blank beating a young woman, Jessie Bishop, on North Clark Street. He personally chased the man into an Ohio Street saloon, collared him, and gave him a taste of his own medicine while an approving crowd looked on. Collins earned the approbation of women's groups when he declared that Bishop's assault was motivating him to lobby for more aggressive police tactics when it came to attacks on women.[51]

In October 1906 he played a key role in the arrest of Leonard Leopold for the brutal murder of Chicago actress Margaret Leslie.[52] Collins refused to be intimidated by any higher authority when it came to the discharge of his duty: when an elevator accident resulting from negligence occurred at the Ederheimer–Stein factory in December 1907, killing several employees, the company owners actually tried to withhold information from Collins and his officers. The young lieutenant glared at the men who made double his annual salary in a single day and snapped, "Unless you tell us exactly how this happened, I'll have to take you to the police station." They gave in.[53]

The day after he was sworn in as chief, Collins gave a speech to his officers that made his intent to seriously combat bootlegging, vice, and gambling crystal clear. Equally obvious was the fate of any policeman who had contradictory sympathies or plans.

"I want you to close every gambling house in your districts," he ordered. "Every place where commercialized vice and gambling is carried on. Close it and keep it closed. Now, in many instances when an order of that kind has been issued, policemen, in order to make it ridiculous, went out and stopped the fellow from playing euchre, pinochle . . . or some other simple game." He explained that innocent, unconnected card games were not the problem, finishing his speech with, "And where they are playing . . . innocent games of that kind, I want you to make sure that no policeman goes around and says, 'Well, we ought to have a little something out of this game.' If it does, it will mean the end of him."[54]

One of Collins's most diligent police attack dogs was Captain John Stege, a tough officer who had been on the force since 1910. Born Albert Stedge in New York in 1883, he came to Chicago at the age of eleven. Before becoming a policeman, he experienced life on the other side of the tracks, being arrested several times for minor offenses and once for burglary.

On March 26, 1900, when he was seventeen, one of his mother's boarders, a man named William Hobson, verbally abused Mrs. Stedge in a drunken rage. The argument woke Albert, who sprang to his mother's defense with a barrel stave. The ferocity of his attack left Hobson dead in a pool of blood outside the Stedge home at 4414 Ashland Avenue.[55] Although the judge who heard his case was sympathetic to his motive, Albert served eighteen months in Pontiac before being pardoned. Changing his name to John Stege to sever the connection to his wilder past, he joined the Chicago police force in 1910[56] and conducted himself favorably enough to attain the rank of captain by the time Dever took office.

Collins and Stege meant business. When Torrio offered the chief $100,000 a month to let the combine's bootlegging activities continue unmolested, Collins turned him down and padlocked the Four Deuces for good measure. Torrio aimed higher and proposed a daily payment of $1,000 for permission to run 250 barrels of beer through the city each day. Collins's response was to launch a full-force assault on Torrio's bootlegging, gambling, and vice outlets. He arrested more than a hundred Torrio–Capone hoodlums and within six months had closed more than forty-five hundred illegal watering holes. To prove that he was not selective in his zeal, he also closed two hundred handbooks belonging to Mont Tennes, forcing the veteran gambler to take retirement at long last.[57]

While Torrio struggled with a police chief he could not buy off, Nails Morton invested some of his bootleg income in a gentleman's pastime. He had often joined Dean and Viola O'Banion on the Lincoln Park bridle paths for a weekend canter, and in May 1923 he decided to purchase his own horse, which he boarded at the Brown Riding Academy at 3008 North Halsted.

On Sunday morning, May 13, he arrived at the academy at 7 a.m., saddled the horse, and rode off to meet the O'Banions and a friend in Lincoln Park. Suddenly the horse bolted and raced down Clark Street with Morton struggling to regain control. When one of the stirrups broke, Morton gave up and jumped off, landing flat on the sidewalk. Before he could get up, the horse lashed out with its hind legs and kicked him in the head, inflicting a severe basal skull fracture.

One of those who ran to the fallen man's rescue was a police officer, John Keys, who recognized Morton as his lieutenant in France during the war. Keys and some bystanders hurried the gangster to the nearest hospital, where he died while awaiting surgery.[58]

Morton's funeral two days later witnessed a huge attendance from both the underworld and the city's Jewish community. No one could deny that while he had been a gangster, he had also been a decorated war hero and defender of his people against anti-Jewish hostility. While Rabbi Julius Levi officiated and Morton was buried with full military honors, police officers navigated the crowds, keeping their eyes open for potential trouble and their mouths shut about their own thoughts regarding Morton. As one newspaper put it, "The other side of the career that ended was not even mentioned."

Gangster lore claims that Louis Alterie exacted his own form of bizarre retribution by removing Morton's horse from the stable, executing it at a remote spot, and calling the stable owner to tell him where he could find the saddle. This scenario appears to have its origin in a 1925 *Daily News* story, and its veracity is doubtful. No mention of the equine shooting appeared in any of the Chicago papers for 1923, but no one who knew Alterie and his extreme reactions would have been surprised if it had.

While O'Banion dealt with the loss of a close friend and mentor, and pondered his viability as Morton's successor in the business undertakings they had initiated together, John Torrio, Al Capone, and the Saltis–McErlane Gang confronted an adversary as formidable as Morgan Collins, but from the other side of the legal barrier.

Spike O'Donnell came home from Joliet in the summer of 1923, the recipient of a full pardon. His brief time behind bars was long enough for a murderous level of resentment to build, and to formulate plans to act on it.

O'Donnell meant business and was determined to take some back. His agenda included regaining the territory in the Back o' the Yards and Gage Park districts now serviced by the Saltis–McErlane Gang selling Torrio beer.

Spike gathered a small but tough crew of sluggers and beer salesmen that included his rejuvenated brothers Steve, Walter, and Tommy. All of his enlisted men had chilling records. George "Spot" Bucher once headed a gang specializing in stolen automobiles and freight car robberies, and had been arrested in 1921 for the murder of the watchman of the Cooke Brewing Company.[59] George Meegan, one of the best "employees" of the "Steve O'Donnell cartage company," had a handy pair of fists and delighted in using them. Phil Corrigan had been arrested at age seventeen for the murder of fellow Stockyards worker Edward Weidmers,[60] and collected more notches over the ensuing years. Gunman Jerry O'Connor, who had recently been released from Joliet after doing time for murder, was also at the forefront of the O'Donnell resurrection.

They hijacked Torrio beer trucks and peddled the product themselves. Spike and a partner, boxer "Packy" McFarland, acquired two Joliet breweries, the Citizens Brewing Company and the Porter Products Company, giving them direct access to unneedled, quality product. Spike sent "salesmen" into territory controlled by the Torrio and Saltis–McErlane gangs to make the general announcement that there was a new supplier in business, and effective immediately the saloons would be selling O'Donnell beer. Some incentive existed independent of violence: the quality surpassed the Torrio product, and it was cheaper by $5 per barrel.

Torrio initially dealt with the aggressive competition by reducing his own prices. When the O'Donnells could not match his bargain rate of $40 a barrel, they strengthened their sales pitches with fist and firepower. Bucher, Meegan, Corrigan, and their associates would wander into saloons and speakeasies, menace the owners, and advise them to buy O'Donnell brew . . . or else. A refusal meant a temporary shutdown of the place, for however long it took for the bartender to recover or the shattered fixtures to be repaired or replaced.[61]

They got away with it for a few months. Then, on the night of September 7, 1923, their actions caught up with them while they were relishing beer and sandwiches at Joseph Klepka's saloon near Fifty-third and Lincoln, an O'Donnell stronghold. Steve, Walter, and Tommy O'Donnell, accompanied by Bucher and Meegan, had worked up an appetite after demolishing Jacob Geis's place on West Fifty-first Street and five other saloons supplied by Torrio and Saltis. One of their victims called the police as soon as the O'Donnell demolition crew departed, alerting Torrio to the rampage. He then made some calls of his own.

A four-man strike force led by Ralph Sheldon and Danny McFall, a deputy sheriff who also used his gun in the service of the Saltis–McErlane Gang, converged on the Klepka saloon. Weapons drawn, they ordered the bewildered O'Donnell men to raise their hands or be annihilated. The men did neither. When Walter O'Donnell challenged them to take the battle outside and was answered with a shot fired into the roof from McFall's gun, they ran in all directions. Everyone except Jerry O'Connor made it to safety through the rear and side doors. The ex-convict was grabbed and marched outside, where Frank McErlane waited with a shotgun. Before O'Connor had a chance to defend himself or even speak, McErlane blew his head off.[62]

O'Connor's murder was barely off the front pages when Torrio and the Saltis–McErlane forces struck again. Frank McErlane and Danny McFall shotgunned Bucher and Meegan to death at the intersection of Laflin Street and Garfield Boulevard. Their bodies were left in a bloodied tangle in their vehicle.

"It's plainly a beer-runners' feud, and I'm glad no honest citizen was killed," Collins said. "It was just a case of these men being out to get another man and the other gang beat them to it."[63]

Mayor Dever was not so dismissive. He summoned Morgan Collins into his office and informed him that Chicago was going to go dry no matter what it took. The chief, carrying out the open-ended order, suspended Captain Thomas Wolfe of the New City police station, who had pushed O'Donnell beer as a sideline, and replaced him with tough and honest William Schoemaker. He also arrested eleven Chicago gangsters and threw them into police cells.

Collins attempted to snare Torrio in the general roundup, but Torrio had gone into hiding and left his attorney, Michael Igoe, to negotiate the terms of his surrender for questioning. When not rounding up known bootleggers, the chief's men closed a total of one hundred saloons and speakeasies and threw three hundred owners and patrons into jail.[64]

Although an admitted opponent of the Prohibition laws, Dever also acknowledged that liquor and the right to distribute it was at the root of the bloodshed. "This brutal murder tonight is another breaking out into violence of that lawless spirit which seems to pervade the community and which can be combated only by a relentless warfare of those pledged to uphold the law," he told the press on September 18. "Until the murderers of Jerry O'Connor and these two men have been apprehended and punished and the illegal traffic for control of which they battle had been suppressed, the dignity of the law and the average man's respect for it is imperiled, and every officer of the law and every enforcing agency should lay aside other duties and join in the common cause—a restoration of law and order."

Dever confirmed that his anti-Volstead view was not a point of consideration in this particular situation. "As I have said previously, I am not in sympathy with the Volstead Act, but I am heartily and inalterably in sympathy with the rigid enforcement of every law upon the books."[65]

Father John Schuette, officiating at George Bucher's funeral mass at St. Raphael's, blamed Prohibition for the slaughter.

During the coroner's inquest, which was attended mostly by police officers and gangsters, George Bucher's brother Joe, who also ran beer for the O'Donnells, insisted that George's bullet had really been meant for him. Coroner Oscar Wolff took him at his word. The "Line o' Type or Two" column in the September 20 issue of the *Chicago Tribune* ridiculed Wolff's findings. "Coroner Wolff says the beer boys killed the wrong man in George Bucher, thus officially putting it up to them to rectify the error."[66]

The following December, Frank McErlane and one William Channell ambushed two more O'Donnell beer-runners outside the village of Lemont and took them for a one-way ride that one of them lived to tell about. "Shorty" Eagan's harrowing account of being forced into the back seat of McErlane's car, blasted multiple times with a shotgun, and thrown into the icy waters of a frozen ditch revolted the public.[67] No one was brought to trial for any of the slayings committed during the South Side beer war, but Mayor Dever and Chief Collins were not prepared to let up on their determination to end bootlegging in Chicago and drive the gangsters out of town.

John Torrio began to wonder whether "out of town" might be a wiser place to be until the raids and arrests abated. The wisdom of spreading his resources had come to him years ago, when he extended the Colosimo vice empire out of the Levee and into the suburban and village roadhouses. He and Capone needed to temporarily move their headquarters out of the city and into an adjacent town or community, where they could monitor their Chicago operations while lessening the risk of arrest. And as it so happened, Cicero, Illinois, adjacent to Chicago, had an election coming up.

On January 17, 1922, William J. Logan arrived in New York City aboard the SS *Cambrai*, which had sailed from Antwerp, Belgium, on January 6. Logan, thirty years old and an embalmer at Klaner's Funeral Parlor at 1253 North Clark Street in Chicago, was accompanied by his wife, Lucy, or Lucille, an attractive twenty-two-year-old brunette originally from Constantinople, Turkey. Completing their traveling party was the woman's son, Louis Logan, who had been born in Angers, France, on August 3, 1920.[68] After Ellis Island officials admitted Lucy and Louis, the Logans traveled on to Chicago.

Mrs. Logan was looking forward to a future finally stripped of the hardship that had ravaged her life for the past three years. Born Lucy Bilezikdijan in Constantinople, she had come to France after the Armistice, anticipating more opportunities than she would have enjoyed in Turkey. Fate instead dealt her a hand that left her pregnant and jobless in the summer of 1920. On August 3 authorities in the city of Angers made the following notation in their records (translated from the French):

The 3rd of August 1920, at eleven o'clock at night, a male child, given the name of Louis, was born in the Maternity Hospital in Angers to Lucie [sic] Bilezikdijan, born in Constantinople, Turkey, on October 26, 1899, unmarried, without visible means of support, living in Angers at the Hotel de France.

Being unmarried and unemployed, Lucy may have left Louis in the care of parish authorities after her discharge from the hospital, for they monitored his whereabouts until December 1921, when another notation was made on the sheet containing his birth record. The surname of Bilezikdijan was crossed out and replaced with "Logan" beneath the notation "Legitimized by William James Logan and Lucie Bilezikdijan following their marriage celebrated in Paris on December 27, 1921."

Whether or not Logan was the actual father is not known, but the marriage granted Lucy and Louis American citizenship. After settling in Chicago, the couple headed off anti-foreigner prejudice by telling friends and neighbors that Lucy's olive complexion, dark hair, and French accent derived from a Creole ancestry and childhood spent in New Orleans. She also modified her name to Lucille.

Within a year the couple had separated, for reasons that have been lost to time. When and how Lucille met George Moran is not known for sure. One James McCauley (or McCarthy), who also resided in the apartments over 1253 North Clark, was frequently questioned by police in connection with bank and payroll robberies,[69] and he may have been an acquaintance that Moran visited.

Moran, who loved children, did not balk at the prospect of raising another man's son. After he became infatuated with the outgoing Lucille, who loved a good drink and a better card game, and more importantly, spoke the language he had been raised in,[70] he proposed marriage. When she accepted, little Louis went through a dramatic name change, becoming John George Moran.

"George would have done anything for that kid," recalled a family friend. "Christmas, birthdays, John got at least ten each of whatever he wanted. George was worried about disappointing him by getting the wrong thing. All the extra stuff would go to the Catholic orphanages or the kids' hospitals. I think George went a little overboard with the presents, but maybe he was just trying to make up for not being the average parent."[71]

His heart was also touched by the small boy whose native language and his own were identical. Moran did not conceal his ability to speak French, telling Lucille that his mother had been from Quebec, and eased the child's transition into English by reading him stories and conversing with him in both languages. In time John George Moran would forget his infancy in Paris, and even the French language itself, but the bond he shared with the man he would forever view as his father only strengthened with time.

8

O'BANION IN THE NEWS, MORAN IN ST. PAUL

A S 1923 CONCLUDED WITHOUT ANYONE being indicted for the murders committed during the O'Donnell uprising, and 1924 dawned bright and chilly, cops and
reporters who made it their business to watch and assess gangland's strongest leaders agreed that Torrio, Capone, and O'Banion were the Big Three of the Chicago
underworld. They had the strongest political connections, commanded the largest
number of armed killers, and O'Banion in particular had a harmonious relationship
with the police. Chief Collins personally believed that O'Banion was the top dog of
the trio, and had a standard response to any news of a gangland crime or killing:
"Find Dean O'Banion."[1] He reasoned, probably correctly, that if the North Sider was
not behind the incident in question, he knew who was and condoned it.

O'Banion took the routine pickups and questioning sessions with a combination
of grace and amusement. Unlike Weiss, Moran, or Drucci, he never had a harsh
word for the police officers who knocked on his door at 3608 North Pine Grove
Avenue, dropped by the shop, or stopped him on the street. He could afford to be
amiable, as the legal talent he had at his disposal could produce habeas corpus writs
before he and his escorts even arrived at the detective bureau.

O'Banion had less tolerance when it came to perceived harassment from his
contemporaries. On the night of January 20, 1924, he tangled with Davey Miller,

brother of Nails Morton ally Hirschie Miller in a bullets-flying exchange that made the front pages the next day.

The Miller brothers wielded influence on the West Side and had partnered with Nails Morton in bootlegging and other enterprises for years. By 1924 Hirschie Miller was making a name for himself in the increasingly turbulent field of cleaning and dyeing. He purchased the Acme Cleaning and Dyeing establishment[2] on North Clark Street, a bankrupt dye plant, and announced a scale of extremely low prices, which he imposed and maintained until nervous competitors bought him out for an exorbitant sum to stop the competition. He left a legacy in the form of unscrupulous men who imitated his tactics and began one wave after another of garment industry price-cutting and terrorism.

Brother Davey was a prizefight referee and a man handy with his own fists. Other siblings included Harry, a policeman, and the youngest, Maxie, who could also hold his own in dangerous situations. Maxie had been charged with the murder of Abe Rubin in April 1922 but was acquitted after witnesses to the poolroom attack refused to identify him.[3]

Prior to Morton's untimely passing, relations between O'Banion and the Millers had been cordial. But when the North Sider tried to present himself as the departed Nails's replacement, Hirschie and his brothers backed off. Violence had yet to erupt, but the North Siders and the Millers regarded each other with a tension and hostility that had all the makings of a potential disaster.

It was a situation that Julius "Yankee" Schwartz turned to his advantage. Schwartz, a former pugilist and hanger-on in the Miller camp, fell out with the brothers after double-crossing Davey in a liquor deal and ingratiated himself with O'Banion by reporting all the derogatory comments that Hirschie and Davey had been making about the North Sider. He had his own agenda, something O'Banion's dislike of the Millers motivated the gang leader to overlook.

On the night of the twentieth O'Banion, Weiss, and Schwartz attended the performance of an airy comedy, *Give And Take*, at the La Salle Theatre.[4] Unbeknownst to them, Davey and Maxie Miller were also in the audience. After the curtain dropped and the attendees began spilling out of the auditorium into the lobby, the O'Banion and Miller parties encountered each other. They paused and exchanged indifferent greetings while theatergoers in evening dress conversed in small groups nearby or hurried out into the night, using fur wraps and heavy cloaks to protect themselves against the minus-eight-degree-Fahrenheit chill.

When O'Banion noticed that Davey Miller was making a point of snubbing Schwartz, he took him aside and demanded to know what his problem was. Miller replied stiffly that as far as he was concerned, Schwartz was no good and he wanted nothing to do with him. When he attempted to end the conversation and walk outside in search of a cab, O'Banion caught him by the arm and retorted, "He's as good as you are, you bastard."

"I can lick all three of you fellows," Miller responded, "but this isn't the place."

O'Banion was less selective about where he brawled; he shoved Miller, who pushed back. Believing that Davey was going for a gun, O'Banion drew his own and fired several rounds into Miller's stomach. Maxie jumped forward and received a bullet too, but it bounced off his belt buckle and only froze him in his tracks.

O'Banion, Weiss, and Schwartz made their escape during the pandemonium that followed. An operation saved Davey Miller's life, and Maxie pressed charges while his wounded brother recovered in Los Angeles. Cops and reporters braced themselves for an outbreak of gang violence until O'Banion diffused the tension, albeit it in a menacing fashion.

"If I'd wanted to bump this Miller off, do you think I'd have done it in the middle of the Loop?" he said. Pausing, he added, "I'd have fixed him out in some dark alley on the South Side." The threat made, O'Banion adopted a conciliatory air. "That [the shooting] was a misfortune. It was a hotheaded affair, and I had hoped it would blow over. But a fellow can't lose a bad break, I guess."[5]

On January 22 a police squad led by Lieutenant William O'Connor came across O'Banion, Dan McCarthy, and Hymie Weiss in the act of hijacking 251 cases of Haveland Rye whiskey intended for the Corning Distillery Company in Peoria. The officers' suspicions were aroused when they spotted a truck stalled near Nineteenth and Indiana and a car parked nearby. When they and O'Banion saw one another at the same time, a car chase commenced and continued until the police overtook the North Siders near State and Twentieth. Huddled in the back seat of the gangsters' vehicle were two terrified truck drivers who all but wept with relief at the police intervention.[6]

O'Banion, Weiss, and McCarthy surrendered and posted $10,000 bail each after the grand jury indicted them for conspiring to sell liquor. The scheduled trial date was July 7, giving the North Side Gang a head start on the bribery and intimidation game plans.

At the end of February, a double homicide captivated a city normally hardened to random acts of murder. The victims were a young married couple, also not unusual in Chicago, but when the husband was exposed as a murderer from Philadelphia who had crossed O'Banion, the newspaper-buying public flooded the newsstands to read every detail.

John Duffy had arrived in Chicago in July 1923,[7] a refugee from two murder investigations back in Philadelphia. He met North Side hanger-on Yankee Schwartz via their mutual connection to the boxing world, Duffy's uncle, a noted referee. Schwartz introduced him to the Miller brothers, who distrusted him and refused to take him into their confidence. Undeterred, Duffy assembled a small gang of unconnected hijackers and rumrunners and began seizing liquor shipments consigned to Chicago gangs. They sold the stolen booze to random saloonkeepers.

No one on the Chicago police force was surprised when Duffy's body, the skull containing three bullet holes, was found in a snowdrift along Nottingham Road on February 20, 1924.[8] But when officers went to the dead man's home at 1216 Carmen Avenue and found his wife, former prostitute Maybelle Exley, lying on a divan with two gunshot wounds to her own head, the case took a pathetic and mysterious twist.[9]

A major break in the investigation occurred when William Engelke, a former policeman and acquaintance of the slain couple, was picked up. An informer had hinted that the young man had been directly involved in the double murder, and the tip turned out to be invaluable. Engelke, frightened at being a prisoner in the type of station where he had once been employed, began talking. He claimed that John Duffy had killed his own wife in a drink-induced rage, then been lured to his own death by Potatoes Kaufman and Dean O'Banion.[10]

Engelke explained that Duffy had attempted to profit from the Miller–O'Banion feud by informing Hirschie Miller that he would kill the North Sider and Yankee Schwartz for $10,000, and that O'Banion had likely learned of it. Either too drunk or too desperate to remember this lethal misstep, Duffy called Julian Kaufman, whom he had met through Yankee Schwartz, and begged him for money and a car so that he could get out of town. Kaufman promised to help, but it took several phone calls and aborted plans before a meeting could be arranged.

John Duffy and Bill Engelke met Kaufman and Dean O'Banion near the Four Deuces on the night of the twentieth. The Philadelphia killer was so distraught because of his own predicament that he thought nothing of pleading with O'Banion, his proposed victim a few weeks back, for a $1,000 loan. The North Sider assured him that money and salvation were forthcoming before escorting him into a waiting Studebaker. When Engelke tried to follow, Kaufman stopped him and warned him in low tones to get lost before he became mixed up in a murder.[11]

After concluding his story, Engelke surveyed the officers witnessing his statement and said glumly, "You might as well take my carcass out to Twelfth and Newberry and bury it now."[12]

When newspapers published the information about the Four Deuces being in the neighborhood of the fatal rendezvous, Capone went to the police voluntarily, lawyer in tow. "I'm a respectable businessman," he said firmly. "I own a furniture store adjoining the place, and for no reason at all somebody is always trying to drag me into something." He also denied knowing the Duffys or Engelke, and while he admitted an acquaintance with O'Banion, Capone added that he had not seen the North Sider for three weeks.[13]

Kaufman was arrested immediately, but O'Banion proved more elusive. He had given an interview to a *Tribune* reporter when the Duffys' bodies were discovered and the earliest details, such as the Philadelphia gangster's association with Schwartz and Kaufman, became known.[14] But since then he had gone missing from all of his usual haunts. O'Banion remained at large, despite the best efforts of the police to locate him, until March 12, when he called Assistant State's Attorney John Sbarbaro and arranged to surrender. Detective Joseph Geary took him into custody at his office above the florist shop.[15]

O'Banion never lost his smile and relaxed demeanor, even when the interrogation took so long that he was sequestered in the Briggs House with detectives overnight. He denied knowing Duffy or having anything but a friendly acquaintance with Kaufman and Yankee Schwartz. His good mood was strengthened when Engelke, brought to the detective bureau to identify him, suffered a paralyzing attack of amnesia.

"If that's O'Banion," Engelke babbled, "he ain't the fellow I thought he was. I never met O'Banion, but I understood he was the man I saw climbing into a sedan with Duffy the night after Duffy killed Maybelle Exley. This ain't that guy though."[16]

O'Banion and Potatoes Kaufman walked free, while the former star witness found himself charged as an accomplice to murder. The charges were later dropped, but Engelke was neither chastened nor contrite after his close brush with imprisonment and possible death. In October 1924 he was found guilty of stealing a $2,238 payroll from Earl Ward of the Shipman-Ward Manufacturing Company and sentenced to a prison term of ten years to life.[17] Errors in the record led to a new trial, but Engelke, not wanting to prolong the experience, pleaded guilty and went to Joliet.

The events of that winter further soured Kaufman's already combative attitude toward the police. Two months later, on May 16, he indulged in the private satisfaction of nearly running down two traffic officers, Edward Healy and Patrick O'Brien, at the corner of Randolph and Clark streets. When Healy remonstrated with him, Kaufman lunged out of his car, hurled himself at the officer, and beat him around the head and face with a revolver butt. O'Brien raced to his brother officer's aid just as the gambler pressed the muzzle against Healy's chest in what looked to be a prelude to murder.

The wounded man was taken to Iroquois Hospital to be treated for a skull fracture and facial lacerations, while Kaufman ended up cuffed to a chair in the First Precinct station. He showed his disdain for the proceedings by displaying a justice of the peace permit to carry the weapon. "I'm a friend of their captain," he sneered, referring to Healy and O'Brien. "I'll get both of their jobs, you wait and see."

Healy recovered, and Kaufman got off with a fine.[18]

Coroner Oscar Wolff concluded the Duffy-Exley inquest on September 15, 1924, and his findings, instead of clearing up the mystery, confounded it. He claimed that Duffy's killers had not been Chicago gangsters at all but a single police officer, Leo O'Neill, who had been acting desk sergeant at the Englewood station.[19]

Wolff said that the Philadelphia gangster had killed his wife in William Engelke's presence, as the latter had claimed. But there the official inquest finding and Engelke's version went their separate ways. "Duffy needed money to get out of the city before the body was discovered," the coroner explained. "Orlando Horton and

Freddie Curtiss [members of the renegade Duffy gang] had robbed him of what money he had accumulated as a bootlegger. So Duffy planned to steal the whiskey that he knew was cached in O'Neill's garage." He added that a well-known rum-runner had been paying O'Neill $600 a month for the use of the garage as a storage facility.

During the robbery Officer O'Neill surprised Duffy and his three confederates, all crooked Cicero cops, in the garage. The gangster, not wanting to be arrested while the body of his wife still lay in the Carmen Avenue flat, bolted and was shot dead. Why his police accomplices were spared the same fate was not explained, but they were permitted to take his body away and dump it where it was found.

"O'Neill called up the police station that night and notified the sergeant he had fired some shots at some burglars," Wolff concluded. "They must have overlooked that report next morning, for the killing of Duffy was not connected with O'Neill's report until I heard about it." O'Neill, who had once been cited for bravery after capturing a black holdup man who had shot him in the shoulder, had recently been arrested as a bootlegger.

This version of events did not explain why Engelke drew the names of O'Banion, McCarthy, and Kaufman into the murder investigation when doing so was potentially fatal. If O'Neill had been the killer and Engelke, by Wolff's own admission, was not in the officer's garage that night, why say that he had seen the Philadelphia gangster take his last ride, and risk being viewed as an accomplice?

With the publication of the coroner's findings, the Duffy case faded into obscurity, as did all of its key players except for O'Banion, McCarthy, and Kaufman. William Engelke was sentenced to Joliet Prison, but even after his release he persisted in making a living through burglary. A small article in the *Tribune* of September 27, 1938, noted that he was questioned in connection with a series of mysterious robberies of North Side homes.[20]

In March 1924, just as the heat over the Duffy case simmered to a lukewarm level, George Moran left Chicago for St. Paul.[21] His mother, Marie Diana, had just returned from Winnipeg with Laurette, now a strapping young woman of twenty, and Cyrille, who had Anglicized his name to Cyril, in tow. Two family members failed to make the journey back to Minnesota: Jules Cunin had died in Winnipeg in 1920, and Josephine had married a Canadian.

Moran did not take his wife and son with him. Although Lucille knew that her husband employed aliases as an occupational necessity, she had no inkling of Adelard Cunin's existence or history. Details are vague on what he did actually tell her about his childhood and family, but at no time did the loved ones of Adelard Cunin and George Moran encounter each other.

The nighttime reunion in Diana Cunin's kitchen at 409 Park Avenue was an emotional one on both sides. Although fourteen years had passed since that momentous escape from Red Wing, Moran initially feared possible re-arrest if his mother's neighbors realized that her wayward son had come home. By prior arrangement he arrived at the house after dark, after everyone else had gone to bed. After much hugging and sobbing, they sat in the kitchen for hours, Diana talking about the death of Jules and the Winnipeg years, and Adelard/George telling her a version of his recent past that he felt she would be able to handle. When daylight came, he took his leave. It was a nocturnal visiting pattern that he would repeat over the years.

Moran visited other St. Paul acquaintances during the Minnesota sojourn. Some, like Dan Hogan, had achieved dizzying heights of power since he had seen them last.[22]

Hogan, a husky and ambitious Irishman, had done time in San Quentin prison as well as various jails in Wisconsin, South Dakota, and Minnesota before finding his niche as a fence, fixer, and all-around criminal mastermind. Insulated by the laissez-faire environment that St. Paul offered, he planned one high-profile crime after another. In 1924 he plotted and supervised the robbery of $13,000 from the Finkelstein and Ruben collection wagon, which made the rounds of local movie houses and picked up the daily receipts. Hogan made sure to launch the attack on a Monday, as the bigger weekend receipts would be included in the day's pickup.

He increased his profile and influence when he allied with his Minneapolis counterpart, "Big Ed" Morgan, which the FBI commented on in a 1926 memo: "It is common knowledge in Minneapolis and St. Paul that Dan Hogan and Edward Morgan harbor criminals from other parts of the United States."[23]

Everywhere Moran walked in St. Paul and Minneapolis, there was no sign that the three dozen Prohibition agents assigned to Minnesota were making any headway in drying the state. In 1887 Minnesota had been the fifth-largest beer-producing state, thanks to its large German population, and one venerable brewery, Schmidt, continued to pump needle beer into speakeasies while operating under the guise of making ginger ale and other nonalcoholic drinks.

Druggists made their own gin in back rooms and sold it over the counter. Police Chief Michael Gebhardt estimated in 1922 that 75 percent of St. Paul's citizens made moonshine or cheap wine at home.[24] Benny Haskell, who sold the finest wines, champagnes, and brandies from his headquarters at Minneapolis's Radisson Hotel, counted the area's social elite among his best customers and supporters.

Walter Liggett of *Plain Talk* magazine charged that Minnesota in general and St. Paul in particular were "dripping wet; that speakeasies, blind pigs, beer flats, and brothels flourish in abundance . . . that gambling joints operate without fear of molestation; and that police and other local officers protect the bootlegger, the gambler, and the prostitute."[25]

The atmosphere was much like it had been in Chicago before Dever took office and empowered Morgan Collins to throw one bootlegger after another in jail. Corruption still existed in the Chicago Police Department, and Prohibition agents were as easy to fool or buy in Illinois as they were in Minnesota, but when a long-standing and well-connected underworld figure like Johnny Torrio talked about relocating to Cicero, Moran wondered whether his chances of making big money might not be better in the city of his birth. St. Paul certainly had not hardened its unspoken policies toward criminals over the years, and in terms of skills and connections, he was a far cry from the cocky eighteen-year-old who had been arrested in 1909. Although he would have to caution his mother and siblings not to discuss his presence with friends and neighbors, enough time and identity changes had taken place over the past fifteen years to obscure his chances of ever going back to jail on that ancient charge. Dan Hogan would certainly make room for him in the growing Hogan syndicate.

In the end, Moran decided to return to Chicago. Dever and his strict observance of law and order would probably not last another term, and if Johnny Torrio played his cards right, Chicago hoodlums seeking refuge from the Dever raids would find safe haven in a nearby town completely under the rule of the gangster.

9

O'BANION'S FINAL SWINDLE

ORRIO HAD BEEN CULTIVATING CICERO since October 1923, when he leased a house on Roosevelt Road and set up a contingent of prostitutes. The town police, reflecting the citizenry's disdain of the flesh trade, raided the place and arrested the women. Another brothel that Torrio tried to set up at Ogden and Fifty-second met the same end.[1] Johnny's response was to impose a similar disruption on the slot-machine operations that funneled thousands of dollars into Eddie Vogel's pockets: Cook County Sheriff Peter Hoffman and a squad of deputies poured into Cicero and impounded every machine they found. This got Vogel's attention fast and led to a sit-down between Torrio, the West Side O'Donnells, and Eddie Vogel. The only local bigwig who did not participate was Eddie Tancl, who had no use for Torrio and whose spiteful reaction to the conference would alienate him from his former allies.[2]

It was agreed that Vogel would get his slot machines back and the O'Donnells would retain an exclusive Cicero beer franchise. Torrio, in return, would supply all saloons and speakeasies not serviced by the O'Donnells, run gambling houses, and set up a second base of operations that would render his empire less vulnerable to Dever's harassment.[3]

Once negotiations ended successfully and the new arrangements enjoyed an uneventful commencement, Torrio took his wife and mother on a long-awaited trip to Europe. During their stay in Italy he bought his mother a seaside villa near Naples and bestowed a small fortune on her, allowing the elderly woman, who had left her native land in a state of abject poverty, to live out her last days there in palatial grandeur.

Capone, who ran the Syndicate in his absence, spent the early part of 1924 strengthening their presence in Cicero. He established a headquarters at the Hawthorne Hotel at 4823 Twenty-second Street, taking up an entire floor and installing steel shutters on the windows. The Hawthorne Smoke Shop next door was the gang's flagship gambling joint, and others, such as the Subway and the Radio, which shifted locations on a regular basis, later followed. O'Banion joined in when Capone and Torrio bought into The Ship, an establishment at 2131 South Cicero Avenue.[4]

Torrio returned from Italy just in time to seize an opportunity to literally own the town government. Cicero had an election coming up in April, and Eddie Vogel was worried. For three terms Joseph Klenha's bipartisan faction had been in power, but Dever's example had inspired Democrats to advance a separate slate. Ed Konvalinka, a local political figure who had played a key role in Cicero politics since his days spent running a popular soda fountain, discussed the dilemma with him. They didn't trust the electorate to keep reform out, so they went to Torrio and Capone and made them an irresistible offer: ensure a Klenha victory and count on immunity from the law in all their Cicero undertakings except prostitution.[5]

Capone went to O'Banion and obtained his assurance that a team of shock troops would be available from the North Side Gang ranks. O'Banion had also foreseen the possibilities to be had from tight control over Cicero, and he wanted in.[6]

The local Democrats either got wind of the negotiations or suspected that they were taking place. The Election Commissioner removed the names of three thousand election clerks known to be Klenha supporters from the staff list. He mistakenly believed that the loss of three thousand clerks, poll watchers, and judges would cancel the threat of a forced Republican victory.[7]

The moment the polls opened on April 1, the town witnessed a grade of violence its residents had previously only read about in the Chicago papers. Gunmen shot up the headquarters of Rudolph Hurt, former Chicago alderman who now ran on the Democratic ticket for president of the Village Board. Hurt bolted from the building with bullets whizzing past his ears and found refuge in another house, where he cowered until a special detail from the Lawndale station arrived to escort him to Chicago. William Pflaum, Democratic candidate for town clerk, was assaulted in his real estate office on the eve of the election by six men, who pistol-whipped him and fired several shots into the ceiling. Pflaum was entertaining family members in the office at the time, and the attackers donned brass knuckles and struck the male relatives in the face for good measure.[8]

Automobiles loaded with hoodlums supplied by the Syndicate, the North Siders, Ralph Sheldon, and the West Side O'Donnells cruised the streets, beating and kidnapping Democratic election workers. Ten gunmen invaded the polling place at 3200 South Forty-ninth Avenue and chased away seventy-five voters. They even seized a police officer on duty there and searched him for a weapon they could confiscate. Six Democratic supporters, one of them a fourteen-year-old boy, were slugged for passing out handbills. Those lined up outside polling stations had their ballots ripped out of the their hands and examined by gangsters who pounded them to the pavement if the wrong candidates were selected. One Cicero policeman, Anton Bican, attempted to interfere during one such assault and was so badly beaten that he required emergency treatment at Oak Park Hospital.[9]

John Rice, a Democratic precinct worker, told a particularly harrowing tale. "Myself and four others were driving to the polls . . . when we were stopped by five men who were riding in another machine. These men drew guns and forced us into their car. We were pushed down in the tonneau and covered with blankets." They were taken to a plumbing shop at 3614 West Harrison Street, which was owned by Klondike O'Donnell adherent Harry Madigan and his brother Joe. "Every once in awhile we were beaten over the head with guns. . . . After they shoved us into the garage [of the shop] O'Brien [John O'Brien, secretary of the Packinghouse Teamsters Union and one of the kidnappers] slugged me on the jaw and head. I lost consciousness after awhile, and when I came to, I was being carried through the night in an automobile. They finally threw me out near Hammond, Indiana."[10]

Stanley Stanklovitch had a similar experience: he was blindfolded and held prisoner in a basement until eight o'clock at night, when he was finally taken away and tossed out of a car near Harrison Street and Laramie Avenue.[11]

Cook County Judge Edmund K. Jarecki and Morgan Collins gathered seventy uniformed Chicago patrolmen, five squads from the detective bureau, and nine flivver squads at the Lawndale station, where Jarecki deputized them as "special agents" of the county court, thus giving them authority in Cicero, and dispatched them to the rescue of the Cicero voters.

Chief of Detectives William Schoemaker raided the Madigan brothers' plumbing shop and took away seven hoodlums who had been standing guard over twenty prisoners. Blood coated the wooden floorboards, hinting at the vicious treatment the Democratic workers had received while in custody.[12] Schoemaker arrested John O'Brien and another one of John Rice's abductors, Hugh McGovern, both of whom were sent to jail by Judge Jarecki after failing to make $160,000 bonds.

A detective squad car encountered Al Capone's older brother, Frank, and two companions, Capone cousin Charlie Fischetti and gunman Dave Hedlin, near a polling place at Cicero and Twenty-second. Guns were drawn and bullets fired, killing Frank Capone and wounding Hedlin, who still managed to escape.[13]

While Al Capone and his family grieved, the Klenha camp rejoiced when the results were announced. The incumbent president was the victor, with 7,878 votes to his opponent's 6,993. Joseph Klenha's triumph was only a surface one, as Torrio, Capone, and their allies were the de facto Cicero government. If the town councilors failed to grasp the concept, they got quick and brutal reminders. One meeting, during which heavy anti-crime legislation was discussed, was broken up by Capone gangsters who dragged one stubborn councilor outside and beat him. Capone personally slapped Klenha around in the presence of a police officer who merely watched.[14]

This type of sensational intimidation and violence rarely happened after the early, turbulent adjustment period following the election. Torrio and Capone honored their promise to establish no brothels in Cicero, and they actually kept street crime levels low. Although the Syndicate did not try to control all the gaming places in Cicero, those that they did not own or operate paid 25 percent to 50 percent of the weekly take for protection. Few protested the high tribute, as their joints did remain raid-free, and a Capone agent was stationed in each place to guard against interlopers as well as protect the Syndicate's interests.

Torrio gave the North Side Gang a Cicero beer concession in acknowledgement of its important role in the town's takeover. The territory was worth an estimated $20,000 a month in beer and liquor sales, but it speedily yielded $100,000 when saloonkeepers seeking refuge from Morgan Collins's raiding parties flooded into the district. O'Banion was only too happy to set them up in business and supply them.

There was a problem, however. These saloon proprietors had former suppliers back in Chicago who were not happy about losing their patronage. The bootlegging gangs complained to Johnny Torrio about what they perceived as theft of their business. In a first-ditch effort to keep the peace, Torrio went to O'Banion and suggested that he split the profits from the inflated beer concession with the offended parties. It did not have to be a huge cut, just enough to quiet the animosity.

O'Banion refused. He had not invited the additional business, although some accounts would suggest otherwise,[15] and he bristled at what he perceived as Torrio's audacity that he share his good fortune with those who happened to have lost theirs.[16]

Torrio did not press the issue, knowing that O'Banion was technically in the right. But the episode, and O'Banion's unyielding reaction to it, muddied the waters that had always been murky at best. While not the vitriolic Italian-hater that history has painted him to be, O'Banion had a suspicion, ingrained during his childhood in Little Hell, of the secretive, backstabbing nature attributed to Italian and Sicilian criminals. He questioned Torrio's sincerity now, wondering what other concessions and gains might be opened for "renegotiation" or amendment.

As potentially explosive as the situation was, Torrio had decided in O'Banion's favor, and there the issue and its poisonous implications might have ended, were it not for another attack on O'Banion's territory, this one more direct and malicious.

Although the North Side was out of their assigned territory, the Genna brothers knew that a market for their low-price (and lower grade) alcohol existed there. O'Banion sold a safer bottle, but the additional precautions he took to make his cut liquor drinkable were reflected in the higher price he charged for it. Six to nine dollars was beyond the means of poorer North Side residents, who either made their own booze or crossed the river to purchase it from the Gennas and other gangs who scorned quality control.

O'Banion took no notice of those who went to such pains to get cheaper product, but when word reached him that Genna liquor pushers were infiltrating the North Side to cater to this lower-income clientele, he bristled. He ordered an investigation, and when Genna bottles were found in lower-grade saloons, he became furious.

O'Banion took the matter directly to Johnny Torrio, insisting that the Gennas be stopped before their "salesmen" began making return trips in pine boxes. Although O'Banion's belligerent stance in the matter of the inflated Cicero beer route had perturbed him, Torrio had to agree that the Gennas' actions were a violation of the territorial agreement, and he probably tried to reason with the brothers. The flow of rotgut continued northward, however, so O'Banion took a more damaging approach by hijacking a shipment of Genna whiskey with a market value of $30,000.[17]

The North Sider's respect for and trust in Torrio and Capone was eroding. He had seen how quickly the hammer fell on the South Side O'Donnells when they defended their long-held territory, and he was sure that his higher underworld standing and police and political connections were all that stood between him and similar treatment. His mind jumped from one conclusion to another, one fear to another, with the result being tension, anxiety, and the sense of living on borrowed time.

O'Banion knew that any attempts to oust him would reach fruition only with the greatest difficulty. But rather than being reassured by the knowledge, he obsessed over the idea that difficult did not mean impossible.

Unless he acted first.

In early May 1924 one of the police informants on O'Banion's payroll passed along the tip that the Sieben Brewery, in which both Torrio and the North Sider had an interest, was targeted for a raid on the nineteenth.

The Sieben, located at 1470 North Larrabee Street, had once been a focal point of the North Side's German community, servicing a popular—and adjacent—beer garden. Since the passage of the Volstead Act, the Bier Stube was gone, but the brewery continued to operate, having obtained a permit to make near beer. Bernard Sieben had subleased it to the Mid-City Brewing Company, which was actually a front for Torrio and O'Banion.[18]

The Sieben had been producing full-strength beer for over a year until, in August 1923, Prohibition enforcement officials investigated it, found evidence that the output contained eight times the legal alcohol limit, and revoked its license.[19] Torrio, O'Banion, and their partners waited for a few months, and then gradually resumed operations. Their return had been anticipated, hence the intended raid on May 19.

John Torrio could ill afford an arrest for bootlegging. In December 1923 he had been arrested and fined for ownership of a brewery in West Hammond,[20] and a second conviction for violating the Prohibition laws carried a mandatory jail sentence. O'Banion knew that if he declined to warn Torrio, the other man would definitely go to jail for six months at the minimum.

Which is why he remained silent.

O'Banion was emulating Torrio's preferred method of dealing with a rival bloodlessly. The looming reality of imprisonment would weaken the Torrio link in the perceived "Italian conspiracy" until he had decided how to better deal with it. Failure to pass along the raid tip was damaging enough, but O'Banion had always operated in extremes. He also sold his share of the soon-to-be-worthless property to Johnny Torrio for half a million dollars.

The record is not clear on how he explained his desire to sell. By most accounts, O'Banion told Torrio that he was planning to quit Chicago, his millions having been made, and wanted to gradually unload his assets. If so, the reason he also must have given for selling to Torrio instead of passing control of his share of the Sieben to his successors has not survived with the rest of the scenario. It's possible that the normally cautious Torrio was so relieved to see a potential end to the growing tension between himself, O'Banion, and the Gennas that he grabbed the bait without detecting the hook.

At five o'clock on the morning of May 19, both men were supervising the loading of nine trucks, each with a two-hundred-barrel capacity. Five more were backed up to the loading platform, waiting to be filled when the hurrying crowd of brewery workers finished with the first nine. Louis Alterie stood with Torrio and O'Banion, and somewhere in the immediate vicinity were North Siders Johnny Phillips, Nick Juffra, and (for reasons never explained) Daniel J. O'Connor, a Democratic politician publicly aligned with the Prohibition cause.

Suddenly a thirty-man police strike force, led by Chief Collins, burst onto the premises, seconds after taking the armed gangsters on sentry duty outside into custody.[21] Everyone except O'Banion reacted with varying degrees of alarm; some of the employees struggled violently when officers arrested them. O'Banion paused long enough to greet Sergeant Michael Vaughn and tell Captain Matthew Zimmer that he deserved a raise, and then made a general plea for the workers not to resist arrest. The advice was particularly necessary in the case of Alterie, who was purple with fury. Torrio also played a crucial role in preventing violence, but his calm demeanor masked the shock and dismay he must have been experiencing. This was it—the second arrest that was his ticket to jail.

Chief Collins seized 128,500 gallons of beer and thirty-four prisoners, two of whom were policemen who had been tasked with ensuring that the Sieben did not reopen after its padlocking. Writs of habeas corpus were filed in state courts for O'Banion and Torrio, but Collins turned all of the prisoners over to federal agents, robbing the gangsters of their usual route to freedom.

After an arraignment before Commissioner Herman Beitler, Torrio, who gave his name as Frank Langley, peeled $12,500 from a thick wad of bills in his pocket and posted bail for himself and Daniel O'Connor. O'Banion and Alterie had to wait for Ike Roderick to show up to sign real estate bonds, which suggests that Torrio had smelled a rat immediately after the trap was sprung.

Commissioner Beitler set the hearing date for May 28, but the hearing would merely be a formality. Not only was Torrio a second offender when it came to bootlegging charges, but Prohibition agent Bryce Armstrong, who had taken part in the raid, found a black notebook that someone had flung under the loading platform at the first sight of incoming uniforms. It yielded a wealth of detail about the Torrio–O'Banion mob's corruption of the police and was more than enough to cause some department heads to roll.

Torrio knew that he was going down, but he was not planning on going alone.

10

MURDER ON STATE STREET

F OUR DAYS AFTER THE SIEBEN raid, on May 23, Deputy U.S. Marshals and dry agents arrived at the Malt Maid Brewery (formerly the Manhattan) at Emerald Avenue and Pershing Road to execute a search-and-seizure warrant issued by Federal Judge James Wilkerson. Venturing into the "chip cellar" section of the plant, they discovered a veritable lake, two feet deep, of 4.8 percent beer that left the nine-thousand-square-foot floor completely submerged.

Two days earlier, pedestrians in the vicinity of Emerald Avenue had been startled by the sight of a golden, frothing geyser erupting from the slots of a manhole cover. It bubbled for more than an hour and left the pavement smelling like an unwashed beer vat. Suspicion as to its source was focused on the Malt Maid, which had been under surveillance for weeks. It had been licensed to manufacture near beer when the Volstead Act took effect, but the permit was revoked in March 1922 when Prohibition Agent Frank Campbell found more potent product being shipped to consumers.

O'Banion and Torrio, operating as the Malt Maid Company, applied for the restoration of the license, so Campbell returned to the brewery on the night of May 21 to investigate and make a report that officials in Washington could use in the final decision regarding the permit. High board fences topped with barbed wire blocked unwanted visitors from the plant, but Campbell, using a ladder and skeleton key, managed to gain entry. He was confronted in the dark by an O'Banion–Torrio minion who advised him that he was trespassing and ordered him to leave, but added that if he returned the following morning at ten o'clock, the brewery officials would be prepared to speak with him. Lacking a search warrant, Campbell agreed, and withdrew. An hour later, the alcoholic version of Old Faithful awed nocturnal strollers on Emerald Avenue.

Police officers stationed at the plant recalled that O'Banion had once tried to make a deal with them that would permit the removal of twenty-five hundred barrels of beer stored on the premises. In the wake of the Sieben arrest, that beer and a lot more went down the drain and backed up the sewers. When Campbell and his colleagues arrived on May 23, armed with a warrant from Judge Wilkerson, and discovered the mess in the chip cellar, they reasoned that the brewery operators, spooked by the attention the Emerald Avenue incident drew, had dumped their remaining product wherever they could.[1] O'Banion had no intention of risking a second arrest himself.

While Torrio and O'Banion mulled over the certain and likely complications arising from the Sieben raid, co-defendant Louis Alterie saw his reckless behavior compound his legal difficulties. In July his car collided with that of attorney Kenner Boreman in Lincoln Park. Boreman and his wife were so badly injured that they required emergency hospitalization. Alterie displayed a Cicero police badge and left the scene after giving his name as "Lew Aleries" of the Morrison Hotel. His true identity was discovered when the police traced the license number of the car. Attorney Samuel Black, who also represented Viola O'Banion, notified the police that he would produce Alterie if the cowboy gangster was wanted, but the case never came to court.[2]

Alterie racked up more headlines as the summer of 1924 progressed. On the humid night of August 27 he, his brother Bert Varain, North Side gangster Johnny Phillips (who also had been arrested at the Sieben), and a fourth companion sought relief from the heat at the Northern Lights Café at Broadway and Devon Avenue. It was gangster-friendly territory, as the owner was divekeeper and Kenna–Coughlin lieutenant Andy Craig.

Alterie and his companions became more and more intoxicated as the evening progressed, but their behavior was not openly disruptive until a flashy brunette named Dorothy Kester took the stage. When she began to sing, Johnny Phillips started shouting obscenities. Finally he lurched to the stage and grabbed her. When she tried to fight him off, he slugged her. Other café patrons rose from their seats to interfere, but Alterie and his two associates drew their weapons and fired warning shots into the ceiling.

A riot call was received at the nearby Summerdale station. Officers O'Connell, Hogan, and Sobel drove to the scene in a patrol wagon. While Sobel remained with the vehicle, his brother officers entered the café. Alterie, Phillips, and their companions descended on them, disarmed them, and marched them out of the establishment toward a waiting car. Their intent clearly was to drive off with the policemen for a purpose that can now only be surmised.

Officer Frank Sobel saw the cop–hood procession emerge from the noisy café. He drew his pistol and opened fire, killing Johnny Phillips with a single shot to the head. The gangsters returned the shot, clipping off the end of Sobel's finger with a bullet, but the officer persisted, and the Alterie party ended up fleeing. One of them stumbled as if wounded but made it into their car and sped away.[3]

Acting Chief of Detectives William O'Connor obtained warrants charging Alterie and his brother with kidnapping and assault to kill. The Northern Lights was padlocked pending further investigation, and a citywide search conducted for the fugitives. Three months later, in November, Superior Court Judge Joseph David ordered the café license restored, ruling that the corporation counsel had failed to substantiate the charge that the place had been a gangster dive.

Judge David was not so beneficent in his assessment of Alterie personally. When he learned that the grand jury had recently been dismissed without Alterie's indictment for assault and kidnapping being secured, he could barely contain his wrath.

"Someone is covering up for this seemingly powerful desperado," he said. Referring a previous grand jury's failure to indict on the same charges, he added, "Some gracious influence protected Alterie then. It seems like the same influence is a protecting hand over him now. He has been treated like a pampered child."

Assistant State's Attorney Gorman defended Alterie's liberation by saying that none of the witnesses had been able to positively identify him. "I think the state's attorney is reluctant to injure the feelings of the notorious gunman," Judge David responded tightly.[4]

While Chicagoans followed the exploits of his cohorts in the daily papers, Moran's profile remained low. He was in and out of the city during the spring and summer months, making flying visits to St. Paul and on at least one occasion taking his wife and son to Montreal. Not long after the Sieben raid, O'Banion sent him on a particularly important assignment.

By the winter of 1924 the North Side Gang had solid rumrunning contacts in Canada and the border towns through which illegal liquor was funneled, such as Windsor and Detroit. But because O'Banion catered to the carriage trade as well as the beer-drinking working men, he wanted to tighten his links to the good French wines and brandies being shipped from the French islands of St.-Pierre et Miquelon.

Prohibition had made the islands, located a dozen or so miles off the coast of Newfoundland, change overnight from a poor fishing center to a distribution point for Canadian as well as French liquor. The formerly deserted docks were suddenly crammed with stacks of liquor cases and armies of workers loading them onto boats destined for U.S. shores. In one month alone, a local historian recorded, more than three hundred thousand cases were loaded on rumrunning boats, and a few houses were even constructed out of the wood from discarded liquor cases.

Fishermen abandoned their trade in favor of pulling in $3 a day plus bonuses serving as stevedores and laborers. The gigantic fish plant on St.-Pierre was closed and converted into a liquor warehouse. The island government rejoiced at the $2 million that the liquor tax garnered in 1924 alone, and visiting mobsters, who created the market for the liquor, were received by wealthy St.-Pierrais with the grace and deference usually reserved for dignitaries.

Jean Busnot, a bar owner remembering those roaring days in 1987, told a Canadian reporter, "On any given night, four or five mobsters would come into this bar [Busnot's], all dressed up with guns and shoulder holsters—real big shots. But they were wonderful; they never hurt anybody." He recalled benevolent gangsters purchasing food for poorer warehouse workers and once giving the local priest $5,000 for a new school.[5]

Most of the larger gangs in U.S. cities either had a direct contact at St.-Pierre or an agent who did. In the summer of 1924 George Moran arrived on the islands to negotiate deals on behalf of the North Side Gang. O'Banion had been acquiring his French liquor through a New York contact up to this point and decided to eliminate the middleman. No records have been preserved to indicate what Moran discussed, or with whom, or what agreement was reached. But one former St.-Pierre resident (who later married a man from Quebec and settled in Montreal) remembered his visit well.[6]

"I was a child at the time," Emilienne Veinot recalled in a 2003 interview, "but I'll never forget that man. When we were children, my friends and I used to play around the old fish plant, which they now used for liquor storage, because Americans frequently came to inspect the product, I suppose, and make deals with local sellers. Sometimes these men would give us a little money, you know, pocket change. So we used to come around.

"One day, we saw two men standing around near the old plant. I could tell immediately that they were visitors, probably American, because they were so well dressed. They had their hands in their pockets and acted like they were waiting for someone. One of them, the taller one, saw us and approached. I was immediately nervous because I didn't speak any English and I was afraid he would ask me something.

"Imagine my shock when he spoke to me in very good French. He had a strange accent and he used some expressions that I'd never heard, but I had no difficulty understanding him. He told me that he and his friend were here to keep an appointment, but the man they wanted to see was late. He asked me if my friends and I could run and get them a couple bottles of ale, I think it was. If we would, we could keep the change from the large bill he showed us. Of course we did it. There was a bar not too far away, and in those days it was not unusual for children to pick up bottles or pails of liquor for their parents.

"I don't think he told us his name, as we were only kids, but he did say he was from America. I guessed him to be Quebeçois from his accent. I forgot about the whole episode and didn't remember it until years later, when I came across a writeup about the St. Valentine's Day Massacre. When I saw the photo of Bugs Moran in the paper, I recognized him as the man who spoke to me in French. I knew him right away from the dimple on his chin and his eyes, which were very soulful, is the best word to use."

It can only be surmised as to who Moran and his companion were meeting that summer morning, and what agreements were reached before he returned to Chicago. O'Banion's trusting him with the task of negotiating directly with the St.-Pierre liquor dealers suggests that he was aware of Moran's pre-Chicago identity, or at the very least Moran may have admitted that he had a French Canadian mother. He was the perfect representative to send into the bargaining ring: a French speaker who did not look like one and had an Irish-sounding last name. Conversations would surely be held in front of him that he was not expected to understand, yielding details and strategy hints that could provide an advantage.

O'Banion spent the summer of 1924 in and out of courtrooms and police stations. When bandits robbed a train of $3 million worth of registered mail near Rondout, Illinois, on June 13, Chicago police acted on Chief Post Office Inspector Germer's announcement in the press that a Philadelphia gang had committed the crime with help from Chicago colleagues. O'Banion, Weiss, and Alterie were picked up, held for a lineup, and then released. On July 7 O'Banion and Dan McCarthy appeared in federal court before Judge Adam C. Cliffe to face charges in connection with the January hijacking.[7]

Weiss was not present in the courtroom, having been admitted to a hospital several days earlier. Never in the best of health, he had been suffering from migraine-intensity headaches for years. Days after the June lineup in connection with the Rondout robbery, he had such a violent attack that he went into a convulsion on the floor of the smoking room above Schofield's.[8] Still recovering at the time of the July 7 court date, he was granted a separate trial.

State's Attorney Crowe had nolle prossed the charges, but a federal grand jury indicted the trio anyway. During the monotonous jury selection O'Banion noticed Genevieve Forbes, a "girl reporter" from the *Tribune*, and grinned at her. "Say," he said, "it's going to take them longer to get a jury than it'll take the Democrats to pick a candidate for president." Forbes had to concede the point when the first day ended without even one juror selected. As he left the courtroom, O'Banion told her, "I'm not guilty. I want to run a florist shop if only they'd let me alone."[9]

The trial was doomed from the start. Star witness Charles Levin, one of the truckers whom the gangsters had kidnapped, suffered a sudden attack of amnesia on the witness stand. He claimed that he could not remember what exactly had happened that January morning and refused to recant even after Judge Cliffe ordered him jailed on perjury charges.[10]

When the jurors retired to deliberate, ten of them favored conviction while two stubbornly refused to consider anything but acquittal, even after they had been arguing for twenty-four hours. The two men, as it turned out, had each received a $25,000 "gift" from the North Siders, which would have motivated them to hold out another twenty-four hours if need be. When a verdict could not be reached, the judge was forced to discharge the jury. Sharing his disgust with the whole affair was Assistant District Attorney Edwin Weisl, who assured reporters that he was going to seek a retrial immediately.

O'Banion left him to it. He and Alterie, who was under fire from the police after the Northern Lights fiasco, left Chicago at the end of September and headed for Colorado, where Alterie maintained a ranch near Jarre Canyon. Their wives, O'Banion's chauffeur, and a woman only identified as Alterie's niece completed the traveling party. They spent a month entertaining neighboring ranchers with one elaborate rodeo after another.[11]

"Short, stocky, and jovial, O'Banion was the life of the party," a reporter for the *Denver (CO) Rocky Mountain News* would recall. "He applauded the longest the feats of his new-found cowboy friends and was the heart of the conversation during the indoor entertainment."[12]

While Alterie, or "Diamond Jack," as the neighbors called him, remained curiously moody and silent, O'Banion delighted in confirming his status as a king bootlegger and gang leader back in Chicago. "This Prohibition stuff is the bunk," he told one rancher. "You can bet your neck I'll keep a lot of breweries going until I'm ready to quit." He showed off some old bullet holes in the tonneau of his car, explaining that Prohibition agent gunfire was responsible. When he tried his hand at hunting, however, he failed miserably and paid a rancher $75 to bag a deer for an evening dinner.[13]

O'Banion took breaks from the horseback riding, cow punching, and bronco busting to visit a local gun dealer, who sold him not only magnificent rifles intended as rodeo prizes, but also a machine gun the likes of which Chicago had yet to see in use. He gave away the rifles, but the machine gun was tucked into one of his trunks for the October 20 homeward journey. Chicago had an election coming up in November, and being an ardent supporter of Bob Crowe and the Republican faction, O'Banion had a huge task ahead of him. His North Side territory had historically voted Democratic, and he needed the means to make hundreds of lifestyle Democrats vote Republican.

No one doubted that the Forty-second and Forty-third ward results were predetermined. A ditty began making the rounds of the clubs and gangster hangouts: "Who'll carry the Forty-second and Forty-third? O'Banion, in his pistol pockets."[14]

The local Democrats did not smile at the joke. Getting wind of O'Banion's grandiose intentions, they went into damage-control mode immediately. At the end of October they hosted a testimonial dinner in the North Sider's honor at the Webster Hotel on Lincoln Park West. It was a gala event, complete with multicolored streamers, top-notch catered cuisine, and liquor on tap. Clinking champagne glasses and rubbing elbows with O'Banion, Weiss, Drucci, Alterie, Frank Gusenberg, and their associates were Colonel Albert Sprague, commissioner of public works and aspiring U.S. Senator; County Clerk Robert Sweitzer; Chief of Detectives Michael Hughes; and others whose positions in the public service were incompatible with their attendance at such an event. The evening climaxed when the Democrats presented O'Banion with a bejeweled platinum watch for past services rendered, and Alterie kept the momentum going by threatening to shoot a waiter for soliciting tips.

Mayor Dever exploded when he heard about the dinner and the high number of public servants who had attended. Chief of Detectives Hughes offered the weak excuse that he had thought someone else was the guest of honor, and claimed that he had left as soon as he recognized former occupants of the detective bureau's basement cells.[15]

At around the same time that the O'Banion testimonial took place, the Italian Republican Club, which the Gennas served as directors, sponsored a similar event in the Morrison Hotel. Jim Genna sat at the speaker's table, and his brothers, Scalise, Anselmi, and Samoots Amatuna chatted over a first-class dinner with such high-profile office seekers as Robert Crowe; Thomas Wallace, clerk of the circuit court; James Kearns, clerk of the municipal court; county recorder Joseph Haas, and county clerk candidate William Scherwat.

Such open fraternizing between known lawbreakers and the men campaigning for positions of public trust led the Better Government Association to complain to the United States Senate, "Chicago politicians are in league with gangsters, and the city is overrun with a combination of lawless politics and protected vice."[16]

O'Banion enjoyed the Democrats' hospitality and cheerfully accepted the platinum watch, but neither succeeded in swaying him from his intended course of action. He had more invested in the outcome of the election than Robert Crowe's gratitude and future complacency. Like Schofield before him, O'Banion was entertaining serious thoughts about a future political career of his own. Pistol-packing politicians were no novelty in Chicago; the names of Big Tim Murphy, Spike O'Donnell, Anthony D'Andrea, and Hot Stove Jimmy Quinn had appeared on both ballots and police blotters throughout their long and varied careers. The North Sider would exercise his powers of voter persuasion for his Republican sponsors in November, but his long-term plan was to eventually employ that ability on his own behalf.

His campaign tactics were nothing if not memorable. In the days leading up to November 4 O'Banion and his associates made a tour of all the North Side speakeasies, gambling houses, and pool halls, announcing their presence by shooting out the light fixtures. After delivering forceful pro-Republican speeches, O'Banion sometimes took the additional step of shattering the doorknobs on the men's room stalls with a few carefully aimed bullets—one never knew where a potential voter might be hiding.

O'Banion's ambition and political-turncoat job would take on an ominous slant less than two weeks later, when his election activities would be examined during the process of a murder investigation.

When the polls opened on November 4, the North Side leader was in an ugly mood that made him tackle his slugging and intimidation duties even more aggressively than usual. The night before, he, Weiss, and Drucci had gone to Cicero to meet Al Capone and collect their share of the profits from The Ship, a gambling house in which they owned a 15 percent interest. As the money was being divided, Capone, who was accompanied by his bodyguard Frank Rio and Frank Maritote (whose brother John would later marry Capone's sister Mafalda), remarked that Angelo Genna had left a $30,000 IOU that should be forgiven, in order that good relations with the Gennas be maintained. O'Banion, who had no special fondness for Angelo and his brothers after the rotgut infiltration into the North Side, not only turned down the suggestion but called Genna in a fit of temper after the meeting broke up and advised him to pay up within a week, or else.[17]

It was the second confrontation he had had with Torrio and Capone in just as many months. Before his trip to Colorado with Alterie, O'Banion had attended yet another meeting, this one concerning his friend "Jew" Bates. Bates was day manager at the Hawthorne Smoke Shop, a gambling spot jointly owned by O'Banion, Alterie, Torrio, Capone, and Frankie Pope. It had come to Torrio's attention that Bates had been betting against the house using inside tips, making $55,000 in September 1924. As a result of his windfall, the Smoke Shop failed to make its usual dividend payments to the owners that month, and Torrio and Capone wanted him out.

O'Banion listened to the arguments, then backed up his friend Bates to the limit. He declared that he and Alterie would block any attempts to remove "the Jew" from his position.[18] Their opposition kept Bates in place (although he was warned strongly enough to renounce his lucky streak) and further deteriorated the personal and professional relationship between the Torrio Syndicate and the North Siders.

Chief Collins, at the behest of the election board, assigned a fleet of detectives in thirty-six automobiles to prevent voting fraud and poll violence. The detective bureau contributed rifle squads to the river wards and sections of the South and West sides known to be particularly turbulent. They had their work cut out for them, and the speediest transportation could not get them to all of the trouble spots quickly enough.

Shooting, slugging, and kidnapping of voters and election officials were hourly occurrences. Anton Rudzinski was shot in the back during a drive-by assault on a polling station on West Forty-fifth Street. Bullets from the same attack grazed Thomas Quinn's head and shattered a window, badly cutting precinct captain George Russell. Sluggers fractured the skull of Nathan Firestone, nearly killing him.[19]

Gangs from rival political factions opened fire on one another in the streets without any concern for bystander safety. O'Banion nearly came to blows with Domenic "Libby" Nuccio, head of the small Gloriano Gang, in front of a polling booth at Wells and Division streets: Nuccio had the sense to flee before triggers were pulled.[20] Hoodlum John Mackey collapsed behind the wheel of his expensive car with eleven bullets in his head and body, and two companions also suffered injuries: Claude Maddox, who headed the Circus Gang, took a slug in the back and Anthony "Red" Kissane sprained his ankle while jumping from the vehicle. Kissane was later found cowering in an alley, Mackey's blood splattered over his face and coat.[21]

Collins's flying squads made one arrest after another, but the police were powerless to stop the violence. The shooting and fighting were too prevalent.

When the polls closed, O'Banion delivered as well as he'd anticipated. Charles Deneen received 17,327 votes to Albert Sprague's 11,389. Robert Crowe defeated Michael Igoe for the state's attorney post by garnering 18,961 votes, 9,315 more than his opponent. "I turned the trick!" the North Sider chuckled to City Sealer Carmen Vacco after the results were announced.[22] He was thrilled at the future he envisioned, never guessing that what he was beholding was a mirage.

On Saturday, November 8, Michael Merlo, president of the Chicago chapter of the Unione Siciliana (Sicilian Union) died after a lingering battle with cancer, effectively sealing O'Banion's fate.

Merlo, who had come to the United States from his native Sicily in 1880, had headed an organization whose outward purpose was to support the local Sicilian community and provide a buffer between new immigrants and their often harsh adopted country. The reality was that the Unione was a political goldmine harvested for the benefit of Merlo's and other chapter leaders' sponsors in city hall. He had attained the presidency after the incumbent Anthony D'Andrea was killed by thirteen shotgun slugs in May 1921.

Merlo did take a sincere interest in bettering the lot of his less-advantaged countrymen, which gained him a devoted following in Chicago's Italian and Sicilian communities. He also had a remarkably level head unfettered by ethnic ties and passionate notions of blood vengeance. One writer noted, "He absolutely rejected violent death as a weapon."[23]

When O'Banion hijacked the Genna liquor truck and conned Torrio out of $500,000 and freedom, his infuriated enemies resolved to kill him. What kept him alive throughout the summer and autumn of 1924 was Mike Merlo's edict that the current trouble not be solved through violence. One could argue that Merlo's pacifism arose from the fact that he and O'Banion had no quarrel between them, but the Unione leader could only foresee further bloodshed resulting from such a drastic move. Not even the wild Gennas dared to defy his order, for he had too many dedicated followers ready to enforce his will.

Torrio and the Sicilian brothers opted to wait, knowing that Merlo would not present an obstacle to their plans for much longer. In the fall of 1923 he had a gland operation on his neck, and follow-up tests revealed the presence of cancer.[24] When he died at his home at 433 Diversey Parkway, the outpouring of grief was as sincere as it was universal. Schofield's received so many orders that floral creations crowded every spare shelf and corner in the Merlo home and had to be piled against the brick walls outside, where the wind caught stray petals and deposited them all over the lawn like so much festively colored confetti.

Schofield, O'Banion, and their assistants were hard at work in the shop all day November 9 and most of the night, taking orders over the phone and struggling to keep their output in sync with the inflow. Torrio alone requested $10,000 worth of flowers, and Capone ordered an $8,000 rose sculpture. After O'Banion left for the night, Jim Genna, City Sealer Carmen Vacco, and a third man came in. Vacco ordered a $750 wreath.[25] As the harried clerk scribbled instructions into the ledger, Genna's eyes wandered over the shop as if memorizing its layout.

Later that night, while the lights were burning in the shop workroom long after neighboring businesses had closed down for the evening, Frankie Yale called. Yale, whose last visit to Chicago had resulted in the murder of Big Jim Colosimo, was the national president of the Unione Siciliana and wanted to place an order for a $2,000 floral piece. He told Schofield that he was in town for the Merlo funeral and would be in at around noon with a couple of friends to pick up the finished creation.[26] Schofield noted the details along with all others amassed during the evening, and then went home.

When O'Banion arrived at the shop shortly after nine o'clock on the morning of November 10, he was in rough shape. He and Alterie had made the rounds of the cabarets the night before, and festivities had not wound down until 3 a.m. O'Banion had escorted his soused friend home and promised to call him in a few hours, but fatigue or concern over the probable size of his bodyguard's hangover resulted in his failure to do so, and he went to the shop alone.[27] He had a busy day ahead of him, and no sooner had he hung up his coat than the shop manager, Victor Young, showed him the stack of wreath orders for the Merlo funeral, all placed via the shop's nighttime phone number the previous evening.

O'Banion shrugged off his fatigue and went to work. Schofield phoned at about 11:15 a.m., explaining that he was at Mount Carmel Cemetery decorating veterans' graves for Armistice Day and would be at the shop by one o'clock.[28] O'Banion chatted with him for a couple of minutes, then hung up the phone and glanced out of the workroom into the now-quiet front area. The hardwood floor was coated with leaves and discarded petals, so he asked the black porter, William Crutchfield, to sweep up the debris. While Crutchfield started the task, the North Sider turned back into the workroom, where he had been clipping the stems off a stack of chrysanthemums. Victor Young and the shop's bookkeeper, Vincent Galvin, were nearby, assisting the delivery driver in loading a mountain of wreaths onto a truck in the alley.

The bell over the shop's front door jingled, heralding the arrival of customers. Crutchfield, the only employee in the public area of the shop, looked up and watched three well-dressed men come in. He figured the two shorter ones to be Italians, but the third, who was taller than his companions and had a smoother, olive-toned complexion, struck the porter as being Greek or Jewish.

Crutchfield might be forgiven for the error in assumption. He had never met Frankie Yale before. And had he recognized John Scalise and Albert Anselmi, the Genna murder twins, he would have hurried into the back room or out the front door.

O'Banion came to the workroom doorway when he heard the bell ring, lighting up when he saw the arrivals. He approached, left hand still gripping florist shears and right extended for a shake. As he passed Crutchfield, who had finished sweeping and was heading to the back room with a heaping dustpan, he asked the porter to close the swinging door that separated the front of the shop from the work area. Taking this to mean that O'Banion wanted to speak privately with the men, Crutchfield complied.

The porter would recall at the subsequent coroner's inquest that roughly fifteen minutes passed before gunfire suddenly punctuated the noontime air. Galvin, Young, and the delivery driver fled into the alley in terror. Crutchfield cringed behind a refrigerator until the noise subsided. Then he hurried into the front of the shop, just in time to see the three men run out the front door onto State Street. They knocked over some schoolboys who had been admiring a window display and made their escape in a car that had been parked in an alley on Superior Street, just west of State.[29] Six automobiles that had been idling in various locations along Superior and State pulled out into the traffic, cutting off other drivers and preventing any possible pursuit of the gunmen.[30]

O'Banion was lying face down on the hardwood floor, the back of his head gaping open from a bullet fired at such close range that the wound bore powder burns.[31] Four other bullets had struck his face, neck, and the right side of his chest, and a sixth had splintered the glass of a showcase along the shop's rear wall. Crutchfield hurried to his side and turned him over with the assistance of the other white-faced employees, but one look at the bloody, still face was all it took to convince them that their boss was beyond help. O'Banion's hands continued to twitch for several seconds, as if seeking one of the guns he always carried on his person. He had gone through life in Chicago ready and able to defend himself, but something about his three visitors had relaxed the vigilance that had kept him alive during his childhood in the slums, his years as a circulation slugger, and during his rise to power on the North Side.

When William Schofield returned from a busy day at Mount Carmel, he was stunned to find the shop crawling with cops and reporters. Captain William Schoemaker, Chief of Detectives Michael Hughes, Captain Daniel Murphy of the East Chicago Avenue police station, and Assistant State's Attorneys John Sbarbaro and William McSwiggin were questioning the employees and schoolboy witnesses while the coroner, Dr. Joseph Springer, examined O'Banion's body in the back room. The portly florist was too shocked and upset to do much more than stand by the phone, picking it up when it rang and numbly telling callers that no more flower orders could be accommodated due to an "accident" on the premises.

William Crutchfield's actions were also mechanical in the midst of bustling blue uniforms, buzzing voices, and jangling telephones. As soon as O'Banion's body had been lifted up and carried into the back room for examination, he retrieved a mop from the utility closet and resumed the process of cleaning, only this time he swabbed blood instead of dirt or water.

While reporters composed their sensational copy, investigators from both the Chicago Police Department and the state's attorney's office examined all of Dean O'Banion's recent affiliations, conflicts, and aspirations. In the wake of a murder, any and all were suspect. O'Banion's growing interest in a political career spawned a short-lived theory that his killing had been accomplished at the behest of wary and nervous incumbents. The "love triangle" possibility resulted in a lengthy interview with Margaret Collins, a feisty blonde whose lovers dropped like flies.[32] Margaret, whose last paramour had been (deceased) North Side adherent Johnny Sheehy, coyly denied the rumor that she had been romantically linked to the married O'Banion, and proponents of the theory had to concede that the dead gangster had not been the type to cheat on his wife. The political and romantic angles had little credence in the face of the clear evidence that O'Banion's killing had been a gangland execution.

As head of this volatile murder investigation, William Schoemaker had a daunting job. He had to pull in both O'Banion's known enemies and angry, grieving friends for interrogations doomed to be failures. Those who had engineered O'Banion's killing were not about to admit it, and Weiss, Drucci, and Moran weren't likely to help the police punish the perpetrators when they had retaliation plans of their own.

At the moment O'Banion fell beneath the assassins' bullets, Weiss and Moran had been in a lunchroom on North Clark Street, meeting with gaming house proprietor Ralph Moss, a longtime friend who had been best man at O'Banion's wedding. Their discussion concluded, the trio walked along Chicago Avenue until they reached State, intending to pick up O'Banion. They were astounded at the sight of the crowds milling on the sidewalk outside of Schofield's and the police officers that hurried in and out. They withdrew before anyone spotted them, and either via taxi or a car belonging to one of them, went to the home of Mary Weiss, Hymie's mother.

As Moran would tell the story to family members, Weiss called the florist shop, asked for O'Banion, and was told about the murder by Schofield. Hanging up without saying another word, Weiss walked into the bathroom and shut the door. Seconds later, Moran, Moss, and Mrs. Weiss heard the dull sound of something heavy hitting the floor tiles. Forcing the door open after calling his name and getting no response, they found Weiss leaning against the bathtub, arms crossed over his chest and a stunned expression in his glazed eyes. The only answer he gave to their frantic queries was, "Everything I have is gone."

He remained in that semi-catatonic state for several minutes, then snapped out of it and gave the others the devastating news.[33] He and Moran, and later Drucci, struggled to deal with the shock and grief while at the same time determining their next course of action and the future of their organization. Decisions made in one area would have a profound impact in the other.

Louis Alterie did talk freely to both cops and reporters, but his story smacked more strongly of soapbox oratory than future courtroom testimony. He claimed to have received death threats over the phone from an ignorant caller who called him a dago. "I am half French and Spanish," he complained.[34] He verbally flogged himself for failing to accompany O'Banion to the florist shop that fatal morning and expressed fear that he was next. With a swarm of reporters within earshot, he issued a challenge to the slayers to meet him at the corner of State and Madison streets and fight it out, Wild West style.[35]

Alterie's theatrics amused the public and probably his enemies, but honest members of the judicial system took his blustering as evidence of the invincibility Chicago gangland had assumed, as well as the corresponding decline of law and order. On November 15 Judge Joseph David listened to testimony in the case of the Northern Lights Café shooting and could scarcely contain himself.

"Have they [Louis Alterie and Bert Varain] been prosecuted?" he demanded. When informed that Alterie had given himself up and been given a "no bill" by the grand jury, the judge exploded.

"What an astounding state of affairs! . . . Here is the place for Mayor Dever to begin his war against gangsters. Let him dig into this rottenness! I understand this Alterie to be the bold bandit who walked into police headquarters after his chief, O'Banion, was killed and said he was going to shoot it out with O'Banion's killers.

You tell Mayor Dever to let him shoot it out in the penitentiary, where he belongs!"[36]

Alterie's indiscretion would come back to haunt him later.

Torrio and Capone, when questioned, claimed that O'Banion had been a close friend. They presented their gigantic orders for Merlo funeral tributes as proof of the high mutual regard they insisted had existed. Angelo Genna, the recipient of O'Banion's "pay up or else" phone call, was let off equally easily when he merely pleaded ignorance.

Davey Miller, now sporting an abdominal scar, did not mince words, telling investigators, "I might as well admit that I'm glad he's dead." Hirschie and Maxie Miller made similar comments, their tight alibis leaving them free to make vindictive statements that would otherwise have rendered them suspect. Libby Nuccio, recipient of O'Banion's rage during the election, and Mike Carrozzo, president of the street sweepers union, whom the North Sider had beaten for striking Margaret Collins at the Friar's Inn, were questioned and released for lack of evidence.[37]

Al Capone spoke candidly to reporters once the wave of interrogations died down, claiming that O'Banion had reached the underworld upper echelon solely through Torrio's support. "Dion [sic] was all right and he was getting along, to begin with, better than he had any right to expect. But, like everyone else, his head got away from his hat. Weiss figured in that. Johnny Torrio had taught O'Banion all he knew, and then O'Banion grabbed some of the best guys we had and decided to be boss of the booze racket in Chicago. What a chance! . . . It was his funeral."[38]

Schoolboys who had seen the killers flee from the shop noticed the license number of the dark-blue Jewett sedan that carried them away. It was traced to Jules Portugais, or Portuguese, a West Side jewel thief and bootlegger, who claimed that the vehicle had been stolen ages ago. He was never prosecuted after his brief detention and interrogation, and his success in living another two years suggested that if O'Banion's successors thought him guilty, it was only marginally so.

The general roundup netted Frankie Yale and a bodyguard, Sam Polaccia, who explained that they were in town for Mike Merlo's funeral. Yale was charged with carrying concealed weapons when officers found a gun on him, but he was released after a brief appearance in night court. However, when Morgan Collins learned of the arrest, he connected Yale's name with the Colosimo investigation, drew the correct conclusion, and ordered him picked up again. Detectives took Yale and Polaccia into custody on November 18, as they were boarding a train for New York.

The national head of the Unione Siciliana claimed that he had not even arrived in Chicago until the day after O'Banion was shot and was in town solely to attend Mike Merlo's funeral. He would have gone home after the burial, but his friend Diamond Joe Esposito had held a banquet in his honor. Although he admitted that he and Capone were friends, Yale denied knowing Torrio and said that he had never heard of Dean O'Banion. When William Crutchfield, the flower shop porter, failed to identify him, Yale and Polaccia were permitted to leave.[39]

Chief of Detectives Michael Hughes voiced the general knowledge that Yale, Scalise, and Anselmi had dispatched O'Banion, and that the chances of obtaining a conviction were practically nil. When Yale was picked up, he said, "Though we know that we are on the right track, I do not believe we can get far enough for a trial with these three men."

That was fine with the North Siders. Frankie Yale, residing on the East Coast, presented a riskier kill in view of the distance and the phalanx of followers and body-guards that his position as head of the Unione warranted. But Scalise, Anselmi, and the Chicago interests that their trigger fingers had represented, were accessible. Weiss did not intend to obtain justice through the courts; he had funerals planned.

The spectacle and ceremony attending O'Banion's funeral was unprecedented in Chicago, eclipsing the opulence of the Merlo and Colosimo burials.

He lay "in state," as the press termed it, for three days in a $10,000 silver and bronze casket that had arrived on an express train from Philadelphia containing no other cargo. Silver angels crouched in frozen sorrow over the head and foot, sur-rounded by heaping blooms and greenery and grasping solid-gold candlesticks. Light from the candles flickered over the marble square supporting the coffin, which bore the inscription "Suffer little children to come onto me."[40] Thousands of people filed through Sbarbaro's funeral chapel at 708 North Wells Street, most of them curiosity seekers, but conspicuous among the wide-eyed and rubberneckers were O'Banion's grieving friends, colleagues, employees, and North Side residents who had benefited from his generosity at one point or another.

Flowers began arriving at Sbarbaro's minutes after the body did. The grief-stricken Viola honored her husband with a floral heart, eight feet high and com-posed of two thousand American Beauty roses. The Teamsters Union sent a gigan-tic wreath, O'Banion's old friend David Jerus provided a basket of blooming chrysanthemums, prizefighter Mickey Walker sent a basket of roses, and an elegant rose arrangement "from Al" occupied a prominent position. As more delivery trucks arrived from Schofield's, bearing pillar-shaped arrangements "from Max's Boys," a blanket of roses, orchids, and lilies which would cover the grave site, and other offerings, John Sbarbaro and his assistants fought to keep the aisles clear and the stained-glass windows, which let in an ethereal golden light, unobstructed.

Viola O'Banion, attended by her sister and a nurse, remained in the chapel con-stantly, her mink-swaddled, shivering figure crouched in the pew at the head of the casket. Charles O'Banion and Louis Alterie took turns sitting with her. On the day of the burial, November 14, she sobbed to *Daily News* reporter Maureen McKer-nan, "He [Dean] was all I have in the world. I don't know what to do now that he is gone. I can't think."[41]

The surviving O'Banions had wanted their beloved son and husband to have a funeral service at Holy Name Cathedral, where he had once been a faithful communicant, but Cardinal George Mundelein forbade it. He indicated through a spokesperson that O'Banion's actions in life had suggested a lack of regard for the teachings of the church and did not entitle him to a Catholic mass when dead. In spite of the edict, Father Patrick Malloy of St. Thomas of Canterbury Church was a conspicuous sight at the chapel, offering words of consolation to the family.[42]

Although the religious rites were absent from the funeral, O'Banion was buried with the pomp and ceremony that the average "good Catholic" never received. Outside the chapel, the sidewalks were jammed with sightseers hoping to get a final glimpse of the celebrity gangster who had been a newspaper name to them for years. Those who could not get into the building when the ceremonies began removed their hats and lowered their heads when the orchestra played soft, haunting melodies. Louis Alterie and Hymie Weiss wept openly, and Drucci, Moran, Eisen, Kaufman, and other primary members of the North Side Gang dabbed at their eyes with handkerchiefs.[43]

While the "Dead March" from Handel's *Saul* played, the pallbearers—Hymie Weiss, George Moran, Vincent Drucci, Maxie Eisen, Frank Gusenberg, Dan McCarthy, and Matt Foley—grasped the coffin handles and carried it outside to the hearse. The fifty or so police officers detailed to preserve order during the funeral procession had a nearly impossible task. Not only did they have to clear the streets so that trolley cars could get through, but they also had to circulate among the mourners, keeping their eyes peeled for any signs of retribution, and chase spectators off the building roofs lining the procession route lest their sheer numbers cause structural damage or worse.[44]

O'Banion's sendoff was of the caliber normally reserved for departed presidents and royalty. Twenty-six cars and trucks containing mourners and flowers respectively, three bands playing dirges, and an honor guard of unformed cops from Stickney jointly composed a spectacle that kept the sidewalks and rooftops choked with the curious. Every streetcar headed for Mount Carmel Cemetery was packed, and when the hearse finally arrived at the grave site, five thousand more people were waiting, and had been for hours. Flowers from the Mike Merlo burial had been disassembled by the brisk November wind, and assorted petals found their way to the future O'Banion resting place, coating the freshly dug hole and mound of earth like confetti.

Because of the Cardinal's edict, there was no graveside mass and the ground prepared to receive the gangster's body was unconsecrated. Father Malloy, who had accompanied the O'Banion family to the cemetery, stepped forward as the coffin was being lowered into the earth and recited a litany, a Hail Mary, and the Lord's Prayer. Malloy had known O'Banion personally and was less dogmatic, telling onlookers, "One good turn deserves another."

The entire spectacle aroused negative comment in the press and pulpits. On the same day that O'Banion was buried, statesman and historian Henry Cabot Lodge was also laid to rest. Where the North Sider's funeral had drawn crowds numbering in the thousands, hundreds had paid tribute to Senator Lodge. The *Tribune* editorialized:

> The comparison has a meaning we had better not neglect. We may allow for the fact that a sensational and violent end like that of O'Banion strikes the imagination of us all and appeals especially to morbid curiosity. Also, O'Banion's popularity, like that of other heroes of the underworld, had something of the Robin Hood flavor about it, in the legend of his acts of liberality and pity. But the significance of the gunman's funeral to this community is not modified by these considerations. It was a demonstration of the power back of organized criminality.[45]

Weiss and the other North Siders returned to their cars and left Mount Carmel after the last clod of dirt had been patted into place. Reporters watched them go and mused about the future leadership of the gang. The earliest, cautiously formulated theory to find its way into print was that there would not be a sole leader, but rather a "governing council" consisting of Weiss, Drucci, Moran, Alterie, McCarthy, and Maxie Eisen.

Eisen and McCarthy were not gang fighters, although they had mastered the art of cowing union officials. They gradually struck out on their own, while maintaining friendly ties with the North Side leadership. Louis Alterie was not destined to last, his public grandstanding and behavior in the wake of O'Banion's murder having turned his former confreres against him. That left Weiss, Drucci, and Moran, the "three Musketeers" as the popular press dubbed them, and through conscious decision or natural evolution, Weiss emerged as the leader.

Weiss and O'Banion had had what Edward Dean Sullivan described as "a Damon and Pythias relationship."[46] The young Polish-American gangster had struggled with a flash-flood temperament since childhood and never enjoyed decent health. He had been diagnosed with arterial cancer earlier in 1924,[47] necessitating at least one trip to Hot Springs, Arkansas, for treatment, and the prospect of a short lifespan compounded his bitterness. O'Banion, although also capable of violence, was more easygoing by nature and could both calm the younger man's rages and make his dour countenance crack a smile.

"Weiss could be a really caring guy," his relative Bob Koznecki remembered. "Whenever he went back to the old neighborhood, he'd stop by the grocery store where his parents shopped and not only pay their tab but the neighbors' too. He didn't feel like that towards everyone, but once he thought you were on his side, there was nothing he wouldn't do for you, or to anyone who hurt you. He really loved O'Banion, and that murder put him over the edge."[48]

Weiss's planned vendetta against the Torrio–Capone Syndicate and the Genna brothers had less to do with protecting the North Side Gang's business interests than it did with his rage over the loss of a cherished friend and essential part of his world. He was less interested in negotiation than annihilation, ultimately earning him a place in Chicago history as the only gangster Al Capone ever really feared.

After O'Banion's funeral, Chief Morgan Collins had a conference with Mayor Dever and emerged with the news that the detective bureau would be reorganized and a "strong-arm" squad created using New York's infamous crimebusters as a model.[49] The chief warned that the new unit would not be a good fit for many of the force's existing officers. "Those detectives who are too ladylike to do business with the gunmen are to be removed," he told reporters. "Too many bureau squads have been joy-riding while the town was being shot up. We are going to stop this promiscuous shooting, these gang murders, and all crimes committed by the hard-boiled."

Collins lambasted his Cicero counterpart, Theodore Svoboda, for failure to prevent Chicago gangsters from turning the town into a safe haven for crooks. Svoboda's response was acidic: "Chief Collins has plenty of dirt at his own back door. He can't keep Chicago clean, but we can keep Cicero clean."[50]

Collins also charged that "rubber-stamp judges" who freed gangsters as quickly as the police could bring them in were to blame for the disdain with which the underworld (and the public) regarded the law. His comment aroused the ire of Chicago's judicial community, which had good reason to be on the defensive. Judge Joseph David branded Collins's accusation "an infamous lie." The judge issued a hot denial that "any judge ever released a prisoner without justification."

No strong-arm squad ever materialized, as it was not a concept that Chicago would have embraced once the sensation surrounding O'Banion's murder and showy funeral had died down.

Almost two weeks after O'Banion died among his flowers, another Torrio opponent bit the dust in his own workplace.

Eddie Tancl, mindful of the fact that he had been calling the shots in Cicero long before the Torrio contingent moved in, felt sure that despite the threats and warnings to get out of town, he would be there long after Torrio got what he surely had coming to him. O'Banion's murder did not shake him from his defiant position in any way.

Tancl himself was no stranger to violent death: on July 6, 1906, he had faced eighteen-year-old Charles "Young" Greenberg in a boxing match held in La Salle, Illinois, and pummeled him so badly that a clot formed in Greenberg's brain and killed him. Tancl and his manager beat manslaughter charges, but the episode finished him as a boxer.[51] Any nostalgia he may have suffered for his fighting days ended when he opened his saloon, as the need to use his fists was a regular occurrence.

Early on the morning of November 23, Myles O'Donnell and gunman Jim Doherty swaggered into Tancl's saloon after a night of drinking and carousing in the nightspots that, unlike Tancl, bought their liquor.[52] They came into this independently operated oasis looking for trouble but were greeted by the waiter, Martin Simet, and served breakfast like any other patrons. Tancl and his wife were sitting at a table at the other end of the room with Leo Klimas, the head bartender, and Maimie MacClain, a cabaret singer who performed nightly. They noticed the arrival of the two O'Donnell men but probably hoped that all they were looking for was a place that served up a decent Sunday breakfast.

Hell broke loose when Simet delivered the $5.50 bill. O'Donnell and Doherty besieged him with curses and accused him of overcharging them. Then O'Donnell threw a punch that barely missed. Tancl was at the table in seconds, demanding to know what the problem was. A raging argument led to both men acting on their long-standing enmity and drawing guns. In the exchange of gunfire that followed, O'Donnell and Tancl were both hit in the chest. When Doherty drew his own weapon and joined in, Leo Klimas seized him and tried to disarm him. A wildly fired bullet struck Klimas and killed him.

In the meantime, Myles O'Donnell and Eddie Tancl continued to blast away at each other until their guns ran out of ammunition. Bleeding from four bullet wounds, O'Donnell, followed by Doherty, staggered out of the saloon into the street. The two disappeared in opposite directions just as the mortally wounded Tancl, who'd snatched up another pistol kept behind the bar, lumbered out the door in pursuit. He chased O'Donnell, gun blazing, and caught up with him after two blocks. At that point, his strength left him and he collapsed, unable to reach his enemy, who fainted from blood loss a few feet away.

When Martin Simet came running up, Tancl used what little energy remained to groan, "Get the rat. He got me." Then his head sagged to the ground, and he died. Simet was only too happy to kick O'Donnell in the head, jump on his back, and then leave him for dead.

Jim Doherty, who had escaped pursuit, went to a hospital to have his wounds treated. When the police determined that Myles O'Donnell had survived both the shooting and beating, they brought him to the same institution, where hours of surgery saved his life.

Mrs. Tancl and Martin Simet gave statements that resulted in the arrest of both men for the murders of Eddie Tancl and Leo Klimas. Coroner Oscar Wolff declared his intention to use the O'Banion inquest jury to hear the evidence in the Cicero killings. The two O'Donnell thugs were indicted for murder but did not stand trial until the following spring, a time span that gave the key witnesses plenty of time to disappear or change their minds as to what they had really seen. Assistant State's Attorney William McSwiggin's prosecution came to naught, and nine minutes was all it took for the jury to bring in a not-guilty verdict.

11

WEISS AT THE HELM

T HE NEW YEAR OF 1925 was less than two weeks old when the North Siders fired their first volley in what became known as the Bootleg Battle of the Marne. Early on the morning of January 12, a sedan with its license plate concealed and side curtains shielding the occupants from outside view cut off Capone's car at Fifty-fifth and State, forcing it to connect heavily with the curb.[1] Capone was not a passenger at the time, so it was his driver, Sylvester Barton, cousin Charlie Fischetti, and a third party who were treated to a volley of pistol and shotgun fire. Barton took a slug in the back, although Fischetti and the other man escaped injury by hugging the floorboard. Capone, rattled by the close call, beefed up his protection by ordering a Cadillac chassis with a steel-armored body and bulletproof glass.[2]

Another certain target of Weiss's wrath, Johnny Torrio, was conspicuously absent from his usual haunts during the first two weeks of January 1925. He supposedly took a trip with his wife to the warmer climates of Hot Springs, New Orleans, St. Petersburg, Palm Beach, Havana, and the Bahamas,[3] O'Banion assassins trailing them from one destination to another. This story is probably apocryphal, at least the shooting gallery part of it, as Torrio's first public resurfacing in Chicago saw him without bodyguards or even the fear that would normally follow such a harrowing flight for life.

On January 17 Torrio and his co-defendants in the Sieben case appeared before federal Judge Adam Cliffe for sentencing. Six truck drivers were fined $500 each, and twenty-two employees and brewery officials went free. Alterie and George Frank, the Sieben's brewmaster, did not show up for court and had their cases continued. The two rogue cops, Sonnenfeld and Warszynski, pled guilty and drew three-month jail sentences. Nick Juffra got six months in the DeKalb County Jail and a $2,000 fine. Torrio, whom Judge Cliffe curtly referred to as an "outlaw gunman," got the stiffest sentence as a second-time offender: nine months in the DuPage County Jail and a $5,000 fine. All those convicted were granted a ten-day grace period to settle their personal and business affairs, a courtesy Judge Cliffe was loathe to give.

"These are the type of men who put the courts to shame," he said. "We might as well close the courts as let them go unpunished."[4]

The following week, on January 24, Torrio returned home with his wife, Anna, at approximately 4:30 p.m. He had spent most of the day taking care of business and wrapping up loose ends while she went shopping. When chauffeur Robert Barton pulled up outside their residence at 7011 Clyde Avenue, the couple climbed out of the vehicle with their arms laden with the results of Anna's shopping trip. She was halfway up the short walkway leading to the building entrance when a movement caught her eye. To her horror, two gunmen had leaped from a gray Cadillac parked on nearby Seventieth Street and were making a beeline for the Lincoln sedan, where Torrio was still gathering parcels. One carried a shotgun, the other a pistol. A third man remained behind the wheel.[5]

Moran, Weiss, and Drucci had been watching the house for most of the afternoon. When they spotted their quarry, Drucci stayed in the car to keep the engine running and watch for interlopers. Moran clenched the .45 while Weiss wielded the shotgun. Moran made for the nose of the Lincoln and Weiss approached the rear fender, intending to trap Torrio between them if he attempted to seek shelter in the car. In the middle of Clyde Avenue they both opened fire, wounding Barton in the knee with a pistol bullet while peppering the body of the car with shotgun pellets.

While Barton slid to the seat, Torrio abandoned the parcels and dashed for the front door of his home. Moran took advantage of the clear shot now offered and fired again, hitting Torrio in the arm. The Italian spun about from the force of the blow and scrambled for his own weapon. Weiss let him have it with the shotgun, shattering his jaw with one slug and sending three more into his chest and abdomen. While Anna watched in wide-eyed horror, Torrio sank to the pavement.

Moran, jubilant, rushed up to his fallen victim, straddled him, and pointed the gun muzzle down at the other man's bleeding head. He squeezed the trigger, anticipating vindication for O'Banion.

Nothing happened. In his haste to get Torrio before the other man could stagger to his feet, he had forgotten to reload his .45.

Back in the Cadillac, Drucci noticed an approaching laundry truck and honked the horn. Cursing but figuring that Torrio was going to suffer a slow death instead of the anticipated quick one, Moran and Weiss ran back to the car and jumped in. Drucci stepped on the gas, sending the vehicle hurtling along Seventieth Street. At Stoney Island Avenue they turned north onto Sixty-seventh Street. The driver of the intrusive laundry truck, Walter Hillebrandt, noted their escape route and later told police that he could identify the gangsters if need be.

Anna Torrio raced to her husband's side, dragged him into the building vestibule, and fought down panic as she worked to staunch the blood flow. Motorcycle policeman Roy Carlson, who arrived on the scene in response to the gunshots, flagged down a passing taxi and had Torrio taken to Jackson Park Hospital.

Despite the knee wound, Robert Barton drove the bullet-riddled sedan to a pay telephone, where he called Capone to report what had happened. No sooner had he completed the call than police officers, noticing the condition of the Lincoln, overtook him at Seventy-first Street and Jeffrey Avenue. When Barton refused to explain how he had been wounded, they arrested him.

"I know who they are," Torrio muttered to Assistant State's Attorney John Sbarbaro. "It's my business. I'll tell you nothing." Mrs. Torrio had a more resigned attitude. When asked for assistance in identifying the attackers, she shrugged and said, "What good would that do?"

Capone was less restrained when he arrived at the hospital. Tears streamed down his round cheeks as he made for Torrio's room at about the same time that Assistant State's Attorney John Sbarbaro showed up. "The gang did it! The gang did it!" he kept repeating. Recognizing Sbarbaro, Capone added, "I'll tell you more when he gets well." It was a promise he broke as soon as he learned that his beloved mentor would live, and his self-control reasserted itself.

As he recuperated from emergency surgery, Torrio made it plain that his attackers would never be convicted with his help. Speaking with difficulty because of his bandaged jaw, he told Lieutenant Charles Egan, "No use bringing anyone here. I won't rap them."

It took an outside party to do the rapping. Seventeen-year-old Peter Veesaert, son of a janitor employed at 6954 Clyde Avenue, was helping his father wash an automobile nearby when the North Siders launched their attack and had seen the entire thing from start to finish. He was afraid, but not enough to keep him from coming forward. When shown a picture of the pallbearers handling O'Banion's coffin, Veesaert picked out Moran as the man with the pistol. He told the detectives that he had seen the North Siders waiting in their car for at least an hour before the Torrios returned home.

Chief of Detectives Schoemaker felt his hope for a conviction rise again. He ordered Moran arrested and brought to the detective bureau. Police officers went to the North Sider's home at 5123 Wolfram Street, where a maid was about to serve dinner. Leaving Lucille and John to enjoy the meal alone, he accompanied the policemen downtown.

Anna Torrio viewed him upon request and denied that he was one of the assailants. Schoemaker sent for Capone, who Moran insisted was a friend. Capone arrived with Jake Guzik, an ex-pimp and financial wizard, and sat across a table from the North Sider. Schoemaker did not expect Capone to actually break the underworld code of silence and make any kind of identification, but he was hoping for a facial expression or similar reaction to give him a sign that he was on the right trail. The experiment disappointed him, as neither Moran, Capone, nor Guzik let any emotion cross their poker faces.

When Veesaert arrived, Schoemaker ordered Moran and eight other prisoners to file into a room, walk around, turn on command, give their names, and put their hats on and off. The teenager watched the procession through a small hole in the wall.

"Do you recognize any of them?" the chief asked.

"Yes." Veesaert indicated Moran. The prisoners were then ordered into another room, where the light was stronger, and the boy was permitted to view them face to face. Quelling any nervousness, he picked out Moran again.

"Me!" The North Sider glared at him.[6]

"Yes," Veesaert nodded, "he's the man."

Judge William Lindsay approved Moran's release on a $5,000 bond when he learned that Torrio would live despite the ferocity of the assault. The police had asked that Moran be held a while longer pending the uncovering of more evidence, but Lindsay ruled against them.

Veesaert's identification of Moran invalidated Capone's insistence that the attack was not an act of retaliation by O'Banion's heirs. So did a predawn visit to Jackson Park Hospital by what could only have been an intended assassin. At around two o'clock on the morning of the twenty-sixth, night nursing superintendent Dorothy Beck was approached by a strange man who asked to see Torrio.

"I told him that it was impossible to see a patient at that hour," she said when recounting the incident to reporters. "He insisted, but I told him Mrs. Torrio was with her husband and would not let anyone but his best friends see him. That did not discourage him, but he left when I told him that two policemen were in the room guarding Torrio."

Her suspicions aroused, she watched as the man left the hospital and walked to the curb, where three automobiles loaded with men were lined up, their engines idling. Beck immediately put in a request for three more policemen to guard Torrio and prevent the hospital from being a prospective shooting gallery.[7]

Chief Collins told the press that the shooting never would have occurred in the first place had it not been for the preferential treatment that the courts accorded gunmen. "Too many men are touring the streets who should be in the penitentiary," he insisted.

Torrio knew that. On February 9, after his condition had stabilized enough for him to leave the hospital, he headed to the Lake County Jail in suburban Waukegan to begin serving his sentence. The original place of incarceration had been changed in view of the ongoing medical treatment he would likely require. Sheriff Edwin Ahlstrom proved to be most solicitous, allowing Torrio to furnish his cell with a brass bed, rich carpets and furnishings, a record player, and a radio. Ahlstrom also permitted him to install bulletproof mesh and blackout curtains on the barred windows to discourage snipers, and to hire deputy sheriffs as bodyguards. Not only Anna Torrio but also colleagues from Chicago were frequent and welcome visitors. Money and influence ensured that he was more a guest than a prisoner.

At some point before his release, Torrio had a special meeting with Capone and his lawyers. Although not a coward, he foresaw what was coming, having gotten a painful and distressing advance preview personally, and did not have the energy or stomach for it. He had made his pile and had no desire to stick around while the cooperative he had helped build dissolved into a cutthroat competition.

It was agreed (according to some accounts) that Torrio would receive a percentage of the Syndicate profits for a time and be available for guidance and consultations.[8] Upon his release from jail, he would leave Chicago, possibly to live in Italy. The future, with its enormous profits and deadly risks, belonged to the younger, more resilient Capone.

With only Peter Veesaert daring to identify Moran, the state's attorney did not bother to indict him for the Clyde Avenue attack. Free of any legal entanglements, Moran now did something he had long wanted to: he sent Louis Alterie packing.

The cowboy gangster had aroused the wrath of the North Side Gang by talking not only to the press (something annoying but not unforgivable, considering that they had their own future headlines planned) but also to the enemy. He had been seen conversing quietly with Torrio and Capone when they arrived at Sbarbaro's on November 13 to publicly pay their respects, and on November 18 caught a train to New York—the same day that John Torrio boarded another train to the same destination.

Had Frankie Yale and Sam Polaccia not been arrested a second time in Chicago, they would have reached their home city mere hours after Torrio and Alterie arrived. A *Herald and Examiner* reporter published the information in the paper's November 19 edition. How Alterie explained himself or for that matter kept himself alive upon his return can only be speculated. On the night of January 28, 1925, Moran finally had a showdown with him.[9]

That evening, the cowboy gangster was in a foul, rowdy mood after a day spent ducking in and out of courtrooms. In his appearance before Judge Emmanuel Eller, he complained that his life was in danger now that police officers had confiscated two automatic pistols he had been carrying. When Eller declined to return the firearms, opting instead to have four deputy sheriffs escort him from the courthouse, Alterie was brimming with indignation. Finding new guns proved easy, as the patrons of the Friar's Inn learned when he strolled into the establishment at six o'clock, brandished the new acquisitions, and invited anyone with the requisite nerve to indulge in a gunfight.

The episode drew citywide attention and focused ridicule on the North Siders, as Alterie was still publicly perceived as a member. Moran, acting for his compatriots, cornered Alterie and delivered a mini-speech with more relish than the occasion called for.

"Nothing hard about you; you talk too much. You'll get us all into trouble, so get out before you're dragged out."[10]

Alterie knew that he had little choice in the matter. If he defied the North Siders and stayed put, it would be too easy for him to turn up dead and be passed off as another casualty in the brewing gang war. He packed his bags and caught the next train to Colorado. Although he would return to Chicago within a month to deal with federal and local indictments against him, and he maintained a friendship with a few people from the O'Banion days, such as Viola O'Banion and the Gusenberg brothers,[11] for all intents and purposes his association with the North Side Gang was over.

On the night of February 21 he and three companions were whooping it up at the Midnight Frolics at 18 East Twenty-second Street, Moran's warning clearly forgotten. They made such an exhibition of themselves with shouting and gun waving that Captain Stege and Lieutenant Edward Birmingham appeared at the club to make arrests. When Alterie menaced him with a pistol, Stege snatched it out of his hand and slapped him across the face. The club went silent for a brief second as the cowboy hoodlum's eyes widened in shock. Then laughter erupted, and followed the policemen and their prisoners all the way to the car outside.

Alterie ended up in a basement cell at the detective bureau, where he was forced to spend the rest of the weekend. He made himself the center of attention the entire time. On Sunday morning, missionaries from the Moody Bible Institute held a service for the inmates in the cells. Alterie joined in on the hymn-singing and read aloud from a Bible that the workers gave him. Seemingly overcome by the moment, he proclaimed that he would:

- Keep out of cabarets.
- Stop carrying guns.
- Give up moonshine.
- Devote his time and attention to his union presidency.
- Give up wine, women, and song.[12]

On Monday morning Alterie's lawyer, William Scott Stewart, persuaded Judge Lindsay to order the police to book his client or release him. Stege charged Alterie with disorderly conduct and carrying concealed weapons. The cowboy hoodlum was found guilty on both charges by Judge Hayes the following month and fined $100.

He continued to draw attention from the Chicago press even when no longer a full-time resident of the city. In January 1926 the newspapers noted that he and his chauffeur, Pete Willis, were in a car accident outside Carroll, Iowa. Their vehicle skidded off the road, rolled down a ten-foot embankment, and came to rest in an upside-down position. Strangely, neither man was hurt.[13] In June 1927 word arrived from Denver that Alterie had been shot in the back by his brother Bert during a quarrel at Alterie's ranch. He was not expected to live, but the efforts of Dr. G. A. Hopkins at the Glenwood Springs Hospital pulled him through.[14]

Hearing that John Stege had been fired from his position by the Civil Service Commission the following August perked him up enough to restore his impish sense of humor. When Big Bill Thompson became mayor again in 1927, Stege had been first suspended and then dismissed, ostensibly for joining the force under fraudulent circumstances (he had neglected to mention his 1900 manslaughter conviction or the fact that his birth name had been Albert Stedge) but in reality because Thompson saw him as a Dever minion.

"Stege fired?" Alterie grinned to reporters when he returned to Chicago. "Well, that tickles me, and I guess none of the boys will be mad either." He added, "I may settle down in Chicago again now."[15]

In 1927 Alterie, who had divorced his wife Mayme, remarried. His new bride was Ermina Rossi, daughter of Denver underworld boss Mike Rossi, who was doing time in the state prison for the murder of his own wife. The father heartily approved of Alterie as a husband for eighteen-year-old Ermina, claiming that any man as handy with a gun as Alterie was a welcome addition to the family.

The cowboy gangster returned to Chicago just often enough to make his job with the janitors union something more substantial than an absentee position. When he did show, he had a knack for making it a newspaper event. In January 1932 he was indicted for alleged complicity in a midwestern kidnapping ring[16] and while appealing that charge had to contend with public exposure of his role in a plot to extort $500,000 from wealthy Illinois residents. One of his accomplices in the latter endeavor was former Cook County Assistant State's Attorney Ward C. Swalwell.

On October 12, 1933, Alterie faced a vagrancy charge under the new "criminal reputation law" that empowered the police to charge anyone recognized as a habitual offender. When a jury found him guilty and Judge Thomas Green ordered him committed to the Bridewell for six months, he launched an appeal and was granted freedom on a $10,000 bond.[17] The Supreme Court repealed the reputation law before he could serve the sentence. Less than a year later, police arrested Alterie at the Auditorium Hotel, where he and another man were covered with knife wounds that they claimed a woman companion had inflicted on them.

He was not on much better behavior in Colorado. On November 8, 1932, he shot two men in a fight in the Glenwood Springs Hotel[18] and received a sentence of one to five years, which was suspended on the condition that he leave the state. Alterie first went to Santa Fe, then returned to Chicago.

Being president of the Theatre and Building Janitors Union, Alterie found himself in the middle of the union strife that shook the movie industry during the early '30s. Gangsters who had gotten rich from bootlegging cast about for a new source of income after Repeal, and they found a promising one in the film industry unions, which were crucial to the production of the movies that the Depression-era public craved. Police knew that Alterie backed up his threats with fists and firepower when defending his turf or adding to it, so when Tommy Malloy of the Moving Pictures Operators Union and a rebellious union organizer and Malloy opponent named Clyde Osterberg turned up murdered, Alterie was brought in for questioning.

Cops and reporters who had been keeping tabs on the Chicago underworld for years marveled that Alterie survived into the thirties when so many of his friends and enemies had not. But those extra years of shooting, union management, and living life on the edge made it a question of when he would finally meet a violent end, not if.

On July 9, 1935, a man named "Sullivan" visited a rooming house run by Mrs. Frances Kern at 927 Eastwood Avenue and rented a room facing the Alterie residence at 922 Eastwood. "He was a nice fellow too," Mrs. Kern would recall. "Looked like an Italian-American."[19]

On July 18 Alterie and Ermina left their sixth-floor apartment so that she could drive him to the union office. When they entered the lobby, she paused to speak to the desk clerk while Alterie continued outside. Mrs. Alterie soon followed, hurrying to catch up. When she was around twenty feet away from him, she heard gunfire. It was emanating from the window of Sullivan's room across the street.

Twelve slugs from an automatic shotgun and a carbine rifle pierced Alterie's body, while five more chipped the stonework of the building entrance, missing Ermina by less than a foot. The gangster crumpled to the curb near his parked car, grasping at his bleeding wounds. While Ermina ran to him, two men in the rooming house bolted from Sullivan's room, passed Mrs. Kern in the corridor, and descended into the basement. It was believed that they fled into a waiting car stationed near the basement's alley door. The weapons used in the shooting were flung, still warm, onto the bed in the room.

Ermina, her face awash with tears, ran to her husband's side, gathered him in her arms, and begged him to rise. He shook his head and whispered, "I'm sorry, but I'm going, Bambino." Stanley Wozny, owner of the apartment building at 930 Eastwood, and two policemen who arrived when they heard gunfire rushed Alterie to the Lake View Hospital, where he died without regaining consciousness.

Ermina met with reporters the next day after formally identifying her slain husband's body at the county morgue. With willful or misguided blindness, she denied that Alterie had been a gunman. "I never saw Lee have a gun," she insisted. "And so far as fearing for his life, he was not afraid of anybody."

"Didn't you know he was a gangster?" one of the reporters queried.

"No. He wasn't." She paused, then added, "Not since we've been married."

Alterie's murder joined Chicago's bulging UNSOLVED file. In September 1940 Matthew Taylor, president of the Chicago Elevator Operators and Starters Union, made a deathbed revelation detailing scores of labor-related murders committed in Chicago over the preceding years.[20] He told State's Attorney Courtney that a certain labor leader, whose name was not published (and who was obviously never prosecuted), engineered Alterie's murder to put him out of the way and take over the janitors union.

"This man told you he put Alterie on the spot?" Courtney asked.

"Yes." Taylor nodded.

Ike McAnally, a reporter for the *New York Post*, advised R. Whitley, special agent in charge at the New York FBI office, that crime overlords Frank Costello and Louis "Lepke" Buchhalter, both of whom were active in racketeering activities in New York, had arrived in Chicago on "important business" during the first week in July and returned home in the wake of the Alterie shooting. In a report to J. Edgar Hoover dated July 22, 1935, Whitley indicated that McAnally's sources were underworld-based and considered "reliable."[21]

Fingerprints were lifted from a rifle used in the Alterie assassination, and no matches came up when comparisons were first made. In 1937 an Inspector Evans of the Chicago Police Department notified the FBI that the gun had been traced through purchase records to a member of the "Dutch Schultz" mob in New York.[22] The prints were run against those of the suspect and other known Dutch Schultz associates, with negative results. The trail went cold and never heated up again.

Weiss and McCarthy appeared in court on April 8, 1925, to face charges stemming from the January 22, 1924, booze hijacking. Charles Levin's memory, which had been diminished by terror in the July 1924 trial, was probably no clearer this time around, but the defendants saved him the stress and the county the cost of a prolonged trial by pleading guilty.

The move surprised everyone in the courtroom. The jury fixing that had freed O'Banion and McCarthy in the first trial could have been duplicated easily enough. Yet they threw themselves on the mercy of the court and were sentenced to six months in the Kane County Jail in Geneva, Illinois, plus a $1,000 fine. The judge granted them thirty days to settle their affairs, but they were ready and waiting when U.S. Marshal Palmer Anderson took them into custody on May 9. Their destination had been changed to the McHenry County Jail at Woodstock, and Anderson delivered them to Sheriff Lester Edinger without delay.

The two North Siders were not destined for a harsh stay if a *Tribune* article published the day of their arrival was any indicator. Reviewing the jails in the northern Illinois federal district, it noted of the McHenry County lockup:

> This is an ancient pile, with the bill of fare and a considerate sheriff about all to recommend it. There are only 13 (prisoners) in now, nine federal, of whom two are bootleggers and six narcotics. Sheriff Lester Edinger sets the best regular table in the district. The boys don't even have to pay for the salad on the bill."[23]

Within two years Sheriff Edinger would be named in an indictment charging conspiracy to violate the dry laws,[24] so there is little doubt that he extended every available courtesy to his newest charges. In the coming months the rumor would arise that Edinger allowed them to leave the jail grounds at will, a likely result of the "felons on the loose" hysteria that erupted after Terry Druggan and Frankie Lake, sentenced to a year in the Cook County Jail for running a brewery after a federal injunction closed it, were discovered in their usual Chicago haunts when they should have been pacing their cells. When the *Chicago American* exposed the arrangement, Warden Westbrook and Torrio's old friend Sheriff Peter Hoffman were sentenced to four months and thirty days respectively behind bars.

There is no evidence that Weiss and McCarthy enjoyed any open-door arrangement with Sheriff Edinger. Although Weiss's name would be linked to the inter-gang carnage that reddened the spring and summer of 1925, he read about it in the papers like the average citizen. Moran, Drucci, and Frank Gusenberg visited frequently,[25] keeping their chieftain apprised of progress. With few exceptions they only had good to report.

Nineteen twenty-five had been a fortuitous year for Angelo Genna from the onset. On January 10 he married Lucille Spingola in a lavish wedding ceremony[26] to which the general public was invited via widely published newspaper ads. Lucille was the kid sister of Henry Spingola, lawyer and Genna associate who had helped map out their alky-cooking venture. Her parents were supposedly less than thrilled with the match, but Genna's influence and Lucille's genuine infatuation saw them engaged. Three thousand people attended the reception at the Ashland Auditorium and enjoyed the sight and taste of a twelve-foot-high, elaborately decorated wedding cake that weighed a ton and took four days to bake in gradual stages.[27]

It was a glittering spectacle befitting a royal union, but Angelo, proud of the way he had fought his way out of humble beginnings and attained a position of power, wealth, and fear, wanted nothing less. He had been named Mike Merlo's successor to the presidency of the Unione Siciliana's Chicago chapter, and the Spingolas were a well-connected family, counting opera stars among their personal acquaintances.

For months the newlyweds lived in a $400-a-month suite at the Belmont Hotel. Then they found a house on South Taylor Avenue in Oak Park[28] that caught their fancy. On the morning of May 25 Genna kissed his wife goodbye, left the hotel, and climbed into his roadster, carrying the $11,000 price for the bungalow in cash.

He had not gone far on Ogden Avenue when a sedan carrying four men drew up and tried to overtake him. Hearing a shotgun go off, Genna hit the accelerator and sent the roadster careening down Ogden at sixty miles per hour. He struggled to control the vehicle and return fire at the same time. He attempted to do a sharp turn onto a road intersecting Ogden to shake his pursuer, but the sudden move sent the roadster crashing into a lamppost near Hudson Avenue.

The Cunin children (from left), Cyrille, Josephine, and Adelard.

BEGINNINGS

Jules Cunin and Marie Diana Gobeil, parents of the future George "Bugs" Moran.

Adelard Cunin (right) at approximately four years of age, with his mother's brother, Cyrille Gobeil.

St. Paul blacksmith and mason Jules Cunin.

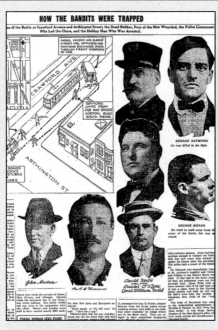

HOW THE BANDITS WERE TRAPPED

The February 1918 shootout that killed George Raymond and saw Moran arrested was front-page news in the Chicago dailies (left).
• The photo above appeared in press coverage following the shooting attack on Johnny Torrio. Moran's intense stare, coupled with his sometimes homicidal temper, spawned the nickname "Bugs."

CHICAGO DAYS

Moran gives the camera a sullen stare after a 1928 court appearance on a bombing charge.

Tommy Touhy and George Moran participated in a failed jailbreak in 1918 but maintained a steady friendship over the years.

George Moran married Turkish-born Lucille Logan in 1922 and became a father to her son, Louis, who was later renamed John George.

Dean O'Banion (above, with wife Viola) brought the North Side Gang to prominence. After his 1924 murder, his successors made Capone's life a nightmare.

Louis Alterie was a key member of the North Side Gang until his antics in the wake of O'Banion's slaying embarrassed his colleagues and led to his expulsion.

Henry Earl Wojciechwoski (left), alias Hymie Weiss, was said to be the only gangster Al Capone ever really feared.
• The October 1926 machine-gun attack that killed Weiss demolished the cornerstone of Holy Name Cathedral, leaving damage that remains visible today (above).

FRIENDS

Lodovico Di Ambrosio (right), alias Vincent "the Schemer" Drucci, took his one-way ride in the back of a police car (below) in April 1927, and ended up in the morgue (below right).

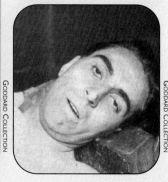

North Sider soldier Pete Gusenberg (right) stands with O'Banion chauffeur and garage owner Jerome MacMahon outside the latter's North Clark Street garage in this rare, candid photo.

Frank Foster (above), was Moran's Los Angeles contact during the early 1930s and the probable killer of *Chicago Tribune* reporter Jake Lingle.
• Vice lord Jack Zuta (right) orchestrated the Lingle hit.

Leo Mongoven (above) was a Moran friend and ally for years.
• Moran never forgave the defection of Ted Newberry (below) to the Capone camp.

Joe Aiello and George Moran had a common goal that led to their partnership in 1928: the elimination of Al Capone.

Julian "Potatoes" Kaufman was a longtime North Sider associate who managed the Sheridan Wave Club for Moran.

ENEMIES

Moran's rivalry with Alphonse Capone (above) would provide 1920s Chicago with one of the bloodiest chapters in its history.

• In September 1926 a caravan of North Siders shot up the Italian restaurant at Cicero's Hawthorne Hotel (below) with Tommyguns while Capone was having lunch there.

Capone mentor Johnny Torrio tried to organize Chicago and was nearly killed by George Moran in an ambush outside his home in January 1925.

John Scalise (left) and Albert Anselmi, Chicago's two-man murder squad, participated in the killing of Dean O'Banion and proved too treacherous even for Capone, who finally invited them to their last supper in 1929.

Pasqualino "Patsy" Lolordo, Capone-backed head of the Unione Siciliana, was shot to death in his home in January 1929. His killers, whom he'd invited in for drinks and conversation, laid his bloody head on a pillow before departing.

After the Gusenbergs failed to kill him on at least two occasions, "Machine-Gun" Jack McGurn fell to assassin bullets in a bowling alley in 1936.

The St. Valentine's Day Massacre shocked a public long accustomed to gang-land violence.

THE MASSACRE

Willie Marks (below) was with Moran (above) the morning that Al Capone's "American Boys" cut down seven North Siders.

Victims in the North Clark Street garage included (top, from left) Adam Heyer; John May; Al Weinshank, whose early arrival and resemblance to Moran saved Moran's life; and Pete Gusenberg (above center) and his brother Frank (above), who lived for hours after the February 14, 1929, hit.

For reasons that remain a mystery, Capone man Frank Diamond (second from right) was arrested in a raid on the Moran gang headquarters in December 1929. He joined Andrew (left) and Domenic Aiello and Leo Mongoven (right) in a subsequent police lineup.

THE THIRTIES

George Moran's duck-hunting excuse for his presence in Lake County received a humorous interpretation in the press.

"STICK 'EM UP!"
[The Evening Telegraph (Providence).]

News item—Bugs Moran, Chicago gangster, tells police he is just a simple duck hunter.

Marvin Apler (above), alias Hart, was Moran's contact in Los Angeles. • At right, Moran as public enemy.

HAVE YOU SEEN THIS MAN?

84684

If you have, call Wabash 4747, the detective bureau, and notify the police he is at large and where he may be found. These are rogues' gallery pictures of George (Bugs) Moran, former convict and leader of north side gangs since the killing of Dean O'Banion, Earl (Hymie) Weiss, and Vincent (Scheme) Drucci. Seven of his followers were killed in the St. Valentine massacre of 1929. He is one of the men listed as public enemies by the Chicago crime commission.

Antioch, Illinois, was a base for Moran and Leo Mongoven's slot-machine ring.

Above, Moran talks with George Bieber, a member of his defense team, during the 1938 trials for forging American Express checks.
• Below, Moran attempts to hide his face during a court appearance.

Moran and Frank Parker consult their attorneys during their trial for forging American Express checks.

From left, James Kelly Renato Lolli, and Lawrence Mazzanars joined Moran in knocking over Syndicate handbooks during the late 1930s and early '40s.

Moran glowers at the camera in this mug shot taken at the Cook County Jail.

Moran in a relaxed mood during the summer of 1941.

Virgil Summers mug shot.

Dayton criminal Al Fouts planned and executed a number of midwestern bank robberies with George Moran and Virgil Summers.

After his December 1943 release from the Cook County Jail, Moran hurries into a waiting cab.

Moran and Summers arrive at the Dayton Jail on July 13, 1946.

Moran and FBI Agent W. McFarlane leave Owensboro City Hall on July 7, 1946, after Moran was finger-printed and photographed.

DAYTON

A weary Moran poses for a mug shot upon admission to the Dayton Jail.

Moran and wife Evelyn Herrell in Dayton on July 13, 1946, after his arrest for the Kurpe payroll robbery.

Virgil Summers (left), Evelyn Moran, George Moran, and Al Fouts (right) contemplate the possibility of conviction during the 1946 trial for the Kurpe payroll robbery.

Upon his parole from the Ohio State Pen in 1956, Moran faced trial for his role in the Ansonia, Ohio, bank robbery (left).
• John George Moran (above), the former Louis Logan, whom George Moran raised as his own.

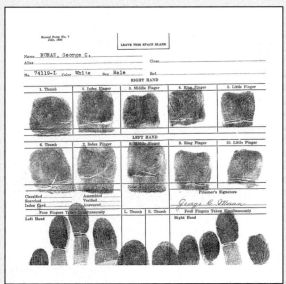

Upon admission to Leavenworth, Moran gave his prints for the last time.

LEAVENWORTH

UNITED STATES PENITENTIARY
LEAVENWORTH, KANS.

February 19, 1957

Mr. Jack G. Moran
c/o Atlantic Ocean House
Box 38
Boca Raton, Florida

RE: MORAN, George C.
Reg. No. 74119-L

Dear Mr. Moran:

With reference to our recent exchange of correspondence, I regret to advise that your father's condition has taken a progressive down-hill course. Our Medical Staff advises us they do not expect him to live more than three weeks to a month, at the longest.

We believe your father is receiving the best of medical care. We have three resident doctors and several consultant specialists on the staff. Inasmuch as our visiting regulations were mailed to your Chicago address, we are enclosing a second copy for your information.

We know this news is distressing, but in our previous letter we advised we would keep you informed of any signifi-cant change in your father's condition. Your father is aware of his critical condition. In fact, prior to a definite diagnosis by our Medical Staff he stated he believed he had cancer.

Very truly yours,

C. H. LOONEY
Warden

Warden Looney's letter to John Moran confirming the presence of cancer.

Barely a month after this mug shot was taken, Moran succumbed to lung cancer.

Hobart Hermansen's Lake Como Inn was a favorite retreat of George and Lucille Moran.

LAKE GENEVA

Hermansen's Geneva Hotel, where John Moran tended bar and was found dead in 1959.

Stunned by the impact, Genna was a defenseless target when the sedan rolled to a halt next to the wreck. More shotgun fire boomed, peppering Angelo with slugs and mangling his spine. He was still alive, although fading fast, when the police arrived. As he lay on the operating table at the German Evangelical Deaconess Hospital awaiting surgery, Angelo spurned Sergeant Roy Hessler's attempts to question him. By the time Sam Genna, the only one he might have confided in, arrived, he was dead.[29]

An agony-stricken Lucille Genna, accompanied by Sam and her brother Henry, sobbed to Chief of Detectives Schoemaker and Captain John Stege that as far as she knew, Angelo "had no enemies." She may have sincerely believed it, but no one else did.

An obvious enemy was the North Side Gang. O'Banion's killing had left Weiss and company with a bone to pick with the entire Genna family. Angelo made a good choice for the first kill because he and brother Mike were the enforcers, the ones who made the Gennas truly dangerous. There was, however, another party who stood to benefit from the death of Angelo in particular, someone who hitherto had been an ally.

When Mike Merlo died, Al Capone recognized an opportunity to assume vicarious control of the Unione, which he as a non-Sicilian could not join. Antonio Lombardo, a commission broker and cheese merchant, was not only a member but also a close friend and someone who could be relied upon to ensure that the Unione was never employed for the purpose of Capone's destruction. But before Lombardo could be maneuvered onto the vacated presidential throne, the Gennas shot forward in true Machiavellian style and placed Angelo there. Capone, stung and worried by the move, did not trust the brothers. They could—and given time and opportunity probably would—break with him and use the Unione's resources against him.[30]

The police, without specifying their sources, announced that the occupants of the killer sedan had been Hymie Weiss (which was unlikely), George Moran, Vincent Drucci, and Frank Gusenberg.[31] Angelo's grieving and furious siblings concurred. After the slain Genna's show-stopping funeral, they went hunting for Moran, Drucci, and anyone else recognized as a North Sider.

On the morning of Saturday, June 13, Drucci and Moran drove east on Congress Street in the latter's Hupmobile. Their moods were darkly jovial; they had reason to believe that before the day was through, John Scalise and Albert Anselmi would pay the price for O'Banion's murder by forfeiting their own lives. The North Siders had approached Genna gendarme Samoots Amatuna, who aspired to the Unione presidency that Angelo Genna had vacated so violently, and by some accounts offered him a bribe[32] to deliver Scalise and Anselmi to a place of execution (another variation claims that they offered to back him in a bid for the position he coveted[33]). As they passed an alley near the intersection of Sangamon and Congress streets, near the northern edge of Little Italy, Moran and Drucci suddenly found themselves targeted for destruction when a car containing Mike Genna, his two prize torpedoes, and another man hurtled out of the shadowy enclosure and peppered the Hupmobile with shotgun slugs.

The two North Siders returned fire. Moran's knee was grazed by a lucky shot,[34] and Drucci may have been injured also. Their car was reduced to junk by the attack, forcing them to abandon it on Congress Street and run for cover. When the police recovered the damaged vehicle and traced it to Moran, he told them that it had been stolen.

An hour later, a detective squad car cruising north on Western Avenue passed the Genna automobile going in the opposite direction. Squad commander Michael Conway, recognizing "Mike the Devil," said, "We'll follow them and see what they're up to." He had not yet learned of the shooting on Congress Street, but noting the direction in which the gangsters were headed, he figured they might be bound for one of the railway yards in the southwestern section of the city to participate in an alcohol pickup or sale. When driver Harold Olson did a U-turn, the occupants of the Genna vehicle noticed, and the chauffeur stepped on the gas.

The two cars raced down Western Avenue at speeds exceeding seventy miles per hour, dodging other motorists and fighting to keep from skidding off the rain-slick pavement. At Sixtieth Street, a truck entered the intersection, and the Genna driver avoided a collision only by hitting the brake so abruptly that his car turned in a screeching semicircle, jumped the curb, and crumpled the right fender against a lamppost. The four gangsters climbed out, clutching their weapons and placing their damaged vehicle between them and the oncoming detective sedan.

The officers halted their car next to the wreck and two got out, one of them calling, "What's the big idea? Why all the speed when we were ringing the gong?"

Detective Harold Olson still had his foot on the running board when shotgun slugs tore into his body, killing him. Officer Charles Walsh collapsed to the pavement next, clutching his breast and groaning. He had sustained mortal wounds and would not survive. Squad commander Michael Conway and Officer William Sweeney, still in the sedan, drew their weapons and returned fire. Conway was shot in the jaw and sank to the floor, badly wounded but alive.

The Genna driver had long since made a run for it, and after shooting Conway, Genna, Scalise, and Anselmi bolted too, across a vacant lot next to the Tourist garage at 5940 South Western Avenue. Leaving the crowd to attend to his fallen comrades, Sweeney snatched up two guns and ran after the killers. Scalise and Anselmi ducked between two houses as the officer converged on them, but Genna spun on his heel, leveled his shotgun at the oncoming policeman's chest, and pulled the trigger. Both barrels were empty, something that had no time to register before Sweeney fired and hit the Sicilian in the thigh.

Genna cried out, turned, and lumbered down the passageway next to 5941 Artesian Avenue. Knowing that Sweeney's next bullet might end up in his skull, he used his shotgun to smash the basement window in a house belonging to Mrs.

Eleanor Knoblauch. He was crawling into the dim, dirty room just as Sweeney arrived, accompanied by off-duty policeman Albert Richert, who had seen the shooting from his seat on a Western Avenue streetcar, and retired officer George Oakey, whose wife had observed the violence and alerted him. The trio broke down the cellar door and confronted Genna, who was bleeding heavily from a damaged femoral artery. He managed to squeeze off a single shot from a .38 gripped in his fist before collapsing and submitting to capture. When an ambulance arrived to take him to the Bridewell Hospital, he used the last remnants of his strength to kick one of the ambulance attendants in the face. He died soon after from blood loss, his body going to Donovan's Morgue.

A flivver squad that had been dispatched to the scene of the shooting hauled Scalise and Anselmi off of a Western Avenue streetcar. Punches were thrown before the Genna hitmen were brought under control and dragged to the station looking like disaster survivors. Reaction to the slaughter of two police officers and the serious wounding of a third was fast and violent. While Chief Schoemaker and Captain Stege were interviewing the battered Sicilians, Officer John Olson, brother of one of the victims, burst into the New City station. "I'm going to shoot my brother's murderer," he shouted as he lunged at the prisoners, and only swift intervention prevented him from carrying out the threat.[35]

A Little Italy resident identified only as "prominent" informed detectives that June 13 would have been Mike Genna's last day on earth even had Conway's squad not intercepted him with fatal results. Scalise and Anselmi had defected to Capone days earlier and were taking their former boss for a one-way ride under the guise of stalking the enemy.[36] The murder twins' open affiliation with Capone after the house of Genna had completely crumbled caused this tip to bear up under scrutiny and gave rise to speculation that Capone gunners, and not North Siders, had chased Angelo to his doom in May. Both Capone and Weiss had strong reasons to see the viperish family annihilated: the North Siders wanted revenge, and Capone coveted control of the Unione and the profitable Little Italy alky-cooking industry,[37] both of which could have enabled the Gennas to take a future stand against him.

On July 8 Tony Genna appeared in front of Charles Cutilla's grocery store on Grand Avenue, in response to a call from Giuseppe Nerone, another of the Genna torpedoes, and one whom he still trusted. As the two men shook hands, a third man stepped from a nearby doorway, automatic in hand, and sent five bullets into Tony's back at close range. The dapper Genna crumpled to the sidewalk while Nerone and the assassin fled.

At Cook County Hospital, Sam Genna pleaded with the dying man to cooperate with the authorities. "Tell the police," he implored. "It's the only hope for me and my kids. Otherwise they kill us too."[38] Gladys Bagwell, Tony's mistress, was also there, imploring. Angelo's widow, Lucille, and two female cousins looked on silently, numb with shock and grief.

Assistant State's Attorney Sbarbaro, who spoke Italian, waited by Tony's bedside for him to speak. When Genna smiled and managed a weak "Hello," Sbarbaro asked, "Who shot you?"

"The gang. Americans. I'd tell you if I knew, but I don't."

He was lying, and the attorney knew it. After the deaths of Angelo and Mike, Tony Genna would never have gone to Grand and Curtis for someone he did not trust or at the very least know.

Succumbing to the pleas from his brother and sweetheart, Genna murmured, "Il Cavaliere," a moniker that police guard John Delaurentis might not recognize but which surely would have meant something to Sam. The officer present thought the name was "Cavallaro," so a fruitless search was ordered for any Sicilian of that name.

Tony Genna finally died at 4:30 p.m., six hours after the fatal attack. After he was buried next to Angelo at Mount Carmel, his surviving brothers dispersed, in fear for their lives.

Pete and Sam went into hiding with their families. Jim Genna boarded a ship for Italy, taking a hefty percentage of the fortune he and his brothers had amassed over the years. He rented a swanky apartment on the Via Monte Grappa in Rome and was a conspicuous sight in the city nightclubs and restaurants, tossing money about like confetti. By November 1925 he was back in Sicily, where he stole the jewels adorning the celebrated Madonna di Trapani statue. Genna was arrested for the theft in Rome in January 1926 and sentenced to two years at hard labor.[39] Upon release, he returned to Chicago and settled in Calumet City, where he engaged in low-level bootlegging. Genna's health took a turn for the worse in 1930, and at the time of his death in November 1931, he had been an invalid for months.[40]

Pete and Sam Genna also went briefly to Sicily, only to return to Chicago and assume lives of comparative obscurity. They were included in routine questioning roundups whenever major gangland killings took place, but authorities viewed them as faded powers. In July 1931 Sam Genna received a bit of unwanted and bizarre publicity when light shining through his lace curtain at 1023 South Ashland Avenue threw a pattern on the brick wall at house 1105, creating a human-like image that a semi-hysterical crowd interpreted as a religious miracle. Genna was astounded to behold hundreds of people, as well as ice cream and hot dog vendors, milling outside his house and responded to a reporter inquiry with, "Miracle? I don't know anything about it. Get out."[41] Pete died in hospital in 1948 after a lingering illness; Sam expired three years later, in 1951. Nicola Genna, the mysterious seventh brother whose long-ago decision to remain in his native Marsala rescued his name from notoriety, lived out his remaining days in obscurity.

Samoots Amatuna, who may have scorned North Sider backing in his bid for the Unione presidency, made a play for the post in his own spectacular, Alterie-esque style. He enhanced his eligibility by becoming engaged to Mike Merlo's niece Rose Pecorara, and overrode the opposition by walking into the Unione headquarters with two decidedly non-Italians backing him up (freelance bootlegger Abraham

"Bummy" Goldstein and West Side saloonkeeper Eddie Zion) and announcing himself as Angelo Genna's successor.

Capone didn't trust Amatuna any more than he did the Gennas, and he fumed at yet another obstacle to the seating of Tony Lombardo. On November 10, 1925, one year to the day after O'Banion died in his flower shop, Amatuna visited Isadore Paul's barbershop on Roosevelt Road, wanting a shave before he took Rose Pecorara and another couple to hear *Aïda*. Just as he was getting out of the chair, two men entered and fired several shots, one of which inflicted a fatal neck wound. Amatuna clung to life for three days before succumbing to the injury.

Eddie Zion attended the funeral, only to be shot and killed on his way home. Three days later someone used a stolen police shotgun to blow away Bummy Goldstein. Underworld rumor supposedly pegged Vincent Drucci and the West Side O'Donnells' Jim Doherty as the duo who wounded the freshly shaven Amatuna, which might have been plausible in Drucci's case after Amatuna set him up for the Congress Street shotgun assault. But the subsequent deaths of Zion and Goldstein, who had done nothing to cross swords with the North Siders, suggest that the Unione office takeover was the motive for the triple killing.

Capone was the one who truly gained from these three murders. The deaths of Amatuna and any followers who might attempt a reprisal cleared the way to his vicarious control of the Unione and Little Italy through Tony Lombardo. According to author Robert Schoenberg, Amatuna's nephew confided to crime historian Bill Balsamo that it was common knowledge in the family that Capone had ordered his uncle put out of the way.[42]

In addition to the Amatuna hit, Vincent Drucci was named as a suspect in Tony Genna's murder, although the theory did not make sense, for nothing Drucci could have said would have persuaded the brainy Genna to meet him alone, even in broad daylight. The call went out to pick him up for questioning. Chief of Detectives Schoemaker located him as he was entering the Criminal Court Building and placed him under arrest when a revolver was found inside his coat pocket.

Drucci was the first gangster to be tried under a new anti-gun law which imposed heavy punishment for carrying concealed weapons.[43] The prior law, known as the Sadler Act, only imposed a maximum penalty of one year in jail. If convicted under the new legislation, Drucci could be sentenced to a year in the county jail or fined $300, or both. If he had a previous conviction for a felony such as murder or manslaughter, the sentence could be upped to one to ten years in Joliet and a heavier fine.[44]

He was booked on a charge of carrying concealed weapons but walked free after posting a $200 bond. He ended up being fined $300 by Judge Howard Hayes[45] but seemed amused by the entire episode—until Chief of Detectives Schoemaker made a point of searching him on sight. As Drucci was leaving the courthouse on October 28, Schoemaker intercepted him and patted him down in full view of an interested crowd. The Sicilian gangster protested, "Is this Russia?" A police official confirmed to the press that the chief intended to frisk Drucci every time they met.[46]

As a precautionary measure, he avoided carrying a gun himself for months, delegating that responsibility to a bodyguard. But the shadow of harassment made his fuse shorter than normal. On November 14, 1925, he entered the Cadillac Motor Car Company on South Michigan Avenue and asked to use the telephone. When employee David Ziedman refused, citing that the phone was not a public one, Drucci stormed outside, where friend and bodyguard Michael "Puggy" White sat in his car, and asked him for his pistol. The North Sider gripped the weapon tightly by the barrel, strode back into the office, and struck Ziedman repeatedly in the head, leaving scalp injuries that required treatment at Mercy Hospital.[47]

Scalise and Anselmi went to trial for the murder of Detective Olson in the fall of 1925, their legal team and other expenses covered by a "defense fund" that had been extracted from Little Italy residents. Attorneys Thomas Nash, Michael Ahern, and Patrick O'Donnell argued that their clients had been defending themselves against unwarranted police aggression. Ahern stated, "If a police officer detains you, even for a moment, and you kill him, you are not guilty of murder but only of manslaughter. If the police officer uses force of arms, you may kill him in self-defense and emerge from the law unscathed."[48]

The press and State's Attorney Crowe had a field day with that remark, although Ahern was correct when it came to confrontations with officers who neither had a warrant nor probable cause to suspect that a detainee had committed a crime. Crowe charged that taking such a view seriously was an open invitation to murder policemen. When Judge Brothers instructed the bailiff during the course of the trial, "If anyone in the courtroom is disorderly, arrest him at once," Crowe piped up sarcastically, "Without a warrant, Your Honor?"[49]

The jury, persuaded by Ahern's merciless logic, returned a verdict of manslaughter and specified a fourteen-year prison sentence. Three months later, Scalise and Anselmi stood trial for the killing of Officer Walsh. When Assistant State's Attorney Gorman told the courtroom, "Either this is a hanging case or a case of justifiable homicide," the jury weighed its options and found the duo not guilty. That verdict signaled an imminent end to their imprisonment.

In December 1926 the Illinois Supreme Court granted Scalise and Anselmi a retrial for Olson's killing, and in June 1927 they were found not guilty. They walked free, to the dismay of the victims' families and the satisfaction of Capone, who welcomed them into his growing Syndicate. Two years later, he would realize his mistake in trusting the murder twins and correct it violently, but in 1927 Capone cherished them as valuable weapons in the war with the opposition.

The year 1925 nearly stained the Chicago air permanently with gunsmoke. Capone and/or the North Siders decimated the Genna family tree. North Sider gunfire took John Torrio out of the game and compelled Capone to order an armored car for his own protection. Spike O'Donnell soared back into action, importing New Jersey gunman Henry Hassmiller and taking on both the Sheldon and Saltis–McErlane gangs. The bodies piled up: the slain Genna brothers, Hassmiller and Spike's brother Walter in June, two Sheldon men outside the gang's clubhouse in October, Samoots Amatuna in November, and three Saltis–McErlane followers in a gun battle in McKeone's saloon at the end of the same month. Three days before Christmas, Ragen's Colts members Joey Brooks and Edward Harmening were found in the back seat of the latter's car in Marquette Park. Their murders were thought to be Frank McErlane's bullet butchery, committed in retaliation for the attack on McKeone's.

On September 25 McErlane introduced the Thompson submachine gun to Chicago as a gangster signature weapon. O'Banion had brought one machine gun from Colorado in 1924, but the fate of that particular weapon is unknown. On that night, Spike was chatting with a newsboy in front of a South Side drugstore when he heard his name called. He turned, saw an approaching car, and reacted on pure instinct, throwing both the boy and himself to the pavement. A shotgun shattered the drugstore window just before McErlane let loose with the machine gun. It left a row of bullet holes just below the window, missing O'Donnell but sending Chicago's veteran reporters into a guessing frenzy as to what kind of weapon could leave such a shot pattern. One scribe suggested that it had been some sort of machine rifle, while another guessed that a firing squad blasting in perfect union had left the damage.

The Thompson weighed about twenty pounds when loaded and could fire eight hundred rounds per minute. It had been intended for use during the Great War, but the Armistice had been signed before the guns could be shipped overseas and they ended up being sold domestically. O'Donnell came close to being its first Chicago victim, a dubious honor that ended up going to Charles Kelly on October 4. Frank McErlane sped past the Ragen Athletic Club, the headquarters of the Ralph Sheldon gang, and riddled it with machine-gun fire, killing Kelly and wounding Thomas Hart.

In the fall of 1925, while the fighting was reaching its peak, Weiss and McCarthy came home from the McHenry County Jail. Weiss intended to pick up the threads of battle, but McCarthy had come to the conclusion that, as close as he had been to O'Banion, he had no stomach for the gang war that had reached a boiling point. He was no coward and had few qualms about meeting adversity with gunplay, but thumping and shooting stubborn union officials was a safer career bet than going toe to toe with Capone and his gunmen.

McCarthy eased himself out of the North Side Gang's inner circle, being careful not to break ties with his former colleagues completely. He maintained control of the Journeyman Plumbers Union and gave George Moran advice about union maintenance and control three years later, when the North Siders were keeping the Central Cleaning Company out of the clutches of the Master Cleaners and Dyers Association. In 1931 a city plumbing inspector named Albert Courchene vocally opposed the Plumbers' current officers and declared his intent to push for a new lineup in the upcoming election. A few days later, three men in a small black sedan that bore no license plates fired fourteen bullets from a submachine gun into Courchene's body as he was directing the work of two plumbers in a building basement. McCarthy was picked up and questioned but released for lack of evidence.[50]

Nineteen twenty-five broke Cook County's previous record for violent deaths, with a total of 389 killings. Not all of them were "beer war casualties," as the press termed them, but enough gangsters and bootleggers contributed to the final tally to suggest that Prohibition, rather than enable law and order, was leading to its irreversible decline. There was no sign that 1926 would be any better.

Three days into the New Year, a scowling Vincent Drucci stormed into Myrtle Fels's dress shop at 515 Diversey Parkway. Fels had accused him of breaking into her establishment the previous Thursday and stealing $5,000 worth of goods. How she came by her information or whether it was indeed accurate are not known, but when Drucci heard the allegations, he was furious. When he arrived at Fels's shop with a husky blond woman at his side, there were seven customers inside, an inconvenience that he dealt with by drawing his pistol and herding them to the rear of the business.[51]

"Now," he said to his blond companion, "do your stuff. Get Myrtle."

The woman lunged at Fels, who was cringing near a display, grabbed her by the hair, and punched her repeatedly in the face, hissing that the proprietress had better change her story about Drucci, or else. When Fels crumpled to the floor, Drucci signaled that the punishment was sufficient and pocketed his pistol. He and the "lady slugger" walked out of the shop and into a waiting cab. Some customers fled while others helped the bruised woman to her feet. Not desiring a repeat performance, Myrtle Fels recanted her accusation the first chance she got.

While the North Siders dealt with an indiscreet dressmaker, Little Italy exploded with violence after months of resentful simmering. Samoots Amatuna had sent the likes of Orazio "the Scourge" Tropea around in 1925 to intimidate the residents into donating money to Scalise and Anselmi's defense fund. Now a second collection was necessary to cover the costs of the murder twins' trial for killing Officer Walsh, and the Scourge, a lean, hawk-faced individual whom the more superstitious Italians accused of possessing the Evil Eye, began knocking on doors again. Tropea may have intended to keep a portion of the proceeds for himself, making him take refusals more personally this time around. On January 10 Angelo Genna's brother-in-law Henry Spingola was shot dead, followed by the double murder of pasta manufacturers Agostino and Antonio Morici.[52]

It was too much. On the night of February 15 Tropea's Evil Eye was closed forever by a shotgun slug issued from a passing sedan. His henchmen and fellow collectors went down one by one in the ensuing weeks. Vito Bascone was found in a Stickney ditch on February 21, a bullet hole between his eyes and the index fingers of both hands shot off, presumably as he raised them in a last defensive gesture. Two nights later, Ecola Baldelli was found dead in an ash heap in a North Side alley, his body bearing the gory signs of a pre-mortem beating.[53] Those who survived assassination attempts, such as Filippo Gnolfo, went into hiding.[54]

While Little Italy continued the decimation job that either Capone or the North Siders (or both) had started the previous spring, Klondike O'Donnell and his West Side followers rose up against their former partner and began pushing O'Donnell beer into Capone's Cicero saloons.

Capone, who had been in New York over Christmas in order to be by his son's side when the boy underwent surgery for a life-threatening mastoid infection, came home to find Chicago gradually going up in gunsmoke. The Sheldon and Saltis–McErlane forces continued to fling bombs and fire guns at each other, and Little Italy was a shooting gallery. Although none of these combatants made advances on Capone's territory, therefore requiring no retaliation from the Syndicate, Klondike O'Donnell may have interpreted the failure to quell the violence as a sign that Capone was weakening and not likely to crack down on interlopers as harshly as before.

Encouraged, he sent experienced "salesmen" like Jim Doherty, Myles O'Donnell, and James "Fur" Sammon into Cicero saloons provisioned by Capone and made them O'Donnell customers under threat of bodily harm. The O'Donnells also allegedly opened a Cicero handbook that siphoned away $5,000 worth of Capone's gambling action per day. It was a paltry loss considering that his Cicero gaming interests took in over $3 million per year, but such a maneuver was an unhealthy example of defiance that could inspire others and create a real problem later.[55]

Something would have to be done about the O'Donnell situation—after the April 13 primary. The Chicago gangs concentrated their resources on getting Robert Crowe's list of candidates elected. A cease-fire for this purpose now would ensure that once warfare resumed later, the threat of punishment from official quarters would be nullified.

An April 10, 1926, edition of the *Tribune* warned against would-be election violence: "Ballot box stealing and other forms of lawlessness will be strictly taboo at the primary election polls next Tuesday if orders issued to the police force yesterday are successfully carried out." Morgan Collins assured voters that the entire force would be on duty for twelve-hour shifts and special details would be assigned to each polling place, ready to halt trouble.[56]

The underworld was not worried. Minutes after the polls opened at 6 a.m. on April 13, gangsters entered the polling station of the Fourteenth Precinct of the Twenty-fourth Ward, grabbed election judge Barney Ehrlich and drove him around town, kicking and slugging him every minute of the ride. After they threw him out of the car at 3437 West Roosevelt Road, he understandably refused to return to his post, and a new judge had to be appointed.[57]

North Side gunmen invaded and took possession of a voting station at 416 West Chicago Avenue. Joseph Caleva, one of the Republican election judges, was forced into a car at gunpoint as he was stepping out for lunch and held captive for nearly six hours. After being robbed of $30, he shakily made his way back to the station, where he learned that gangsters had terrorized his colleagues. Margaret Kipp, the Democratic election judge at that location, later testified that she had been forced to sign false returns. Democratic worker James O'Neill was stabbed and shot in the face in front of a polling place on West Grand Avenue, near the home of Weiss's brother-in-law James Monahan.[58]

Gangsters in three automobiles converged on a voting site on West Madison Street. They had been alerted that a repeat voter had been arrested there, and in the process of rescuing him, they shot the place up, kicked ballot boxes over, and seriously wounded the arresting officer, Charles Saxon. County Judge Edmund Jarecki, who had sent Chicago cops to Cicero's aid in 1924, appealed to Chief Collins for additional policemen to guard the polls. "We have received more than twenty complaints of violence and intimidation in that ward [where Saxon was shot]," he said.[59]

Hymie Weiss, North Sider Frank Foster, and two others went to a polling place at 752 North Wells Street. Foster had been with the North Siders for years. According to Howard Browne, author of the novel *Pork City*, Foster was born Ferdinand Bruna to Romanian parents who settled in San Francisco upon arrival in America. Other sources[60] claim that his birth name was actually Citro, that he was of Sicilian descent and had a brother, John Citro, who was affiliated in business with the departed Samoots Amatuna. He had a minor record—a disorderly conduct charge in 1920 and two days in the House of Correction and a fine of $100 plus costs for driving drunk in 1925.[61] He had been indicted for murder in 1924, but the charges were later dropped.

When election judge Francis Perry recognized Foster and refused to let him vote under the fictitious name of Hoffman, Weiss drew a revolver. Policeman Edward Russell, noticing trouble, headed for the booth. The North Siders fled, but Perry managed to tackle Foster and hold him. Russell arrested Weiss but allowed the other two to go when no weapons were found on them. Both Foster and Weiss were, predictably, discharged in court the next day.

Drucci did his part by leading a gang of gunmen to a booth on Rush Street and punctuating his threats with bullets.[62]

When a poll watcher tried to interfere during an assault on a policeman by West Side O'Donnell thug Jim Doherty, he was stopped by none other than Assistant

State's Attorney William McSwiggin. "Keep your mouth shut," the attorney warned, implying that to do otherwise was a ticket to jail. The precinct worker blinked in shock, for McSwiggin was a legend in Robert Crowe's stable of sixty-nine assistants, having been responsible for seven of the eleven first-degree murder verdicts that Crowe's office had scored in 1925.[63] Of course, none of those convicted had been big-league gangsters.

McSwiggin had questioned Al Capone in May 1924, after Capone killed a small-time bootlegger and thug named Joe Howard for slapping around his buddy and financial advisor Jake Guzik. He was also one of the first on the scene when O'Banion was murdered, and had prosecuted John Scalise and Albert Anselmi for the murder of Officer Harold Olson. He may never have sent a gangster to jail or the gallows, but the public appreciated him for appearing to try.

McSwiggin's threat made sense two weeks later, on April 27. That night, Capone received word that a carload of West Side O'Donnell men had been seen driving along Roosevelt Road, and he seized the opportunity to pull Klondike back into line. He assembled a hunting expedition of five cars and went out looking for the enemy, intending to nullify their threat once and for all.

They spotted Jim Doherty's green Lincoln outside the Pony Inn, a watering hole belonging to O'Donnell ancillary Harry Madigan at 5613–5615 Roosevelt Road, and opened fire. The gunners figured that they'd hit someone, probably multiple someones, but the casualty list did not become public until the next day. Among the dead were Jim Doherty; Thomas "Red" Duffy, a bootlegger and Thirtieth Ward precinct captain; and Assistant State's Attorney William McSwiggin.

Twenty-eight bullets tore away the west wall of the Pony Inn and fragmented a tree in front. Five bullets lodged in Red Duffy's body as he was stepping out of the Lincoln; he crawled painfully into an empty lot next to the inn to hide, and died at a hospital after a passing motorist found him and took him in. Jim Doherty fell to the sidewalk with sixteen bullet holes in his body. McSwiggin made it to one of the inn's entrances before collapsing. The ravaged car's other occupants, Myles O'Donnell and driver Edward Hanley, dragged the bodies of Doherty and McSwiggin into the vehicle and drove away. Both corpses were later stripped of identification and dumped in Berwyn. The blood-spattered Lincoln was abandoned in Oak Park.[64]

McSwiggin, who lived at home with his parents and four sisters, had been close friends with both Doherty and Duffy since childhood and saw their diverging career paths as no reason to break off the comradeship. His father, Sergeant Anthony McSwiggin, a veteran officer with thirty years' experience, begged his son to reconsider his shadier associations, all to no avail. The young assistant state's attorney did prosecute Myles O'Donnell and Jim Doherty for the November 1924 murder of Eddie Tancl, but their acquittal came as no surprise to anyone.

Robert Crowe attempted damage control by telling the press that his murdered assistant had been doing undercover work in relation to another case they were investigating. "When he [McSwiggin] was on a case, he worked twenty-four hours a day. I am sure he was in Cicero seeking evidence against Martin Durkin, who hid there for some time after he killed Edwin Shanahan. It was his big case, and he went there despite the fact that he knew there were numerous enemies he had made in his prosecutions."[65]

The explanation proved embarrassingly weak when additional details came to light, such as McSwiggin's visit to Capone at the Hawthorne Hotel after the April primary. Sergeant McSwiggin admitted that the meeting had taken place but refused to divulge details. "If I told what that business was, I'd blow the lid off Chicago. This case is loaded with dynamite. It's dangerous to talk about it." Capone was less reticent. "Of course I didn't kill him. Why should I? I liked the kid. Only the day before he was up to my place and I gave him a bottle of scotch for his old man."

Five grand juries failed to bring the killers to justice. The public gradually came to understand that McSwiggin, although a brilliant lawyer, had not been the paragon of social justice that his office implied. Capone validated their doubts by stating, "I paid McSwiggin. I paid him a lot, and I got what I was paying for."

"Those shots were never meant for my boy," Anthony McSwiggin claimed when he first learned about the tragedy.[66] Capone could second that. He'd had no idea that the young prosecutor was one of the green Lincoln's passengers, had not even gotten a good look at him during the attack, although the story made the rounds that Capone had indeed seen the attorney and mistaken him for Hymie Weiss, whom McSwiggin was said to casually resemble.

Capone went into hiding, fearing, and with good reason, that the police would shoot him on sight. While the press cried, "Who killed McSwiggin?" the Chicago police under Morgan Collins and William Schoemaker attacked Capone-owned brothels and gambling joints, going as far as to acquire county deputy status so that they could damage his holdings in Stickney, Forest View, and Berwyn. They cost him an estimated $1 million in property damage and lost revenue before the fervor subsided.

It wasn't until July 28 that Capone agreed to surrender himself for questioning. He met federal agents at the Illinois–Indiana state line, and after appearing briefly in Chief Justice Thomas Lynch's court, was freed due to lack of evidence. William Schoemaker was frustrated but philosophical.

"I am satisfied that Capone was at the bottom of these murders," he said. "But it is one thing to be satisfied in your own mind and another to prove it beyond a reasonable doubt."[67]

Exactly.

In May 1926, while Capone was still a refugee from police interrogation, George Moran's old benefactor, Major M. A. Messlein, saw his stock-selling scheme become public knowledge and the subject of an investigation headed by Attorney General Oscar E. Carlstrom and State's Attorney Crowe. Included in the spotlight were Will Colvin, head of the board of pardons and paroles; Moran himself; fellow parolee Walter Stevens; and numerous others.[68]

Crowe and Carlstrom got their first break in the case when Lucas Pollack, whose nephew Ralph Steiner had been sent to Joliet for auto theft in 1923, came to them with an incredible story. He was casually acquainted with Joseph "Yellow Kid" Weil, a well-known con artist, and through Weil learned that Messlein was the key to Steiner's release.

"He said to me," Pollack recounted, "'Oh, go and see my friend Major Messlein. He can fix you up.' So I went to Messlein's engineering office and talked to him about it. He made several trips to Springfield, he told me, and I paid all his expenses. I presented his wife with an expensive beaded handbag."

Messlein showed Pollack a prospectus for his company, which listed Will Colvin as a shareholder, and explained that recipients of pardons and paroles usually bought stock in the corporation. When Pollack mentioned this to Weil, the Yellow Kid told him not to buy any stock, that he would ask Messlein to intercede as a personal favor. The major came through, and Steiner was released.

While Messlein strenuously denied that he required stock purchase as a prelude to parole, investigators from the state's attorney's office went through his records and found, among other incriminating documents, a copy of a letter from Will Colvin to O'Banion's old partner William Schofield. Dated June 24, 1924, and headed "Subject: Michael Cunningham, No. 5219, Joliet," it read:

> My dear Mr. Schofield,
> I regret I did not know you came to the Joliet prison today upon the invitation of Major Messlein. The Cunningham case has been reviewed time and again. The last review was in April of this year, when a no change order was entered.
> Under ordinary circumstances it would be too soon to again review the case in June.
> However, if it had been called to my attention that you were here upon the invitation of Major Messlein, I would have been glad to give you such time as you desired to discuss the case.
> I am asking Major Messlein to make a personal explanation and to express my regrets over the incident.
> Very truly yours,
> Will Colvin[69]

Michael Cunningham had been indicted for the murder of one Frank Madison in Peter Reinmuller's saloon in 1916. Why Schofield was interested in obtaining his release is not known.

Moran and Walter Stevens ducked out of sight to avoid giving testimony in the inquiry. Even without their reluctant cooperation, Carlstrom and Crowe succeeded in forcing Governor Small to dismiss Colvin from his post on the parole board. It proved to be a hollow triumph, for Small gave Colvin another job, with the Illinois Commerce Commission. A *Tribune* editorial noted sarcastically:

> Mr. Small saw nothing in Colvin's relations with Messlein, nothing in the parole of droves of hardened criminals, to suggest that Colvin was anything but a fit public servant. The governor has therefore given Colvin a job with the commission which fixes streetcar fares and electric light and telephone rates throughout the state. Fortunately, the governor does not appoint the judges of the Supreme Court, which has yet to fix, finally, the sum due from Small to the state treasury.[70]

Messlein escaped indictment; he was perceived as a greedy opportunist as opposed to a public servant abusing a position of responsibility. And by 1926 more than five thousand Joliet alumni had him to thank for their freedom.

While Capone and Moran were hiding from the authorities, Weiss and Frank Foster attended a party on June 23 for Eddie Vogel, Cicero slot-machine king, at the Rienzi Hotel. Vogel's coming wedding was the impetus for the festivities, which were in full swing at the time that a deputy U.S. marshal arrived to serve a warrant on Vogel for violation of the Mann Act. Weiss ran him off at the point of a shotgun. When the marshal returned with three policemen in tow, all the revelers were gone, but they had left a liquid goldmine in Rooms 301, 302, and 303. Piled against the walls were forty-eight pints and twenty-four quarts of Cliquot champagne, jugs and bottles of whiskey, and a fifth of first-class brandy.[71]

The officers alerted Special Intelligence Officers Pat Roche and Clarence Converse, who went to the Rienzi with two Prohibition agents. They confiscated everything and charged Weiss, Foster, and Vogel with conspiracy to violate the Volstead Act.

Before leaving the premises, Converse picked up some jewelry, a gold desk pad, and an assortment of books, keys, and papers to prevent their being stolen from the deserted rooms. His thoughtful gesture gave the gangsters an idea, and in July they sued for the return of the valuables and a lot more, charging that neckties, hats, and underwear were also missing. They also demanded the return of the booze, claiming that it had been taken from a lawful residence.

The government denied all knowledge of missing underwear and such and shot down the idea that the Rienzi rooms could be legally classified as a private residence. The three defendants remained at liberty after posting $2,500 bonds; Weiss's had been signed by his Canadian partner, J. J. Stewart of Montreal.

Weiss had many such partners outside of Chicago. Since his release from the McHenry County Jail, he had been concentrating on making and strengthening contacts with bootleggers in Canada and other U.S. cities. He had a boat, the *Half*

Moon, anchored off the coast of Florida to receive and smuggle in Cuban liquor, as well as booze purchasing and transportation arrangements with counterparts in Detroit and Cleveland.

Drucci and Pete and Frank Gusenberg came to the attention of the authorities next. On July 12 the president of a New York jewelry concern, Wilbur Brown, contacted the police to report that three men had broken into his room at the Congress Hotel, tied and gagged him, and stolen $80,000 worth of jewelry from his suitcase. He cursed his bad luck, claiming that he had kept the valuables in the hotel safe until that morning, when he withdrew them and brought them to his room.

While he pored over mug shots at the detective bureau, Sergeants Frank Johnson and William Crot volunteered the information that they had seen Drucci in the vicinity of the hotel not long before the robbery. An elevator operator at the Congress identified Drucci and the Gusenbergs as passengers in his conveyance that morning.

When he got wind that he was wanted, Drucci told a reporter friend at the *Tribune* that he would give himself up to Captain Stege and take part in an identification lineup. "If I can get in touch with the others mentioned as suspects," he said, "I will have them appear at the same time." He admitted to having encountered Detectives Johnson and Crot near the Congress, but grinned, "I rarely go out on the street without meeting a policeman I know."[72]

That was not exactly true. If it were, two young boys would not have made a grisly discovery on August 3.

John and Joseph Novak, a pair of young brothers, went into a forest preserve near Ninety-third Street and 100th Avenue in Palos Township, to water their horses. When the animals shied from a particular cistern, the boys investigated, detected a human form in the murky water, and notified the police. County highway policemen from Willow Springs gingerly extracted the body of a man, aged about thirty-five by their estimation, who had been bound hand and foot and weighted with stones and bricks from the nearby ruins of a burned house. They estimated that he had been in the cistern for a month, maybe more.[73]

The dead man, who had been tortured before bullets in the skull put him out of his misery, was identified as Anthony Cuiringione, alias Ross or Rossi, Capone's chauffeur, who had replaced the wounded Sylvester Barton. He had been missing since July, which was when the North Siders abducted him with the intention of making him divulge information about Capone's daily routine. When Capone learned of the gruesome discovery, he was genuinely appalled.

"They call me heartless, eh? Ross was tortured to make him tell my business secrets. He knew nothing whatever about my affairs."[74]

On August 10 the North Siders received Capone's answer to Cuiringione's murder. That morning Drucci and Weiss had breakfast in the former's suite at the Congress Hotel, where he had taken up residence, and strolled down Michigan Avenue,

191

en route to the Standard Oil Building. Drucci was carrying $13, 200 in his pocket, which he would claim was intended for use in closing a real estate deal. In actuality he had business with Morris Eller, Chicago Sanitary District trustee and Twentieth Ward boss, who had an office in the Standard Oil Building. The day was calm, and the duo, figuring that any enemy gangsters were usually nursing hangovers at that time of morning, relaxed their customary vigilance for the walk.

When they reached Ninth Street, in the shadow of their destination, the ear-splitting screech of a suddenly halted car assailed their ears. Gunfire boomed, sending commuters scrambling for cover and bringing traffic to a standstill.

Weiss reacted instinctively and threw himself facedown on the sidewalk. Drucci ducked behind a mailbox, drew his own weapon, and returned fire, shooting blindly into Ninth Street. More than thirty bullets smashed car windows and chipped holes in concrete walls. Only one spectator, a James Cardin, received a minor wound.

Two gunmen jumped from a car jammed against the curb, pistols drawn, and closed in on Drucci, circling the mailbox in order to trap him and pick him off. Before any fatal bullets could be fired, a police car roared into view, spooking the driver of the assault vehicle. He took off, leaving his colleagues behind.

All of the targets/combatants fled, Weiss into the Standard Oil Building, one of the gunmen into the crowd. Officers caught the second gunman when he threw his gun to the pavement and bolted. He gave his name as Paul Valerie of 3533 Walnut Avenue, a nonexistent address. His real name was Louis Barko, and he was a gunner for Capone.

Drucci ran into the street and hurtled onto the running board of a car that had slowed down in the tangle of traffic. He thrust his warm pistol against the startled driver's temple and ordered, "Take me away and make it snappy." No sooner had he spoken than policemen surrounded the vehicle and hauled Drucci off. The North Sider initially reacted with a flurry of curses, but once his temper cooled, he gave his name as Frank Walsh, real estate agent. The ruse didn't work, and when confronted with his real identity, he grudgingly admitted it, but insisted that the battle had nothing to do with booze or revenge.

"It wasn't no gang fight!" he explained. "A stickup, that's all. They wanted my roll [money]."

When Louis Barko was brought before him for identification, Drucci held true to the code of the underworld, saying, "Never saw him before." Barko went free, and Drucci was arrested on charges of carrying concealed weapons and assault with intent to kill. Mary Weiss, Hymie's mother, signed the $5,000 bond required for him to evade jail.

E. D. Jackson, a self-styled cowboy who had recently traveled from Wyoming to Chicago to perform in a rodeo, witnessed the entire episode from start to finish. He could barely curb his enthusiasm. "I sure wish I'd had a gun," he said. "This is more fun than I've seen since I left Wyoming."[75]

One of the earliest hints of a North Side Gang/Saltis–McErlane alliance became public on September 17, 1926,[76] when a police squad led by Lieutenants John Sullivan and Joseph McGuire came across George Moran, Frank Gusenberg, Vincent McErlane (brother of Frank) and Charles George as the quartet was lingering in front of the Commonwealth Hotel at Diversey Parkway and Pine Grove Avenue. Following Captain Stege's general directive to arrest known gangsters "on suspicion," the officers patted down foursome and found revolvers on McErlane and George.

"The McErlane–Saltis crowd has disintegrated, scattered, with its leaders . . . in jail awaiting trial for murder," Stege told the press when news of the mass arrest spread. "There has been a consolidation, probably brought around by Vincent McErlane, with the remnants of the old O'Banion gang on the North Side."

Moran and Gusenberg walked free after their lawyer, Milton D. Smith, filed a petition for a writ of habeas corpus before Judge Lindsay. McErlane and George were charged with carrying concealed weapons but were never prosecuted.

Just as Capone had allied with Sheldon during the South Side turf wars, the North Siders forged a connection with the Saltis–McErlane crew. Joe Saltis had done enough to make Weiss agreeable to a partnership. On July 14 he had supposedly arranged a one-way ride for Jules Portuguese, by then a Ralph Sheldon adherent,[77] whose car had been used in O'Banion's murder. Because Portuguese was a jewel thief, the police initially supposed that he had been killed as the result of a fight over the division of the jewels stolen from Wilbur Brown at the Congress Hotel, the same crime attributed to Vincent Drucci and the Gusenbergs.[78] There was also the old adage that any enemy of Capone was a friend of Weiss, and Capone's support of Sheldon did not endear him to Saltis and McErlane.

The North Siders, in the process of building up and strengthening their organization, made other alliances during this period, one of which they never would have considered in less precarious days.

It was with Jack Zuta, a Polish-born[79] vicemonger from the West Side who made the acquaintance of Moran and Drucci through Billy Skidmore. They despised Zuta as a pimp and he knew it, but they did value his uncanny financial acumen and tolerated him as a business advisor, the North Side's equivalent of Capone's bookkeeping genius Jake Guzik. Zuta for his part was soft, a physical coward incapable of intimidating anyone save nerve-wrecked prostitutes (again, not dissimilar to Guzik), so he welcomed an open association with the hard-hitting North Siders.

Zuta had been running a chain of brothels and saloons on the West Side even before Prohibition. His resorts at the Home, Newport, Florence, and Harvard hotels were rarely raided, thanks to his political connections, although Robert Crowe had recommended them for closure in a 1921 vice report.[80] He'd had some trouble with local authorities; in January 1925, James Bell, whom Zuta had detailed to guard a resort at Randolph and Green streets, shot and killed another black man in an alley beside the building. Zuta was arrested for supplying the gun to Bell, but the charge was dropped.[81] He may have been a pimp, but he was a pimp with pull, making him someone the North Siders could use.

Capone only had to wait a month for Weiss's response to the Standard Oil Building ambush. On September 20 he and bodyguard Frank Rio were sipping coffee in the Hawthorne Restaurant, three doors away from the Hawthorne Hotel. It was 1:15 p.m., and both men were killing time until 2:30, when the first race of the day was scheduled at the nearby track. On the street outside, cars belonging to other racing buffs lined the curb and attendees strolled on the sidewalk, browsing their programs and adopting an air of leisure.

Suddenly, the intrusive sound of rapid gunfire chattered in the distance, gradually becoming louder. Rio and Capone listened as the firing noise, accompanied by the brassy clanging of a police gong, intensified until it sounded as if it were coming from outside the café door, then faded into silence, leaving a deserted street and bewildered, scared citizens wondering what had been afoot.

Capone got slowly to his feet and headed for the doorway. Rio, however, suspected that the worst was yet to come and pulled his boss down seconds before the worst arrived.

Several sedans[82] drove down West Twenty-second Street, each one loaded with men and high-powered weapons. The occupants opened fire as soon as the lead car drew up to the Anton Hotel, and they continued blasting as the motorcade rolled to a halt outside the restaurant. Chairs scraped on the tile floor and cutlery rattled as the restaurant patrons dropped to the floor. Those who had ventured cautiously back into the street after the first car whipped past threw themselves to the pavement or ducked behind parked cars.

Hundreds of bullets tore into the exteriors of the Hawthorne Hotel, the café, and the adjacent buildings, smashing windows and opening the interiors to near-complete demolition. Plaster fragments, shattered light fixtures, and destroyed porcelain cups and plates rained onto the backs of those hugging the diner floor.

One of the doors on the next-to-last car in the procession opened, discharging a man in overalls and a khaki shirt. While his comrades covered him with pointed weapons, he knelt on the sidewalk in front of the restaurant, aimed his machine gun, and squeezed off a hundred rounds into the silent café in less than ten seconds. After destroying almost everything that had survived the first fusillade, he returned to his car and got in. A horn blew three times, motors chugged back to life, and the procession continued east, back toward Chicago. It was later estimated that more than a thousand rounds had been fired from start to finish.

Amazingly, only four people suffered any real injury. A racing buff from Louisiana was sitting in his car when the shooting began, and a bullet grazed his knee. His small son's scalp was scraped by another shot, and glass from the family vehicle's shattered windshield lodged in his wife's eye. Capone, taking responsibility for the attack clearly meant for him, paid to save the woman's sight and compensated the owners of all the businesses along the block that had been damaged.

The fourth wounded party was Louis Barko, the Capone gunman who had tangled with Drucci outside the Standard Oil Building the month before. He had been entering the Hawthorne Hotel when the strike force came calling, and he survived the attack with minor neck and shoulder wounds. Adhering to the gangster code of silence/ignorance, he viewed Drucci and the other North Siders in a police lineup afterward and denied seeing them that day.

The boldness and violence of this daylight attack unnerved everyone, even the police who were accustomed to investigating the aftermath of gang skirmishing. No one doubted that the North Siders were responsible: glass and brick fragments were still littering the sidewalks when a call went out to pick up Weiss, Drucci, Moran, and the Gusenbergs. Others slated for questioning were Vincent McErlane, Frank Foster, the Applequist brothers, Drucci's pal Puggy White, and Dingbat Oberta.[83]

The police responded to the act of deadly audacity by clamping down on gangland businesses again, forcibly closing speakeasies and gambling spots that Capone had slowly built back up after the heat generated by McSwiggin's death. Something had to be done, before the authorities were enraged and embarrassed beyond the point of no return.

It was time to put to use more of the lessons Capone had learned from Torrio. Through an emissary he sent word to Weiss that he wanted to talk peace. The North Sider agreed to a sit-down at the Hotel Sherman on October 4 and met with Tony Lombardo, president of the Unione Siciliana since the murder of Samoots Amatuna. Lombardo was authorized to offer the North Siders any peace terms within reason, but what Weiss wanted, Capone would not consent to: the murders of Scalise and Anselmi.

The Sicilian torpedoes were still in Joliet in October 1926, but all that could really amount to was a stay of execution until their appeals got them released. When an uncomfortable Lombardo phoned Capone with Weiss's terms and requested further instructions, he was given a message to pass on: "I wouldn't do that to a yellow dog."

Bloodshed was what it would take to end the abductions, the daylight shootings, the explosive street battles, the daily threat of murder. It just remained to be seen whose blood signaled the final outrage.

Weeks before the Hotel Sherman showdown, a young man appeared on the doorstep of a boarding house at 740 North State Street, directly beside Schofield's. The three-story stone building belonged to Harry Stephen Keeler, best-selling author, but the man seemed more interested in obtaining accommodations than admiring the house's connection to celebrity. He politely requested a room overlooking the street, but when the landlady, Anna Rotariu, told him that all were occupied, he consented to take a hall room until one with a front view became available.

While the man was moving his few belongings into the threadbare room, an attractive young woman who gave her name as Mrs. Thomas Schultz from Mitchell, South Dakota, showed up at another boarding house, this one at 1 East Superior Street, and rented a room whose window overlooked the front of Schofield's as well as the alley behind.

Weiss was too busy to pay attention to who was moving in and out of the neighborhood in September. He made a brief trip to Montreal, Quebec, soon after Labor Day, and came back with a bigger souvenir than intended: flaxen-haired, French Canadian singer and dancer Josephine Simard. She would later tell friends and reporters that she and Weiss had gone to Florida after leaving Montreal and married there, but would never be able to prove to anyone's satisfaction that the union was a legal one.

The two moved into a luxury suite at the Congress Hotel, where they kept other guests on their floor entertained with lively arguments and late-night parties. Josephine, who performed under the stage name Josephine Libby, was the perfect foil for Weiss's serious, aggressive demeanor, being bubbly and easygoing. Their disputes, a natural outcome of two hyperkinetic individuals living together, sounded more serious than they really were, and the union was a happy one.[84]

The North Side leader was also preoccupied with the upcoming murder trial of his ally Joe Saltis. On August 6 Saltis had struck out at Ralph Sheldon yet again by killing labor official John "Mitters" Foley, one of Sheldon's beer-runners, near Sixty-fifth and Richmond streets. Two witnesses who refused to be intimidated saw him do it, and Foley's seventeen-year-old brother, Thomas, blurted, "Joe was my brother's most dangerous enemy!"[85] Now he and henchman Frank "Lefty" Koncil were facing a murder trial.

Frank McErlane was in jail, fighting extradition to Indiana, so Hymie Weiss stepped in to pull the strings necessary to get Saltis and Koncil off. Special prosecutor Charles McDonald was dismayed, but not really surprised, when witnesses began switching their original testimony and dodging court appearances, and files in his office bore the signs of after-dark perusal. Weiss was spending an estimated $100,000 to ensure Saltis's acquittal, and that kind of money threw up roadblocks that made McDonald doubt that justice would prevail.

On October 8 Oscar Lundin received the good news that a room with a window overlooking State Street was now available. He moved in, paying the landlady a week's rent in advance. Down the street, Mrs. Schultz made a similar advance payment. She and Lundin then vanished, yielding their rooms to strangers whom the landladies, strangely, did not confront or question. Mrs. Rotariu recognized the two new tenants as friends of Lundin and probably did not care who stayed in the room as long as the rent was paid regularly, while two men of apparently Italian descent took over Mrs. Schultz's accommodations.

On October 11 Weiss and his colleagues lingered about the Criminal Court Building, watching the gradual process of jury selection for the Saltis–Koncil trial. When court adjourned for the day, the group climbed into two cars and drove to Schofield's, intending to meet in the upstairs rooms that had been maintained as offices since O'Banion's day. The entourage consisted of Weiss; his bodyguard Patrick "Paddy" Murray, brother of Rondout train robber Jimmy Murray; Sam Pellar, who had criminal records in Alabama and Indianapolis and strong ties in Chicago to both Hymie Weiss and Twentieth Ward boss Morris Eller; Eller lieutenant Ben Jacobs, whose own record included a 1915 manslaughter indictment in a gang murder case; and W. W. O'Brien, a slick courtroom orator who formed part of the Saltis–Koncil defense team.

Upon reaching their destination, they parked one car in front of Holy Name Cathedral and the other around the corner on East Superior Street. After regrouping in the street, they walked toward Schofield's, likely evaluating the selected jurors, discussing the progress they had made thus far, and formulating the next step in saving Joe Saltis. No one noticed the curtains parting at Lundin's rooming house window, revealing the grim barrels of a shotgun and a machine gun.

State Street exploded with noise and buzzed with flying lead. Paddy Murray had no time to reach for a weapon before seven bullets lodged in his body and killed him. Lawyer O'Brien froze for a millisecond in terror. "I turned," he later recalled, "and it's a good thing I did or I would have been killed, as I heard them [bullets] whizzing around my head. Then I was hit again, and again, and I ran down a stairway."[86] He crouched there until the way was clear to limp to a doctor's office at 748 North State. Sam Pellar and Ben Jacobs ran for their lives, Pellar with a groin injury and Jacobs with a wound to the foot. Both sought treatment in a doctor's office at 720 Cass Street.

Hymie Weiss, the primary target, was shot ten times, one slug entering his skull over his left eye and leaving an ugly, gaping wound. He fell onto his face, breaking his nose, and lay there in the gutter, unconscious but still alive. Behind him, the cornerstone of Holy Name Cathedral bore ravaged witness to the attack. Its original inscription, which had read "At the name of Jesus every knee should bow— those that are in heaven and those on earth" now bore the chipped and fragmented words "every knee . . . should . . . heaven and earth."

While priests from the cathedral were running to the dead and wounded men to render what spiritual aid they could, the two gunmen in Anna Rotariu's rooming house hurried down the building's back stairs and vaulted out a rear window. They threw the machine gun on top of a dog kennel at 12 West Huron Street and made it to Dearborn Street, where they disappeared.

Squad No. 1 of the Chicago Fire Department was on its way from answering an alarm when it came across the scene of the shootings. Weiss was still breathing, so firemen called an ambulance to take him to Henrotin Hospital. He died on the examination table, after the staff had removed $5,300 in cash, a $6,000 check, a loaded .45 automatic, and a packet of letters confirming his identity. Those documents would provide interesting reading, for in addition to a letter from Terry Druggan in Miami, Weiss happened to have a copy of the veniremen list for the Saltis–Koncil murder trial. This particular discovery led to the opening of the gangster's safe in his office over Schofield's, revealing a list of the prosecution witnesses in the Saltis trial, among other pieces of personal and professional correspondence.

Capone, attired casually in house slippers and shirtsleeves, received reporters at the Hawthorne Hotel. His face was a mask of regret and outward sorrow as he said, "I'm sorry that Weiss was killed, but I didn't have anything to do with it. I telephoned the detective bureau that I would come in if they wanted me to, but they told me they didn't want me. I knew that I would be blamed for it, but why should I kill Weiss?"

Chief of Detectives Schoemaker was not fooled. "He knows why," he told reporters. Chief Collins was even more blunt. "Capone played safety first by importing the killers, expert machine-gunners, and then hurrying them out of town," he said. "It's a waste of time to arrest him. He's been in before on other murder charges. He has his alibi. He was in Cicero when the shooting occurred."

Referring to the murder itself, he said, "We knew it was coming sooner or later. And it isn't over. I fully expect that there will be a reprisal, then a counter-reprisal, and so on. These beer feuds go on in eternal vicious cycles. I don't want to encourage the business, but if somebody has to be killed, it's a good thing the gangsters are murdering themselves off. It saves trouble for the police."

When Drucci learned of the attack, he hurried from his suite at the Bentmere Hotel on Diversey Parkway, jumped into his car, and headed for the scene of the shooting. A friend flagged him down near Lincoln Park, advised him that Weiss was dead instead of injured, and told him that he should avoid the State Street area. Drucci returned to the Bentmere, collected his personal effects, and went into hiding. He dodged police interrogation until October 17, when detectives found him in a box seat at the Cubs Park, watching a Cardinals–Bears football game with Potatoes Kaufman and Harry Sorg, who had once been arrested in Los Angeles with Terry Druggan.

While Kaufman enlivened the hallways of the detective bureau with shouts that his constitutional rights were being violated, Drucci was uncharacteristically calm. He told John Stege that he was in New York at the time of the State Street shooting and had not seen his friend Weiss for a month. Flicking his cigarette and smirking as the ashes cluttered his interrogator's desk, he said that he was in the real estate business and knew nothing of rum warfare. Harry Sorg acted frightened, only confirming that he was a former Druggan associate. Stege, desiring to hold them, booked them for disorderly conduct after Kaufman became too mouthy, and sent them to a cell overnight.

"All those fellows could tell us a lot—if they would," Schoemaker told reporters. "Drucci, at least, should know all about the Weiss murder."[87]

The Weiss inquest revealed little more than an animosity between Captain Daniel Murphy of the East Chicago Avenue station, who had been among the first officers at both the O'Banion and Weiss slayings, and Coroner's Physician Dr. Joseph Springer. When Deputy Coroner Kennedy asked Springer to describe the wounds in Paddy Murray's body, the doctor replied in disgust, "We could tell better about such things if the bodies were left alone and the captains were not so dumb."

"Which captains do you mean?" Murphy challenged.

"You know very well what captain I mean," Springer retorted. "His name is Murphy."

"Remember, Doctor," Murphy warned, "you are not the coroner, you are just the coroner's physician."

"I am the coroner's physician in Cook County, and you are dumb."[88]

Frederick Weiss appeared to testify about the family history and his brother's vital statistics. He replied "Not known" to practically every question and signed a death certificate that only confirmed Earl Weiss's name and last known address. He became talkative when he described how his brother had shot him in 1920 and said that they had not seen each other since Christmas 1923, but his general demeanor was contrary and hostile. He gave the impression that the Wojciechowskis had been an emotionally estranged, feuding lot, neglecting to mention that both Mary Weiss and Earl had lived with Violet Monahan and her husband at 3808 West Grand Avenue, where Bernard and Walente were also regular guests.

The coroner's jury announced on October 21 that Sam Pellar and Benny Jacobs must have been implicated in the murder: "They were present and armed and had foreknowledge of the shooting." This conclusion must have been reached by the fact that the two survived the shooting and one witness claimed he saw Pellar discharging his weapon in Weiss's general direction. They were arraigned on murder charges, but Mary Weiss came forward to sign their $15,000 bonds.[89]

Earl Weiss was laid to rest in Mount Carmel Cemetery on October 15. Where O'Banion's funeral had been a public spectacle, fewer than than two hundred people came to Sbarbaro's to view Weiss's remains, and the funeral cortege, consisting of the hearse, eight carloads of flowers, and automobiles containing mourners, attracted little attention on the street. Most people turned their heads to read the signs that had been affixed to some of the cars: John Sbarbaro for municipal judge, Joseph Savage for county judge, and Morris Eller for sanitary district trustee.

A minor sensation took place when Moran suddenly disappeared from the cemetery. Policemen and detectives who had been circulating among the mourners, alert for an outbreak of violence, noticed him missing, and no one admitted to having seen him leave. A concerned North Sider, thinking he might have been arrested, hurried away from the cemetery to locate the nearest telephone.[90]

"George is sneezed," the man exclaimed excitedly when he placed a call to the office of North Sider attorney W. W. Smith, who was also a partner of famed lawyer Clarence Darrow. "Get a writ [of habeas corpus] quick!"

Smith wasted no time in calling Judge William Lindsay. Lindsay contacted the detective bureau to confirm that Moran was in fact in custody. When a negative response came back, Smith and the North Siders began to fear that something worse than arrest might have befallen Moran.

Drucci was overheard voicing two concerns: one that enemy gangsters posing as policemen might have lured Moran away from the graveside on the pretext of arresting him, and the other that the government, the "feds," might have him in its clutches. In what must be considered a classic case of jumping the gun, reporters crowded into the offices of Smith and Darrow, hoping that the missing gangster would either check in momentarily, or that Smith would receive a call asking him to join Lucille Moran in identifying a body.

It was more than an hour before someone thought of calling the Surf Hotel, where the missing gangster had moved with Lucille and John after the Torrio assassination attempt. He had taken the rooms under the name "G. O. Heitl and wife." To everyone's consternation, Moran's voice came on the line when the receiver was picked up. While he expressed his surprise at the dire conclusions that had been drawn about his whereabouts, Chief of Detectives Schoemaker ordered Lieutenant Joseph McGuire to go pick him up.

"Aw, I drove home from the cemetery with my wife and two other people in my Lincoln," Moran explained to Schoemaker at the detective bureau. "I'm out of the booze racket. I'm a real estater now, and I have my own subdivision fourteen miles out of Chicago."

"What is it, a private cemetery?" John Stege inquired sarcastically.

In an editorial titled "New Gang Chief Replaces Slain Weiss in War on Capone," the *Tribune* noted:

> George Moran now takes the scepter torn by murder first from the fist of Dean O'Banion, and lately the grasp of Hymie Weiss, and he becomes ruler of the bootleg domain of Chicago.
>
> As this information came last night to Deputy Chief of Detectives John Stege, he learned that all the gang-booze forces of Chicago have united against a common enemy, Al Capone, chief of the Cicero, Stickney, and Chicago Heights bootleggers.
>
> Thus there are two gangs where once there were eight. Capt. Stege heard that a peace would be sought between these two forces, but he questioned that information, for with the helm of the old O'Banionites guided by Moran, he doubted that Capone would even parley. For Moran, a fearless tough, is hated by the Cicero aliens, who call him "the Devil."[91]

Within mere weeks after the funeral, Josephine Simard began her bitter struggle with Earl's parents and siblings over his estate. The Weiss family, particularly Mary

Weiss and Violet Monahan, suspected that Josephine had been a kept woman, and demanded proof of marriage before they would relinquish their claim on Weiss's estate. Simard retorted that the marriage had taken place in Florida the previous September, after they had arrived from Canada, but she could not remember exactly where.

The vague response fueled the suspicions of Hymie's mother, who then sought to repossess the expensive automobile that had belonged to him but remained in Simard's possession. Josephine insisted that he had bought it for her but again failed to provide documentation listing her as the titular owner. One morning in early December, she awoke at her home at 3520 Sheridan Road to discover the vehicle gone from its usual spot. It was found later that day tucked away in James Monahan's garage.

Josephine Simard charged Monahan with the theft of the car. On December 21 she appeared in the Pekin court to press charges, only to be served with a citation from the probate court.[92] Mary Weiss was refusing to give an inch and demanding that the former actress prove her claim against Weiss's estate. The battle ended in 1927, when Probate Judge Henry Horner concluded that Simard's claim had no merit, and the dead gangster's estate, which legally amounted to $11,000, was divided equally among his parents and siblings.[93]

After Weiss's death, Schofield no longer let the upstairs offices to gangsters for headquarter purposes. Two murders of men he had known and liked resulted in a decision to separate his florist business from the underworld element that had made it thrive for so long, although he remained friendly with Weiss's successors. Schofield continued to run the shop, which later moved to 731 North State, until October 1947, when failing health forced him to retire and hand the business over to his son Steven. Three months later, in December, he died at home, aged sixty-eight.[94]

In August 1960 the old shop location at 738 North State was razed to make way for a parking lot. Five years later, police arrested Steven Schofield and two associates for running an illegal gambling operation. The judge who sentenced him to six months in the county jail called professional gambling a "national calamity" and refused his request for a thirty-day stay of sentence so that a temporary replacement could be trained for the florist shop.

Joe Saltis had a lot of thinking and worrying to do after Weiss's death. Ralph Sheldon had been gunning for him with renewed enthusiasm after Mitters Foley's murder became public knowledge. On August 7 Sheldon and Hugh McGovern were found cruising along Michigan Avenue, holding revolvers and a shotgun and scanning the streets as if they were hunting someone.[95]

The copious amounts of cash that Weiss had spent gave him a spectacular chance at an acquittal, but he was more concerned at what he and his co-defendants would be walking into after they left the courtroom—probably a lead-packed greeting card like Weiss had gotten on October 11. Saltis was no coward, and the new North Side leadership had shown no signs of deserting him, but the prospect of an abbreviated future now left him weary.

He turned for advice to John "Dingbat" Oberta, who was also on trial for the murder of Mitters Foley. Oberta knew of one man who was affiliated with the North Siders yet managed to retain the respect of the Capone–Sheldon faction: Maxie Eisen.

12

"YOU'RE A BUNCH OF SAPS"

ISEN HAD EMBARKED ON A worldwide sightseeing tour after O'Banion was killed, and returned to Chicago in the summer of 1925. Although he employed violence when the situation demanded, he shared Torrio's view that in the long run, vendettas and murder caused more trouble than any lust for revenge could justify. When Oberta approached him on Saltis's behalf, Eisen was of the opinion that Polack Joe's hope for salvation lay in a gangland armistice.[1]

"The idea is to call the war off," he said. "You're a bunch of saps, killing each other this way and giving the cops a laugh. There's plenty of jack for everybody, as long as Prohibition lasts. I'll talk to the boys."

Eisen went to see Tony Lombardo, knowing that Lombardo was valued and trusted by Capone, and sold him on the idea of a peace conference. The next day, the Sicilian reported that Capone desired nothing more than a chance to meet with the North Siders and the other primary gang leaders in safe territory and negotiate an armistice. More talks between Eisen and Lombardo followed, and the final result was a convergence of the gangland bigwigs at the Hotel Sherman on October 20. The Sherman had been the site of the ill-fated peace conference with Weiss, but this time around, the chances of failure were much less.

They all came without weapons or bodyguards. Moran, Drucci, Potatoes Kaufman, and Frank Foster represented the North Side interests. Accompanying them was Jack Zuta. Capone attended with his brother Ralph, Tony Lombardo, Jake Guzik, and Eddie Vogel, whose association with Capone had not been weakened by his arrest with Weiss and Foster the previous summer. Myles and Klondike O'Donnell came to safeguard their interests, as did Ralph Sheldon, and longtime underworld figures Billy Skidmore and Barney Bertsche put in an appearance. Skidmore had a thriving bail-bond practice and a gambling concession on the side; Bertsche had been a political fixer since the turn of the century and operated casinos on the Northwest Side. They had no real role in the bootlegging hierarchy but attended the conference to ensure that their own interests were not adversely affected by the outcome.

Everyone had his chance to speak, but Capone's speech summed up what was on the mind of almost all the attendees. "We're making a shooting gallery out of a great business," he said. "It's hard and dangerous work, aside from any hate at all, and when a fellow works hard at any line of business, he wants to go home and forget about it. He doesn't want to be afraid to sit near a window or open a door."

Among the peace terms agreed on by all were:

- No more killings or beatings.
- All past murders and shootings attributed to gunmen affiliated with Chicago and Cicero mobs would be looked on as closed incidents.
- All ribbing incited by malicious cops and reporters or the discovery of old correspondence written prior to the peace treaty would be disregarded.
- All gang leaders would be responsible for the conduct of their own men. Any infractions by the rank and file would be dealt with by the malefactor's boss.
- Each gang would retain the territories that had originally been assigned to it during the original Torrio-inspired arrangement.[2]

After the meeting ended, the attendees went to Diamond Joe Esposito's Bella Napoli Café en masse. Everyone was in such buoyant spirits after the apparent end of the two years of bloodshed that old killings and past battles were discussed with as much good-natured animation as one would employ when recounting a recently seen play or movie.

"Remember that night eight months ago when your car was chased by two of ours?"

"I sure do."

"Well, we were going to kill you that night, but you had a woman with you."[3]

The peace brought on by Saltis's trepidation about the future prevailed even in the face of two disruptions. The first was another comeback attempted by Spike O'Donnell and his followers. After a skirmish that left two of his brothers at death's door, O'Donnell realized that bucking Capone was a fight he could never hope to win. He backed off and posed no further problems for the Capone organization. The second was the December 16, 1926, disappearance of Ralph Sheldon bootlegger

Hillary Clements. When his body was found in a shallow grave two weeks later, Sheldon declined to retaliate.

"Just like the old days," Capone said. "They (the North Siders) stay on the North Side and I stay in Cicero, and if we meet on the street, we say hello and shake hands. Better, ain't it?"

It was. Maxie Eisen, his duty done, went back to his union management and periodic terrorism. In April 1927 the United Kosher Sausage Company sued the Kosher Meat Peddlers Association, which Eisen represented, for throwing poison about in sausage stores that sold United Kosher product. Eisen and partner John Cito, representing the Poultry Dealers Union, were indicted the following October for attacking David Trabush. When Trabush sold a pound of chicken at a lower price than ordered to a woman who happened to be a union spy, Eisen and Cito pistol-whipped him and left him with injuries requiring sixteen stitches.[4] They were acquitted in Judge Harry Miller's courtroom the following January, but not before Eisen commented to Mrs. Trabush, "I should have killed your husband when I had the chance."

In July 1928 a fish shop owner, Mrs. Mamie Oberlander, accused him of preventing her from conducting her business unless she paid $3,000 up front and kicked back $50 a month to Eisen's union. Eisen and Charles Solomon were arrested when she pressed charges.[5] Nine months later, while still on bail awaiting trial, Eisen beat up another fish peddler, David Wolcoff.

The state's attorney's office thought it was experiencing a belated April Fool's joke in April 1931, when a man identifying himself as Max Eisen called and demanded protection. It really was Max Eisen, but not the racketeer. This distraught individual, who owned the Humboldt Radio Company, had been getting threatening phone calls from those who had a grievance against the union agent because the two of them had the same name, and he was the only one with a listing in the phone book. He'd even been hauled from his home to the Federal Building by mistake and had been blacklisted from a lodge until he convinced the members that he was not the notorious Eisen.[6]

"I am going to change my name to Pete Jones or something like that unless something is done to the real Maxie Eisen," he wailed.

O'Banion's former union advisor received periodic writeups in the press over the years. He made the papers when a group of orthodox Jewish butchers protested his election to the head of the Hebrew Butchers Union in 1931, and in 1936 the scandal gourmets fell over themselves with delight when Freda Snyder, his former bookkeeper, accused him of stalking her.[7] Eisen died sometime in the late 1950s, his conscience scarred by a lifetime of crime.

On Tuesday, November 30, Vincent Drucci and George Moran, accompanied by Pete and Frank Gusenberg, strolled into a garage at 2901 Lawrence Avenue, where Albany Park police had recently seized fifty cartons of bottled beer. Pending its removal by federal authorities, officers were guarding the liquor bonanza in pairs. Sergeant William Messett and patrolman D. J. Clifford were on duty at the time of the North Siders' 4 a.m. arrival. A black employee, Ulysses Calvin, was at work on a car nearby.[8]

According to Pat Roche, chief investigator for the state's attorney's office, Drucci identified himself to the policemen as a federal officer and snapped handcuffs on both before relieving them of their guns. Calvin, who later identified Drucci from a mug shot on file at the detective bureau, protested and was pistol-whipped so severely that his lacerated scalp required hospital treatment.

Strangely, the North Side gangsters did not touch the confiscated liquor. While Messett and Clifford watched tensely and Calvin pressed a towel to his bleeding head, they rifled through the files in the garage office, selected some papers, and took them. Their mission clearly completed, Drucci adopted a kindly, even apologetic air, uncuffed the officers, and returned their firearms to them. He, Moran, and the Gusenbergs sauntered out into the frigid November air, clutching the files under their arms.

When news of the ambush became public knowledge, everyone gasped or laughed except the Chicago Police Department and Prohibition officials. It seemed unreal that gangsters masquerading as federal officers could disarm police guards and rifle a protected premises so easily. Sergeant Messett protested that Drucci, whom he did not know by sight, had flashed credentials that looked real enough, although he and Clifford were silent as to why they had submitted to being handcuffed and disarmed.

Drucci was soon picked up, minus the fraudulent credentials, charged with impersonating a federal officer, and released on a $2,000 bond. An order went out to pick up Moran and the Gusenbergs, but no charges were ever brought against them.

The purpose of their predawn visit to the Lawrence Avenue garage remains a mystery. All they seemed concerned about obtaining was an assortment of files whose import was never determined. Although newspaper readers laughed off what the *Tribune* called a "serio-comedy," the police department had been publicly embarrassed and Chicago's face to the world had received another black eye.

The North Side Gang's outlandish leadership and unregimented membership style attracted other underworld denizens of like mind. Willie Marks, whom the press would be describing as the North Side Gang's second-in-command before two years had passed, was a short man, standing just five foot four, and dark-complected. The son of a British immigrant father and Canadian mother,[9] he had a long history of arrests for suspicion of payroll theft, assault, and even murder. In early 1918 he and two cohorts, Joseph Dunn and William Wilson, had stood trial for the shooting of one John Byers, a crime for which the state's attorney had demanded the death penalty. After nine hours of deliberation, the jury returned a not-guilty verdict, and Marks went free.[10]

He was visibly connected with Moran's North Siders by 1928, but his ranking status within the gang suggests that he was a key member for a long time before that. As early as 1916 he and Moran had a friend in common—William Wilson, who had been arrested along with Moran in the Peter Bulfin murder case.

Another Moran gang stalwart was Leo Mongoven, who had been a peripheral member of the North Side Gang since O'Banion's day but became more prominent under Drucci and Moran. He had a briefer criminal record than Willie Marks, but murder and violent death featured prominently in what notations did exist.

On March 31, 1926, the 140-pound Mongoven got into a fistfight with Andre Anderson at Tonneman's café in Cicero. Anderson, a hulking bruiser once regarded as a contender for heavyweight champion of the world, was in the midst of beating his smaller opponent to a pulp when Mongoven drew a pistol and killed him. Mongoven had supposedly threatened Anderson for failing to "throw" the victory to his opponent William Munn during a match the previous December, as ordered.[11]

A year and a half later, in November 1927, Mongoven's car crashed into a vehicle driven by Bert Finstad on a road outside Libertyville. Fog was the primary culprit, but the two men preferred to blame each other, and words led to a violent brawl, which attracted an interested crowd. It was this gathering that the chauffeur of a car bearing Chicago banker John J. Mitchell and his wife tried to avoid when he came upon it suddenly in the fog. The roads were slippery, and the Mitchell car flipped into the ditch, killing the banker and Mrs. Mitchell. Mongoven bolted but was soon found hiding out at a Bluff Lake hotel near Antioch, Illinois. He was arrested in both the Anderson and Mitchell deaths but never prosecuted.

Albert Kachellek, who preferred the alias of James Clark, was an enforcer on a par with the Gusenbergs. A native of Krojencke, Germany, Clark had anglicized his name to spare his mother, Anna, any grief that could associate from his notoriety. He had a long criminal record, having been arrested in 1905 for robbery and running a confidence game. After four months in the Bridewell, Clark went back to his old ways and was arrested again later in the year and sentenced to a four-year term at Pontiac Reformatory. He got out in 1909, none the wiser for the lengthier sentence.

Early on the morning of March 6, 1910, Clark broke into a three story stone house at 923 East Sixtieth Street, the residence of the Alpha Tau Omega fraternity. The porter came upon him as he was loading valuables into his pocket and floored him with a stick. Clark bolted out the window, with the porter and twenty pajama-clad youths in hot pursuit, but only got a block and a half away before they surrounded him and pinned him.

In retrospect, Clark probably wished that the police had caught him instead. Singing their college songs in full voice despite the early hour, the young men dragged him back to the frat house, put him in the bathtub, and, in the words of the *Tribune*, "gave him the treatment usually accorded unwilling and recalcitrant freshmen. Then they called a doctor to fix up Mr. Burglar. About 6:30 a.m. . . . Lieutenant John L. Hogan and Officers Curtin and Loey . . . saved Mr. Burglar from further punishment à la college."[12]

Clark received a sentence of one year to life at Joliet and was paroled in May 1914. In October of the same year he and two friends, William Hogan and Frederick Corrigan, attempted to hold up the Franklin Park State Bank. Clark shot and wounded cashier Walter L. Joss. The three young men were found guilty in Judge McDonald's courtroom on November 25, 1914, and Clark returned to prison.[13] Upon release he evaded further punishment at the hands of the law, and by 1927 was a close friend of Moran. He would be erroneously described as Moran's brother-in-law, although no kinship between the two ever existed.

Albert L. Weinshenker, normally called Al Weinshank, was a friend and associate dating back to the days of O'Banion, whom he had met when both worked in the "circulation department" of the *Herald and Examiner*.[14] He ran a speakeasy called the Alcazar at 4207 Broadway and had special talents as a union slugger and organizer, making him someone the North Siders could use. He had a striking resemblance to Moran, with his dimpled chin, square face, and stocky build.

Edward Newberry, more commonly called Ted, came originally from the Northwest Side. After completing high school, he went to work for a grocery store as a delivery driver,[15] and when Prohibition took effect Newberry acquired a North Side liquor franchise from O'Banion. He became an independent bootlegger, selling booze to customers on his old grocery route. He also worked as a cab driver and was a suspected ringleader in the "taxi cab wars" that flared up periodically.

In September 1924 he and two companions, Leonard Tarr and Arresti Capolla, were charged with assault to kill after a partner, Harry Callan, was shot near Lincoln Park, but the trio went free when Callan refused to cooperate with the prosecution.[16] One of Newberry's many moneymaking endeavors was posing as a Prohibition agent and soliciting payoffs from unsuspecting saloonkeepers. In December 1924 an intended victim named Homer Finch resisted and ended up dead.[17] Newberry was indicted for murder, but the charges were dropped.

Newberry and Moran got along especially well, both possessing a sometimes-crazy sense of humor. One of Moran's relatives[18] remembered a stunt that they were particularly fond of, but which must have left the victims having nightmares for months. They would drive along the roads leading from the suburbs and outlying areas into Chicago, looking for "tramps" or anyone heading into the city on foot. Pulling over, they would offer him a ride—and treat him to a performance worthy of vaudeville. While one drove, the other would turn into a lunatic before the new passenger's eyes, giggling, chattering about nonsense . . . and extolling the glories of murder. With few exceptions the newcomer panicked and was dropped off. Once, a terrified tramp lost control of his bladder and urinated all over the seat, bringing the days of the Moran–Newberry free-ride service to an end.

The year 1927 started out as a busy one for the North Siders. The aldermanic primaries took place in February, and their prime objective was to see to it that O'Banion's old political protector and North Side ally, Titus Haffa, was re-elected in the Forty-Third Ward. Opposing him was A. F. Albert, formerly connected to the Crowe faction but recently affiliated with Charles Deneen's camp.

The days preceding the primary were full of the usual political vitriol. "Haffa is a political chameleon—he changes color every election," Albert said. Haffa responded with, "He is a reformer—when reform helps him. More than that, Albert is a fake lawyer. He never went to school a day in his life after he left grammar school."[19]

Albert charged that his workers were being intimidated by Haffa-backed gangsters, who sidled up to them and threatened them with one-way rides should their sponsor lose the election. He also accused Haffa of bringing a thousand nonresidents into the ward to pad the voter registration list. The Municipal Voter's League, when endorsing Albert, warned that electing Haffa would be a "calamity."

Haffa's response was that he had it on good authority that Albert was hiring ex-cops and Prohibition agents as sluggers, and pointed out that the alderman's chauffeur, Eugene MacLaughlin, had been wanted for murder.

The primary, which took place on February 23, proved that the accusations on both sides had a boulder of truth to them. Six months later, mayoral candidate Edward Litsinger testified before a city council judiciary committee, saying, "Armed gangsters ran rampant in the district. These guerrilla bands drove Deneen workers from the polls and in several instances took possession of the voting places and superintended the ballot counting. Among them I recognized Vincent Drucci and Fur Sammon."[20]

Michael Wolf, also an aldermanic candidate, talked of a stunning example of fraudulent voting. When he went to cast his ballot, the official at the polling station informed him that, according to the record, he had already voted.

"Why, I haven't even been here," Wolf exclaimed.

"Then somebody voted for you," the judge replied. Wolf, in recounting the incident, could not keep the disgust out of his voice. "Think of that—me, a candidate—an outrage!"[21]

After the polls closed and the votes were counted, Haffa was the loser by a tiny margin. Not willing to concede defeat, he challenged the results and insisted, although he did not disclose how he came by the information, that he was really the victor by seventy-seven votes. Alderman Albert said that if those votes were cast at all, they were likely fraudulent. A series of hearings into the matter commenced in the summer and ended on August 31, when the city council, urged by Mayor Thompson, backed Haffa's claim, ousted Albert, and seated Haffa.

Albert was forced to accept the council's decision but opted not to do it gracefully. "They're putting me on the political auction block," he told the packed council chamber. "I'm making a sacrifice for my conscience. But I go down fighting." He cast a scornful glare at Thompson. "You boast that your grandfather fought for this country and his blood runs in your veins. I don't know anything about my grandfather, but I'm a better representative of this country than you are. You shout 'Down with King George' and wave the Constitution with one hand and tear it up with the other."

What gangland narrowly missed accomplishing, Thompson brought to fruition. In a sense, the February primary outcome had been inevitable.

Just as the April mayoral race would be.

Big Bill Thompson had not been idle during the years after his defeat by William Dever. He spent $25,000 constructing a sailing boat that he called the *Big Bill.* Even the figurehead was a bust of Thompson's own profile. He announced that he would assemble a crew and sail the ship down to the South Seas, where he intended to photograph a unique species of tree-climbing fish. The expedition made it as far as New Orleans, with Thompson pausing to give speeches at numerous riverside towns en route.

On December 11, 1926, he announced his intention to run again for mayor in the 1927 election. Gangster supporters and political opportunists rounded up and presented him with 433,000 signed pledge cards, which he accepted with a grandiose show of humility.

It was support he needed. He had broken with his old sponsor, Fred Lundin, and Lundin in turn backed Dr. John Dill Robertson, whom Thompson had made city health commissioner during his previous administration. When he began to seriously entertain thoughts of re-entering the mayoral race, his first public move was to ridicule the enemy. He held a noon rally in the Cort, a Loop theater, a year before the election and treated the audience to what has gone down in local and political history as "the Rat Show." Two big gray rats named "Fred" and "Doc" (after Lundin and Robertson) were displayed in cages and castigated for the sins of their human counterparts.[22]

"The one on the left here is Doc," Thompson said. "I can tell because he hasn't had a bath for twenty years." Leaning over "Fred," he asked sorrowfully, "Fred, let me ask you something. Wasn't I the best friend you ever had? . . . Isn't it true that I came home from Honolulu to save you from the penitentiary? Well, what gratitude could you expect from rats?"

When Robertson withdrew from the primary in February, Thompson and Dever faced off. Big Bill was at his finest level of Anglophobia, calling Dever's superintendent of schools "King George's stool pigeon . . . leader of a plot to undermine patriotism in Chicago's children." He suggested that King George might have been partly to blame for the Volstead Act "so that all their [English] distillers can make fortunes selling us bootleg liquor. . . . If George comes to Chicago, I'll punch him in the snoot."

Dever could scarcely contain his annoyance with Thompson's obsession with the British monarch. "I have tried to confine this campaign to the issues and inter-ests of Chicago, but in that I have found no combatant. I thought the square thing to do was get into the ring with Bill with the gloves, but he would not come into the ring. He has been throwing tacks from the outside. I have never respected him. I do not respect him now. I shall not respect him whether he wins or loses."

Judge Harry Miller was more to the point. "If Thompson wins," he said, "Chicago will have a Fatty Arbuckle for mayor."

Jack Zuta contributed $50,000 to the Thompson campaign chest, boasting, "I'm for Big Bill, hook, line, and sinker, and Big Bill's for me, hook, line, and sinker." Capone contributed a sum that variously estimated at from $100,000 to $260,000.

Dever, in contrast, had to rely on his unquestioned integrity and dedication to enforcing the law when appealing to voters. His campaign slogan was "Dever and Decency." The problem was, he advocated enforcement of laws that no one wanted. He and his police force had padlocked thousands of speakeasies and gam-bling joints, which the public initially welcomed as corrective measures against what was perceived at the time as an embarrassing gangster menace. Four years later, the people wanted them open again. They listened with enthusiasm as Thompson promised, "When I'm elected, we will not only reopen places these peo-ple have closed, but we'll open ten thousand new ones." He even turned Dever's accusation of hoodlum support to his advantage by addressing wealthy women vot-ers as "my fellow hoodlums." They loved it.

Drucci and Moran had one thing in common with Capone as election day neared: they wanted Dever out of office and Thompson elected. Two days before the polls opened, Drucci led a team of thugs into the office of Forty-Third Ward Alderman Dorsey Crowe, a Dever minion. Finding him away, they settled for roughing up the night watchman and demolishing the place. When word of the attack reached Chief Collins, he ordered the immediate roundup and detention of all known gang leaders.

On April 4 a detective squad spotted Drucci and two companions, Henry Finkel-stein and Albert Singel, coming out of the Hotel Bellaire. Finkelstein was the owner of the Silver Slipper Cabaret and a partner in the Rendezvous Café on Diversey; Sin-gel was a Peoria resident who owned a distillery there. The officers had no particu-lar interest in anyone but Drucci, but Finkelstein and Singel were guilty by associa-tion and stopped as well. All three men submitted to a search, which turned up a .45 tucked into the North Side leader's waistband. The officers ran them in to the detective bureau, booked them, and returned them to the car for a trip to the Crim-inal Courts Building, where habeas corpus proceedings were scheduled.[23]

As they approached the vehicle, one of the officers, Danny Healy, held Drucci's arm a little too tightly. Drucci yanked free and cursed him. Healy pulled out his service revolver and warned, "You call me that again and I'll let you have it."

Healy, who at age thirty-one had been a policeman for eight years, had a repu-tation for playing hardball with gangsters. Earlier in the year he had killed a bandit during a public shootout on Armitage Avenue, and the previous November he had nearly shot Joe Saltis during a raid on a Stockyards saloon. Healy's squad leader, Lieutenant Liebeck, stepped in before Saltis became a casualty. Drucci probably knew of Healy's record, and no sense of discretion could mask his disgust. As he climbed into the car, he snarled over his shoulder, "You kid copper, I'll get you. I'll wait on your doorstep for you."

"Shut up," the detective ordered. Albert Singel took a seat next to Drucci, and Healy followed him.

"Go on, you kid copper," Drucci taunted. "I'll fix you for this." When Healy, whose own restraint was evaporating, repeated the order to shut up, the North Sider challenged, "You take your gun off me and I'll kick hell out of you."

The car pulled away from the curb as the arguing continued. Albert Singel, feeling more like a clay pigeon with each passing minute, leaned as far back into the seat as possible. He was scared, and with good reason. Healy and Drucci were becoming more abusive to each other as the seconds passed, and no one was close enough to intervene in the moving car. Sergeant Daniel Keough and Henry Finkelstein were in the collapsible seat in front of them, while squad head Lieutenant Liebeck was in the front passenger seat with the driver, Sergeant Matthew Cunningham.

The car proceeded along Wacker Drive. By the time it neared the Clark Street bridge, Drucci was so irate that he began punching holes in the side curtains. The police officers would later claim that after the punching episode, the gang leader leaped at Healy with a yell of "I'll take you and your tool! I'll fix you!" The thug-hating detective, needing no more encouragement than that, shot him.

Drucci's companions would remember the fatal moment differently. Finkelstein said that a scuffle had been initiated when Healy threw the first punch. The driver pulled over to the Clark Street curb. Healy opened the door, got out, and shot Drucci while the North Sider was sitting with his hands in his lap. Albert Singel said that both men had exchanged blows and that Healy shot after Drucci challenged him to put his gun away and fight it out.

No source could dispute that Drucci was badly wounded by Healy's gunfire. He had been hit in the arm, belly, and leg, and was losing blood at an alarming rate. Liebeck ordered Keough to drive to Iroquois Hospital, which specialized in emergency cases, but the physicians there pronounced Drucci's condition too serious for their resources and sent him by ambulance to the county hospital. He died just before arrival.

Singel and Finkelstein, both badly shaken after witnessing their colleague's execution, were taken to the original destination of the Criminal Courts Building. Like Drucci, they had friends ready to secure their immediate release. In the case of Finkelstein, Judge Lindsay was approached by State Representative Harry Weisbrod, Alderman Jacob Arvey, and Moe Rosenberg, whose brother Stanley was sanitary district trustee.

When Maurice Green, the gangster's attorney, learned that his client was now a stiffening corpse, he and the now-widowed Cecelia Drucci demanded that Detective Healy be charged with murder. After she identified her husband's body at the morgue amidst sobs and cries of "my great big baby" and "my poor boy," Cecelia made it plain that she wanted revenge, judicial or otherwise. Chief of Detectives Schoemaker responded to both of them via the press. "I don't know anything about anyone being murdered. I do know that Drucci was killed trying to take a gun away from Healy. We're having a medal made for Healy."[24]

On Thursday, April 7, Drucci was interred in Mount Carmel Cemetery with full military honors.[25] His silver and aluminum casket was adorned with an American flag and $30,000 worth of flowers, which included a heart of roses inscribed "To my darling husband," a circlet of pink roses from Drucci's widowed mother, and a mountain of white and purple blooms fashioned in the shape of a chair. That particular tribute was from Moran and the North Siders.

Viola O'Banion stood with the sobbing widow and the di Ambrosio family at the graveside, offering silent support. The service itself was brief, as the coroner's inquest was scheduled to commence that day and the family was anxious to attend. As she left the cemetery, the pale, blonde Cecelia Drucci parted her red lips in a weary smile for reporters. Pride mingled with grief in her expression. "A policeman murdered him," she said, "but we sure gave him a grand funeral."[26]

It was a grand funeral, although the rites of the Catholic Church were withheld as usual. Among the mourners were George Moran, Al Capone, Maxie Eisen, the Gusenberg brothers, Frank McErlane, Joe Saltis and his wife, Potatoes Kaufman, and Dan McCarthy.

Now the North Side leadership was no longer divided. Moran was exclusively in charge.

On April 5 Chicago elected Big Bill Thompson to a third term, defeating Dever by a plurality of 83,072 votes. Over 1,000,000 votes had been cast out of a total registration of 1,146,000 eligible voters, setting a record.

It had been a quiet election too. Police squads and an extra five thousand armed guards hired by Dever discouraged open violence, and the voting took place in the midst of only two bomb explosions and random cases of attacks on election officials.

While Thompson broadcast a jubilant victory speech from the Hotel Sherman, thousands of his supporters flocked to the Loop and commandeered the sidewalks, turning the central business district into one cheering, rollicking Thompson rally. Fire alarms were triggered deliberately so that engine sirens could intensify the din. Later that night, Thompson and a crowd of followers took the party to the Fish Fans clubhouse, a boat moored off Lincoln Park. The sheer number of celebrants proved to be more than the vessel could handle, and it sank to the bottom. The water was only six feet deep where the boat was anchored, so no one suffered more than a mild case of alarm.

Dever, accepting that the citizens of Chicago preferred drinking to decency, said, "The people of Chicago have made their choice, and that is all there is to it. So far as my personal future is concerned, I am perfectly happy because I am relieved of a very onerous task."[27]

The inquest into Drucci's death, with Deputy Coroner Kennedy presiding, commenced on April 7, the day of the funeral. John di Ambrosio, his brother, took the stand to blindly deny that Drucci had been a bootleg baron in possession of a $500,000 personal fortune. On the contrary, he insisted, Drucci had left no estate at all.

Charles S. Wharton, appearing for Cecelia Drucci, declared that he was going to press for a murder investigation. "We never did figure out how an unarmed man in a police squad car surrounded by armed policeman can be shot to death without the act being called murder."

Healy took the stand to give his version of the shooting, and concluded his testimony with "I felt I had to kill him or he would kill me." Deputy Chief Zimmer had received a letter suggesting that the young officer was now living on borrowed time, so he posted extra guards in the courtroom the entire time Healy was present.

Albert Singel told of cringing between Healy and Drucci when the cursing match started and admitted that when tempers began escalating, he became so frightened that he could not remember much of the actual shooting. When questioned by Mrs. Drucci's lawyer, Singel said that the only insult he could recall Drucci using was "kid copper."

Singel was followed to the stand by the other officers who had been in the squad car, who corroborated Healy's account.[28]

The members of the public passed their own comments on the Drucci killing in the *Chicago Tribune*'s Voice of the People column. A woman signing her name "Mrs. L. Meters" wrote, "Any four policemen that can't take care of one unarmed man without killing him is a menace to the city. Probably our mayor will see punishment meted out to Dan Healy. And see that the police use their guns when necessary, not whenever they meet someone they don't like. We have a law to punish; it isn't up to the police to take the law into their own hands to do as they like."

"R.H.D." saw it differently. He/she wrote, "The headlines tell us that the widow of Vincent Drucci will devote the rest of her life to bringing to justice "the murderer" of her husband. . . . I don't think Chicago has reached the point yet where it will stand for seeing a man like Healy persecuted for ridding the community of a gunman like Drucci. If it should come to pass, then Chicago will have gone beyond redemption."[29]

Chicago was not beyond redemption, at least not in this case. The coroner's jury ruled the killing a justifiable homicide, and Danny Healy went on to a long and illustrious career in police work. In 1964, when he retired from the force, Healy became chief of police of Stone Park, a West Side suburb where Syndicate-owned motels, clubs, and gambling joints abounded. There is no record that he seriously inconvenienced their operation in any way.

Thomas Maloy had been business agent of the Motion Picture Operators Union in Chicago since 1920. His peers had viewed him as a prime candidate for the position after a memorable incident that took place during Maloy's own tenure as a projectionist: two armed hoodlums intent on muscling into the union climbed the stairs to his booth, ready and eager to do damage. Maloy wrested their weapons from them, kicked both men in the teeth, and chased them out of the building. He was not a newcomer to the seamier side of life, as he ran a small gambling operation in the same building that housed his theater. His toughness and head for business made him rich and the union strong.

By 1927 the union was pulling in enough money to attract Moran's attention. The North Siders knew Maloy, who had been friendly with Dapper Dan McCarthy and Cornelius "Con" Shea, but not well enough to avoid his operation on "friendship" grounds. Each year Maloy negotiated new labor contracts with the theater owners on behalf of the union and never failed to obtain wage increases that indirectly found their way into his own pocket. His job was an enticing target for gangsters, but Maloy stood his ground as tenaciously as he had during the booth brawl and even sent Big Tim Murphy running in 1922.

Henry Gusenberg, younger brother of Pete and Frank, already had a job as a projectionist, so in 1927 the North Siders put him forward as a contender for Maloy's elected position. Moran and the Gusenbergs had the influence and the firepower to make the imminent election a deadly one, and detective squads began to infiltrate union meetings. Maloy, recognizing a very real threat, arranged a truce and agreed that in exchange for his guaranteed re-election, Henry Gusenberg would get a "fat assignment" as an operator. It must have been an extremely generous concession, as the North Siders accepted the proposal. They may have been opting to wait things out and try again, when the stakes were even higher, or giving Henry's initial candidacy a chance to create a fissure in the membership that would gradually widen to their advantage.

Maloy, shaken by the close call, vented his fury on those who had encouraged the rebellion. Ten days after the sit-down, four operators who had supported Gusenberg were driving near Lincoln Park when gunmen curbed their vehicle and shot one of them, Arthur Devent. Devent recovered, but the attack chastened his fellow projectionists and resulted in no further trouble for Maloy for another four years.[30]

While Moran took stock of the gang's future after April 1927, Capone had another adversary waiting to challenge his control of Little Italy and its alky cooking cottage industry.

Joseph Aiello had originally been a partner of Capone's friend and associate Tony Lombardo. During Prohibition's early years they realized a minor fortune selling sugar and other home-cooked alcohol components to the Genna brothers. Aiello also ran a bakery that did a brisk business. Between the booze and bread riches, he was able to afford a three-story mansion in Rogers Park, an elevated neighborhood that he would never have even passed through during his earlier years in America. He had been dirt poor when he left his homeland of Bagheria, Palermo, Sicily, in July 1907, at the age of seventeen, and arrived in New York City on the *Cretic*. He had made his way to Chicago with his brothers, cousins, and widowed father, Carlo Sr., after working a series of menial jobs in Utica, New York, and Buffalo.[31]

But for the ambitious Aiello, who stood out in a family of at least nine brothers and a phalanx of cousins, money alone was not enough. He craved recognition and prestige, two goals that the Unione Siciliana presidency could have attained for him. When that coveted post went to Tony Lombardo instead, Aiello severed all personal and professional ties with his old partner and vented his anger and disappointment on Capone, without whom Lombardo would not have come across such a stroke of fortune.

Aiello allied with the Billy Skidmore–Barney Bertsche–Jack Zuta combine of vice and gambling house operators. They were nursing grievances against Capone as well, resenting how they had to cut him in on the rackets they had once exclusively controlled. They were receptive to Aiello—until Capone approached Skidmore privately at his gambling and bail bondsmen headquarters and warned him to have no part of the vengeful Sicilian's scheme . . . or else. Contrary to popular belief, Aiello was not actively backed by Moran's North Siders during this early phase of the so-called "War of the Sicilian Succession." He may have been approached, but Moran pledged no support.[32]

Learning that his scarfaced nemesis dined regularly at a restaurant called the Little Italy, he offered the chef $10,000 to put prussic acid in Capone's minestrone soup. When the chef valued his own life more highly and told Capone, Aiello upped the ante to $50,000 to anyone who could send his foe on a one-way ride to Mount Carmel. At least ten gunmen, some from out of town, tried for the brass ring and ended up, according to legend, clutching nickels in their hands instead. With or without such a parting token, they were definitely dead.

The nickels were supposedly the calling card of Vincenzo Gibaldi, alias "Machine-Gun" Jack McGurn, a Sicilian born gunman and jazz sheik who stepped into his vocation by killing the murderers of his father and stepfather. By 1927 McGurn was one of Capone's best gunmen, being young, nervy, and accurate with any firearm he used. He was, in the words of one crime historian, "a professional killer who killed professional killers."

Capone gunmen also shot up the Aiello Brothers Bakery on May 28, sending two hundred machine-gun bullets into the building and wounding Joe's brother

Antonio.[33] The windows were perforated, the interior was shot into kindling, and icing from rows of exploded wedding cakes coated the pocked walls.

In November 1927, acting on a tip, a police sergeant raided an apartment in the Aiello locale of Rogers Park. He found a huge cache of dynamite and documents that sent suspicious investigators to the Rex Hotel on North Ashland Avenue. They netted a young hoodlum named Angelo Lo Mantio and four Aiello gangsters, who had rifles and boxes of ammunition on them. Searching Lo Mantio's pockets, they found rent receipts for an apartment on Washington Boulevard that faced Tony Lombardo's house at 4442 Washington, and a room at the Atlantic Hotel on South Clark Street. The apartment was a machine-gun nest; the hotel room window had rifles clamped to its sill, with the barrels trained on Michael "Hinky Dink" Kenna's cigar store, which Capone visited almost daily.

Angelo Lo Mantio admitted, after a session in the basement of the detective bureau, that Joe Aiello had hired him to kill both Lombardo and Capone. His jabbered confession resulted in Aiello's pickup and transportation to the bureau.

Less than an hour after he was put in a cell, a flood of taxis pulled up outside the building and disgorged several men. One officer glanced out the nearest window, saw them, and assumed that they were plainclothes detectives bringing in prisoners. But instead of coming in the front door, they surrounded the detective bureau by slipping into the surrounding alleys and stood guard over the front and back entrances. Finally, perhaps tired of waiting, three of the men headed for the doorway, one slipping a .45 from a shoulder holster to his coat pocket. When one was recognized as a Capone gangster, officers seized them, confiscated their weapons, and put them into a cell adjacent to Aiello. A policeman who understood Sicilian was nearby, posing as a prisoner, and listened as Capone gunman Louis Campagna began hissing threats at the terrified Aiello.

"You're dead, friend, dead. You won't get up to the end of the street still walking."

Aiello quaked. "Can't we settle this? Give me just fifteen days and I'll get out of town and stay out."

"You have broken faith with us twice now. Now that you have started this, we'll finish it."

After his release on bail, Aiello asked for, and got, a police escort into a taxicab with his wife and son. He did not flee to Sicily, as the police had hoped, but went into hiding in Trenton, New Jersey, with his family and brothers Antonio and Domenic.

Capone let him go but made it plain that future attempts at reprisal would be punished without hesitation or mercy. When Domenic Aiello returned to Chicago in January 1928, he received a telephone warning, and the Aiello Brothers Bakery at 473 West Division Street was shot up, frightening his wife, Grace, and their three little girls.

What made things personal, and brought Moran actively into the conflict, was the December 28, 1927, murder of John Touhy, brother of his old friend Tommy, at the Lone Tree Inn at 6873 North Milwaukee Avenue, near Niles. Capone had been eyeing the Northwest territory claimed by the Touhy brothers, and the Lone Tree Inn, with its chateau-like structure and steady clientele, was an especially attractive prize. A Capone beer-runner, Charles Miller, began supplying his boss's product there, the consent of owner Bob Freebus being a nonissue.

Touhy was prepared to make an issue of it. At three o'clock on the morning of December 28, he and some followers stormed the Lone Tree and opened fire, killing Miller and sending Freebus scurrying for cover.[34] Miller fired some return rounds before succumbing to his wounds.

An hour later, a man was taken to University Hospital by friends, who told the night attendant that he had been injured in a car accident. After seating him, they said that they would go out to their car to bring in his coat and hat. They never returned, and the attendant discovered that the man's bloody face was caused by a bullet wound in the left temple. Because he had papers in his pocket identifying him as John Davis, John Touhy's real identity did not come to light until several county highway patrolmen viewed the body and recognized him as the brother of the notorious Tommy.

Prior to Touhy's killing, Moran had been cheering on Joe Aiello without actively participating in the revolt. His failure to give Capone lead poisoning when Aiello had been plotting to feed his target prussic acid led to the misconception that the "Bugs Moran gang" was in tatters, a shadow force that did not act because it lacked the backbone and the firepower. Nothing could be further than the truth: Moran had ambitious and fearless gunmen in his camp—men like the Gusenberg brothers, Willie Marks, Ted Newberry, Leo Mongoven, Frank Foster, and James Clark—ready to back him up. Moran had been content to watch from the sidelines as Aiello went about his scheming, letting the Sicilian get his hands dirty and deal with killers like Jack McGurn on his tail.

Moran's personal loathing for Capone, whom he refused to stop seeing as the murderer of O'Banion and Weiss, was later evidenced in an interview he gave to the Reverend Elmer Williams, who ran an exposé publication called *Lightnin.* "The Beast," he called Capone, preferring name-calling to name-dropping, "uses his muscle men to peddle rotgut alcohol and green beer. I'm a legitimate salesman of good beer and pure whiskey. He trusts nobody and suspects everybody. He always has guards. I travel around with a couple of pals. The Behemoth can't sleep nights. If you ask me, he's on the dope. Me, I don't even need an aspirin."[35]

John Touhy's murder shook George Moran into a grieving fury he had not experienced since Weiss's killing. Hotel Sherman peace conference or not, he wanted Capone out of the way. He always had, but Touhy was the catalyst for the series of rebellions that would eventually end in massacre.

13

"BOMBS BURSTING IN AIR"

T HE WEEKS LEADING UP TO the April 1928 Republican primary conventions were literally explosive. On the night of January 27 bombs wrecked the homes of Charles Fitzmorris, Thompson's former chief of police and now city controller, and Dr. William Reid, commissioner of public service. Commissioner Mike Hughes assured the public that the terrorists would be dealt with accordingly. "When we go out after our men," he said, "we'll know who we want and we'll get them. You may be sure they won't be handled with kid gloves either."[1]

Apparently no one was afraid of Mike Hughes. On February 11, bombers targeted the home of Bob Crowe's brother-in-law Lawrence Cuneo, who was also his secretary, and on the eighteenth, John Sbarbaro's funeral parlor, the final public outing for many a Chicago gangster, was wrecked. On March 21, 1928, Diamond Joe Esposito, who was backing Crowe's opponent, Judge John A. Swanson, was shot dead in the street while walking home from a meeting at the Esposito National Republican Club. He had been warned via telephone to "Get out of town or get killed," and two Capone lieutenants dropped by the same day to repeat the message, but he had paid serious attention to neither.[2] The day after his funeral, more bombs devastated the homes of Republican Senator (and Thompson adversary) Charles Deneen and Judge Swanson.

On the morning of February 29, 1928, a team of police raiders included Moran and James Clark in a series of arrests made in the aftermath of that month's bombings.[3] Interestingly, Danny Healy, who had killed Drucci, headed the squad performing the mass roundup. He and Moran reportedly exchanged insults before Moran, remembering his friend's fate, quieted down and realized that the presence of the other officers would be no deterrent to Healy if the latter became irate enough to start shooting.

Moran, Clark, and three others (one of whom was a woman) were taken to the detective bureau and hurriedly booked on charges of robbery, vagrancy, and disorderly conduct. When news of the arrests became public, the report circulated that the charge was based on the theft of $80,000 from the Ravenswood National Bank. Reporters contacted bank officials for comment, only to learn that the police had sent no word of any kind to the bank about suspect arrests. A subsequent report revealed the real reason: the bombings. It was believed that the bank-robbery connection was a subterfuge allowing the police to hold the prisoners in custody until further investigation into the bombings could be conducted.

No sooner was Moran in custody and arrangements were being made for his arraignment before Judge Lyle than his attorney, Israel Goldberg, appeared before Chief Justice William Brothers of the criminal court and requested a writ of habeas corpus. The police, learning of the move, quickly booked Moran, Clark, and the other three on the robbery charge. Goldberg, like most gang-retained lawyers, was undaunted; he announced his intention to go before Chief Justice Harry Olsen of the municipal court and demand that Moran be arraigned before the judge presiding over the district in which he was arrested, as opposed to John Lyle's Grand Crossing court, where he'd likely be subjected to one of Lyle's infamous high bails.

Moran's friends were a conspicuous presence at the detective bureau, bearing checkbooks and property deeds to furnish bail. Detective Commissioner William O'Connor, who had arrested O'Banion, Weiss, and Dan McCarthy on the robbery and kidnapping charges in January 1924, declared to reporters, "If they get him loose on that bond, let me know and we'll arrest him again on another charge as soon as he leaves the station. We'll keep on arresting him until they run out of bond money."

A member of the North Side Gang gave his own opinion on the mentality that motivated the mass arrests. "This bank-robbery charge is a frame-up," he insisted. "They booked him on that so they could hold him for something else. Now they want Judge Lyle to put a 'rap' on him that will keep him in jail. George is the only one of the big boys on the North Side who hasn't been picked up since these bombings broke loose. They want to see what he knows." He pointed out that Moran had returned from Canada only the night before.[4]

Goldberg's attempt to save Moran and his co-defendants from an appearance before Judge Lyle failed. The irascible judge, knowing that the robbery charges were not likely to stick due to lack of evidence, concentrated on the vagrancy charge instead. Peering down at Goldberg and his client from the bench, Lyle first indicated that he would fix the bond at $25,000 and queried, "Do you think you will be able to raise that amount?"

"Why, Judge," the attorney replied, "I don't anticipate any problem in raising that amount."

Lyle smiled and responded, "Fine. Then we'll just make it $50,000."[5]

Goldberg's smile was sheepish, but Moran, behind the railing, glared. James Clark, because of his long record, was also assessed a $50,000 bail. The other defendants fared far better: the woman and one of the men, George Desur, were discharged, and the third, Adam Sklodowski, was fined $15 plus costs. Learning that Moran had cursed out Danny Healy, Lyle tacked on an additional $400 for a disorderly conduct charge.

Israel Goldberg hurried before Judge Emmanuel Eller, who reduced the $50,000 bond to $1,000 (the $400 bond was allowed to stand). It was a swipe at Lyle, who was far from popular among his judicial brethren. Chief Justice Harry Olsen had announced his intention to remove him from the criminal branch of the municipal court and install him in the civil branch instead. Olsen, hearing of the original arrests of Moran's group and the police's intention to bring them before Lyle specifically, declared that Lyle's propensity for fixing abnormally high bail amounts had resulted in the police taking cases from other judges' districts and presenting them to the Grand Crossing court.

Meanwhile, the political sniping continued. Thompson, who was backing Judge Bernard Barasa for the Cook County Board of Review, met his match in Barasa's opponent Edward Litsinger. A week before the primary, Thompson appeared on Litsinger's home turf and regaled a meeting with stories of how the candidate had regarded his old neighborhood and his mother as incompatible with his Gold Coast ambitions and deserted both. He would have gotten away with it had Litsinger's sister not jumped up and proven him a liar in front of the entire crowd. The next night, Litsinger told a packed house at the Olympic Theater that he had dozens of affidavits "relating to the life of the big baboon [Thompson]," but that he would not read them out of respect to the memory of his departed mother.

That primary went down in history as the "Pineapple Primary" (pineapple being slang for bomb), prompting a columnist to lampoon the national anthem:

> The rockets' red glare, the bombs bursting in air
> Gave proof through the night that Chicago's still there.

When the polls opened it was the voters' turn to be threatened and terrorized. A black attorney, Octavius Granady, who ran against Morris Eller in the Twentieth Ward, was killed by shotgun fire after the voting ended, capping a day of gunsmoke, bloodshed, and terror.

Normally, firepower brought about the desired results, and by an overwhelming majority; therefore, it came as an eye-opener for Thompson, Capone, Moran, and veteran politicos when the violence elicited the exact opposite effect. Robert Crowe lost the state's attorney nomination to Judge Swanson, 265,371 to 466,598, and Litsinger beat Thompson's favorite, Barasa, 307,941 to 417,527. More Chicagoans had turned up at the polls than anticipated, the consequence of a citizenry sick of front-page gangsters and a mayor obsessed with King George, and there were just too many voters to "scare up" a Thompson–Crowe–Small machine victory.

The all-around defeat, which included a trouncing of Governor Len Small at the state level, left Thompson mentally and physically at rock bottom. In the summer, he left the city in the hands of Acting Mayor Samuel Ettelson and fled to a Wisconsin retreat, where he drank heavily and gave little thought to the reality that he had a city to run for three more years. Capone left Chicago too, returning to his newly acquired Palm Island estate in Miami, Florida, after the election. He had his own future to contemplate too, and it included at least one murder, that of an old friend who committed the one sin Capone could never forgive: betrayal.

Moran left the venue issues, courtroom intrigues, and post-election damage control to those paid to worry about it all. He was ready to commence the first of many offensives against Al Capone. In March he struck.

On the night of March 7 Jack McGurn and a friend, Nick Mastro, were in the Smoke Shop in the McCormick Hotel at Ontario and Rush Streets. The story would later make the rounds that they were there to surreptitiously place slot machines in North Sider territory. By some accounts, McGurn was making a call in a public telephone booth;[6] by others, he was sitting in the lounge when a sedan bearing three men halted outside.[7] Two got out, one cradling a submachine gun. McGurn saw them, but not before the machine gun began spitting. At least a dozen shots were fired before the duo left the hotel, the second gunman covering their exit with a .45, got back in their car, and drove away.

Mastro staggered into the lobby, his face ashen, and begged the house physician for aid. Dr. Lamb sent him to Henrotin Hospital. A few minutes later, a bellboy summoned the doctor to Room 906, where McGurn lay bleeding from multiple bullet wounds in his chest and arm. He was immediately sent to Alexian Brothers Hospital by ambulance. While convalescing, he admitted that he knew the identities of his attackers but refused to name them, saying that he had been shot before and would be taking care of his own affairs once he was discharged. The police charged him with vagrancy and disorderly conduct.[8]

McGurn had indeed recognized Pete and Frank Gusenberg. A month later, on April 17, they tried again. McGurn was driving along Morgan Street in his sedan when a touring car containing the Gusenbergs and two others swung onto Morgan Street from the east.[9] As they drew alongside the sedan, machine guns rattled. McGurn abandoned his riddled automobile at Morgan and Harrison Streets and ran for cover.

When not gunning for Capone's top killers, Moran was moving into yet another racket—the clothing business.

By 1928 the battles between the unions, gangs, and shop owners in the various aspects of Chicago's cleaning and dyeing industry were being fought with the violence and intensity of a civil war. Bombs were tossed like confetti, pro and anti-union workers shared an equal risk of being beaten up on the job, and the price of cleaning one's clothes in Chicago rose so high to cover the cost of enforced union "dues" that residents began carting their dirty laundry out to the suburbs for processing.

The industry was originally a monopoly run by the Master Cleaners and Dyers Association, which owned or controlled most of the city's cleaning and dyeing plants. It operated in conjunction with the Retail Cleaners and Dyers Union and the Laundry and Dyehouse Chauffeurs, Drivers, and Helpers Union, which was headed by John G. Clay. Clay, a powerhouse in the industry for more than seventeen years, had played a primary role in elevating the union from a small band of drivers to a strong unit with a $300,000 treasury.[10]

The Master Cleaners targeted the small, independent laundries and tailoring shops, threatening the owners into joining and kicking back money to the association. The fees demanded forced these smaller operators to raise their prices, while their own costs remained the same, and the end result was that the Chicago public began to bypass the local businesses in favor of sending their cleaning and dyeing work out to the suburbs. It did not take long for the situation to become so intolerable that the independents turned to local gangsters for the protection that the police and state's attorney's office had failed to provide.

Morris Becker was one such ex-victim who made a deal with the devil and emerged unscathed. In May 1927 a representative from the Master Cleaners, Sam Rubin, a self-styled "good convincer," went to Becker's plant and informed him that he was going to raise his prices or else. Becker, a veteran businessman with more than forty years in the trade, responded that such coercion violated his constitutional rights. Rubin sneered that he was "a damned sight bigger than the Constitution."[11]

Becker refused the demand, and three days later a bomb exploded in his plant. A strike left him without workers. One F. Crowley from the Master Cleaners told him that paying the $5,000 fee to join the association and running his business according to their rules would end his troubles. Becker pretended to comply in order to buy enough time to file a complaint with the state's attorney's office. A grand jury handed down indictments against fifteen officials of the Master Cleaners and Dyers Association, but they were all acquitted when only Becker and his son appeared as witnesses at the trial—no one had told the plant owner that he was responsible for obtaining his own witnesses. The assistant state's attorney responded to a demand for an explanation by snapping, "I'm not a process server."

Exasperated, Morris Becker took his dilemma to Al Capone. He emerged from the meeting with smugness and relief evident on his face. He told reporters, "I now have no need of the state's attorney, the police department, or the Employers Association. I have the best protection in the world."

With Al Capone as a partner in Becker's independent concern, Sanitary Shops Inc., he certainly did. Capone had accepted Becker's partnership offer readily, finding the cleaning and dyeing business and its attending perks and hazards to be similar enough to his union racketeering endeavors. When a lawyer representing the Master Cleaners tried to use legalese to discourage Capone from supporting price cuts for cleaning services, the gang chief's response sent him scurrying: "Get the hell out of my office. You try to monkey with my business and I'll throw you out of the window."

Becker could scarcely contain his glee. "You know Mr. Capone," he said. "And so does the Master Cleaners and Dyers Association." He never had cause to regret his decision for the two years he and Capone remained partners in Sanitary Shops Inc.[12]

When the assessments and demands from the Master Cleaners became too much, a hundred small cleaning and dyeing shops on the North and Northwest Sides banded together to form the Central Cleaning Company, with offices at 2705 Fullerton Avenue. To ward off the likes of Sam Rubin, they hired Moran at $1,800 per week, and President Benjamin Kornick agreed to accept James Clark and Willie Marks as company vice presidents.[13]

Like Becker, Kornick had been threatened with personal injury and financial ruin, and the lives of his employees were constantly at risk. In 1928 terrorists repeatedly hid small quantities of explosives in old clothes before sending them to his plant to be dry-cleaned. The garments passed safely through the cleaning process, but when they were hung in the drying rooms they exploded, resulting in $15,000 worth of damage to clothing and property in the four-month period spanning January and April. Kornick complained, "So frequent were these bombings that an insurance company would pay us off only on a 35 percent basis and finally canceled our policies."[14]

In early April, Kornick received a phone call warning him that the Central Cleaning Company's headquarters was targeted for a bombing guaranteed to level it, forcing him to secure both police and private protection. Armed guards stationed at every entrance averted the bombing, but the Master Cleaners merely broadened its method of attack. Two weeks later four men hijacked a Central Cleaning delivery truck carrying $2,500 worth of clothing and administered crippling beatings to the driver, William Goldstein, and his assistant, Charles Foreman.[15] Foreman managed to flee despite his injuries, but Goldstein was thrown into the back of the truck, doused in gasoline, and set on fire along with the garments just before the doors were locked. He kicked his way to safety, but not before suffering third-degree burns.

On May 9 three thugs in a sedan forced a truck driven by Albert Robbins to the curb near 7625 East End Avenue. They hustled Robbins and his assistant into an alley, robbed them of $500 in cash and company checks, and torched the truck, incinerating $5,000 worth of garments.[16]

Ben Kornick and the other officials of the Central Cleaning Company felt their backs hit a figurative brick wall in early June, when a police squad led by Sergeant Thomas O'Malley took them into custody at the plant offices. They were transported to the state's attorney's office and subjected to an all-night grilling by an assistant prosecutor, Joseph Nicolai. Nicolai implied that he had it on good information that the company was deliberately inflicting damage on its own property and injuring its own employees in order to discredit the Master Cleaners. The bewildered officials finally obtained their freedom at five o'clock the next morning after being told to keep their "mouths shut, especially to reporters."[17]

Kornick obliged: he did all his talking to Moran.

After their agreement, Moran's North Siders talked to the Master Cleaners goons in a language both sides understood, and the Central Cleaning Company members stopped getting threatening visitors. But according to Fred Pasley, Kornick soon became convinced that the Moran gang's real intention was not to provide ongoing, contracted protection, but to muscle him out of the presidency and take over the entire operation.

Pasley wrote in *Al Capone* that Kornick switched his previous perception of who was the lesser of two evils and went to the Master Cleaners to seek its help in ousting the North Siders. When told that he and his associates would have to unionize the Central Cleaning Company's help in order to re-affiliate with the Master Cleaners, Kornick allegedly made plans to see John Clay for the necessary approval and instructions.[18]

Pasley went on to write that the Moran gang learned of Kornick's intentions and tried to preempt him by sending Willie Marks to Clay first, with an offer to unionize the Central Cleaning Company's drivers. Far from being a sign of surrender, an agreement of this nature with first Clay and then the Master Cleaners would give the North Siders a foothold in these two additional organizations, with the ultimate objective being control over the Master Cleaners and the score of businesses they represented, as well as the $300,000 treasury of Clay's union. When a suspicious Clay asked Marks to provide authorization for negotiation from Ben Kornick, the gangster balked and became aggressive. John Clay was used to dealing with mutinous and threatening characters and refused to be intimidated. He showed Marks the door.

Master Cleaners officials did confirm that this meeting occurred, but the fact that Ben Kornick and George Moran remained business partners for years after those turbulent months suggests it was not motivated by duplicity on Kornick's part. Moran did not want to work with Clay. His intention was to assume the same ironclad control over the Master Cleaners and Clay's own union that he enjoyed with the Central Cleaning Company.

Although Pasley characterized Clay as honest, contemporary press reports described the union organizer as anything but. A 1928 *Tribune* article presented a less noble picture:

> Clay's position as head of the drivers union was powerful in that he had control of the distribution among the Masters' cleaning plants of the garments collected from the small tailoring shops. He really was a dictator in his field . . . police records showed that Clay was an old-timer in racket circles and regarded as a dangerous man. He has been indicted on charges of conspiracy but was able to elude prison.

Being a "dangerous man," Clay lived every day with the knowledge that the time might come when he would not survive an encounter with other, more dangerous men. Ordering Willie Marks out of his office in effect set that date.

The third Thursday of every month was stewards' night at the Laundry and Dyehouse Union offices, located in a former residence at 629 South Ashland Boulevard. John Clay arrived early in the evening on November 16 and took a seat at his desk, which faced the first-floor windows looking out onto the street. Union President Joseph Iwaniec, Vice President George Bendel, and five stewards were in an adjoining room, separated from Clay's office by a pair of folding doors.

At 7 p.m., an automobile pulled up outside the building. Two men climbed out, walked up the short flight of steps leading up to the front door, and paused on the stone landing, where they had a good view of Clay at his desk. Passersby froze when they saw the men produce an automatic pistol and a shotgun from beneath their heavy coats. Gunfire shattered the windows, bringing the building's occupants racing toward the front door, but not quickly enough to save Clay, who slumped onto his desk with eight bullet wounds in his chest. A fountain pen he had been using at the time of the attack shattered in the fusillade and leaked ink all over the desktop.[19]

Police investigation of the murder confirmed that John Clay had been a man with multiple enemies. Some time prior to when he himself was murdered, Big Tim Murphy, accompanied by notorious police character Abe Shaffner, visited the union man at the South Ashland Boulevard offices. The *Daily News* wrote, "Forcing Clay to look into the business end of a revolver, Murphy advised him to get out of the organization." Three weeks later, Big Tim was dead and Clay was one of the many suspects questioned in the aftermath.[20]

Edward N. Nockels, secretary of the Chicago Federation of Labor, denounced those who viewed the murdered labor leader as a criminal. "Clay was as clean as a hound's tooth," he snapped. "To say he has a criminal record is a libel and a slander. For many months criminals who found the booze-running game less prosperous have threatened his life. He defied them, and his murder last night is his reward for that defiance."[21]

At the inquest, Deputy Coroner Joseph Dorfman told officials of the Laundry and Dyehouse Chauffeurs, Drivers, and Helpers Union, "It is up to you gentlemen of organized labor to clean the city of racketeers. . . . The time has come when the only place for them to muscle themselves in is in the chamber where the electric chair is kept."

Clay's body lay in state at the union headquarters on South Ashland Avenue, the first time in Chicago history that a murdered labor leader had been publicly laid out in his office. Mourners and those who came to pay their respects numbered in the hundreds, requiring an extra police detail around the building to keep order. Clay went to his grave a martyr, his own misdeeds cloaked by a posthumous glory.

The murder of John Clay was never officially solved. The questions died down after the coroner's jury handed down a verdict of murder by person or persons unknown, but it would all arise again a mere three months later . . . in February 1929.

Moran's success in dominating Kornick and crushing the opposition impressed George Gartler, owner of the Hollywood Cleaners and Dyers Inc. in Los Angeles, sufficiently to send one of his officials, Paul Mitchell, to Chicago. Mitchell was asked to meet with Moran and get his advice on how to cope with a cleaning and dyeing war going on in Los Angeles at the time.[22]

When asked about this conference in a courtroom eleven years later, Mitchell declined to state how the North Sider had been compensated for his words of wisdom, but Moran's advice was put to good use, as Gartler and his allies tossed bombs at competitors and threw acid on clothing trucks belonging to the opposition. In December 1931 a night watchman, John Stockman, was shot during a midnight assault on a rival cleaning plant in the East End, and an eight-year legal wrangle ended with Gartler and his confederates being shipped to San Quentin.

Joe Aiello came back to Chicago in the summer of 1928, around the time that Frankie Yale, murderer of Big Jim Colosimo, Dean O'Banion, and countless others, finally fell victim to someone more resourceful and determined than he was.

Yale had favored Aiello to ascend to the Chicago chapter's Unione presidency after Samoots Amatuna died, but Capone's man Tony Lombardo ended up in that seat. Under Lombardo's direction, the payments from the alky-cooking and gambling operations run under the aegis of the Unione, usually remitted to Yale's national office in healthy amounts, dwindled to mere token kickbacks.[23]

Capone received intelligence from New York that Aiello was now there, meeting regularly with Yale and plotting yet another overthrow. Trucks carrying liquor consigned to Capone, loaded in Brooklyn, were being hijacked before they even left the state, compounding his suspicion that his former comrade and mentor had turned on him. He asked an old friend from his Brooklyn days, James DeAmato, to look into it. DeAmato was shot to death soon after confirming that Yale was indeed behind the hijackings.[24]

On the afternoon of July 1, 1928, Frankie Yale was driving home from his café at Sixty-fifth Street and Fourteenth Avenue, having received a phone call that something was wrong with his wife. He suddenly noticed a black Nash trailing him and swerved west onto Forty-fourth Street. As he crossed Tenth Avenue, the Nash caught up and its occupants poured pistol, shotgun, and machine-gun fire into his coffee-colored Lincoln, which crashed into the stoop of a residential building. Stunned and wounded by the impact, Yale was helpless to resist as a gunman jumped out of the Nash, .45 in hand, and finished him off.[25]

The Nash was abandoned blocks away, the still-warm weapons inside. Police traced two handguns to a batch of twelve sold in Miami to a Capone contact, Parker Henderson, and a machine gun, complete with hundred-round drum, to Peter von Frantzius, a Chicago sporting goods dealer whose name would be dragged into an even more spectacular crime before the decade was out.

Losing Yale's support was a blow to Aiello, but the Sicilian now had other options. In Chicago he had a probable ally in Moran, whose relationship with Capone had degenerated to mutual distrust and gunfights in the streets. When Aiello talked this time around, Moran listened.

On September 8, 1928, Capone's Unione man, Tony Lombardo, was shot and killed as he and two bodyguards, Joseph Ferraro and Joseph Lolordo, arrived at Madison and Dearborn Streets, the famed "World's Busiest Corner." Ferraro received a mortal bullet wound in the back, and a police officer apprehended Lolordo when the bodyguard attempted to chase the assassins.

Theories for Lombardo's assassination included payback for the murder of Frankie Yale in July, and that Moran and Aiello had jointly planned and made a move which proved that however ineffectual they were against Capone as separate forces, together they were a power to be reckoned with. Either version is plausible, although the speed and precision of the attack was contrary to the usual North Sider method. Regardless of who actually orchestrated the Lombardo hit, the Moran–Aiello forces would be responsible for more losses in the Capone camp in the coming months.

On November 3, 1928, while John Clay's fate was being plotted, Pete Gusenberg, Frank Foster, Leo Mongoven, and North Sider Clarence Gleason were arrested in connection with a robbery that had occurred the previous week. Three wealthy Chicago matrons—Mrs. George Levee, Mrs. William Leahy, and Mrs. George Arquette—had been ambushed in front of the Arquette home by partially masked bandits and relieved of $14,000 worth of jewelry. Mrs. Levee's black chauffeur positively identified Gusenberg and Gleason. They secured their freedom on $65,000 bail each and appeared in court on the morning of the fifth. After obtaining a continuance until the seventeenth, Mongoven, Gusenberg, and Foster drove to the Rookery Building at Adams and La Salle Streets.[26]

What happened next is a matter of record, although what brought it on is a matter of conjecture.

Abe Cooper had been one of many independent bootleggers who operated on the North Side with the O'Banion gang's approval. He told the police that he and a partner made wine for sacramental purposes, but it's more likely that they either supplied a designated client list with booze and kicked back a percentage to the O'Banions, or functioned as salesmen for North Sider product. By 1928, Cooper claimed, the personal and professional relationship with the gang had deteriorated, although he was vague as to the reason.

On April 2 Cooper was standing on Independence Boulevard, about to get into his car, when Mongoven drove by and fired eight shots at him. Cooper, his anger larger than his five-foot-two, 110-pound frame, jumped behind the wheel, chased Mongoven's vehicle, and rammed it from behind. "They all jumped [out[and ran," he recalled. "They let me alone for a week." The last time he saw them before November 5 was the day after the jewelry theft, when they waylaid him and demanded $5,000, relenting only when he pleaded for time to get the money together.

When Mongoven, Foster, and Gusenberg arrived at the Rookery Building, Cooper was in a brokerage house there. Mongoven stalked in, located him, and propelled him outside, where Foster and Gusenberg waited in the idling car.

"Get in and we'll take you for a ride," Mongoven ordered. Realizing that this was no mere extortion attempt, Cooper yanked out his revolver and put two bullets into his would-be attacker. When Mongoven dropped to the street, police officers who had been patrolling nearby sprinted onto the scene, prompting Gusenberg to flee. Foster also tried to run but was caught.

At the station, the police complimented Abe Cooper for his bravery at the same time that they were forced to charge him with attempted murder. When he related the story of the April 2 attack, they encouraged him not only to charge Gusenberg, Foster, and Mongoven with extortion, but also to charge Mongoven with attempted murder. All charges ended up being dropped, bringing the escalating fiasco to an end.

On December 4 Moran got word from St. Paul that his old friend Dan Hogan had been badly injured by an explosive charge wired to the starter of his Paige coupe.[27] The force of the blast had thrown the vehicle out of the Irishman's garage into the alley and torn his right leg off. Although Hogan protested from his deathbed that he had no enemies, Moran was concerned enough to offer his services to Hogan's family as a bodyguard after the funeral. He was seen pacing back and forth in front of their residence on West Seventh Street, puffing a cigarette as his eyes scanned oncoming cars and pedestrians. He remained in the city for a week, going back to Chicago in mid-December. Too much was happening there for him to be absent for long.

In an article titled "Jupiter Gives General Forecast for the Year 1929," the *Tribune's* resident "star-gazer" wrote:

> Whatever else the year 1929 might turn out to be, of one thing we can all be certain, it won't be dull, for the intermittently frenzied spirit that has swept the country since the world war will reach its zenith in the months to come . . . .
> The oncoming period will be one of great tribulation. Aside from the world of science, reason and sanity apparently will have fled . . . This country will face hate, suspicion, and jealousy. And during this crisis, internal strife against crime, corrupt practices, and protected vice rings will reach such proportions that it will practically become internecine warfare.

"Jupiter" predicted that Chicago and some other major U.S. cities would experience spectacular instances of crime and gang violence during the summer months, saying, "Ghastly and horrible murders will mark the sway of Mars and Neptune at this period. . . . New and heretofore unheard of methods of killing will be used. Cunning, cruelty, and fiendishness that has not been exercised by mankind since the Dark Ages will be brought to light in the trail of victims left by the slayers."[28]

Although Jupiter's forecast would be off the mark in terms of time span, the rest, in retrospect, was eerily accurate. The end of 1928 would be the end of an era.

14

BLOODY VALENTINE

J OE AIELLO MISSED HIS CHANCE for the Unione presidency yet again when Al Capone installed Pasqualino Lolordo, brother of Lombardo bodyguard Joseph Lolordo, in the post. He only lasted four months, his tenure ending on January 8, 1929. On that afternoon, Lolordo and his wife returned to their apartment on the top floor of a three-story building at 1921 West North Street. Two men whom the couple knew (although the wife later denied remembering their names) were waiting at the door. Mrs. Lolordo laid out food, drink, and cigars and busied herself in the kitchen until three, when she heard the men leave. Five minutes after their departure, another knock came at the door, which Lolordo answered. He seemed pleased to see the newcomers but acted as if their visit required privacy, closing the door to the kitchen.

After an hour of discussion and bouts of good-natured laughter, Aleina Lolordo heard a volley of shots. She burst out of the kitchen in time to see three men bending over the bloodied body of her husband, which lay in front of the fireplace. Not bothered by her presence, one of them slid a pillow under Lolordo's fractured head before they took their leave. The killers seemed unconcerned about the possibility of being caught; one tossed his still-warm .38 on the living room floor, and another threw his weapon away on the second-floor landing.

Early stories circulated that Aleina Lolordo named Joe Aiello as one of the visitors, a claim that John Stege disputed, saying, "She didn't identify anyone. I don't know how the report got started."[1]

Other reports named the trio as James Clark and Pete and Frank Gusenberg, a suspect list that gained credence when Mrs. Lolordo confirmed that the killers were not Italians.[2] How they acquired Lolordo's trust so completely that he welcomed them into his home without the presence of bodyguards can only be conjectured.

No one was charged with the murder of Patsy Lolordo, but Capone blamed the North Siders. Moran had to go, for without him, his followers would either be left aimless or with a new leader who might be less pugnacious in defending the North Side against the gradual inflow of Capone slot machines and liquor. Without Moran, Joe Aiello's wings would be clipped long enough for him to be hunted down and dealt with accordingly. The glory days that the North Side Gang had known under Dean O'Banion and Hymie Weiss were long over, but Moran was a resourceful and fearless enemy, and worse still, he had shot up Jack McGurn, played a role in Lolordo's murder, and continued to help himself to incoming liquor shipments consigned to Capone.

Moran's death would change things—it had to be arranged.

On January 13, 1929, a deadly cold snap seized Chicago, freezing the surface of the river, covering windows with blinding layers of frost, and turning the streets into the scene of many a life or death struggle. Three people, one of them a seventy-year-old widow, collapsed and died of exposure, and firemen who had to answer 175 alarms in a twenty-four hour period dealt with the double peril of frostbite and water freezing in their hoses.

As soon as the intensity of the cold relented, Moran and friend Israel Alderman took refuge in the Club Chez Pierre, a nightspot located at 247 East Ontario Street that catered mostly to the after-theater crowd.[3] After enjoying a quiet dinner, they collected their coats, bundled themselves against the cold, and went outside. Their breath fogged the air as they conversed on the way to Moran's car. Alderman, whose real name was Edelstein, had known Moran for years, and the two were close. One Chicago paper even referred to him as the North Sider's best friend.

He was definitely a lifesaver that night. The two had almost reached Moran's vehicle when Alderman noticed another car cruising along East Ontario Street, picking up speed as it approached. He reacted on instinct, grabbing Moran and hurling him sideways just before gunfire punctuated the frigid air. The two men tumbled over an iron railing headfirst. Alderman suffered only bruises, but Moran, when falling downward, was shot in the right thigh. The bullet sliced the skin, leaving a deep flesh wound, a discomfort that the North Sider could deal with considering that his head had been the intended target.

Other restaurant patrons who had been walking behind them hurried forward and helped them to their feet. Alderman, supporting Moran, assured them that he was taking his friend to a hospital. If anyone called the police, no officers arrived in time to prevent the two gangsters from climbing into Moran's car and seeking treatment from a physician who forsook the annoying practice of reporting gunshot wounds to the police.

This shot in the dark was probably Capone's response to the execution of Patsy Lolordo. Moran, shaken, sought private medical treatment for the injury and stayed off the streets for more than two weeks, confining himself to the Parkway Hotel suite that he shared with his wife and son.

Finally he sent word that he was ready to meet with the key members of his North Side Gang and discuss what form their answer to the shooting and business encroachment would take. The Parkway was too conspicuous a location, and one likely to be under scrutiny. It was the same with the Wigwam in the Marigold Hotel on North Broadway, and the gang's office at 127 North Dearborn. Too much was happening on all sides: the shooting, Capone's pushing slot machines into the North Side, and the Circus Gang, Capone associates lodged in North Sider territory, bombing speakeasies and stills under the joint protection of Moran and Aiello.[4] Moran told his key lieutenants that he had an informer in the enemy camp, someone who had warned him about what the enemy planned on doing and when.[5] An action plan had to be formulated.

At last a location was decided upon, a garage and impromptu liquor storage depot that Adam Heyer had leased the previous fall. When Moran sent word out at the beginning of February that a meeting was being called for the fourteenth, the news went beyond his immediate circle, a miscalculation he would not realize until it was too late.[6]

The one-story brick building at 2122 North Clark Street was outwardly unassuming. It measured about twenty-five feet wide by one hundred fifty feet deep. The upper half of the street window was painted black to conceal the interior from curious passersby, and additional disguise took the form of a dirty sign bearing the name SMC Cartage Company, which covered up the unpainted glass. Anyone who entered through the front door found themselves in a threadbare office with only a few desks, chairs, and a counter with telephones. A battered partition separated this small working area from a large garage that always seemed to have a truck or two parked alongside the brick walls. A heavy set of wooden doors opened out into the alley behind the building.

Adam Heyer, using the alias Frank J. Snyder, leased the garage in October 1928, and despite the signage advertising it as the home of a modest moving company, the building was used by the Moran gang as a liquor storage site and maintenance depot for their trucks. Crates of booze acquired from Detroit through Nails Morton's brother Paul were briefly stored in the rafters before undergoing the usual dilution transformation and ending up in the hands of the consumers.

Most days John May could be found working there, clad in grease- and oil-spot-ted coveralls as he repaired and tuned the gang's trucks. May was on the payroll as a mechanic at $50 a week, a job he welcomed because he had an ill wife, Hattie, and seven children to support. The fact that he had a minor record, having been charged (but not indicted) for burglary in 1913 and larceny in 1917,[7] would have led him to accept gangster money without qualms even if he had not been so finan-cially desperate.

At the beginning of February, Mrs. Michael Doody and Mrs. Frank Arvidson, who ran rooming houses at 2119 and 2135 North Clark Street, let two street-front rooms to men who passed themselves off as cab drivers working nights. The win-dows at both locations looked out over 2122, enabling the roomers to keep tabs on who was coming and going. It was a prelude to assassination that Capone had used in the Weiss murder, and now it would do just as well for Moran. There was only a slight chance of tying him to this one, for Capone was at his Palm Island estate, and had been since December.

On the morning of February 14 May was probably the first to arrive at the garage, having work to do on the trucks. He brought along his Alsatian dog, High-ball, and tied the animal's leash to a truck axle. Soon afterward, James Clark, Adam Heyer, Pete and Frank Gusenberg, and Reinhardt Schwimmer[8] joined him.

Schwimmer had been one of the North Side Gang's most stalwart pilot fish for years. An optometrist who had taken over—and mismanaged—his father's eyeglass business, Schwimmer had first made the acquaintance of O'Banion and then ingra-tiated himself with each successive leader. He was especially friendly with the Gusenbergs. Dr. Karl Meyer, chief surgeon at Cook County Hospital, would recall him constantly attending Peter Gusenberg when the latter was operated on for appendicitis in 1928.[9]

Schwimmer's marital and professional life matched each other for disaster. He experienced two short and tumultuous marriages, to Fae Johnson and a wealthy widow named Risch, and his father's business failed under his direction. In 1929 he, like Moran, lived at the Parkway, with his eccentric and doting mother, Josephine, both paying the rent and giving him "walking-around" money. He used his association with the North Siders for personal aggrandizement, telling anyone who would listen that he shared in their profits and could have anyone who aggra-vated him marked for death.

The six men made coffee on a gas ring, smoked, and conversed as they waited for the others—Al Weinshank, Ted Newberry, Willie Marks, and Moran. Frank Fos-ter may or may not have been due to drop by as well.

Weinshank finally showed up, clad in a tan hat and gray winter coat that, from a distance, gave him a strong resemblance to Moran. The watchers at the rooming house windows, who had been maintaining their post for almost two weeks, made the instant decision that Bugs Moran had joined his followers, and made a call.

Elmer Lewis, a driver for the Beaver Paper Company, was peering about for the address of his next delivery when he ran into potential disaster at North Clark and Webster. A seven-passenger Cadillac, coming down Webster, swerved left onto North Clark and collided with his truck, its left rear fender thumping solidly into his left front bumper. When Lewis got over the shock and took a good look at the other vehicle, his heart sank; the siren, gong, and rear gun rack signified its police issue, and two uniformed officers were among the five men in the car. A man wearing a blue suit and an elegant chinchilla overcoat got out, glanced at the minor damage, and to Lewis's surprise and relief, just laughed and motioned him to move along.

After Lewis forged gratefully onward, the Cadillac continued along North Clark, sliding to a halt in front of the garage at 2122. He delivered his package and returned to his truck in time to hear loud popping noises that he shrugged off as car backfires, a common enough sound on Chicago's busy streets.

Jeanette Landesman, a thirty-four-year-old housewife who lived over Sam Schneider's tailor shop at 2124 North Clark with her husband, son, and aging mother, was ironing clothes in her kitchen, when she heard a rapid-fire series of noises coming from somewhere in the garage next door. Curious and concerned, as the sounds were too prolonged to be mere car backfires, she waited until silence reigned again and then went to her living room window, which overlooked North Clark. Mrs. Landesman saw a small group of men get into what looked like a police vehicle, which pulled quickly away from the curb and went south on the street, narrowly missing collision with a trolley car.

Just before Mrs. Landesman reached her window, Moran and Willie Marks rounded the corner of Griffin and North Clark.[10] They had been scheduled to arrive at the garage fifteen minutes earlier, but Moran's appointment at the Parkway Hotel's barbershop had run overtime.[11] They stood there, watching a pair of uniformed cops marching two strangers at gunpoint out of the garage into a waiting police car. What conclusion, if any, they came to can only be surmised. Moran would comment later that the sight of the police uniforms did not alarm him half as much as the fact that he did not recognize the men in their custody, men being herded out of the garage where his colleagues were supposed to be waiting for him.[12]

Ted Newberry and Henry Gusenberg, by various accounts, either stumbled across the same scene or were warned away personally or via telephone once Moran and Marks retreated. Foster's whereabouts that morning are unknown.

In the meantime, Jeanette Landesman's curiosity had gotten the better of her. She left her apartment, went down two flights of stairs, and stepped out onto the icy sidewalk. As she tried to peer through the SMC Cartage Company's front window, the sound of a dog howling somewhere in the dim interior unnerved her, especially in the wake of the suspicious noises that initially had drawn her attention. She tried the door, but it refused to budge. Returning to her building, she went back up the stairs, stopping at the room of self-employed sign painter Clair McAllister. At her request, he agreed to check out the source of the dog's agitation.[13]

The first thing that McAllister noticed as he forced open the front door was the searing scent of gunpowder. Following the direction of the dog's yelping, he crossed the vacant front office, entering the acrid, smoky garage area. The noises from the distressed canine and the pungent air were clear signs that something out of the ordinary had taken place minutes before, but McAllister could hardly have been prepared for the butchery that met his horrified stare when he emerged from between two parked vehicles.

Six men were lying against the garage's north wall, flesh and clothing torn by bullets, blood from their mangled heads and bodies puddling on the filthy concrete floor. An overhead lamp cast a sickly yellow glow over the entire spectacle, making the dead men's pallor even more ghastly and darkening the rivulets of blood that coursed lazily toward a floor drain. In sharp contrast to their stillness was the sight of a barking gray Alsatian dog that struggled against the cheap yellow rope binding it to a jacked-up truck.

A seventh man was still moving, feebly attempting to extricate himself from his lifeless colleagues. Looking up and seeing the white-faced painter, he croaked, "Who is it?"

McAllister stammered, "I just came to help you out." Then he turned, ran back outside, and staggered up the stairs of his own building, calling for Mrs. Landesman to phone for the police and a doctor.

Josephine Morin, who lived across the street at 2125 North Clark, also saw the "cops" and their apparent prisoners depart the garage, climb into the Cadillac, and drive away. So did James Wilcox, who had been delivering coal in the vicinity. He gave in to curiosity and entered the death scene, coming across the still struggling Frank Gusenberg when the first police officers arrived in response to Jeanette Landesman's frantic call.[14]

Sergeant Thomas J. Loftus and two other policemen attached to the Thirty-Sixth district station, George Love and Thomas Christie, reached the scene at around 10:45 a.m. Loftus entered the garage first, ordering Wilcox out before taking in the worst carnage he had encountered in his thirty-eight years on the force. Managing to contain his horror for the sake of the one survivor, he leaned toward Gusenberg and asked, "Do you know me, Frank?"

The North Sider's reply was barely audible. "Yes, you're Tom Loftus." When the sergeant asked him what had happened, he whispered, "I won't talk." A pause, then he added, "Cops did it." Gusenberg fended off further questions with a plea of, "For God's sake, get me to a hospital."[15]

Loftus stayed with him until the wagon arrived and carted the injured gangster to Alexian Brothers Hospital. The wagon men responded to the sergeant's order for a physician by fetching Dr. Frederick Doyle, who owned the Northern Hospital and dispensary at 2314 North Clark Street. Doyle tried the pulses of the six men against the bullet-ravaged wall and confirmed that all were dead.

Doyle was really only officially stating the obvious. The bodies were badly ripped up, indicating a machine-gun attack so savage that it was a miracle Frank Gusenberg had survived it. Slugs of the .45-caliber variety had been sprayed across their lower backs and at the level of their shoulders and heads. The left side of May's skull was gone, and Schwimmer's back bore a huge "cluster wound" from a shotgun blast.[16]

While the police tried to bag evidence (which included a snub-nosed .38 that likely had fallen out of Frank Gusenberg's pocket) and the photographers who soon showed up made the garage even smokier with flash powder, Police Commissioner William Russell and Coroner Herman Bundesen arrived. After they surveyed the scene, the six corpses were loaded onto stretchers and conveyed via police wagons to Braithwaite's, a private mortuary at 2219 Lincoln Avenue.

Gusenberg clung to life at Alexian Brothers for hours, Officer James Mikes assigned to question him during lucid moments. He responded to the repeated query of "Who shot you?" with a weak but stubborn "Nobody shot me." After declining an offer of a priest, he died at 1:30 p.m., bringing the North Clark Street massacre death toll to seven.

The failure of the seven men to fight back was attributed to the police uniforms worn by two of the assassins. Just four days previously, on February 10, Pete Gusenberg, along with Frank Foster, had been rounded up along with roughly five hundred other known characters and paraded before robbery and burglary victims at the South State Street district police station.[17] When death came calling on the morning of the fourteenth, the North Siders' fight or flight instincts were subdued by annoyance and resignation.

Theories for the multiple murder proliferated. One scenario that persists to the present day is that the North Siders had agreed to meet in the garage that morning to receive a hijacked shipment of Old Log Cabin whiskey and been slaughtered by the rightful owner. Other angles that were thoroughly investigated were a supposed conflict with Detroit's Purple Gang, a rupture between the North Siders and the Aiellos, payback for the murder of John Clay, additional payback for Lombardo and Lolordo, and a Canadian distillery war. None of them stood up under close scrutiny.[18]

"I can tell you one thing," a Moran relative who was seven at the time remembers, "there was no meeting with out-of-town gangsters or any plans to unload bootleg. They were there to meet George because he'd been shot and they were losing their territory to Capone. George was always thinking his [phone] lines were tapped and they were waiting for their chance to find out where he'd be and finish him off."[19] Incidentally, early news reports indicated that a telephone repairman had been to the garage numerous times during the days leading up to the mass killing, making sure that the phones were not tapped. His last visit was supposedly the morning of the fourteenth, not long before the shooters made their appearance.[20]

Because Moran could not immediately be found in any of his normal haunts, the initial assumption was that he had been one of the "prisoners" seen coming out of the garage by the witnesses. Word of his body being found in a ditch or alley was anticipated hourly, and the period of uneasy expectation did not end until he came forward, albeit indirectly.

Prostrated by grief and shock, Moran had checked into the St. Francis Hospital in Evanston later on the day of the fourteenth, after spending hours secluded in his suite at the Parkway. He notified Chief of Detectives Eagan that he had no idea what had brought on the bloodshed, adding, "We're facing an enemy in the dark."[21] He remained in the hospital until February 18, although reports reached police headquarters that he was seen outside its walls on the fifteenth,[22] and upon checkout went first to Detroit, then crossed the Canadian border into Windsor. Lucille and John remained at the Parkway, with Leo Mongoven assuming responsibility for their protection and welfare.[23] Ted Newberry and Willie Marks were among the small contingent that accompanied the shaken gang boss.

The small band of refugees stayed at the King Edward Hotel in Windsor and no doubt spent many a late night grieving the loss of so many comrades and wondering about the future of their own lives and the organization. In the end, everyone returned to Chicago to safeguard what gambling, union, and bootlegging interests remained, while Moran, knowing that he was the principal target of the Capone Syndicate, the police, and the press, decided to make himself "unavailable" for the next few months. After exiting Windsor, he made his way to Montreal, where he booked passage on a ship bound for Europe. He had decided to hide out in Paris until the storm passed, and his nerves had steadied.[24]

Capone, when contacted by the press in Florida, told one reporter, "That fellow Moran isn't called 'Bugs' for nothing. He's crazy if he thinks I had anything to do with that killing."

The killers' chances of going to the chair for the massacre, providing they could be found, tried, and convicted in the first place, were distressingly minimal. Fred Pasley noted in *Al Capone*, "In Chicago (in 1928) there were 367 murders, 129 of which were either unsolved or the principals not apprehended. Of those arrested, 37 were acquitted, 39 received jail sentences, 16 were sent to insane asylums, 16 committed suicide, and 11 [gangster cases] were killed. There were no executions. In other words, on the 1928 record, a murderer had a 300–to–0 chance that he would not be sentenced to death in Chicago."

Well, not by the courts anyway.

Police Commissioner William Russell promised the shocked and revolted public, "It's war to the finish. I've never known a challenge like this—the killers posing as policemen—but now that the challenge has been made, it's been accepted. We are going to make this the death knell of gangdom in Chicago."[25] Assistant State's Attorney David Stansbury, assigned by his office to head the inquiry into what the press called the "North Clark Street Massacre," said, "I've heard of brutal slayings in

Chicago but never anything quite equal to this. The gangsters, by their very bold-ness, have written their own doom." Pat Roche spoke for federal authorities when he said, "Never in the history of feuds or gangland has Chicago or the nation seen anything like today's wholesale slaughter."[26]

Commissioner Russell and State's Attorney Swanson competed in the press with promises that their men would wipe out booze drinking and selling in Chicago. Between them, they damaged so much business in that field that saloonkeepers began complaining bitterly about how the gangsters had gone too far this time. "Why can't the big shots go along and be satisfied making thousands while we make dollars?" one complained.

Police investigators searched the homes of the victims, taking a loaded gun from Schwimmer's room at the Parkway and finding two men, one of them his brother-in-law Patrick King, in Frank Gusenberg's place. They also interviewed family mem-bers, all of whom yielded no clues but provided a colorful cast of characters at the inquest presided over by Coroner Bundesen.

Maurice Weinshank, uncle of Al and an attorney with offices at 110 West Washington Street, took the stand at the inquest to testify that he knew nothing of any illegal activities that his deceased nephew might have been involved in. All he knew for sure was that he and Al had planned to meet later that morning and discuss an intended Florida trip to see a prizefight between Jack Sharkey and Young Stribling.

He was followed to the stand by Henry Gusenberg, who said that he was a motion-picture projectionist with two now-deceased brothers that he rarely saw, making him no expert on what they did for a living. Pete's widow, Myrtle, who sobbed that she had married the gangster the previous June, insisted that she had known him as "P. J. Gorman," a prosperous real estate broker.

Two women showed up for questioning, claiming to be the widow of Frank Gusenberg. The gangster had married Ruth five years previously, then wed Lucille while his first union was two years old. The two women glowered at each other and refused to disclose details about their late husband's affairs on the wit-ness stand.

Adam Heyer's seventeen-year-old son, Howard, cringed from photographers as he testified that his father had been general manager of the Fairview Kennel Club. Mrs. Marie Neubauer, sister of James Clark, drew universal sympathy when she told the coroner's jury that she had lost her husband in an accident in late January and, less than a month later, was suffering from the additional shock of losing her wayward brother.

The most pathetic witness of the day was Reinhart Schwimmer's aged mother, Josephine, who paid the rent for his Parkway Hotel room and gave him the money he needed to maintain the lifestyle he was used to. Tears actually welled in the eyes of many courtroom onlookers as the elderly woman mourned the loss of her only child: "He was always a good boy, my son, until he got to going around with that

North Side Gang about a year and a half ago [sic]. I pleaded with him and warned him to break away from them, but he seemed to like to boast about knowing reputed 'toughs' and having an 'in.'"

The last witnesses of the day were James May and Mrs. Lucy Powell, John May's brother and sister. James said vaguely that as far as he knew, his deceased brother had been a truck driver and mechanic. Mrs. Powell said that Hattie May, the widow, was at home, too hysterical to testify. In the wake of their testimony, some reporters with no sense of decency or decorum cracked jokes about the bullet-chipped St. Christopher medals that had been taken from May's corpse, wondering what protective use they had served.[27]

Major Frederick D. Silloway, assistant administrator of the Prohibition Unit in Chicago, made an early and sensational claim that the killers had been real cops. He said that six weeks previously, five hundred cases of liquor consigned to Moran had been hijacked on Indianapolis Boulevard by men from "a West Side gang led by Billy Skidmore, Jack Zuta, and Frankie Pope," and that the ease with which the theft was accomplished strongly indicated the hijackers had police protection. According to Silloway, Moran retaliated by cutting off the regular flow of protection payments. "The result of this move," he said, "was the machine-gun killing of yesterday."[28]

Commissioner Russell blanched at the accusation but publicly maintained his composure. "If Major Silloway has any evidence in this case, he ought to come to us with it. . . . I'm going to go through with this investigation. We are going to find out who committed this crime. As far as Major Silloway is concerned, I would just as soon prosecute policemen, if they are guilty, as anyone else."[29]

Chief of Detectives John Egan echoed his chief's hostility. "It is all very well for Major Silloway to hatch theories and give them out for publication," he said, "but we will pay more attention when he can produce facts." Silloway, unable to produce any, was transferred from his post and eventually fired.

Young George Arthur Brichetti (Brichet by some accounts) offered the police more than just conjecture. He claimed to have seen a car in the alley behind 2122 North Clark, pulling up to the garage's rear doors. Two of the four passengers were in police uniforms. Brichetti, curious, watched three of them go into the building and, guessing that a raid was in progress, ran down the alley and around to the front, hoping to see more. He got there in time to see the men walk out.

He would recall that one of the men in civilian garb was missing a finger and said to a companion, "All right, Mac." Brichetti's story was indirectly supported by a statement from Jeanette Landesman's elderly mother, who claimed to have seen two detective squad cars pull up in front of the SMC Cartage Company, although one left before the shooting began.[30]

William J. Helmer and Art Bilek, in their book *The St. Valentine's Day Massacre: The Untold Story of the Gangland Bloodbath that Brought Down Al Capone*, noted that the young man's statement threw new light on how the killers had gained entry to the garage.

240

> What now made sense, although it was not reported, was that the killers didn't just go in and out the *front* door, as virtually every account describes.
>
> For one thing, the front door almost certainly was locked, and a uniformed policeman, especially a stranger, was not likely to be invited in . . . . It would have been much simpler for the men in uniform to enter from the alley, disarm the seven victims, and then open the door for the shooters. . . .[31]

On the strength of Brichetti's story, police began looking for James Belcastro, Capone's master bomber, who had a missing finger, and Jack McGurn, the only "Mac" they could think of with a connection to Capone, who was already universally suspected as the mastermind behind the killings.[32] Their names were integrated into a wanted list, to which fifteen other names were soon added.

On February 21 Commissioner Russell announced that, as part of the police drive to dry up Chicago, investigators would be searching garages, barns, sheds, and any other outbuilding large enough to house an alky-cooking still. Hours later, neighbors living in the vicinity of 1723 North Wood Street saw smoke drifting lazily out of a garage at that address and called the fire department. What the firemen found resulted in a hurried call to the police.

Inside the smoky building was a 1927 Cadillac seven-passenger sedan that had been partially dismantled by a hacksaw, ax, and acetylene torch. A police siren had been removed from the car and discarded in a corner. A charred coat and hat lay on the floor, and a nurse at a nearby doctor's office recalled their probable owner, a man who came in with burns that he claimed resulted from a still explosion. When told that he would have to wait until the doctor finished with another patient, the man took off. Assistant State's Attorney Harry Ditchburne stated his firm belief, as did one deputy chief, that the murder car had been found.[33]

Investigation revealed that the garage had been rented on February 12 to "Frank Rogers," who gave his address as 1859 West North Avenue. It was a locale familiar to the police, as the Circus Café, headquarters of Capone ally Claude Maddox, was right next door. Witnesses would recall seeing Maddox and two helpers in dirty overalls in the vicinity of the Wood Street garage, but that alone was not enough to make a case against him, automobile abuse not being a crime. A known opponent of Moran and the Aiellos by 1929, Maddox's name joined Belcastro's and McGurn's on the "wanted list," along with Joseph Lolordo, Capone's future brother-in-law Frank Maritote, and, bizarrely enough, Joe Aiello and one of his brothers.

Six days later, another car, this one a black 1926 Peerless touring car, went up in flames in suburban Maywood.[34] The explosion woke up the entire neighborhood. Like the Wood Street car, this one had a police gong lying nearby, as well as two spent shotgun shells like those used in the massacre, license plates with a Chicago detective squad prefix that had been stolen two months before, and a red notebook that had belonged to Al Weinshank. The discovery lent powerful credence to the theory that two cars had been used in the murder plot.

McGurn was picked up at the end of February and indicted in mid-March, but the police could only go on the assumption that he had helped plan the massacre without actively taking part. His alibi was too good—blonde, sultry Louise Rolfe insisted that on the morning in question, she had been in bed with him at the Stevens Hotel. Without getting explicit, she did purr, "When you're with Jack, you're never bored."[35]

Her testimony kept McGurn from being tried as a killer, but it got him charged under the Mann Act, a law dating from the white-slavery days that prohibited a woman from being taken across state lines for immoral purposes. The crime? Taking Rolfe, a woman not his wife, to Florida for an erotic holiday. He married her, presumably to prevent her from being forced to testify against him, but the state went ahead and charged him anyway—and Louise too, for the unusual crime of conspiring to debauch herself.

The police announced that they were looking for two former members of the St. Louis-based Egan's Rats gang: Frederick "Killer" Burke, a fugitive since 1927, when he skipped bail on a 1925 bank robbery charge, and James Ray, the usual alias of Gus Winkler, another ex-Rat with whom he usually worked. They were fugitives from Ohio justice at the time of the massacre, being wanted for bank robbery and murder, and both were known to use police uniforms as a disarming ruse in their crimes.[36]

The two had recently robbed the American Securities Company in Toledo, along with Chicagoan Fred Goetz and Toledo native Ray "Crane-Neck" Nugent. They transported the company's safe to Nugent's garage to blast it open, and Burke shot a policeman who had followed them to their lair.[37] In fleeing the scene Goetz left behind his coat, which contained the Cicero address where he was living with his wife and Byron Bolton, a cohort.

Other suspects named and sought were Joseph Lolordo, brother of the slain Patsy, and Scalise and Anselmi. To investigate *any* spectacular gang murder without adding the murder twins to the suspect list was practically a misstep.

Scalise and Anselmi were found, charged with murder, and appeared in court on March 8. Their lawyer, Thomas Nash, got the arresting officer to admit that he had no "just and reasonable" grounds for assuming that the pair had anything to do with the Moran gang slaughter, and they eventually walked.

On March 20 Commissioner Russell conferred with the corporation counsel's office to ascertain whether they could dissolve an injunction issued by Judge Harry Fisher that prohibited police from raiding a Moran gambling house, the Sheridan Wave Tournament Club at 621 Waveland Avenue. It was a more upscale resort that raked in money under the shrewd management of Joey Josephs and Julian "Potatoes" Kaufman. A Mr. and Mrs. Feigenheimer claimed that bandits had followed them when they left the place the previous morning, and robbed them of $30,000 in diamonds.

The Sheridan Wave had been operating under Fisher's injunction since the previous June. Reverend Elmer Williams, who published the brazen reform broadsheet *Lightnin*, noted of the judicial rescue:

> Al Capone may be our greatest civic leader, when it comes to developing and encouraging greyhounds, but he is not the only idealist who is unselfishly giving himself for our Metropolis. George "Bugs" Moran is a close second.
>
> When attorney Martin L. Callahan appeared before Judge Harry M. Fisher on June 7, 1928, seeking an injunction [to protect the Sheridan Wave], he presented the sworn statement that this club was "organized for the higher and better ideals in sporting contests and tournaments." Judge Fisher, always alert to encourage civic enterprises, issued the injunction. . . .
>
> Mr. Moran, having a great beer business to look after, could not give the Sheridan Wave much of his personal attention. But he placed "Potatoes" Kaufman in charge. . . . But on February 14, 1929, a mob of uncouth barbarians who have no appreciation of the culture fostered by Bugs Moran by the grace of Judge Fisher, invaded the private garage of Mr. Moran at 2122 N. Clark Street, where he kept a lot of culture in storage in kegs, and standing seven men up against a wall, including some of Moran's leading artists, cut them in pieces with a machine gun.
>
> This incident of St. Valentine's Day directed attention to the civic activities at the Sheridan Wave and greatly interfered with the "higher and better ideals in sporting contests and tournaments" going on there.[38]

The club ended up padlocked, and issues surrounding its re-opening would bring another scandal upon Chicago over a year later.

Soon after the coroner's jury opened for the second time, on February 23, Bundesen created a sensation by announcing that Calvin Goddard, who worked at the police ballistics bureau that he had helped establish in New York, was being hired to examine the shell casings and bullets taken from the garage and from the victims' bodies. Goddard's testimony was as impressive as promised. After conducting a detailed examination, he told the jury on April 13 that the massacre gunmen had used two machine guns and two shotguns, both pump automatics. The Chicago

Police Department was relieved of a public relations burden when Goddard said that he had tested the weapons owned by the Chicago and Cicero forces and not found the murder guns among them.[39]

Impressed by his evidence, two of the jurors, wealthy business owners Burt Massee and Walter Olson, helped fund the Scientific Crime Detection Laboratory, which was affiliated with Northwestern University. Goddard was named its director, his talents being of the caliber that violence-ridden Chicago needed at that point.

When the inquest jury reconvened in April, Pete Von Frantzius, whose sporting goods store at 608 West Diversey Parkway had been a regular destination for Hymie Weiss and other members of the North Side Gang (as well as their enemies) found himself on the hot seat. On April 19 he described how he had gotten into the "arms" business by running a small mail-order operation out of his mother's house until he opened the shop on Diversey in 1925. Among the items he kept stocked were Thompsons, of which he admitted to selling around fifty since 1925, one of which canceled the life of Frankie Yale.

He did not seem concerned about his product falling into the wrong hands, stating coolly on May 1, "We are in the business of selling firearms." Much as he may have wanted to, Bundesen could not touch him, the selling of machine guns being legal, even to criminals with records the size of the Bible.

Frank Thompson of Kirkland, Illinois, who was one of the underworld's major suppliers of Thompson submachine guns, took the stand on May 30. He was an excellent machine-gun salesman because he made good use of the weapon himself. In 1927 he became so incensed after a quarrel with his wife that he shot up her parents' home in Kirkland. The stunt earned him a conviction for assault with a deadly weapon and a six-month sentence in the DeKalb County Jail.[40] His testimony increased the sinister element of the proceedings, when he talked about the deliberate removal of serial numbers from weapons he sold and purchasers whose identities were unknown.

While burning garages were being investigated and his own whereabouts remained a source of mystery for those not in the know, Moran arrived in Paris, where he took accommodations at the newly built, elegant Hotel de Montalembert in the Left Bank. The hotel, built in 1926 and named after Charles Forbes Montalembert, writer and member of the prestigious Academie Française, was a favorite destination for artists and writers. It is not known who, if anyone, accompanied him on the trip, as the postcards he sent to Lucille only went into detail about his own exploits. Moran even mentioned an attempt at robbing him on the Boulevard St-Germain during the early morning hours.

"At first I let them [commit the holdup] because I thought they had rods," he wrote to Lucille in a letter dated March 1929. "Then I saw that they just had knives." He flung off his coat, hurled it over one of the two would-be robbers, and launched himself at them. "I walked back to the hotel with just a shiner, and they were carried off to the station in an old cart," he concluded proudly.[41]

He was one of millions who thronged the sidewalks of Paris to watch the somber, magnificent funeral procession of Marshal Ferdinand Foch, French war hero who died on March 20, 1929. On March 26 the procession left Notre Dame Cathedral and wound through the streets toward the temple that Louis XIV had erected for the interment of war heroes. Among the mourners were the French president, American politicians, statesmen and royal personages from other European countries, and prominent men in the fields of art and science. While a band played "La Marseillaise," onlookers cast their awed gaze over the gun carriage, drawn by six coal-black horses, containing Foch's regal, silver-handled oak casket. More than two hundred people were injured in their eagerness to take in the spectacle, falling off roofs, cornices, canopies, and other precarious vantage points.[42]

After watching for awhile, Moran retreated either to his room at the hotel or a café and penned another letter to Lucille.[43] "That whole show was like the old days in Chicago," he wrote, clearly referring to the showy funerals of O'Banion, Colosimo, and Angelo Genna. "I don't think I'll have anything like that when my time comes though."

France would have a restorative effect on him. When he boarded a ship for the return trip at the end of May, his old nerve and determination had returned.

Moran missed the May 1929 conference in Atlantic City that was attended by almost every other Chicago gang leader of note, as well as delegates from other cities in the East and Midwest. John Torrio helped preside over a crowd that included New York crime figures Frank Costello, Meyer Lansky, Charles "Lucky" Luciano, and Dutch Schultz; New Jersey boss Abner "Longy" Zwillman; Abe Bernstein, leader of Detroit's Purple Gang; Max "Boo Boo" Hoff from Philadelphia; and Charles "King" Solomon from Boston.

When Capone addressed them, he emphasized that the killings had to stop, that they had to look on their businesses as blue-collar workers regarded theirs, something to be worked at and then forgotten at quitting time. "It wasn't easy," he later remembered, "for men who had been fighting for years to agree on a peaceful business program."[44]

In the end, they agreed with his logic and signed their names on the dotted line. The St. Valentine's Day Massacre, a blatant symbol of bootlegger violence that inflamed citizens and authority figures previously inclined to be tolerant, had shamed the nation. There was a lot of damage to be repaired, and the conference was a crucial first step.

Ironically, Capone, who spoke so forcefully and persuasively about nonviolence being the key to future prosperity, left a decidedly gory—not to mention *violent*— sign of his wrath for Indiana law enforcement officials to find before he headed to Atlantic City. Perhaps the contract he would sign had special clauses applying to betrayal.

At about one-thirty on the morning of May 8, 1929, two Indiana police officers came across a coupe parked in a lonely spot called Spooner's Nook, just across the Illinois state line, near Hammond. It yielded a grisly cargo. John Scalise and Joseph Guinta, who had beaten out Joe Aiello for the Unione presidency, were slumped in the rear seat, bodies blackened from a recent and savage beating. Albert Anselmi, who was also bruised and swollen almost beyond recognition, lay in the road, about twenty-five feet away from the silent vehicle. All three men were dead, although the apparent cause was a toss-up between the bullet wounds in their heads and the blunt violence applied to their bodies.

The Hammond Police Department solicited the aid of Coroner Bundesen and Deputy Commissioner Stege once investigating officers concluded that the trio had been murdered in retaliation for the St. Valentine's Day Massacre. The general consensus was that they had been killed somewhere in Chicago and transported in two vehicles to Spooner's Nook.

"The three men killed today were not small-fry members of the Capone–Lombardo outfit," Stege said. "I believe it is a serious attempt on the part of the Moran gang, especially the Aiello faction of it, to wipe out the leaders of the Capone gang, including Capone himself."[45]

Other theories included the suggestion that the trio had been the victims of Little Italy residents whose resentment at being squeezed for contributions to the Scalise–Anselmi defense fund had fermented over time into a murderous rage. The appalling condition of the bodies did point toward an emotionally charged assault. Someone else brought up the possibility that the killings had been committed during the robbery of said funds. The latter notion arose primarily from the fact that the pockets of all three corpses had been turned inside out, an unusual state for a gangland murder victim to be found in.

The truth took a while to come to light, but when it did, it revealed an intricate network of double-crossing that would have made Machiavelli yield his title.

John Scalise had long been showing signs of being deluded by a sense of invincibility. As a merciless torpedo valued first by the Terrible Gennas and now Al Capone, he knew and relished that he inspired fear. The magnitude of the defense fund that had been raised for him and Anselmi suggested that his status and reputation could squeeze blood from a stone. His success in walking free after a double cop killing only added to the awe with which he was regarded. Not long after the massacre, he was heard to boast, "I am the most powerful man in Chicago."

At least powerful enough in his own mind to consider betraying Capone the way he had discarded his loyalty to the Gennas.

Two versions exist of Scalise's plans for treachery and Capone's discovery of them. The first contended that the ambitious killer met Joe Aiello at a Waukegan restaurant and accepted the latter's offer of $50,000 to kill Capone. A waiter overheard the plot and conveyed the details to the intended victim. The second suggested that Capone's loyal bodyguard Frank Rio caught scent of a plot being hatched by Scalise, Anselmi, and Joe Guinta, and to get concrete proof, feigned a quarrel with his boss to gain the plotters' trust. The trio told Rio about their plans to murder Capone, use their position within the Unione to assume control of the Outfit, and grant the North Side to Joe Aiello (no mention of Moran) to ensure his continued support. When Rio presented his evidence, Capone did some scheming of his own. Either way, the Sicilians' intentions were not as camouflaged as they believed, something they never realized until they had nowhere to run.

On the night of Tuesday, May 7, Scalise, Anselmi, and Guinta joined Capone and an assortment of Outfit members at The Plantation, a Torrio–Capone roadhouse near Thirty-fifth and Indiana on the South Side. After a banquet during which the trio, believing themselves to be guests of honor, feasted on mountains of pasta and veal and washed it all down with the finest wines, liqueurs, and coffee, Capone dropped the gaiety act and informed them that he was aware of what they had been planning. He held back long enough for the terror to set in, then picked up a cut-down baseball bat and beat all three to a pulp, reserving the most violence for John Scalise.

Once Capone was too exhausted from spent fury to strike any longer, his henchmen (and probably Capone as well) finished the job with bullets. Scalise, miraculously still alive after the brutal attack, raised one hand to ward off the bullet aimed at his head. It tore off his little finger before embedding in his eye.

George Meyer, who was on guard duty in the roadhouse anteroom, told author Robert Schoenberg, "They said Capone got so worked up they thought he had a heart attack."[46] The proof was in the end result: a pathologist who examined the victims declared that never before had he seen such badly beaten corpses.

Guinta's murder allowed Joe Aiello to acquire the Unione presidency that he had coveted for years. He would hold the position until October 1930, when Capone got around to dealing with him at long last.

On May 16 Capone left Atlantic City, accompanied by Frank Rio and two other bodyguards, and headed for Philadelphia, where they planned to catch a train to Chicago. Car trouble caused them to miss their connection, and the next train did not leave for three hours, so they decided to take in a movie at the local cinema.

The film was a detective picture, and what happened when they left the theater could have been a continuation. Two Philadelphia detectives, one of whom claimed to have seen Capone in Florida and recognized him as he was going into the cinema, flashed their badges, and Capone and Rio surrendered their weapons. The two bodyguards, who had been following at a distance, slipped into the crowd.

Charged with carrying concealed weapons and being "suspicious characters," Capone and Rio appeared before Judge John E. Walsh and pleaded guilty. Walsh then sentenced them to a year in jail, the maximum penalty allowed for that offense. The two prisoners evidenced surprise, the typical punishment for gun toting being ninety days maximum. But Capone just sighed to a bailiff, "It's the breaks, kid," as he and Rio were led away.[47]

The story circulated that the whole episode had been prearranged, that Capone agreed, in view of the still-hot furor over the massacre, to allow himself to be jailed. Frank Loesch of the Chicago Crime Commission claimed that he wanted to escape the wrath of Moran and/or Sicilians who were inclined to avenge Scalise, Anselmi, and Guinta. Even the *Philadelphia Record* noted, "Scarface Al Capone went deliberately to jail." Probably. The knowledge that Capone was behind bars could be expected to lower the heat being applied to his Chicago interests because of the recent bloodshed.

When Moran returned from France, one of the first things he did was place an undisclosed amount of money in trust for Peter Gusenberg Sr., to ensure that the old man would have a comfortable old age despite the loss of two of his sons in the massacre.[48]

The third son, Henry, was not scared onto the straight and narrow path after the slaughter of his brothers. On May 15, 1933, Gusenberg reported his car stolen, and collected $1,400 in insurance money. It was later found in the possession of Harry Burns, an ex-convict with a record dating back to 1918, who was taken to felony court for arraignment. When Gusenberg failed to appear, the case was dismissed.

Assistant State's Attorney Charles Dougherty, suspecting that something much deeper was afoot, took Burns before the grand jury. The man panicked during questioning and confessed that Gusenberg had offered him $100 to steal the car so that insurance money could be obtained. He added resentfully that he had only been given $20 of the promised fee so far.[49] True bills were voted against Gusenberg and gambling house proprietor Paul Kuhn, who had acted as the go-between in the plot.

They appeared before Judge Harry Miller on April 19, 1934, charged with conspiracy to defraud the insurance company, but were acquitted on the twenty-third.[50] The rest of Gusenberg's life was comparatively uneventful, and he died in March 1978.

On May 20, 1929, while the echo from the North Clark Street Massacre gunfire was still being heard figuratively if no longer literally, President Herbert Hoover established the National Commission on Law Observance and Enforcement.[51] Chaired by George W. Wickersham, who had served as U.S. attorney general under President Taft, the committee consisted of ten individuals prominent in American law enforcement and/or public affairs, such as Frank Loesch, leader of the Chicago Crime Commission; Roscoe Pound, dean of Harvard Law School and leading expert on American criminal justice; and Newton D. Baker, reformer during the Progressive Era and secretary of war under President Wilson.

Among the subjects selected for scrutiny were Prohibition; Enforcement of the Prohibition Laws of the United States; Criminal Statistics; Prosecution; Enforcement of the Deportation Laws of the United States; the Child Offender in the Federal System of Justice and the Federal Courts; Criminal Procedure; Penal Institutions, Probation, and Parole; Crime and the Foreign Born; the Cost of Crime; the Causes of Crime (two volumes); and the Police. Modeling its aims on that of the Cleveland Survey of Criminal Justice, which published its report in 1922 (and which had been co-directed by Roscoe Pound), it not only investigated the primary components of the criminal justice system (police, courts, and corrections) but also investigated new areas, such as theoretical criminology, criminal statistics, and the costs of crime.

Chicago was a fertile ground for such a study, considering that gangsters such as Moran and Capone carried more weight there than the police and politicians. Reporter Lemuel Parton wrote, "It may be reported, without cynicism, that Al Capone, the Aiello Brothers, Jack Cusick [sic], and George "Bugs" Moran wield far greater influence in Chicago than Dr. Merriman, and Dr. Goode, and all the other high-minded and indefatigable university professors who have been frantically swinging red lights across the track since the university started. If the Wickersham Report should bring law violators to an issue in Chicago, and it should devolve upon the city to do something about it, no one can deny that the decision would be influenced more by the gangsters than by the teachers."

The Wickersham Report, when finally released, contained observations and recommendations that were never acted on, as the country was more focused on coping with the social and economic devastation accompanying the Depression. It did little more than state the obvious: that the Volstead Act had given the nation's gangsters a leg up out of the immigrant ghetto and into the economic, social, and political life of the nation.

On June 12 three raids targeting dog tracks run by the Capone Syndicate, Moran's North Siders, and the Chicago Heights Syndicate were executed.[52] The state's attorney's office celebrated the assaults directed at the Hawthorne Kennel Club, Fairview Club, and the Illinois Kennel Club as a "smashing blow at the dog-racing racket."

The Fairview at Lawrence Avenue and Mannheim Road, which the Morans operated, was practically deserted when the police raiders arrived. About fifty customers stood around, looking at the rain-swept track with little enthusiasm while thirty-four tellers idled in their booths. Everyone submitted quietly to arrest, but William J. O'Brien, president of the club, warned the raiders to expect trouble in court. "You'll have to answer to Judge Fisher for this," he said, "and I wouldn't want to be in your shoes. But then this stunt may give us some good publicity. We can afford to shut down for one night if folks will learn that we're open for business. And we will be open—soon." Gang members netted included Solly Vision, a Zuta associate, and Clarence Gleason, Willie Marks's brother-in-law.

O'Brien was not making idle threats. A year earlier, Judge Harry Fisher of the circuit court had issued an injunction restraining the police from interfering with dog racing. In May the state had announced its intention to have Master in Chancery Max Korshak dissolve the injunction, but attorneys for the tracks vowed a fight against any such appeals. As of June 12, Fisher's order remained in effect, so Lewis Jacobson, attorney for Capone's Hawthorne Kennel Club, announced the next day that he intended to appear before Judge Fisher with a petition asking that State's Attorney Swanson and the raiders be charged with contempt of court.[53]

Fisher did not cite anyone for contempt, but he did issue another, temporary injunction. Pat Roche suggested that a grand jury be impaneled to investigate the connections between highly placed politicians and the gangsters who owned the tracks. He also pointed out that over the past two years, the number of dog tracks in the Chicago area had plummeted from seven to three, the end result of hoodlums muscling out the competition. On June 22 it was announced that a grand jury would indeed be called to look into the matter. Roche, elated, elaborated on his suspicions.

"One report," he said, " is that one official is interested to the extent of $60,000 and another to the tune of $5,000 in the dog tracks. The grand jury will be asked to call for the bank accounts of these men, as well as look into the reports that gangsters and beer-runners are really behind the tracks."[54]

The Moran gang's ownership of the Fairview Kennel Club became public knowledge on June 27, when the grand jury voted true bills against sixteen men connected with the track. The Fairview, which went into receivership in 1927, had been operating under an order granted by Judge Michael Feinberg of the circuit court and financed by the now-deceased Adam Heyer. Feinberg denied that he had authorized the operation of the club, and when shown a copy of his July 1928 order, maintained that he did not actually agree to the racing of the dogs. Judge Fisher postponed the proceedings until August 5 pending a final investigation and decision on the matter, but warned Swanson and Sheriff Traeger, who had conducted the June 12 raids, that they could be charged with contempt of Judge Feinberg's order.

While the issue of dog racing's legality kept the courts busy throughout the summer of 1929, underworld slayings continued to make headlines. On June 27 two men shot and killed Samuel Muscia, a gangster and alcohol peddler who had been operating under the Aiello banner. The killers tossed their emptied weapons beside his bloodied body before fleeing on foot.[55]

Late on the night of November 30, Ted Newberry was walking toward the Wigwam Café at 3750 North Broadway, one of the Moran gang's favorite hangouts, when two men in a moving sedan opened fire on him. A bullet clipped him on the wrist, slowing his retaliation long enough for them to escape. Newberry, blood streaming down his arm, made it to his own vehicle and drove to a doctor's office to have the wound treated.[56]

Another North Sider was not so lucky three days later. On December 3 the body of Patrick King (real name John Voegtle), brother-in-law of the dead Gusenbergs, was found in the building at 426 South Wabash Avenue, the first floor of which housed the popular Club Royale. The fourth floor, where King's bloody remains were discovered, was vacant but had once contained an elaborate gambling den run by O'Banion friend Jerry O'Connor. King had been struck in the chest, face, and shoulder by five bullets, but a pistol with two shots evidently fired laid near his body, suggesting that he had fought back.[57] The success of his resistance is debatable, however, as his was the only corpse found.

By December 1929 the trail was going cold in the massacre investigation. Then a break in the case occurred, literally by accident.

On the night of December 14 a minor collision took place between two cars outside city hall in St. Joseph, Michigan. The damage was negligible, but both drivers argued hotly anyway. Officer Charles Skelly intervened and ordered them to drive to police headquarters. When he stepped up onto the running board of one car, its driver took out a pistol and fired three times.

Skelly fell to the road—he would die in a local hospital three hours later. The assailant tried to drive away, but his wheel broke on an obstacle in the road. Getting out, he flagged down a passing motorist, took over the car at gunpoint, and escaped.

The town police searched the abandoned vehicle and found papers that led them to a bungalow belonging to a Fred and Viola Dane. Going through the place, they uncovered an unusual assortment of items for a middle-class couple to own: two machine guns, two bulletproof vests, handguns, ammunition, and $319,850 in bonds, at least $112,000 of them stolen. A laundry mark, with the initials, FRB, pointed suspicion toward the still-wanted Frederick Burke.

Calvin Goddard tested the machine guns, with the astonishing result that bullets from one matched those taken from Reinhart Schwimmer, and the other bore the ballistic evidence of having been used on James Clark. What was more, one of them had also been used in the Frankie Yale hit of July 1928.

The last session of the coroner's inquest was held on December 23, after Goddard presented his ballistics evidence confirming that Burke had possessed two of the murder weapons. The jury declared in its verdict:

> [The victims] came to their death on the fourteenth of February in premises known as 2122 North Clark Street as a result of gunshot wounds received from bullets fired from a machine gun in the hands of a person or persons at present unknown to this jury at above location on February 14 at about 10:30 a.m. From testimony presented to us, we, the jury, recommend that the said Burke, now a fugitive from justice, be apprehended and held to the Grand Jury on a charge of murder as a

participant in the said murder and that the police continue their search for the other said unknown person or persons and when apprehended that he or they may be held to the Grand Jury on the charge of murder until released by due process of the law.[58]

After a manhunt lasting over a year, Burke was captured in March 1931 in Green City, Missouri, at the home of his in-laws. Michigan got him for the Skelly murder, beating out Illinois and the other states who wanted him for murder, robbery, and a roster of other charges. Chicago prosecutors succeeded in questioning him about the massacre, but his answers were predictably ignorant and useless. He received a life sentence in the Michigan State Prison but died there of a heart attack in July 1940, never facing justice for his probable role in one of Chicago's goriest mass murders.

On December 29, while the search was still on for Burke, the police responded to the back-and-forth fighting between the gangs by raiding one of the Moran gang's primary headquarters, in the American Bond and Mortgage Building at 127 North Dearborn. The North Siders had rented Suite 517 a while back and camouflaged its real use by employing respectable-looking "office girls" and fixing a plate on the door that read "ACME SALES COMPANY—Insurance, Investments, and Mortgages."[59]

The police raiding party, led by Lieutenant Joseph Ronan, netted eleven suspects. They included Andrew and Domenic Aiello, the latter of whom gave his name as Mike Perra to the arresting officers; Leo Mongoven; Joseph and Louise Fernandez, caretakers of Moran's summer cottage in Antioch, who were allowed to go after they explained that they were in the office to collect their wages; trucking contractor Si Gorman, who explained that he was there to see about selling Moran a truck; and A. B. Margolis, a lawyer for the Checker Cab Company. One other suspect, like Domenic Aiello, gave a false name, but when he identified himself as an investigator for the office of Corporation Counsel Samuel Ettelson, he was permitted to go without justifying the reason for his presence in the "Moran den," as the newspapers called it.

Deputy Commissioner Stege took over the investigation after the suspects were rounded up, and his thorough search of the premises yielded some very interesting results. In one of the desks, a detective found half a dozen enlarged news photos of the St. Valentine's Day Massacre crime scene. In the same envelope were pictures of five Purple Gang members, one of which was torn across the middle. When Stege tracked down the identity of the man in the mutilated photo, he learned that the man had recently been murdered.

One suspect's presence, and the reason for it, baffled the police. He was Frank Maritote, alias Diamond. What was a ranking Capone lieutenant doing in the midst of the Moran gang's operational nerve center? All he would say to account for being on the premises was that he was there to see someone about a building contract, and he displayed legal documents proving that he had borrowed $170,000 from a Loop bank, ostensibly for that purpose. The probable truth was that he was there as a spy, keeping an eye on who came into and left the Moran office.

Stege and Assistant State's Attorney Harry Ditchburne spent hours interrogating the suspects, to no avail. The Aiellos were polite but cold, Leo Mongoven glared, Diamond offered nothing. In order to hold them for extended questioning, Stege ended up charging them with, oddly enough, being inmates of a disorderly house. When Mongoven mentioned that the North Side Gang was about to embark on a new enterprise selling punch boards all over the United States, Stege looked into the possibility of charging them with mail fraud.

"I don't know whether this use or some other use of the mails by these men constitutes using the mails for fraudulent purposes," he said. "I am going in the morning, however, to see K. B. Aldrich, chief post office inspector, and lay before him what evidence was obtained in the raid."[60]

On December 31 the four men who had been retained on the disorderly house charge—Domenic and Andrew Aiello, Leo Mongoven, and Frank Diamond— appeared before Judge William Fetzer. The prosecutor asked for a continuance in order to give the government more time to examine the gang's financial records and other evidence obtained in the raid. Fetzer granted the continuance, and shortly afterward Circuit Judge Daniel Trude issued a search warrant to open a vault found in the gang's suite of offices.

Mongoven had originally offered to open the vault and make its contents available for inspection, but he backed out and told a story about the "office girl who had the combination" being out of town. The investigators were positive that the vault contained records that would give the police and state's attorney's office insights into the workings of the Moran–Zuta–Aiello combine.

Leo Mongoven protested when Judge Fetzer granted the continuance. "It's a frame. They just want to keep us around so the young coppers can get a good look at us."[61]

Armed with the search warrant signed by Judge Trude, Lieutenant George Barker, a technician who would open the mysterious vault, and a small detachment of officers returned to 127 North Dearborn. Moran was in the lobby when they arrived but did nothing except watch the men go upstairs to the offices.

"Why don't you go in?" a reporter inquired.

"Because there are four quarts of scotch in the vault, and I don't want to get the rap for it," the gangster replied. He then walked out of the building, got into his car, and drove away.

When opened, the vault yielded some interesting contents. One hundred sixty-five punch boards, with premiums, occupied a shelf along with a pile of financial records. A casual glance at the latter revealed a stack of canceled checks signed by Arthur Elrod, former assistant to Corporation Counsel Ettelson, a bank account under a probably fictitious name that showed a balance of $11,929 for the month of October, another account with a $300,000 balance, and four bottles of whiskey.

As the decade closed, Prohibition and its failure (although some continued to applaud it as a success) was a topic in almost all the New Year's Eve editions of American newspapers. Even some of the staunchest drys despaired of successful enforcement. Senator William E. Borah from Idaho, himself a Prohibition advocate, claimed that "practically open saloons" were running everywhere, right under the noses of agents sworn to close them.

"When I say this, I do not mean simply New York or Chicago," he said. "I mean to state a condition that prevails throughout the country. I do not assume that you can catch every bootlegger. But the open flaunting, defiant, persistent disregard of the law day after day and month after month, with no effort being made to stop it, calls for discussion."

Attorney General William D. Mitchell issued a general directive to all district attorneys that said they were not to nolle pros prohibition cases without specific consent from the Department of Justice, "except in the case of emergency." Almost at once, a state of emergency hit most DA case lists. Very few applied for the requisite permission.

In their extensively researched study of the massacre, William Helmer and Art Bilek conclude that the North Clark Street murder team consisted of former Egan's Rats members who were collectively referred to by the Italian segment of Capone's organization as the "American Boys." They were Fred Burke; Gus Winkler, whose widow, Georgette, would shed light on the mystery in her memoir of the period; Ray "Crane-Neck" Nugent; Bob Carey, alias Newberry or Conroy; and Fred Goetz.

Winkler, who knew Claude Maddox, arrived in Chicago in May 1927, followed by Nugent and Carey. The three nearly had their visit cut short by murder when they kidnapped one of Capone's lieutenants with the intention of holding him for ransom. Winkler's close friend, Fred Burke, was a past master in the art of snatching bootleggers and gamblers for profit.[62] According to Georgette Winkler, Capone called the enterprising trio into his office to discuss the release of his lieutenant, and instead of punishing them for their effrontery, offered to help set them up in something less small-time and hazardous.

In time, their circle expanded to include Fred Goetz and Byron "Monty" Bolton, both Capone associates, and Fred Burke, whose success in the snatch racket made Detroit a dangerous place for him to be.[63] They hung out at the Hawthorne Hotel, coming into contact with Jack McGurn, Louis "Little New York" Campagna, Claude Maddox's Circus Café partner Tony Capezio, and other Outfit notables in the process. They participated in one major hit for Capone prior to wielding the massacre weapons. According to Georgette Winkler and a confession later made by

Byron Bolton, Burke, Winkler, and Goetz accompanied Campagna to New York in 1928 and rubbed out Frankie Yale.[64]

One by one the American Boys fell victim to their own lifestyle. Bob Carey turned up dead in New York in 1932, shot to death along with his girlfriend. "Crane Neck" Nugent simply vanished after following Al Capone's brother Ralph to Miami and opening a tavern; twenty years after his disappearance, his wife initiated paperwork to have him legally declared dead. Burke spent the rest of his life in prison.

Gus Winkler, who appears to have enjoyed Capone's confidence, joined turncoat North Sider Ted Newberry in overseeing gambling and bootlegging in areas of the North Side that were gradually wrested from Moran. By the autumn of 1933 he had fallen out of Frank Nitti's favor, although one could debate whether he had ever possessed it to begin with, since his elevation had been Capone-directed. He had also been forced into negotiations with federal agents after local police arrested him in September 1930 for alleged complicity in the robbery of the Lincoln National Bank and Trust Company in Lincoln, Nebraska. The charges were dropped after he posted a $100,000 bond and convinced the culprits, the Bailey Gang (whom he knew) to surrender the loot to him for return. This incident, coupled with the fact that he told federal agents where to find his homicidal former friend Verne Miller in Chicago, led to speculation that he might be turning full-time informer.

On October 9, 1933, six blasts from automatic shotguns killed Winkler as he walked to the front door of the Weber Beer Distributing Company. He was followed to the grave the following March by Fred Goetz, who was leaving the Minerva Restaurant in Cicero when shotguns ended his long and bloody career. His killers, like those of Winkler, were presumably Syndicate gunmen finishing off the last of the massacre shooters.

Lookout Byron Bolton was taken into custody on January 8, 1935, when federal agents, hunting down the Barker–Karpis Gang, laid siege to an apartment building at 3920 North Pine Grove Avenue. Three weeks into his stay as a "guest" of the federal government, the *Chicago American* announced that it was publishing the inside story of the St. Valentine's Day Massacre, citing a Bolton confession as its source. How the *American* came across this particular scoop is still a mystery, but it created a sensation.

Because the former lookout was in federal custody at the time, being questioned about bank robberies, the immediate assumption was that the FBI was investigating the six-year-old crime. It was not, murder not being a federal offense. Hoover, bewildered and irate, scrambled to discover the source of the story, wondering if the bureau's phone lines were tapped or his field offices were not sharing their intelligence with him. While he did an in-house investigation, he denied the truth of the story to the press.

It may not have come from Bolton to begin with. Helmer and Bilek note that the paper credited the source as Bolton's "friends," who may not have been friends at all but former associates from the Barker–Karpis Gang or even a defense attorney seeking to discredit the ex-lookout as a potential witness in an upcoming kidnapping trial. But in the end, the story drew a real confession out of him.

He told Chicago detectives about purchasing one of the phony squad cars in a lot near the Lexington and Metropole hotels, using the alias of James Martin, a close enough match to the "James Morton," whom the dealer recalled having sold the car to. Bolton also claimed that the murders had been plotted in October or November 1928 at a lodge at Cranberry Lake in rural Wisconsin. The attendees were Al Capone, Gus Winkler, Louis Campagna, Fred Burke, Fred Goetz, and two Chicago politicians with Capone connections, Danny Seritella and William Pacelli. After Capone left for Florida, Frank Nitti assumed responsibility for the project, with the details being attended to by Frank Rio, a devoted Capone bodyguard.[65]

The principal lookouts, who rented their rooms from Minnie Arvidson at 2051 North Clark, were Byron Bolton and Jimmy "the Swede" Morand or Jimmy McCrussen.[66] Morand and McCrussen knew George Moran by sight, and they were relied on to signal his arrival at the garage. Mistaking Al Weinshank for Moran, they called the killers into action prematurely that morning and spared Moran's life. The shooters and their drivers were at the house of Capone henchman Rocco de Grazia, from which they came forth when the lookouts phoned in the signal.[67]

Georgette Winkler claimed that Fred Burke and Fred Goetz had donned the cop uniforms that fooled the North Siders. She wrote that after the massacre, Winkler and Carey hid out at the Winkler home, becoming agitated when the afternoon newspapers informed them that none of the blood spilled that morning had been Moran's.

Mrs. Winkler put together a manuscript detailing her knowledge of the massacre and other crimes in which her husband had played a role, intending it to be a morality piece as opposed to an exposé. Publishing houses rejected it initially because of her static writing style, and later because she named gangsters who were alive and likely to retaliate. The story was finally published in installments in a detective magazine, but the market at the time was glutted with true crime stories, and its impact was slight.

Although Bolton's information was valuable, he had played too small a role in the massacre for the FBI to let an investigation into a six-year-old murder case hamper the federal proceedings in which he was a key witness. When Bolton claimed that John Stege had been on the Capone payroll in 1929, earning $5,000 a week, the Chicago police lost interest in what he had to say, and the case officially went cold.

On February 8, 1956, the *Chicago Sun-Times* ran an article titled *Bugs Moran Recalls Valentine's Day, 1929.*[68] Supposedly based on information supplied by Ohio State Penitentiary convicts who conversed with Moran and fed the stories back to the press, Moran was quoted as saying, "I saw two men dressed as policemen and two in civilian clothes come out of the garage that day. Newberry [sic] and I were only half a block down the street. . . . We stored Prohibition alcohol in the garage, and I figured it was a raid, so I took a walk around the block."

The same article, still naming Moran as its source, listed the shooters as Byron Bolton, Fred Burke, Gus Winkler, Fred Goetz, and Jack McGurn. Claude Maddox and Murray "the Camel" Humphreys, a Capone man, were seen by witnesses in the neighborhood but "probably not in the garage."[69]

"George never spoke of Humphreys, but those other names I definitely remember him mentioning," G. J. Moran remembered seventy-five years later. "He knew who did the shooting, found out soon after it happened. He also talked about walking to the garage with Willie Marks—not Ted Newberry—and running late because his barbershop appointment ran overtime."

Moran's accusation of Bolton, Winkler, Goetz, Burke, and McGurn coincides with what history has stated in general and what Art Bilek and William Helmer claimed in particular. One name was neglected when discussing the tragedy with family, and as it turns out, Bob Carey might have been overlooked in conversation for a reason.

At the end of July 1932, a double homicide occurred in New York City that, on the surface, looked like a murder-suicide but was possibly Moran's retaliation against one of the key figures in the St. Valentine's Day Massacre.

Alexander Gordon, a cab driver who lived in the top apartment of a five-story tenement at 220 West 104th Street, became concerned when he noticed that the lights had been burning for two days nonstop in the downstairs flat occupied by a couple he knew as "Mr. and Mrs. Sanborne." On July 31, after the lights failed to go out and the Sanbornes had yet to emerge from their apartment, he called Patrolman Arthur Miller in from the street. When knocking on the Sanbornes' door yielded only silence, Miller and Gordon let themselves into a vacant flat next door, climbed out a window, and gained entry to the premises through another open window.[70]

Since the apartment was a six-room "railroad-style" model, they immediately saw Mrs. Sanborne, a petite blonde in her late thirties, lying across the threshold of the bathroom door. Behind her, Mr. Sanborne was slumped over the bathtub. Both were dead, the woman with three bullet wounds in her head, chest and arm, and the man with a single shot to the head.

A quick inspection of the premises indicated that the Sanbornes had not been model citizens. In a small room off of the bedroom, a printing press, rolls of counterfeit $5 notes, and plates used to stamp the phony currency were found. Photographs of the woman in the company of various men were tacked up all over the walls, the angle of the shots suggesting that the men had not been aware that they were being photographed. Although it disappeared after its initial discovery, a little black book containing the names of U.S. Senators and other influential men was found in a bureau drawer.

The clear evidence of a blackmail and counterfeiting operation prompted the New York police to check the slain couple's fingerprints against those on record.

257

Robert Sanborne, as he called himself when he rented the apartment, was none other than Bob Carey, the lookout who had called the North Clark Street killers into action three years previously. The woman, Rosemary Sanborne, had been a cigarette girl at a West Side cabaret in Chicago.

The New York police, lacking evidence to the contrary, concluded that, for reasons which could only be surmised, Carey had killed his girlfriend and then shot himself. The reason for the murder-suicide was never given, and no one found it unusual that Carey would do something so drastic when he was making a small fortune blackmailing wealthy married men and turning out counterfeit notes that one New York police lieutenant grudgingly admitted were the most authentic-looking he had ever seen.

The probable reason for Carey's death was revealed in a dark Waukegan tavern five months later. E. Barnett, a former North Side booze hauler who had left the gang's employ after O'Banion's funeral, had gone on to work for an interstate trucking company and ended up in Waukegan during a delivery run. He stopped at a place that had been pointed out to him as a tavern, and there he encountered George Moran, whom he had not seen in seven years. Moran appeared to be the worse for drink but was amiable when Barnett reminded him of the old O'Banion connection.

"We talked for a bit," Barnett remembered, "and then I felt I had to say something about the massacre. I said, 'Shame about Clark Street, George, those were good boys.' He said he hadn't forgotten that, that in fact he had evened the score part way. He said that he'd gone to the coast—he didn't say which coast—and taken care of some guy named Bob Carey. I didn't know who it was, never heard the name before. And I didn't want to ask questions in case he was drunk enough to tell me something that might get me in hot water later."[71]

How Moran learned of Carey's role in the massacre and why he waited three years to act on that knowledge remains a mystery. Also lost to time is the name of the Judas figure who called Moran regularly during the days leading up to the mass killing. Those calls stopped afterward, with Moran never elaborating as to why, or even who the person was.

15

"GOOD FOR YOU, BAD FOR . . ."

O N JANUARY 9, 1930, DETECTIVES Roy Van Herik and William Murphy arrested Moran and Mongoven in the lobby of the Hotel Sherman. When he saw the officers approaching, the North Side leader demanded to know who they were. Van Herik and Murphy displayed their stars, which Moran eyed with derision.

"Stars don't mean nothing," he said. "Fellows with badges like that killed seven men up on Clark Street on Valentine's Day. Besides, my name ain't Moran. It's George E. Q. Johnson."[1] (The name was that of a federal attorney—Moran's idea of a joke.)

He balked at riding to the detective bureau in a patrol wagon, so the officers agreed to hail a cab if he would pay the fare. He and Mongoven spent four hours in a cell before appearing in Judge Otto Kerner's court and securing their freedom on a $1,400 bond. They appeared in Municipal Judge Joseph Schulman's court-room as ordered the next day for arraignment on disorderly conduct and vagrancy charges.

"What were these men doing?" Schulman asked the detectives.

"Nothing," they admitted. "But they are notorious characters, and here are their records."

Schulman shook his head. "That may be," he said, "but there's nothing to do but let them go."[2]

Moran and Mongoven beamed as they shook hands with their attorney and departed from the courtroom.

Less than two weeks later, Sergeants Bill Drury and John Howe picked them up in the lobby of the Sherman yet again. Mongoven bristled with visible annoyance, but Moran merely smiled as he was patted down for a weapon.

"We don't carry guns any more," he informed Drury, who replied, "I'm not interested. Let's go."

Within two hours a writ of habeas corpus was filed, and after another two hours in a cell, Moran paid $200 to obtain their release pending their vagrancy hearing the next day. When they appeared, the charges were promptly dismissed.

At the end of February, gunmen burst into a room at the German Evangelical Deaconess Hospital where Frank McErlane was recovering from a bullet-induced leg fracture. They opened fire on him, wounding him in the chest, groin, and wrist, but he had a weapon of his own stashed under his pillow and returned fire, forcing them to retreat.[3] More than a week later, Saltis's ally Dingbat Oberta and his chauffeur/bodyguard Sam Malaga were found murdered outside the city limits, near Chicago Ridge. Oberta was in the front seat of his car, slumped against the door, his head a bloody mess, while Malaga was partly submerged in the frozen water of a ditch. The police had heard that Saltis and McErlane had fallen out, and both the hospital shooting and ditch murder looked like opening shots in another gangster feud.[4]

John Stege, to head off such an event, ordered yet another pickup of any known gangsters found in the Loop. Police officers found Willie Marks and three companions driving about in the "forbidden territory" on the night on March 10 and gave chase, finally catching them on the West Side. Caught in the net were Moran, Mongoven, and Potatoes Kaufman. Kaufman was particularly indignant as he strode into Stege's office, where the veteran officer was waiting with Assistant State's Attorney Harry Ditchburne to interview him.

"Can Drury and Howe [the arresting officers] arrest me every time they see me?" he demanded. When Stege coolly replied, "I guess they can," Kaufman snarled, "There's got to be a stop to this as far as I'm concerned. I'm no ex-convict or bootlegger. My father left me my money. My kids are getting so big now that I don't want them to be always hearing that their father was picked up as a suspect in this or that."

Moran and Mongoven were more relaxed, telling reporters that they had been arrested so many times they were used to it. "But we aren't doing anything wrong," Moran scolded Stege and Ditchburne in mild tones. "You'd be surprised how much money I'm paying out to fellows who are broke, and it's only me that keeps them out of trouble." He confirmed that he had placed money in trust for the ailing father of Pete and Frank Gusenberg.

"Why don't you put all your hoods to work in that big cleaning plant of yours up north?" Stege wanted to know.

"I have," he replied. Acting amused by the whole episode, Moran turned to Mongoven with a sober expression that his aide quickly copied. "If it's orders, well, I guess we'd better stay out of the Loop."[5]

Jack Zuta ended up in the "disreputables" net two weeks later. Zuta, like Moran, had been fighting to protect his assets and stay alive during the past two years. In 1928 Capone vice operators Mike "de Pike" Heitler, Rocco Fanelli, and Johnny and Joseph "Peppi" Genaro moved in on his West Side vice holdings and began trying to wrest them from him. He appealed to Moran for aid that was not forthcoming, probably due to the fact that Moran had no sympathy for pimps (although he valued the financial advice of a smart one) and the West Side was out of his sphere of influence.

When he heard that a $30,000 price tag was on his head, Zuta fled Chicago and hid in Ohio. One of his attachés, Jack Hartnett, tried to run Capone man "Two Gun Patsy" Tardi out of Zuta's Sterling Hotel, resulting in shootouts that brought more Capone ire on Zuta's head. The Polish vicemonger did not return to Chicago until the massacre took place and gave him reason to hope that Moran needed friends and allies badly enough to be less morally selective. He was successful in making a formal alliance with Moran and later Aiello.[6]

Confronted with John Stege's relentless questioning, he deflated. "I haven't an enemy in the world," he complained.

"Yes, you have; I'm your enemy," Stege replied. "Every decent man is your enemy. The mother of every girl whose virtue you sullied and sold is your enemy."

"I'm not what you think I am," Zuta protested.

"I'll call you by your proper term—the worst word that can be applied to man— at the corner of State and Madison Streets in the presence of five hundred witnesses, and you can sue me if you want," Stege challenged him. "I know your history."

"You got me painted wrong. I'm in the real estate business," Zuta countered. When asked about his connection to Joe Aiello, he admitted it with pride, acquiring some spirit in the process. "Joe Aiello is a fine man. He does a lot for widows and orphans. You'd be surprised how much."

"Yes, he makes widows and orphans," Stege said. "Look out for him. He has no use for your kind. You make your living out of women's shame, and you're a doomed man."

A lawyer produced a writ of habeas corpus, forcing Stege to release Zuta on a $100 bond that night.[7]

Although the harassing arrests and vagrancy warrants were annoying for Moran, they were problems that his high-priced legal team could handle. He had no courtroom redress available when a mysterious fire broke out at his Fairview

Kennel Club, at Mannheim Road and Lawrence Avenue, on the night of April 10. The entire grandstand, which measured three hundred feet long, and the dog sheds were completely destroyed, and the Schiller Park and Franklin Park fire departments had their hands full trying to contain the blaze and cope with the smaller fires started on the roofs of nearby houses when the wind carried sparks in all directions.

The club had been "officially" closed since the raids and federal injunction of the previous summer, and August Sikowski, owner of the property, assured reporters that he had not renewed the Moran lease for another year.[8] He pretended ignorance when confronted with signs that the operation had been creeping back to life. The fire, almost certainly arson, signaled the end of Moran's investment in dog racing.

On April 24, 1930, the Chicago Crime Commission released a list of the city's twenty-eight greatest "public enemies," coining a term that would be applied universally to first the city's and later the nation's foremost and "celebrity" criminals. Al Capone topped the list at number one: George Moran ranked twelfth. Jack Zuta, strangely enough, was number nine, and Mongoven bottomed out the roster at twenty-six.

Although the gangsters and the police considered the concept of the list a joke, the nation's imagination was captured, and *public enemy* became a popular enough catchphrase to be used as the title of a James Cagney movie in 1931. When the Crime Commission issued its 1931 list, a new name was on it: Ted Newberry, who in less than two years suddenly found himself elevated from Moran minion to successor.

It is unclear exactly when Newberry shifted his allegiance from the North Siders to Capone and the Outfit. By some accounts, it happened in the wake of the massacre, but he was publicly identified as a Moran man until the spring of 1930, when a Zuta-directed hit made North Side affiliations a risky thing to brag about.

Although Newberry was not the only North Sider to abandon ship, Moran reacted to his departure with a bitterness that made its way into his voice anytime he mentioned the other man's name over the years. "Ted Newberry was someone he hated to his dying day," G. J. Moran remembered. Probably because Newberry, working with Gus Winkler to further Outfit interests in the North Side, had crossed the gulf from friend to enemy, a transition that Moran, like Capone, considered unforgivable.

On May 21, 1930, police arrested Leo Mongoven at the Madison–Kedzie State Bank. Patting him down, they found two .45 pistols strapped under his coat. Moran was allegedly across the street when the arrest took place. Mongoven had been trying for several days to convince bank officials to buy $5,000 worth of bonds at face value, although in reality they were worth less than half that amount, and police believed that at the time of his arrest, he was been planning to use the guns to force the purchase. After posting bond on the concealed weapons charge, he disappeared from the public eye, not to return for another two years.

His disappearance would arouse speculation that he had been murdered. But Mongoven simply avoided the Chicago area, dividing his time between Bemidji, Minnesota, which was a destination/clearing house for the booze Moran smuggled in from Manitoba, and cloak-and-dagger-style visits to a property he owned on Bluff Lake, in Lake County.

He may have stopped over for a night at Fox Lake, Illinois, more than a week into his "disappearance" and come close to vanishing for good.

Fox Lake, Illinois, fifty miles northwest of Chicago, was one of Lake County's more popular vacation destinations. The resorts were all avid customers of Chicago beer and liquor, and a favored stopover for gangsters from the city. Although the Moran gang supplied the booze through Ray Pregenzer, who owned his own spot on Grass Lake, Capone gangsters stopped there without fear of molestation.

At 1:40 a.m. on June 1, that changed. A small party consisting of Terry Druggan's brother George, former Hymie Weiss bodyguard Sam Pellar, old-time gangster and safeblower Joseph Bertsche, and Mrs. Vivian Ponic McGinnis were sitting in an enclosed porch at the Manning resort overlooking Pistakee Lake. The bartender, a man named Capella, was sweeping around their table, hoping that they would take the hint and leave, but they ignored him and continued to talk.[9]

Suddenly, a single gunshot rang out from somewhere in the darkness beyond the porch. Capella dove behind the bar. More shots followed; when they ceased, the bartender peered out. He saw pure carnage everywhere. Klondike O'Donnell gangster Michael Quirk, who had been upstairs and come down when the shooting began, was lying dead in front of the bar. George Druggan, covered with blood, was running toward the stairs, which led to the room where his uncle lay sleeping. Pellar collapsed while heading for the kitchen area, and Bertsche made it into one of the bedrooms before dropping dead. Mrs. McGinnis was on the floor beside the table, seriously wounded. She and Druggan both survived.

Among the theories that arose to account for the sudden and vicious attack was that Al Capone had been moving in on Moran's Lake County territory and waging terror against Moran-supplied resorts like Manning's. This scenario discounts the fact that the injured parties (with the exception of Michael Quirk, who had just come downstairs when the shooting started) were either specific targets or sitting too close to one. Druggan, Pellar, and Bertsche were Capone allies in June 1930 and not likely targets for assassination from that quarter.

Another, more plausible theory, is that it was a Moran assault on encroachers. Early coverage of the Fox Lake Massacre brought forth the information that local alderman James Manning, who owned the hotel, had supposedly switched from

Moran booze to a product being shipped in by George Druggan.[10] However, there are unconfirmed reports that Leo Mongoven was in the place that night, drinking in the same general area as the victims, and barely escaped getting shot.[11] If this were the case, Moran would not have exposed him to risk.

A third possibility exists. The Fox Lake Massacre, according to author and crime researcher Brad Smith, was the sole work of an individual bent on revenge: former policeman turned outlaw Verne Miller.[12]

Miller had two friends, Bob McLaughlin and his younger brother Eugene, otherwise known as Red. Bob was the president of Chicago's Checker Cab Company, a position he had seized for himself through the usual means of bribery, intimidation, and murder. Red McLaughlin served as enforcer and by all accounts did an effective job. He was the chief suspect in five murder cases, all involving officers and employees of Checker Cab who had loudly opposed Bob McLaughlin.

At the end of May 1930, Red returned from a Miami sojourn, dropped in at his brother's office, and said that he was going to visit their mother. Not only did he fail to make the visit, he seemed to disappear off the face of the earth. A concerned Bob McLaughlin made discreet inquiries and learned that after leaving the office, Red had been observed in the company of George Druggan and Joe Bertsche. Incidentally, Bob was at Manning's resort when the shooting commenced, but safely upstairs, having long since retired. He was particularly defensive when Lake County State's Attorney A. V. Smith questioned him about the incident.

One week later, on June 8, Red McLaughlin's body, decomposed and gruesomely attired in chains and seventy-five pounds of iron weights, was brought to the surface of the Chicago Sanitary Canal in Summitt, in a tugboat's wake. He had been shot twice through the back of the head, execution-style.[13]

In a jailhouse interview '30s outlaw George "Machine-Gun" Kelly claimed that Miller had been the Fox Lake shooter. He said that Miller had organized the shooting expedition after learning through the underworld grapevine that Druggan and Bertsche had been involved in Red McLaughlin's death. Kelly opined that Miller really had no business getting involved, but he "did it because he liked Red."

Local authorities did not seem to be too interested in solving the case. Just four days after the bloodshed took place, A. V. Smith announced he was satisfied that the killers, whom he believed to be professionals from New York, were long gone and that he was abandoning the investigation.

Verne Miller biographer Brad Smith summed up the Fox Lake Massacre succinctly in *Lawman to Outlaw*: "The men who stayed up that night drinking on the porch of Manning's Resort learned too late what others would also come to learn. It was hazardous to your health to cross a friend of Verne Miller."

On June 8 Frank Thompson, whom the press had nicknamed "the Armorer of Gangland," drove into a filling station in New Milford, Winnebago County. He stumbled out of the car, blood spreading across the front of his shirt from a chest wound, and groaned to the startled attendant, "I'm dying—get a doctor." At the hospital, Sheriff Harry Baldwin asked him who had shot him. Thompson, although physically weak, was mentally stubborn.[14]

"Listen, Harry," he said, "I've seen everything, done everything, and got everything, and you're smart enough to know that I won't talk. Go to hell."

He never did talk. But the police investigators speculated that his involvement in the St. Valentine's Day Massacre, which had only entailed his selling the weapons to the killers, had triggered the assault.

On the morning of June 9, while Thompson was fighting for life in a Winnebago County hospital, veteran *Tribune* reporter Alfred "Jake" Lingle, walking on Randolph, headed for the west entrance of a pedestrian underpass that tunneled under Michigan Avenue. He was on his way to catch the 1:30 Illinois Central train to the Washington Park racetrack in Homewood, his eyes on a copy of the *Racing Form* and his mind on the day he planned to spend at the races.

Lingle paused when a man in a nearby car called, "Hey, Jake." When the reporter looked at him, the man said, "Don't forget to play Hy Schneider in the third." Lingle nodded, smiled, and ventured down into the darkness of the underpass. He was so absorbed in the racing sheet that he did not notice a tall young man, clad in a gray suit and wearing a straw hat over blond or light brown hair, hurrying up behind him. A snub-nosed .38, aimed at the back of the absentminded reporter's head, went off once, sending a bullet into his brain. Lingle pitched forward, killed so quickly that his cigar remained between his teeth and he still grasped the paper.[15]

Witnesses differed as to whether one or two men had been involved. Most had seen the blond man, who doubled back through the tunnel at a brisk pace and upon reaching the intersection of Randolph and Michigan, ran like hell. Others claimed to have seen another killer, this one a shorter individual, with dark hair and wearing a blue suit. This man supposedly continued east after Lingle fell, exiting the underpass on the other side and escaping. A traffic policeman noticed the blond man when those who followed him out of the subway cried, "Stop that man!" Officer Anthony Ruthy gave chase but was soon outdistanced.

The *Tribune* and its powerhouse publisher, Colonel Robert McCormick, reacted to Lingle's murder with the righteous fury normally expected after the slaying of a martyr. McCormick secured the services of a special prosecutor, *Tribune* lawyer Charles Rathburn, and Pat Roche was retained as chief investigator. Rewards offered by not only the *Trib* but other Chicago papers totaled more than $50,000. The universal belief was that Lingle had known too much about something, probably gang-related, and was murdered to prevent publication of his findings.

Jake Lingle's martyr status dissipated as soon as inexplicable financial records came to light. He was found to be in possession of much more money that his sixty-five-dollar-a-week job brought in legally, as well as a diamond-studded belt buckle that Al Capone was known to give to his friends. Further investigation forced a red-faced McCormick to note in a personally written editorial, ". . . Alfred Lingle was killed because he was using his *Tribune* position to profit from criminal operations and not because he was serving the *Tribune* as it thought he was. Events will prove that this newspaper has nothing to cover in this connection."[16]

Calvin Goddard restored the serial numbers on the murder weapon, which had been dropped in the subway, enabling the police to identify it as one of six guns shipped to gangland armorer Peter von Frantzius. The weapons dealer, sweated by investigators when they located a sale in his books with no name recorded, admitted that he had sold the .38 to North Sider Frank Foster, who came to his shop with Ted Newberry.[17]

While the police hunted high and low for the two North Siders, Chicago's other dailies began examining the activities and associations of their own reporters in the wake of the Lingle revelations. One casualty of this journalistic witch-hunt was Jimmy Murphy, one of Chicago's colorful old breed of newsmen, a contemporary of Charles MacArthur and Ben Hecht (who would parody him in their wildly successful play *The Front Page*). Murphy, who'd been a reporter for twenty-eight years, had admitted that three years previously, he had been a partner in a neighborhood speakeasy for six months. The revelation resulted in his paper, the *Daily Times*, terminating his employment. A published statement justifying the dismissal ended with "The *Daily Times* has nothing but good wishes for Jimmy Murphy." It is not a matter of record how Murphy responded to the feeble attempt at sentiment.[18]

On July 17 Harry Brundidge, a reporter for the *St. Louis Star*, announced his intention to appear before the Cook County grand jury and give extensive testimony regarding the tight alliance between certain members of the press and the underworld. One person he planned to expose in detail was *Herald and Examiner* crime reporter Ted Tod, who was on the payroll of Moran's Fairview Kennel Club.[19]

Tod certainly fit the profile of the double-faced reporter that Lingle had coined. He maintained a lavish apartment at 1400 Lake Shore Drive, where his neighbors came from old-money families. At his grand parties, for which he was renowned, he served first-rate liquor that he freely admitted to be Moran product. Investigators from the state's attorney's office determined that he had entered the North Side Gang's employ at the time that Swanson had been hitting the Fairview with one raid after another. While Moran arranged for an injunction to stop the raids, he hired Tod as a publicity agent, which involved sending race information to the papers, taking care of advertising, and in general making sure that the track received positive press.

Moran's name was also mentioned in connection with another of Brundidge's exposés: a crooked lottery run by O'Banion's old associate Matt Foley.[20] Foley, assistant circulation manager at the *Herald and Examiner*, used newsboys in need of extra cash to sell $50,000 worth of "Kentucky Derby Sweepstakes" tickets to hundreds of Illinois Central Railroad employees. Although there were only twelve big cash prizes, Foley's salesmen assured buyers that anyone holding a ticket for a horse that ended up participating in the derby would automatically win $50.

When Foley not only refused to honor the winning tickets but also left town, attorneys representing the fleeced railroad employees wondered if they had recourse in suing Moran. A *Herald and Examiner* representative was quoted as saying, "I think Bugs Moran is behind this thing." Clyde Hoffman, chairman of the grievance committee that the conned ticket buyers had formed, dismissed the notion. "I told Cornell [the *H&E* rep] that I did not think Moran had anything to do with the racket because if he had, he would be honorable enough to pay up." Moran was never officially questioned in the matter.

At the end of June 1930, raiders from the state's attorney's office invaded the North Side Gang's Loop headquarters, which had been under surveillance for some time. Among the ten arrested (one of them a woman) was Grover Dullard, a Moran gangster whom underworld rumor hinted had been trailing Jake Lingle on the day of the reporter's murder. During the uproar that followed the explosive entry of the state's attorney's men, one of the office's occupants snatched a ledger off of a table and hurled it out the window. It was later recovered and discovered to contain more than 150 names and contact information for North Side gangsters. Two more raids immediately followed, one of which caught Jack Zuta.[21]

On July 1 Los Angeles police arrested Frank Foster and his twenty-three-year-old wife, Moran's Hollywood bootlegging contact Marvin Hart, and three other men in connection with the Lingle case. Also present when the arrests took place was a man who gave his name as Herbert Williams but was identified as Herbert Woellter, Moran's Chicago brewmaster, whom the North Side Gang had sent out to Los Angeles a month earlier to establish a chain of breweries and distilleries in partnership with Marvin Hart.

Hart, real name Marvin Apler, was a former North Sider who had moved to Los Angeles in 1925, around the time that Hymie Weiss was expanding the gang's list of contacts to include Ohio, New York, Florida, and probably California. He and George Davis, another native son in the liquor-selling business, scouted out the prospects in the county and sent reports back to Moran. Letters found in the possession of both Foster and Hart confirmed to investigators that the North Side Gang was solidifying an alliance with the leading Hollywood bootleggers. These letters, along with confiscated maps depicting brewery-building plans, were turned over to Chicago investigators.[22]

The *Los Angeles Times* noted:

> Moran has been in Los Angeles on one occasion, the Chicago investiga-
> tors (Dudley and Scherping, who had been sent to Los Angeles by Pat
> Roche) said, but they believe he is now in Florida. They have no trace,
> they said, of him having been here for some months. (They) assert that
> Foster was to pave the way for the moving of the Moran beer-running
> activities here, and that the "big boss" would arrive here to make his
> headquarters only after the preliminary details had been worked out and
> the "business" operating on a Chicago-like basis.[23]

Woellter admitted that the North Siders were planning to construct a large beer plant in Los Angeles, saying that he had been engaged on salary to oversee the beverage production. "I'm not a gangster or killer," he said firmly. "And that's all there is to it."

The public exposure of the Moran gang's infiltration preparations and Foster's arrest temporarily aborted the operation. Not only the police were relieved. One local bootlegger was overheard commenting to another, "Well, there's one thing certain, anyway. If they'd ever put it over, we'd have had to fold up and get us another racket, pronto, 'cause we wouldn't have a Chinaman's chance of staying in business. No sir, not with that kind of competition!"[24]

That kind of competition continued to exist, as evidenced by the October 2 seizure of a beer shipment from Chicago. It had arrived two weeks previously, consigned to a fictitious organization called the United Wholesale Varnish Company. A man who identified himself as Mr. Johnson claimed it and then divided it up into two parts, 125 barrels being stored in a warehouse at 1320 Margo Street and 53 barrels delivered to a warehouse at 440 Seaton Street. Detective Lieutenant Sears of the Los Angeles Police Department's vice detail said that the evidence stored at the Seaton Street location proved that the beer had come from Chicago, but he was reluctant to confirm that Moran's gang had originally sent it. Sears admitted that it was first-class product, much in demand among Los Angeles's "exclusive set," who gladly paid upwards of $2 a pint.[25]

Sheriff Bannick of Seattle was much less reticent about naming the Moran gang as suppliers of bootleg liquor along the Pacific Coast. In June 1931 Bannick told reporters that a local bootlegger, menaced by the invaders who had been running their wares from San Francisco to Portland and Seattle, had appealed to him for protection from men he insisted were Bugs Moran gangsters.[26] While Moran's West Coast operations were in effect, competition was unhealthy.

When Deputy Chief of Detectives John Ryan received a telephone tip on July 1 that a gang was headquartering at 807 Lakeside Place, he sent squads of detectives to investigate. They arrived to find Jack Zuta; his bodyguard Solly Vision; Albert Bratz, a Moran–Zuta associate employed at the Central Cleaning Company plant; and a woman, Leona Bernstein. The policeman arrested all four and took them to the detective bureau,where Pat Roche interrogated them about the Lingle murder.[27]

Zuta was a prime suspect. If underworld sources had the story right, Moran, Potatoes Kaufman, and Joey Josephs had been planning to reopen the Sheridan Wave Club, which had been padlocked in the wake of the St. Valentine's Day Massacre. Engraved invitations had actually gone out for its intended June 9 re-opening. Jake Lingle, who for years had been close friends with Police Commissioner Russell, supposedly demanded either 50 percent of the take or $15,000 up front to "clear" the opening with his police contacts. When the managers turned him down, he warned them to expect "more squad cars in front ready to raid it than you ever saw in your life before." Judging from his bank balance, Lingle made a lot of money talking like that, but the threats ended when the harassed managers appealed to Zuta. Frank Foster and the vicemonger were long-term associates, a fact that added more pieces to the puzzle.[28]

When Zuta's attorney, Richard Gavin, produced a writ of habeas corpus, they were released, which they viewed as a mixed blessing. It soon became obvious that the Lakeside location had been a hiding place, not a headquarters.

Zuta accosted Lieutenant George Barker as the officer was leaving the bureau. His broad features were sweaty and pale with fear. "Lieutenant," he pleaded, "I'll be killed if I go through the Loop. When you arrested me you took me from a place of safety and you ought to return me to a place of safety."

Barker responded with contempt, telling him to run along. Zuta indicated his woman companion, Leona Bernstein, and begged that the policeman help out for her sake. Barker relented. He agreed to drive him as far as the Loop and let his party find a taxi there.

While Barker got behind the wheel, Zuta, Bratz, Vision, and Bernstein piled into his car. They drove north on State Street. As they passed Jackson Boulevard, someone shouted, "We're being followed!"

The lieutenant turned to look. As he did so, a car pulled alongside his vehicle's right side. A man hung onto its running board with one hand and aimed a gun at them with the other. Barker jammed on the brakes, drew his service revolver, and leaped into the street. He was no stranger to combat; a marine during the war, he had been one of only eight survivors of a 250-man company slaughtered in France, and had twice suffered serious battlefield wounds. Zuta's party had a fraction of his fortitude; they scrambled from the car and bolted for safety. All four escaped unharmed, but two innocent bystanders were not so lucky. A stray bullet killed a motorman, Elbert Lusader, and one Olaf Svenste received a leg wound.[29]

While Barker shot at the man perched on the running board, another police officer appeared on the scene. The lieutenant, who was in plainclothes, flashed his star in time to avoid being shot. The two officers got into Barker's now-vacant car and pursued the escaping would-be assassins. Near Quincy Street, they ran into a new weapon in gang warfare, as a smokescreen issued from the back of their quarry's car, obstructing their vision and forcing them to abandon the chase. This ruse had been used frequently in the past to deter hijackers. A substance was put in the engine of liquor trucks or escort cars that caused huge clouds of dense smoke to belch from the exhaust when the driver's foot set off a device. On this occasion it proved equally effective in preventing police pursuit.[30]

Zuta and his companions failed to show up for their appearance before Judge Joseph McCarthy the next morning. Attorney Benjamin Cohen explained that they feared assassination if they emerged from hiding. The annoyed judge ordered him to have them present for another appearance the following Saturday "even if you have to bring them in an armored car."

Albert Bratz alone came to the detective bureau. He told Chief Norton that he had no idea why they had been fired upon in State Street and said that he had not seen the others since they escaped from the barrage of bullets unwounded. When pressed for more information, Bratz insisted that he did not know where Zuta and the others had gone.[31] There was no point holding him for questioning; at this stage he feared a police cell less than the world beyond the station doors.

George Moran was still wanted for questioning. On July 3 Pat Roche from the state's attorney's office seized a load of Moran liquor that had just been shipped from Boston. The investigator had been informed that Frank Parker, the "airplane bootlegger" and ex-Chicagoan who now directed his liquor-selling operations from Canada, was the original consignor. The shipment, which consisted of twenty-four crates of gin and Old Colonel whiskey valued at $80 per case, had been left in a freight car placed on a siding at Clinton and Fulton streets, so Roche's men waited for an entire day for someone to come pick it up, in order to net bootleggers and booze at the same time. When no one showed, they had to settle for the liquor alone. Roche told the press, "It was apparent the syndicate knew we had learned of the car's expected arrival, and they abandoned it."[32]

Better to lose a shipment than one's freedom.

After Governor C. C. Young signed the necessary papers, Foster blocked his extradition to Illinois by suing to obtain a writ of habeas corpus. He and his lawyers appeared before California Superior Court Judge McComb on July 15, intending to prove that he had not even been in Chicago at the time of Lingle's death.[33] When he took the stand, his lawyer asked him when he had last been in Chicago. Foster pursed his lips as if trying to recall, and finally replied, "Oh, around June sixth or seventh."

"And where did you go, Mr. Foster, when you left Chicago?"

"Santa Fe. I didn't have any business out there, just a pleasure trip, see? I like the country in New Mexico."

Deputy District Attorney Tracy Becker stood up to cross-examine. "You took a berth on this alleged trip to Santa Fe?" Foster crossed his legs, nodded, and drawled, "Sure, do you think I took a boxcar?"

Becker let that one pass. "Remember the name of the Pullman car?" he asked. Foster scowled and shook his head. Nor could he recall the name of the porter, the meals he ate, or the towns he passed through en route to his claimed destination. When he left the stand, the North Sider's face was a study in fear and irritation. He was followed to the witness chair by Donald Wilson, room clerk at the St. Clair Hotel on East Ohio Street in Chicago. Both Wilson and the hotel's secretary, Mary Micklin, testified that they had seen Foster in the lobby of the St. Clair on June 11, placing him in Chicago after Lingle's death, and not in Santa Fe as he had claimed.

Judge McComb had heard enough. He entered an order denying the writ of habeas corpus. Foster was manacled and put in the custody of the Los Angeles Sheriff's Department pending his return to Illinois. He finally boarded a train, accompanied by investigators from Pat Roche's office, arriving in Chicago on July 19. By prior arrangement with railway officials, the train made an unscheduled stop at Thirty-first Street Street and Western Avenue, and Foster was hustled into a detective squad car by Roche and a contingent of detectives.

After more than a week of questioning, his attorneys Harold Levy and Emmett Byrne succeeded in getting their client into Judge Daniel Trude's courtroom for a bail hearing. Drama abounded when Officer Anthony Ruthy, who had chased Lingle's slayer, identified Foster as the man he had pursued. Judge Trude continued the case until September 9, warning that if the state was not prepared to go to trial by then, he would order Foster's release on a $25,000 bond.[34]

While Bratz feigned ignorance in Norton's office, Zuta fled to Wisconsin, registering first at the Rockstead Hotel on Pewaukee Lake on July 4. He remained there for several days, until a couple arrived from Chicago and signed the register "Al Rosen and wife." The vicemonger spied them in the hotel, ducked out of sight before they could see him, and checked out as soon as he could pack his valises. Who they were and why their presence frightened Zuta is not known.[35]

He ended up at the Lake View Hotel, a roadhouse on Upper Nemahbin Lake, twenty-five miles west of Milwaukee. The hotel employees would recall that he was accompanied by a woman and two men who signed the register as Charles Stern and Charles Gordon Jr. They may have been Albert Bratz and Solly Vision, as underwear later found in a suitcase in Zuta's quarters had the initials S. V. stitched on them.

Checking in under the alias of J. H. Goodman, Zuta quickly ingratiated himself with the resort staff by dispensing lavish tips. He was especially charming with the female employees, treating them to apple turnovers and other desserts when their shifts ended. He spent a lot of time in the Lake View's bar, buying drinks for other guests and feeding one nickel after another into a coin-operated player piano.[36]

The seriousness of his situation never left his mind. Lingle's death had made him a marked man, and he succumbed to periodic bursts of terror. On the morning of August 1 a sixteen-year-old girl saw him come into the Rexall drugstore in Pewaukee, his agitated expression and mannerisms grabbing her attention. She listened in as he stepped into the store's phone booth and placed a call to Chicago. She recalled, "I didn't catch the name of the party he talked to, but he was highly excited. He said, cursing, 'You better send someone up here damn quick. I want a bodyguard and an escort back to Chicago, and you'd better send them here in a hell of a hurry!!'"[37]

He had calmed down by nightfall, possibly reassured that help was forthcoming, and made a visit to the Lake View barroom. He eventually grew tired of watching half a dozen couples hopping and swaying in the heat, and walked over to the player piano. He fished a nickel from his pocket and fed it into the slot. Zuta did not notice five men filing silently into the room, one carrying a Thompson and the others clutching sawed-off shotguns and revolvers.

Just as a popular tune of the day, "Good For You, Bad For Me," began playing, the armed newcomers emptied their weapons into him, the combined firepower hurling him against the piano keys. Sixteen bullets were later extracted from his body. One had passed through his mouth, splitting the lip and shattering several teeth.

While Zuta fell to the dance floor that was now empty of waltzing couples, the killers ran outside, brandishing their guns and warning bathers on a nearby beach to keep back. They entered two automobiles and drove off.[38]

One of the Lake View guests identified Ted Newberry, whom rumor credited as defecting to Capone in the wake of the Lingle furor, as one of the assassins after perusing a stack of photographs. A waitress gave a description that tallied almost exactly with that of Drucci's old comrade Henry Finkelstein.[39] Neither was charged with the crime and may not even have been involved.

On August 2 police investigators arrived at a cottage along the shores of Lake Nagawiska, about a mile east of Delafield, acting on a tip that it had been the rendezvous for Zuta's assassins. Waukesha County District Attorney Herman Salen learned that the property had been rented on July 23 by "Ralph Ross," who had paid $100 in advance for a four-week rental.

A maid in a nearby resort cabin gave the authorities a clue. Sophie Oninski told investigators from both Wisconsin and Chicago that on July 23, she saw one of the men occupying Ralph Ross's cottage carry what looked like a machine gun into the house. Anywhere from two to eleven men were on the premises at any given time. Oninski described another man in the party as blonde and left-handed, the latter feature being obvious when she watched him tossing a ball at the beach. The Chicago investigators pricked up their ears:, for that particular description matched early witness reports of Jake Lingle's killer.

The maid, upon being shown a photo of Zuta, recalled having seen him walk along the beach. The incident stuck in her memory because the men from the Ross cottage were also there, and seeing him coming at a distance, dove into the lake to avoid a meeting.[40]

Calvin Goddard's tests concluded that slugs taken from Zuta's body matched one from a gun taken from Danny Stanton, a Capone gunman.[41] On September 30, police investigators arrested Stanton on a warrant charging him with Zuta's murder. Stanton was leaving a courtroom, where he'd appeared for a vagrancy hearing and been informed that he'd stand trial on the charge on October 16. He fought extradition to Wisconsin, and in October 1931 the Supreme Court decided in his favor, which drew widespread criticism in view of Goddard's ballistics evidence. The judges justified their decision by stating that it had been proved to their satisfaction that Stanton had "not been in Wisconsin when the crime was committed."[42]

A male cousin of Zuta named Ginsberg claimed the body. He said that Zuta had left a will, which would be read in Middlesboro, Kentucky, where the vicemonger had lived before coming to Chicago. The $1,900 taken from Zuta's remains by the police would not be included in the estate; it was seized by internal revenue officers who were investigating his tax returns.[43]

Another cousin, Mrs. Reve Sabel of Milwaukee, announced that she would assume the daunting task of telling Zuta's mother back in Poland what had befallen him. Mrs. Sabel told reporters that he had not been a dutiful son. "When I left Poland years ago, the last word I had from Zuta's mother was for me to find her son in the new country," she said sadly. "She thought he was a horse trader and feared his business wasn't prospering, for he never wrote nor sent her money as the emigrant sons of her neighbors did to their mothers."[44]

The mass of records taken from Zuta's safety deposit boxes yielded a who's who of Chicago's police and public servants and detailed who was taking what from whom. Five hundred canceled checks, IOUs and notes that might have intentionally gone uncollected, an assortment of letters and memos from judges, police officers, and aldermen were among the box's contents. One notation mentioned a weekly $3,500 payment to the East Chicago Avenue station, and a letter commencing with "Dear Jack" and requesting a $400 loan was found . . . from the police chief of Evanston.[45]

Among Zuta's effects was an account book that aroused much comment and excitement on the part of the investigators. One section, apparently an accounting of division of profits, suggested that the North Side Gang and their allies had split more than $36,000 among themselves the week ending June 23, with "D" (presumed to be Domenic Aiello), "George" (Moran), "Jack" (Zuta), and "Solly" (Vision) getting $4,000 each. A legal advisor marked only as "lawyer" got $1,500, and a mysterious personage identified only as "Who" received $3,221, bringing "Who's" take for the month of June to $16,261.

Another section of the book detailed receipts from speakeasies, nightclubs, and resorts, with totals ranging from a mere $22 to more than $1,800. One pile of receipts that covered an unspecified period revealed a total syndicate take of $429,046.78. Among the payouts was $108,469 to "M. K." (probably Matt Kolb), who distributed protection bribes to the police and city and county officials.[46]

Jack Zuta functioned as a one-man loan company, if the notes and canceled checks were an accurate measure. Among the men who paid him or owed him money were Judge Joseph Schulman of the municipal court; Judge Emmanuel Eller, son of Morris Eller; Nate De Lue, assistant business manager of the board of education; Illinois State Senator Henry Starr (who claimed that the $400 check was for legal services), and former Illinois State Senator George Van Lent.

Of particular interest was a letter from onetime Capone minion Louis La Cava, who had lost favor with his former boss and been exiled. Dated June 1927 and sent from New York, the message was a plea for Zuta to help him form a united front against Capone: "Dear Jack—I'd help you organize a strong business organization capable of coping with theirs in Cicero." In a written confession that somehow found its way from the police files into Zuta's possession, a nineteen-year-old New York girl talked of how she had been hired as decoy to lure Zuta into the clutches of kidnappers who planned to hold him for $50,000 ransom. She named Mops Volpe and Joeseph Genaro as the plot's instigators.[47]

Pat Roche could barely conceal his satisfaction. When asked if he was ready to make arrests or serve grand jury subpoenas, he replied, "A lot of men will be leaving town. . . . We are following the trail of many of Zuta's dollars, and there is no telling where it will end."

While Roche exposed the dead vicemonger's secret benefactors, Zuta's heirs began a six-month battle to claim his estate.[48] On March 22, 1931, Zuta's will was refused probate in Illinois by Probate Judge Henry Horner's assistant, Oscar Caplan. Caplan pointed out that it lacked the signature of two witnesses, making Zuta legally intestate when he died. Caplan's decision quashed the hopes of twelve cousins hoping to share an estate valued at $150,000, awarding it instead to his brother, Hirsch Zoota, and a half-brother, Elza Szmul, both residing in Poland.

In August federal agents hit one of Moran's breweries, a 16,000-gallon operation on the Near North Side that they had been watching for some time. When they failed to detect anyone entering the premises during several days of observation, the Prohibition officials moved in, making no arrests but confiscating 14,000 gallons of freshly brewed ale, as seven of the eight 2,000-gallon vats were full. It was their second coup in recent history. On July 30 a 1,250-gallon alcohol-cooking plant and a 2,000-gallon moonshine still, both belonging to Moran and hidden in an old grain elevator at 1911 North Laramie Avenue, were raided and 45,000 gallons of mash dumped. Exploring the building, agents observed that tins of alcohol

274

were conveyed to a loading platform by means of an escalator, and that the gang had attempted to minimize the chances of detection by installing an electric blowing apparatus that propelled any alcohol fumes high into the air.[49]

Moran was not in Chicago at the time. In the immediate wake of Zuta's murder, he packed Lucille and John off to a resort north of Brainerd, Minnesota, and then continued to St. Paul. His plan was to hide out from the Chicago authorities and tighten his alliances with the St. Paul–Minneapolis gangs who bought the liquor he imported from Canada or brewed in his Cook and Lake County properties.

He came at an opportune time. Muscle power was needed in a war with the Weisman Gang of Kansas City, a wildcat crew that did little on its own but made a profitable living hijacking liquor trucks consigned to Moran's Minneapolis allies or kidnapping members of the same gang for ransom. The members inflicted such terrible tortures on their victims before releasing or killing them that the mere rumor of an intended abduction sent the potential victim hurrying to the Weisman Gang's Minneapolis representative, Russian-born gangster Sammy Stein, to pay the ransom in advance. Twenty-five-year-old Stein was a vicious character long wanted by the Kansas City Police Department for the 1928 murder of a traffic policeman who interfered with the robbery of the Home Trust Company.

The week of August 7, Minneapolis police officers learned from gangland informants that the notorious Bugs Moran had been seen in the company of a local gang leader who had lost multiple booze shipments to the Weismans. The leader was never identified, but the public association assumed a special significance the morning of August 14.[50]

At around ten thirty the previous evening, General W. F. Rhinow, director of the Minnesota Bureau of Criminal Apprehension, accompanied by five operatives, was cruising slowly south on Long Lake Road, near Wildwood (outside St. Paul) when they spotted a small sedan parked along the side of the road, its lights on and engine idling. Rhinow and his team were on the alert for the perpetrators of a recent bank robbery, so they pulled over to investigate. They immediately discovered two men, one lying dead beside the sedan, the other unconscious and mortally wounded in the tall grass about twenty-five yards away. The victims, who'd been struck with .45-caliber slugs, were identified as Mike Rusick and Frank Coleman, both of Kansas City and known Weisman gangsters. Coleman was still breathing but died at St. John's Hospital in St. Paul five hours later. At 6 a.m. the body of Sammy Stein was found in a thicket close to the scene of Rusick's and Coleman's murders. He too had been shot with a .45 in the head.

Underworld rumor had been suggesting that Stein and his Kansas City confederates had been marked for death for some time by the gangs who'd lost liquor shipments or had their men terrorized by them. Popular suspicion connected Moran's recent arrival with the murder of "Doc" Miller, another of the Weisman Gang's Minneapolis connections. One informer told the police that the Minneapolis gangster seen in Moran's company had recently paid $2,000 to Sammy Stein to avert the threat of a kidnapping. "He said to his pals," the stoolie claimed, "that he thought this was the best policy and that he would bide his time."

Then came Moran.

The following week, Minneapolis police arrested a Chicago gangster (who remained unidentified in the papers) recognized as a Moran man, questioned him, and reluctantly released him for lack of evidence. At roughly the same time that he was undergoing interrogation, underworld informers passed on the information that four carloads of first-class Moran liquor from Chicago had recently arrived in Minneapolis, supposedly the first big shipment in months to come through successfully without molestation from hijackers.[51]

Machine-Gun Kelly revealed the supposedly true story behind the Wildwood triple slaying years afterward. He claimed that Verne Miller, alleged Fox Lake shooter, and Sammy Stein had been members of a gang that robbed a bank in Willmar, Minnesota, approximately a hundred miles east of St. Paul. Harvey Bailey, another Depression-era bank robber, insisted that Miller did not join the gang in question until several weeks afterward but was close friends with two key members, Tommy Holden and Francis "Jimmy" Keating. In either event, Stein, as the story went, unfairly distributed the $140,000 booty from the Willmar job, arousing the wrath of Verne Miller or his friends, which was pretty much tantamount to insulting Miller personally. Another black mark against Stein was his threat to kidnap bootlegger Harry Jaffa, a Miller comrade.[52]

The remote location of the killing, along a road surely frequented by bank robbers going furtively from hideout to hideout, suggests that Kelly had the correct version of events. But the theory that Moran was involved cannot be completely discounted. Stein's activities seriously inconvenienced his St. Paul customers and created a problem that he would have had no qualms about solving in a homicidal way.

After Lingle's murder brought intense police crackdowns, Moran began shifting his operations into Lake County. He came to an agreement with Tommy Touhy, his old jailbreak buddy, who had been operating in Lake County since Prohibition became law, and went about constructing smaller breweries in the more isolated homesteads.

Lake County offered prime prospects that showed promise of helping Moran recoup the financial losses he'd incurred with the erosion and takeover of his North Side businesses. There were dozens of resorts in Lake County and the Chain o' Lakes area, as well as Lake Geneva and other destination parts of Wisconsin, all serviced by local bootleggers such as Ray Pregenzer, who sold liquor at his own resort, Pregenzer's, near Grass Lake. Fox Lake alone had such popular watering holes as the Mineola Hotel, the Helvetia Hotel, Harry McElvoy's tearoom, Robert Velisek's saloon, Frank Votava's dance hall, and the Willis Inn. In Antioch, the Wedeen Hotel and Pavilion saloon sold beer and liquor as quickly as it could be brought in, and more remote but still thriving "booze oases" were Charles Walker's at Grass Lake, Roy Sorensen's at Channel Lake, and Henry Challenger's at Cary.[53]

Frank Cantwell is a former Lake County resident who became acquainted with the Moran family in the spring of 1930. Nine years old at the time, he became friendly with Jack Moran when the latter's parents visited the Channel Lake cottage of a liquor-selling contact. The boys' friendship led to their parents meeting and visiting back and forth. Cantwell has especially fond memories of George Moran.

"He loved kids," he recalled in a 2003 interview. "George was always giving me money, five-dollar bills, ten dollars. I think once he gave me a twenty. My mother knew that that was way too much for a kid to be carrying around, so she'd always make me give it to her to hold on to. She'd give it back to me in smaller amounts, a quarter here, a quarter there. When my bike broke down, she bought me another one using money from George."

One day, a group of Purdue alumni made a trip to Lake County, choosing a cottage on Channel Lake for a rowdy celebration.

"My God, they started at dinnertime and got worse as it got darker," Cantwell remembered. "I don't know why the sheriff didn't get after them; you could tell that they were liquored up. Just as my mom was putting me to bed, they started yelling *'Long Live Purdue!'* Over and over again."

Cantwell's father was in the cottage's back yard, drinking iced beer and talking to Moran and Leo Mongoven, while their wives busied themselves in the kitchen. When the cheering students became too loud to ignore, the gangsters reacted with scarcely more decorum.

"Moran and Mongoven went down the slope, to the water," Cantwell recalled, "and started screaming across the lake at the frat boys. My God, what a racket! The college crowd was hollering *'Long Live Purdue!'* and Moran and Mongoven were shouting back *'Shut the Fuck Up!'* I think it got to be a pissing contest, with each side trying to outdo the other. I was at my bedroom window, where I could see everything, but my mother came in and shut the window so that I couldn't hear the curse words as clearly. I waited until she left and then got out of bed and opened it again.

"My dad was just standing there, not knowing what to do. Suddenly one of the college boys yells something Moran and Mongoven don't like, so Mongoven says to Dad, 'We're borrowing your boat to go teach those punks a lesson.' I don't know what Dad said to them, but they disappear from my view and come back five minutes later dragging the boat from the dry dock next to our place. I watch them push it into the water and get in. Moran says something about 'You got your piece on you?' I was sure they were going to go shoot the frat boys, so I could not tear myself away from the window."

Cantwell noticed immediately that the rowboat was wobbling heavily as the two gangsters started to row toward their cheering quarry. "Then suddenly, *Splash!* The boat goes down nose first, and Moran and Mongoven are sitting on the bottom of the lake. It was maybe a couple feet deep where they were. All I see are these two heads sticking out of the water."

Unbeknownst to the gangsters, Lucille Moran, anticipating disaster, had reached the boat before they did and removed the plug. The men were too drunk to notice until it was too late, and they were the recipients of an unexpected dip.

"They started blaming each other," Cantwell laughed. "Moran accuses Mongoven of sinking the boat, and Mongoven tells him to shut his face. Their wives went down to the water and persuaded them to come out. They were the sorriest looking spectacle as they headed back up toward the cottage, a pair of drowned rats."

The Morans also went on excursions to Lake Geneva, Wisconsin. When scouting out the area with the intention of building a summer home, George and Lucille became friendly with local resort owner Hobart Hermansen, who ran the Lake Como Inn and later the Geneva Hotel. The amiable but tough as nails son of a Danish hotel owner, Hermansen had plenty of experience handling visiting gangsters. Al Capone had been a guest at the Lake Como property, and in the not-too-distant future his place would become the hideout of choice for Baby Face Nelson, John Dillinger, and Roger Touhy. The Lake Como Inn was equipped with elegant guest rooms, a gambling den that had all the trappings of a mini-casino, a restaurant, and a speakeasy that served quite palatable liquor in spite of its name: The Sewer.[54]

Hermansen's gaming facilities earned him the nickname of the "slot-machine king of Walworth County." He was rarely raided, thanks to regular kickbacks to the local police force, but when an "official police visit" was unavoidable, he improvised.

Hermansen and Moran hit it off especially well. After staying briefly at the inn as a regular guest, the Morans were invited to stay at Hermansen's home, further down the lake. It was not long before other gangsters, many of them Moran's own men, realized the allure of the Lake Geneva–Lake Como area and began coming en masse to relax or plot outside the Cook County jurisdiction. Local legend has it that only one waitress on Hermansen's staff had the nerve to serve Moran and his crowd when they entered the dining room on one occasion. She proved to be such a good sport, taking their ribbing and liquor demands with such humor and grace, that Moran requested her by name on subsequent visits.[55]

Lucille Moran was especially taken with the area, and with Hermansen personally, as Moran was destined to learn before the year was out.

When September 9 arrived, the prearranged date for Frank Foster to be either tried or let out on bail, Judge Daniel Trude agreed to another continuance, until October 20, so that California witnesses could be brought to Chicago. Foster's attorney Byrne protested, "I was told by Mr. Rathburn, the assistant state's attorney, who is also a *Tribune* attorney, and who is handling this investigation, that it would be a long, long time before Foster got a trial. I'm beginning to think so. But I'd like to know who's running this community—the officials or the *Tribune's* attorney?"

After another continuance, Levy and Byrne finally succeeded in getting their client released on $20,000 bail in early December. Foster walked free, only to be annoyed by a trip to Judge Lyle's court to answer a vagrancy charge. He posted a $5,000 bond in that case.[56]

Foster did not keep the peace while out on bond. On February 21, 1931, he was charged with holding up hotel proprietor John Wesley Gray and his wife and robbing them of $7,600 worth of Mrs. Gray's jewelry. He beat that rap and got even better news on June 19, when Judge Fisher of the criminal court finally dismissed the murder charge against him, in view of the capture of Leo Vincent Brothers.

Brothers, a union terrorist, had been in Chicago as a refugee from bombing, arson, and murder charges back in his native St. Louis. Charles Rathburn and Pat Roche had hired a "reformed" gangster to move through the underworld and get a lead on who the Lingle killer had been. Brothers's name came up, and when seven of the Lingle witnesses identified him after his arrest, he was charged with murder.

He went to trial in March 1931 and was convicted by a narrow margin, the jury being on the verge of announcing itself hung. Their hesitation was understandable, for seven prosecution witnesses had testified to seeing him in the tunnel when Lingle was murdered, but not one could say that he or she had actually seen him pull the trigger. There was also the prevailing suspicion that Brothers was a fall guy, hired or forced to take the rap for the real killer. The jury finally declared him guilty but imposed the minimum sentence of fourteen years' imprisonment instead of the death penalty that first-degree murder convictions usually called for.[57]

Although the evidence strongly suggests that Zuta and Foster, with North Sider backing, had planned and carried out Lingle's execution, Brothers has been historically regarded as having taken the fall at the request/order of Al Capone. If so, Capone had not been consciously doing the North Siders a favor. Lingle's death had brought on a heat that matched the post-massacre furor degree for degree, and Zuta had paid for that gaffe with his life. That satisfied Capone's sense of justice, and Brothers's conviction was what the public and the police needed to see to bring things back to normal.

Foster opted to return to Los Angeles to live. He became a bail bondsman for the Pacific Surety Bonding Company, but having a semi-legitimate occupation did not stop the police departments in both Los Angeles and San Francisco from attacking him with vagrancy warrants and, on one occasion, an arrest for having a gun in his expensive coupe. In April 1932 San Francisco police Captain Dullea pointed Foster out to a group of younger officers while the ex-North Sider was part of a lineup and said, "Take a good look at him, and every time you boys see him on the streets of this city, lock him up and lock up everyone you see with him."[58]

Despite the police's hostility to his presence, Frank Foster called Los Angeles home until he died of a heart attack in Studio City on April 22, 1967.[59] Author

Richard Lindberg states, probably correctly, in his excellent *Return to the Scene of the Crime* that the secret of who really killed Jake Lingle died forever when Foster did.

On October 13, 1930, two young men rented a second-story apartment at 202 Kolmar Avenue, across the street from Pasquale "Patsy" Prestogiacoma's house at number 205. Prestogiacoma was Joe Aiello's partner in the Italo-American Importing Company and was currently playing host to the nervous Unione head. Aiello had been in hiding since Capone returned from Philadelphia, but it did not take long for Capone's coldly efficient network to track him down. Soon after the two men moved into number 202, another man rented a third-floor apartment at 4518 West End Avenue, which overlooked the rear entrance to Prestogiacoma's home.

At eight thirty on the night of October 23, their vigil paid off. Aiello, a train ticket to Brownsville, Texas in his pocket, emerged from the house with Prestogiacoma and headed down the walkway to the curb, where a cab waited. Machine-gun fire rained across the street, missing Patsy and the cab driver but riddling Aiello. Bleeding and moaning, he staggered around the corner of the building, only to be struck by bullets fired from the West End Avenue outpost. He collapsed and died, yet another Chicago gangster to be murdered by "person or persons unknown."[60]

16

VAGRANT

A IELLO'S DEATH BROUGHT ON AN all-points-bulletin for Moran, who had disappeared from all of his usual haunts. The police had some idea of where he was, thanks to an arrest made two days before. Early on the morning of October 21, Colonel A. V. Smith, state's attorney for Lake County, received word that the gangster had arrived at Elizabeth Cassidy's resort on Bluff Lake, five miles southwest of Antioch, at about ten o'clock the previous night. Smith knew the Cassidy place well; it was a favored stopover for gangsters on vacation or on the lam from Chicago, and he raided it regularly to sour their welcome.

In June 1929, after a band of Chicago gangsters had indulged in machine-gun practice in the woods behind the house and accidentally wounded some farmers, he had the resort closed temporarily by an injunction. Smith worried that Chicago gangsters were intending to set up a headquarters in Lake County, the same way they had done in Cicero, and he was determined to keep his jurisdiction from acquiring similar infamy. In mid-October the state's attorney had received the tip that Moran would be arriving at Mrs. Cassidy's place any day and enlisted the assistance of the Hargrave Detective Agency in Chicago in watching the premises day and night.[1]

Now their quarry had arrived, so Smith contacted Hargrave immediately. The state's attorney had also been tipped off that Leo Mongoven, whose mysterious disappearance had yet to be explained by a body or a capture, was not only alive and well but heading for Cassidy's to reunite with Moran. For all they knew, he might already have arrived unnoticed. The detective, along with five colleagues, hurried up to Lake County and met with Constable George Stried, who would represent local law enforcement.

The small raiding party made its way quietly to Bluff Lake and surrounded the resort. Hargrave and Stried entered the premises while the others waited outside to block any possible escape attempts. The two men first encountered Elizabeth Cassidy and her son, who were sullen and hostile but did not attempt to interfere. They searched the resort and found Moran asleep in bed. He woke with a start when they shook him but did not resist when they ordered him to get dressed and come with them to answer a vagrancy charge.

While the angry gangster removed his pajamas and dressed in clothes he'd brought—a hunting outfit consisting of a tan cap, black leather coat resembling a bomber jacket, gray flannel shirt, olive-green corduroy knickers, and knee-high black leather "tramping boots"—Hargrave and Stried searched the room and found a .22 revolver hidden under Moran's pillow. Satisfied that Mongoven was not on the premises, Stried charged Moran with carrying concealed weapons and vagrancy, and brought him before Judge Harold Tallett.

The gangster was silent except when addressed directly, but his cold stare spoke volumes. He paled slightly when Tallett fixed his bail on the concealed weapons and vagrancy charges at $50,000 but said nothing as Lake County officers escorted him to the jail at Waukegan pending his release on bond. His trial date was scheduled for October 24. When his counsel, Claire Edwards, petitioned for a bail reduction by reminding the judge that the Supreme Court had recently fixed $5,000 as a reasonable bail amount in such cases, Tallett accordingly reduced Moran's bond, which was immediately posted by Waukegan bondsman Joe Oltusky.

The concealed weapons charge was brought before Judge Perry Persons. As soon as the judge noticed that Oltusky was offering bond in this case as well, he asked Colonel Smith, "Is the state satisfied with this surety?" Smith voiced no objection. Persons then asked Moran whether Oltusky was bailing him out at his request. When Moran replied in the affirmative, Persons explained the question.

"There is a rule in the court," he said, "that when bail is offered by a professional bondsman who is given a fee by the defendant, the bond will not be approved except for definite reasons."

Moran's counsel, former Judge Claire Edwards (who had presided over Governor Len Small's trial years previously) explained that his client had no friends in Lake County who could offer bail for him, forcing him to resort to the services of a bondsman. Satisfied, Persons approved the bond.[2]

After court was adjourned, Lake County officials delivered Moran into the custody of Lieutenant Phillip Carroll of the Chicago Detective Bureau, who had been sent to bring him back to Chicago. Although he did not create a scene, he made it clear that he did not intend to cooperate. Chief of Detectives Norton got nothing out of him, nor did Pat Roche, chief investigator for State's Attorney Swanson, who was especially anxious to interview him about the Lingle murder.

"I knew Lingle and thought he was a regular fellow," Moran offered. "I don't know why he was killed, or who killed him."

Reporters with access to the gangster asked him about the rumor that he had been negotiating with Capone for a safe return to the rackets, the proposed arrangement being that he reclaim control of the liquor and gambling businesses and operate under the aegis of Capone. Newberry, the defector, was apparently doing that job poorly.

"I am trying to make a deal with no one," Moran asserted. "I've been out of the rackets for four years, and I've been living the life of a respectable businessman. I'm going to continue as such." He downplayed his well-known enmity with Capone, insisting that he had never actually accused Capone of ordering or masterminding the St. Valentine's Day Massacre. "I never accused Capone of that."

He made light of the vagrancy charges. "How can they make a vagrant out of me? I'm a businessman. I am vice president of the Central Cleaners and Dyers, and have entered actively in the business. The records will show that I have attended directors meetings monthly." He told the reporters that his salary at the union was roughly $5,000 annually, but dividends paid him an additional $22,000.

Moran explained his presence in Waukegan by insisting that he was only at Bluff Lake to do some duck hunting. "I am a lover of the outdoors, and I spend much of my time hunting and fishing. . . . Yesterday I got a hunting license at Antioch, and today I expected a bunch of my friends up there to go hunting with me."[3]

He was expecting at least three, as it turned out. Reporters who hovered around the Cassidy place after the arrest spotted a limousine winding its way along the road leading to the resort. When it stopped, three men whom the newsmen did not recognize got out. Upon learning that Moran had been taken into custody, they hastily climbed back into the car and drove off. The vehicle's license plates were traced to Ben Kornick.

The *Tribune* reporter asked Moran about Mongoven. The North Sider paused for a brief second, then gave a decidedly sly smile. "To the best of my knowledge, he's dead," he replied. When another reporter asked him who had killed his friends and colleagues in the massacre, his smile slipped and he answered tersely, "Santa Claus."

At 10:30 a.m. on October 22, Moran and his Chicago lawyer Richard Gavin appeared in Judge Lyle's courtroom to answer a vagrancy charge. When the defendant's name was called, there was a stir in the crowd, which consisted mostly of reporters, bailiffs, and courtroom hangers-on who followed the daily case rosters like soap opera addicts. Clad in his leather jacket and hunting costume, Moran moved with Gavin toward the bench and listened as the attorney presented a petition for a change of venue.

Lyle had expected it, of course. Few gangsters were willing to throw themselves on his mercy, as he was notorious for jailing outlaws who failed to pay the abnormally high bails he set. Appearing before Lyle could land one behind bars as quickly as a murder confession. But for all his severity when it came to handling career criminals, John Lyle had a soft spot for Moran which he wrote about at length decades later in *The Dry and Lawless Years*.

Lyle leaned forward and stared across the bench at the North Sider, who met his eyes with no small amount of apprehension. "What's the matter?" he inquired, as if he didn't know. "Don't you like me, Moran?"

The gangster cracked a smile, recognizing and responding with amusement to the mild baiting. "I like you, your honor," he replied, "but I am suspicious of you."

Lyle suppressed a smile. Moran's quick replies entertained him more than his position on the bench allowed him to safely show. In his biography Lyle would recall Moran approaching him at a ballpark, noticing an expensive ring on his finger, and saying, "Judge, that's a beautiful diamond ring you're wearing. If it's snatched some night, promise me you won't go hunting me. I'm telling you right now I'm innocent."[4]

The banter over, Lyle declined to approve or deny Gavin's petition. Instead, he asked a series of questions that must have made Adelard Cunin's blood turn to ice in his veins. Lyle informed the now-nervous defendant that he had it on good authority that George Moran was not his real name but rather a pseudonym that masked a probably lurid past.[5]

"Is Moran in fact your actual surname?"

"Yes, it is."

"That's the name you were born with?"

"Yes—but how do you expect me to remember that far back?"

The courtroom erupted in laughter. Even Lyle was amused in spite of himself. But he was determined not to let Moran out of his clutches. Word had reached him that immigration authorities were on their way to interview Moran in regard to his citizenship status. Next to vagrancy, deportation was now law enforcement's favorite method of eradicating the gangster problem, and investigators had noted the Canadian birthplace that Moran had claimed during his second incarceration at Joliet.

Switching tacks, the judge shuffled the papers on his desk and picked up a copy of the gangster's criminal record, which he dryly described as "as long as the Delaware River." He called for Clerk John A. Passmore of the criminal court, and requested him to do a thorough search of his records to determine if Moran had any charges pending. A similar request was dispatched to James A. Kearns of the municipal court. In the meantime, he ordered Moran held until the following day, when another hearing would be scheduled to examine the outcome of the records search.

Shortly after leaving the courts building at 5 p.m., Lyle satisfied himself that Moran was one of a dozen prisoners awaiting transfer to the Cook County Jail. He queried the clerk, Thomas Loftus, as to whether preparations for the transfer had been completed. Loftus confirmed that he had finished the requisite paperwork and that they would be taken over to the jail within the hour.

Lyle had underestimated Moran's resources. Perhaps the "leader without a gang" description had been bandied around so often by October 1930 that Lyle thought he was dealing with a feisty but deflated has-been. Therefore, it came as an unwelcome surprise when he learned later that night that just after he left, a mysterious visitor had arrived at the criminal court clerk's office at city hall and posted $10,000 cash as bond for Moran. Bailiff Carmen Viviano was leading the handcuffed gangster to a holding cell when he was stopped and shown both the bond and the release order.

Loftus, the clerk who had filled out the transfer paperwork, claimed to be as baffled as Lyle. "I knew nothing of any bond for Moran," he insisted to reporters. "Moran must have found some other judge just after I left and before the prisoners were started to jail."

Gavin, as it turned out, had made a bond application for Moran before Municipal Judge John Sbarbaro, who made a second living from burying gangsters and was more amenable to their plights than was Lyle. Sbarbaro, who had buried Dean O'Banion, Hymie Weiss, and Vincent Drucci, speedily approved a $10,000 bond, which the mystery savior had paid in cash.

Henry L. Kane, attorney for the Central Cleaners and Dyers, confirmed Moran's release when reporters telephoned him, but he declined to name the man who had paid the bond. "Someone took $10,000 in cash to Kearns's office in the city hall," he said, "and all Moran had to do was sign his name on the bond. No, I won't tell you where the money came from. I promised Moran I wouldn't, but he'll be in court again at 5 p.m. tomorrow."

Lyle vented his wrath on Viviano, the bailiff who had allowed the gangster to leave his custody: "You had no right to turn Moran loose. I told you to take him to jail, and you should have followed my orders. I don't like bailiffs who make it easy for hoodlums in my court. You released one of the worst criminals in the United States."

Viviano protested that he had been between a rock and a hard place, as refusal to release Moran would have put him in contempt of Judge Sbarbaro. Lyle knew he was right but fumed all the same.[6]

Moran arrived at the courthouse at 5 p.m. for the scheduled hearing before Lyle, who reluctantly approved a change of venue and a jury trial. Before he could depart the courtroom, however, two immigration officials pushed their way through the crowd, identified themselves to Moran, and asked to speak to him in

Lyle's chambers. By now the rumor about a potential deportation had reached almost everyone, and there were whispers as eyes followed gangster and officials into the private room.

"They're going to deport Bugs Moran," someone said wonderingly.

What was said during the interview is not a matter of record, but when the door finally opened, Moran emerged with an ear-to-ear smile. Behind him, the officials signaled to Lyle that the interview was over. Adjusting his tie and smoothing the thick folds of his black overcoat, he cast his gaze over the onlookers and waited until the hum had subsided. Then he declared, after the dramatic pause due the occasion, "They haven't a thing on me. I am a citizen of the United States."[7]

Flanked by his attorneys, Moran made his way out of the Criminal Courts Building and headed for a Packard parked near the curb. Lucille Moran sat inside, pale but brightening when she observed her husband's jovial and triumphant demeanor. She shifted across the seat to the passenger side as he opened the door and settled behind the wheel. The Morans drove off, but not before George introduced Lucille to the sea of reporters.

"Gentlemen," he said amiably, "my wife. If anyone comes looking for me, you can tell them that this is our wedding anniversary and we're going roller skating."[8]

Days later, on October 26, Lake County State's Attorney Smith learned with astonishment that Moran had returned to Bluff Lake and taken a room at Cassidy's. George Hargrave and Constable Stried went to the resort to investigate a tip that Mongoven had holed up there after Moran's arrest, and again found Moran in bed, this time wide awake and reading the Sunday paper while lounging in his pajamas. A shotgun leaned against the bed headboard, and the men eyed it warily while they confronted the gangster.

"We didn't expect to find you back in Lake County," Stried said, annoyed. "Come along, Bugs."

The gangster lowered the paper but refused to budge. "I'm out on bail now. I've got some rights as an American citizen. You can't pinch me."

They ignored his protests and took him before Justice of the Peace Tallett. He stood accused of concealing Mongoven and conspiring to defeat justice. For good measure, another vagrancy charge was thrown in.[9]

"What are you trying to do, pull some Lyle stuff?" Moran demanded, his sense of fight not dampened in the least by the sudden and harsh capture. "This is double jeopardy or something. You can't do it."

Justice Tallett, whose tolerance for arrogant criminals was on a par with Lyle's punitive outlook, warned him that he could indeed, and that he would add a contempt of court charge to the existing ones if Moran's courtroom defiance continued. Colonel Smith added insult to injury when he said to Moran, "You're going to be taught to stay out of this county. You'll be arrested every time you're found here."

"I was only up here for some innocent little duck hunting," Moran said, standing his ground. Tallett reminded him that he was due to appear in court later that day in relation to the first Waukegan vagrancy charge leveled against him, and the concealed weapons charge the following Tuesday. As to the conspiracy charge, Tallett imposed a $5,000 bond, which was guaranteed by local businessman and Moran friend Tom Thames. A hearing on the conspiracy and second vagrancy arrest was scheduled for November 5.

After Moran, his wife, and his counsel left Tallett's courtroom, reporters surrounded them.

"What do you know about the murder of Joe Aiello?" one of them asked.

"That double-crosser?" Moran said with disdain. "I haven't seen him for eight months. I haven't been in the rackets for four years. I'm a respectable guy."

When asked whether he was in the process of re-organizing the gang that had received a mortal blow from the St. Valentine's Day Massacre, the gangster laughed out loud. "I'm out of it all. I'm not after anybody and no one is after me. Don't get me wrong, though. I'm not afraid of anyone, Capone or whoever it is."[10]

On December 9, after a continuance had been granted, Moran stood trial in Waukegan for vagrancy. The Lake County jury consisted of three farmers, three salesmen, two carpenters, a cab driver, a retired merchant, a laborer, and one man currently unemployed. Moran, a conspicuous yet elegant sight in a green suit, was in good humor, and his personality dominated the courtroom, creating a jovial atmosphere despite the judicial surroundings.

The defense attorneys, Claire C. Edwards and Richard Gavin, listened to State's Attorney Smith explain the vagrancy offense with which the nattily dressed gangster stood charged.

"Moran is a vagrant not in the sense of one penniless and unemployed," he clarified, in case the gang leader's suave and prosperous appearance instilled doubts in the minds of the jury, "but as a habitual criminal engaged in no honest occupation and with a criminal record, in his case as a burglar and robber."

Edwards and Gavin, in their opening statement, reminded the jury that their client did have a criminal record but was now an official of the Central Cleaners and Dyers company, owning approximately one-third of the business's $300,000 worth of stock. With salary and dividends combined, he earned $25,000 a year from his position as vice president.

Smith responded to the portrait of reformation and respectability by suggesting that leopards did not change their spots that easily. "He was the associate of such men as Dean O'Banion, Frank and Peter Gusenberg, and Hymie Weiss, all shot down in gangland quarrels. He shot a policeman named O'Hara and once shot John Torrio, notorious gangster. He used aliases whenever arrested."

The state opened its case by calling Detectives John Howe and William Drury to the stand. They recounted the January 9, 1930, arrest of Moran at the Hotel Sherman in the company of the still-missing Mongoven. Howe recalled, "Moran gave his name as G. E. Q. Johnson." The gangster grinned, and a titter ran through the courtroom.

"Who was Mongoven?" Smith asked, for the record.

"A gangster."[11]

Edwards and Gavin leaped to their feet, objecting strenuously. Judge Persons sustained the objections and ordered the question repeated.

"A racketeer," was Howe's second attempt at a reply, and the defense table thundered with objections again. Moran and the onlookers erupted in laughter as Howe fumbled for an acceptable way to answer. Finally he ventured tentatively, "He was a beer peddler." Edwards and Gavin did not challenge that response.

Howe testified to seeing Moran in a Chicago jail on two additional occasions. "In 1929 he was pinched with John [sic] Clark, who was later killed in the Valentine Day Massacre."[12]

The next day, the defense called its first witness: Moran himself. So great had been the anticipation of the gangster's testimony that one of the courtroom doors was broken when the crowd surged back in after a brief recess. Tastefully dressed in a gray pinstriped suit and blue tie, Moran rose from where he had been sitting with his wife and Elizabeth Cassidy when his name was called, and made his way calmly to the stand.

"State your name and age, please," the clerk requested.

"George Clarence Moran, thirty-seven years old, vice president of the Central Cleaners and Dyers," he responded with a visible touch of pride. He shot a triumphant look at the prosecutor's table while the crowd giggled at the mention of his comically refined middle name.[13]

In response to questions from Edwards and Gavin, Moran told the court that his income from the company itself came to roughly $100 per week, and that he held two hundred of its six hundred shares. He listed as additional assets seven lots in Berkley Lawn valued at $12,000 to $16,000 each, and fifty shares in the American Telephone and Telegraph Company.

Smith declined to cross-examine directly, choosing instead to impress Moran's recorded misdeeds on the jury and raise doubt that the gangster was capable of going straight. He called Sheriff James Reeder and jailer Herbert Loer, both of McLean County, who testified to Moran's 1912 and 1913 arrests in Bloomington for theft and larceny. When Reeder told the jury that the theft had been of a horse and buggy, the audience laughed and Moran looked embarrassed. They were followed to the stand by Chief of Detectives John Norton, who recounted Peter Veesaert's identification of Moran as one of John Torrio's assailants in the January 1925 attack, and Captain William Schoemaker, who showed the jury photos of Moran acting as a pallbearer at O'Banion's funeral.

The last state witness before adjournment was George Kargonis, a private detective who had once been hired by Smith to get evidence of illegal booze being sold at Cassidy's. His testimony was intended to prove that the so-called "respectable businessman Moran" was not averse to frequenting places where the law was disregarded like yesterday's newspapers.

When Kargonis testified that he had seen Elizabeth Cassidy serving liquor at her house, she leaned forward in her seat, ignoring Lucille Moran's restraining grip in her arm, and hissed, "You lie!" When Judge Persons announced an adjournment, the irate resort keeper got out of her chair, lunged at Kargonis, and screamed, "You liar, I'll get you!" Bailiffs restrained her before her nails and fists could do any damage and escorted her firmly from the courtroom.[14]

The following morning, Smith took his opportunity to cross-examine Moran. He addressed the gang leader's employment with the Central Cleaners and Dyers, asking specifically how he had gotten the job.

"Isn't it true that you elbowed your way into the firm?" the state's attorney demanded.[15]

"It certainly isn't," Moran retorted.

"What did you do as an officer of this company?"

"I arbitrated the differences they had."

Smith persisted. "What do you mean by arbitrate?"

"I kept things moving in a harmonious way."

The state's attorney was skeptical. "How could you settle these differences in a lawful manner?" Moran gave a response disturbingly accurate: "I was in a position to settle any little matters that came up."

When asked whether it was true that many cleaning and dyeing establishments had been terrorized and bombed during the strife that saw Moran join the company, Moran admitted, "There may have been some trouble. I don't know how much."

"Well, after you got into the business, the trouble stopped, didn't it?" Smith queried sarcastically. Moran met his stare and answered, "I guess it died down a little." When asked, he said that he showed up at the office at least once a month.

The last day of the trial was perhaps the most explosive. During a recess Moran and George Hargrave encountered each other in the hall outside the courtroom, and insults were exchanged. Hargrave barely missed having his jaw broken by the enraged gangster's flying fist, and before Moran could try again, the bailiff and friends of both men separated the combatants.

Another sensational moment took place when Ben Kornick was seized after leaving the witness stand, where he gave cursory information about his dealings with Moran in the Cleaners and Dyers offices. Federal agents ordered him to produce the company's books and records before the grand jury the next day, as a possible prelude to tax evasion charges aimed at Moran and/or the company.

Captain John Stege noticed a North Side gangster loitering in the corridor outside the courtroom and ordered him seized. The man fled but was apprehended after a brief chase. When Stege identified him as Mike Douvich, alias Doorman, a known North Sider who had been with the gang for at least eight years, he was arrested for vagrancy. Moran, upon learning of the arrest, said calmly, "We'll see whether he [Stege] can get away with that."

It was up to Moran's own lawyer to give him a reality check. "Everyone's against you in this state," Richard Gavin was heard whispering to him before closing arguments. "You'd better leave. Their prejudice will never give you a chance." Lucille burst into tears, and her husband lost his cocky grin.[16]

In his closing argument Colonel Smith described Bugs Moran to the jury as a "bloodthirsty tiger who should be treated as all dangerous animals are treated." His assistant, prosecutor Sidney Block, insisted that the gangster was not a vagrant in the unemployment sense but because of the fact that he made his money from criminal activities.

"He said he was a businessman," Block observed in a voice thick with sarcasm and contempt. "What a businessman he was! Every time he registered at a hotel, it was under an alias. He served time in prison. He was convicted of burglary and robbery."

The jury retired to deliberate at about 5 p.m. Five hours and eight ballots later, the members announced that they had reached a verdict: not guilty. They later told reporters that the evidence did not convince them that Moran was a vagrant in the legal sense. His testimony, as well as that of Ben Kornick, satisfied them that he was a businessman with a regular and legal income.

Moran was all smiles as he shook hands with the jury and his attorneys. Beside him, Lucille sobbed quietly with elation and relief. "Now that this is cleared up," he told reporters, "I want to be cleared of all charges in Chicago. Then I'm going to get back in the cleaning and dyeing business." Smiling mysteriously, he added, "I have some important plans for the improvement of the trade."

When that statement was printed in the papers, the Master Cleaners and Dyers responded with a public announcement of their own. "Assuming that George Clarence Moran has been correctly reported by the press," said their spokesman, "the Master Cleaners and Dyers Association wishes to point out that it has recently put into operation a new plan of its own for the improvement of the industry in this vicinity to the benefit of the public and industry alike. This new plan was announced by the newspapers of Chicago this week and is available to all members of the industry who can qualify for its requirements."[17]

Attorney Henry Kane, who represented the Central Cleaning Company, told reporters that he was planning on meeting with federal authorities the following day to discuss and reach a settlement over Moran's income tax problems. Rumors had been circulating that federal agents were waiting to arrest the gangster after the trial, based on his testimony about his income, but it was pointed out that Moran had only given details about his 1930 earnings, which he did not have to report and pay taxes on until the following March.

The year 1930 did not end in triumph for the North Sider, despite the successful battle against a vagrancy conviction. Lucille, who had stood by him throughout his rise to power in the North Side Gang, had been badly shaken by the massacre and her husband's narrow escape from joining the body count. The advice from Moran's own counsel—to leave Lake County—was the last straw. She refused to run or hide any more, and at the end of 1930 she had him served with divorce papers.[18]

As soon as the decree, which Moran did not contest, became final, Lucille returned with John to Lake Geneva, where she assumed management of a tiny resort called The Doll House,[19] which adjoined Hobart Hermansen's Lake Como Inn. She took to the business naturally, having organized numerous poker games for Moran and his cohorts in the same area, and her discretion, the byproduct of her years spent married to one of America's most notorious gangsters, made her "hotel" a favorite stopover for Baby Face Nelson and members of John Dillinger's gang of wandering outlaws, such as Tommy Carroll and his girlfriend Jean Delaney Crompton.

In 1932 Lucille married again, this time to Hobart Hermansen. Oddly enough, Moran did not turn on his old drinking and gambling crony when Hermansen married his ex-wife and assumed partial responsibility for raising John. Relations between the two men might not have been as warm as before, but they remained cordial, and George dropped by periodically to visit his son.

His presence was particularly welcome the time Lucille found "French postcards" in John's schoolbag. The pictures were not explicit but were risqué enough to warrant a phone call to Chicago. Moran and John spent an hour by the lake, having the "talk" that all parents and teenagers anticipate with unease, and when they returned to the house, both had faces the color of boiled lobster. "I hope I never have to go through that again!" Moran sputtered to Lucille. The veteran of many a heavy-handed police interrogation, talking to his son about sex had unnerved him completely.[20]

He remarried in 1931, his second bride being twenty-one-year-old Chicago nightclub entertainer and Tennessee native Evelyn Herrell. The ceremony took place in La Crosse, Wisconsin.[21] Evelyn, who was recently divorced and had a small child being raised by relatives, had dark blonde hair, a heart-shaped face, and a cupid's-bow mouth that she loved to paint in fiery shades of red lipstick. She was feminine but tough, carrying her own gun if and when the occasion demanded and evidencing none of the stress Lucille had experienced as an outlaw's wife. For more than twenty years, she would not only be Moran's spouse but also his confidante and, in all likelihood, partner in crime.

On December 26 Mongoven emerged from the dead, figuratively speaking. Reporters learned that he had come out of hiding and showed up at his home in Villa Park, DuPage County, where he played Santa Claus to his two boys. On Christmas Day a neighbor out walking his dog did a double take when he saw Mongoven doing the same thing. The Moran aide just smiled, nodded, and carried on.[22]

The sighting nullified the rumors that he had been murdered[23] and intensified the search for him. By the time the police arrived at the Mongoven bungalow, he had gone again, and would evade capture for another two years.

During the first week of January 1931, Los Angeles police received a tip that Moran had recently arrived in the city to confer with Marvin Hart and his other West Coast partners. A thorough search of known gangster hangouts in the city failed to turn up any sign of him.

Moran's Los Angeles expansion had never really passed the primary stage, and it ended entirely when Marvin Hart was murdered at the end of December. The former Chicago gangster was stepping out of his car in the garage of his home at 453 North Orange Drive when two men whom witnesses described as "slim and undersized" ambushed him and sent four bullets into his brain and upper body.

In seeking a motive for the killing, Los Angeles police recalled that an elaborate dinner had been held at a Hollywood hotel several days previously and was attended by Frank Foster, Hart, and "some eastern liquor men."[24] They learned that Hart had recently approached his probation officer to seek permission to leave California briefly, and theorized that he may have stiffed the easterners in a liquor deal and was planning to flee. Whatever the motive, his death quelled Foster's enthusiasm for the venture, and Moran had to change his mind about a possible move to California's sunny but deadly climes.

He may have had something to fall back on. On February 27, 1931, the *Milwaukee Journal* published an article declaring the belief that Moran had assumed control of all the bootlegging and gambling in the southern part of Wisconsin. "Since Moran's fortunes have waned on Chicago's North Side, he and his followers are daily extending their fields northward," the paper said. "With the exception of the cities, these gangsters are almost entirely in control of the racketeering operations in Kenosha and Walworth Counties."[25]

The paper blamed lax Prohibition agent activity for the foothold that Moran had acquired in Wisconsin and used as a launching pad to develop his bootlegging network. "There has been little or no official activity in Walworth and Kenosha counties during the last two years by W. Frank Cunningham, deputy administrator, and his men. When the expensive private cars of federal Prohibition agents leave the Milwaukee federal building, they are almost never headed in a southerly direction," it concluded acidly.

Although Moran did not enjoy exclusive control in these endeavors, as he had during his tenure as boss of Chicago's North Side, his liquor-running contacts and reputation made him welcome among bootlegging gangs in other cities and states, unless said gangs were allied with Capone. His name would come up often as the 1930s progressed, as one or another of his short-lived partnerships became common knowledge. Sometimes a body or two was left in his wake, but murder was an occupational hazard.

On October 17, 1931, Al Capone, sitting in a courtroom in Chicago's Federal Court Building, listened to a jury of his peers find him guilty of tax evasion after a trial that lasted eleven days. The following week, Judge James H. Wilkerson sentenced him to eleven years in prison and fines and court costs totaling thousands of dollars.

Leaving the building in the custody of a U.S. marshal and several deputies, he offered a resigned smile to photographers. "Get enough, boys. You won't see me for a long, long time." In the taxi on the way to the county jail, where he would be held pending his transfer to a federal prison, he said philosophically, "It was my own fault. Publicity—that's what got me."[26]

He would have been more accurate if he'd said notoriety. The St. Valentine's Day Massacre, and crimes like it, killed not only rival gangsters but whatever tolerance the public may have had for the bootleg barons who had been enjoying public-benefactor status for too long. Other gangsters got prison time for tax evasion:— Frank Nitti, Jake Guzik, and Ralph Capone, to name a few—but Capone's downfall symbolized the triumph of the law over the "gangster menace."

Capone served part of his sentence in Atlanta and became one of the earliest inmates of the notorious Alcatraz Federal Penitentiary. In 1939, his brain affected by the unchecked spread of syphilis, he was released. He died at his estate in Palm Island in 1947, his name, in writer William J. Helmer's words, "still synonymous with the Chicago Syndicate. Scarface Al Capone learned the hard way that Crime Does Not Pay—but it can be a shortcut to immortality."[27]

17

WANDERING OUTLAW

I T WAS MAY 1931, AND six-year-old Doretta Hoehne was back in St. Louis for her second round of treatments for the infantile paralysis she had been diagnosed with when she was barely a year old. She lived with her parents and younger brother in Lincoln, Nebraska, but since 1930 had been coming to the McLain's Orthopedic Sanitarium for a May to August series of rehabilitative treatments that included massage, weight machines, and alternating applications of cold and heat. Although the disability had been severe at the onset, by 1931 she was able to walk with the aid of a leg brace.[1]

Each year, Doretta and her mother made the trip alone, as her father had to remain in Lincoln for employment reasons. Mother and daughter stayed at a boarding house, but unfortunately the only affordable accommodations within walking distance of McLain's was cheap for a good reason. Mrs. Hoehne routinely shook out the bedsheets before turning in for the night to get rid of the bedbugs that had accumulated during the day.

Every day, right after breakfast, Doretta and her mother would walk the few blocks to the sanitarium. One bright morning, a black touring car pulled up to the curb, and the driver spoke to Mrs. Hoehne while the little girl stared at the polished doors and fixtures in fascination. All windows except those on the driver's side were dark and rolled up, concealing the car's other occupants from view.

"He asked Mother if we wanted a ride to wherever we were going," Doretta recalled in a 2004 interview. "She thanked him but said no."

The touring car rolled away and re-entered the morning traffic flow, but the encounter was not destined to be unique. The next day, at approximately the same time, Doretta and her mother were stopped again, this time in front of their boarding house.

"It was the same car, same driver," Doretta remembered. "They offered us a ride again. Mother became nervous and refused again, so away they went a second time."

When mother and daughter returned to the house that night, their landlady informed them that they had had a visitor who identified himself as George Moran, from Chicago. Moran must have explained the two ride offers to the woman, for she said, "He wanted to reassure you that he wasn't trying to pull anything funny. He just felt bad seeing the little girl"—she nodded down at Doretta—"hobbling with her leg in a brace. He said to tell you he'll be back tomorrow, and if you really wouldn't like a lift to the sanitarium, he won't bother you again."

Mrs. Hoehne must have been impressed by this gesture of honest intention, for the next morning, when Moran and his driver pulled up in front of the house, she and Doretta agreed to get into the touring car's cool interior and be chauffeured to their destination. The little girl had never been in such a luxurious vehicle in her life and sat completely still, running her small palms over the rich-smelling leather. It wasn't until she had been riding in it for over a week that she began to relax.

Exactly what Moran was doing in St. Louis that summer is uncertain, although he may have been visiting with the Hill Mob, a rogue segment of the Cuckoos who happened to be allied with the anti-Capone Shelton Gang.[2] He and Evelyn had taken up residence in the affluent Roosevelt Hotel in the Central West End of the city. It was an area in which nightclubs, theaters, and exclusive supper clubs flourished. Moran had been supplying liquor from his own resources to one of the local gangs and held regular meetings in his hotel suite.

When he visited the Hoehnes' boarding house, what he saw appalled him. Before they realized what was happening, mother and daughter found themselves whisked out of their substandard accommodations and given a small suite at the Roosevelt. Moran's generosity extended to buying Doretta stylish dresses and a child's pearl necklace. What Mrs. Hoehne thought of the lavish presents can only be conjectured, but she never objected to seeing her daughter receive and delight in such finery, and she accepted the gangster's offer to pay for the Roosevelt suite as long as it was required. Moran's motivation in assisting them was beyond reproach. He conducted himself like a gentleman, and did so with Evelyn by his side, in case anyone was inclined to suspect an attraction to Doretta's mother.

It was actually Doretta's childish prattle that threw a shadow over the arrangement. One morning, she and her mother were sharing a table in the crowded dining room with some wealthy Jewish women. The summer heat had already descended upon the city, and the little girl was impressed by the fact that her milk had ice cubes in it. While she stirred and play with them, she half-listened to the adults converse. One of the women asked Mrs. Hoehne about her husband. Doretta perked up.

"My mom and dad aren't married—I wasn't at the wedding!" she piped. She had only meant to add to the conversation, but it had definitely been the wrong thing to say in the wrong company, at the wrong time. Young women with children and no sign of a husband were viewed askance, even with suspicion. The Jewish ladies started at the remark but collected their composure and resumed talking, although with less friendliness directed toward Doretta's mortified mother.

It didn't take long for Moran to hear about the incident from his wife and act on it. Doretta, who alternately cringed and laughed when remembering the incident years later, said, "He arranged for my father to fly up from Lincoln to spend a long weekend. It was a chance for Father to see how Mother and I were getting on, where we were living, and it was a chance for Mother to prove that she was indeed a respectable married lady."

The Morans took Mr. and Mrs. Hoehne on a grand tour of all of St. Louis's finest speakeasies, which basically were the places that bought and sold Moran's Chicago stock. During one stopover, Moran observed Mrs. Hoehne's open admiration of the silver fox stole that Evelyn had draped around her shoulders.

"You like it?" he asked. Upon receiving an answer to the affirmative, he queried, "Do you have one already?"

She admitted that she didn't. Evelyn, knowing her husband well, unclasped the pins holding it in place, allowing Moran to slide it off her own body and across that of Doretta's startled mother.

"It's yours then," he said grandly.

When the weekend was up and Mrs. Hoehne had satisfied her breakfast companions that she was not the victim of an unfortunate past, things went back to normal . . . for a while.

"Then one day something happened," Doretta remembered. "Mother and I were walking down the street, heading for our hotel, when we saw a man come out of a restaurant a little further down the street. Suddenly a car came toward him, opposite the direction we were walking in, and I heard a horrible noise. The man fell to the sidewalk, dead. He'd been shot.

"Mother froze, holding my hand. Then we saw another man come out of the same restaurant, look around, and see us. He was one of Mr. Moran's friends that I remembered seeing, and I know he recognized us, because he ran over to us, grabbed Mother's arm, and hurried us into the restaurant. I remember him getting us to sit in an empty booth, and grabbing dirty dishes from a nearby table so that he could pile them on ours and make it look like we'd all been eating there for a while. He told Mother that when the police arrived, she was to say that we'd been eating with him when the shooting took place. She did what he said."

Whatever violence Moran may have been involved in that summer, there weren't enough perks included for him to stay in St. Louis. He left in September and returned to Chicago, where problems in the cleaning and dyeing industry were about to culminate in murder yet again.

On January 11, 1932, Benjamin Rosenberg, who ran a small dry-cleaning establishment and had been relentlessly vocal in his defiance of the Master Cleaners and Dyers and Moran's Central Cleaning Company's business practices, was ambushed near his Maywood home by a band of thugs who slugged him senseless and fired six bullets into his body while he lay on the sidewalk.[3] The murder surprised no one, for months before, Rosenberg had self-published a pamphlet claiming that racketeers were extorting an estimated $2 million annually from Chicago dry-cleaning concerns.

The International Cleaners and Dyers Inc., which Rosenberg served as manager, employed non-union help, cut prices, and refused to join any of the cleaning company associations. Vandals had attacked his plant on numerous occasions, once destroying $20,000 worth of clothing with acid. Rosenberg had been scheduled to testify against two gangsters, Philip Mangano and Louis Clementi, who'd been charged with instigating one of the raids on his plant. His widow told the press that her husband had received threats on a regular basis because his firm had refused to charge "regulation" prices, hire union help, or join the Master Cleaners or Moran.

State's Attorney Swanson summoned the trustees of the Cleaners and Dyers Institute and officials of three unions affiliated with the institute to his office. Chief of Detectives Schoemaker and Assistant State's Attorney E. C. Duffy of the "racket bureau" stood by as Swanson conducted his interrogations.

Morris Kaplan, attorney for the Cleaners and Dyers Institute, reminded the state's attorney that gang control of the industry was a small percentage of the actual problem. Discord and cutthroat business practices had mandated the underworld's entry into the fray. "The hoodlums didn't force their way into the picture," he said. "They were invited in. The cleaners are now discovering that they have created a Frankenstein monster, which threatens to destroy them." Swanson heard him out, and then asked about the truth of a story that Kaplan had personally warned Rosenberg to get out of the business. The attorney looked startled but quickly denied it.

On January 20, stench bombs exploded in two Berwyn shops. One, the Berwyn Dry Cleaning Company, belonged to Abarbanell Brothers, a cleaning and dyeing concern that had recently sought an injunction against three unions that had been terrorizing its officials and employees.[4] Despite the acres of newsprint spent exposing and decrying the subject, the "Cleaner's and Dyer's" war showed no evidence of abating.

On March 30 Leo Mongoven made his first appearance in court since his "disappearance" two years earlier. Although a neighbor had seen him return home earlier, he'd eluded police detection until now. The night before, his attorney notified Chief of Detectives Schoemaker that Mongoven was in his office and intended to surrender himself the next day on the gun-carrying charge.[5]

The gangster showed up at the Criminal Court Building as promised. He explained to reporters that he was there to post bond on two old charges—one a generic vagrancy warrant that had been sworn out against all public enemies in 1930, and the other the concealed weapons charge related to his arrest at the Madison–Kedzie bank in May 1930. The police sergeant who was the principal witness in the weapons case had died two weeks previously, an event universally suspected to have been Mongoven's reason for coming out of hiding.

Mongoven looked pretty much the same as the Chicago police remembered, except for a huge V-shaped scar on the side of his face. He declined to say where he had been during the past two years but did quip that he'd been "doing lots of reading." His attorney, Milton Smith, merely said, "My client has been in business."[6]

A representative of the Public Indemnity Company, a bonding concern, was also present to post the $10,000 bail. Judge Prystalski stunned everyone present by refusing to accept it.[7]

"I ordered an investigation of this company several weeks ago," he said, "and I want to make sure this bond is all right." Judge Prystalski explained that Public Indemnity had yet to pay the $10,000 bond that had been forfeited when jewel thief Ernest Levy skipped town.

Mongoven was too surprised to offer his usual vehement protest as he was led off to jail. James Alex, a friend and restaurant owner, hurried to his aid when news of the bail failure reached him and applied to schedule property on Mongoven's bond. The bond department of the state's attorney's office investigated the application and notified Judge Prystalski that it was bona fide. Prystalski approved it, and Mongoven went free.

He soon attended a funeral. On April 7 two veteran North Side Gang members, Benjamin "Red" Applequist, and his brother Ernest, fell victim to assassins' bullets while drinking in a West Side speakeasy that both managed. They had been struck in the head by shotgun slugs at close range, apparently after drinking with their killers, as four glasses of beer were on the bar where they fell. An untouched cash register ruled out robbery as the motive.

Ernest, who had been especially close to O'Banion and Moran, had until recently been head of the City Chauffeurs Union, so police investigators looked into the possibility that the murders had been labor-related. Ben Applequist told a friend a few days before the attack that Capone henchman "Dago" Lawrence Mangano had warned him to quit selling beer and get out of the business. Posters of Francis M. Tuite, Republican candidate for state senator, were plastered all over the speakeasy walls, and Ben assured his concerned friend that once Tuite was elected, he would have the resources to keep Mangano at bay.[8]

Moran put in an appearance at the funeral, his mood and expression somber as he witnessed the burial of yet more friends and colleagues from the old days. As soon as the weather became warm enough to trigger a mass exodus to the cool waters and lush greenery of Lake County, he and Mongoven headed up to the Chain o' Lakes area and its swelling summer population of beer drinkers. He now had at least one brewery in full operation in the region, and Mongoven was looking into acquiring a monopoly over the slot machines that cottagers loved spending their spare change on.

On June 12, 1932, four FBI agents from the Chicago office left the city in two separate vehicles and arrived at a pre-arranged meeting spot near the Chain-o-Lakes Golf Course near Antioch. The bureau had received a tip that escaped federal prisoner Frank Nash might be hiding out in Lake County. They interviewed a female witness who provided some possible hideout information relating to Nash and then regrouped at the Phillips 66 Service Station on Highway 57, across the street from the golf course. By that point it was close to 7 p.m.[9]

No sooner had the FBI team parked both cars when two men approached them from the direction of the service station. One, a swarthy individual of middle height and aggressive demeanor, walked up to one of the automobiles, a Chevrolet in which two agents were sitting, while the other made his way over to where the other two agents were standing. The swarthy man drew a pistol from inside his shirt, pointed it at the FBI men in the car, and ordered them to get out. "Go to hell," one of them retorted. Before the armed individual could react violently, another agent asked, "Who are you?"

"I'm James Marr, deputy sheriff of Lake County," the man responded. His companion, who was standing on the other side of the Chevrolet, facing the two agents who'd been standing around, asked them who they were and what they were doing in the area. When asked if he was a law enforcement officer, he replied in the affirmative. When the FBI team identified itself to both men, they became nervous, tucking their weapons away but shaking hands only with the greatest reluctance. The agent in charge asked who they were with, but Marr's companion replied dismissively, "That's all right, we won't go into that matter." The two mysterious law officials walked off, one calling over his shoulder, "You fellows are lucky you didn't get your goddamned brains blown out," adding that there had been a number of killings in the area in the recent past.

Mystified by the semi-assault and more than a little peeved, the agent in charge contacted Sheriff Tiffany of Lake County and asked him if he had a deputy sheriff by the name of James Marr. Tiffany could not recollect such a man but advised the agents that he had many deputies whose names he did not personally know and, strangely, he kept no record of deputies.

The mystery would be solved exactly a month later. On July 13 George Moran was picked up for questioning in connection with the June murder of labor slugger and Capone union man George "Red" Barker. He insisted to policemen Roy Van Herik and James Bresnahan that he was a country gentleman living at Bluff Lake and that complicity in Chicago gang killings was a figment of his past, but they ignored the assumed respectability and took him in.

Chief Schoemaker also collected Leo Mongoven, who'd been discharged by Chief Justice Harry M. Fisher of the municipal court on the charge of carrying concealed weapons. Fisher had suppressed the evidence on a defense motion when Mongoven's counsel was able to prove that while he was accused of carrying two concealed .45 pistols on his person during the Madison–Kedzie arrest, the truth was that the closest guns to the gangster were in a safety deposit box. When he saw Schoemaker approaching, Mongoven snapped at him, "Why don't you learn what it's all about before you pick up me and George?"

Two of the FBI agents who had been seeking Nash in Lake County were in the Chicago Police Department headquarters when Moran and Mongoven were brought in, and recognized them as the "deputy sheriffs" who had given them a potentially deadly welcome. The other two agents were summoned, but by the time they arrived, the two gangsters had been released. They had to content themselves with viewing the photos stored in the identification records, and agreed with their colleagues that they had been tricked by two hoodlums posing as lawmen.

Uncertain of what steps, if any, the bureau should take in response to the incident, the special agent in charge, M. A. McSwain, forwarded the details to Hoover, who responded on July 23. He wrote:

> I do not believe that we should allow matters of this kind to pass provided there has been any violation of Federal Law by any individual with whom the Agents of this Bureau come in contact. If Moran has been guilty of any violation of Federal Law I believe he should be prosecuted to the limit. Proper inquiry should be made of the United States Attorney's Office along these lines and in the event it is decided that he may be prosecuted, appropriate investigative activity should be made by the Bureau with a view to procuring all possible evidence.

McSwain's response was sent to Washington five days later. He seemed anxious to let the whole incident pass, writing in a memo:

> I believe it would be extremely judicious to consider the incident closed and not endeavor to initiate prosecution against George "Bugs" Moran and his accomplice Leo Mongoven for two reasons. First Agent (name withheld) is the only one who has personally viewed "Bugs" Moran and identified him. The identification of this person on the part of the other agents is based on a photograph and second, it would create a great deal of notoriety and perhaps react unfavorably towards the Bureau. . . . The Agents in question were conducting an undercover operation with a view to locating Frank Nash, an escaped Federal Prisoner.

His excuses were weak. Those who identified Moran and Mongoven via photograph could easily have viewed them in a lineup that Schoemaker would have been all too happy to arrange. But his recommendation stood. J. Edgar Hoover agreed that news coverage of any attempts at prosecution would draw attention to the bureau's pursuit of Frank Nash, and the less Nash and his protectors knew, the better.

Moran was luckier than Capone had been when a target of federal scrutiny. At least this time around.

On the sweltering night of July 21 Willie Marks finally kept the date with death that he had missed three years previously.

Earlier that day, Marks and his brother-in-law, Clarence Gleason, drove from Chicago to the Lime Kiln Hill Inn, a small resort five miles east of Shawano, Wisconsin. They were there to meet Patrick Berrell, vice president of the International Teamsters Union, whom Marks sometimes served as a bodyguard. Berrell had been staying at a Shawano Lake cottage with an attractive young woman, Betty Davis. The purpose for the conference with Marks and Gleason was never clear (Gleason later told authorities that he had never met Berrell before that night), but the three men drank beer in Bud Haupt's bar at the Lime Kiln Hill Inn and conversed until well after midnight, when Berrell complained of feeling sick. Marks accompanied him outside to get some fresh air while Gleason remained at the bar, chatting with bartender George LaValle.[10]

The two men walked out the back door and had gone only a few feet into the yard when machine-gun fire rattled through the night air, followed by the ominous boom of shotgun blasts. Patrons in the bar screamed or ran for cover as bullets chipped the bricks outside. Gleason and the bartender ran into the yard with weapons drawn as soon as the noise subsided, but the gunmen had escaped in their car, taking County Road T onto Highway 29.

The scene in the roadhouse yard was sheer carnage. Patrick Berrell, head and body riddled with machine-gun slugs, was slumped against his big Lincoln coupe, where he had tried to seek shelter. The running board was slippery with blood, although the car itself was undamaged. Willie Marks had four holes in his head from shotgun pellets and lay near the Inn wall, unconscious but still alive. Berrell was breathing too, but he died just as the men from the sheriff's office arrived on the scene.[11]

While an agitated Gleason and Betty Davis, who had also been present, gave statements to the police, Marks was loaded into an ambulance and rushed to the nearest hospital. Five minutes after arrival, as emergency physicians were cutting away his blood-soaked clothing, he died. The *Shawano (WI) County Journal* reporter, after viewing the body, wrote, "William Marks is about 45 years old. He was wanted in Chicago by the police for implication in the hold-up of the Drake Hotel over a year ago, and also for the notorious Valentine murder in which seven gangsters [sic] were killed. . . . Even in death his profile showed a snarling, snickety smile of the hardboiled. He is alleged to have been a much-hunted killer. His hair was black, gray hair curtaining the temples. A rather slick fellow, well-dressed."[12]

Berrell's brother and Mrs. Lillian Marks came from Chicago to claim the bodies, the valuables (Marks had $143.11, a gold ring, and expensive watch; Berrell possessed $5,671 in cash, a $10,000 note, and some diamond jewelry), and the cars. Clarence Gleason and Davis, who had been jailed as material witnesses, gave inconsequential testimony at the inquest and then caught the next train to Chicago.

District Attorney Louis Catteau told reporters that he believed the killers were from Chicago and had been shadowing Marks. "There's no other way that they could have known that Marks and Berrell were meeting," he insisted. "This is a typical Chicago killing, and presumably [afterward] the gang headed for Illinois."

Back in Chicago, the police and state's attorney's office blamed the double murder on James "Fur" Sammon. Chief of Detectives Schoemaker and Pat Roche were unanimous in their opinion that Sammon, who had been released from Joliet Prison only two days before, was behind the killings. Schoemaker pointed out that the recent murder of George "Red" Barker, former President of the Chicago Teamsters Union and a Capone man, would have aroused the ire of Sammon, as Barker had helped raise the $50,000 fund that led to Sammon's release after a long legal battle. He also noted that Berrell was heard threatening Barker for racketeering activities in the labor unions that the former controlled.[13]

Edward N. Nockels, vice president of the Chicago Federation of Labor, insisted that Berrell, who had been a protégé of the murdered John Clay, had been a vocal opponent of racketeer influence and control in the labor unions. He and Red Barker had been seen quarreling bitterly on numerous occasions. But nothing was ever proven. Sammon would have had as good a reason as anyone to see Berrell dead, but the fact that there were multiple "anyones" in the labor struggle guaranteed there were no convictions.

Moran's reaction to the news of Willie Marks's death can only be surmised, as he never spoke publicly on the subject. He could not have been pleased with the aftermath, though. In the wake of the Shawano double homicide, federal agents swooped down on one resort after another in Lake County and the cottage colonies in Wisconsin. Chicagoans visiting Fox Lake, Antioch, and similar locations looked on in wonder and some dismay as the raiders rushed into the speakeasies and hotel bars, seized beer and liquor and arrested the proprietors. In the Mineola Hotel at Fox Lake, everything, including the furnishings, was loaded onto trucks for a trip back to Chicago. When the dry agents burst into the Helvetia Hotel at Pistakee Bay and arrested the owner, Fred Elter, Elter's wife collapsed in a dead faint and required a physician to revive her. All those arrested were taken to the Prohibition Bureau's Chicago headquarters, where they were arraigned before U.S. Commissioner Walker.[14]

The raids persisted, although less frequently with time, until December, when State's Attorney Mason announced that they would cease. "There will be no more beer raids under my regime except where there are flagrant violations," he said. "And in any raids that are made, there will be no fines. I will try to get injunctions. These . . . raids were made more or less to ascertain if the syndicate, through Bugs Moran or Leo Mongoven, is trying to come up here. We'll keep them out and also keep out any other hoodlums who are finding Mayor Cermak's campaign in Chicago too warm."[15]

(Anton Cermak had defeated Big Bill Thompson by almost 200,000 votes in the April 1931 mayoral election and soon incurred the Chicago Outfit's wrath by supporting labor organizer Roger Touhy and, by some accounts, attempting to have Frank Nitti assassinated by a pair of Chicago policemen. In December1932 Cermak was mortally wounded while talking with President-elect Franklin Roosevelt after a speech in Miami, perhaps in retribution for the attack on Nitti.)

Lake County imposed less heat and danger than Chicago, in spite of Mason's vow. In the predawn hours of September 2, 1934, Prohibition agent Eliot Ness, who had waged a campaign to dry up Al Capone's beer and liquor supply and render Capone vulnerable, made his move on the brewery Moran maintained on a farm owned by Lake County resident Laura Yopp. He and his raiders had had Moran's Lake County bootlegging activities under surveillance for weeks; agents had infiltrated the locale but failed to find the brewery until airplane surveillance finally pinpointed its location. Moran himself was not present, but three brothers— Frank, Peter, and Fred Wolf—and Peter Yopp, son of Laura Yopp, were. They were taken into custody, and Ness confiscated brewing and icing equipment, two cars, a truck, and ten thousand gallons of freshly brewed beer ready to be delivered to Labor Day weekend crowds.[16]

The Yopp brewery represented a fraction of Moran's investment in Lake County. He and Mongoven, who took up residency at Bluff Lake, began purchasing slot machines in Chicago for use in the same hotels and resorts that bought his liquor. In August 1933, county authorities seized 138 machines, 50 of which were found in the barn of a Bluff Lake farm Mongoven owned. Sheriff Tiffany asserted that he had evidence to prove that Moran owned the machines, although Mongoven, who was arrested and promptly released on a $2,000 bond, claimed that they belonged to some "higher-up" living elsewhere in the county. Justice of the Peace Harry Hoyt fined him and three associates $100 each for possessing slot machines, a paltry sum that they paid with a smirk.[17]

Slot machines were not a new phenomenon, but in the earliest years of the Depression the "get rich for a nickel" potential that they represented made them especially attractive and addictive. An article called "We Bet 5 Million," published in the *Tribune* in November 1936, outlined the allure of the "slots" for the average player who sauntered up to a Moran–Mongoven machine with his or her pocket full of nickels:

Some time or other you've probably stepped up to a slot machine and
fed it a coin, then kept on feeding until you finally broke away, kicking
yourself for an idiot.

Why did you do it? . . .

It's simple. Anybody can play it. You don't have to know any rules—
don't have to know even the combinations that pay off. The money
comes jingling down anyway.

The payoff system keeps you playing once you start. There's first the
jackpot—the long shot chance such as attracts lottery players. Second,
frequent payoffs of small sums keep you trying. Third, the "almost wins"
suck you in for one more play. . . .

There's the primal urge of all gambling—something for nothing. . . .

George Moran and Leo Mongoven would supervise slot-machine rackets in
Lake County until approximately 1936, when Moran's newer business interests
took him elsewhere. They remained close despite the dissolution of their working
relationship, and up until his death in the early 1980s, Mongoven stayed fiercely
protective of his friend's memory.[18]

Although now running the show alone, Mongoven assumed such a tight control over the slots that he was commonly referred to as the slot-machine king of
northern Lake County. Frightened residents who claimed that they had been threatened for protesting the county's wide-open gambling brought up his name often.
When Claude Warner, volunteer leader of a series of gambling raids in the summer
of 1938, was arrested for grand larceny, he claimed that the charge was a trumped-
up one formulated by Mongoven and his allies to quell reform activity in Lake
County. The slashing of his car tires while he was inside the police station offered
mute support to Warner's assertions.

Two Lake Forest mothers, who pressed for suppression of the slot machines
after their children repeatedly lost bus fare on them, received threatening letters
until they backed off. Newspaper publisher Ralph Miller told of seeing three cars
loaded with gangsters, machine guns in hand, lying in wait on a town street for a
rival group delivering slots.[19]

No one doubted Miller's story after deputy sheriffs and special constables from
Waukegan descended on Mongoven's home in December 1938 and seized eighteen guns and more than a hundred rounds of ammunition. The ex-Moran aide paid
a $1,200 fine for possession of firearms whose serial numbers had been filed off.

When not tangling with the law and civic-minded Lake County residents, Mongoven would visit his old friend Billy Skidmore at Skidmore's Pistakee Bay mansion
for a round of golf, or make trips down to Chicago, where he ran some minor handbook and slot-machine action[20] that Frank Nitti, who had been directing the Outfit's multiple enterprises since Capone's incarceration, did not interfere with or prevent. He died in January 1980, a rare survivor from the North Sider ranks.

On January 7, 1933, Ted Newberry turned up dead alongside a road outside of Chesterton, Indiana, a bullet hole in his head confirming that he had taken a one-way ride. He had been reported missing that morning, prompting his lawyer, Abraham Marovitz, to file a petition for a writ of habeas corpus on the off chance that cops instead of enemy gangsters had him in custody. Chief of Detectives Schoemaker informed the attorney that Newberry was not a guest of the Chicago Police Department, but that the body of a man matching his description had just been found in rural Indiana. Marovitz drove to the spot, took one look, and formally identified his former client.[21]

There was evidence that Newberry had struggled with his killers. One of his hands was crushed, and his head bore signs of a heavy blow. A platinum watch he habitually wore was missing, although the diamond-studded belt buckle that Al Capone had given him was left untouched.

Theories as to the reason behind his murder included alleged involvement in a plot to murder Frank Nitti; trouble with Teamsters unions controlled by Outfit leaders Murray Humphreys and Three-Fingered Jack White, and retaliation for warning unnamed gangster friends that the Outfit had marked them for a one-way ride. Georgette Winkler, whose husband had worked with Newberry in overseeing the North Side, wrote that he had gotten into debt with Nitti and the Outfit by making a liquor order and not paying for it.[22] In the end, the Chicago police reverted to using a quote that Newberry himself had been fond of using whenever questioned about a gangland homicide: "He must have done something. They don't kill you for nothing."

On February 21, 1934, Sergeant Andrew Carroll spotted Moran at the corner of Randolph and Dearborn streets and arrested him for vagrancy. The North Sider obtained his freedom on a $10,000 bond after agreeing to appear in court for arraignment on the twenty-fourth. He protested to Chief of Detectives Schoemaker that he was a reputable businessman, with a position and shares in the Central Cleaning Company, and said that he had actually been on his way to the U.S. Courthouse to pay his income taxes when Carroll grabbed him.

"I'll get an injunction to keep the police from molesting me," he warned. "I know a city judge, and I'll have him issue the injunction."

"That won't do you any good," Schoemaker replied pleasantly. "Because we can get a new vagrancy warrant for you any time."

Moran reddened but kept his temper in check. "Why do you keep picking on me all the time? You know I'm legitimate."[23]

"I guess it's because you look so much like Spike O'Donnell with those spats on."

The vagrancy warrant lost its sting for Moran and Chicago's other "public enemies" in April 1934, when the Illinois State Supreme Court declared the "criminal reputation law" invalid. Louis Alterie, Maxie Eisen, Jack McGurn, James Belcastro, and five other gangster defendants breathed a collective sigh of relief when their convictions were overturned, rescuing them from the mandatory six months of imprisonment. Attorneys James Burke and George Crane argued that no person could be deprived of liberty because of his reputation alone, and took exception to the section of the vagrancy law that read, "All persons who . . . are reputed to be habitual violators of the criminal laws of this state or of the United States . . . shall be deemed to be, and they are declared to be, vagabonds."[24]

Burke and Crane insisted that this wording in effect placed the burden on the defendant to prove that he or she was not "reputed" to be a habitual violator. The state's attorney's office and the judges who supported what was now called the "reputation law" replied that convictions should be allowed to stand if the record provided proof of repeat crimes.

The Supreme Court sided with the defense attorneys. In their decision, the justices noted:

> However worthy the purpose of this act, and notwithstanding the argument that the general assembly has the power to protect the public against those whose reputation as law violators is alone sufficient to compel innocent persons to accede to their demands, yet it is necessary that before liberty or property may be taken from anyone, regardless of his reputation, there must be proof that he is in fact a habitual criminal. This is essential to compliance with the due process requirements of the state and federal constitutions. For this reason indicated . . . this act is invalid.[25]

One habitual criminal received a long-overdue reckoning at about one o'clock on the morning of February 15, 1936. Jack McGurn, who had not been liked by all of his fellow Outfit members even during Capone's day, had spent the period immediately following Capone's sentencing practicing his golf swing and rethinking his prospects. At last he decided he wanted back in, only to learn that, as far as Capone's successors were concerned, he no longer had a place. It was a snub that he did not take lying down.

He was at a bowling alley at 805 Milwaukee Avenue with two friends, too absorbed in the game to notice a pair of men who walked into the place, came up behind him, and shot him several times in the head and back. A comic Valentine that was a clear stab at his fall from grace was located beside the body:

> *You've lost your job*
> *You've lost your dough*
> *Your jewels and handsome houses*
> *But things could be worse, you know*
> *You haven't lost your trousers*[26]

Moran's name was brought up as a suspect by those lovers of poetic justice who thought it might be his revenge for the massacre of his seven friends seven years previously. If Moran did kill anyone in 1936, it was not McGurn, whose slayers had almost certainly been sent by Frank Nitti, new chief of the Capone Outfit.

Another 1936 murder, this one in Minneapolis, did bring Moran's name into a courtroom. In December 1937 Walter Frank, financial secretary and business agent for Lathers Union No. 190, told the coroner's jury investigating the murder of labor leader Patrick Corcoran that his recent past had been a nightmare of telephone threats, cars cruising ominously past his home, and steel shafts thrown through his windows. On one occasion several men waylaid him and beat him unconscious with fists and clubs. Frank said that he believed the deadly harassment "came from the enemies of labor and their business agents who don't like to see the trade union movement progress." Strangely, he made a point of insisting that he did not believe those enemies included gangsters.[27]

A milk truck driver, Frank Dorrance, followed him to the stand and refuted the zero-gangster-involvement statement. He insisted that he had known Patrick Corcoran well, as the latter had been with the Milk Drivers Union for a while, and that the labor leader had confided in him about threats made by one gangster in particular, Bugs Moran. Moran allegedly had warned Corcoran to quit organization work or be taken for a one-way ride. Dorrance said that his friend, fearing retaliation, had sworn him to secrecy.

No further investigation was made regarding Moran, primarily because Dorrance was the only one to make an accusation of involvement in Corcoran's murder. He was in the St. Paul-Minneapolis area at the time of Corcoran's murder, visiting his mother, but only the milk driver put forth his name as an aggressor in the Minneapolis labor struggle.

By 1937 Moran was through with all aspects of union racketeering. He and Ben Kornick went their separate ways sometime during the early 1930s, with Kornick forming a new cleaning and dyeing concern, the Majestic Dye House. The protection that Kornick hired for that business paled in comparison to that which Moran had offered. In 1953, while the night watchman answered a phone call, four burglars forced open a window in the company's headquarters and made off with $1,500 from the safe.[28]

18

THE COUNTERFEIT TRIALS

I N JANUARY 1938 MORAN AND Frank Parker, the airplane bootlegger with whom the North Siders had done business during Prohibition, joined ex-policeman Frank Hicketts, alias Frank Ross, in hatching a scheme to print and sell counterfeit American Express checks.

Parker and Moran had a history dating back to 1926, when he supplied the North Siders with quality liquor from his Montreal plant, Dominion Distilleries Limited. Before being an American bootlegger on Canadian soil became his direct line to a $5 million fortune, Parker headed an automobile theft ring. His record at the Chicago police identification bureau matched Moran's in recidivism rate:

- September 1911—confidence game charge.
- April 4, 1913—unspecified charge. Fined $15 and sentenced to ten days' imprisonment.
- October 3, 1914—sentenced to Joliet penitentiary for five to twenty-five years for burglary.
- October 16, 1915—paroled on technicality in mittimus.
- March 13, 1917—returned to Joliet for parole violation (stealing automobiles).

- April 9, 1920—reparoled.
- September 20, 1920—discharged from parole.
- January 11, 1926—crime against nature. Charge stricken off.[1]

Parker fled to Canada when a Chicago grand jury indicted him in July 1926 for ownership of the Archer Products Brewery. He assumed control of the Montreal distillery and purchased five planes to fly the liquor to its U.S. destinations, giving rise to his nickname. He passed himself off as a respectable and ambitious member of Montreal business circles until Chicago law enforcement authorities alerted Canadian officials to his shady past. The information threatened his Canadian residency, as upon entry in 1926 Parker had sworn that he had never been an inmate of a penitentiary. He got out of it by presenting a pardon from Governor Len Small, which his lawyer assured Canadian authorities legally wiped the slate clean as far as a man's Illinois criminal record went. He returned to Chicago in January 1932 and embarked on an assortment of counterfeit-money schemes with various partners.

Hicketts was also a Joliet alumnus. In August 1925 he had shot and killed bootlegger Edward Olsen in front of the victim's Surf Street home. Although he claimed that he had fired in self-defense after Olsen threatened to take him for "a ride," a jury found him guilty of murder and he received a fourteen-year sentence, which ended up being reduced to eight.[2]

On January 3 Carl Silver, a Moran associate who agreed to be part of the plot, approached Berger Hansen, an engraver with thirty-eight years of experience, who ran a printing and engraving shop at 538 South Clark Street. Silver and Hansen had worked together on minor counterfeiting schemes over the past two years.

The gangster showed the engraver a genuine $100 American Express check and asked if he could duplicate it successfully. Hansen, who had been experiencing a slump in business thanks to the Depression, agreed to try for $600. Silver supplied him with legitimate checks in $10, $20, $50, and $100 denominations. Hansen photographed them, using the images to make six zinc plates—one for the watermark, two for the backgrounds of both sides, one for color printing, one for lettering, and a sixth for the serial numbers.[3]

While Hansen and his assistants worked, Frank Parker dropped into the office of attorney Emil Van Bever in the Reaper Block on February 20. Van Bever, who had known Parker since the previous November, was a portly, silver-haired man in his fifties. His past was a checkered one; he had lost his license to practice in California in 1932 after fraud charges were laid against him there, although he was never disbarred in Illinois. He spent seventy-eight days in a Texas jail on an unspecified charge in 1934. Van Bever had represented Parker in a lawsuit that the former bootlegger had launched against Edward Litsinger, former Republican leader and member of the county board of tax appeals, and Parker often visited him to discuss the ongoing case or to dictate a letter to the lawyer's secretary.

During this particular visit Parker mentioned that he was working on a deal in which some "paper would be circulated" and considerable money made. Nothing more was said about it until Van Bever encountered Frank Hicketts in early March and asked if he knew about the "paper deal." When the attorney nodded, Hicketts said, "If you want to get in, I can take care of you in the deal."[4]

The conspirators seem to have targeted Van Bever as a distribution source for their forgeries. On March 14 Parker asked him, "Do you know any right people?"

"What do you mean?"

"Some people who might be interested in handling this paper."

"I don't think so."

Hansen and his assistants finished running off $20,000 worth of checks by March 24. After cutting and perforating them, he sent a package of the freshly printed phonies to Jack Campbell, a Kansas City, Missouri, tavernkeeper whom Carl Silver had named as their distribution contact there. The engraver met Moran in a handbook by prior arrangement on the twenty-sixth. The North Sider accepted the checks but complained that they were not ideal. He made some suggestions that Hansen used in creating another set of plates.[5]

Frank Parker was less discriminating. Later that same day, he met Emil Van Bever in the lobby of the Reaper Block. The ex-bootlegger's mood was buoyant as he showed his counsel two bogus checks, one for $50 and the other for $100.

"How do you like these?" he asked proudly.

"I don't know a great deal about ink and coloring," Van Bever answered. He did admit that they looked genuine enough.

Parker and Moran met Van Bever for lunch soon afterward. During the discussion Parker handed $1,050 in forged checks to the attorney, who paid him $150 and agreed to sell them in turn to professional "check passers." Van Bever also consented to hold on to an additional 150 checks until Parker came for them.

Unbeknownst to the conspirators, Van Bever revealed every detail of the meetings and operations to Sergeant Walter Paradowski at the detective bureau and asked for his advice. Why Van Bever betrayed his former client Parker is unclear. Perhaps he believed that Parker's insistence on his cooperation made refusal risky, and was looking out for himself. Paradowski advised him to approach American Express directly and inform them what was happening. Van Bever did so, and an official at the company requested that he continue working with Moran, Parker, and their confederates, all the while feeding details back to American Express and the police, until more evidence could be obtained. When Parker reclaimed the 150 checks the lawyer had been holding for him, American Express had already obtained and registered the serial number of each one.[6]

A week after the meeting in the diner, Parker met with Van Bever again in a restaurant on Van Buren Street and handed him a chilling bit of news: the gang was convinced that a "rat" was in their ranks. The attorney was not alarmed, figuring that if he were the object of suspicion, Parker would not be giving him the courtesy of a hint. He knew that despite the surface solidarity required to pull off such a major scheme, some of the gang members mistrusted one another. Frank Hicketts had warned him, "Watch out for Parker. He'll put you in the middle every time." Two days later the former bootlegger had complained, "What the hell are you running around with that rat Ross [Hicketts] for? He's no good." The men had been nourishing spite for each other after Hicketts tried selling some forgeries for fifteen cents on the dollar while Parker wanted twenty.[7]

Moran met with Berger Hansen in a handbook on April 2 and informed him that he had found a customer for $11,000 worth of checks, but he insisted that the merchandise had to be flawless. He added that he personally wanted $25,000 worth for distribution. Hansen wired Del Bruno, who was in Kansas City with Jack Campbell: "George wants thirty-six thousand. Shall we make them? Will be in office tonight." Bruno advised him to go ahead with it, so Hansen heated up the presses.[8]

On April 17 Hansen and Bruno met Moran, who was sitting alone in his parked car, near the corner of Harrison and Clark streets. The printers handed over the checks, which had been securely bound in brown paper, and agreed to meet Moran in a handbook the next day to be paid.

The forgeries that Hansen turned out were excellent imitations of the real thing. Experts might have pronounced them fakes because of the different quality of paper used, but to the layman's eye, nothing aroused suspicion unless one looked closely enough to observe the absence of underscoring beneath a couple of figures. Moran, Parker, and their accomplices offered them to check-passing rings in Chicago, New York, Pittsburgh, and Philadelphia at twenty cents on the dollar.

On April 20 three members of the gang cashed a $50 fraudulent check in a Loop shoe store, buying $10 worth of shoes and hose and receiving $40 in change. As soon as American Express checked the serial number against the master list of phonies and found a match, detectives arrested Frank Quigley, Robert Sexton, and D. J. Driscoll in Pittsburgh, where they had gone immediately after their purchase. They were picked up with $21,800 worth of counterfeit checks in their possession.

News of their arrest forced the Chicago Police Department's hand. Captain Daniel "Tubbo" Gilbert, who had headed the massacre investigation and was known to have ties to the Capone mob, claimed later that he had wanted to wait until more phonies turned up, but the Pittsburgh arrests forced him to abandon the "watch."

Frank Parker was grabbed first, in an office at 30 North La Salle Street. Another gang member, Walter Nolan, and his wife, Marian, were arrested in a North Side hotel. When detectives located Moran strolling in the 3700 block of North Lake Shore Drive, he submitted to arrest without protest. It was approximately 2 a.m. when detectives brought him to the state's attorney's office, where Frank Parker was also being held.

"Well, I see they've got you too," Moran chuckled to Parker, who merely smiled wryly. When a photographer moved too close, the North Sider released his pent-up aggression and tension by hurling a milk bottle at him.[9]

Both men were quizzed until 3 a.m. but refused to tell the state's attorney the name and location of the printing shop that had produced the bogus checks. They sued for a writ of habeas corpus, prompting Chief Justice Harrington of the criminal court to order the state's attorney's office to lay charges or release them. The office delayed laying charges until eleven o'clock on a Friday night, hoping to keep Moran and Parker in custody over the weekend, but friends found a judge willing to accept a house visit and supplied the $33,000 bond required.

Detectives raided the engraving shop on South Clark Street and arrested Berger Hansen, Emil Ahrens, and Del Bruno. Hansen had destroyed the check plates when he learned of the mass arrests, but the raiders found fragments and retained them as evidence.

On September 27, after months of gathering evidence and interrogating the more malleable witnesses, Assistant State's Attorney Robert Wright told reporters that the signed confessions of the engraver and two printers forged the final link in the chain of evidence tying Moran, Parker, and their cohorts to the elusive counterfeit securities ring. Moran, along with Frank Parker and five others appeared before Judge Robert Dunne on October 28, 1938, (Quigley, Sexton, and Driscoll would stand trial in Pittsburgh) charged with conspiracy to forge $62,000 worth of American Express checks. The only one who appeared to have escaped the net was Carl Silver, who was hiding out in San Antonio, Texas. The legal team of Roland Libonati, Joseph Burke, and Harold Levy represented Moran, Hicketts, and Parker.[10]

When Moran failed to make the $30,000 bond ordered by Dunne, he was remanded to the county jail. He and Parker acquired the necessary funds a week later, while Frank Hicketts remained behind bars. Six cases, including theirs, were set for trial on November 28, but the date was later changed to January 3. State and federal authorities continued to pursue leads indicating that the ring had also been involved in the counterfeiting of revenue stamps for liquor and cigarettes.

While in the Cook County jail awaiting bond, Moran received a letter that the jailer intercepted and passed on to the police. Investigators puzzled over it before reluctantly—in view of Moran's known St. Louis connections—deciding that it was cryptic enough to be worthless:

> Say Bugs, why don't youse come clean and tell em about the St. Louis crowd on river at quarry near workhouse at end of Wyandotte and Dakota Streets. No, of course youse won't. All your gang want to protect this outfit so as to have a secur [sic] hideout where any of youse can go any time and be protected by police, mayor. Them St. Louis fellers kin even make maps as well as stamps and youse knows if anyone finds it out and squeals on em they are put on the spot and nobody will do a thing about it that is why youse wants to protect youse all good old hideout. They are jest [sic] as good convincing liars as Hitler is. Tell em about their big underground dugouts. They have been getting a little scared

lately and have filled most of them up with clay rock concrete dirt sand and so forth and so forth and some grass weeds and bushes are growing in them. Where the old cave was that run in the quarry they did have a lot of them stetalites [sic] made of concrete to look like a real cave. Then youse knows there is another real cave about a block south of Dakota Street and a boy got killed in there a year or two ago but guess youse knows about that, youse was here I guess. If youse has to tell on us Kansas City people tell on all youse other friends, make a clean break while youse is about it.[11]

It soon became obvious how Moran planned to fund his defense. Early on the evening of December 16 Lieutenant Thomas Kelly led a raid on the headquarters of the Wholesale Grocery Workers Union at 702 Fulton Street, in response to complaints from merchants. Grocery store owners had notified the police that the union was using strong-arm methods to sell tickets and program advertising space for a dance that the union planned to hold on February 5. Lieutenant Kelly had heard the rumor that the proceeds from the ticket and ad sales would be used to fund Moran's defense.[12]

Moran was in the headquarters building when the police arrived, leading Kelly to suspect that the defense fund was no myth. But he explained his presence by saying that he had merely dropped by to visit friends, and the others present backed him up. Kelly had no alternative but to release him.

When the trial opened on January 3 with jury selection, Moran started the proceedings by pleading with attorney James Burke, who represented Parker, to have the nickname "Bugs" banned from use in the courtroom. He insisted that being called by the old moniker might plant prejudicial thoughts in the minds of the jury.

"*Bugs* is a slang word which designates a person as being insane," Burke explained to the judge. "The inference of the jury would be that that kind of person would commit any crime."

Judge Fardy agreed. He ruled that since the defendant's actual name was George, not "Bugs," the nickname was not to be used during the trial.[13]

Berger Hansen, Del Bruno, and Emil Arends presented guilty pleas by prior arrangement. The state's attorney's office had agreed to nolle pros the forgery charges against them in exchange for their testimony against Moran, Parker, and Hicketts. Emil Van Bever, who had been in voluntary custody for months, was the state's star witness, but Assistant State's Attorney Wright felt that the testimony of the three accomplices would strengthen the case enough to justify their evading punishment.

Emil Van Bever was the chief witness for the state when testimony began on January 9. He testified that he had joined the gang in a conspiracy to produce and pass the checks while really acting as a spy for the police and American Express Company. Defense witnesses produced by Moran's counsel offered rebuttal evidence that he had been disbarred in California and jailed in Texas, casting shadows over his credibility as a witness.[14]

Del Bruno told the courtroom that the bogus checks had been prepared at Hansen's shop and delivered to Moran personally on April 18. Upon cross-examination, Bruno admitted to having committed other forgeries in the past. When Moran's counsel demanded, "Is it not true that you were on WPA by day and a thief by night?" he replied tensely, "That's right."

Frank Parker took the stand on January 18. After giving a sanitized and abbreviated version of his history, he denied being involved in the forgery scheme. When asked what his connection was with the state's star witness, Emil Van Bever, Parker testified, "In January, Percy Adix [a mutual friend] told me that Van Bever needed a job and had threatened to jump out of a window if he didn't get one. He asked me to give Van Bever some work. [He] had done some work for Adix, trying to square some raps on oil dealings."

Parker said that he had retained Van Bever to represent him in his lawsuit against Litsinger over shares in a brewing company that Litsinger had promised and allegedly reneged on. The former airplane bootlegger was followed to the stand by his wife, Nellie, who denied that Van Bever had ever been in touch with her husband about forgeries of any kind.[15]

Harold Levy, Moran's counsel, asked, "Did Moran ever say, 'I'll bump somebody off' after the plot was exposed?"

Nellie Parker recoiled. "Oh no, sir."

On January 21 the state lost its first attempt to convict Moran, Parker, and Frank Hicketts on the conspiracy charge. The jury, after deliberating less than four hours, acquitted all three. The defendants and their wives were elated, momentarily forgetting that this trial had been merely in the connection with the $50 forged note that had been disastrously passed in the shoe store. The prosecution was prepared to file other charges related to the case.

"I certainly want to thank the jurors," Parker beamed. "Their decision was a fair and just one."

"This verdict is a tremendous blow to me," Wright said. "I can't understand it. I thought we had an airtight case. I will certainly move for trial of the other indictments."[16]

The other indictments he referred to were forgery of other checks besides the one cashed in the shoe store; conspiracy to forge and pass said checks; and two indictments, each alleging forgery of a New York Central Railroad bond and conspiracy to forge the bond. Wright explained that, if found guilty on any of the forgery charges, the defendants could receive one to fourteen years in Joliet. The conspiracy charges potentially drew a one- to five-year sentence or a $2,000 fine.

Wright kept his word. He moved for a February 6 retrial, but Judge Fardy consented to the defense counsel's motion for a month's continuance. Moran and Parker remained free on bond, while Hicketts, who lacked resources, returned to jail.

On March 8 an old counterfeiting scheme of Frank Parker's came back to haunt him.[17] In 1933 he and August Englehardt, who ran a saloon on Clark Street near the Cubs baseball park, had joined forces with renowned swindler and counter-feiter Victor Lustig and engraving plant owner William Davis to counterfeit more than a million dollars in currency. Lustig ended up doing a twenty-year stretch in Alcatraz after his capture in New York, but Englehardt and Parker, against whom there was no conclusive evidence, were not charged. They took more than $18,000 worth of the counterfeit cash, stuffed the bills in glass jars, and buried them on the Tam O' Shanter golf course in Niles.

On January 23, 1939, as Moran and Parker were celebrating their first court-room victory, the treasure was discovered and dug up. Englehardt was arrested in California for passing some of the counterfeit notes and sent to the penitentiary to serve an eighteen-month sentence. Discovery of correspondence between himself and Parker, which included a crudely drawn map of the golf course, resulted in Parker's arrest.

The former bootlegger had jumped out of one frying pan into two fires now. While awaiting the second conspiracy trial, he appeared in federal district court for arraignment on the charges of possession and sale and conspiracy to possess and sell the spurious $20 bills. Judge Charles Woodward set the trial for April 10. Six days later, on March 20, Judge Fardy granted yet another continuance in the second American Express forgery trial, setting the new date for April 17. Two of the "Pitts-burgh trio"—Daniel Driscoll and Robert Sexton—had just completed short sen-tences in Pittsburgh for possession of the forged checks (Frank Quigley had been acquitted) and were en route to Chicago to face trial with their co-conspirators, which required more defense preparation time.[18]

The week of April 15 saw many Prohibition-era heavyweights headed for state or federal prisons. Johnny Torrio pleaded guilty to charges of income-tax evasion, was ordered to pay $86,000 in back taxes and fines, and received a two-and-a-half-year sentence in a New York prison. On the same day that Torrio, accompanied by fed-eral marshals, left semi-retirement to begin his term, Terry Druggan borrowed a nickel from a friend and called Assistant U.S. Attorney David Bazelton and, accord-ing to Bazelton, complained, "I'm broke. I can't even hire a lawyer." Unimpressed by the plea of poverty, the assistant U.S. attorney obtained a judgment against Drug-gan for more than $61,000 in back taxes, interest, and penalties.

On April 30, 1939, after twenty-five hours of deliberation, the criminal court jury convicted Moran and Frankie Parker of conspiracy to create and cash $62,000 worth of American Express traveler's checks. The other three defendants—Hicketts, Driscoll, and Sexton—were acquitted. Moran's and Parker's attorneys immediately requested a new trial; Judge Fardy agreed to hear arguments on the motion on May 11.

Assistant State's Attorney Wright was jubilant. "Moran's luck has run out," he said. He evidenced no disappointment at the three acquittals, making it obvious that the former North Side Gang leader and Frank Parker had been the primary targets.[19]

Moran remained free on his $30,000 bond in the interim, while Parker, who in a separate trial had been found guilty of conspiring to possess the counterfeit money found on the golf course, was accompanied back to jail by a federal marshal. He was already facing a two-year sentence in Leavenworth, and how much extra time this newest guilty verdict would bring him remained to be seen. The jury had not specified a sentence length when it announced its verdict, which meant that he and Moran could serve anywhere from a day to a year in the Cook County Jail and/or pay a fine ranging in amount from $1 to $2,000. As conspiracy was defined by statute to be a misdemeanor and not a felony, punishment was comparatively light.

On May 25, after listening to arguments from both sides, Judge Fardy set the sentence at the maximum for both men: one year in jail and a $2,000 fine. The next day Parker joined nineteen other convicts on a Leavenworth-bound train to begin serving his two years. He would serve the year for conspiracy upon his release. Moran, refusing to concede defeat, announced through Harold Levy that he was presenting his case to the appellate court. Fardy permitted him to remain free on the $35,000 bond that had insulated him from jail time for months.

On November 27 the time limit for his freedom on that bond expired, and the trial judge ordered Moran committed to the Cook County Jail. The former North Side Gang leader was behind bars for just eight days before the Illinois Appellate Court issued an order for his release on a $5,000 bond pending a review of his appeal.[20]

Moran was still free on bond on May 31, 1939, when he got word that his old crony from the O'Banion days, Potatoes Kaufman, had died in New York of a heart attack.

When Jake Lingle was murdered in June 1930, Kaufman, worried about being connected with the case, had fled to New York. He operated briefly there under the paid protection of Vincent "Jimmy Blue Eyes" Alo. In the mid-'30s, he headed south and found a new business venture in Hallendale, Florida. Kaufman struck up a partnership with bookie Claude Litteral, who had the outlet for the local wire service. The two men ran a bookmaking operation out of a tomato-packing shed, and as the money rolled in, they added gambling equipment such as a craps table and roulette wheel. They called their new haven The Plantation. When Jimmy Alo and Meyer Lansky joined Kaufman and Litteral as partners, The Plantation became a well-protected gambler's paradise.[21]

Kaufman died young, aged forty, but without being hastened to his grave by bullets. The target of Lingle's extortion attempt when he had an interest in the Sheridan Wave Club, he was another one who probably took the truth about Leo Vincent Brothers's guilt with him.

On Tuesday, December 3, 1940, Berger Hansen locked himself in his engraving shop and took out a homemade pistol he'd fashioned from a six-inch piece of pipe and loaded it with a .45 caliber cartridge. Positioning it carefully on his workbench and firing it using a hammer and nail, he sent a bullet into his head. A colleague found him, and he was taken to the hospital, alive but mortally wounded. He regained consciousness long enough to tell the police that his attempt at suicide had been motivated by despondency over financial difficulties that occurred in the wake of the forgery and conspiracy trials. He then sank into a coma and died the following Friday.[22]

On January 15, 1940, Assistant State's Attorney Wright dismissed the charges of conspiring to forge $230,000 worth of New York City Railroad bonds against Moran, Parker, and their co-defendants in the previous trials. Wright cited the inability to locate Carl Silver as his reason behind the move, but in actuality there was not enough evidence to go to trial, and the four-term act called for dismissal of charges if demand for trial was not made in four successive grand jury terms.[23]

Moran took a break from the attorney meetings to travel to St. Paul in March 1941. He had gotten word that his long-suffering mother, Marie Diana, had died on March 7, after a short-lived battle with heart disease. Following her burial in Calvary Cemetery, he made a solitary visit to the grave, adding a few extra layers of flowers to the small pile covering the soil. Her loss was no small one in his life, even though he had not lived under her roof in thirty-two years. Marie Diana's love for her eldest son had never diminished despite the separation and her worrying over his safety as a ranking Chicago gangster.

Frank Parker was released from Leavenworth in April 1941 and immediately remanded to the Cook County jail. Like Moran, who was still at liberty, he posted a $5,000 bond to go free while the appellate court reviewed his case. When the court decided against both men, they persisted in taking their case to the U.S. Supreme Court. Their counsel claimed that Moran and Parker had been placed in double jeopardy, pointing out that they had been acquitted at their first trial and convicted in a second trial related to the same case. The Supreme Court refused to review the appeal, which meant that they now had no more recourse to evade imprisonment.

No more recourse existed except refusal to report to the jail. Parker admitted defeat and surrendered to the police, but Moran simply disappeared. In May 1942 the rumor arose that he was in hiding, recovering from a leg fracture. He managed to stay out of sight for almost a year and a half, until a night of boozing revealed his whereabouts.

On the night of January 28, 1943, Ensign Alexander Hansen of the Coast Guard was approaching the busy intersection of Clark and Madison streets. The air was brisk and cold, so he wrapped his head securely in a scarf that left his vision free in front but impeded on the sides. Hansen, therefore, did not see the man who lurched unsteadily up to him until the stranger had him firmly by the arm.

"What do you want?" the ensign demanded warily. He did not recognize the accoster as the notorious Bugs Moran, hence his hostile tone.

Moran, whose breath reeked heavily of liquor, tugged on him. "Let's go out and make a lot of money," he slurred. When Hansen tried to break away, Moran exploded and began punching and shaking him. The fifty-two-year-old gangster was administering a sound thumping to the younger man when a police squad car drew up. When he saw the officers get out of the vehicle and run toward him, Moran released Hansen and fled into a tavern at 18 North Clark Street. Detectives chased him inside and collared him after he had taken a seat in a darkened corner and ordered a crème de menthe. As they led him outside, he tried to toss a .32-caliber automatic into the gutter, resulting in another struggle. At the station, he gave flippant answers to police questions. When asked what he did with a living, he tugged on the material of his bright-green suit and smirked, "I'm an asparagus salesman."[24]

He spent the night passed out in the drunk tank and awoke feeling sick and garrulous. He grumbled to reporters, "I have been drinking too much moko" [slang for *moko loko*, or moonshine, so named during Prohibition because of its brain-numbing effects]. When the lockup supervisor asked Moran what he wanted for breakfast, Moran paled and replied, "Five aspirin tablets."

He was charged with three counts of assault (scrapping with the police officers and the Coast Guard ensign), one count of disorderly conduct, and one of carrying a gun. When he was arraigned before Judge Gibson E. Gorman, the judge noted that he had yet to begin serving his year in jail on the conspiracy conviction. Because Moran demanded a jury trial, his case was continued until February 11, but Gorman ordered him taken to the county jail to begin serving his earlier sentence.[25]

Moran remained behind bars until December 21, when he was released a month early for good behavior. Reports of his doings while inside continued to make the papers. In March investigators from the state's attorney's office administered a lie-detector test to determine whether he had been involved in the October 22, 1942, murders of Mrs. Lillian Galvin and her maid, who had been killed in their Evanston home during a robbery. The results of the test absolved him of complicity to the state's attorney's satisfaction.[26]

Warden Frank Sain confirmed to the press that Moran was a model prisoner. "He has been working in the prison chapel, and he really worked. He got on his knees to scrub it every day. I don't know whether he absorbed any religion, or what his plans are."

At the end of October the gangster collapsed while working in the chapel and was found unconscious by a guard. He was rushed to the jail infirmary, where doctors determined that he had suffered a heart attack.[27] By the time of his released in December, he had recovered. When photographers tried to take a picture of him as he left the Criminal Courts Building, Moran, dressed in an elegant brown suit and green shirt, outran them and ducked into a taxicab in which Evelyn sat waiting.

When Warden Sain told reporters that he had no idea what Moran's plans for the future were, he was sincere. Otherwise, he would have lost his job or been committed to his own jail, in view of events destined to unfold.

19

BREAKING THE BANKS

VIRGIL WILSON SUMMERS WAS A lanky six-footer with angular features and a head of thick black hair that he wore slicked back in the style of the day. Originally from Mount Vernon, Illinois, Summers had been an incorrigible youth despite his father's position on the small town police force. When Henry Summers died in 1929, soon after his son turned seventeen, Virgil followed the path of lawlessness with more determination than ever. He left the family farm on the outskirts of Mount Vernon and spent more time within the town proper, hanging around with other youths who were just as aimless.

On December 8, 1933, Virgil Summers and three companions went to the home of Rozier Green, a farmer who maintained a small property outside Bluford, near Mount Vernon.[1] A treacherous neighbor had told the young men that Green had hidden his life's savings, an estimated $3,000, on the premises, so they arrived at his farm that chilly night with the intention of robbing him.

The plan went awry when Green reacted to the sight of their weapons by running away and yelling instead of showing the gang where his money was hidden. His brother, Wiley Green, who happened to be visiting for the evening, rushed out with a revolver, and suddenly bullets were flying everywhere, nicking one of the gang members in the ear and killing Rozier Green.

Summers and his three accomplices were turned in by a gang member who had turned state's evidence to avoid being charged as an accessory to Green's murder and stood trial in February and March of 1934. The *Mount Vernon Register–News*, covering the proceedings, reproduced a segment of Summer's cross-examination by Special Prosecutor Hart, after the former insisted that on the night Green died, he had been home in bed suffering from a headache:

Q: Do you remember trying to escape from the Benton jail? (referring to an attempt Summers had made in January).

A: I didn't try to escape.

Q: Didn't you use saws and try to cut your way out?

A: No.

Q: Well, wasn't a bar sawed in your cell in your presence and didn't you tie a blanket from your bunk to the bar?

A: Yes, but I didn't try to escape.

Q: (sarcastically) Do you mean to say that if the sawing had done any good you wouldn't have left?

A: Oh no, if I'd found any hole I'd have left all right.[2]

The jury found all four defendants guilty, and Judge Joseph Hill sentenced them to seventeen years in the Southern Illinois Penitentiary at Menard. Many felt the sentence was too light, considering that the gang members had previously been arrested for auto theft and armed robbery, but Hill probably took the youths' ages (Summers was nineteen) into account. In 1935 he was transferred to Joliet, from which he was finally discharged in 1943.

Albert Fouts (born Pfautz) had been spending more of his life outside the law than within its boundaries. Born October 7, 1891, in Dayton, Ohio, Fouts experienced his first arrest for suspicion of having committed robbery in 1905, when he was fourteen. He beat that rap but was not so lucky three years later, when the evidence in a burglary and larceny trial was more convincing and he was sent to the Ohio State Reformatory. He violated parole twice, on each occasion returning to the reformatory, but finally walked free in January 1914. His brother, Pete Fouts, also had a criminal record, and the Dayton police considered the two violent and ruthless.[3]

Fouts, visually, was a Dickens prototype. Standing five foot two and averaging his weight at 109 pounds, he was apple-cheeked and habitually wore a benign expression. Only his eyes, which were cold and blue, hinted at his unrepentant criminal leanings. He was a burglar and apprentice safecracker, racking up one arrest after another but managing to evade punishment aside from that first juvenile sentence.

Then, in December 1916, he was charged with murder.

On December 2 a Dayton police officer was passing the residence at 922 East Fifth Street when he spotted a man stumbling across the sidewalk, blood-soaked fingers clutching a throat wound. It was Al Fouts. The policeman subdued him and called for reinforcements and an ambulance.[4]

Investigating officers went behind the building, which housed a shoe store on the ground floor, and climbed a rickety stairwell to access the apartment on the second floor. Picking their way carefully along a blood-spattered hallway, they entered the front room and found the body of a woman on the sofa. She was later identified as Edith Mullen, aged twenty-seven, wife of gangster Mike Mullen, who was currently serving time in the Ohio State Penitentiary. The apartment belonged to her parents, Mr and Mrs. Charles Coll, with whom she lived. Fouts, the police learned, roomed there.

The Colls and Fouts, once he regained consciousness at the hospital, told the police that the previous Tuesday, November 28, Mrs. Mullen and Fouts had gotten into a terrible verbal battle. He claimed that she was infatuated with him and jealous of a woman he had been seeing. When he declared he was leaving and began to pack a suitcase, she snatched up a butcher knife left on the kitchen counter and lunged at him, cutting him in the left arm. Infuriated, Fouts grabbed the knife when Edith dropped it and struck when she lunged at him again, stabbing her in the right breast.

What happened from that point until her death just before 3 a.m. the following Saturday was nothing less than bizarre. Shocked by the damage he had inflicted, Fouts helped the woman's hysterical parents get her into bed and called a local physician, Dr. D. C. Litchliter, who had a small practice at 809 East Fifth Street. The doctor arrived, directed that Mrs. Mullen be carried into the front room, and dressed her wound there. He observed that her pulse was weak and her general condition "not good." When he suggested that she be taken to the hospital, she, her parents, and Fouts unanimously refused. He left reluctantly but returned two more times during the week, noticing each time that she seemed to be improving.

When asked why he did not notify the police of the stabbing, he replied nervously that he was afraid of Fouts. "He did not threaten me," Litchliter admitted, "but for some reason I was afraid of him."[5]

Mrs. Mullen took a turn for the worse on Friday night and died early Saturday morning. Rather than face a murder change, Fouts attempted to cut his own throat with a razor. The patrolman found him seconds later.

The two detectives investigating the incident found a jagged hole in the left sleeve of Fouts's coat, which supported his contention that she had attacked him first. He was in critical condition for days but finally rallied, only to be charged with the murder of Edith Mullen. Because of extenuating circumstances, the prosecutor reduced the charge to manslaughter, but Fouts did receive an indefinite term at the Ohio State Penitentiary.

On June 15, 1920, he was paroled, and, finding the Midwest too hot for his liking, went to Los Angeles, where he resumed his perfected craft of burglary and larceny. Los Angeles police arrested him on suspicion of burglary in April 1921, but he was released for lack of evidence. He was not so lucky the following year, in July 1922, when he was arrested for burglary and received a one- to fifteen-year sentence at first San Quentin and then Folsom Prison.[6]

Fouts returned to Ohio upon his discharge from Folsom, but his experience in one of the nation's most desperate prisons did nothing to decrease his determination to make his living via dishonorable means. He was arrested repeatedly throughout the 1930s in Ohio, North Carolina, Tennessee, and Kentucky on burglary and larceny charges.

On December 16, 1943, Thomas Alex, proprietor of the Silver Star restaurant at 1260 West Third Street, notified the police that Al Fouts was in his establishment, behaving erratically. Patrolman A. Durham investigated and found Fouts in possession of a .38-caliber revolver, extra bullets, and three bottles of strychnine, all stuffed in a paper sack. When Durham demanded to know the purpose of the unsettling collection, Fouts refused to offer an explanation. He surrendered the items for ballistics testing (in the case of the bullets) and walked away. But Ohio had not heard the last of him.

In the late autumn of 1943 Robert Loughran from the United Press wrote a column in which he suggested that bootlegging, and all of the wanton lawbreaking and violence that accompanied it during Prohibition, was on the verge of a comeback, Repeal be damned. E. C. Yellowley, who headed the Chicago alcohol tax unit, stated that the big-time gangsters had not been linked with any recent bootlegging activity, but should the revival be successful, that would probably change.

"The illicit alcohol traffic can be traced to the little guys who were allied with Capone during Prohibition and are now trying to be big shots," Yellowley said. "Once they get established and start turning a comfortable profit, we can expect the return of some of the mobs which flourished in the dry era." He named Moran and Jake Guzik as likely contenders for the bootlegging throne.

The alcohol tax unit had figures that did support the suggestion of a return to bathtub gin and stovetop stills. Federal agents had been raiding stills on a steady basis for months. The revival was ascribed to wartime liquor rationing, and according to the authorities, was held in check only because the sugar needed to make the alcohol was too scarce for the output to be plentiful. What alcohol could be cooked up was in demand by saloonkeepers who wanted to cut their legitimate liquor stock and make more money from it.

The latter half of 1943 had, according to Yellowley's records, seen $300,000 worth of liquor hijacked in the Chicago area, ostensibly by bootleggers looking for the "good stuff" to mix their homemade creations with, just as it had been in the good old days.

The unit head tried to calm public fears about the return of "jake leg" and alcohol poisoning deaths. "The bootleg stuff now is much better than during the first few years of Prohibition," Yellowley said. "The boys learned a lot about making alcohol."

Whether Al Fouts had been inspired by that article or was already onto something that Loughran had merely happened to select for his column is not known, but in early 1944 he traveled to Chicago to visit a former Daytonian who now resided there. His intention was to acquire contacts in the liquor business and arrange the smuggling of Grade A Canadian liquor into Dayton and the surrounding area. His expatriate friend, who now ran a saloon, introduced him to Moran.

Since his release from the Cook County Jail, Moran had been fulfilling Yellowley's prediction by reverting to his 1920s bootlegging roots. He operated primarily by hijacking legitimate liquor shipments or pilfering government warehouses and selling the goods to local bootleggers who needed bona fide ingredients for their home-cooked output. He welcomed Al Fouts as a potential long-term customer, but the two hit it off after their first meeting. Moran agreed to supply the visitor with as much liquor as needed.

When Fouts returned to Dayton, he and Moran remained in touch via telephone and letter, their conversations not always confined to business matters. A friendship grew and persisted even after the ex-North Sider left the bootlegging field. Moran made sure that Fouts maintained a strong connection to the liquor smuggling network by introducing him to Johnny Alexs, who operated a roadhouse on the Illinois–Indiana state line.[7]

They would be engaged in a different type of business before the year was out.

On May 28, 1944, a beautiful, exotic-looking brunette walked into the Austin Avenue police station, teary-eyed and clutching her purse. Approaching the front desk, she pleaded to the sergeant on duty, "Please . . . you have to help me find out who I am." Taken aback by the unusual request, the officer called Lieutenant Edward LeFevour, who questioned her.

The woman claimed that the conductor had awakened her on a Madison Street trolley car at around 9 p.m. To her shock and terror, she could not remember getting on the streetcar or even what her own name was. She disembarked, feeling dazed, and wandered into a bowling alley at Madison and Austin Avenue. "Do you know me?" she asked an employee. When he said that he did not, she went back outside, hired a cab, and asked driver Harry Riedy to convey her to the nearest police station.[8]

Going through her purse, the police discovered a thick bundle of newspaper clippings mentioning a woman by the long-winded name of Mrs. Pluma Louise Lowery Abatiello Palmer Struck. She evidenced no recognition as she glanced over them. The mystery was not solved until Lieutenant Nat Ruvell came on duty and did a double take. He identified her as Louise Moran, widow of Potter D'Orsay Palmer of Chicago's illustrious Palmer family, and currently the wife of George Moran's son John.

Ruvell drove her to the Moran apartment at 3300 Warren Boulevard but found John gone, along with his clothing and personal effects. Louise wandered from room to room for several minutes before shaking her head and confessing that nothing was familiar to her. The lieutenant then took her to Psychopathic Hospital, where either the treatment or a change of heart restored her memory.

The twenty-seven-year-old beauty, who had married John Moran the previous January, had a flair for short-lived and dramatic marriages. In December 1938 she had married Potter D'Orsay Palmer in Florida, where she had been a waitress at a Sarasota sandwich stand, but the couple spent more time apart than together. They argued often, and Palmer preferred the company of his cronies to that of his neurotic wife, who would call the police in a fit of hysterics whenever he stayed away for too long.

In early 1939 Louise filed suit for $500,000 in damages against her wealthy in-laws, claiming that their meddling had alienated her husband's affection for her, but reconciliation with Palmer led her to drop it. When he died in May 1939 from a brain hemorrhage incurred after a fistfight at a party, the Palmer family cut her off without a cent, having disapproved of the marriage. She married again, this time to Ellsworth Struck, but the union barely lasted a year. Struck went home to Ohio, and Louise made her way to Chicago.

She met John Moran in the fall of 1943 at the Chez Paree nightclub, where she had been working as a hatcheck girl.[9] It did not take long for the relationship to sour; Moran responded to her fits of rage and tearful tantrums by simply packing his bags and going to stay with his father or checking into a men's hotel. Her May 1944 "amnesia attack" had been preceded by a particularly nasty quarrel.

George and Evelyn Moran interceded when they could, but the marriage did not last. While Evelyn took the irate young woman to a coffee shop to calm down and talk after one knock-down, drag-out argument, George Moran spoke frankly to his son.

"She's a gold-digger, and nuts," he insisted. "Get rid of her. If she won't divorce you, lock her up in a nuthouse. I'll pay for it."[10]

John Moran, a bartender, was less vindictive and rejected the offer. In the end, the marriage terminated of its own accord. The couple divorced in April 1946, with Pluma Louise charging desertion and waiving alimony. By that point she and John were glad to see the last of each other.

Although the charge proved to be unfounded in this particular instance, George Moran's arrest in December 1944 for the alleged holdup of a Gary, Indiana, dice game foretold the type of activity that he would soon be involved in.

Detectives Arthur Williams and George Harms said that they entered the Central restaurant at 1305 Washington Street in Gary at 2:45 a.m. on December 3, intending to have coffee, and noticed a holdup in progress. Forty men who had been taking part in a dice game in a back room were being held at bay by four men wielding pistols. One of the robbers noticed the detectives and escorted them back to their squad car at gunpoint while the others collected the $3,500 that the game had racked up so far.

Williams and Harms thought they recognized one of the gunmen as Bugs Moran and checked the photo on file at headquarters to be sure. They swore out a complaint, leading to Moran's arrest in Chicago. The detectives traveled to the city to view him in a lineup and successfully picked him out. Moran indignantly denied the charge and fought the extradition proceedings that instantly commenced. The charges were dropped the following May, when Indiana authorities admitted that they "could not substantiate" the charges.[11]

It was around this time that Moran's association with the infamous Bookie Gang began. He joined a small but tenacious crew of former robbers, gangsters, and strong-arm men: Virgil Summers and his brother Neal, aka Monk; ex-convict and armed robber James Joseph Kelly; thief Eugene "Red" Smith; West Side hoodlum Richard Todd; Steve "the Greek" Manos; Lawrence "Tiny" Mazzanars; and Renato Lolli. Moran reunited with Grover Dullard, a North Sider from the old days, who knew the locations of Chicago's various handbooks, or had ways of finding out.[12]

The gang headquartered in a lunchroom at Madison and Paulina, and selected their first target in the early summer of 1945: the Outfit-controlled slot machines and handbooks of Cook and Lake counties, which were being managed by the venerable Eddie Vogel. In August 1945 they made their first attack on a Vogel handbook on the North Side, and began knocking them over at a rate of one a week.

The gang's robberies not only caused the Outfit some financial losses but also drew police attention to their gambling operations. The police began cracking down in the fall of 1945. Casual gang member Eugene Duggan was netted during one raid and in exchange for his freedom told Detective Emil Smicklas all he knew about Bookie activities. Duggan turned up murdered, but the gang's troubles did not end there.

Red Smith fatally shot two police officers, Charles Brady and George Hellstern, on September 2 when they interrupted him during a robbery on the North Side. This was a major faux pas, as cop killings guaranteed relentless police harassment. The Bookie Gang made a preemptive strike to avert possible legal annihilation: Mazzanars and Lolli killed Red Smith and buried his body in a field just outside the city proper.[13]

Assistant State's Attorney Alexander Napoli filed murder charges against Mazzanars and Lolli and secured confessions from them. By that point Moran and Summers had left the city, wisely sensing that the Bookie Gang's reign of Syndicate harassment had finally been brought to a bloody end.

In June 1945 George and Evelyn Moran arrived in Owensboro, Kentucky, a small but thriving community on the Ohio River. It is not known where they initially stayed, but in October they rented a house at 1921 Littlewood Drive, in what is now the Dogwood Azalea Trail. The owner, H. C. Farmer, was planning to winter in Florida and signed a rental agreement with Mrs. Moran, which stipulated that when they returned from Florida on May 1 of the following year, the Morans had to seek accommodations elsewhere. Farmer found Moran affable and not particularly memorable in his appearance and habits. "He appeared to be an ordinary fellow," the oil producer would later recall.[14]

Moran told his new neighbors that he was in the oil business. They noticed, though, that he had some odd personal habits. One they found especially bewildering was how he would pull into the nearest available parking space after rounding a corner and wait until other automobiles which had previously been behind him passed before continuing on his way. He would leave the Littlewood Drive house by car during the night, sometimes not returning until two or three days later, also under cover of darkness. The Morans had no shortage of visitors who would remain for days at a time, and more observant (or bored) neighbors noticed that their milk deliveries varied from three to six quarts a day, depending on how many guests they happened to be entertaining at the moment.

One of the neighbors was Grady Herrald Jr., a pharmacist who lived at 2001 Littlewood. His impression of Moran was not a favorable one. Almost sixty years later he recalled, "He [Moran] was in the yard one day. I walked over to say hello, and he turned and went into the house." Grady was, however, favorably impressed by the gangster's appearance. "He was a nice-looking, short, heavyset fellow."[15]

In November, Herrald was at work in his pharmacy when he received a visit from A. Hamby Jones, Owensboro's resident FBI agent. With him were two men whom the pharmacist did not recognize but had the look of being agents as well.

Jones told Herrald that Littlewood Drive's newest resident was none other than the notorious Bugs Moran and requested permission to use the house at 2001 as a surveillance point. Herrald, taken aback by the request and more than a little nervous, asked what would happen if he refused.

"We'd get a court order to move in," Jones replied, giving the pharmacist little choice but to agree.

For the next four months, three FBI agents were stationed in the Herrald house around the clock. Grady and his wife had three small children, who asked their parents who the strange men were. "Bugs exterminators," Herrald joked.[16]

The agents were brought in from one of the bureau's West Coast offices to avoid recognition by Moran. They worked in two twelve-hour shifts and maintained their watch from the dining room and an upstairs bedroom. They brought their own food and kept to themselves but occasionally talked to their host about recent cases they had been on. One thing they warned Herrald about was the fact that Moran's crew of interstate bank robbers was at war with an East St. Louis gang.

One day, one of the agents hurried over to Herrald and demanded that he get his three children out of the front yard, where they were playing. They had spotted a man who fitted the description of an East St. Louis hit man parked on nearby Ford Avenue, watching 1921 Littlewood. The local police were called, the FBI being unwilling to tip its hand to deal with the situation, but the man drove away as soon as the police car turned onto Littlewood.

During the autumn of 1945 three bank robberies occurred that aroused FBI suspicion because of the common modus operandi applied to each.

Sometime during the early morning hours of October 17, unknown thieves broke into the Lake State Bank in Richland, Indiana, and stole $13,000 in currency as well as $158 in rolled nickels and pennies from the teller tills. Investigators determined that the burglars had gained entry through a jimmied window and gotten into the vault using an acetylene torch and tools stolen from a blacksmith shop in a nearby town. A truck that had been reported stolen earlier was found abandoned near the bank, suggesting that it had been used to transport the equipment to the scene. The police did not succeed in lifting any clean fingerprint samples and deduced that it had been a professional job.[17]

The following month, on November 9, the Citizens State Bank in Ansonia, Ohio, was broken into and $24,195 in cash and $100,000 worth of war savings bonds stolen, along with stocks, property deeds, and insurance policies. The burglars entered the premises by prying open the front door and then jimmying the lock on a partition door leading into an office area where the vault was located. They cut through the steel door using a blowtorch and tools stolen from a hardware store in the vicinity. It became apparent that before tackling the bank, they had broken into a grocery store down the street, stolen $3,000 from the safe, and made off with some market baskets and water pails, likely for use in carrying off the bank loot.[18]

The third of a possible series of robberies committed by the same gang took place at the West Point Bank in West Point, Kentucky. On the frigid night of December 8, unknown parties used a blowtorch to get into the vault and steal $7,574.19 in currency. Tools of the type found in hardware stores were used to force open the safety deposit boxes and remove $144,124 in U.S. war bonds.[19]

The FBI got its first real break in the bank robbery epidemic in December, when agents arrested a man (his name has been blacked out in the surviving FBI reports) in Missouri after discovering him in possession of a 1941 Buick loaded with safe-cracking tools, an acetylene torch, and two revolvers, one of which was reported stolen during the August 1, 1945, burglary of the Vergennes State Bank in Vergennes, Illinois.

This individual, anxious to curry favor and earn a less severe charge, told agents that he had been brought to George Moran's home at 1921 Littlewood Drive in Owensboro that fall and met with not only Moran but also Al Fouts, Virgil Summers, James Mitchell, and a man named Roy Montgomery Foster. During the conversation that followed, Mitchell told the informant that the gang, headed by

Moran, had burglarized "over sixty banks and had plenty more work to do." The gang had directed him to buy the Buick in Evansville, Indiana, where Summers was living under the pseudonym of "Clarence Sefried," and have it ready for them whenever they might need it. One of them gave him the revolver later identified as one stolen from the Vergennes State Bank and stated that they had "just knocked over a bank down the road in Indiana," a probable reference to the Lake State Bank of Richland.

The Vergennes robbers had been Virgil Summers, his brother Cornelius, Roy Montgomery Foster, and St. Louis gangster Lawrence Drewer, and the informant's intelligence pointed the FBI in the right direction. None of the four was destined to be punished for the crime, however. Foster was arrested in Chicago on December 2 for the interstate transportation of a stolen vehicle, and Cornelius Summers was nabbed for a freelance holdup in Mount Vernon.[20]

Another FBI informant hinted that Al Fouts had been a direct participant in the Ansonia bank job, and Fouts's known connection to Moran intensified the attention and suspicion of the bureau. On January 8, 1946, the Louisville Field Office requested authorization to put a wiretap on the telephone at Moran's Owensboro residence. Phone company records had proven that Fouts repeatedly called 1283–W, Moran's number.

J. Edgard Hoover approved the request for telephone surveillance and justified the decision in a memorandum to the Attorney General:

> Inquiries in the vicinity of George "Bugs" Moran's residence at 1921 Littlewood Drive, Owensboro, Kentucky, reflects that while Moran claims to be in the oil business, he obviously has no business at all. He has numerous visitors at all hours of the night who drive automobiles bearing out-of-state license plates.[21]

Although the Herrald residence continued to be a surveillance point, the FBI set up a wiretap listening post in the basement of 2007 Littlewood. It yielded little.

"Moran didn't trust telephones," Agent Jones would remember half a century later. "He would go uptown and use the pay phone outside Gabe's" (a dining establishment in the 300 block of Frederica Street).[22]

His shadows noted that Moran, when in Owensboro, spent considerable time downtown, in the area between Third and Fifth streets on Frederica, which was notoriously wide open. "You could get anything there back then," Jones recalled. "There was a lot of gambling . . . Bugs used to shoot dice in the in the basement of the Hotel Owensboro with a .45 on his hip. He was losing a lot of money, but it didn't bother him."

Sometimes Evelyn accompanied him. The FBI considered her only slightly less formidable than her husband. While she was at a doctor's appointment, agents briefly obtained and searched her purse. It contained a wallet stuffed with money, cosmetics . . . and a .32-caliber revolver and a knife. They winced at the daintily hidden arsenal and returned everything without Evelyn suspecting anything.[23]

On January 4, 1946, Lawrence Drewer was shot and killed in St Louis by two unknown gunmen who, according to witnesses, waited until the woman whom Drewer had seized as a human shield had kicked free before opening fire.[24] No one mourned his passing, least of all his own followers. Gang members George Tyson, Ethel Sparks, and William Ruemker were found shot to death, and the St. Louis underworld grapevine had it that Drewer had killed them to obtain their share of the loot from bank heists. With his passing, the leadership of the gang he had commanded fell on Moran's shoulders. Among those who enlisted under the Moran banner were brothers Joseph and Edward Burnett, ex-convict Robert L. Robertson, Lou Hannon, and Robert Hannon, who had extensive experience robbing banks in Missouri.

On April 24 Moran and Summers met with Al Fouts in Evansville. Fouts claimed to be in possession of knowledge regarding payroll deliveries to a plant just outside of Dayton. He admitted that more investigation would be required as to the frequency and times of the shipments. On May 5, he sent a letter to Summers in Evansville, urging him and Moran to come to Dayton.[25] They arrived, but the plan Fouts proposed had to be postponed, as his mother, Mrs. Emma Smith, had fallen dangerously ill, and doctors predicted that she probably would not last the month. Assuring Fouts that the job could be explored further at a later date, Moran and Summers went back home.

At the end of May, H. C. Farmer and his wife returned from Florida to regain possession of the Littlewood Drive house. Because of the housing shortage that was prevalent during the 1940s, the Morans were unable to find new accommodations in Owensboro and were forced to relocate to Henderson, roughly thirty miles away.

They succeeded in finding a stately three-story stone house at 514 Center Street that was, ironically, owned by a police officer, Richard Stites, and his wife, Mary Lynn.[26] The top floor, which had formerly been the servant's quarters, was for rent. Evelyn Moran once again made all of the arrangements and signed the rental agreement, but no sooner had they settled in than a call came from Dayton, Ohio. It was Al Fouts, who told Moran that a big score had been pinpointed and decided upon.

Little did George or Evelyn know that, after they had agreed to take the apartment and made a date to return to sign the lease, FBI agents had been to the house to speak to Stites and his wife. The agents urged the police officer to accept the gangster as a tenant, explaining that they wished to maintain the surveillance that had been established in Owensboro. Stites had some misgivings but agreed.[27]

While the FBI was setting up the Henderson surveillance, Moran was actually in another state. Everyone converged on Fouts's residence at 502 West Fourth Street in Dayton on June 25. Moran slept in Fouts's bed, which was just off the living room on the first floor, while Summers and Johnny Alexs shared one of the upstairs rooms. Fouts's cook, Mary Elizabeth Hamblin, provided one lavish chicken dinner after another while the men sat around the dining room table and discussed the upcoming robbery in low tones amid a bluish haze of cigarette and cigar smoke.[28]

Al Fouts informed his confederates that he had received a tip about an upcoming payroll shipment. On the twenty-eighth, he said, John Kurpe Jr. would be stopping at the Winters bank branch at West Third Street and Broadway to collect about $10,000 in payroll money destined for employees of Frigidaire's Moraine City plant. Kurpe followed the same route from his home to the bank, and then to the Moraine City location, every payday. Moran and Summers needed no special encouragement to support a robbery plan.

To obtain a getaway vehicle, they drove to Middletown, Ohio, on the evening of June 27 and stole the first unattended parked car that they could locate, which turned out to belong to Dr. Anson Hayes, head chemist at the American Rolling Mill research laboratory. Upon arriving back in Dayton and noticing that the gas tank was low, they drove from Fouts's home to a filling station at West Fifth Street and Broadway in Dayton, purchasing fourteen gallons of gas from night manager Roderick Upton. Moran and Summers, who were in the stolen vehicle while Al Fouts drove the other car, chatted briefly with Upton during the transaction and told him that they were en route to Chicago. They then took drove back to Fouts's home to apply phony license plates to their new acquisition and hide it in a nearby garage until it was needed.[29]

At 10 a.m. on June 28, thirty-year-old John Kurpe Jr., a recently discharged Navy veteran and father of three small children, stopped at the Winters bank branch at West Third Street and Broadway, as the plotters had anticipated. He picked up $10,000 in $10 bills for use in cashing checks for employees of the Moraine City Frigidaire plant. Friday the twenty-eighth was a "double payroll day" at Frigidaire, as factory employees and those only paid twice a month all got their checks that day, so Kurpe made sure to withdraw enough money. Kurpe told the teller that he wanted all new bills, explaining, "The old bills don't stick together when you count 'em. We have to count the bills out in a hurry."[30]

When she handed him the money, Kurpe left the bank, climbed into his green coupe, and headed for Moraine City. He intended to stop at the tavern that his father-in-law, Gabor Silas, ran across from the Frigidaire plant, as the plant owners had an arrangement with Silas to cash employee paychecks there.

At the intersection of South Broadway and Donna Avenue, the ex-sailor noticed a large truck turning onto Donna, so he slowed down. Glancing in the mirror, he saw a large black car coming up behind him at increasing speed. "That driver must be crazy if he tries to make the curve," Kurpe thought. Suddenly the black car, a Buick, passed him and swerved sharply to the side, cutting him off. Before he could do much more than hit the brakes, two men got out of the Buick and approached, brandishing guns.[31]

Both men wore striped workman's hats and old clothes obviously intended for physical labor. One opened the car door on the driver's side and took over the wheel, sliding Kurpe over. A second man got in on the other side, forced Kurpe's head between his knees, and warned him not to yell. The frightened young man felt a gun muzzle press against the back of his neck and nodded jerkily. The macabre two-vehicle motorcade proceeded to Vance Road, south of Maddin Park. When Kurpe noticed that they were picking up speed, he ventured to say, "Don't drive so fast; my brakes are no good." They ignored him.

After stopping, the bandits forced John Kurpe out of the car. As he was climbing out, some of the payroll money, which he had stuffed inside his shirt, fell to the grass. His captors searched him eagerly, taking everything. When satisfied that he was not hiding any more, they hustled him into the woods. Fighting down a growing fear, he asked if he could smoke and was granted permission. But before he had taken more than a few puffs, the cigarette was knocked from his mouth and he was ordered to lie down. The bandits stripped him of his shoes and secured his mouth, wrists, and ankles with surgical tape. When they began to walk back toward the cars, Kurpe looked over his shoulder at them, only to have one yell, "Look forward or we'll stretch you out!" They left him there and returned to the parked cars. A fourth accomplice, driving another vehicle, arrived in the interim to cart his comrades off to safety, abandoning Kurpe's coupe and the robbers' own car.[32]

As soon as the motor sounds faded into the distance, John Kurpe used his tongue to force the tape off his mouth and wriggled free of his bonds. He made his way back to Vance Road and saw the two empty automobiles there, but he refused to touch them for fear of damaging fingerprint evidence. He walked down Vance until a passing motorist gave him a lift into town, and there called the sheriff's office and the police.

The FBI had had Moran, Fouts, and Summers under almost constant surveillance during the days prior to the payroll robbery. When Kurpe reported the incident to the Dayton Police Department, the agents looked at both the modus operandi, and the span of time just before the assault when the trio had evaded surveillance. Putting two and two together and getting the right number, the FBI obtained the necessary warrants and moved in.

20

"I ALMOST BEGAN TO FEEL SORRY FOR HIM"

I N THE PREDAWN HOURS OF Saturday, July 6, the FBI agents moved in to make their arrests. Summers was woken from a sound sleep in the bedroom of the house on the outskirts of Henderson, which he had rented for himself, his wife, and two-month-old daughter, Patricia Ann. At 4:30 a.m., a second, nine-man team quietly infiltrated the Center Street apartment.

Moran did not awake until the agents entered his bedroom and roused him. Henderson folklore claims that the FBI team hauled George and Evelyn out of bed by their feet to prevent either from grabbing a hidden weapon, but in actuality the agents only ripped the covers from Moran, although machine guns were trained on both husband and wife. Both were permitted to get up and dress after displaying empty hands as ordered.

After Moran was handcuffed and prepared for a trip to the jail in Owensboro, two agents remained to search the apartment. Evelyn made coffee after the pot had been inspected, and swallowed her resentment enough to make breakfast for the two men as well as herself, perhaps worried that hostile behavior on her part might result in difficulty for her husband later. A search of the apartment turned up a .32-20 Colt revolver, a .22 automatic-loading Ranger Rifle, and an H&R .22 revolver.[1]

Police descended on Al Fouts's West Fourth Street home shortly before noon, arresting him as he was about to eat lunch. When Detective L. F. St. Pierre searched the bedroom, he made an incriminating discovery. Prying up some suspiciously loose floorboards in Fouts's clothes closet, he found several hundred dollars, all in $10 bills, secreted in a sealed box. He confiscated it in the hope that it could be identified as a portion of the Kurpe payroll loot. When arraigned before Judge Cecil, Fouts, through his attorney Herbert Eikenbary, asked for a preliminary hearing. Cecil set a date of July 16 and approved Fouts's release on a $25,000 bond.

Moran and Summers were brought to Owensboro and placed in the Daviess County Jail. Charged with unlawful flight to avoid prosecution in the Kurpe payroll robbery, they were arraigned Saturday afternoon before U.S. Commissioner J. E. Walters, who held them under bonds of $25,000 each for an examining trial set for the following week. Neither entered a plea.

FBI agents brought Summers from the jail to Owensboro police headquarters, where they used Chief Bidwell's office for interrogation purposes. He refused to talk, except to say that he knew neither Bugs Moran nor Al Fouts, so after a while they gave up and turned him over to local officers to be photographed and fingerprinted. Then it was Moran's turn, but the middle-aged gangster responded to the agents' questions with a cool but stubborn front. He refused to confirm or deny his association with Summers and Fouts, or tell where he was on June 28. When it became obvious that the session was not going to achieve its intended purpose, he too was fingerprinted, photographed, and returned with Summers to the county jail.[2]

While Evelyn Moran fought desperately to raise the $25,000 bond under which her husband was being held, jailer A. C. Reisz told reporters that Moran and Summers were "just another pair of prisoners" to him. The fame of the two offenders, as well as the crime of which they stood accused, warranted incarceration in the jail's bullpen, which was reserved for those who had committed more serious offenses. It was unlike ordinary cells in that it had no windows of its own, the only light provided by dim overhead bulbs and the pale sunlight that filtered in from windows located several feet away from the cell's unyielding bars.

Reisz was relieved to note that Moran and Summers appeared to forgo escape plans in favor of reading and chatting with the other inmates, who regarded them with awe. When the jailer asked Moran about the charges he faced, the fifty-five-year old gangster gave the same answer he had given the arresting officers: "I don't know what it's about, and I have nothing to say."[3]

Sheriff Carl Harrison received a telegram from the sheriff of Franklin Parish, Louisiana, in which the latter voiced his suspicions that Moran and Summers had been behind the gang that robbed $4,000 from a Wisner, Louisiana, bank on September 29, 1945. Harrison questioned the two prisoners and received emphatic denials from both that they had had anything to do with the crime.

Back in Dayton, on July 8, Detective Sergeant Teeter and Detective E. R. Pendell interviewed Fouts's cook, Mary Hamblin, and housekeeper, Fay Lavon Wilson.

Mary confirmed that Moran, Summers, and a man they could only identify as "Johnny" had been at the Fouts residence together from approximately June 26 until the day of the Kurpe robbery. She said she would see the four men leave the house at the same time, at various hours, but was not sure whether they all went to the same destination once out of the house. She admitted to serving them whiskey, beer, and fried chicken dinners, and that they ate at irregular times.[4]

Wilson merely recounted her employment history with Fouts and described the sleeping arrangements. Neither woman was of much help to the police inquiry.

Fouts was the most challenging interview subject of all. He sat before Sergeant Teeter and stenographer Gladys Roehm, his normally sly features cold with pretended boredom.

"Would you state your name please?" Teeter requested.

"Albert G. Fouts, 502 West Fourth Street, Dayton, Ohio. That is all."

How old are you Albert?"

"You have all that," Fouts replied testily. "I don't care to make any more statement or have any more conversation."

"Are there any comments which you care to make at this time?"

"No, I don't care to make any at this time."

For the record, the officer asked, "Have you been mistreated or threatened in any way?"

"I have not been threatened or mistreated," the dwarfish hoodlum conceded. "That is correct."

"Are you willing to sign this?"

"No, I don't care to sign it."

On Friday, July 12, Moran and Summers appeared with their attorney, Beckham A. Robertson, before Police Judge John F. Wood on the warrant charging them with being fugitives from justice. The previous Wednesday, Commissioner Walters, at the request of U.S. Attorney General Hobson L. James, had dismissed the federal charge of unlawful flight to avoid prosecution. It was hardly a victory, as a contingent of Dayton police officers had just arrived in town to take custody of the two and return them to the Ohio city to face the payroll robbery charges.[5]

The Dayton policemen—Sergeants Teeter (who had interrogated Fouts), R.K. Pfoul, and Herbert Gaylor, and Detectives E. R. Pendell, R. G. Reed, and Lester St. Clair—had obtained extradition papers for Moran and Summers the previous day, while en route to Owensboro. Sergeant Teeter appeared before Judge Wood and City Solicitor Earl Winter on Friday morning, while the prisoners were appearing before Commissioner Walters, and obtained a fugitive warrant against them. Owensboro police Captain W. M. Gabert served it on the two men as they stepped from the car in which Deputy U.S. Marshal Denton, Sheriff Harrison, Deputy Sheriff Estes, and jailer Reisz had transported them to and from the jail.

Teeter took the witness stand in Judge Wood's courtroom and testified regarding the warrant the state of Ohio had issued against Moran and Summers. The prisoners sat with their lawyer at the defense table, handcuffed to each other. "They have been positively identified," he explained, when Robertson asked him if he himself had ever seen Moran and Summers on the streets of Dayton.

Immediately after the hearing, the two men were taken from Owensboro by the Dayton police team and an escort from the Kentucky Highway Patrol. The patrol officers, it had been agreed, would accompany the Dayton men and the prisoners to Cincinnati, where a detachment of Ohio state police would take over for the remainder of the journey to Dayton. The delivery went without a hitch, and at 7:13 p.m. on Friday, July 13, Moran and Summers arrived in Dayton with their escorts. They were booked at police headquarters and taken to the central police station to spend the night. Detective Sergeant E. L. McEthany told the bevy of reporters outside the station that the duo would be arraigned in the common pleas court the following Monday on the armed robbery charges.

A crowd of some three hundred people clustered in front of police headquarters at nine o'clock Saturday morning, when an armed guard of seven detectives and police officers took the prisoners from their temporary accommodations and transported them to the county jail on West Third Street. A similar crowd was waiting by the jail entrance. While Summers attempted to shield his face with his manacled hands, Moran smiled and nodded at friendly faces. He explained to one of his guards that he'd "been arrested a few times" and was not rattled.[6]

Evelyn Moran arrived in Dayton later in the morning with Bertha Summers, eleven-week-old Patricia Ann, and Summers's sister Gail Emmer. When reporters learned that the women were conferring with local attorney Albert Scharrer, they hurried to his office to obtain details. Scharrer denied having been hired to represent the prisoners but did admit that he was planning to go to the jail with Evelyn and Bertha later in the day to talk to the men. He said that Beckham Robertson in Owensboro had telephoned him and requested that he consider taking the case.

At the jail, Bertha, cradling Patricia Ann, stood silently outside the bars, waiting for her husband to emerge from behind the massive iron door that hid the jail interior from the outside world. Evelyn sat in a chair, her right ankle bandaged from a sprain that had occurred when she fell in the Henderson home. Both women impressed *Dayton Daily News* reporter Joan Bryan, who wrote, "Neither Mrs. Moran nor Mrs. Summers had the look of hardened gun molls. There was no air of arrogance about them, nor did they put on a great display of emotionalism. They were quiet, controlled, and had the appearance of the average Mrs. Housewife." Evelyn spent a few minutes chatting with Bryan but refused to comment on her husband's arrest, saying, "I don't know of anything I could say that would do any good."

An officer soon unlocked the door, and Summers appeared first. The tall, lanky ex-convict embraced his family and gave his sister a quick hug. He then hurried up the steps, where the conference room was located, with the two women and Albert Scharrer. The baby began to cry as the small group ascended. "It's her feeding time," Bertha said apologetically.[7]

For five minutes the Summers party conferred with Scharrer behind a closed door inaccessible to reporters. When they finally came down and Virgil was returned to his cell, Moran appeared with a police guard. He seemed dejected, refraining from looking Evelyn in the eye and passively accepting her kiss on his cheek. The Morans also met with Scharrer in the upstairs room. After the meetings, Scharrer confirmed to the press that he had been hired to represent the prisoners.

Satisfied that they now had competent legal counsel, Moran and Summers refused to make any statements to their police interrogators. When asked to make one, Moran smiled at Detective Sergeant Gaylor and asked, "Do you know any more funny stories?"

At the Monday morning arraignment Scharrer entered a plea of not guilty for each man and requested a preliminary hearing. Judge Lester Cecil set it for 9:30 a.m. on Thursday, July 18, and imposed a bond of $25,000 per prisoner. Moran and Summers were brought in separately, escorted from the jail into the courtroom via an overhead passage that connected the two buildings. They slumped and stared at the floorboards when they heard the bail amount that the judge set. Their wives watched tearfully as deputies led them back to their cells, where it looked like they would be staying until the outcome of the trial. Fouts, who had been bailed out by a friend who owned a café, remained at liberty.[8]

The preliminary hearing commenced at 9:45 a.m. on the eighteenth. When word got out that Judge Cecil would be presiding, eager spectators hoping for a ringside seat crowded into his courtroom as soon as the building opened to the public. By the time they realized that the proceedings would instead take place in a small room borrowed from Judge Don Thomas, all of the primary participants and journalists had arrived and the doors were closed.

Among the first witnesses were Fay Wilson and Mary Hamblin, who repeated their statements about Moran, Summers, and "Johnnie" staying at the Fouts residence around the time of the robbery. Roderick Upton, the filling station manager, told of the 1:30 a.m. stop at his gas pumps. Detective St. Pierre recounted the discovery of the money in Fouts's closet during the post-arrest search.

The reporters and few onlookers listened to the testimony with interest, but when John Kurpe Jr. took the stand, everyone sat up straight in their seats. An excited buzz arose, subsiding when the state's attorney began asking questions. Moran, Fouts, and Summers, flanked by Sheriff's Deputy Joe Holthouse and Sheriff Harry Kinderdine, remained immobile except for a few nervous gestures. Fouts rubbed his chin, Moran ran his palm repeatedly over his left ear, and Summers kept throwing his stare between the witness stand and the floor.[9]

Bertha Summers's lower lip trembled convulsively when Kurpe pointed at her husband and positively identified him as the man who had taken the wheel of his car after the ambush. When he admitted that he could not identify Moran or Fouts, Evelyn's eyes shot toward the courtroom ceiling in what looked like a prayer of thanks. When cross-examined by Scharrer, Kurpe admitted that he had initially told the police he could not identify his assailants, but seeing a photograph of Virgil Summers at the police station had jogged his memory.

On July 27 Albert Scharrer and Fouts's attorney Herbert Eikenbary requested that the trial be delayed until the September court term. They argued that the publicity which had attended their clients' arrest and the extradition of Moran and Summers from Kentucky would make jury selection difficult. "It will be hard to find a jury that hasn't read the papers," Scharrer said.

Judge Robert U. Martin denied the motion and set August 12 as the trial date. He continued the $25,000 bond for each man, with Fouts alone posting it. The following Monday, Fouts filed a motion in common pleas court requesting a separate trial. It had been his contention all along that he did not know or associate with Moran and Summers, despite the preponderance of evidence to the contrary, and the motion was a clear attempt to distance himself from them in the eyes of prospective jurors.

Jury selection began on Monday, August 12. Ninety-seven jury veniremen filled Judge Martin's courtroom at 9 a.m., and the proceedings were closed to all except those directly involved in the trial and a handful of members of the public who had managed to find seats. Al Fouts was the first defendant to arrive, followed by Moran and Summers, who were escorted by Sheriff's Deputies Cliff Bolender and Joe Holthouse. Evelyn Moran and Gail Emmer were seated behind the defense table. Bertha Summers had occupied a chair next to Mrs. Emmer, but the young woman had to leave when Patricia Ann became too fretful.

Two new attorneys joined the defense team that morning: George Hurley joined Eikenbary as co-counsel for Fouts, and Harold Bandy of East St. Louis represented Summers. Hurley was a well-known figure in the Ohio legal community, having run in the May primary as a Democratic candidate for state attorney general.

Through their attorneys, all three defendants filed their intention of using alibi as a defense. Fouts contended that he was at his home on West Fourth Street and later in a café on West Third Street at the time Kurpe was robbed. Summers and Moran claimed that they had been in Aurora, Indiana, en route to Henderson.

Albert Scharrer's first motion was to ask Judge Martin to excuse the entire assembly of prospective jurors because his clients had been brought into the courtroom in handcuffs. Herbert Eikenbary made a similar motion on behalf of Fouts. Martin ruled against them but agreed to consider a subsequent motion that the defendants not be handcuffed in the courtroom in the future. "The act prejudices the jury," Scharrer explained.[10]

By Wednesday, August 14, the jury of eleven women and one man had finally been selected and sworn in. The process of selection had been a contentious one, with the defense exercising all twelve (four for each defendant) peremptory challenges and the state using eleven. Judge Martin took a few minutes to explain two important points of law to the newly impaneled jury: first, that a person is equally guilty of a crime if he aids and abets it in any way, although he may not actually commit the deed itself; and second, that since Moran, Summers, and Fouts intended to use alibi as their defense, they bore the burden of proving said alibis.[11]

The jury members then boarded a bus for a trip to the scene of the robbery, following the route Kurpe had taken up until the moment of the robbery and abduction. They also visited Fouts's home and the White Owl café, where he claimed to have been eating when the robbery occurred. When they returned, Assistant Prosecutor Fred Kerr and the defense counsel made their opening arguments.[12]

"We will prove," Kerr began, "that Moran and Summers drove here from Kentucky on June 25, where they were joined by a man named "Johnny," and that the trio went to the home of Al Fouts and slept there. We will prove that the next day they drove in an automobile over the route they traveled in the holdup." The state would also prove, he added, that the trio had been acquainted for some time before the robbery, despite claims to the contrary.

Kerr promised to produce witnesses who could prove that Moran, Summers, and Fouts left Fouts's home on June 26, arrived in Middletown between 8:30 and 9:00 p.m., and stole Dr. Hayes's car from his open garage. The garage attendant at the filling station where they had "gassed up" at 1:30 a.m. on the twenty-seventh would testify that he had seen them in two cars. He related the details of the holdup itself, which would be bolstered by John Kurpe's testimony.

The defense attorneys then said their piece. "My client," Scharrer said, indicating Moran, "came to Dayton with Summers to visit Fouts. We do not deny that. But we will prove that Moran and Summers left Dayton at 8 a.m. on June 28, and we will prove where they were every minute after that time for the rest of the day."

Scharrer admitted that Moran had a prison record but had long since gone straight. He told the jury that his client had gone to Owensboro in 1945 to purchase and develop oil leases outside of the city. Moran, he said, had known Virgil Summers and Al Fouts, and stated that in August 1945 Fouts and his mother, who had died the following June, had visited George and Evelyn in Owensboro for a week. The attorney added that Virgil Summers had also come for a short stay at the same time, but that it was strictly a friendly visit.

He admitted that Moran arrived in Dayton on June 25, 1946, in response to news of Fouts's mother passing away on the sixteenth, but made the trip with Summers because his own car had bad tires. "Moran drove around Dayton in the three or four days he was here," Scharrer explained, "but he left for Evansville, Indiana, at 8:30 a.m. on the day of the robbery, which took place after 10 a.m."

"John Kurpe," he continued, "repeatedly told a number of persons that he could not identify any of the men who held him up. Even after seeing the pictures in the newspapers, he was unable to identify his assailants. He could not even identify Moran when he was called out of the cell block of the county jail by name."

When he pointed out that Kurpe's memory had been restored around the time that the insurance company denied a claim that Kurpe and his father-in-law had made and refused to compensate them for the lost money, Fred Kerr leaped to his feet and shouted an objection. Judge Martin said he would reserve his ruling on the matter.

Eikenbary, when it was his turn to address the jury, called the robbery "quaint." He warned them that his witnesses might not include such estimable people as professors, ministers, and Red Cross campaigners, but that did not diminish the value of their testimony.

"You will hear a lot about $10 bills," he went on. "Fouts paid his mother's funeral bill in $10 bills [before the robbery]. He carried a lot of money on his person. He has been in the liquor business intermittently, but not as big as Capone." At that comment, Moran cracked a chuckle and rolled his eyes, and even some of the jury smiled. "He has served time in penitentiaries, but that time was bought and paid for." In concluding his opening statement, Eikenbary said that at the time of the holdup, Al Fouts "was truly the little man who wasn't there."

The next day, the state called its first witnesses: Robert L. Bell of Louisville and Willam Van Landingham Jr. and John McKenna of Evansville. All three had one important thing in common; they were FBI agents who had been maintaining surveillance on George Moran and Virgil Summers on June 28. McKenna had also participated in Moran's predawn arrest in Henderson.[13]

Van Landingham told Fred Kerr that on April 22, he had seen Moran and Summers together in Evansville, near the latter's home on West Louisiana Street, and two days later observed Al Fouts, driving a car with Ohio license plates, in the vicinity.

McKenna testified that he had seen Moran and Summers together four times: on April 22, in a restaurant at the corner of West Louisiana and First Streets in Evansville, where Summers had been living; on May 10, driving about in Moran's car; on May 22, walking from the Summers residence at 604 West Louisiana toward Moran's vehicle; and the fourth time, on June 7, at the same location. He corroborated much of the testimony of Van Landingham. McKenna identified state's exhibits that had been taken from the house for use as evidence, including a photo of Virgil and Bertha Summers in front of the former's car, a letter addressed to "Doc," an envelope that had originally contained the letter, and a repair bill, dated April 22, for work on Summers's car.[14]

Detective St. Pierre took the stand to describe the discovery of the payroll loot in Fouts's closet and the finding of Kurpe's vehicle and the stolen Hayes car off Vance Road on the morning of June 28. He was followed by Cincinnati FBI agent James C. Montgomery, who testified that, while monitoring the Fouts residence on June 25, he had seen Summers and Moran arrive and stay till late. Two other Cincinnati agents, Richard Smith and Joseph Ziegler, said they had followed Summers and two other men whom they did not recognize to the scene of the holdup, the inference being that the entire operation was being rehearsed in advance.

Wayne W. Bradley, a "document examiner" attached to the FBI laboratory in Washington, confirmed that a letter addressed to "Clarence Sefried" at Virgil Summers's Evansville address had been written by Al Fouts. The message, dated May 5, 1946, read:

> Dear Friend (Doc etc)
> I received your note after I returned from the Derby—so congratulations folks upon your new arrival.
> Doc and "Pop"—I would very much like for you and "old" man to be over this way by 9:30 a.m. Wednesday—starting Wednesday a.m. the issue starts to roll.
> I want you folks to see those conditions for the one week—I and also the author will check on last Wed, Thurs, and Friday's events, to see if things are regular. (By the way- bring with you also a working man outfit—like you did up Ft. Wayne way—it will make it better to see things.)
> I would like you to stay over Wed a.m. till Fri noon—I'll arrange for you folks lodging so be here by 9:30 a.m. Wed—then we'll go into details.
> I'll be waiting here at the house Wed so give me a ring when you get in and I'll meet you—so get in touch with the "old" man.
> Regards from all to all.

The signature was illegible, but Bradley confirmed that the handwriting matched specimens he had been able to obtain from Fouts.

"What that letters means," Judge Martin advised the jury, "is up to you to decide." Kerr said that the letter would be taken up again later in the trial.[15]

On Friday, August 16, William Jahn Jr., an FBI agent assigned to the Dayton office, gave testimony that struck a potentially fatal blow at the defendants' case. After Dr. Anson Hayes took the stand to describe the theft of his car from Middletown sometime between 8 p.m. on June 26 and 8 a.m. on the twenty-seventh, when he discovered it missing, Jahn said that he and a partner had been maintaining surveillance on the Fouts home on June 26, arriving at 9 p.m. and parking their car across the street. A few minutes after 1 a.m., two cars drove speedily up West Fourth Street and pulled to a sudden stop in front of number 502. The two automobiles were parked so closely together that Jahn and his partner could not make out the license plates of the first one, although they could discern the Illinois plates on the second, which was later traced to Virgil Summers.[16]

While the agents watched from the shadows that enveloped their car, Summers got out of his vehicle, followed by Moran, who stood on the curb for a few minutes and smoked. A third man, whom Jahn did not identify but was presumed to be Fouts, got out of the third car, and all three men went into the house. As soon as the front door closed, the agents emerged from their hiding place and scurried across the street to read the license plate number they had not yet been able to make out. They copied it down: A–31–H.

It was the same plate number given by Dr. Hayes when he reported his car missing.

In response to a question posed by Scharrer, Jahn admitted that he had never seen Moran in person before that night, but said that he had been carrying the gangster's picture in his pocket for the last four or five months.

"Had you ever seen Summers before?" Harold Bandy asked.

"It was the first clear look I had, but I'm sure it was him."

Special Agent Clarence Swearington, also on a stakeout of the Fouts home, said that the three suspects left the house about twenty minutes after Jahn and his partner had seen them arrive. Swearington followed them as they drove the two automobiles to the filling station. After leaving the station, he said, they headed toward Dayton View by way of North Broadway, Harvard Boulevard, and Salem Avenue. He admitted that after they turned onto Red Haw Road at 1:50 a.m., he lost them.

The most entertaining witness of the day was Mrs. Gertrude Thompson, who had been a neighbor of Emma Smith, Fouts's deceased mother. She said that during the early morning hours of June 28[t] her dog awakened her by barking at the sound of an approaching car. She looked out her window and saw two cars pull into the garage adjoining Mrs. Smith's home. Fouts, she said, was in the first vehicle. After leaving it in the garage, he drove away in the other vehicle with two other men. She estimated the time to be 2:15 a.m. Mrs. Thompson identified Virgil Summers as the driver of a car she had seen in the vicinity of the Smith home at least twice in the days prior to the robbery.[17]

The defense team did its best to shake her testimony, suggesting that she had been on bad terms with Mrs. Smith and the Fouts family. She indignantly denied it, saying that although she and Emma Smith had not been close, they had been "neighbor-friends."

Harold Bandy was particularly relentless when questioning FBI agent John Vicars, who had been maintaining surveillance with William Jahn. The lawyer tried to elicit an admission from the agent that the night had been a rainy one, and that his view of the men on the front lawn was not crystal clear. Vicar replied that he could not remember.

"Don't you know that it is customary to have more clear nights than rainy ones at that time of year?" Bandy queried.

"I am not a weatherman, sir!" Vicars shot back.[18]

Albert Scharrer was equally terse when cross-examining Clarence Swearington, who had been one of the agents detailed to tail Moran, Summers, and Fouts at the very time John Kurpe was being held up. "Where were you then during the robbery?"

"We were trying to find 'em!" Swearington retorted, insisting that he had not been able to locate the trio since they had given him the slip on Red Haw Road.

At the end of the day, Judge Martin adjourned the proceedings until the following Monday. Moran and Summers embraced their wives before filing out in the custody of deputies, while Fouts joined the crowd that spilled out of the humid courtroom into the afternoon air. The diminutive ex-convict was sweating profusely, although from nerves or the heat was the question.

On Saturday, the seventeenth, an Ansonia resident contacted the *Dayton Daily News* with information that put Al Fouts in the town at the time that the Citizens State Bank there was robbed.

George Klipstine, a lumber dealer, told the *News* that when he saw a photo of Fouts the paper had published on its front page, he recognized him as one of three men he had seen in Ansonia a few hours before the robbery. He said that he and his wife had driven into town at 11:15 p.m. on November 9, after spending part of the day in nearby Greenville, and noticed three men standing on a street corner, two tall and of average build, while the third was short and stocky. From a distance Klipstine took them to be local men and drew up alongside them to say hello. The taller men averted their faces but the third was not so quick, and Klipstine got a good look at him.

"I saw I didn't know him, so I drove on home and thought nothing more about it," the lumber dealer said. He was sure that the man was Al Fouts.

Another Ansonia resident, real estate broker John Harrison, corroborated Klipstine's story. He too had seen three men of the same description on a street corner, but he admitted that he had not seen their faces and would not be able to identify them.[19]

The *News* contacted George King, agent in charge of the FBI's Cincinnati office, to confirm the theory that the bureau had been keeping Moran and his colleagues under surveillance in order to collect the evidence necessary to link them to the Ansonia bank robbery. King's response was noncommittal.

"It is not the policy of the bureau to comment on cases until they are actually brought to prosecution," he explained. "In the event that charges are brought against these men for another offense, any facts the bureau may have concerning that offense will be brought to light."

Ripples of excitement set the courtroom abuzz on August 20, when John Kurpe Jr. took the stand. He recited for the jury's benefit the whole story of drawing the payroll money from the bank and the gangsters' car forcing his vehicle to the curb as he was driving to his father-in-law's tavern. "He's one of them," Kurpe told the court, pointing at Summers, who kept his eyes lowered and refused to meet his former victim's accusing stare.[20]

Albert Scharrer precipitated a war of words with the prosecution when he asked Kurpe to confirm the allegation that he had reported a similar robbery, this one entailing $5,000, in 1941. Kurpe hotly denied it.

"Do you mean to tell me," the lawyer said with exaggerated disbelief, "that you don't remember telling your father-in-law that you were robbed of $5,000 five years ago?"

"No, it never happened."

Fred Kerr leaped to his feet. "Let me hear you prove that slander, Mr. Scharrer."

"I will."

"You are trying to slander our respectable citizens," Kerr accused, to which Scharrer replied coolly, "I am a citizen too."

Christine Gooden, whose house was located a half-block away from the Donna Avenue bypass where Kurpe was ambushed, claimed to have witnessed the entire episode. She told the court she had been watching traffic from her front porch that day and had seen Kurpe's green coupe drive into view, but that she had turned away until a screeching of brakes assailed her ears and made her look again.

"A big black Buick had driven up," she testified. "Two men got out of the Buick with guns and got into the coupe." She said saw them climb into the coupe and force the driver's head down before both coupe and Buick drove on. Mrs. Gooden did not make out the assailants' features but said that both had worn caps similar to those sported by railroad brakemen.[21]

Other witnesses heard that day included Roderick Upton, the filling station operator, and Harold Hotopp, an FBI agent who had been riding in Clarence Swearington's car during the post-midnight tailing of the suspects.

August 21 saw a bigger crowd than usual jostling for seats, as the defense was scheduled to call its star witness, George "Bugs" Moran. He was preceded to the stand by two witnesses who had been brought all the way from Kentucky to prove his claim that he had been in another state at the time of the payroll heist.

Melville L. Nicely, who ran a service station in Owensboro, testified that at 2 p.m. on the twenty-eighth, he had sold Moran two new tires for his car. Scharrer reminded the jury that with Owensboro 278 miles away, the likelihood that his client had robbed Kurpe at 10:40 a.m. and been in Kentucky four hours later was nil.

Nicely went on to say that Moran's reputation in Owensboro was that of a respectable citizen and good neighbor. "They all [the residents] thought awfully well of him," the filling station operator said. "They thought nothing but good about him."[22]

In response to a question from Kerr, he said that he had known the former Chicago gangster for over a year and that as far as he knew, Moran had interests in an oil-drilling operation near Utica, Kentucky, fifteen miles south of Owensboro. He denied knowing anything of Moran's previous reputation as a Chicago gang chief and said that he did not know Virgil Summers.

He seemed unusually anxious to have the jury believe his story. "I go to church. . . . I'm trying to tell the truth as nearly as I can. . . . This is the honest truth. . . . I'm just trying to give you the honest picture."

The second Owensboro witness was Henry Thomason, who drilled oil near Utica. He said that he saw George and Evelyn Moran drive past his house at 4:30 p.m. Kentucky time (5:30 p.m. Dayton time). Kerr questioned him as to why he was so sure of the date. Thomason answered that his sister had visited him that day and borrowed his car.

All chatter in the courtroom ceased when Albert Scharrer called the next witness for the defense: Moran. Wearing a double-breasted blue suit, white shirt, and striped tie, the former gang leader took the stand and sat down. Onlookers remarked on how pale and thin he appeared. When he spoke, it was slowly, and in a monotone.[23]

Through leading questions posed by his attorney, he gave a brief history of his activities in the Chicago area prior to his gradual withdrawal in 1930. He said that he had been an official in the Central Cleaning Company for years, and prior to that, "not much."

He said that he had first met Al Fouts when the Daytonian, interested in entering the liquor business, came to Chicago in 1944 and asked him for connections. Summers, he explained, looked him up the following year in Owensboro and asked him for information about two local liquor distillers. He introduced the two men to each other, and a friendly as well as professional relationship developed.

When Scharrer asked him about the letter taken from Summers's Evansville residence, which referred to "Doc," "Pop," the "old man," work clothes, and an imminent trip to Dayton, Moran replied that he had never seen it. He said that he had arrived in Dayton with Summers at about 4 p.m. on Tuesday, June 25, and looked up Fouts at the White Owl Café. The trio went out to Emma Smith's former residence, where Johnny Alexs was waiting with a case of liquor in his trunk. Fouts unlocked the garage at the rear so that Alexs could park his car in a sheltered area.

"Did you have anything at all to do with the robbery of John Kurpe?" Scharrer asked for the record.

"Absolutely not."

On the twenty-sixth, after a few drinks, he became sick, Moran said. He admitted that he'd had gall bladder trouble for three years that had left him with severe headaches and nausea. He did manage to chat briefly with Fouts about an oil lease back in Kentucky before going to bed, he said, adding that he was sick all day on the twenty-seventh. On the twenty-eighth, he left Dayton with Summers at around 8:30 a.m., arriving in Evansville at 1:15 p.m. After a brief stopover they continued to Kentucky, reaching Owensboro and Melvin Nicely's filling station at 2 p.m. After the tire change, the two men went to Utica to check on an oil well, passing the house of defense witness Henry Thomason, who had drilled the well. They stopped in an Owensboro restaurant for dinner and made it home to Henderson at 8 p.m.

Before concluding his examination, Scharrer asked, "How old are you, George?"

"Fifty-four years old. Today."

"Happy birthday," the lawyer grinned. Moran smiled back while the courtroom erupted in laughter.

When Fred Kerr cross-examined, Moran made his contempt for the FBI's handling of his July 6 arrest clear.

"Why, they came to my home at four in the morning, with shotguns and machine guns, like the Gestapo, pushed me around, handcuffed me, and took me to jail in the next county. It was like the Gestapo.

"I made no admissions and denied nothing. I didn't know why I was being arrested, but when they came in at four thirty in the morning with machine guns and shotguns, I knew it must be for something I knew nothing about."

"Why did you decline to admit that you knew Al Fouts when you were questioned?" Kerr asked.

"I've been arrested before and went through a lot of experiences. I don't like to reveal anything until I talk to my attorney."

The assistant state's attorney persisted. "Why did you lie about having been in Dayton?"

Moran explained that he thought the arrest might have been in connection with his old liquor deals with Fouts. "I knew about that raid at Fouts's house a month or so before, when they got seventeen or eighteen cases of whiskey. I thought they might try to charge me with that. That was about the only thing I could remember about Dayton." He added, "I didn't try to conceal anything, just kept my mouth shut."

"So why did you deny knowing Virgil Summers?"

"Just kept my mouth shut."

Moran refused to give too many details away about Johnny Alexs, other than to say that he had known him since 1944, and that he had introduced him to Fouts in the hope that Alexs's previous experience running roadhouses on the Illinois–Indiana state line might make him a useful contact for Fouts in the liquor trade.

He dismissed the testimony of the FBI agents claiming to have tailed him in the days before the robbery. "I heard all the testimony, and it is all mistaken, as far as I am concerned."

When he recalled having dinner at Gabe's restaurant in Owensboro at 6:30 p.m. Kentucky time on June 28, Kerr asked him how accurate his time estimate was.

"It might be off by ten or twenty minutes at the most," was the reply.

"Maybe as much as four or five hours?"

"No."

When Kerr indicated that he had no further questions for the time being, the jury and spectators let out a collective sign and relaxed. They had been leaning forward in their seats, trying to catch every word of testimony despite the loud traffic noises that entered the courtroom through an open window. Judge Martin had to temporarily halt proceedings during Thomason's stint on the witness stand because someone drove a creaking cart through the alley, creating a noise that made everyone's skin crawl.

Once the noise subsided, Evelyn Moran took the stand.[24] She struck reporters as pleasant and cheerful as she gave her testimony. She corroborated the arrival time of her husband and Virgil Summers in Henderson on June 28 (2:30 p.m. Dayton time) and confirmed that she had accompanied the men to Utica and Owensboro, waving at Henry Thomason at one point. When talking about the arrival of the FBI agents at her home on July 6, her cheery tones grew heavier and she frowned in spite of herself. When asked if she thought the raid should have been handled differently, she snapped, "Why, of course." She muttered something about the "early hour of the morning, the noise, and humiliation."

Kerr tried to get her to publicly admit her knowledge of her husband's nationwide reputation, but she evaded answering while Scharrer fought to have the questions ruled out.

Virgil Summers took the stand in his own defense on Thursday, the twenty-third. He corroborated Moran's account of their activities of June 28. He insisted that he and Moran had reached Henderson at about 1:30 p.m. Kentucky time, and after inspecting the Utica oil well and having dinner at Gabe's restaurant, went to Moran's house on Center Street in Henderson. After a brief visit, he headed for his own home in Evansville. A careful questioning by Albert Scharrer elicited the admission that, although he was an ex-convict who had done thirteen years in prison for murder, he was trying to go straight. When he saw Fred Kerr rise from the prosecutor's table and approach, his expression darkened and he frowned.[25]

Kerr asked him about the cryptic letter referring to "Doc" and bringing along work clothes like they "did up Fort Wayne way." "I guess that letter was meant for me," Summers admitted. He said he used Clarence Sefried and other aliases, such as B. W. Wallace and Raymond Bailey, because he was an ex-convict trying to cover up his past.

"Isn't it a fact that you didn't reach Henderson until 6:05 p.m. in your car?" the prosecutor asked.

"No."

"Isn't it a fact that you didn't return to Henderson after eating at Gabe's restaurant, Owensboro, until 11:38 p.m.?"

"No."

"Isn't it a fact that you did not get home at 1025 West Indiana Avenue in Evansville until 12:17 a.m. Saturday?"

"No."

Summers steadfastly denied that he had ever laid eyes on John Kurpe before the young man went to the county jail on July 13 with the aim of identifying his attackers. He said that after viewing him, Kurpe had said something along the lines of "He doesn't look like the man."

When Kerr asked him if he completed the liquor deal he claimed to have come to Dayton on June 26 to help Fouts with, Summers replied that his help had not been necessary, as Fouts had made other arrangements.

349

"What did you do?" Kerr asked.

"I didn't do anything."

"Does it take three days to do nothing?"

"Well, Moran talked to Fouts and I talked to him too," Summers offered.

Bertha Summers followed her husband to the stand. She smiled and simpered at the jury as she backed up the testimony of her husband and the Morans.[26]

Thursday afternoon, Herbert Eikenbary paraded one witness after another before the jury to prove Al Fouts's offered alibi. The defense got off to a bad start when it was revealed that an "alibi party" had been hosted at Fouts's home on August 5 and was attended by those who agreed to back him up on the witness stand. It smacked too strongly of staged performances, but Eikenbary forged ahead anyway.

Doris Larsen, a voluptuous blond who worked in the kitchen of the White Owl Café, said that Fouts had been in the restaurant with his pet Airedale, Pat, at the time of the robbery. Kerr let her finish her statement, then suggested that he was aware of all conversations that had taken place at the alibi party, including hers.[27]

Bringing up a discussion of the time period just before the assault, he asked, "Didn't you tell Fouts, 'Well, Al, didn't you leave about that time and take the dog home?'"

Larsen looked startled but denied it. She also denied that Fouts had responded, "Don't bring that up. Just forget that. There's no point in that."

George Moore, bartender at the Friendly Inn, another Fouts hangout, flinched when Kerr asked him if he had indeed said at the party, "What would the answer be if the prosecutor asked how they could carry thirty-four cases of whiskey from Chicago in one auto?" When Moore fumbled for a response, the prosecutor assured him that whiskey running had nothing to do with the trial, so the rehearsal had been for naught.

One witness, Stanley Pence, was outright laughable. A housepainter by trade, he lived in a rooming house Fouts owned. When asked how many rooms the house contained, he scratched his head and said, "Must be about twenty-two rooms. Must be about twenty-two roomers." He paused for a moment, then added, "Some are doubled up, may be a few more." He admitted accompanying Fouts in whiskey-collecting trips to Chicago but admitted that his boss always left him in Danville, Illinois, before carrying on to the Windy City. "I'd play bingo in Danville until Fouts came back for me," he grinned. Judge Martin banged his gavel to quiet the laughter.[28]

George Sepean, the bartender at the White Owl, offered testimony more relevant to the case but was visibly nervous. He said that John Kurpe had told him, White Owl owner John Hanos Jr., and Sheriff's Deputy James Griffin that he "would not know them [the assailants] if they walked through the door right now."

The fiasco continued the next day, when John Hanos took the stand. He said he could not remember if Fouts had been in his café on the morning of June 28, and after a few minutes of testimony, reversed his story and said Fouts had definitely been there.

"So he *was* there that morning?" Kerr inquired.

"Well . . ." Hanos mopped his sweating brow. "What do you mean by morning?"

"Most people consider morning up until twelve noon," the prosecutor replied coldly.

"I think I saw Fouts around eleven o'clock."

"Didn't you tell Detective Sergeant Teeter that you were in the café all morning, except for a trip to the bank? Didn't you tell him that you hadn't seen Fouts until twelve noon?"

"I don't remember."[29]

Cross-examined by George Hurley, Hanos admitted having seen John Kurpe at the Winters National Bank at ten thirty that morning, as he himself banked there. When Kerr asked whether he had discussed with Fouts the operation of the Silas tavern, where Kurpe assisted his father-in-law as co-manager, the defense objected. John Hanos, knowing that the question was an attempt to link him to the robbery plot, was trembling as he left the stand.

Kerr recalled Edward Ruckman, who had testified briefly Tuesday afternoon, to the stand. Ruckman, day bartender at the White Owl and another alibi party attendee, said that he had seen Fouts on two occasions on the morning in question. The prosecutor wanted the jury to see how unusual it was that he could remember Fouts's comings and goings on that particular day but no other.

"Isn't it a fact that Mr. Eikenbary told you that the prosecutor will ask you how you can remember it was that particular day [that Fouts had arrived and departed twice]?"

"Yes," Ruckman admitted.

"And isn't it a fact that you told Mr. Eikenbary that on the next day you picked up a newspaper [detailing Fouts's arrest] and you told your wife that it couldn't have been Fouts because he was in the café on that day?"

Relaxing a little, the bartender nodded and said yes.

"Really? Because Al Fouts's name never appeared in the paper the day after the robbery. It was one week later, following his arrest, that his name first appeared in print in connection with this case."

Ainsley Nunn, the farmer who had found the dazed Kurpe by the side of the road after the assault, testified for the defense. He said that when he first laid eyes on him, Kurpe was "looking like he'd lost something." Nunn pulled over, offered him a lift, and took him to a telephone in the 1600 block of South Broadway. He said that during the ride, Kurpe had said that he didn't know his attackers.[30]

The defense rested its case that day, as the Friday afternoon session began. The state had a few more whacks ready. Patrolman Pat Walsh testified that his beat included the White Owl, and on the morning of June 28 he was in and out of the place at least three times, never seeing Fouts once. The first time he noticed Fouts's presence at one of the tables, it was 2:30 in the afternoon.

FBI agents Polk Young and John McKenna, along with Henderson police officer Glyn Seward described the surveillance they had maintained on Moran's Center Street residence on the afternoon of June 28. Seward said he had been watching the house from 12:55 p.m. (1:55 p.m. Dayton time) and seen no activity, so he went for dinner at six. When he returned at 6:35 p.m., Summers's car was parked in the Center Street driveway, next to Moran's own car, the one with the bad tires. A few minutes later, Summers, Moran, and their wives came out of the house, got into Moran's car, and drove away. When they returned at 11:40 p.m., Seward was still on watch, although no longer by himself, as four FBI agents had joined him.

Agent Young said he had been keeping watch since 3 p.m., and that Moran and Summers arrived at around five minutes after six. McKenna, who joined the surveillance team at 8:45 p.m., recalled that the two suspects and their wives came home for the night at 11:38 p.m. The Morans went inside, so McKenna tailed Summers back to Evansville.

With that, the state rested its case. After both sides summed up on Monday, the fate of the defendants would be in the hands of the jury.

On Friday the *Dayton Herald* had published the previously withheld information that the FBI was probing the possibility that Moran, Summers, and Fouts had been involved in the Midwest bank robbery spree of the previous year and first half of 1946. The *Daily News* had had access to the same intelligence but, at the request of the FBI, had agreed not to publish details until after the trial, to avoid prejudicing the case against the defendants. Why the *Herald* did not extend a similar courtesy is not known, but on Saturday morning Herbert Eikenbary announced to reporters that he was seeking a mistrial on behalf of his client. Later that evening, Scharrer and Harold Bandy confirmed that they would file similar motions on Monday.[31]

At about ten thirty on Saturday night, the manager of the Gibbons Hotel in Dayton called the police to report the presence of a drunken female guest in Room 429, where he insisted she was not registered and did not belong. The room itself was registered to Paul Holmes, a reporter for the *Chicago Tribune* who was in town covering the Moran–Fouts–Summers trial.

Sergeant R. G. Smith arrived with two patrolmen, Riley and Maroney, and found the woman lying on the floor next to the bed, too intoxicated to give them her name or any other information. When they checked her purse, they found papers identifying her as Virgil Summers's sister Gail. Smith called the station immediately with news of the discovery, and spoke to Captain Kirkpatrick, who sent two detectives to the hotel. Several notes found in Mrs. Emmer's purse pertained to the trial. The officers placed her under arrest for being drunk in a public place and conveyed her to the station, where she fended off all questions with boozy belligerence.[32]

On Monday, Judge Martin overruled two motions filed by the defense: one for a mistrial, the other for a directed verdict of not guilty. As the state and defense were preparing to sum up, Bertha Summers gave in to nervous exhaustion and collapsed in the hallway outside the courtroom. She was carried to an adjoining office by Evelyn and an onlooker, and revived.

Eikenbary was the first of the defense attorneys to give a closing speech, and practically all of the thirty minutes allotted to him were spent shooting verbal arrows at the FBI and their supposedly incompetent, malicious agenda.

"They must have all been Eagle Scouts when young and then graduated into Master Scouts," he said scornfully. Other descriptions included "professional witnesses" and "the Gestapo." When he became a little too enthusiastic, Judge Martin warned him to stick to the facts of the case. Eikenbary heeded him, but just barely.[33]

"Are the taxpayers of Montgomery County running a kindergarten for FBI agents?" he queried. "Who is paying for the training the FBI has received here over the last fifteen days? Are we interested in the dictatorship of J. Edgar Hoover or investigation by the local sheriff and police?"

He explained that Al Fouts had refrained from taking the stand not because of fear over a guilty admission during cross-examination but to protect the privacy of some of Dayton's leading citizens.

"There is honor among a small group of people. There is honor among the select group of bootleggers. If Al went on the stand, he would be subject to cross-examination. He would have to divulge the names of thirty or more of your best local citizens and hotels- who have used his product. Al has honor."

He dismissed the evidence of the Evansville letter to "Doc" and "Pop," saying that his client did write it, but the intent was not what the state would have the jury believe. He pointed out that someone planning to do a payroll robbery would not write such a letter five days before the deed.

Eikenbary seemed oblivious to the frowns from the eleven female jurors when he addressed many of his remarks to the sole male juror, Jesse Noffsinger, by name.

Albert Scharrer pleaded with the jury "not to guess, not to gamble, with George Moran's future." An audible sniffle sent all eyes shooting to the defense table, where a tear was seen rolling down Moran's cheek. When he realized that he was under scrutiny, the former gangster brushed it away quickly and averted his eyes.

Assistant prosecutor William Wolff addressed the jury on behalf of the state. He suggested that guilt had kept Fouts off the witness stand, saying, "If he told you the truth, he would have to tell you that he is part and parcel of the story."

He reviewed the testimony from Moran and Summers, dissecting it and pointing out the flaws as the state viewed them. In closing, he said, "To these people, robbery is a business. They make clever plans and plan well. They don't want to get caught. If they're caught, they're out of business. There is no other conclusion that can be reached by you except that all three are guilty as charged."

The case was finally submitted to the jury at 5:57 p.m.

Reporters mobbed all three defendants as they left the courtroom to await the verdict. "How do you feel about the outcome?" one asked Moran.

"Oh, they'll acquit me. All this stuff is just a frame. They haven't anything on me." He chatted a bit about the trip to Paris that he had made in the aftermath of the St. Valentine's Day Massacre, the first time he had publicly admitted to his whereabouts in the wake of that infamous event, and recounted his discovery of an English-language newspaper with his picture on it. "Guess they follow you wherever you go," he commented.

Moran evidenced some concern about the Ansonia investigation details published by the *Herald*. "What do you hear around from the people about those pictures in the paper?" he asked. "The FBI have released that . . . they thought they had the psychological moment, I guess."[34]

After retiring to the jury room, the jurors elected Jesse Noffsinger as foreman. They left the building to have dinner at six thirty, returning at a quarter past eight. Deliberations went on until 9:44 p.m., when Noffsinger knocked on the door to indicate to the bailiff that a verdict had been reached. Fouts, informed that his bond was now at an end, joined Moran and Summers in the courtroom at 10:25 p.m.

Dead silence reigned, broken only by the judge's request as to whether a verdict had been reached. Noffsinger replied in the affirmative and said, "Guilty."

The courtroom sprang back to life with the excited buzz of the spectators and the stampede of reporters rushing to telephone the story in. Evelyn Moran burst into tears, as did Gail Emmer and Bertha Summers, who had insisted on attending the night session despite her earlier breakdown. The guilty verdict carried an automatic indeterminate ten- to twenty-five-year sentence in the Ohio State Penitentiary. Moran, Summers, and Fouts would be required to serve the minimum ten before applying for parole.

After the judge thanked and dismissed the jury, the members filed out of the courtroom, passing within a foot of Evelyn Moran. Tears running down her fatigue-whitened cheeks, she hissed at them, "I hope you have bad luck for the rest of your lives." Mrs. Summers and Gail Emmer continued to cry. Only the defendants appeared completely unaffected, as they calmly submitted to being handcuffed and led away by deputies as if they'd been watching someone else's fate being decided.[35]

At 2:40 p.m. the following day, Judge Martin sentenced Moran, Summers, and Fouts to ten to twenty years in the Ohio State Penitentiary, after dismissing yet another set of motions from the defense team seeking new trials. After pronouncing sentence, he directed Sheriff Harry Kinderdine to remove the men to the prison within five days, as directed by law. Kinderdine indicated that he would take them as soon as he received the commitment papers.

No sooner was sentence passed than the U.S. district attorney's office announced that it was filing a federal warrant charging the three men with staging the Ansonia bank robbery. The officer's representative also indicated that federal detainers would also be filed, thereby preventing any future release of Moran, Summers, or Fouts until they faced federal action on the warrant, and excluding them from making bond should Judge Martin grant them new trials on the payroll robbery charge. The FBI also charged Roy Montgomery Foster and James Mitchell in the warrant. No court date was named, but the *Daily News* pointed out that no trial could occur until winter, as the men would first have to be indicted by a federal court jury during its November term.

Gabor Silas indicated that he too was filing suit against the newly convicted trio. He and his insurance company, the Great American Indemnity Company of New York, launched a civil suit to recover the $10,000 that the men had been found guilty of stealing. The action stated that they had "conspired together in planning, arranging, and agreeing" upon the robbery. The insurance company had paid Silas $8,000 compensation for the payroll loss and wanted its money back.

While Moran, Summers, and Fouts held hurried conferences with their attorneys in the county jail and did their best to cheer up their wives and Summers's sister, Fred Kerr received reporters at his home. Reclining in an armchair and surrounded by his wife, Mary, and children, Bob and Nancy (Bob crowed with joy about how he'd been allowed to play with the emptied revolvers used as evidence at the trial), he answered questions about his professional history and his thoughts during the trial.

"When did you feel you had the case in the bag?" a reporter from the *Daily News* asked.

"I believe it was when the defense shifted from denial of Moran and Summers having ever been in Dayton to the alibis that they got home at a certain time in the afternoon. They didn't know that we could prove they got to Henderson much later than that." When asked to elaborate on additional advantages he had obtained, Kerr replied, "The defense never satisfactorily explained what the defendants were doing in that stolen car which was used in the robbery."

"One more question," the *Daily News* reporter said. When Kerr nodded assent, the man asked, "Don't you think Summers about the worst witness you ever saw? The way he kept saying, 'I don't remember . . . I could have been but I can't say for sure.' Did you ever hear anything like it?"

Kerr chuckled. "Yes, he was so bad that I didn't question him as much as I could have. I almost began to feel sorry for him."[36]

21

FINAL DESTINATION: LEAVENWORTH

N MORAN'S ADMISSION INTERVIEW AT the Ohio State Penitentiary, he told the representative of the Classification Committee (which compiled his file and recommended his work detail) that he was not guilty of the Kurpe robbery. "All I know about it is what I read in the papers," he insisted. When asked about his family history, he spoke of his marriages to Lucille and Evelyn, and named John as his next of kin, but the rest of his statement was pure fiction.

He said that his father, George Moran, had emigrated from Ireland and made his living as a pharmacist before dying of cancer in 1915 at the age of fifty-five. His mother's name was Julia, and she had been a Canadian by birth. He claimed that she died of a heart disorder in 1920. He said he had a brother who recently passed away at the age of forty from a heart disorder, and a sister who'd been carried away by a fatal illness while still in her teens.[1]

"Good attitude," a prison official noted in his report. "Recommend mills and factories." A physical examination, which included a serology test, revealed no major illnesses. The Classification Committee recommended his placement in the print shop and ordered that he be housed separately from Fouts and Summers.

Moran remained in the print shop job for over five months. In December the personnel officer and the chief medical officer approved his transfer to the hospital as a nurse. The position, which he retained for the duration of his time in the prison, entailed the supervision and handling of mental cases being treated on site or awaiting transfer to the Lima State Hospital. The prison psychiatrist, Dr. J. J. Alpers, considered him dependable, conscientious, and possessing a flair for handling the mentally ill. Moran, unlike many high-profile prisoners, made no attempt at ringleading and was never cited in disciplinary court.

One of his duties was pushing a "medicine cart" around the various cellblocks, dispensing medication to inmates who had had it prescribed to them. A guard escorted him on these rounds but never intervened or even seemed to notice when prisoners would slip Moran notes for delivery to those in other sections of the institution.[2]

Marion Koslowski, a former warden, told the *Columbus Dispatch* in 1984, "There were no more perfect gentlemen than the Wop, Joe Sinatra, and Bugs Moran. When they had charge of the psych range, you didn't have inmates diddling anyone."[3] "The Wop" was Joe English, who with Serafina "Joe" Sinatra, were associates of Toledo mobster Yonnie Licavoli. Domenic Marzano, an inmate barber, elaborated in the same interview, "I worked on the psych range for seven years with old George Moran and Yonnie Licavoli. We were there to keep them [psychopaths] from getting hurt . . . so the guards wouldn't get to them."

The FBI continued to gather evidence about their bank-robbing spree during the 1945–46 period. Moran, Fouts, and Summers were indicted on December 9 by a federal grand jury for violation of Section 588, title 18 of the U.S. Code in connection with the Ansonia, Ohio, robbery. In effect, this meant that the moment they were released from the penitentiary, they would find themselves back in custody and facing a second trial. Another dose of bad news arrived on April 30, 1947, when the Ohio Supreme Court upheld their armed-robbery convictions. No further appeals were filed. The trio resigned themselves to the estimated ten-year prison term, and whatever lay beyond it.

In July 1947 Joe Saltis finally took the one-way ride that had been reserved for him for so long.[4] Suffering from an acute liver ailment, he was taken by ambulance to the county hospital from the skid row hotel on the North Side that he had been occupying for years. The days of making more than $5,000 a week and giving $50 tips to cigarette girls had been over for decades; by 1947 Saltis was a confirmed charity case. Police officers who had known him during the 1920s told reporters, "He was one of the toughest hoodlums of them all. When Joe was big time, Capone stayed the hell out of the Stockyards."

When Repeal dawned on America, Saltis had still been in possession of a considerable fortune, having made close to a $3 million personal profit over the years.

But Capone's downfall at the hands of the federal government had driven him to safeguard his assets by placing them in his wife's name. What he had not considered when making this move was the fallibility of his marriage. During one explosive marital dispute, Saltis fired a shotgun at his wife and missed, the inevitable outcome being that she filed for divorce. At the time of Saltis's death, she, her sons, and daughter were living in a $50,000 mansion in Beverly Hills. He died penniless, alone, and mostly unheralded except for a few press mentions.

In June 1947 Warden Ralph Alvis told reporters that Moran had turned down $50,000 from the *Chicago Tribune* to tell his life story. Hollywood movie columnist Louella Parsons had made an earlier offer of $100,000 for movie rights to the same subject, but the gangster turned both down with a firm, "No soap." Moran told the warden that his life "would not be worth a plugged nickel" if he cooperated with either endeavor.[5]

He underwent two surgeries in 1948, one to repair an incisional hernia that had been troubling him for years, the other a hemorrhoidectomy. That same year, a severe case of pneumonia struck him and left him so weak that he remained bedridden in the prison hospital for weeks. He had a second operation on the hernia in 1954, when the first one failed to correct the discomfort.

Around this time, letters from Evelyn stopped coming. She had moved to Chicago from Henderson soon after his arrest, and although her correspondence with him had been faithful and regular for the first few years of his imprisonment, by 1954 it had become sporadic. Although no divorce papers were ever served on him, Moran sensed that to all intents and purposes she was part of his past.

John remained a faithful figure in his life, visiting at least once a year. The younger Moran had married again, to an attractive Polish girl, and divided his time between an assistant hotel manager job in Chicago and bartending at Hobart Hermansen's Geneva Hotel in Lake Geneva, Wisconsin.

Prior to his second marriage, the debonair John Moran, though heavyset, sustained a reputation for being a spendthrift and a ladies' man, and would often "catch it" from Hermansen for enjoying female company a little too noisily while staying at the Lake Como property. Age and responsibility sobered him, and as his father's parole neared, the two of them would discuss the possibility of living together again under the same roof for the first time in more than twenty years. Such an idyllic arrangement was not likely, given the Ansonia robbery indictment, but it was a conversation both enjoyed.

At the end of September 1957 the press announced that Moran and Summers would be released on parole from the Ohio State Penitentiary on November 8, but that their freedom would be short-lived. Albert Fouts, who had already been released on September 20, had been immediately indicted for the Ansonia bank robbery, and secured his freedom by posting a $15,000 bond.[6]

At 8:25 a.m. on November 8, Moran and Summers, both wearing the prison-blue suits given to all newly paroled men, walked out through the open penitentiary gates. Waiting for them were Howard Bott, federal marshal for the Southern Ohio District, and Deputy Ralph Collet. The two parolees, who had been expecting them but were subdued all the same, allowed themselves to be handcuffed together and led into Bott's car. By 10 a.m. they were standing before Judge Lester L. Cecil in Dayton.

Asked how he wished to plead, Moran answered tiredly, "We just got out of the penitentiary this morning, Judge, Your Honor, and this is the first I've heard of this thing." This was actually not the case, but Judge Cecil did not debate the issue. He directed the bailiff to show both men, who were not represented by legal counsel, a copy of the indictments against them. Moran perused it briefly before handing it back, and said, "The only plea I can make is not guilty. I am speaking for myself."

Taking his cue, Summers told the judge, "I'm in the same position your honor. I wish to enter a plea of not guilty."

After their pleas were entered into the record, Cecil imposed a bond of $25,000. When they were unable to post it, deputy marshals escorted the two men out of the federal courtroom and back into Bott's automobile for the one-block ride to the Montgomery County Jail. Moran told his escort, "It's been a long time since I've been out."

At the jail, Moran and Summers surrendered $455 and $136, their respective prison earnings, and were turned loose among the other prisoners in the second-floor bullpen. The jailer told reporters that both were considered "maximum-security prisoners" and would be locked in their cells at night.

While in the county jail, Moran's coughing, which he'd always passed off as an annoying byproduct of his incessant smoking, became worse. He began to run a fever that left him tired and without appetite, and lost weight at the rate of ten pounds a month.

Both men, together with Al Fouts, appeared for trial before Judge Cecil in U.S. district court on January 7, 1957. Roy Montgomery Foster, their former accomplice, who had completed his eight-year sentence for the Ansonia crime but was now a guest of the Indiana prison system for assaulting a policeman, testified for the state.[7] He recalled that the crime had been planned at Fouts's Dayton home on November 5, 1945, and that he, Moran, Fouts, Summers, Lawrence Drewer, and James Mitchell had all been present. They left Dayton in three vehicles, two men to a car, on November 8, arriving in Ansonia at 11 p.m. that night. While everyone else hid in a graveyard, Moran went into town alone and scouted the locale. While the robbery took place, he said, Moran had functioned as the lookout, standing in the doorway of a hotel across the street.

Moran's court-appointed attorney, J. H. Patricoff, attacked Foster's credibility. "[He] is a liar who got something concocted in that crooked, dishonest, corrupt brain of his and seized the opportunity to help himself by testifying here."[8]

On January 10 the jury of seven men and five women returned a verdict of guilty, and the following day Judge Cecil sentenced them to serve a term of five years in the federal prison at Leavenworth. Moran accepted the blow with a strangely resigned air, and stranger still, declined to appeal. He looked ill and coughed repeatedly throughout the trial, sometimes to the point of near-strangulation.

On January 14, 1957, he and Summers arrived at Leavenworth. Moran's sentence was five years, but he would be eligible for parole in September 1958. Fouts remained free on bond awaiting appeal.

Moran requested that John be notified in event of his illness or death, the estrangement from Evelyn being complete. The standard questionnaire submitted to the family members of newly arrived inmates was never returned or even acknowledged by her, although John had replied soon after receiving the documents at his address in Boca Raton, Florida, where he was working at Hobart Hermansen's Atlantic Ocean House. He wrote:

> I am . . . (the) son of George C. Moran. . . . In 1930 my mother, who died ten years ago,[9] divorced my dad and since that time I probably haven't seen him twenty times. I remember him being very kind and generous to me and all those who associated with him in business or personal. . . . I am very much interested in his behalf and welfare, although we have our limitations here at home. I assure you I will do everything I can to make his position and situation in Leavenworth as pleasant as possible.[10]

Many of the items that Moran brought in he was not permitted to keep, in view of his status as a federal prisoner, including a belt, a Ronson lighter, a razor set, and belt, among others. These were packaged and sent at his request to Virgil Summers's brother, Lorne, in Kansas City, to be held pending his release.

Associate Warden Virgil Breland found one item in Moran's personal effects that raised some questions: a business card from H. M. "Mike" Siebert of the Ohio State Department of Probation and Parole. While in Pensacola, Florida, in November 1956 to testify in a federal case being heard there, Breland met J. A. Callahan, a postal inspector from Atlanta, whom Breland summed up as a "very brilliant and conscientious officer." During their conversation, Callahan asked if any inmates in the associate warden's custody had ever requested to correspond with Mike Siebert. Breland could not recall any such requests and asked why. Callahan explained that Siebert was suspected by his peers of conspiring with "thugs" to get their cases assigned to him upon parole. In a memorandum to Warden Looney, Breland wrote that Siebert would "allegedly permit them to function in widespread and large-scale criminal activity with whatever official cover-up assistance he could afford them."

The tone of his note implied that Moran had cultivated Siebert's acquaintance in the event that a subsequent sentence for the Ansonia robbery was not imposed following his release from the Ohio State Penitentiary. Neither Looney nor Breland questioned Moran about it, as it did not look like he would ever be in a position to take advantage of Siebert's services.

Moran gave clear evidence of ill health upon arrival. His color was ashy gray, he coughed until a choking fit seized him, and although coherent, a low-grade fever left him tired and listless. An X-ray revealed an orange-sized mass on his left upper lung. Looney directed that he be sent to the prison hospital for observation.

On February 5 the chief medical officer, Dr. Russell Settle, penned the following memo to Warden Looney:

> The . . . prisoner was received at Leavenworth on January 14, 1957, to serve a five year sentence for bank robbery. He has been continuously hospitalized to date and has presumptive findings of advanced bronchogenic carcinoma of the left upper lung. . . . He is continuing to lose weight, is intermittently febrile, has a consistently elevated sedimentation rate and secondary anemia. We are currently awaiting a report from the National Institute of Health at Washington, D.C., on bronchoscopic washings sent in about ten days ago. Biopsy of cervical lymph nodes was done this morning and this report should be available in a week or so. The X-ray on admission showed an orange-sized mass above and to the left of the entire hilus, which has increased in size and led to a dense infiltration of the entire upper lobe.

Settle concluded the memo on an ominous note:

> If the diagnosis of bronchogenic carcinoma is correct, as we believe it is, it means that this prisoner's prognosis is quite poor and that he has but a few months to live.

On February 7, the report from Washington arrived confirming the diagnosis. George Moran was in an advanced, untreatable stage of lung cancer, and the remainder of his life could be measured in days.

Warden Looney sent a letter to John Moran in Florida, advising him of the diagnosis and assuring him that his father was receiving the best medical treatment available. In mid-February, after George Moran took a turn for the worse, Looney dispatched another letter.

Dear Mr. Moran,

With reference to our recent exchange of correspondence, I regret to advise that your father's condition has taken a progressive downhill course. Our Medical Staff advises us they do not expect him to live more than three weeks, to a month, at the longest . . . .

We know this news is distressing, but in our previous letter we advised we would keep you informed of any significant change in your father's condition. Your father is aware of his critical condition. In fact, prior to a definite diagnosis by our Medical Staff he stated be believed he had cancer.

> Very truly yours,
> C.H. Looney
> Warden

On February 14, twenty-eight years to the day since the slaughter in the North Clark Street garage that he so narrowly missed, Moran received the sacraments of Penance and Extreme Unction from Father O'Connor. The end came at 7:55 on the dim, gray morning of February 25. George Moran, after rallying briefly during the night, took one final deep, labored breath and died.

Warden Looney took it upon himself to call John Moran and give him the news before the newspapers could. A few hours after the conversation, John sent him a telegram thanking him for his condolences and giving permission for an autopsy.

As soon as word of Moran's death reached the press, the warden's office was besieged with requests from United Press, Associated Press, and individual newspapers for permission to send representatives to cover and photograph the funeral. Looney advised all applicants that while reporters were welcome, photographers were not. Father O'Connor and John Moran had vigorously objected to any pictures being taken during the funeral service.

Satisfied that he had laid down inviolable guidelines, on the morning of the funeral, February 27, Looney sent Acting Lieutenant Temple and Record Clerk Zarter to the Davis Undertaking establishment to officially identify the body (as required by law) to avoid having to open the casket at the graveside and run the risk of a hidden camera snapping a picture. When he called to advise the funeral home that the two prison employees were en route, Davis informed him that two reporters from United Press had just left the premises, having made their way in while he was on his lunch break, and he was sure that they had snapped several pictures.

Looney, furious, managed to track down one of them, a man named Feeback from Kansas City, who admitted to having gone to Davis's establishment with his photographer, Paul McWilliams, with the intention of taking pictures of the casket and the hearse as it left the undertakers. Feeback appeared to relent and handed over four negatives showing Moran in the casket to Davis, who subsequently turned them in to Record Clerk Zarter.

363

A few minutes after 1 p.m. the casket with octagon-shaped hinges was carried out of the Davis Funeral Chapel into a hearse. The three-car funeral procession, which consisted of the hearse, a prison carry-all truck, and a station wagon driven by photographers, moved along the highway toward the graveyard, a bleak gray sky overhead. The photographers were not permitted to pass the highway entrance to the cemetery grounds, although two representatives of the press—A. Moretti Jr. from KCLO, the local radio station, who was present on behalf of United Press, and Johnny Johnston Jr., a reporter with the *Leavenworth Times*, who came by prior arrangement with the warden—were waved through.

The small caravan proceeded to the prison cemetery, where everything rolled to a halt next to the burial spot. Warden Looney joined the group at 1:20 p.m. "We're all set, are we?" he asked as he stepped out of his car. Receiving an answer in the affirmative, he gave the signal for the burial to begin.

Six prisoners acting as pallbearers removed the cloth-covered wooden casket from the hearse and carried it up four steps that had been carved out of the frozen earth, the grave having been dug on a hillside. Besides the warden, Father O'Connor, the pallbearers, and the media men, the ceremony was witnessed by Acting Lieutenant Temple, a guard named Wacker, and Record Clerk Zarter. As the casket was being lowered into the ground at 1:29 p.m., Father O'Connor recited prayers.

"Graciously grant to thy servant departed the remission of all his sins," he intoned as he blessed the casket. He then recited an Our Father and Hail Mary. He concluded the prayers with "Remember, man, that thou art dust, and unto dust thou shalt return."

"OK, I guess that takes care of it," the warden said after a few seconds of silence were observed. A plain wooden lid was laid across the casket before the inmates began the laborious task of shoveling earth into the hole. Looney, O'Connor, and the media representatives left the inmates and guards to complete the task.

Moran's few meager possessions (two pairs of glasses, two bars of soap, one razor with matching case, and one pad of legal paper) were destroyed, but John made an application to obtain the $99.84 that had been credited to his father's account in the Prisoners' Trust Fund. In July, he received a lengthy letter from the comptroller general's office, notifying him that his claim had been disallowed. It explained that since Moran had died intestate, the disposal of his property had to be done according to the laws of the state of Kansas, and said laws stated that his widow was the primary heir to the money.

"While you indicated on your claim that no widow survived your late father," the letter continued, "the record showed that he was separated from his wife, Evelyn Moran. . . . Although you allege that your father had said that Evelyn Moran divorced him and she, in turn, told you she could not remain his wife, no evidence that they were in fact divorced or statement from her has been submitted in support of your claim."

What became of Evelyn Moran is not known. She did not attend the funeral and made no claim to the funds that had been denied John. When last heard of she was living in Chicago, supposedly divorced and tight-lipped about her years with Moran, regarding that period of her life with a mixture of genuine love, grief, and sorrow.[11]

Virgil Summers completed his sentence and was freed in 1960. Fifteen consecutive years in prison had made him more reliant on a criminal lifestyle than ever, with fatal results. On the night of December 1, 1962, he was walking toward his apartment building in East St. Louis. It was late—3 a.m.—and the street apparently deserted. As he was about to enter the building, three shotgun blasts boomed from the shadows of a nearby vacant house, and the forty-eight-year-old ex-bank robber and gangster slumped to the ground, dead. His killers were never apprehended.

After his father's burial, John Moran returned to Chicago, where he and his wife had a small home on North Austin Avenue. Unlike Al Capone's son Albert Francis, the younger Moran had succeeded in avoiding media attention. News accounts of the Leavenworth burial that confirmed his existence came as a surprise to those who had never read the *Tribune* accounts of his marital difficulties with his first wife. Thanks to his years spent in Lake Geneva, very few who did not remember his Chicago childhood even knew that the infamous Bugs Moran had raised a child.

He worked a series of hospitality-related jobs, mostly at Hermansen-owned hotels—at the time of George Moran's death, John had been looking after one of Hobart's Boca Raton properties.[12] He spent summers in Lake Geneva, working at the Annex Bar connected to the Geneva Hotel. Gifted with his mother's outgoing and gregarious nature, he was popular with guests, customers, and co-workers. He was never known to start fights or even show excessive anger, suggesting that George Moran's influence on him was minimal.

Roberta Kelter, whose father, Robert ("Red"), was one of John Moran's closest friends, remembers him fondly, saying, "He was the life of the party wherever he showed up."[13] Moran had a particular fondness for children, buying Roberta small trinkets and toys and lavishing attention on his own son when the boy was born. One New Year's Eve, he and his wife threw a party intended for a small group of friends, but Moran, loving a full house, inflated the guest list by inviting a virtual crowd.

Noticing that Roberta was the only child present except for the sleeping baby, he rummaged in his record collection until he found the old Ram Trio record "Hokey Pokey." When the music came on, he cleared a space on the living room floor, took Roberta by the hand, and went through the dance moves dictated by the outlandish lyrics.

"Everyone was howling," Roberta recalls. "John was a big man, overweight, and the sight of him dancing the hokey-pokey got the whole room laughing." They only stopped when John's wife called from the kitchen that the noise might wake the baby.

His good humor sometimes made him the brunt of teasing. He had been solidly built but in good shape during his younger years, but too many late-night, post-shift sparerib-and-baked-potato dinners shared with other employees at the resorts where he worked had added pounds until he bordered on obesity. Red Kelter nicknamed him "Wimpy" after the *Popeye* comic strip character who had a hamburger obses-sion, and once had him convinced that his weight made him an airline liability.

"John was going with my dad to California by plane," Roberta remembers, "and my dad told him that because of his size, the seats wouldn't fit him and they had to make arrangements to put him in the cargo hold. John believed him and was really upset before Dad admitted he was kidding."

John Moran had his father's ambition to live well and make money, but he lacked the criminal inclination to illegally acquire the necessary funds for the "good life." He was honest, and that honesty motivated him to seek his fortune by work-ing long hours for his stepfather.

Long and late working hours and relentless money worries took their toll on his health, despite John's easygoing nature. In mid-July 1959, when particularly upset, he ranted to Red Kelter that he wondered whether his mother's estate had been worth more than he was led to believe. What planted this notion in his head can only be surmised now, but when Moran insisted that he planned to go into Hobart Hermansen's office after hours and rifle through his documents, among other things, Kelter became concerned.

"If you're really going to do that," he told John, "for God's sake don't go by yourself. Wait till I come back to town." Kelter and his family lived in Chicago at that time and made frequent visits to Lake Geneva. Perhaps he was hoping that John would calm down and lose interest in the idea. If not, someone had to be around to talk him out of it, or at the very least be on hand if an ugly confronta-tion occurred.[14]

A couple of days later, on July 18, Roberta and her father were watching televi-sion in their Chicago apartment when the phone in the kitchen rang. Mrs. Kelter answered it, spoke to the caller, and came into the living room a few minutes later, her face ashen.

"It's [John's wife]," she said slowly. "John is dead."

"At first Dad thought it was some kind of joke," Roberta remembers. "But he soon realized it wasn't. After he got off the phone, he went into my parent's bed-room, and I saw him lie across the bed, crying nonstop. It was the first and only time I've ever seen my father cry."

Earlier that day, John had not been seen around his usual haunts at the Geneva Hotel. Allen Hermansen, Hobart's nephew and a close friend of Moran, became concerned when morning rolled into afternoon and there was no sign of him. He finally walked through the hotel office and entered the small bedroom where John stayed whenever summer work called him to Lake Geneva.

Moran was lying motionless on the floor beside the bed, blood caked in his nostrils and his face deathly still. Hermansen, failing to rouse him, called for an ambulance, but John was beyond medical help and had been for some hours.[15]

Dr. E. D. Hudsen estimated that he had been dead since about 6 a.m. Filling out the death certificate, he noted the primary cause of death to be coronary thrombosis, with obesity and heart disease listed as contributing factors. The bloody nose was attributed to his fall from the bed when cardiac arrest hit.

John Moran, born Louis Logan, was laid to rest next to his mother, Lucille, in Oak Hill Cemetery. Twenty-five years later, Hobart Hermansen joined them in the same plot. The Geneva Hotel, where Moran was found, was razed during the 1970s, and the former site now hosts the Geneva Towers high-rise. Hermansen's other principal property, the Lake Como Inn, was sold in 1971 to Sam Argento, a former policeman from the Chicago suburbs who spoke of having served Hobart as a chauffeur and bodyguard.

Argento ran the place as the Red Chimney Inn for years, during which time he became convinced that the property was haunted. He told a writer for *At The Lake* magazine in 1998 that after he began renovations, workmen complained of hearing footsteps and other unexplained noises. At first he scoffed . . . then he spent the night there and was so spooked that he kept a gun handy at all times. Another time, he heard music coming from an unoccupied shoreline cottage. The manifestations ceased when Argento had a priest bless the place and built a tiny chapel on the front lawn.[16]

In 1986 Anthony Navrilio bought the property and renovated it to create a relaxing and elegant atmosphere reminiscent of Europe's grandest resorts. Today he and his wife run it as the French Country Inn. Hobart Hermansen's house, where George and Lucille Moran used to visit and where Lucille eventually called home, is now a bed and breakfast called The Water's Edge.

EPILOGUE

OST CHICAGO GANGLAND HISTORIES CLOSE the chapter on Moran after the St. Valentine's Day Massacre. The more thorough ones note in a sentence or two that he masterminded a check-counterfeiting ring in the late 1930s and made his round of the Midwestern banks during the '40s, but the general consensus is that the massacre finished Moran as a gangland power.

In Chicago that was partly true. After 1929 the Outfit spawned by Johnny Torrio and maintained/expanded by Al Capone, Frank Nitti, and their successors had become so omnipotent that few could operate without its backing and permission. Moran courted neither, which gradually ended his days as a ranking gangster in the city that had vaulted him to infamy and fortune. But he did not back down in the face of insurmountable opposition and instead moved his operations elsewhere, to the fertile and less organized playing fields in Lake County, Los Angeles, and rural Minnesota and Wisconsin. His Canadian liquor running connections made him useful as well in St. Paul, the city of his birth, where he may also have helped out old friends by dispatching annoying predators like Sammy Stein and his cohorts.

With Repeal, Moran moved into freelance union terrorism, slot-machine distribution, counterfeiting, knocking over handbooks, and bank robbery. "The Man

Who Got Away," the title of this book, was Al Fouts's nickname for George Moran and stems from his success at evading gangland assassination and serious punishment . . . until 1946. Then he became "The Man Who Got Caught, But Good."

"What's ironic," G. J. Moran insisted, "is that if George had been killed in that Clark Street garage along with his men, he might be remembered today in a different light. But he lived to see his territory be taken over, and his failure to hold on to it is blamed on stupidity, incompetence, you name it."

George Moran's historical record has, until now, been a bewildering melange of legend and outright lies of his own making. When Adelard Cunin fled Minnesota in 1909 to escape the consequences of a juvenile burglary conviction, his repeated name changes threw a smokescreen over his pre-Chicago past, a screen made so dense by police records, newspaper fallacies, and popular folklore that only yellowing records on file at the St. Paul–Minneapolis Archdiocese and the Minnesota Historical Society, not to mention the memories of those who knew him personally, prove that Adelard Cunin ever existed.

To the crime historian and gangsterphile at large, George Moran was the native-born son of Irish, or Polish, or both, parents. The boy who raced through the streets of Frogtown, cursed his teachers in French, and roamed nighttime St. Paul in search of robbery opportunities disappeared from the public record in 1909, and it has taken ninety-five years to find him again.

Although more than a few gang historians have dismissed him as a post-massacre failure, George "Bugs" Moran retains a mystique as Capone's last great challenger in the Chicago bootlegging wars. Moran collectibles, when they appear on Internet auction sites such as eBay, draw premium bids. An original, framed newspaper headline from his 1946 Owensboro arrest had a reserve price of $250 that was quickly met. A leading manuscript and autograph seller, History For Sale (www.historyforsale.com), listed a legal document that the gangster had signed, and it carried a $9,000 price tag.

Moran's Owensboro, Kentucky, home remains a tourist attraction, according to the current owner, a Joy Horton who, ironically, is a district supervisor for the Kentucky Division of Probation and Parole. She joked to the local press, "I wasn't a parole officer when we bought the house. And no, we haven't found any hidden money."[1]

The St. Valentine's Day Massacre continues to be the focus of television specials and magazine articles, was the subject of one 1967 movie and one manuscript, and is a key ingredient in any book or TV treatment of Chicago's gangland era. Moran remains in the public eye as the intended target of that bloody event. His whereabouts that morning, the reason for the meeting, and what he did during the tumultuous aftermath have been puzzled over along with the identities of the killers. William J. Helmer and Art Bilek brought forth evidence to answer the second question in their book *The St. Valentine's Day Massacre: The Untold Story of the Gangland Bloodbath That Brought Down Al Capone.* In this book, Moran's relatives have shared their personal reminiscences to answer the first.

"They called him 'Bugs' because he could go berserk when provoked," G. J. Moran recalled, "but there was another side to him that came more to the front in his old age. He was tough, make no mistake about that. But he also had the softest heart. He loved kids—I went through college on the money he gave me over the years. And when he worked in the psych ward, he was patient and gentle with all of the head cases."

Judge John Lyle, who delighted in distressing the gangster community with his vagrancy warrants, knew Moran's darker reputation all too well. Yet he detected a contradiction in the North Sider's makeup—streaks of emotion, sentimentality, and humor beneath the dour, sullen courtroom façade—and believed that if any gangster were capable of regretting his violent livelihood, it would one day be George Moran. When he learned of Moran's death, he wrote a letter to the prison chaplain, expressing his thoughts and wondering if the former gang chieftain had indeed repented before dying.

Father O'Connor, who was at Moran's bedside when he took his final breath and tried to shield his funeral from photographers, was happy to confirm that Lyle's prediction had been accurate. "George Moran died a very peaceful death and was strengthened with the full Last Rites of the Catholic Church while he was fully conscious," he wrote in a return letter. "This happened some days before he died and was not a 'last-ditch' stand. Your theory certainly proved to be very satisfactory in his case. I am sure that God in His mercy was very kind to him in judgment."

NOTES

Chapter 1

1. E-mail correspondence with Jeanne Coonan
2. E-mail correspondence with Pat and Jeanne Coonan
3. An excellent synopsis of Parrant's life can be found at http://www.lareau.org/pep-p.html
4. St. Paul Web site at www.ci.stpaul.mn.us
5. 1890 St. Paul City Directory
6. Baptismal record, on file at the Archdiocese of St. Paul and Minneapolis
7. Interview with Carol Horan
8. E-mail correspondence with Pat Coonan
9. Ibid.
10. Paul Maccabee, *John Dillinger Slept Here*, pp. 8-12
11. St. Paul City Directory 1909
12. Citypages.com, vol. 24, issue 1200, Dec. 3, 2003
13. Ibid.
14. Interview with Carol Horan
15. E-mail correspondence with Jeanne Coonan
16. George Moran's admission interview at Leavenworth Penitentiary, 1956
17. Interview with G. J. Moran, who heard the story directly from Moran. George Moran confirmed during his admission interview at Leavenworth that he had been wounded by gunfire in 1910.
18. Information obtained from the Web site at http://www.jolietprison.com
19. *Chicago Tribune*, July 2, 1910, p. 5
20. Federal Bureau of Investigation file on George Moran.

Chapter 2

1. *London Daily Mail* article, n.d.
2. Herbert Asbury, *The Gangs of Chicago*, p. 3
3. Kenan Heise and Ed Bauman, *Chicago Originals*, p. 3
4. Asbury, p. 25
5. Ibid., p. 31
6. Ibid., p. 53
7. Ibid. p. 156
8. John Kobler, *Al Capone*, p. 41
9. Ibid. p. 56
10. Robert Schoenberg, *Mr. Capone*, p. 46
11. Asbury, p. 207
12. Douglas Bukowski, *Big Bill Thompson, Chicago, and the Politics of Image*, p. 3
13. Curt Johnson with R. Craig Sutter, *Wicked City—Chicago: From Kenna to Capone*, p. 9
14. Ibid., p. 10
15. Bukowski, p. 5
16. Schoenberg, p. 43
17. Bukowski, p. 12
18. Schoenberg, p. 44
19. Bukowski, p. 13
20. Ibid., p. 14
21. Kobler, pp. 61-62
22. Ibid., p. 63
23. Details about the Bloomington trials of 1912 and 1913 are on file in the archives of the circuit court clerk of McLean County, Ill.
24. William J. Helmer and Arthur J. Bilek, *The St. Valentine's Day Massacre: The Untold Story of the Gangland Bloodbath that Brought Down Al Capone*, p. 121
25. John Kobler, *Ardent Spirits: The Rise and Fall of Prohibition*, p. 198
26. Ibid., p. 35
27. Ibid., p. 70
28. Ibid., p. 200
29. Ibid., p. 205
30. Ibid., p. 207

Chapter 3

1. Harvey Warren Zorbaugh, *The Gold Coast and the Slum*, p. 28
2. *Chicago Tribune*, July 6, 1917, p. 12
3. *Chicago Tribune*, Sept. 1, 1917, p. 1
4. Zorbaugh, p. 111
5. *Chicago Tribune*, July 15, 1917, p. 14
6. *Chicago Tribune*, July 14, 1917, p. 1
7. *Chicago Tribune*, July 15, 1917, p. 14
8. Interview with G. J. Moran
9. Robert Schoenberg, *Mr. Capone*, p. 34
10. Rose Keefe, *Guns and Roses: The Untold Story of Dean O'Banion, Chicago's Big Shot Before Al Capone*, pp. 59-60
11. Frederick Schoeps death certificate
12. Keefe, pp. 27-28
13. Ibid., pp. 11-12
14. For a thorough description of Little Hell, read Zorbaugh's *The Gold Coast and the Slum*, pp. 159-181.
15. O'Banion's school record, on file at Holy Name High School
16. *Chicago Tribune*, Jan. 8, 1908, p. 8
17. Keefe, p. 25 (based on interview with former O'Banion employee E. Barnett)
18. *Chicago Tribune*, Sept. 27, 1909, p. 1
19. 2003 interview with John Stewart
20. George Murray, *The Legacy of Al Capone*, p. 40
21. *Chicago Tribune*, Nov. 30, 1914, p. 13
22. Edward Dean Sullivan, *Rattling the Cup on Chicago Crime*, p. 121
23. Interview with Weiss relative Bob Koznecki
24. Illinois census of 1910
25. *Chicago Tribune*, Aug. 25, 1894, p. 8
26. *New York Times*, Aug. 25, 1894, p. 1
27. 1910 Illinois census (ages of children). Mary Wojciechowski is listed as head of the household, after Walente's name is crossed out.
28. Interview of Mary Weiss during proof of heirship hearing after Weiss's 1926 murder. This interview is part of the probate records archived at the office of the circuit court clerk of Cook County.

29. This signed prayer book is in the possession of Bob Koznecki
30. Murray, p. 48
31. Ibid., p. 43
32. Illinois census 1910
33. John di Ambrosio's death certificate, on file at the Cook County clerk's office
34. *Chicago Tribune*, April 9, 1927, p. 4 refers to Drucci's two years in the Navy.
35. *Chicago Tribune*, Feb. 3, 1918, p. 1
36. *Chicago Tribune*, Feb. 2, 1918, p. 1
37. *Chicago Tribune*, Feb. 3, 1918, p. 1. This article covers the shooting of George Raymond and capture of Moran in detail.
38. *Chicago Tribune*, Feb. 5, 1918, p. 2
39. *Chicago Tribune*, May 5, 1918, p. 1
40. *Chicago Tribune*, July 13, 1918, p. 13
41. 1920 Illinois census
42. *Chicago Tribune*, Aug. 10, 1918, p. 5

Chapter 4

1. Jack McPhaul, *Johnny Torrio: First of the Gang Lords*, pp. 38-40.
2. Robert Schoenberg, *Mr. Capone*, p. 24
3. Ibid., pp. 24-25
4. Schoenberg p. 46 names Torrio as the cousin of Colosimo's wife Victoria Moresco, while Kobler p. 37 states that he was Big Jim's nephew. Colosimo's obituary in the *Chicago Tribune* (May 14, 1920, p. 15) states that he was survived by a sister named Maria, which was also the name of Torrio's mother. Given the fact that Maria is a common Italian name, this is not a conclusive piece of evidence regarding a blood relationship.
5. Schoenberg p. 47 points out that gang warfare in Manhattan and aggressive Irish control of the Brooklyn dockyards were instrumental in Torrio's willingness to relocate to Chicago, even if only temporarily.
6. Schoenberg, p. 47
7. John Kobler, *Capone*, p. 55

8. *Chicago Tribune*, Feb. 10, 1916, p. 13
9. *Chicago Tribune*, Oct. 26, 1912, p. 2
10. *Chicago Tribune*, March 14, 1900 p. 16
11. Kobler, p. 44
12. Ibid., pp. 38-40
13. Ibid., p. 64
14. Ibid., p. 56
15. Schoenberg, p. 48
16. *Chicago Tribune*, May 19, 1919 p. 17
17. *Chicago Tribune*, May 29, 1919 p. 17
18. Kobler, p. 69
19. Schoenberg, p. 59
20. George Murray, *The Legacy of Al Capone*, p. 37
21. *Chicago Tribune*, May 14, 1923 p. 1
22. Former O'Banion employee E. Barnett maintained that Morton had strong ties with the Little Jewish Navy at the onset of Prohibition.
23. Murray, p. 39
24. John Kobler, *Ardent Spirits: The Rise and Fall of Prohibition*, p. 12
25. Ibid., p. 13
26. Ibid., p. 16
27. Ibid., p. 17
28. Paul Maccabee, *John Dillinger Slept Here*, p. 24

Chapter 5

1. John Kobler, *Ardent Spirits: The Rise and Fall of Prohibition*, pp. 222-223
2. Ibid., p. 223
3. *New York Times*, Jan. 1, 1921, p. 3
4. John Kobler, *Al Capone*, p. 68
5. Kobler, *Ardent Spirits*, p. 223
6. Ibid., p. 239
7. Interview with E. Barnett
8. *Chicago Tribune*, Feb. 10, 1920, p. 6
9. *Chicago Tribune*, Feb. 27, 1920, p. 1
10. *Chicago Tribune*, Jan. 31, 1925, p. 5
11. Kobler, *Ardent Spirits*, pp. 334-335
12. Kobler, *Capone*, p. 69
13. Ibid., p. 65
14. *Chicago Tribune*, Jan. 29, 1917, p. 17
15. *Chicago Tribune*, May 12, 1920, p. 3

16. Ibid.
17. *Chicago Tribune*, March 30, 1920, p. 10
18. Robert Schoenberg, *Mr. Capone*, p. 63
19. Kobler, *Capone*, p. 75
20. Schoenberg, p. 65
21. John Landesco, Illinois Crime Survey, p. 199
22. *Chicago Tribune*, June 26, 1941, p. 10
23. *Chicago Tribune*, June 18, 1920, p. 17
24. *Chicago Tribune*, April 4, 1926, p. 1
25. *Chicago Tribune*, March 3, 1920, p. 9
26. *Chicago Tribune*, March 5, 1920, p. 2
27. *Chicago Tribune*, March 7, 1920, p. 1
28. *Chicago Tribune*, May 30, 1920, p. 10
29. Ibid.
30. Rose Keefe, *Guns and Roses*, p. 132
31. *Chicago Tribune*, Oct. 1, 1921, p. 17
32. *Chicago Tribune*, March 29, 1922, p. 21
33. *Chicago Tribune*, Nov. 6, 1942, p. 15
34. *Chicago Tribune*, June 25, 1920, p. 10

Chapter 6
1. *Chicago Tribune*, July 23, 1925, p. 5
2. John Kobler, *Capone*, p. 87
3. Ibid., p. 90
4. *Chicago Tribune*, May 11, 1929, p. 1 refers to Scalise's birthplace as Castelvetrano, refuting the common belief that the Gennas welcomed him because he was also from Marsala.
5. Kobler, p. 88
6. Ibid., p. 94
7. *Chicago Tribune*, Feb. 25, 1921, p. 1
8. *Chicago Tribune*, April 11, 1921, p. 17
9. *Chicago Tribune*, July 21, 1921, p. 16
10. Interview with Larry Raeder
11. *Chicago Tribune*, March 11, 1930, p. 1S
12. *Chicago Tribune*, March 25, 1913, p. 11
13. *Chicago Tribune*, Jan. 30, 1918, p. 17
14. *Chicago Tribune*, July 16, 1918, p. 13
15. *Chicago Tribune*, May 10, 1920, p. 1

16. Interview with Larry Raeder
17. Kobler, *Capone*, p. 109
18. *Chicago Tribune*, April 4, 1926, p. 1
19. Robert Schoenberg, *Mr. Capone*, p. 83
20. *Chicago Daily News* May 18, 1943
21. Schoenberg, p. 83
22. *Chicago Tribune*, March 30, 1916, p. 12
23. *Chicago Tribune*, Feb. 28, 1917, p. 8
24. *Chicago Tribune*, March 24, 1918, p. 8
25. *Chicago Tribune*, April 10, 1918, p. 11
26. Interview with Larry Raeder
27. Schoenberg, p. 55
28. *Chicago Tribune*, Sept. 17, 1920, p. 5
29. Curt Johnson and Craig Sautter, *Wicked City*, pp. 162-163
30. *Chicago Tribune*, Aug. 24, 1920, p. 1

Chapter 7
1. George Murray, *The Legacy of Al Capone*, p. 55
2. *Chicago Herald and Examiner*, March 9, 1924
3. *Chicago Tribune*, July 20, 1928, p. 2 refers to the price scale
4. *Chicago Tribune*, July 30, 1929, p. 13
5. Chicago newspaper clipping, n.d.
6. *Chicago Tribune*, Dec. 4, 1911, p. 1 covers Mrs. Kaufman's murder, additional family information supplied during interview with Julian's grandson Richard.
7. *Chicago Tribune*, Sept. 27, 1909, p. 9
8. *Chicago Tribune*, June 6, 1912, p. 4
9. *Chicago Tribune*, Dec. 12, 1916, p. 11
10. *Chicago Tribune*, Feb. 15, 1929 p. 2
11. *Chicago Tribune*, May 13, 1921, p. 1 refers to the ball game, although it incorrectly names Frank as an additional participant
12. *Chicago Tribune*, July 13, 1921, p. 17
13. *Chicago Tribune*, Aug. 7 1922, p. 7
14. Interview with Doug Hawke, who has a manuscript about Alterie in the works
15. *Chicago Tribune*, June 19, 1922, p. 1

16. Ibid.
17. FBI File No. 320989
18. *Chicago Evening Post*, Oct. 7, 1921. This article mistakenly credits Moran with having a record dating back to 1893.
19. George Murray, *The Legacy of Al Capone*, p. 45
20. *Chicago Tribune*, June 1, 1921, p. 3
21. *Chicago Tribune*, June 5, 1921, p. 5
22. Rose Keefe, *Guns and Roses: The Untold Story of Dean O'Banion, Chicago's Big Shot Before Al Capone*, p. 129
23. Indictment 24784, records on file at the county clerk's office.
24. Murray, p. 49
25. Dean O'Banion and Helen Viola Kaniff were married at Our Lady of Sorrows Basilica on Feb. 5, 1921.
26. Robert Schoenberg, *Mr. Capone*, p. 73
27. Douglas Bukowski, *Big Bill Thompson, Chicago, and the Politics of Image*, p. 134
28. Ibid.
29. *Chicago Tribune*, Oct. 19 1921, p. 1
30. *Chicago Tribune*, Oct. 20, 1921, p. 15
31. *Chicago Tribune*, Oct. 22, 1921, p. 1
32. *Chicago Tribune*, Dec. 8, 1921, p. 17
33. Murray, p. 45
34. *Chicago Tribune*, Nov. 21, 1926, p. 16
35. Ibid.
36. Murray, pp. 57-58
37. Indictment record 28982, on file at the county clerk's office; and Murray, p. 58
38. *Chicago Tribune*, June 25, 1922, p. 17
39. William Shanley was killed in December 1933 in a North Broadway garage by John Hamilton of the Dillinger Gang.
40. Ibid.
41. *Chicago Tribune*, Sept. 1 1922, p. 17
42. *Chicago Tribune*, Aug. 31, 1922, p. 3
43. FBI File No. 320989
44. *Chicago Tribune*, May 6, 1926, p. 1
45. *Chicago Tribune*, Jan. 22, 1924, p. 9
46. John Kobler, *Al Capone*, p. 169
47. Schoenberg, p. 85
48. Bukowski, p. 149
49. Ibid.
50. *Chicago Tribune*, April 14, 1923, p. 3
51. *Chicago Tribune*, June 3 1906, p. 2
52. *Chicago Tribune*, Oct. 20, 1906, p. 5
53. *Chicago Tribune*, Dec. 1, 1907, p. 5
54. *Chicago Tribune*, April 18, 1923, p. 1
55. *Chicago Tribune*, March 28, 1900, p. 2
56. *Chicago Tribune*, July 6, 1927, p. 16
57. Schoenberg, p. 86
58. *Chicago Tribune*, May 14, 1923, p. 1
59. *Chicago Tribune*, Dec. 18, 1921, p. 3
60. *Chicago Tribune*, Oct. 6, 1924, p. 1
61. Schoenberg, p. 87
62. Ibid., p. 90
63. *Chicago Tribune*, Sept. 18, 1923, p. 1
64. *Chicago Tribune*, Sept. 19, 1923, p. 1
65. *Chicago Tribune*, Sept. 18, 1923, p. 1
66. *Chicago Tribune*, Sept. 20, 1923, p. 8
67. Kobler, p. 107
68. Ship's manifest for the SS *Cambrai* is among the records stored at the Statue of Liberty–Ellis Island Foundation, Inc.
69. *Chicago Tribune*, April 22, 1922, p. 5
70. G. J. Moran believes they were married in Wisconsin, although he erroneously gave a May 1921 date. Lucille was still married to Logan at that time and not even in the United States. The exact date of their marriage is not known, as no certificate has been tracked down to date.
71. Interview with Frank Cantwell

Chapter 8
1. *Chicago Herald and Examiner*, Nov. 11, 1924 p. 2
2. *Chicago Tribune*, March 14, 1924, p. 1
3. *Chicago Tribune*, April 15, 1922, p. 6
4. *Chicago Herald and Examiner*, Jan. 22, 1924 p. 1

5. *Chicago Tribune* March 1, 1924 p. 1
6. *Chicago Tribune*, Jan. 23, 1924 p. 13
7. *Chicago Daily News*, n.d.
8. *Chicago Herald and Examiner* Feb. 23 1924 p. 1
9. Ibid.
10. *Chicago Herald and Examiner* March 8, 1924 p. 1
11. *Chicago Herald and Examiner*, n.d.
12. *Chicago Herald and Examiner* March 9, 1924 p. 1
13. Robert Schoenberg, *Mr. Capone*, p. 109
14. *Chicago Tribune*, March 1, 1924, p. 1
15. *Chicago Herald and Examiner* March 13, 1924
16. Schoenberg, p. 109
17. *Chicago Tribune*, Oct. 4, 1924, p. 2
18. *Chicago Tribune*, May 16, 1924, p. 1
19. *Chicago Tribune*, Sept. 15, 1924, p. 1
20. *Chicago Tribune*, Sept. 22, 1938, p. 1
21. Interview with G. J. Moran. Cunin family stories confirm that Adelard was a frequent visitor to his mother's home after she returned from Canada.
22. Paul Maccabee, *John Dillinger Slept Here*, p. 2
23. Ibid., p. 3
24. Ibid., p. 25
25. Ibid., p. 26

Chapter 9
1. Robert Schoenberg, *Mr. Capone*, p. 92
2. John Kobler, *Capone*, p. 110
3. Ibid.
4. Schoenberg, p. 97
5. Fred Pasley, *Al Capone*, pp. 38-39
6. Kobler, p. 124
7. *Chicago Tribune*, April 2, 1924, p. 1
8. *Chicago Tribune*, April 1, 1924, p. 1
9. *Chicago Tribune*, April 2, 1924, p. 1
10. *Chicago Tribune*, April 4, 1924, p. 3
11. Ibid.
12. *Chicago Tribune*, April 3, 1924, p. 9

13. Schoenberg, p. 98
14. Ibid., p. 99
15. Kobler p. 124 has O'Banion persuading fifty Chicago saloonkeepers to relocate.
16. Interview with former O'Banion beer trucker E. Barnett, who remembered this period well.
17. Kobler p. 125. E. Barnett recalled O'Banion finding the Genna bottles and complaining to Torrio to no avail.
18. *Chicago Tribune*, May 23, 1924, p. 3
19. Criminal Case 12475 and Equity Case 4006 at the National Archives, Great Lakes Branch, contain extensive files on the Sieben raid and subsequent attempts to close it as a public nuisance.
20. *Chicago Tribune*, Dec. 8, 1923, p. 3
21. *Chicago Tribune*, May 20, 1924, p. 1

Chapter 10
1. *Chicago Tribune*, May 24, 1924, p. 3
2. *Chicago Tribune*, July 4, 1924, p. 1
3. *Chicago Tribune*, Aug. 28, 1924, p. 7
4. *Chicago Tribune*, Nov. 30, 1924, p. 19
5. *Halifax (NS) Chronicle-Herald* article, n.d., circa 1987-88
6. Interview with Emilienne Veinot, Montreal
7. *Chicago Tribune*, July 8, 1924, p. 5
8. Interview with E. Barnett
9. *Chicago Tribune*, July 8, 1924, p. 5
10. *Chicago Tribune*, July 10, 1924, p. 11
11. *Denver (CO) Rocky Mountain News*, Nov. 12, 1924, p. 1
12. Ibid.
13. Ibid.
14. Fred Pasley, *Al Capone*, p. 43
15. Ibid., pp. 50-53
16. Ibid., pp. 97-98
17. John Kobler, *Capone*, p. 127
18. Chicago newspaper, n.d.
19. *Chicago Tribune*, Nov. 5, 1924, p. 5
20. *Chicago Herald and Examiner*, Nov. 13, 1924, p. 1

NOTES

21. *Chicago Tribune*, Nov. 5, 1924, p. 5
22. Pasley, p. 54
23. Schoenberg, p. 111
24. *Chicago Tribune*, Nov. 14, 1924, p. 2
25. Pasley, p. 54
26. Schoenberg, p. 117
27. *Chicago Herald and Examiner*, Nov. 12, 1924
28. *Chicago Tribune*, Nov. 11, 1924, p. 1
29. *Chicago Herald and Examiner*, Nov. 11, 1924, p. 1
30. *New York Times*, Nov. 11, 1924, p. 1
31. Some accounts claim he was shot in the face, but O'Banion's morgue photo fails to reveal any facial injuries save a temple laceration probably caused by his fall.
32. *Chicago Tribune*, Nov. 11, 1924, p. 1
33. Interview with G. J. Moran
34. *Chicago Daily News*, Nov. 13, 1924
35. *Chicago Herald and Examiner*, Nov. 13, 1924
36. *Chicago Tribune*, Nov. 16, 1924, p. 1
37. *Chicago Herald and Examiner*. Nov. 11 and Nov. 13, 1924
38. Edward Dean Sullivan, *Rattling the Cup on Chicago Crime*, pp. 48-49
39. *Chicago Tribune*, Nov. 19, 1924, p. 1
40. Pasley, p. 58
41. *Chicago Daily News* Nov. 15, 1924, p. 1
42. *Chicago Tribune*, Nov. 15, 1924, p. 1
43. *Chicago Herald and Examiner*, Nov. 15, 1924
44. Ibid.
45. *Chicago Tribune*, Nov. 16, 1924, p. 8
46. Edward Dean Sullivan, *Rattling the Cup on Chicago Crime*, p. 48
47. Interview with Weiss relative Bob Koznecki
48. Ibid.
49. *Chicago Tribune*, Nov. 22, 1924, p. 1
50. Ibid.
51. *Chicago Tribune*, July 8, 1906, p. 3
52. *Chicago Tribune*, Nov. 24, 1924, p. 1

Chapter 11
1. *Chicago Tribune*, Jan. 13, 1925, p. 5
2. Robert Schoenberg, *Mr. Capone*, p. 123
3. John Kobler, *Capone*, p. 134
4. *Chicago Tribune*, Jan. 18, 1925, p. 5
5. *Chicago Tribune*, Jan. 25, 1925, p. 5
6. *Chicago Tribune*, Jan. 27, 1925, p. 1
7. *Chicago Daily Journal*, Jan. 26, 1925
8. Schoenberg p. 127 suggests that Torrio's share would be 25 percent over a ten-year period but admits that this is speculation.
9. *Chicago Tribune*, Jan. 29, 1925, p. 3
10. *Chicago Tribune*, Jan. 30, 1925, p. 3. Although Moran is not named here as the deliverer of the bad news, Pasley p. 74 names Moran.
11. Alterie allegedly hid Frank Gusenberg at his Colorado ranch during the first week of January, when both were being sought for questioning in connection with the Northern Lights Café shooting: *Chicago Daily Journal*, Jan. 6, 1925
12. *Chicago Tribune*, Feb. 23, 1925, p. 1
13. *Chicago Tribune*, Jan. 31, 1926, p.A7
14. *Chicago Tribune*, June 5, 1927, p. 9
15. *Chicago Tribune*, Aug. 16, 1927, p. 4
16. *Chicago Tribune*, Jan. 7, 1932, p. 4
17. *Chicago Tribune*, Oct. 19, 1933, p. 2
18. *Chicago Tribune*, Nov. 8, 1932, p. 3
19. *Chicago Tribune*, July 19, 1935, p. 1
20. *Chicago Tribune*, Sept. 7, 1930, p. 1
21. FBI file on the Louis Alterie murder, made available through the Freedom of Information Act
22. Ibid. The name is blacked out in the FBI correspondence.
23. *Chicago Tribune*, May 9, 1925, p. 11
24. *Chicago Tribune*, Oct. 1, 1927, p. 4
25. Interview with G. J. Moran
26. *Chicago Tribune*, May 27, 1925, p. 2
27. Kobler, p. 134
28. *Chicago Tribune*, May 27, 1925, p. 2
29. Ibid.

379

30. Fred Pasley, *Al Capone*, pp. 100-101
31. Schoenberg, p. 131
32. Kobler, p. 157
33. Chicago newspaper article, n.d.
34. Schoenberg p. 131 has Drucci being grazed by the shot, while Kobler p. 157 writes that both men were injured badly enough to require hospitalization. G. J. Moran confirms that Moran was injured, and Moran admitted in his 1956 Leavenworth Prison admission interview that he had suffered a shotgun wound in 1925.
35. *Chicago Tribune*, June 14, 1925, p. 1
36. Kenneth Allsop, *The Bootleggers*, p. 96
37. Kobler, p. 158
38. *Chicago Tribune*, July 9, 1925, p. 1
39. *Chicago Tribune*, Nov. 2, 1926, p. 1
40. *Chicago Tribune*, Nov. 9, 1931, p. 1
41. *Chicago Tribune*, July 16, 1931, p. 1
42. Schoenberg, p. 136
43. *Chicago Tribune*, July 21, 1925, p. 6
44. *Chicago Tribune*, Feb. 25, 1925, p. 5
45. *Chicago Tribune*, Aug. 21, 1925, p. 12
46. *Chicago Tribune*, Oct. 29, 1925, p. 14
47. *Chicago Tribune*, Nov. 15, 1925, p. 12
48. Schoenberg, pp. 134135
49. *Chicago Tribune*, Nov. 8, 1925, p. 3
50. *Chicago Tribune*, Feb. 19, 1931, p. 3
51. *Chicago Tribune*, Jan. 3, 1926, p. 1
52. Schoenberg, p. 146
53. John Kobler, *Capone*, p. 165
54. Filippo Gnolfo, otherwise known as Philip, was finally killed on May 31, 1930
55. Schoenberg, p. 147
56. *Chicago Tribune*, April 10, 1926, p. 5
57. *Chicago Tribune*, April 13, 1926, p. 1
58. *Chicago Tribune*, April 14, 1926, p. 5
59. Ibid.
60. John Landesco, Illinois Crime Survey, p. 237, and Kenneth Allsop, *The Bootleggers*, p. 159
61. Landesco p. 237
62. *Chicago Tribune*, April 14, 1926, p. 5
63. *Chicago Daily Journal*, Dec. 3, 1925

64. Schoenberg, p. 151
65. *Chicago Tribune*, April 28, 1926, p. 1
66. *Chicago Daily Journal*, April 28, 1926
67. Schoenberg, p. 155
68. *Chicago Tribune*, May 6, 1926, p. 1
69. Ibid.
70. *Chicago Tribune*, July 22, 1926, p. 6
71. Criminal Case File 14678, on file at the National Archives, Great Lakes Branch
72. *Chicago Tribune*, July 13 1926, p. 2
73. *Chicago Tribune*, Aug. 4 1926, p. 2
74. Schoenberg p. 158
75. *Washington Post*, Aug. 11, 1926, p. 1 The *Tribune* for the same date also describes the attack but does not mention Weiss's presence.
76. *Chicago Evening Post*, Sept. 17, 1926
77. Jules's brother Alex was a Sheldon follower also
78. *Chicago Tribune*, July 14 1926, p. 1
79. Zuta is often erroneously described as Russian born. His death certificate confirms his Polish ancestry.
80. *Chicago Tribune*, June 1 1921, p. 5
81. *Chicago Tribune*, Jan. 26 1925, p. 5
82. *Chicago Tribune*, Sept. 22 1926, p. 17 puts the number of cars at eight, while other sources say ten.
83. Ibid.
84. Interview with Sarah Simard
85. *Chicago Tribune*, Aug. 8 1926, p. 5
86. *Chicago Tribune*, Oct. 12 1926, p. 1
87. *Chicago Tribune*, Oct. 18 1926, p. 3
88. *Chicago Tribune*, Oct. 14 1926, p. 2
89. *Chicago Tribune*, Oct. 22 1926, p. 20
90. *Chicago Tribune*, Oct. 16 1926, p. 1
91. *Chicago Tribune*, Oct. 15 1926, p. 4
92. *Chicago Tribune*, Dec. 21 1926, p. 3
93. Probate files related to the Weiss estate are on file at the office of the circuit court clerk of Cook County, probate division
94. *Chicago Tribune*, Dec. 4, 1947, p. 1
95. *Chicago Tribune*, Aug. 8 1926, p. 5

.

NOTES

Chapter 12

1. The previous suppositions have been that Saltis sought peace because he feared Capone's wrath upon being revealed as a North Sider ally. This would have been common knowledge in the Chicago underworld in 1926.
2. Fred Pasley, *Al Capone*, p. 143
3. John Kobler, *Capone*, p. 194
4. *Chicago Tribune*, Oct. 8, 1927, p. 7
5. *Chicago Tribune*, July 20, 1928, p. 5
6. *Chicago Tribune*, April 3, 1931, p. 6
7. *Chicago Tribune*, Nov. 13, 1936, p. 7
8. *Chicago Tribune*, Dec. 4, 1926, p. 4
9. 1920 Illinois census. Marks and his wife and daughter Lillie were living in Chicago, Marks's occupation is noted as steamfitter for a telephone supply company.
10. *Chicago Tribune*, Jan. 9, 1918, p. 3
11. *Chicago Tribune*, Nov. 14, 1927, p. 6
12. *Chicago Tribune*, March 7, 1910, p. 3
13. *Chicago Tribune*, Nov. 26, 1914, p. 22
14. Helmer, William J., and Art Bilek, *The St. Valentine's Day Massacre*, p. 120
15. *Chicago Tribune*, Jan. 8, 1933, p. 1
16. *Chicago Tribune*, Sept. 27, 1924, p. 1
17. *Chicago Tribune*, Dec. 20, 1924, p. 3
18. Interview with G. J. Moran
19. *Chicago Tribune*, Feb. 17, 1927, p. 5
20. *Chicago Tribune*, Aug. 16, 1927, p. 5
21. *Chicago Tribune*, Aug. 16, 1927, p. 5
22. Pasley, p. 157
23. *Chicago Tribune*, April 5, 1927, p. 1
24. Kobler, p. 200
25. *Chicago Tribune*, April 8, 1927, p. 7
26. Pasley, p. 162
27. *Chicago Tribune*, April 6, 1927, p. 1
28. *Chicago Tribune*, April 13, 1927, p. 17
29. *Chicago Tribune*, April 11, 1927, p. 10
30. *Chicago Tribune*, March 29, 1936, p. D1
31. Ship's log of the *Cretic*. Also interview with Mario Gomes, who corresponded with Aiello's great-granddaughter.
32. G. J. Moran, remembers Moran discussing this period and saying that contrary to newspaper reports, he did not ally with Aiello until the latter's return from New Jersey.
33. *Chicago Tribune*, May 29, 1927, p. 1
34. *Chicago Tribune*, Dec. 28, 1927, p. 1
35. John H. Lyle, *The Dry and Lawless Years*, p. 202

Chapter 13

1. *Chicago Tribune*, Jan. 28, 1928, p. 1
2. John Kobler, *Capone*, p. 217
3. *Chicago Daily News*, Feb. 29, 1928, p. 1
4. Ibid.
5. *Chicago Daily News*, March 1, 1928, p. 1
6. Robert Schoenberg, *Mr. Capone*, p. 206
7. *Chicago Tribune*, March 7, 1928, p. 1
8. *Chicago Tribune*, March 9, 1928, p. 7
9. *Chicago Tribune*, April 18, 1928, p. 1
10. Fred Pasley, *Al Capone*, p. 249
11. Schoenberg, p. 200
12. Ibid., p. 201
13. Pasley, p. 250
14. *Chicago Tribune*, April 2, 1928, p. 3
15. Pasley, pp. 250-251
16. *Chicago Tribune*, May 15, 1928, p. 7
17. *Chicago Tribune*, June 2, 1928, p. 9
18. *Chicago Tribune*, April 21, 1928, p. 1
19. *Chicago Daily News*, Nov. 17, 1928
20. Ibid.
21. *Chicago Evening Post*, Nov. 17, 1928
22. *Los Angeles Times*, April 5, 1939, p. A2
23. Kobler, p. 223
24. Robert Schoenberg, *Mr. Capone*, p. 202
25. Ibid.
26. *Chicago Tribune*, Nov. 6, 1928, p. 3
27. Paul Maccabee, *John Dillinger Slept Here*, p. 2
28. *Chicago Tribune*, Dec. 30, 1928, p. E5

Chapter 14

1. Robert Schoenberg, *Mr. Capone*, p. 206
2. Fred Pasley, *Al Capone*, p. 238
3. G. J. Moran, who remembers this incident, does not recall the exact date, only that it occurred during the last week in January.
4. William J. Helmer and Art Bilek, *The St. Valentine's Day Massacre: The Untold Story of the Gangland Bloodbath that Brought Down Al Capone*, p. 132
5. Interview with G. J. Moran
6. Interview with G. J. Moran, who heard details from Moran years afterward
7. *Chicago Tribune*, Feb. 15, 1929, p. 2
8. Schwimmer probably learned of the meeting location from the Gusenbergs, as it's hard to imagine Moran contacting him directly for that purpose.
9. *Chicago Tribune*, Feb. 15, 1929, p. 1
10. Contrary to most published accounts, it was Willie Marks, not Ted Newberry, who accompanied Moran to 2122 North Clark the morning of Feb. 14. Interview with G. J. Moran
11. Moran confirmed in his admission interview to Leavenworth federal prison that a haircut was the cause of his delay.
12. Interview with G. J. Moran
13. William J. Helmer and Art Bilek, *The St. Valentine's Day Massacre: The Untold Story of the Gangland Bloodbath that Brought Down Al Capone*, p. 5
14. Ibid., p. 6
15. Ibid., p. 7
16. In early news reports, Schwimmer would be erroneously identified as Frank Foster
17. *Chicago Tribune*, Feb. 11, 1929, p. 2
18. Helmer and Bilek, p. 107
19. Interview with G. J. Moran
20. Helmer and Bilek, p. 129
21. *New York Times*, Feb. 17, 1929
22. *Chicago Tribune*, Feb. 25, 1929, p. 1
23. Interview with G. J. Moran
24. Interview with G. J. Moran
25. *New York Times*, Feb. 15, 1929
26. Helmer and Bilek, p. 108
27. Ibid., pp. 123-124
28. *New York Times*, Feb. 16, 1929
29. Ibid.
30. Helmer and Bilek, p. 130
31. Ibid., p. 131
32. Schoenberg, p. 220
33. Ibid., p. 222
34. Helmer and Bilek, p. 142
35. *Chicago Tribune*, March 1, 1929, p. 5
36. John Kobler, *Capone*, p. 251
37. Helmer and Bilek, p. 137
38. *Lightnin'*, Sept. 1929, p. 4
39. Schoenberg, p. 225
40. *Chicago Tribune*, June 9, 1930, p. 1
41. This letter is in the possession of G. J. Moran
42. *Chicago Tribune*, March 27, 1929, p. 1
43. These letters and notes were addressed to a family friend, who would pass them on to Lucille
44. Schoenberg, p. 234
45. *New York Times*, May 9, 1929, p. 17
46. Schoenberg, p. 234
47. Ibid., p. 238
48. *Chicago Tribune*, March 11, 1930, p. 1
49. *Chicago Tribune*, April 20, 1934, p. 9
50. *Chicago Tribune*, April 24, 1934, p. 26
51. *Chicago Tribune*, May 21, 1929, p. 2
52. *Chicago Tribune*, June 12, 1929, p. 1
53. *Chicago Tribune*, June 13, 1929, p. 7
54. *Chicago Tribune*, June 23, 1929, p. 7
55. *Chicago Tribune*, June 27, 1929, p. 3
56. *Chicago Tribune*, Dec. 3, 1929, p. 17
57. *Chicago Tribune*, Dec. 4, 1929, p. 2
58. Helmer and Bilek, pp. 182-183
59. *Chicago Tribune*, Dec. 29, 1929, p. 1
60. *Chicago Tribune*, Dec. 30, 1929, p. 1
61. *Chicago Tribune*, Dec. 31, 1929, p. 1

62. Helmer and Bilek, p. 80
63. Ibid., p. 84
64. Ibid., p. 91
65. Ibid., p. 232
66. Ibid., p. 104
67. Ibid., p. 232
68. *Chicago Sun-Times* Feb. 8, 1956
69. Ibid.
70. *New York Times*, Aug. 2, 1932, p. 34
71. 1988 interview with E. Barnett

Chapter 15

1. *Chicago Tribune*, Jan. 10, 1930, p. 7
2. *Chicago Tribune*, Jan. 11, 1930, p. 17
3. *Chicago Tribune*, Feb. 25, 1930, p. 1
4. According to author William J. Helmer, the bullet wound that originally sent McErlane to the hospital may have been inflicted by his common law wife, Elfreda Rigus, whom he terror-ized on a regular basis. She was later found in the back seat of her car, shot to death along with her two dogs, supposedly as payback for shooting McErlane.
5. *Chicago Tribune*, March 11, 1930, p. 1
6. *Chicago Tribune*, March 25, 1930, p. 6
7. Ibid.
8. *Chicago Tribune*, April 10, 1930, p. 1
9. *Chicago Tribune*, June 2, 1930
10. Ibid.
11. Richard Lindberg, *Return Again to the Scene of the Crime*, p. 239
12. Brad Smith, *Lawman to Outlaw: Verne Miller and the Kansas City Massacre*, pp. 57-59
13. *Chicago Tribune*, June 8, 1930, p. 1
14. *Havre (MT) Daily News*, June 9, 1930
15. Schoenberg pp. 277-278
16. Ibid., p. 279
17. Ibid.
18. *New York Times*, July 17, 1930
19. *Chicago Tribune*, July 18, 1930 p. 5
20. *Chicago Tribune*, July 22, 1930 p. 4
21. *Chicago Tribune*, July 1, 1930 p. 1
22. *Los Angeles Times*, July 2, 1930, p. 3
23. *Los Angeles Times*, July 2, 1930, p. 1
24. *Los Angeles Times*, July 2, 1930, p. 3
25. *Los Angeles Times*, Oct. 2, 1930, p.A2
26. *Los Angeles Times*, June 22, 1931 p. 5
27. *Chicago Tribune*, July 2, 1930, p. 1
28. Schoenberg, p. 280
29. *Chicago Tribune*, July 2, 1930, p. 1
30. *Chicago Tribune*, July 3, 1930, p. 1
31. Ibid.
32. *Chicago Tribune*, July 4, 1930, p. 1
33. *Chicago Tribune*, July 16, 1930, p. 1
34. *Chicago Tribune*, July 31, 1930, p. 1
35. *Chicago Tribune*, Aug. 6, 1930, p. 1
36. *Chicago Tribune*, Aug. 3, 1930, p. 1
37. *Chicago Tribune*, Aug. 8, 1930, p. 5
38. *Chicago Tribune*, Aug. 3, 1930, p. 2
39. *Chicago Tribune*, Aug. 8, 1930, p. 5
40. *Chicago Tribune*, Aug. 13, 1930, p. 7
41. *Chicago Tribune*, Sept. 24, 1930, p. 1
42. *Chicago Tribune*, Oct. 24, 1930, p. 2
43. *Chicago Tribune*, Aug. 5, 1930, p. 1
44. Ibid.
45. *Chicago Tribune*, Aug. 19, 1930, p. 1
46. *Chicago Tribune*, Aug. 16, 1930, p. 1
47. *Chicago Tribune*, Aug. 22, 1930, p. 2
48. *Chicago Tribune*, March 22, 1931, p. 7
49. *Chicago Tribune*, July 31, 1930, p. 3
50. *St. Paul Dispatch*, Aug. 14, 1930, p. 1
51. *St. Paul Dispatch*, n.d.
52. Smith, pp. 69-71
53. For an excellent history of Lake County, check out Diana Dretske's *Lake County, Illinois, an Illustrated History* (Heritage Media Corp., 2002)
54. *Spirit of Geneva Lakes* magazine, Feb. 2004
55. Ibid.
56. *Chicago Tribune*, Dec. 3, 1930, p. 5
57. John Kobler, *Capone*, pp. 302-303
58. *Los Angeles Times*, April 12, 1932
59. Richard Lindberg, *Return to the Scene of the Crime*, p. 68
60. *Chicago Tribune*, Oct. 23, 1930, p. 1

Chapter 16

1. *Chicago Tribune*, Oct. 21, 1930, p. 1
2. *Chicago Tribune*, Oct. 22, 1930, p. 2
3. Ibid.
4. John H. Lyle, *The Dry and Lawless Years*, p. 202
5. *Chicago Tribune*, Oct. 23, 1930, p. 1
6. Ibid.
7. *Chicago Tribune*, Oct. 24, 1930, p. 1
8. Ibid.
9. *Chicago Tribune*, Oct. 27, 1930, p. 1
10. Ibid.
11. *Chicago Tribune*, Dec. 10, 1930, p. 1
12. Ibid.
13. *Chicago Tribune*, Dec. 11, 1930, p. 2
14. Ibid.
15. *Chicago Tribune*, Dec. 12, 1930, p. 1
16. Ibid.
17. Ibid.
18. Interview with G. J. Moran
19. Ellen Poulsen, *Don't Call Us Molls*, p. 309
20. Interview with G. J. Moran
21. Moran named the year and location in his 1957 admission interview at Leavenworth Prison. A search of marriage records fails to turn up a certificate, suggesting that either he was mistaken about the La Crosse location or assumed a false name for official purposes.
22. Charleston, West Virginia *Daily Mail*, Dec. 26, 1930
23. Capone gunman Sam "Golf Bag" Hunt was credited with an attempt on Mongoven's life. See *Chicago Tribune*, Nov. 10, 1930, p. 1
24. *Los Angeles Times*, Dec. 24, 1931 p. A2
25. *Milwaukee Journal*, Feb. 27, 1931
26. Robert Schoenberg, *Mr. Capone*, p. 326
27. William J. Helmer and Art Bilek, *The St. Valentine's Day Massacre: The Untold Story of the Gangland Bloodbath that Brought Down Al Capone*, p. 241

Chapter 17

1. Interview with Doretta Hoehne
2. E-mail correspondence with Walter Fontane, St. Louis crime expert
3. *Chicago Tribune*, Jan. 12, 1932 p. 1
4. *Chicago Tribune*, Jan. 20, 1932 p. 1
5. *Chicago Tribune*, March 30, 1932, p. 3
6. *Lima (OH) News*, March 31, 1932
7. *Chicago Tribune*, March 31, 1932 p. 14
8. *Chicago Tribune*, April 18, 1932 p. 1
9. FBI file on George "Bugs" Moran
10. *Shawano (WI) Leader-Advocate*, July 28, 1932, p. 1
11. *Shawano (WI) County Journal*, July 28, 1932, p. 1
12. Ibid.
13. *Chicago Tribune*, July 22, 1932 p. 1
14. *Chicago Tribune*, July 23, 1932 p. 1
15. *Chicago Tribune*, Dec. 24, 1932 p. 4
16. *Chicago Daily News*, Sept. 2, 1932
17. *Chicago Tribune*, Aug. 4, 1933 p. 4
18. Mario Gomes, webmaster of the Al Capone Museum (www.alcaponemuseum.com) received an e-mail from an individual who had known Mongoven during the former gangster's later years. Mongoven would apparently fly into a rage when questioned about Moran.
19. *Chicago Tribune*, July 16, 1938 p. 1
20. *Chicago Tribune*, Oct. 26, 1941 p. 1
21. *Chicago Tribune*, Jan. 8, 1933 p. 1
22. William J. Helmer and Art Bilek, *The St. Valentine's Day Massacre: The Untold Story of the Gangland Bloodbath that Brought Down Al Capone*, p. 201
23. *Chicago Tribune*, Feb. 22, 1934 p. 1
24. *Chicago Tribune*, April 22, 1934 p. 11
25. Ibid.
26. Robert Schoenberg, *Mr. Capone*, p. 357
27. *Chicago Tribune*, Dec. 3, 1937 p. 11
28. *Chicago Tribune*, July 27, 1953 p. C7

Chapter 18

1. *Chicago Tribune*, May 17, 1930, p. 2
2. *Chicago Tribune*, Jan. 26, 1926, p. 9
3. *Chicago Tribune*, Jan. 18, 1939, p. 8
4. *Chicago Tribune*, Jan. 11, 1939, p. 1
5. *Chicago Tribune*, Jan. 10, 1939, p. 1
6. Ibid.
7. *Chicago Tribune*, Jan. 11, 1939, p. 1
8. *Chicago Tribune*, Jan. 18, 1939, p. 8
9. *Chicago Tribune*, April 22, 1938, p. 1
10. *Chicago Tribune*, Jan. 21, 1939, p. 1
11. FBI file on George "Bugs" Moran
12. *Chicago Tribune*, Dec. 17, 1938, p. 4
13. *Chicago Tribune*, Jan. 4, 1939, p. 12
14. *Chicago Tribune*, Jan. 11, 1939, p. 1
15. *Chicago Tribune*, Jan. 19, 1939, p. 2
16. *Chicago Tribune*, Jan. 21, 1939, p. 1
17. *Chicago Tribune*, March 9, 1939, p. 1
18. *Chicago Tribune*, March 21, 1939, p. 5
19. *Chicago Tribune*, May 1, 1939, p. 1
20. *Chicago Tribune*, Nov. 28, 1939, p. 11
21. Interview with Julian's grandson, Richard Kaufman
22. *Chicago Tribune*, Dec. 5, 1940, p. 5
23. *Chicago Tribune*, Jan. 16, 1940, p. 5
24. *Chicago Tribune*, Jan. 28, 1943, p. 1
25. *Chicago Tribune*, Jan. 31, 1943, p. 1
26. *Chicago Tribune*, March 12, 1943, p. 11
27. *Chicago Tribune*, Dec. 20, 1943, p. 11

Chapter 19

1. *Mount Vernon (IL) Register–News*, Dec. 9, 1933, p. 1
2. *Mount Vernon (IL) Register–News*, March 1, 1934, p. 3
3. Al Fouts file, available through the Ohio Historical Society
4. *Dayton (OH) Daily News*, Dec. 3, 1916, p. 1
5. Ibid.
6. Al Fouts file, available through the Ohio Historical Society
7. *Dayton (OH) Daily News*, Aug. 21, 1946, p. 1
8. *Chicago Tribune*, May 29, 1944, p. 8

9. *Chicago Tribune*, Sept. 4, 1943, p. 1
10. Interview with G. J. Moran
11. *Chicago Tribune*, May 16, 1945, p. 11
12. Halper, Albert, editor. *The Chicago Crime Book*, p. 420
13. *Chicago Tribune*, Dec. 14, 1945, p. 1
14. Owensboro *Messenger*, July 9, 1946, p. 1
15. *Owensboro (KY) Messenger–Inquirer*, May, 1991
16. Ibid.
17. FBI file on George "Bugs" Moran
18. Ibid.
19. Ibid.
20. Ibid.
21. Ibid.
22. *Owensboro (KY) Messenger–Inquirer*, May, 1991
23. Ibid.
24. *Chicago Tribune*, Jan. 5, 1945, p. 14
25. *Dayton (OH) Daily News*, Aug. 16, 1946, p. A17
26. *Evansville (IN) Courier*, Feb. 25, 1987
27. Ibid.
28. Dayton Police Dept. police interview with Mary Hamblin, on file at the Ohio Historical Society
29. *Dayton (OH) Daily News*, Aug. 15, 1946, p. 4
30. *Dayton (OH) Daily News*, Aug. 20, 1946, p. A1
31. Ibid.
32. Ibid.

Chapter 20

1. *Chicago Tribune*, Aug. 22, 1946, p. 13
2. *Owensboro (KY) Messenger*, July 7, 1946, p. 1
3. *Owensboro (KY) Messenger*, July 9, 1946, p. 1
4. Dayton Police Dept. interview with Mary Hamblin, Fay Wilson, and Al Fouts
5. *Dayton (OH) Daily News*. July 14, 1946, p. 1

6. Ibid.
7. *Dayton (OH) Daily News.* July 14, 1946, p. 1
8. *Dayton (OH) Daily News.* July 15, 1946
9. *Dayton (OH) Daily News.* July 18, 1946, p. 1
10. *Dayton (OH) Daily News.* Aug. 12, 1946, p. 1
11. *Dayton (OH) Daily News.* Aug. 14, 1946, p. 1
12. *Dayton (OH) Daily News.* Aug. 15, 1946, p. 1
13. *Dayton (OH) Daily News.* Aug. 15, 1946, p. 1
14. *Dayton (OH) Daily News.* Aug. 16, 1946, p. 1
15. Ibid.
16. Ibid.
17. *Dayton (OH) Daily News.* Aug. 17, 1946, p. 1
18. Ibid.
19. Ibid.
20. *Dayton (OH) Daily News.* Aug. 20, 1946, p. 1
21. Ibid.
22. *Dayton (OH) Daily News.* Aug. 21, 1946, p. 1
23. Ibid.
24. *Chicago Tribune*, Aug. 22, 1946, p. 13
25. *Dayton (OH) Daily News.* Aug. 22, 1946, p. 1
26. Ibid.
27. *Dayton (OH) Daily News.* Aug. 23, 1946, p. 1
28. Ibid.
29. Ibid.
30. *Chicago Tribune*, Aug. 24, 1946, p. 1
31. *Dayton (OH) Daily News.* Aug. 25, 1946, p. 1
32. Dayton Police Dept., report on file at the Ohio Historical Society
33. *Dayton (OH) Daily News.* Aug. 26, 1946, p. 1
34. *Dayton (OH) Daily News.* Aug. 27, 1946, p. 1
35. *Dayton (OH) Daily News.* Aug. 27, 1946, p. 1
36. Ibid.

Chapter 21
1. Ohio State Penitentiary file on George Moran
2. While appearing at the Golden Age of Gangsters convention in Itasca, Illinois, in Sept. 2004, I met an attendee whose friend had done time at the Ohio State Penitentiary during the time Moran was incarcerated there. The friend, a black man, recounted this story about the Bugs Moran delivery service.
3. *Columbus Dispatch*, Oct. 28, 1984
4. *Chicago Daily News*, July 2, 1947
5. *Washington Post*, June 5, 1949, p. 12
6. *Dayton (OH) Journal-Herald*, Nov. 9, 1956, p. 16
7. *Chicago Tribune*, Jan. 9, 1957, p.A9
8. *Chicago Tribune*, Jan. 11, 1957, p. 4
9. Lucille Hermansen, her health deteriorating from excessive drinking, briefly left Hobart Hermansen and went to New Orleans. She died there in 1946, aged 46. Her body was returned to Wisconsin for burial in the Hermansen family plot in Oak Hill Cemetery.
10. Leavenworth Prison file on George Moran, courtesy of G. J. Moran
11. Interview with G. J. Moran
12. 2004 phone conversation with Allen Hermansen
13. 2004 interview with Roberta Kelter, now Roberta Bajoreck
14. Ibid.
15. 2004 phone conversation with Allen Hermansen
16. *At The Lake* magazine, Autumn 1998 issue, page 51

Epilogue
1. *Owensboro (KY) Messenger–Inquirer*, Sept. 21, 2004

BIBLIOGRAPHY AND SOURCES

BOOKS

Allsop, Kenneth, *The Bootleggers and Their Era*. London: Hutchinson, 1961

Asbury, Herbert, *The Gangs of Chicago*. New York: Thunder's Mouth Press, 1986

Binder, John J., *The Chicago Outfit*. Chicago: Arcadia Publishing, 2003

Bukowski, Doug, *Big Bill Thompson, Chicago, and the Politics of Image*. Chicago: University of Illinois Press, 1998

Cowdry, Ray R., *Capone's Chicago*. Kusnacht: Northstar Maschek Books, 1987

Dretske, Diana, *Lake County, Illinois*. Carlsbad: Heritage Media Corp., 2002

Heise, Kenan and Ed Baumann, *Chicago Originals*. Chicago: Bonus Books, 1990

Helmer, William J., and Art Bilek, *The St. Valentine's Day Massacre: The Untold Story of the Gangland Bloodbath that Brought Down Al Capone*. Nashville: Cumberland House, 2004

Johnson, Curt, with R. Craig Sautter, *Wicked City: Chicago from Kenna to Capone*. Highland Park, IL: December Press, 1994

Kobler, John, *Ardent Spirits*. New York: Putnam's, 1975

Kobler, John, *Capone: The Life and World of Al Capone*. New York: Putnam's, 1971

Landesco, John, *Organized Crime in Chicago: Part III of the Illinois Crime Survey 1929*. Chicago: University of Chicago Press, 1929

Lindberg, Richard, *Return to the Scene of the Crime*. Nashville: Cumberland House, 1999

Lindberg, Richard, *Return Again to the Scene of the Crime*. Nashville: Cumberland House, 2001

Lyle, John H. *The Dry and Lawless Years*. Englewood Cliffs, NJ: Prentice-Hall, 1960

Maccabee, Paul, *John Dillinger Slept Here: A Crooks' tour of Crime and Corruption in St. Paul, 1920–1936*. St. Paul: Minnesota Historical Society Press, 1995

Murray, George, *The Legacy of Al Capone: Portraits and Annals of Chicago's Public Enemies*. New York: Putnam's, 1975

Pasley, Fred D., *Al Capone: The Biography of a Self-Made Man*. (Originally published 1930, 1971 reprint). Salem, NH: Ayer Press, 1971

Poulsen, Ellen, *Don't Call Us Molls: Women of the John Dillinger Gang*. New York: Clinton Cook Publishing Corp., 2002

Schoenberg, Robert, *Mr. Capone*. New York: William Morrow and Company, 1992

Smith, Brad, *Lawman to Outlaw: Verne Miller and the Kansas City Massacre*. Bedford, IN: JoNa Books, 2002

Sullivan, Edward D. *Rattling the Cup on Chicago Crime*. New York: Vanguard, 1929

Sullivan, Edward D., *Chicago Surrenders*. New York: Vanguard Press, 1930

Walter N. Trenerry, *Murder in Minnesota*. St. Paul: Minnesota Historical Society, 1962

Zorbaugh, Harvey W., *The Gold Coast and the Slum: A Sociological Study of Chicago's Near North Side*. Chicago: University of Chicago Press, 1929

PERIODICALS
Chicago Daily News
Chicago Evening Post
Chicago Herald and Examiner
Chicago Tribune
Dayton (OH) Daily News
Denver (CO) Rocky Mountain News
Los Angeles Times
Mount Vernon (IL) Register
New York Times
Owensboro (KY) Messenger–Inquirer
St. Paul Dispatch
Shawano (WI) County Journal
Shawano (WI) Leader-Advocate
Spirit of Geneva Lakes magazine, Feb. 2004

OFFICIAL DOCUMENTS
Ohio State and Leavenworth prison files on George "Bugs" Moran
FBI file on George "Bugs" Moran
United States Census records, 1910-1920
Ellis Island arrival records (ship's manifests) www.ellisisland.org

INDEX

389

INDEX

INDEX

INDEX

INDEX

INDEX